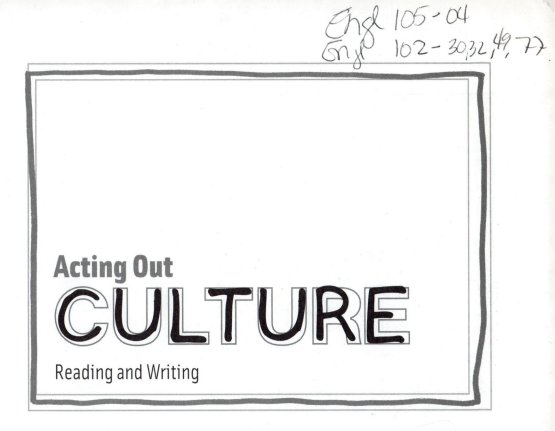

Acting Out
CULTURE
Reading and Writing

James S. Miller

University of Wisconsin, Whitewater

Bedford/St. Martin's   Boston ◆ New York

For Bedford/St. Martin's

Executive Editors: Leasa Burton and Stephen A. Scipione
Developmental Editor: Adam Whitehurst
Production Editor: Kerri A. Cardone
Production Supervisor: Andrew Ensor
Senior Marketing Manager: Karita dos Santos
Editorial Assistant: Abby Bielagus
Copyeditor: Lisa Wehrle
Text Design: Tom Carling/Carling Design
Cover Art and Design: Billy Boardman
Composition: TexTech Inc.
Printing and Binding: R. R. Donnelley & Sons Company

President: Joan E. Feinberg
Editorial Director: Denise B. Wydra
Editor in Chief: Karen S. Henry
Director of Marketing: Karen Melton Soeltz
Director of Editing, Design, and Production: Marcia Cohen
Assistant Director of Editing, Design, and Production: Elise S. Kaiser
Managing Editor: Elizabeth M. Schaaf

Library of Congress Control Number: 2007934304

For information, write: Bedford/St. Martin's, 75 Arlington Street, Boston, MA 02116
(617-399-4000)

ISBN-10: 0–312–45416–3

ISBN-13: 978–0–312–45416–6

Acknowledgments

Acknowledgments and copyrights are continued at the back of the book on pages 660–62 which constitute an extension of the copyright page. It is a violation of the law to reproduce these selections by any means whatsoever without the written permission of the copyright holder.

Sasha Abramsky. "Return of the Madhouse." From *The American Prospect* 11, no 3: February 11, 2002. Reprinted with permission from Sasha Abramsky. The American Prospect, 11 Beacon Street, Suite 1120, Boston, MA 02108. All rights reserved.

Adbusters. Excerpt from "Buy-Nothing Christmas." Copyright © 2006. Courtesy *Adbusters.* www.adbusters.org.

For Henry, Eliza, and Hope

Preface for Instructors

"WHADDAYA GOT?"

In the 1953 film *The Wild One,* Marlon Brando, playing Johnny Strabler, the leather-jacketed leader of a motorcycle gang that invades a small town, utters one of the most famous lines in movie history. Asked "Johnny, what are you rebelling against?" Brando arches an eyebrow and replies, "Whaddaya got?"

Acting Out Culture encourages students to cultivate a "Whaddaya got?" stance toward American culture — although not, of course, in the belligerent and self-destructive vein of Johnny Strabler. Rather, it takes as a given that students have already internalized countless rules, and are bombarded every day with media messages that dictate how they should think, feel, and behave. *Acting Out Culture* urges them to recognize these rules and prescriptions that they may adhere to unthinkingly, probe them, and imagine alternatives. Unlike an actor in a Hollywood movie, students have options. Although scripts for their lives abound, the endings are not written in stone. Working with the readings and assignments in *Acting Out Culture* gives students the opportunity to think critically about the norms and roles handed to or imposed on them, and, as it were, devise their own scripts in response to what they discover. On the stage of a composition classroom where popular culture is the subject of inquiry, they have the chance to "act out" through writing that positions them as citizens making informed decisions about their world.

WHY THESE CHAPTERS?

Because they start where students are and encourage them to exceed their own comfort zones of belief and action. The thematic organization of *Acting Out Culture* focuses students' attention not only on *what* our culture tells us but also on *how* it establishes those rules and disseminates those norms. The chapter themes explore questions of what and how we believe, watch, eat, work, fight, learn, and talk — questions that get to the heart of who students are and how they behave. Do they count themselves among the "we"s? As students evaluate, negotiate, and resist the roles and stances reflected in the chapters, their "Whaddaya got?" responses begin to emerge.

Moreover, the specific topics and readings within the chapters use students' own knowledge of popular culture as a springboard to deeper analysis. For example, Chapter 5, "How We Fight," covers several types of conflict, making connections between the simulated and the real. Students are asked to draw on *what* they know about online conflict and violent TV and video games as a first step in considering broader questions of *how* this knowledge might connect to the culture at large. Does our society need war to give us purpose? Is the pervasive use of combat metaphors to describe action on the sports field morally appropriate?

WHY THESE READINGS?

Because they are exceptional models of writing and thinking by contemporary authors who have important things to say about issues students care about. Each chapter includes academic pieces that support sustained reading and model in-depth critical analysis, as well as more popular pieces that go beyond trend-spotting to tackle the question"How does America tick? — with often surprising conclusions. The authors include academics such as Michael Eric Dyson (writing on the news media's characterization of the African American victims of Hurricane Katrina), journalists such as Barbara Ehrenreich (who brings readers along on her search for a white-collar job) and activists such as Naomi Klein (who objects to sex being sold to women as a form of empowerment). Although the authors approach the book's main themes from different angles, the overall focus on making and breaking the sometimes unspoken rules that govern our everyday lives creates a dialogue that will challenge students' critical thinking skills.

WHY THESE FEATURES IN EACH CHAPTER?

Because they introduce a variety of approaches to thinking and writing about cultural norms and rules. To analyze culture, students need to notice what they often overlook or take for granted, so each chapter opens with a photograph or sign that captures for analysis the rules that often fly beneath students' radar. Another recurring feature that makes the often-invisible visible is **"Everybody Knows That . . . ,"** which appears in the margins of the introductions. These call-outs list common rules that reflect conventional wisdom and invite students to move what's in the margins of their awareness to front and center, better to unpack and examine the assumptions nested in the norms.

Students also need to see that cultural analysis moves beyond binary thinking — the impulse to frame issues in black-and-white terms. Therefore, each chapter introduction closes with **Rule Maker/Rule Breaker** boxes, which present opposing points of view on a cultural issue in the opponents' own words. By looking into debates such as whether the proliferation of mega-retailers like Wal-Mart is beneficial or harmful, and whether the U.S. Military's "Don't Ask, Don't Tell" policy is necessary or pernicious, students can discover that there are more than two sides to every issue, which prepares them for the multiple perspectives and complex dialogues in the ensuing chapter.

Because students increasingly receive their daily doses of popular culture via visual media, *Acting Out Culture* presents advertisements, movies, television, and news photos as objects of analysis. Throughout, the book provides opportunities for students to respond to images as conductors of cultural messages.

The images in **Then and Now** depict popular thinking from the past to the present. Students can compare and contrast the images, but they can also use the accompanying contextual information to think further about what *hasn't* changed over time. In the "How We Watch" chapter, for example, a news photo of a Cold War-era duck-and-cover air raid drill is paired with a recent news photo showing bottles of shampoo and mouthwash being confiscated at the airport. Students are asked to consider, then and now, "What's more important? To feel safe or to be safe?" Do the images suggest similarly futile responses to overwhelming perils? If not, why not? If so, what are some alternatives?

Scenes and Un-Scenes track cultural norms in visual media by juxtaposing images on a central topic. These topics range from patriotic symbols in political speeches to the importance of victory as an American ideal. Students are encouraged to see the images as texts, composed to persuade audiences to interpret the world in a certain way. Discussion and writing prompts then direct students think about how visual media portray, navigate, and re-frame social rules and norms. What's in the pictures, and what's been left out?

Why These Writing Assignments?

Because writing is the best way for students to harness their own thinking and take control of what the culture wants them to believe. Writing is one of the most powerful tools for participating as active members of society, and the assignments in *Acting Out Culture* help students get a grip on the issues and construct sturdy arguments for action and change. After reading each selection, students are asked to identify the norms the author address, think critically about the issues at hand, and take a stand on these topics by analyzing an author's argument, examining the point of view, or evaluating the effectiveness of the language.

In particular, the **Putting It into Practice** assignments that close each chapter put students in the driver's seat. Often rooted in field research, these assignments urge students to consider how the issues in a chapter play out in their communities and in their personal lives. For example, in the "How We Work" chapter students are asked to research mean salaries for a range of jobs and write about why we "value" different types of work in different ways, using what they've discovered by reading the chapter selections to frame their own thoughts.

What Resources Are Available to Support Teaching and Learning?

Resources for Teaching Acting Out Culture: Reading and Writing
ISBN-10: 0–312–47474–1   ISBN-13: 978–0–312–47474–4
Designed for both new and experienced instructors, this manual supports every selection in the book and includes overviews, discussion starters,

suggested responses to the writing prompts, and ideas for clustering readings into topical or thematic units. An online version of the instructor's manual is available at bedfordstmartins.com/actingout.

AN INTEGRATED COMPANION SITE, BEDFORDSTMARTINS.COM/ACTINGOUT

Because many of the quotes and artifacts excerpted in *Acting Out Culture* can be found online, the book's companion site has compiled all the links to these resources into a **Weblinks** section in order to allow students to read excerpts in context and promote research. In addition, the site features **TopLinks,** a dynamic database of annotated links related to the topics in the book and well as access to **Re:Writing,** a free collection of our most popular online materials for writing, grammar, and research — including Diana Hacker's *Research and Documentation Online,* with expert and student-friendly advice for finding, evaluating, integrating, and documenting sources; and *Exercise Central,* the largest collection of editing exercises available online offering more than 8,000 items, with instant scoring and feedback. Instructor access to **Re:Writing** also provides an online gradebook, access to bibliographies and online journals, and much more.

TEACHING AND LEARNING VISUAL RHETORIC, RESEARCH, AND ARGUMENT: I·CITE, IX, AND I·CLAIM

i·cite, visualizing sources.   Do your students need help working with sources? This research and documentation CD-ROM brings research to life with animation and four interactive tutorials that explore fundamental concepts about working with sources. Students get concrete practice recognizing, evaluating, incorporating, and citing a wide range of real-life sources from across the disciplines. To order *Acting Out Culture* packaged free with i·cite, use ISBN-10: 0–312–48198–5 or ISBN-13: 978–0–312–48198–8.

ix visual exercises.   Do your students need help working with visuals in their writing? This ground-breaking CD-ROM allows students to analyze and manipulate the elements of visuals, giving them a more thorough under-standing of how visual rhetoric works. To order *Acting Out Culture* packaged free with ix, use ISBN-10: 0–312–48931–5 or ISBN-13: 978–0–321–48931–1.

i·claim, visualizing argument.   Do your students need help writing persuasively? Supporting their arguments? With six tutorials on the fundamental qualities good arguments share, this student-friendly CD-ROM also provides an illustrated glossary that defines 50 key terms from argument theory and classical rhetoric and includes a visual index providing access to more than 70 multimedia arguments. To order *Acting Out Culture* packed with i·claim, use ISBN-10: 0–312–48199–3 or ISBN-13: 978–0–312–48199–5.

ACKNOWLEDGMENTS

As befits its focus on "acting," this book owes its existence to the contributions of a truly ensemble cast. First, there are the friends and colleagues whose encouragement in the early stages helped keep this project alive when I had little (if any) idea about where it was going. To Alanya Harter, my first friend at Bedford, many thanks for steering this project my way in the first place and for sticking with me through months of initial dithering. Thanks as well to Leasa Burton whose early insights and guidance helped get this project off the ground, as well as to Joan Feinberg, Denise Wydra, Karen Henry, and Steve Scipione, whose combined wealth of experience and ideas added immeasurable depth and purpose to the book.

To Andrew Hansen and David Zimmerman, my gratitude for allowing themselves to be my sounding board; their feedback about what students might truly want from a book like this — and what they wouldn't — proved invaluable. In the same vein, I want to express my appreciation to the many reviewers whose insight helped shape this book throughout its many, at times seemingly endless, stages of development: Amy Braziller, Red Rocks Community College; Liz Canfield, Virginia Commonwealth University; Cherie Post Dargan, Hawkeye Community College; Daniel L. DeSanto, (formerly) University of Vermont; Danielle Nicole DeVoss, Michigan State University; Stephanie L. Dowdle, Salt Lake Community College; Robert Dunne, Central Connecticut State University; Heather Eaton, Daytona Beach Community College; Richard Fine, Virginia Commonwealth University; Thomas A. Hamill, Wilkes University; Amy Hawkins, Columbia College, Chicago; Kristina Heiks, Appalachian State University; Tom Henthorne, Pace University; Deborah Kirkman, University of Kentucky; Alison A. Knoblauch, University of New Hampshire; Fern Kupfer, Iowa State University; Matthew Marx, University of Nebraska at Omaha; Randall McClure, Minnesota State University; Geraldine R. McNenny, Chapman University; Terry Nienhuis, Western Carolina University; Jennifer Reich, University of Denver; Rhonda Schlatter, Mesa Community College; Scott Stevens, Western Washington University; Deborah Coxwell Teague, Florida State University; Danica Natalia Vukovic, George Mason University; Cynthia L. Walker, Faulkner University; Christopher Wilkey, Northern Kentucky University; and Lee Zickel, Cleveland State University.

Monumental thanks go out to my editor, Adam Whitehurst. Few collaborations in my professional experience have better warranted the term. Adam joined this project at a point when this book was little more than a loose collection of ideas and for well over a year did yeoman work to keep a rookie author on the right path. And of course, this book would have never made it past manuscript without the careful work of production editor Kerri Cardone and copyeditor Lisa Wehrle as well as the work of Elizabeth Schaaf and Rosemary Jaffe. And there'd be very little in it without Sandy

Schecter and Fred Courtright to hammer out the text permissions and without Martha Friedman and Martha Shethar applying the expert research skills to the visuals.

Also, my thanks to all the lovely people at EVP Coffee in Madison, whose strong brew and good company made for the most congenial work environment I could have imagined. And finally, to Emily Hall, whose contributions to this project were at once subtle, ongoing, and I am sure, vastly underappreciated. From sharing her own thoughts about performance and role-playing to supplying an emergency fax machine, Emily not only kept me moving along at something more than my usual glacial speed, she also offered a daily reminder of what made sticking with a project like this worthwhile to begin with. My love and thanks.

Contents

3 How We Eat   167

CONTENTS

Introduction for Students

THESE ARE THE RULES

Why do you act differently at a job interview than on a night out with friends? Why do we so rarely see people wearing their pajamas to church? What accounts for the fact that you're far more likely to be on a first-name basis with a classmate than with a professor? Why does your Thanksgiving dinner conversation with a grandparent sound so different from your e-mail exchanges with friends? Whether sitting in class or working an off-campus job, chatting with family on the phone or meeting a roommate for coffee, it's hardly a secret that different situations require different standards of behavior. And while this may seem like a fairly obvious observation, it is also an important one because it raises other questions whose answers aren't nearly as simple or straightforward. Namely, why do we accept *these* standards instead of others? Why do we regard only certain ways of acting, talking, and dressing as acceptable, appropriate, *normal?* Who, or what, teaches us to be normal?

This book invites you to look at and think more deeply about the countless rules that operate in our world: where they come from, how they shape our individual actions and attitudes, and whether ultimately they can be questioned, challenged, or even rewritten. From the shopping mall to the classroom, from the jobs we hold to the parties we attend, from family holidays to first dates, our world abounds with an almost endless array of instructions: different collections of "dos" and "don'ts" that, while generally unspoken, nonetheless play a formative role in influencing how we act. This book asks you to consider writing about the world around you by asking yourself a series of questions:

- *What* is it that producers of popular culture want me to do?

- *How* do they use our common cultural beliefs, identities, or fears to persuade me to do it?

- How do I *really* want to do it?

Unlike other books that focus on popular culture, this book asks you to begin by examining the ordinary details of our daily lives. Rather than exploring the texts and products of pop culture in isolation, you will be asked to uncover and make sense of the complex connections between this material and your personal actions. It is the goal of this book to direct your attention not just to what our popular culture *says* but to what it asks us to *do* as well. You probably already know quite a bit about some of the ways that popular culture attempts to influence you. For example, you already have a working understanding of what mass media has as its primary goals: ads exist to sell you products, political commentary wants you to vote a certain way, and TV producers want you to watch their programs. But deciding for yourself which pitches to tune in and which to tune out means looking deeper, beyond *what's* being sold to us to *how* it's being sold. How do writers, advertisers, politicians, and activists use our common cultural ideas about normality to influence the ways we believe and behave?

NORMS, SCRIPTS, ROLES, RULES: ANALYZING POPULAR CULTURE

Although you are surrounded by the messages of popular culture every day, the act of talking and writing about it can seem a little foreign. How do we talk about something we all experience, but none of us experience the same way? Because this analysis of popular culture emphasizes how it influences us to "act," this book invites you take up your investigation of culture by using a set of terms borrowed from the theatre as well as cultural studies. What happens, we ask, when we begin looking at our daily actions and choices as if they were highly choreographed *performances?* When we begin thinking about the rules that define the different settings in our world not just as instructions per se, but as *scripts* to be followed? When we start redefining our own individual behavior as *roles* we have been assigned to play? What do we gain, in sum, by thinking about our world as a kind of *stage* on which we are encouraged to *act out* parts written for us in advance?

To get a handle on what this work actually looks like, let's turn to one of those typical or everyday situations we might use as a case study. Imagine for a moment you're sitting in a college composition classroom on the first day of the semester. If we wanted to attempt the kind of analysis of our lives as performances described above, we might begin by itemizing all of the different **rules** that, while often not spelled out explicitly, nonetheless govern within this particular environment: sit attentively, listen to the instructor, write down all the information we are told is especially important, agree to complete the readings, compose the essays, hand in other assignments on firm due dates. Likewise, there are an equal number of rules that set the standard for how we may and

> **Rule:**
>
> **A spoken or unspoken directive for how people should or should not act in a given situation.**

may not talk: no interruptions or random interjections; respond on point when questioned by the instructor; speak in a measured tone of voice and make sure to use a formal, more academic vocabulary than you might elsewhere; restrict your conversation to topics and issues that fit the course themes.

Rather than conclude our investigation here, however, we would next delve more deeply into these rules in search of what ideas they invite us to accept as **norms**, or widely held cultural ideas about what is proper thinking or behavior in a given situation. For example, we might focus on the rules around student speech in order to figure out the more fundamental messages they simultaneously convey, such as "real" learning happens only when power is shared unequally within the classroom or "quality" education requires that instructors lead and students follow. In a similar vein, we could view the rule establishing formal standards for classroom discussion as an effort to impose a value system on different types of talk: one that defines so-called personal stories as being less legitimate than more abstract forms of argumentation. When figuring out what the norms are for a given situation, it is often helpful to think about what they *aren't*. In this case, you might ask yourself what you'd think about a classmate who constantly interrupted others or an instructor who told you you'd be graded solely on your penmanship.

Norm:

A widely-held cultural belief about what is appropriate in a given situation.

Conducting this kind of analysis sets us up nicely for the next step in a performative approach: one that involves defining these classroom rules as **social scripts**, the ways that following the rules and accepting the norms require us to behave. Building on the connection uncovered between rules and norms, following a social script in the classroom would be performing a task like reading the assigned selections in this book — both because the rules require it and the norms tell you that reading the assigned selections will help you in your quest for education. Doing this would then allow us to move to the final phase of this analysis: thinking of one's actions and choices within the classroom as if you are performing a **role**: that is, "acting out" a social script for a given situation as part of your relationship to the larger culture. In this class, for example, your role as student means that you will most likely perform the social script of participating in class because the norms tell you that education is valuable and rules of the course require your participation. The relationship between these four terms can be applied to an analysis of any topic in this book, and the more you practice them in your writing, the more second-nature this analysis will become.

Social script:

a set of behavioral instructions reinforced by norms and rules.

Role:

How people act in relation to their standing or environment.

EXERCISE:

Think of two or three roles you are often required to play in your life (for example, student, sibling, friend, consumer) and write a paragraph for each in which you describe the scripts you follow as a part of performing these roles. What norms and rules do you think influence how effectively you play these roles?

The World in Words

So, what can we gain by reading about all these rules and norms that we are powerless to change? If we're all cogs in the pop culture machine, what can we gain from learning just how powerless we are? One of the primary goals of this book is to show that we are, in fact, anything *but* helpless. The ways we think about and respond to popular culture are constantly changing, and these changes are often brought about by one common act: questioning the norm through writing. To see examples of how writing helps us question and rewrite what is or should be the norm, you need look no further than the selections in this book. Only by reading and writing about the world we live in can we understand it and learn to navigate it on our own terms.

The selections in this book are designed to challenge the ways many of us think about a wide range of current topics. What they're *not* designed to do is to inspire you to agree with everything their authors say. Each of the authors in this book is using writing as a way to explore, influence, or protest against different aspects of our larger culture. By responding to their ideas with your own writing, you are entering a larger dialogue in which you begin to defend and define your place as part of that culture.

As you read the selections, you may find it helpful to approach each one with a set of questions in mind to assist you in positioning your own opinion.

- **Question the Author:** Who is this author? What is her level of expertise about this topic? What else has she written? Is she an academic, a journalist, an activist, a politician? How do those roles influence the way she communicates her opinions?

- **Question the Audience:** What prompted the author to write this piece? Who is this piece aimed at? What examples in the language or tone tell me about that?

- **Question the Rules:** What rules, norms, or scripts is this author writing about? Is he writing in support of them or in opposition?

- **Question the Argument:** What are the main points of this piece? How does the author support his point of view? Are his examples scientific, derived from interviews, or part of his own experience? What are the possible counterarguments? How does the author anticipate and refute them?

- **Question Yourself:** How do I react to this piece? Does it support or go against my own experience and exposure to this topic?

READING VISUALS

More and more frequently, the messages we receive about popular culture come in visual form. News photos, cartoons, films, and advertisements are composed in much the same way that text is. Subjects are carefully considered and captured in a visual medium in order to communicate a message. With visual art like film or painting, many of these messages are on the surface and can be seen plainly. However, certain images, like advertisements, are often composed for a purpose in which the message is sometimes deeply embedded, even secondary. For example, take a look at this ad for make-up:

You've probably seen similar ads in magazines before. But how do you go about *reading* the visual messages of an ad as typical as this? Here are a few categories you might consider when analyzing a visual message:

- **Layout:** Think about the different elements of the ad. Here, there is only one figure, a model in close-up. Visually, how does focusing on the model's face help you understand the message of this ad?

- **Audience:** Who is the target audience of this ad? The model in the ad is made up to look like screen icon Audrey Hepburn. Who is likely to see and respond to this resemblance? How does invoking the image of Audrey Hepburn appeal to this audience?

- **Purpose:** Obviously, this is an advertisement, and advertisements are designed to sell products. Can you imagine using this image for another purpose? What would be your response if, instead of in a magazine, you saw this in a museum? How would your reaction be different?

- **Text:** The headline of this ad says, "Inside every woman is a star," and at the bottom of the ad, the text says, "Celebrate glamour. Celebrate 50 years of star-making make-up." How does the addition of text clarify the composition of this image? Without the text, would it be as effective?

- **Message(s):** Of course, as an ad, this image is designed to sell you make-up. But how does it do that? How does the message use some common attitudes about wanting to look like celebrities to convince us to use Max Factor make-up? What do the advertisers gain from associating celebrity with cosmetics?

Most of the images in this book can be read independently, or as part of a series. Just like with texts, considering images side by side can show you a larger picture about how our culture depicts as normal any action or belief. Imagine if you were to look at this cosmetics ad, which tells us that using make-up will make any normal woman look like a celebrity, side by side with an image of a celebrity being made up by a team of professionals. If you consider both images as a set, one that examines the topic of beauty, how would looking at the second image influence how you read the first?

MAKING YOURSELF HEARD

The bulk of this book consists of readings from a range of writers who've accepted the job of analyzing the rules we live by. You will be familiar with many of these topics, but some may be new to you. Whether you've had any exposure to these topics or not, each selection is organized into chapters that examine the issues as part of roles we all play: believers, watchers, eaters, workers, fighters, learners, and talkers. The writing assignments in this book will ask you to take what you know about these topics and consider it side by side with these authors so that you can ultimately decide for yourself how *you* want to play life's roles.

Why should we ultimately care about analyzing popular culture? Consider this: In January 2007, Senators Hillary Rodham Clinton and Barack Obama both announced that they would seek the Democratic nomination for president of the United States. But rather than call a press conference, both politicians did something unprecedented. They posted videos on the Internet. Whereas sites like YouTube and MySpace were once designed for killing time watching clips of strangers' home movies or making new friends across the globe, the power of popular culture has forced contenders for the biggest job in the United States to use the methods of dissemination perfected by popular culture to spread very serious promises about the future of America itself. By writing about popular culture, you become a part of the fabric of cultural conversation. This book will ask you to analyze and write about the world around you, but more importantly, it will ask you to use that analysis to make a decision about how to rewrite the world on your own terms. You're not only about to read the writing of people who have used words as a way to navigate through thousands of competing media messages. You're about to become one of them.

Acting Out Culture

Reading and Writing

1 How We BELIEVE

Introduction

BELIEVING IN "BELIEF"

Imagine yourself as the central actor in the following scenarios:

- First-time voter contemplating the choice for president in this year's election
- Pacifist member of the National Guard summoned to active duty in Iraq
- Graduating senior considering employment offers from both the Peace Corps and Goldman Sachs
- Juror weighing evidence of corporate fraud in the Enron trial
- Student in a college physics class who has happened onto the answers to an upcoming midterm exam
- Shopper deciding whether to spend rent money on a new outfit
- Pedestrian on a city street approached by a homeless person asking for money
- Journalist ordered by a judge to divulge a confidential news source

Although these examples touch on different issues, they are alike in one crucial way: Each situation requires you to make a value judgment, to choose between what matters more and what matters less. In other words, each choice hinges on *what you believe.*

The concept of belief turns our attention to what lies *underneath* the choices we make: to the embedded, unspoken, and often subconscious assumptions that make these choices feel natural or normal. It's easy for most of us, given a set of circumstances, to say *what* we believe. But how often do any of us stop to think about *how* we came to hold the beliefs we take for granted? When we really stop to think about it, *how* do we make up our minds about what are the right and wrong things to do? Who or what teaches us to draw these kinds of distinctions? And how do these lessons come to feel so natural to us? Beliefs are not hypotheses. Grounded as they are in faith, in our intuitive or instinctive conviction that something is so, they require no recourse to empirical proof, factual data, or concrete evidence in order to stand in our minds as truth. Indeed, it might be said that belief encompasses all the things in our lives we're convinced are true simply because they *feel* right.

Of course, this is also what makes explaining or defending our beliefs such a tricky matter. If ultimately we can't prove the validity of our beliefs, then how can we ever hope to make others understand, accept, or share them? This dilemma — which in many ways seems hardwired into the very concept of belief — explains in part why our society is marked by so many disputes and controversies over what is and is not proper for us to believe. If beliefs are not hypotheses that can be proved but rather convictions that are "right" because they feel so to their believers, how can different members of society ever establish common ground?

Although it is often assumed that belief applies only to questions of religion, it lies at the heart of some of our most urgent and intractable debates: from gay marriage to abortion to the war in Iraq. Belief also underlies countless decisions we confront every day in our personal lives: from how (or even whether) we vote to where we shop, from the work we perform to the money we earn, from the movies and television we watch, the books and magazines we read to the clothes we wear. Whatever the individual focus or context, belief always boils down to the same basic questions: What are the ideas and values we feel most committed to? Which ones end up just feeling right?

If we are not born already hardwired with ingrained assumptions about what is and is not right, then how did it happen that our beliefs feel like second nature to us now? By what process did we learn to regard only certain viewpoints and values as articles of faith?

Everybody Knows That . . .

PERSONAL BELIEFS, CULTURAL NORMS, AND SCRIPTING BELIEF

To pose questions like these is to begin connecting belief to the broader question of social *norms*. Stated differently: it is to wonder about the ways our own assumptions about right and wrong intersect with — perhaps even derive from — the standards and instructions mapped by our larger culture.

Indeed, such questions might even prompt us to rethink the idea of *personal* belief altogether. To be sure, we are far more used to thinking of our personal beliefs as things that belong exclusively to ourselves: those values, ethics, and priorities that, in the final analysis, remain beyond the influence of our larger culture. This definition is an attractive one because it not

Everybody Knows That . . .

❝One World, One Dream❞

— *Slogan for the 2008 Olympic Games in Beijing, China*

only reaffirms our faith in our individuality but also seems to confirm our irreducible *agency*: our ability to control and determine the choices we make. But this conceit misrepresents our fundamental relationship to the larger culture around us. Far from being tangential or irrelevant, our culture plays a central role in shaping what we come to believe, suggesting that the values we consider to be our own private domain do not belong to us alone.

We do, after all, live in a world that promotes very specific messages about what is right and what is wrong, a world in which countless instructions get issued telling us what we should and should not care about. From the Patriot Act to the Home Shopping Network, from *Cosmopolitan* magazine to the *New York Times* business section, our cultural landscape is littered with sources that tell us, often in very authoritative tones, which things truly matter

5

Everybody Knows That . . .

"I believe in . . . an America that lives by a Constitution that inspires freedom and democracy around the world. An America with a big, open, charitable heart that reaches out to people in need around the world. . . . An America that is still the beacon of light to the darkest corner of the world."

> — *Colin Powell, "The America I Believe In"*
> *from the National Public Radio*
> *series* **This I Believe**

and which things do not. To compile even so cursory a list as this is to shift the terms of our conversation from individual or personal *choice* to cultural and social *power*; to confront the possibility that our own distinctions and value judgments are better understood as *scripts* we are encouraged, even enjoined, to follow. In attempting to make sense of all this, our goal is less to "pick sides," to vote up or down on the validity of a given belief, than to better understand how beliefs take shape in the first place, how certain ideas come to acquire this special status as unexamined and cherished norms. Stated a bit more abstractly, our job is to assess the process of *legitimation*: the operations through which only select ideas and actions come to be promoted as the proper role models for the rest of us.

"PLEDGING ALLEGIANCE:" ACTING ON AND ACTING OUT OUR COMMITMENTS

An example from our everyday life will clarify the kind of work this involves, as well as the implications for us in undertaking it. Virtually all of us are familiar with reciting the Pledge of Allegiance. The Pledge offers an especially useful case study because it underscores how intimately connected belief is to issues of social scripts and role-playing. From the reverential pose we are supposed to maintain toward the flag, to the obligatory "hand-over-the-heart" gesture, to the language itself through which we express our "allegiance," the rules by which this ritual is defined couldn't be more detailed. One way to better apprehend the values underlying this performance is to ask what kind of objectives stand behind this kind of mandatory performance. Why have schoolchildren been required to recite the Pledge as a daily part of their scholastic lives? This line of inquiry leads us to wonder next about the particular assumptions this ritual reinforces — assumptions defining what our proper duties to the nation are supposed to be or the role that such patriotic expressions are supposed to play in our educational system. Building on this, we then consider the implications of endorsing these assumptions. We ponder, for instance, what it means for children to memorize and recite the loyalty oath at the center of the Pledge. What would be different if the words of the

Everybody Knows That . . .

"I pledge allegiance to the Flag of the United States of America, and to the Republic for which it stands: one Nation under God, indivisible, with Liberty and Justice for all."

Pledge were different, if students were allowed to recite the oath silently or even to opt out from it altogether? Finally, we ask where else in our culture we are presented with opportunities to demonstrate our "allegiance" to the nation.

It is precisely this kind of work that each of the selections included in this chapter invites us to conduct. Referencing a wide range of contemporary issues — from patriotism to consumerism, stereotypes about gender and the body to the idealization of science and technology — this collection shows how complex and overlapping the connection between personal beliefs and social scripts can be. Sarah E. Igo starts us off with a discussion of how the popularity of surveying American beliefs in the early twentieth century came to influence what we actually believe today. James Twitchell offers an impassioned and surprising defense of consumerism as both an individual and a social ideal. Defending shopping both as a quintessentially American undertaking and a laudable personal undertaking, his essay seeks to resuscitate our faith in materialism as a legitimate belief system. Modeling a very different viewpoint, Ian Frazier also focuses on our cultural penchant for shopping. In this case, however, he does so in order to dismantle some of our most entrenched conceits about consumerism and patriotism, questioning the (often unspoken) equation between shopping and citizenship that our culture so often proposes. Moving from the political to the scientific arena, Rebecca Saxe mounts her own investigation into entrenched belief, questioning our long-standing faith in the supposedly limitless powers of scientific "expertise" to resolve every societal problem. Pursuing her own investigation of science within a racial context, Debra Dickerson offers a similarly compelling challenge to our assumptions about scientific knowledge. Chronicling the long history of scientific racism in America, she wonders aloud about the implications of accepting any such findings about race at face value. David Brooks, on the other hand, works to reframe our current racial thinking from a different vantage, challenging what he claims is our unthinking embrace of "diversity" as a social ideal. Catherine Newman, meanwhile, redirects our attention from race to gender, training a similarly jaundiced eye on the clichés and assumptions that conventionally define marriage. Recounting her own decision to eschew the traditional rituals and rewards of the "wedding ceremony," she offers a strikingly different way to think not only about marriage per se, but also about the social and emotional consequences of taking up this particular social script.

"EVERYBODY KNOWS THAT" EXERCISE

Choose one of the images or quotations featured in the margins on the previous pages and answer the following questions:

1. What does this image or quotation ask you to believe?

2. What are the particular ideas/values/attitudes it invites us to accept as *normal*?

3. What would it feel like to act upon or act out these norms in our personal lives?

Rule Maker > > > > > > > > Rule Breaker

❝ 2006 Holiday Fun Facts
This year, most malls will begin decorating for the holidays on . . . November 1
The percentage of malls that include décor for Christmas . . . 95 percent
The percentage of malls that include décor for Hanukkah . . . 7.2 percent
The percentage of malls that include décor for Kwanza . . . 1.2 percent
100 percent of malls have extended holiday hours, on average, they begin on . . . November 24, Day after Thanksgiving
— INTERNATIONAL COUNCIL OF SHOPPING CENTERS, INC. (ICSC)

❝ Dreading the holiday season? The frantic rush and stress? The to-do lists and sales hype? The spiritless hours trapped in malls? This year, why not gather together your loved ones and decide to do things differently? With the simplest of plans you can create a new rhythm, purpose, and meaning for the holidays. Why not try a Buy Nothing Christmas? If that's too extreme for grandma and the kids, maybe try a Buy Less Christmas. Or a Buy Fairer Christmas. Or a Slow-Down Christmas. Whatever you decide, 'tis the season to reclaim our celebration from the grip of commercial forces."
— BUY NOTHING CHRISTMAS HOMEPAGE, ADBUSTERS.ORG, 2006

It seems like every holiday season brings a fresh batch of criticism about the pairing of commercialism and seasonal or religious festivities. Many of us gripe about overcommercialization at the same moment a store clerk is swiping our credit card. Television news reports on decreases in holiday sales and then airs stories on the amount of personal debt the holidays bring. And then it cuts to commercial, offering the audience a fresh onslaught of ads urging them to finish their holiday shopping. It could almost be said that holiday shopping is as much a part of our beliefs as the holidays we're shopping for. However, the two quotes above underscore how contested a belief system consumerism actually is. As these examples make clear, we don't all work through these messages in exactly the same way.

In the first quotation, the International Council of Shopping Centers presents some of its "Fun Facts" about holiday shopping (you can find more at http://holiday.icsc.org). What do these quotes tell you about how closely our American "belief" in shopping is tied to our larger religious beliefs? What are the attitudes about shopping that these facts take for granted? What do these facts tell you about holiday shopping as a cultural phenomenon? Compare this quotation to the second, from Adbuster's "Buy Nothing Christmas" initiative, in which we are encouraged to ignore advertisers' calls to buy, buy, buy. How is this second quotation critical of the ideas expressed in the first? How is it critical of us and our roles as holiday shoppers?

FIND THE RULES: Make a list of the different attitudes about consumerism that each of these quotations is expressing. Then write a paragraph for each one that examines how it "sells" its point of view. What does each quotation say, and how does it say it, in order to appeal to its intended audience?

MAKE YOUR OWN RULES: Write a brief essay in which you analyze your own opinions about holiday shopping. Which of the two perspectives in this feature strikes you as most appealing? Why?

Buy Nothing Christmas
RETHINK THE SEASON
ADBUSTERS MEDIA FOUNDATION <www.adbusters.org>

SARAH E. IGO

"Statistical Citizens"

Surveys, Citizens, and the Making of a Mass Public

Why do Americans so eagerly answer surveys and respond to opinion polls? What explains our enthusiasm for statistical data that purports to document public attitudes and national trends? Whether it concerns voting preferences or shopping habits, it seems as if we have become obsessed with defining ourselves against the statistical "average." Trying to make sense of this curious phenomenon, Sarah E. Igo explores the ways in which Americans' personal behavior and private beliefs have been influenced, perhaps even scripted, by surveys, tests, and polls by examining the rise in popularity of polling that began with the study of social norms in Muncie, Indiana ("Middletown") by Robert and Helen Lynd and continued with Alfred Kinsey's controversial findings on sexual norms. Igo is an assistant professor of history at the University of Pennsylvania. She received her undergraduate degree from Harvard University and her PhD from Princeton in 2001. In 2006–2007 she was a visiting fellow at the Whitney Humanities Center at Yale University, and she has also received fellowships from the Institute for Advanced Study and the Mellon Foundation. Her book, *The Averaged American: Surveys, Citizens, and the Making of a Mass Public* (2006), examines the relationship between statistical indexes and modern views of the self. She is currently working on a cultural history of privacy.

A SOCIETY SATURATED BY FACTS ABOUT ITS MEMBERS — "KNOW-able" through the aggregated answers to surveys — was a curious one, and one first imaginable in the twentieth century. Modern surveys were built out of private information told to a stranger. Yet they permitted citizens to know what their metaphorical, if not their actual, neighbors were thinking and doing. More oddly still, they permitted some individuals a flicker of recognition or communion with statistics displayed in charts and graphs — even when they themselves had been excluded from the making of those numbers. The kind of public created by the dissemination of such knowledge about itself was at once highly intrusive and completely anonymous, self-scrutinizing and other-directed, familiar and impersonal. In a word, it was the backdrop for some of the peculiar tensions of life in a "mass" society: between being "oneself" and being known as a member of a group, between being an individual and being a statistic.

In the concrete techniques of the questionnaire and the interview, in public debates over survey findings, and in encounters between researchers and the researched, a new mode of knowing "ourselves" took shape in the twentieth-century United States. Robert Lynd understood in 1939 that "the characteristics of American culture" and the "current focus and methods in social science research" were intertwined. But we have not yet reckoned with the work polls and statistics performed in constituting that culture: Americans' sense of what their society is and how they belong to it. . . . [M]odern survey methods helped to forge a mass public. They also shaped the selves who would inhabit it, influencing everything from beliefs about morality and individuality to visions of democracy and the nation. Social scientific representations underwrote entities as abstract as "the typical American" and as intimate as an individual's self-understanding. Concepts as resonant as "mainstream culture," "public opinion," and "normal sexuality" were brought into being, at least in part, by surveyors and their toolkit of empirical techniques. That such constructs gained new social reality — for surveyors and laypeople alike — attests to the powerful effects of an aggregated America. They offer a partial explanation for the official, if not actual, cohesion of "the American public" in the middle decades of the century.[1]

As such, social scientific ways of ordering the world fed an anxious dialogue about mass society. The impersonal techniques of survey production privileged the national over the local, the aggregate over the individual, the average over the unique. Moreover, a sociologist's 1953 definition of the "mass" — it was heterogeneous, "composed of individuals who do not know each other," made up of "spatially separated" people, and without any organized leadership — described quite precisely the public created by midcentury social surveyors. Robert and Helen Lynd's subjects, after all, had been an actual community of neighbors before they were transformed into archetypical Americans. But George Gallup and Elmo Roper forged a purely statistical public from groups of randomly selected strangers. This shifting concept of community provoked worries about U.S. culture and society: over the bandwagon effect and "statistical morality." Such concerns about the "mass" are compelling proof of its recognition by, and visibility to, contemporaries.[2]

The questions surveyors posed — not the specific ones about cereal brands or sexual habits, but the underlying ones, such as Who can stand for America? Where is the majority? How do "we" behave? — were weighty. By asking them, community studiers as well as opinion pollsters helped to define who was part of the nation and the normal and who was relegated to the fringes or extremes. It is not coincidental, then, that the issues that most distressed the surveyors' critics — representation and influence — were political in nature. Americans who wrote to Gallup and Roper to complain about their lack of inclusion in the polls, or who deplored

> **Opinion pollsters helped to define who was part of the nation and the normal.**

Alfred Kinsey's influence on mores, understood the cultural weight of social data. Facts that appeared to be merely empirical were always also freighted with the moral and the evaluative. What is clear in listening to the anger, skepticism, and relief of those ordinary citizens who wrestled with survey findings is that their understandings of themselves as members of a mass public flowed from such knowledge as well as from the techniques that produced it.

What surveyors aimed to do and what their facts *did* once they moved into radio broadcasts, newspaper reports, and common knowledge were not always or even usually congruent. Adopting the stance of the anthropologist to critique dominant trends in contemporary culture, Robert and Helen Lynd in fact fashioned a powerful marker of the "typical." George Gallup and Elmo Roper employed scientific sampling to better hear the voice of the "man in the street" but instead created an averaged-out and abstracted public opinion that severed attitudes from their source. Alfred Kinsey sought to uncover how ordinary Americans actually behaved in their sexual lives so as to liberate them from social conventions, but one of the key consequences of his *Sexual Behavior* studies, and the national discussion surrounding them, was the public shaping of "normal" private selves. Surveys may have transformed American culture; but Americans always also transformed the surveys.

There were plenty of citizens who refused to accept social scientific ways of knowing, of course, such as one of Kinsey's anonymous correspondents who mocked the scientific classification of human experience by signing his or her letter "Case #45697234 1/2, Age 23, no premarital sex, Catholic," as if the writer defied being summed up by these standard pieces of information. Or another who simply wrote, "I do not fit in any of you're catagories [sic] and pray to God I never will." But the distinctive characteristic of modern social surveying was the junction it created between knowledge and norms, permitting data points and percentages to penetrate individuals' lives in meaningful ways. Across the twentieth century, *Middletown's* readers and even Muncie residents were learning to trust distant experts rather than their own perceptions of contemporary life, believing that "outside" assessments of the culture could best reveal it. Pollsters' multiple audiences were growing dependent, no matter how warily, on the kind of information opinion research proffered. All but Kinsey's fiercest critics ultimately accepted sex as a legitimate subject for surveyors, some importing his statistics into their very definitions of themselves. Americans, that is, were coming to objectify modern culture, to envision the public through the prism of majorities and minorities, and to find themselves in social scientific aggregates.[3]

Indeed, ordinary citizens' vigorous challenges to particular findings and the techniques used to reach them may have revealed their understanding of the power of the new surveys, or at least their sense that important questions would be determined by them. Individuals' bids for inclusion in the very statistics they distrusted and even condemned suggests that disagreement blended easily with accommodation to social surveying practices. The best evidence that the public was being remade by scientific surveys can be found in the sometimes reluctant, sometimes eager, embrace of their tools and vocabulary by a broad array of citizens. If many Middletowners resented being under the gaze of the Lynds in the mid-1920s, other Americans complained bitterly about being overlooked by Gallup and Roper in the following decades, and Kinsey had to turn away scores of volunteers who hoped to be interviewed for his Reports in the 1940s and 1950s. Becoming a statistic represented by midcentury a uniquely modern way of being.

Survey technologies never worked simply to normalize their subjects in the service of a consensus society, however. This would not account for their widespread appeal. Surveys could also encourage and give new weight, through numbers, to nonnormative habits, beliefs, and identities. Social statistics, highlighting both inclusion and exclusion, prompted some to imagine themselves into new collectives or to forge a minority consciousness. Kinsey's statistics, for example, would be a resource for the gay rights movement, preparing the ground for one form of modern "identity politics." The seemingly private and atomized act of divulging personal information to a surveyor, in other words, could have significant political effects. In such ways, social scientific data created novel possibilities for community and self-assertion even as they placed new constraints on self-fashioning. If this constituted a mass society, it was different from any we have known before, encouraging new links between strangers even as it eroded older bonds of family, religion, and locale.[4]

Social data . . . played a critical role in the cultural life of the midcentury United States. Surveyors' bold accounts of the "typical," "average," and "normal" ensured that statistics were at the very heart of major public controversies. But modern surveys were moving targets, much like the society they both reflected and defined. For all their homogenizing tendencies, they did permit challenge and revision. If the United States could be represented by a community of native-born whites in the late 1920s, it was also known through pollsters' aggregate majorities and minorities in the 1930s and 1940s and the Kinsey Reports' variegated normal in the postwar years.

The particular mass public of fifty years ago — characterized by an iconic Americanism, a majoritarian emphasis, and a fixation on the normal — does not exist in quite the same way today. Numbers can present conformity, but they can also project strife. Beginning in the mid-1960s, surveyors, influenced by new social movements, more

Numbers can present conformity, but they can also project strife.

emphatically called attention to the nation's fractures than had their predecessors. Just as a popular audience had developed for studies of "typical" American life several decades earlier, a new market composed of policy-makers but also lay readers would emerge for inquiries such as Michael Harrington's *The Other America* of 1963, the Moynihan Report of 1965, and the Kerner Commission Report of 1968 — studies that, like their nineteenth-century predecessors emphasized class stratification and cultural and racial differences. The significant departure here was the later studies' pessimistic conclusions about the deep and perhaps unbridgeable divides among various groups of Americans. Social investigations into diversity and conflict had never waned since the height of the Chicago School, but general audiences for them had. The fact that in the 1960s volumes on race and poverty attracted more national attention than studies of the "mainstream" indicated that something substantial in the relationship between Americans and their surveyors was changing.

Indeed, after a decade that witnessed the "discovery" of poverty, major civil rights mobilizations, and then Black, Red, Gray, and Gay Power, it would be difficult to speak credibly, either politically or scientifically, of a unitary America. Those taking the measure of nation in the 1960s and beyond sought to explain the United States less as a singular bundle of beliefs or an easily calculated center point than as a contending set of publics. Investigators wrote about "two societies, one black, one white." Pollsters recalibrated their strong majoritarian frame, detecting new significance in how men and women, young and old, Latinos and Asian Americans assessed presidents and purchases differently. Marketers, convinced that niches and "complexity" were becoming more relevant than the broad sweep, talked of "nine American lifestyles," inventing new psychographic categories of citizens such as "survivors," "belongers," and "emulators." Others mapped new "regional-culture" areas — "MexAmerica" in the Southwest and "Ecotopia" in the Pacific Northwest — onto the old singular nation.[5]

In the years following the Kinsey Reports, social scientific attention to diversity and variety would explode. The population, it seemed, could be fissured into ever smaller and more specific fragments for reasons of profit as well as politics. Market researchers were once again in the vanguard, discovering that their object was not anything so vague as "the public," but women between the ages of eighteen and forty-nine, or still more focused demographic groupings. Using methods of "narrowcasting" and "microtargeting," they searched as fervently for the niche as earlier surveyors had sought the mass. One of the "best business books of 1988," Michael Weiss's *The Clustering of America,* employed a technique called cluster analysis to distill forty distinct "neighborhood types" in the United States. What is more, he found this sort of national segmentation to be accelerating. When Weiss looked again at the purchasing habits as well as the "demographics, intellect, taste, and outlook" of different U.S. "consumption communities" in 2000, he no longer saw forty "lifestyle types" but sixty-two "modern tribes" (Rustic Elders, Young Literati, Greenbelt Families, and Grey Collars, to name a few) — a neatly summarized 55 percent increase in social differentiation in twelve short years. "For a nation that's always valued community," he intoned, "this breakup of the mass market into balkanized segments is as momentous as the collapse of Communism." Weiss surely overstated the case. Subdivision of this kind was the outgrowth of the ways minorities and majorities, but also more defined communities, were being stitched together statistically in the age of Gallup and Kinsey. In any case, it is worth asking: Had techniques like cluster analysis, enabled by powerful hard drives and updated marketing theories, turned up a newly diverse America? Or did they instead reveal a multiplicity that had always been there but was shielded from view by the assumptions and technological limitations of earlier surveyors? Or was there yet another explanation: that the confluence of new cultural currents and new social scientific techniques to elaborate them had *created* the new "tribes" and "lifestyles"?[6]

As surveyors' descriptions of new kinds of citizens — and a new sort of society — suggest, post-1960s developments may have made the search for the "typical American" and a singular public more problematic, but this did not mean that survey techniques lost their cultural force. On the contrary, the arrival of widespread focus group and personality testing allowed ever-more intricate methods of measuring citizens' preferences and selves to take root. Oddly enough, as with marketers' cluster analysis, this move away from a national "mass" returned surveyors to a world of face-to-face contacts and a form of data gathering that was more like the Lynds' than Gallup's, in their search for detailed, qualitative, and embedded knowledge about individuals. This move from the mass to the niche, in market and social research, underscored the flexibility of survey instruments, which both responded to and amplified the cultural sea change.

Significantly, new survey technologies, such as the popular Minnesota Multiphasic Personality Inventory, came with a more pronounced individualist rhetoric and psychological flavor. The Myers-Briggs Type Indicator, for example, developed in 1943 but not published until 1962 and not widely distributed until 1975, offered sixteen categories — through the matched pairs of Thinking-Feeling, Perceiving-Judging, Extraversion-Introversion, Sensation-Intuition — for Americans to slot themselves into. This was perhaps the logical path from the Kinsey Reports, which in one fell swoop did away with the normal curve *and* reassured individuals

15

that they were normal. The Myers-Briggs, among the most frequently administered, and self-administered, tests today, was certainly a testament to the grip of popular psychology on Americans and their employers in the late twentieth century. But its appeal to consumers was also a reaction to the standardizing, indeed massifying, tendencies of modernist social science.[7]

Writing in 1979 and looking out upon a landscape pervaded by self-help literature running the gamut from "personal growth" to "creative divorce," two observers argued that the "applied behavioral and social sciences . . . have assumed an unprecedented role in what might be termed the 'consciousness industry,'" a broad constellation of professional and institutional entities devoted to "changing some aspects of the lives or identities of their clients." This of course had been true since the earliest days of surveyors' interventions in the lives of the poor, the criminal, and the sexually deviant. What was new was that consumers now paid for scientific expertise, not in the service of social knowledge but in the hope of individual, intimate transformation. In this sense, the late twentieth century saw the deepest penetration yet of social survey tools into everyday conversation and self-categorization. Corporate managers, popular experts, media figures, and ordinary citizens speak in a social scientific language that has become virtually indistinguishable from American culture at large.[8]

Consumers now paid for scientific expertise.

Survey techniques of the late twentieth century were certainly more personal, more individualized, and more intrusive than Middletowners could have imagined. This did not necessarily mean that they were less reductive. Political researchers, for example, following marketers' lead, hunted for the hidden link, whether the car model or the gardening habit, that could predict an individual's likelihood to vote Democratic or Republican. For this they depended on correlations pulled from vast databanks, themselves culled from "state voter-registration rolls, census reports, consumer data-mining companies, and direct marketing vendors." This was a sort of aggregating that was also infinitely segmenting. In a parallel development, striving to solve once and for all Kinsey's problem of unreliable human subjects, market researchers invented techniques of "passive" rather than "active" measurement: innovations such as "portable people meters" that could record television watchers' viewing habits without having to depend on accurate reports from human beings about those same habits. Roper and Gallup had argued for the civic potential of their surveys on the ground of participation. But taking part in surveys is not what it used to be. Some investigators have begun to test the appeal of political platforms not by querying citizens about their opinions but by watching flashes of activity on subjects' MRI (magnetic resonance imaging) brain scans. The dawn of "neuromarketing" — whether of presidential candidates or soft drinks — to some seems, not (social) science fiction, but very close at hand.[9]

From the 1930s onward, Americans had not always liked being polled, but they did believe their own responses were critical to the project of a representative public. New developments in surveying the population suggest that in the future citizens might no longer be asked, at least not directly. Writes an expert on recent trends in commercial and security data-mining, the scope and depth of information gathering "took on dramatic new dimensions in the 1990s," as the Internet and high-powered computing were brought to bear on old questions about who was doing what, for the joint purposes of law enforcement and commercial gain. "Much of this," he notes, "took place out of the public's view, and largely without the public's direct consent."[10]

Faced with such profuse variety in the public — and in the instruments employed to take its pulse — the strand of midcentury social surveying that had gained traction from its claims to define the culture *in toto* found few toeholds. The few social scientists who continued to work in this vein, notably Robert Bellah in his *Habits of the Heart* and *The Good Society*, tended in fact to decry the lack of a coherent body of binding American values and habits. Others proclaimed that the public itself had vanished, subsumed by self-interest and private rather than civic engagements. Headline-grabbing studies of social trends convinced many that the nation had lost any sense of common commitment, that its inhabitants were isolated from one another and "bowling alone." As historian Wilfred McClay has noted, where social thinkers of the 1950s worried about the dangers of conformity, those of the 1970s and 1980s reversed course, their writings full of "concern for the nurturance of community and solidarity rather than individualism and autonomy."[11]

The mass public of the Gallup polls and the Kinsey Reports was born of a specific conjunction of cultural preoccupations and social scientific innovations. The same is true of the differentiated America found in survey research today. The recasting of "the public" into alternative publics, subcultures, and counterpublics is not un-problematic, however. Like older social scientific representations of the nation as a collection of typical whites or majority views, the new ways of picturing the population leave much out and congeal dynamic social processes. It remains difficult to find a public vocabulary that recognizes differences but also allows citizens to perceive the social or the whole in a complex fashion. Categorizations like "welfare queens," "angry white males," "soccer moms," and "security moms" demonstrate the allure of simplifications of the American public even as finer labels for subgroups are devised. These composites owe a debt to niche market thinking, but also to the inherently flattening tendencies of survey formats and terminology. The notion that the nation is fundamentally fractured into "red states" and "blue states" or that a clean 22 percent of the populace had turned to voting their "moral values" — as revealed by an exit poll — in the aftermath of the 2004 presidential election, are just the most obvious of these fictions. Misreadings of "the public" via the powerful conjunction of media narrative and quantified support seem just as likely in the twenty-first century as they had been in the twentieth.[12]

Amidst such talk of divisions and segments, some Americans began to look back nostalgically to the midcentury as a time of national unity and mass markets. In a series of works in the late 1990s and early 2000s, commentators bewailed not just the fraying of the citizenry, but the passing of the "greatest generation." Fantasies of a singular nation and culture — in part generated by older social surveys — continued to percolate, both in politicians' statements about "the American people" and in attempts to fashion icons representative of a multitudinous population. Publicizing the "new face of America" in 1993, *Time* magazine proposed that the future nation could be glimpsed in a computer-generated amalgam of the demographic average of the population, one slightly darker and less Anglo than the "typical" citizen of Middletown. Cultural theorist Lauren Berlant, noting that this image arrived on the heels of the widely reported finding that European Americans would soon be eclipsed as the statistical majority, wrote that it was "suffused with nostalgia for . . . a stable and dominant collective identity." A growing recognition of national disaggregation did not prevent, and could even promote, a desire for a unitary Americanness.[13]

> *Americans began to look back nostalgically to the midcentury as a time of national unity and mass markets.*

The hunt for the "Average American" hobbled along. In a quixotic 2005 book by that name, the search for the "nation's most ordinary citizen" entailed locating a person who matched the U.S. statistical majority in 140 discrete, and rather idiosyncratic, categories. The individual had to be of average height and weight, own an electric coffeemaker, go to sleep before midnight, regularly use a seatbelt, live within three miles of a McDonald's, own a suburban house valued between $100,000 and $300,000, and so on. But this was no return to Middletown. (In fact, reasoning that the "ordinary citizen" had to live in a statistically normal community, the author bypassed Muncie for its lower-than-average marriage rate, its submedian household income, and its dearth of Hispanic residents.) Unlike the Lynds' "Middletown Spirit," this checklist did not add up to a meaningful bundle of characteristics that aimed to describe a culture. In fact, the statistically "average" American was so elusive as to be an oddity, as peculiar as the "exotics" to whom the Lynds had compared Middletowners in 1929.[14]

Others searched more intently for an index to the whole, sometimes retracing the steps of earlier surveyors to do so. Middletown still lures marketers and pollsters, even if the seemingly atypical city of Las Vegas is now its competitor as a testing laboratory for consumer products and television shows. Ongoing political studies of Muncie, for example, contend that the community continues to predict the nation's vote. The city remains "typical," some claim, in its economic profile as well as its divorce, robbery, and book-borrowing rates. A recent survey, going by the name of Middletown Media Studies and inspired by the Lynds' work, sought, via telephone questionnaires, diary studies, and direct observation, "to determine how digital and other media were used on a daily basis in typical American homes." Other researchers returning to Middletown, and aware of the city's riches in longitudinal social data, are at long last trying to make the Lynds' study more demographically representative, including black Middletowners in their sights. A team of social scientists is currently attempting to retrieve baseline data on Muncie's African American community from 1924 to 1977.[15]

If "Middletown" was gradually becoming more representative, many were coming to believe that Kinsey's Reports were less so. Kinsey's figures on sexual behavior, used not only by gay advocacy groups but also by the Centers for Disease Control to estimate and track the spread of the Human Immunodeficiency Virus (HIV) in 1986, were vigorously challenged in the closing decades of the twentieth century. New scholarship revealing Kinsey's less-than-neutral stance on the topic of homosexuality provided a ready avenue for casting doubt on the surveyor's entire research program — and perhaps sexual science itself. But Americans still could not stop talking about the scientist, as dramatized accounts of his career as a sex surveyor appeared in print, on stage, and on the big screen. Controversies over Kinsey's research — the "sex panic" unleashed by the female Report triggering a congressional inquiry in 1954 and costing Kinsey his Rockefeller funding, for example — never wholly subsided. They again became news in 2004, when a panel of conservative scholars and policy-makers, voting on the thirty most "dangerous books" of the previous two centuries, ranked the Kinsey Reports fourth, just after works by Marx, Hitler, and Mao. A major follow-up study to the *Sexual Behavior* research in the 1990s by a man dubbed "the new Kinsey" faced some of the same foes as had the Reports of 1948 and 1953. Working with the National Opinion Research Center at the University of Chicago, Edward Laumann's sex survey — initially intended to gather information on HIV transmission — became the subject of yet another congressional debate, after which the administration of the first George Bush withdrew its funding. Private foundations took up the slack, and the first of three studies was published in 1994. Heralded as the first comprehensive and reputable scientific study since the *Sexual Behavior* reports, *The Social*

Organization of Sexuality was said to prove that Americans enjoy happier marriages and are more faithful to their spouses than had previously been supposed. As Miriam Reumann writes, "The news media were quick to note that the 1990s survey, in contrast to Kinsey's, offered a portrait of American sexual practices that repudiated the apparent triumph of a major 'sexual revolution,'" an event that the scientist was often blamed for causing.[16]

Meanwhile, the production of political and market research intensified. By the mid-1960s, national opinion polling had spread throughout the world. The Gallup Poll itself boasted thirty-two affiliates and conducted surveys in nearly fifty countries. A 1983 study found that 23 percent of U.S. respondents had been interviewed in the past year at least once and that twenty million citizens were polled annually. Questions continued to surface, however, about the capacity of polls to measure and inform public opinion. Political scientist James Fishkin, urging more deliberative and nuanced ways of researching attitudes, was just one who argued that the "people's voice" had been lost because of — not despite — the welter of public opinion polls. The paradoxes of the polling enterprise linger. Over half of Americans surveyed in 1985 did not trust the representativeness of random sampling, and the response rate to telephone surveys has steadily declined since 1952. The "golden age of the household survey," with in-person interviews and relatively cooperative subjects, has ended. Yet, Susan Herbst writes, "few candidates run for office, express their views on current issues, or change campaign strategy without consulting opinion polls." At the same time, many Americans demonstrate a persistent desire to voice their opinions in patently unscientific and unrepresentative Internet surveys and other so-called SLOPs (selected listener opinion polls). Whether for entertainment or strategic impact — as during the 2004 election, when political action committees urged the like-minded to use electronic surveys to spin the reportage on presidential debates — polls continued to offer at least the simulacrum of civic participation in a statistical public.[17]

At the turn of the twenty-first century, arguments about how we quantify and characterize ourselves as a national population are alive and well, even if the terms of those arguments have changed. The very linking of "representative" and "democratic" survey technologies to "the public" across the midcentury decades guaranteed that numerical skirmishes would continue to be waged in the years that followed.

One such statistical battle, perhaps appropriately, has taken place around the oldest official survey of the population, and the only one that claims to count every member of the nation. Census data have always triggered controversy. But the 1990 census provoked a major lawsuit, spearheaded by New York City, even before that year's questionnaires had been placed in the mail. At issue was the "differential undercount" of minorities and the poor in inner cities, a problem quite familiar to early pollsters. In this case, however, neglecting such groups incurred the loss of political representation as well as funding for major metropolitan areas. Ten years later, the national census sat at the center of yet another legal and congressional battle, this time over the legitimacy of representing those same uncounted Americans by scientific sampling instead of physical tabulation. Here it was evident that the techniques that had so troubled Gallup's and Roper's correspondents at midcentury remained fundamentally mysterious to some in the halls of government. In a lawsuit against the U.S. Department of Commerce it was charged that by "using statistical methods commonly referred to as sampling" the census would "include millions and millions of people who are simply deemed to exist based upon computations of statisticians."[18]

Debates over who counts and how to count have not been confined to official number crunching. Having promoted quantitative data as an avenue not just to political but also to cultural visibility, surveyors like Gallup and Roper paved the way for many groups — especially those who had been rendered invisible in earlier surveys — to embrace the statistical banner. Biracial and multiracial Americans who wanted to count in their own particular way on the 2000 census forms were one striking example. But there were many others. In 1977 the National Gay Task Force had used Kinsey's findings on the prevalence of homosexuality in the 1940s and 1950s United States to pronounce that 10 percent of the population was homosexual. In subsequent decades, gay advocacy organizations gladly took up a numerical slogan. "One in Ten" became a rallying cry, a favorite name for support groups, youth organizations, and cultural festivals as well as the tag of the first commercial radio program, on Boston's WFNX station, devoted to gay and lesbian listeners. The 10 percent claim in turn triggered a virtual cottage industry devoted to debunking that purportedly inflated number. The two sides of this demographic dispute, one suspects, had little in common beyond a belief in the rhetorical sway of numbers about "ourselves." Those who sought to dislodge the figure, like those who hoped to cement it, suspected that it worked to persuade others — politicians, journalists, marketers, and maybe even the man in the street — to bestow civic and cultural legitimacy upon a sexual minority significant enough to register as a double-digit percentage of the population. An implied equation between numerical strength and citizenship was seldom challenged, as if fewer rights were deserved by a gay population just 5 — or 3 or 1 — percent of the whole.[19]

An implied equation between numerical strength and citizenship was seldom challenged.

Struggles over what we might call "statistical citizenship" were often proxy wars for representation in other realms of U.S. society. The tabulating of protesters and ralliers raised this issue repeatedly. In the wake of the 1995 Million Man March in Washington, D.C., organized as a show of "protest and unity" of African American men, the Nation of Islam threatened to sue the National Park Service for deflating the number of marchers in its reports. The decision soon after by Congress to bar the Park Police from giving official crowd estimates indicated that some numbers were too political to calculate. Equally illuminating was the formation of a watchdog coalition calling itself "Don't Count Us Out" in 2004, aimed at remedying "the consistent undercounting of minorities" by the Nielsen Media Research corporation. Asserting that a new technology for measuring television viewing did not adequately capture the presence of Hispanic and African American audiences and therefore illegitimately dampened their market power and cultural clout, Don't Count Us Out called upon Congress to regulate the raters. "Join us," its Web site urged the potential underrepresented, "and make sure your voice is counted." This seamless alignment of the consumer and civic voice was of course foreshadowed by the merger of commercial and political opinion research in the 1940s. When it turned out that the coalition was not a grassroots protest group at all but an effort engineered by the News Corporation to preserve its viewership ratings, Nielsen set up its own defense under the banner "Everyone Counts." This contretemps revealed the high stakes involved in representing the U.S. population in an age when just about everyone understood the politics of numbers. In the strategic corporate use of minority underrepresentation, it also suggested just how complicated statistical citizenship had become.[20]

A number of scholars and journalists have recently contended that the rapid growth of entrepreneurial, ideological, think-tank, and corporate-sponsored data, not just in the United States but around the world, has made social research even more fragile and less trustworthy than it was previously. Yet how can we get along without these measures, incomplete and distorted though they may be? The fact that dependence on and distrust of surveyors' data continue to come fused together, in the era of the Middletown studies and the Kinsey Reports but even today, indicates that perhaps this too is a characteristic of a modern public. Not sure of the information we live by — where it comes from, how to verify or challenge it — we nonetheless do live by it. As one Frenchman relayed to a journalist during the outbreak of Muslim youth riots in Paris in late 2005, many of his compatriots believed that "surveying by race or religion is bad, it's dirty, it's something reserved for Americans and . . . we shouldn't do it here." He continued by musing, "But without statistics to look at, how can we measure the problem?" Although disavowing the impulses behind survey knowledge, this man acknowledged that numbers allow societies to track inequalities and gaps, to apprehend things they have no other easy way of knowing.[21]

Who are we? What do we believe? Where do we fit? Social surveys entered Americans' lives promising to answer these questions. The truth is that we still want to know. And so statistical struggles over how to aggregate and disaggregate the United States will remain with us. And we will continue to live in a world shaped by, and perceived through, survey data.

NOTES

[1]Robert Lynd, *Knowledge for What? The Place of Social Science in American Culture* (Princeton: Princeton University Press, 1939), ix.

[2]Eliot Freidson, "Communications Research and the Concept of the Mass," *American Sociological Review* 18 (1953); 313. By the 1950s, prominent social commentators and cultural critics were also coming to recognize the shaping force of social surveys and market research on the culture at large. C. Wright Mills's *White Collar* (1951) and William F. Whyte's *Organization Man* (1956), for example, charged commercial research and personality tests with creating a population of bureaucratically minded individuals who were keenly aware of social norms and eager to adjust themselves to them.

[3]"Case #45697234 1/2" to Kinsey, 2 Sept. 1953; anonymous (Champaign-Urbana, IL) to Kinsey, undated; both in KCF.

[4]Jeffrey Escoffier, "Homosexuality and the Sociological Imagination: Hegemonic Discourses, the Circulation of Ideas, and the Process of Reading in the 1950s and 1960s," in his *American Homo: Community and Perversity* (Berkeley: University of California Press, 1998), 79–98; John D'Emilio, *Sexual Politics, Sexual Communities: The Making of a Homosexual Minority in the United States, 1940–1970* (Chicago: University of Chicago Press, 1983).

[5]United States Kerner Commission, *Report of the National Advisory Commission on Civil Disorders* (Washington, DC: U.S. Government Printing Office, 1968); Arlene Dávila, *Latinos, Inc.: The Marketing and the Making of a People* (Berkeley: University of California Press, 2001); Donald R. Kinder and Lynn M. Sanders, *Divided by Color: Racial Politics and Democratic Ideals* (Chicago: University of Chicago Press, 1996); Arnold Mitchell, *The Nine American Lifestyles: Who We Are and Where We're Going* (New York: Macmillan, 1983); Ronald D. Michman, Edward M. Mazze, and Alan J. Greco, *Lifestyle Marketing: Reaching the New American Consumer* (Westport, CT: Praeger, 2003); James Atlas, "Beyond Demographics," *Atlantic Monthly*, Oct. 1984, 49–50; Martha Farnsworth Riche, "Psychographics for the 1990s," *American Demographics* 11 (July 1989): 24–31, 53; Joel Garreau, *The Nine Nations of North America* (Boston: Houghton Mifflin, 1981).

[6]Karen S. Buzzard, *Chains of Gold: Marketing the Ratings and Rating the Markets* (Metuchen, NJ: Scarecrow Press, 1990), 86–88. Michael J. Weiss, *The Clustering of America* (New York: Harper and Row, 1988) and *Clustered World: How We Live, What We Buy, and What It All Means about Who We Are* (Boston: Little, Brown, 2000), 10–11, 14. Ian Hacking has provided an accounting of how new categories create new people in "Making Up People," in *Reconstructing Individualism: Autonomy, Individuality, and the Self in Western Thought*, ed. Thomas C. Heller, Morton Sosna, and David E. Wellbery (Stanford: Stanford University Press, 1986), and "The Looping Effects of Human Kinds," in *Causal Cognition: A Multi-disciplinary Debate*, ed. Dan Sperber, David Premack, and Ann James Premack (New York: Oxford University Press, 1995).

[7]Isabel Briggs Myers, *Manual: Myers-Briggs Type Indicator* (Palo Alto, CA: Consulting Psychologists Press, 1962). Self-help books based on the Myers-Briggs typology include David Keirsey and Marilyn Bates, *Please Understand Me: Character and Temperament Types* (Del Mar, CA: Prometheus Nemesis, 1978) and *Please Understand Me II: Temperament, Character, Intelligence* (Del Mar, CA: Prometheus Nemesis, 1998). For the history of the MMPI and Myers-Briggs instruments, see Annie Paul Murphy, *The Cult of Personality: How Personality Tests Are Leading Us to Miseducate Our Children, Mismanage Our Companies, and Misunderstand Ourselves* (New York: Free Press, 2004), 45–73, 105–137. Murphy notes, in an intriguing parallel to *Middletown,* that the MMPI was based on an all-white, nearly all-Protestant group of Americans of largely Scandinavian descent.

[8]Burkart Holzner and John H. Marx, *Knowledge Application: The Knowledge System in Society* (Boston: Allyn and Bacon, 1979), 320–321. Others have traced the therapeutic as a dominant theme of twentieth-century life, including Philip Rieff, *The Triumph of the Therapeutic: Uses of Faith after Freud* (London: Chatto and Windus, 1966); Christopher Lasch, *The Culture of Narcissism: American Life in an Age of Diminishing Expectations* (New York: Norton, 1978); T. J. Jackson Lears, *Fables of Abundance: A Cultural History of Advertising in America* (New York: Basic Books, 1994); and Ellen Herman, *The Romance of American Psychology: Political Culture in the Age of Experts* (Berkeley: University of California Press, 1995).

[9]See, for example, Jon Gertner, "The Very, Very Personal Is the Political," *New York Times,* 15 Feb. 2004; and Jon Gertner, "The Mismeasure of TV," *New York Times,* 10 Apr. 2005. On MRI imaging, see John Tierney, "Using M.R.I's to See Politics on the Brain," *New York Times,* 20 Apr. 2004. In his *Strangers to Ourselves: Discovering the Adaptive Unconscious* (Cambridge, MA: Harvard University Press, 2002), Timothy D. Wilson gives a concise overview of developments in contemporary psychological research that have convinced some social scientists of the real limits on what human beings know about their own thoughts and perceptions.

[10]Robert O'Harrow Jr., *No Place to Hide* (New York: Free Press, 2005), 4–5.

[11]Robert N. Bellah, et al., *Habits of the Heart: Individualism and Commitment in American Life* (Berkeley: University of California Press, 1985); Robert N. Bellah, et al., *The Good Society* (New York: Knopf, 1991); Robert D. Putnam, *Bowling Alone: The Collapse and Revival of American Community* (New York: Simon and Schuster, 2000); Wilfred M. McClay, *The Masterless: Self and Society in Modern America* (Chapel Hill: University of North Carolina Press, 1994), 288. See also Robert Wuthnow's *Loose Connections: Joining Together in America's Fragmented Communities* (Cambridge, MA: Harvard University Press, 1998), itself a product of extensive survey research.

[12]Morris P. Fiorina with Samuel J. Abrams and Jeremy C. Pope, *Culture War? The Myth of a Polarized America* (New York: Pearson Longman, 2005). Debates over the extent of political and cultural polarization in the contemporary United States are taken up in James Davison Hunter's *Culture Wars: The Struggle to Define America* (New York: Basic Books, 1991); Alan Wolfe's *One Nation, After All: What Americans Really Think about God, Country, Family, Racism, Welfare, Immigration, Homosexuality, Work, the Right, the Left and Each Other* (New York: Viking, 1998); and Thomas Frank, *What's the Matter with Kansas? How Conservatives Won the Heart of America* (New York: Henry Holt, 2004). For a critique of the "moral values" finding, see Larry M. Bartels, "What's the Matter with *What's the Matter with Kansas?*" working paper prepared for presentation at the annual meeting of the American Political Science Association, 1–5 Sept. 2005.

[13]See, for example, Cass Sunstein, *Republic.com* (Princeton: Princeton University Press, 2001); Putnam, *Bowling Alone;* and Tom Brokaw, *The Greatest Generation* (New York: Random House, 1998). "The New Face of America," *Time,* 18 Nov. 1993; this was part of a special issue devoted to immigration and multiculturalism, including the implications for marketers of the "new ethnic consumer." For Berlant's incisive analysis, see her *The Queen of America Goes to Washington City: Essays on Sex and Citizenship* (Durham, NC: Duke University Press, 1997), 191–208, quotation on 203.

[14]Kevin O'Keefe, *The Average American: The Extraordinary Search for the Nation's Most Ordinary Citizen* (New York: Public Affairs, 2005), 110.

[15]"Leaving It in Las Vegas," *New York Times*, 7 June 2004; Graham Fraser, "Bellwether City Leans toward Clinton," *Toronto Globe and Mail*, 24 Sept. 1996. Ball State University sociologist Stephen Johnson has argued that Muncie's voting patterns are representative of the nation's. Editor's note, *International Digital Media and Arts Association Journal* 1, no. 1 (Spring 2004): 1; for the Middletown media study, see, in the same issue of that journal, Robert A. Papper, Michael E. Holmes, and Mark N. Popovich, "Middletown Media Studies," 5–55. Theodore Caplow, afterword, in Luke Eric Lassiter, Hurley Goodall, Elizabeth Campbell, and Michelle Natasya Johnson, eds., *The Other Side of Middletown* (Walnut Creek, CA: Alta Mira Press, 2004), 270. The marked absence of minority populations in the Lynds' work has inspired a number of corrective studies, including Hurley Goodall and J. Paul Mitchell, *A History of Negroes in Muncie* (Muncie, IN: Ball State University, 1976); Dwight W. Hoover, "To Be a Jew in Middletown: A Muncie Oral History Project," *Indiana Magazine of History* 81 (1985): 131–158; Dan Rottenberg, *Middletown Jews: The Tenuous Survival of an American Jewish Community* (Bloomington: Indiana University Press, 1997); and Lassiter et al., *Other Side of Middletown*.

[16]Julia Ericksen and Sally Steffen, *Kiss and Tell: Surveying Sex in the Twentieth Century* (Cambridge, MA: Harvard University Press, 1999), 196–197. For recent Kinsey scholarship challenging the surveyor's neutrality, see James H. Jones, *Alfred C. Kinsey: A Public/Private Life* (New York: W. W. Norton, 1997); and Jonathan Gathorne-Hardy, *Alfred C. Kinsey: Sex the Measure of All Things* (London: Chatto and Windus, 1998). T. Coraghessan Boyle, *The Inner Circle* (New York: Viking, 2004); Sally Deering and Larry Bortniker, *Dr. Sex: A New Musical Comedy* (2005); Jason Zinoman, "That Sexual Researcher Again, This Time Played for Laughs," *New York Times*, 22 Sept. 2005; *Kinsey*, dir. Bill Condon (20th Century Fox, United Artist Films, 2004). PBS also made a documentary about Kinsey for its *American Experience* series (*Kinsey*, dir. Barak Goodman and John Maggio [Twin Cities Public Television/TPT and Ark Media, 2005]). Peter Gorner, "U. of C. Sex Study Sees Love, Loneliness," *Chicago Tribune*, 9 Jan. 2004. Edward O. Laumann et al., *The Social Organization of Sexuality: Sexual Practices in the United States* (Chicago: Chicago University Press, 1994). The other two books to come from the study are Edward O. Laumann and Robert T. Michael, eds., *Sex, Love and Health in America: Private Choices and Public Policies* (Chicago: University of Chicago Press, 2000), and Edward O. Laumann et al., *The Sexual Organization of the City* (Chicago: University of Chicago Press, 2004). Miriam Reumann, *American Sexual Character: Sex, Gender, and National Identity in the Kinsey Reports* (Berkeley: University of California Press, 2005), 209.

Kinsey has been a prime target for the Concerned Women of America and other conservative groups such as Phyllis Schlafly's Eagle Forum. For a sense of the conservative critique, see Judith A. Reisman and Edward W. Eichel, *Kinsey, Sex, and Fraud: The Indoctrination of a People* (Lafayette, LA: Huntington House, 1990), which charged (inaccurately) that information about children's sexual responses, obtained from adult pedophiles by Kinsey, and Kinsey's purported sexual experimentation with children, were the basis for modern sex education. In 1995 the Family Research Council similarly attacked Kinsey's data on preadolescent orgasm. This latter charge was taken up by Representative Steve Stockman of Galveston, Texas, who called for a congressional hearing. In 1997 the Concerned Women for America renewed the call for investigation. See News Bureau, "Bancroft Responds to Allegations from Family Research Council," 6 Sept. 1995, and "Statement by John W. Ryan, Chairman, the Kinsey Institute Board of Trustees, and Former President of Indiana University, 1971–1987," 7 Dec. 1997; both are University News Releases, Bloomington, Indiana. See also John Bancroft, letter to the editor, *Washington Post*, 28 Dec. 1995.

[17]W. Phillips Davison, "Public Opinion," *International Encyclopedia of the Social Sciences*, ed. David L. Sills (New York: Macmillan, 1968), 13:189; James S. Fishkin, *The Voice of the People: Public Opinion and Democracy* (New Haven: Yale University Press, 1995), 80; Susan Herbst, *Numbered Voices: How Opinion Polling Has Shaped American Politics*

(Chicago: University of Chicago Press, 1993), ix, 124, 127. On the "golden age," and on "pseudo-surveys" such as SLOPs and news television 900 polls, see Martin R. Frankel and Lester R. Frankel, "Fifty Years of Survey Sampling in the United States," *Public Opinion Quarterly* 51, pt. 2 (1987): S129, S135–S136.

[18]On the 1990 and 2000 censuses and the conflicts leading up to them, see Margo J. Anderson and Stephen E. Fienberg, *Who Counts? The Politics of Census-Taking in Contemporary America* (New York: Russell Sage, 1999), esp. 1–10, 191–213, quotations on 5 and 200. Anderson and Fienberg note, however, that Congress has "long accepted the results from statistical sampling for population surveys other than the census, such as the employment rate that comes from the Current Population Survey" (200). Eric Schmitt, "Census Bureau against Use of Adjusted 2000 Count," *New York Times*, 1 Mar. 2001; Steven A. Holmes, "Los Angeles Will Challenge Bush on Census," *New York Times*, 21 Feb. 2001.

[19]The 10 percent figure, argue Julia Ericksen and Sally Steffen, "transformed Kinsey's data on sexual behavior during three years of adult life into a measure of unchanging sexual identity" (*Kiss and Tell*, 160). For WFNX, see www.fnxradio.com, accessed Dec. 2005. Katherine Sender, *Business, Not Politics: The Making of the Gay Market* (New York: Columbia University Press, 2004), esp. 139–173.

[20]Philip Kennicott, "500,000? 750,000? 1 Million?" *Washington Post*, 1 May 2004; Monte Reel, "Crowd Estimates: 30,000 to 500,000," *Washington Post*, 19 Jan. 2003. The Web site for Don't Count Us Out can be found at www.dontcountusout.com, and Nielsen's can be found at www.everyonecounts.tv; both accessed Dec. 2005. Raymond Hernandez and Stuart Elliott, "The Odd Couple vs. Nielsen," *New York Times*, 14 June 2004; Lorne Manly and Raymond Hernandez, "Nielsen, Long a Gauge of Popularity, Fights to Preserve Its Own," *New York Times*, 8 Aug. 2005. The charge of media underrepresentation of minority groups was not new; in fact, special collection and weighting techniques for African American and Hispanic broadcast stations were developed as a consequence of critiques in the mid-1960s (Buzzard, *Chains of Gold*, 158–159). On the merging of consumers and citizens more generally, see Lizabeth Cohen, *A Consumers' Republic: The Politics of Mass Consumption in Postwar America* (New York: Alfred A. Knopf, 2003).

[21]See Lisa Anderson, *Pursuing Truth, Exercising Power: Social Science and Public Policy in the Twenty-first Century* (New York: Columbia University Press, 2003); Cynthia Crossen, *Tainted Truth: The Manipulation of Fact in America* (New York: Simon and Schuster, 1994); and Arjun Appadurai, "The Research Ethic and the Spirit of Internationalism," *Items: Social Science Research Council* 51 (1997): 55–60. Craig S. Smith, "What Makes Someone French?" *New York Times*, 11 Nov. 2005.

DISCUSSION

1. Igo writes about the allure of "typicality," arguing that Americans today are taught to measure themselves against some kind of statistical "average." What do you make of this claim? In your view, is it now the norm to use survey information and poll findings to define what we ourselves believe? Is this something you do yourself?

2. Igo also talks about the role opinion polls and statistical surveys play in *sanctioning* different ideas and beliefs: that Americans nowadays need the proof of the "finding" to feel as if their own individual points of view are valid. Do you agree? Are we, as Igo suggests, so dependent on polls that we need them to "know" whether our own views are right?

3. Much of the power of statistical surveying rests on its claim of neutral or "scientific" objectivity. How legitimate is this claim? Can you think of any ways that such surveys function as a more subjective form of inquiry? And if so, should this fact alter the ways we think about their findings?

WRITING

4. How have we been taught to define the "average American"? And what role does this construct play in shaping how we act and think? In a short essay, write out a description or profile of the different attributes (for example, attitudes and background, hobbies, and values) that, in your view, captures the way the "average American" gets defined. How closely does this description match your own self view?

5. Visit a major news website and take note of how many news stories on the front page use polling data to propose what "average" Americans think of a given issue. Write an essay in which you argue whether the inclusion of such data gives the story additional weight that strict reporting on the issue wouldn't. According to Igo, why might the news media use polling data in its stories?

6. Igo writes about the evolution of surveying as something that initially excluded minority points of view, but has recently begun to see these points of view as opportunities to explore niche marketing. How do you think Debra Dickerson, based on her writing in "The Great White Way" (p. 73), would respond to this development?

JAMES TWITCHELL
Two Cheers for Materialism

How are we taught to define the successful life? And do we create these definitions for ourselves? Taking up these questions, James Twitchell explores how firmly "materialism" has come to anchor our prevailing definitions of "success." Rather than bemoan this fact, however, he offers a spirited defense of this cultural logic, pointing instead to the "creative" and "emancipating" effects of consumerism. Twitchell is a professor of English and advertising at the University of Florida, and he has published several books in each field. His studies on Romantic and Gothic literature include *Living Dead: A Study of the Vampire in Romantic Literature* (1981) and *Dreadful Pleasures: An Anatomy of Modern Horror* (1985). He has also written several books on consumerism, including *Adcult USA: The Triumph of Advertising in America* (1995) and *Living It Up: Our Love Affair with Luxury* (2002). His most recent work is *Shopping for God: How Christianity Moved from in Your Heart to in Your Face* (2007). The following essay is adapted from *Lead Us into Temptation: The Triumph of American Materialism* (1999).

OF ALL THE STRANGE BEASTS THAT HAVE COME SLOUCHING INTO THE 20th century, none has been more misunderstood, more criticized, and more important than materialism. Who but fools, toadies, hacks, and occasional loopy libertarians have ever risen to its defense? Yet the fact remains that while materialism may be the most shallow of the 20th century's various -isms, it has been the one that has ultimately triumphed. The world of commodities appears so antithetical to the world of ideas that it seems almost heresy to point out the obvious: most of the world most of the time spends most of its energy producing and consuming more and more stuff. The really interesting question may be not why we are so materialistic, but why we are so unwilling to acknowledge and explore what seems the central characteristic of modern life.

When the French wished to disparage the English in the 19th century, they called them a nation of shopkeepers. When the rest of the world now wishes to disparage Americans, they call us a nation of consumers. And they are right. We are developing and rapidly exporting a new material culture, a mallcondo culture. To the rest of the world we do indeed seem not just born to shop, but alive to shop. Americans spend more time tooling around the mallcondo — three to four times as many hours as our European counterparts — and we have more stuff to show for it. According to some estimates, we have about four times as many things as

Middle Europeans, and who knows how much more than people in the less developed parts of the world. The quantity and disparity are increasing daily, even, as we see in Russia and China, the "emerging nations" are playing a frantic game of catch-up.

This burst of mallcondo commercialism has happened recently — in my lifetime — and it is spreading around the world at the speed of television. The average American consumes twice as many goods and services as in 1950; in fact, the poorest fifth of the current population buys more than the average fifth did in 1955. Little wonder that the average new home of today is twice as large as the average house built in the early years after World War II. We have to put that stuff somewhere — quick — before it turns to junk.

Sooner or later we are going to have to acknowledge the uncomfortable fact that this amoral consumerama has proved potent because human beings love things. In fact, to a considerable degree we live for things. In all cultures we buy things, steal things, exchange things, and horde things. From time to time, some of us collect vast amounts of things, from tulip bulbs to paint drippings on canvasses to matchbook covers. Often these objects have no observable use.

> ## *Human beings love things.*

We live through things. We create ourselves through things. And we change ourselves by changing our things. In the West, we have even developed the elaborate algebra of commercial law to decide how things are exchanged, divested, and recaptured. Remember, we call these things "goods," as in "goods and services." We don't — unless we are academic critics — call them "bads." This sounds simplistic, but it is crucial to understanding the powerful allure of materialism.

Our commercial culture has been blamed for the rise of eating disorders, the spread of "affluenza," the epidemic of depression, the despoliation of cultural icons, the corruption of politics, the carnivalization of holy times like Christmas, and the gnat-life attention span of our youth. All of this is true. Commercialism contributes. But it is by no means the whole truth. Commercialism is more a mirror than a lamp. In demonizing it, in seeing ourselves as helpless and innocent victims of its overpowering force, in making it the scapegoat du jour, we reveal far more about our own eagerness to be passive in the face of complexity than about the thing itself.

Anthropologists tell us that consumption habits are gender-specific. Men seem to want stuff in the latent, arid, post-midlife years. That's when the male collecting impulse seems to be felt. Boys amass playing marbles first, Elgin marbles later. Women seem to gain potency as consumers after childbirth, almost as if getting and spending is part of a nesting impulse.

Historians, however, tell us to be careful about such stereotyping. Although women are the primary consumers of commercial objects today, they have enjoyed this status only since the Industrial Revolution. Certainly in the pre-industrial world men were the chief hunter-gatherers. If we can trust works of art to accurately portray how booty was split (and cultural historians such as John Berger and Simon Schama think we can), then males were the prime consumers of fine clothes, heavily decorated furniture, gold and silver articles, and of course, paintings in which they could be shown displaying their stuff.

Once a surplus was created, in the 19th century, women joined the fray in earnest. They were not duped. The hegemonic phallocentric patriarchy did not brainwash them into thinking goods mattered. The Industrial Revolution produced more and more things not simply because it had the machines to do so, and not because nasty producers twisted their handlebar mustaches and whispered, "We can talk women into buying anything," but because both sexes are powerfully attracted to the world of things.

Karl Marx understood the magnetism of things better than anyone else. In *The Communist Manifesto* (1848), he wrote:

> The bourgeoisie, by the rapid improvement of all instruments of production, by the immensely facilitated means of communication, draws all, even the most barbarian nations into civilization. The cheap prices of its commodities are the heavy artillery with which it batters down all Chinese walls. . . . It compels all nations on pain of extinction, to adopt the bourgeois mode of production; it compels them to introduce what it calls civilization into their midst, i.e. to become bourgeois themselves. In one word, it creates a world after its own image.

Marx used this insight to motivate the heroic struggle against capitalism. But the struggle should not be to deter capitalism and its mad consumptive ways, but to appreciate how it works so its furious energy may be understood and exploited.

Don't turn to today's middle-aged academic critic for any help on that score. Driving about in his totemic Volvo (unattractive and built to stay that way), he can certainly criticize the bourgeois afflictions of others, but he is unable to provide much actual insight into their consumption practices, much less his own. Ask him to explain the difference between "Hilfiger" inscribed on an oversize shirt hanging nearly to the knees and his rear-window university decal (My child goes to Yale, sorry about yours), and you will be met with a blank stare. If you were then to suggest that what that decal and automotive nameplate represent is as overpriced as Calvin Klein's initials on a plain white T-shirt, he would pout that you can't compare apples and whatever. If you were to say next that aspiration and affiliation are at the heart of both displays, he would say that you just don't get it, just don't get it at all.

If you want to understand the potency of American consumer culture, ask any group of teenagers what democracy means to them. You will hear an extraordinary response. Democracy is the right to buy anything you want. Freedom's just another word for lots of things to buy. Appalling perhaps, but there is something to their answer. Being able to buy what you want when and where you want it was, after all, the right that made 1989 a watershed year in Eastern Europe.

Recall as well that freedom to shop was another way to describe the right to be served in a restaurant that provided one focus for the early civil rights movement. Go back further. It was the right to consume freely which sparked the fires of separation of this country from England. The freedom to buy what you want (even if you can't pay for it) is what most foreigners immediately spot as what they like about our culture, even though in the next breath they will understandably criticize it.

The pressure to commercialize — to turn things into commodities and then market them as charms — has always been particularly Western. As Max Weber first argued in *The Protestant Ethic and the Spirit of Capitalism* (1905), much of the Protestant Reformation was geared toward denying the holiness of many things that the Catholic church had endowed with meanings. From the inviolable priesthood to the sacrificial holy water, this deconstructive movement systematically unloaded meaning. Soon the marketplace would capture this off-loaded meaning and apply it to secular things. Buy this, you'll be saved. You deserve a break today. You, you're the one. We are the company that cares about you. You're worth it. You are in good hands. We care. Trust in us. We are there for you.

Materialism, it's important to note, does not crowd out spiritualism; spiritualism is more likely a substitute when objects are scarce. When we have few things we make the next world holy. When we have plenty we enchant the objects around us. The hereafter becomes the here and now.

We have not grown weaker but stronger by accepting the self-evidently ridiculous myths that sacramentalize mass-produced objects; we have not wasted away but have proved inordinately powerful, have not devolved and been rebarbarized, but seem to have marginally improved. Dreaded affluenza notwithstanding, commercialism has lessened pain. Most of us have more pleasure and less discomfort in our lives than most of the people most of the time in all of history.

Commercialism has lessened pain.

As Stanley Lebergott, an economist at Wesleyan University, argues in *Pursuing Happiness* (1993), most Americans have "spent their way to happiness." Lest this sound overly Panglossian, what Lebergott means is that while consumption by the rich has remained relatively steady, the rest of us — the intractable poor (about four percent of the population) are the exception — have now had a go of it. If the rich really are different, as F. Scott Fitzgerald said, and the difference is that they have longer shopping lists and are happier for it, then we have, in the last two generations, substantially caught up.

The most interesting part of the book is the second half. Here Lebergott unloads reams of government statistics and calculations to chart the path that American consumption has taken in a wide range of products and services: food, tobacco, clothing, fuel, domestic service, and medicine — to name only a few. Two themes emerge strongly from these data. The first, not surprisingly, is that Americans were far better off by 1990 than they were in 1900. And the second is that academic critics — from Robert Heilbroner, Tibor Scitovsky, Robert and Helen Lynd, and Christopher Lasch to Juliet Schor, Robert Frank, and legions of others — who've censured the waste and tastelessness of much of American consumerism have simply missed the point. Okay, okay, money, can't buy happiness, but you stand a better chance than with penury.

The cultural pessimists counter that it may be true that materialism offers a temporary palliative against the anxiety of emptiness, but we still must burst joy's grape. Consumption will turn sour because so much of it is based on the chimera of debt. Easy credit = overbuying = disappointment = increased anxiety.

This is not just patronizing, it is wrongheaded. As another economist, Lendol Calder, has argued in *Financing the American Dream* (1999), debt has been an important part of families' financial planning since the time of Washington and Jefferson. And although consumer debt has consistently risen in recent times, the default rate has remained remarkably stable — more than 95.5 percent of consumer debt gets paid, usually on time. In fact, the increased availability of credit to a growing share of the population, particularly to lower-income individuals and families, has allowed many more "have riots" to enter the economic mainstream.

There is, in fact, a special crippling quality to poverty in the modern Western world. For the penalty, of intractable, transgenerational destitution is not just the absence of things; it is also the absence of meaning, the exclusion from participating in the essential socializing events of modern life. When you hear that some ghetto kid has killed one of his peers for a pair of branded sneakers or a monogrammed athletic jacket you realize that chronically unemployed poor youths are indeed living the absurdist life proclaimed by existentialists. The poor are truly the selfless ones in commercial culture.

Clearly what the poor are after is what we all want: association, affiliation, inclusion, magical purpose. While they are bombarded, as we all are, by the commercial imprecations of being cool, of experimenting with various presentations of disposable self, they lack the wherewithal to even enter the loop.

The grandfather of today's academic scolds is Thorstein Veblen (1857–1929), the eccentric Minnesotan who coined the phrase "conspicuous consumption" and has become almost a cult figure among critics of consumption. All of his books (save for his translation of the *Lexdaela Saga*) are still in print. His most famous, *The Theory of the Leisure Class,* has never been out of print since it was first published in 1899.

Veblen claimed that the leisure class set the standards for conspicuous consumption. Without sumptuary laws to protect their markers of distinction, the rest of us could soon make their styles into our own — the Industrial Revolution saw to that. But since objects lose their status distinctions when consumed by the hoi polloi, the leisure class must eternally be finding newer and more wasteful markers. Waste is not just inevitable, it is always increasing as the foolish hounds chase the wily fox.

Veblen lumped conspicuous consumption with sports and games, "devout observances," and aesthetic display. They were all reducible, he insisted, to "pecuniary emulation," his characteristically inflated term for getting in with the in-crowd. Veblen fancied himself a socialist looking forward to the day when "the discipline of the machine" would be turned around to promote stringent nationality among the entire population instead of wasted dispersion. If only we had fewer choices we would be happier, there would be less waste, and we would accept each other as equals.

The key to Veblen's argumentative power is that, like Hercules cleaning the Augean stables, he felt no responsibility to explain what happens next. True, if we all purchased the same toothpaste things would be more efficient and less wasteful. Logically we should all read *Consumer Reports,* find out the best brand, and then all be happy using the same product. But we aren't. Procter & Gamble markets 36 sizes and shapes of Crest. There are 41 versions of Tylenol. Is this because we are dolts afflicted with "pecuniary emulation," obsessed with making invidious distinctions, or is the answer more complex? Veblen never considered that consumers might have other reasons for exercising choice in the marketplace. He never considered, for example, that along with "keeping up with the Joneses" runs "keeping away from the Joneses."

Remember in *King Lear* when the two nasty daughters want to strip Lear of his last remaining trappings of majesty? He has moved in with them, and they don't think he needs so many expensive guards. They whittle away at his retinue until only one is left. "What needs one?" they say. Rather like governments attempting to redistribute wealth or like academics criticizing consumption, they conclude that Lear's needs are excessive. They are false needs. Lear, however, knows otherwise. Terrified and suddenly bereft of purpose, he bellows from his innermost soul, "Reason not the need."

Lear knows that possessions are definitions — superficial meanings, perhaps, but meanings nonetheless. And unlike Veblen, he knows those meanings are worth having. Without soldiers he is no king. Without a BMW there can be no yuppie, without tattoos no adolescent rebel, without big hair no Southwestern glamour-puss, without Volvos no academic intellectual, and, well, you know the rest. Meaning is what we are after, what we need, especially when we are young.

What kind of meaning? In the standard academic view, growing out of the work of the Frankfurt school theorists of the 1950s and '60s (such as Antonio Gramsci, Theodor Adorno, and Max Horkheimer) and later those of the Center for Contemporary Cultural Studies at the University of Birmingham, it is meaning supplied by capitalist manipulators. What we see in popular culture, in this view, is the result of the manipulation of the many for the profit of the few.

For an analogy, take watching television. In academic circles, we assume that youngsters are being reified (to borrow a bit of the vast lexicon of jargon that accompanies this view) by passively consuming pixels in the dark. Meaning supposedly resides in the shows and is transferred to the sponge-like viewers. So boys, for example, see flickering scenes of violence, internalize these scenes, and willy-nilly are soon out Jimmying open your car. This is the famous Twinkie interpretation of human behavior — consuming too much sugar leads to violent actions. Would listening to Barry Manilow five hours a day make adolescents into loving, caring people?

Watch kids watching television and you see something quite different from what is seen by the critics. Most consumption, whether it be of entertainment or in the grocery store, is active. We are engaged. Here is how I watch television. I almost never turn the set on to see a particular show. I am near the machine and think I'll see what's happening. I know all the channels; any eight-year-old does. I am not a passive viewer. I use the remote control to pass through various programs, not searching for a final destination but making up a shopping basket, as it were, of entertainment.

But the academic critic doesn't see this. He sees a passive observer who sits quietly in front of the set letting the phosphorescent glow of mindless infotainment pour over his consciousness. In the hypodermic analogy beloved by critics, the potent dope of desire is pumped into the bleary dupe. This paradigm of passive observer and active supplier, a receptive moron and smart manipulator, is easily transported to the marketplace. One can see why such a system would appeal to the critic. After all, since the critic is not being duped, he should be empowered to protect the young, the female, the foreign, the uneducated, and the helpless from the onslaught of dreck.

In the last decade or so, however, a number of scholars in the humanities and social sciences have been challenging many of the academy's assumptions.[1] What distinguishes the newer thinking is that scholars have left the office to actually observe and question their subjects. Just one example: Mihaly Csikszentmihalyi, a psychology professor at the University of Chicago, interviewed 315 Chicagoans from 82 families, asking them what objects in the home they cherished most. The adult members of the five happiest families picked things that reminded them of other people and good times they'd had together. They mentioned a memento (such as an old toy) from their childhood 30 percent of the time. Adults in the five most dissatisfied families cited such objects only 6 percent of the time.

In explaining why they liked something, happy family members often described, for example, the times their family had spent on a favorite couch, rather than its style or color. Their gloomier counterparts tended to focus on the merely physical qualities of things. What was clear was that both happy and unhappy families derived great meaning from the consumption and interchange of manufactured things. The thesis, reflected in the title of his co-authored 1981 book, *The Meaning of Things: Domestic Symbols and the Self,* is that most of the "work" of consumption occurs after the act of purchase. Things do not come complete; they are forever being assembled.

Twentieth-century French sociologists have taken the argument even further. Two of the most important are Pierre Bourdieu, author of *Distinction: A Social Critique of the Judgement of Taste* (1984), and Jean Baudrillard, whose books include *The Mirror of Production* (1983) and *Simulacra and Simulation* (1994). In the spirit of reader-response theory in literary criticism, they see meaning not as a single thing that producers affix to consumer goods, but as something created by the user, who jumbles various interpretations simultaneously. Essentially, beneath the jargon, this means that the Budweiser you drink is not the same as the one I drink. . . .

The process of consumption is creative and even emancipating. In an open market, we consume the real and the imaginary meanings, fusing objects, symbols, and images together to end up with "a little world made cunningly." Rather than lives, individuals since midcentury have had *lifestyles.* For better or worse, lifestyles are secular religions, coherent patterns of valued things. Your lifestyle is not related to what you do for a living but to what you buy. One of the chief aims of the way we live now is the enjoyment of affiliating with those who share the same clusters of objects as we do.

Mallcondo culture is so powerful in part because it frees us from the strictures of social class. The outcome of

> **Mallcondo culture is so powerful in part because it frees us from the strictures of social class.**

material life is no longer preordained by coat of arms, pew seat, or trust fund. Instead, it evolves from a never-ending shifting of individual choice. No one wants to be middle class, for instance. You want to be cool, hip, with it, with the "in" crowd, instead.

One of the reasons terms like *Yuppie, Baby Boomer,* and *GenX* have elbowed aside such older designations as "upper middle class" is that we no longer understand social class as well as we do lifestyle, or what marketing firms call "consumption communities." Observing stuff is the way we understand each other. Even if no one knows exactly how much money it takes to be a yuppie, or how young you have to be, or how upwardly aspiring, everybody knows where yuppies gather, how they dress, what they play, what they drive, what they eat, and why they hate to be called yuppies.

For better or worse, American culture is well on its way to becoming world culture. The Soviets have fallen. Only quixotic French intellectuals and anxious Islamic fundamentalists are trying to stand up to it. By no means am I sanguine about such a material culture. It has many problems that I have glossed over. Consumerism is wasteful, it is devoid of otherworldly concerns, it lives for today and celebrates the body, and it overindulges and spoils the young with impossible promises.

"Getting and spending" has eclipsed family, ethnicity, even religion as a defining matrix. That doesn't mean that those other defining systems have disappeared, but that an increasing number of young people around the world will give more of their loyalty to Nike than to creeds of blood, race, or belief. This is not entirely a bad thing, since a lust for upscale branding isn't likely to drive many people to war, but it is, to say the least, far from inspiring.

It would be nice to think that materialism could be heroic, self-abnegating, and redemptive. It would be nice to think that greater material comforts will release us from racism, sexism, and ethnocentrism, and that the apocalypse will come as it did at the end of romanticism in Shelley's *Prometheus Unbound,* leaving us "Scepterless, free, uncircumscribed . . . Equal, unclassed, tribeless, and nationless."

But it is more likely that the globalization of capitalism will result in the banalities of an ever-increasing worldwide consumerist culture. The French don't stand a chance. The untranscendent, repetitive, sensational, democratic, immediate, tribalizing, and unifying force of what Irving Kristol calls the American Imperium need not necessarily result in a Bronze Age of culture. But it certainly will not produce what Shelley had in mind.

We have not been led into this world of material closeness against our better judgment. For many of us, especially when young, consumerism is our better judgment. We have not just asked to go this way, we have demanded. Now most of the world is lining up, pushing and shoving, eager to elbow into the mall. Getting and spending has become the most passionate, and often the most imaginative, endeavor of modern life. While this is dreary and depressing to some, as doubtless it should be, it is liberating and democratic to many more.

NOTES

[1]This reconsideration of consumption is an especially strong current in anthropology, where the central text is *The World of Goods: Towards an Anthropology of Consumption* (1979), by Mary Douglas and Baron Isherwood. It can also be seen in the work of scholars such as William Leiss in communication studies; Dick Hebdige in sociology; Jackson Lears in history; David Morley in cultural studies; Michael Schudson in the study of advertising; Sidney Levy in consumer research; Tyler Cowan in economics; Grant McCracken in fashion; and Simon Schama in art history. There are many other signs of change. One of the most interesting recent shows at the Museum of Modern Art, "Objects of Desire: The Modern Still Life," actually focused on the salutary influence of consumer culture on high culture.

DISCUSSION

1. Twitchell uses the term "mallcondo commercialism" to define the type of materialism he sees as characteristic of American culture. What vision of consumer society does it imply? Do you have as approving a view of this term as Twitchell? Why or why not?

2. Much of Twitchell's argument rests on what benefits he associates with shopping. What, according to this piece, are the advantages or payoffs of playing the role of shopper? How do these benefits compare to your own experiences as a shopper?

3. While acknowledging the ways in which the pursuit of things can lead to the homogenization or flattening of public life, Twitchell nonetheless concludes on a very optimistic note, going so far as to connect consumerist beliefs to the prospect of living a democratic life. On what basis do you think he draws this conclusion? What does he claim is inherently "democratic" about being a consumer? And are you inclined to draw the same conclusion? Why or why not?

WRITING

4. According to Twitchell, consumer society has gained such ascendancy within our society in part because it has come to function as a kind of "secular religion." Write a brief essay in which you assess the validity of this claim. In your view, does it make sense to think of consumerism as a belief system? If so, what kinds of belief does it promote, and what sorts of religious meaning do they have? If not, what is a more accurate term to describe consumerism, and why?

5. In defending consumerism in his larger work, *Lead Us into Temptation*, Twitchell makes the following claim: "We live through things. We create ourselves through things. And we change ourselves by changing our things." Describe an experience from your life that you think reflects, at least to some degree, the argument Twitchell advances here. What example from your life can you find in which a thing you owned fulfilled this promise? As you look back on this example now, does it seem to warrant the conclusion Twitchell draws? How or how not?

6. Ian Frazier's essay (p. 39) is similarly preoccupied with the ways we've been taught to think about and value consumerist ideals. But he draws dramatically different conclusions regarding what it means to live out these ideals. Write an essay in which you analyze what you think accounts for the differences in the ways these two writers treat the same question. What aspects of consumerism does each emphasize? And what questions about this set of beliefs does each pose? And finally, which perspective do you find yourself in greater sympathy with, and why?

IAN FRAZIER
All Consuming Patriotism

What does it mean to love one's country? Do we all define being patriotic in
the same ways? Should we? In an essay that explores the increasing
conflation of patriotism and consumerism in American public life, Ian Frazier
presents us with a fresh way to address these questions. More specifically, he
explores the degree to which consumerism — as one of the dominant "belief
systems" in our culture — has come to influence and shape how we think
about issues of nationalism and national identity. Frazier grew up in Ohio, lived
for some time in Montana, and now resides in Montclair, New Jersey. While
completing his undergraduate degree at Harvard, he wrote for the *Harvard
Lampoon* and later went on to become a staff writer for the *New Yorker.* His
published works include both humor writing and more serious nonfiction,
but they all use close observation to reveal neglected aspects of his subjects.
His most recent book is *Gone to New York: Adventures in the City* (2005),
a series of personal reflections on the city from the perspective of a native
midwesterner. Among his nine other books are *Great Plains* (1989), *Family*
(1994), *Coyote v. Acme* (1996), and *On the Rez* (1999). The following essay
was originally published in the March/April 2002 issue of *Mother Jones.*

I THINK OF MYSELF AS A GOOD AMERICAN. I FOLLOW CURRENT EVENTS,
come to a complete stop at stop signs, show up for jury duty, vote. When
the government tells me to shop, as it's been doing recently, I shop. Over
the last few months, patriotically, I've bought all kinds of stuff I have no
use for. Lack of money has been no obstacle; years ago I could never get a
credit card, due to low income and lack of a regular job, and then one day
for no reason credit cards began tumbling on me out of the mail. I now
owe more to credit card companies than the average family of four earns
in a year. So when buying something I don't want or need, I simply take
out my credit card. That part's been easy; for me, it's the shopping itself
that's hard. I happen to be a bad shopper — nervous, uninformed, prone
to grab the first product I see on the shelf and pay any amount for it and
run out the door. Frequently, trips I make to the supermarket end with my
wife shouting in disbelief as she goes through the grocery bags and
immediately transfers one wrongly purchased item after another directly
into the garbage can.

It's been hard, as I say, but I've done my duty — I've shopped and then
shopped some more. Certain sacrifices are called for. Out of concern for

the economy after the terror attacks, the president said that he wanted us to go about our business, and not stop shopping. On a TV commercial sponsored by the travel industry, he exhorted us to take the family for a vacation. The treasury secretary, financial commentators, leaders of industry — all told us not to be afraid to spend. So I've gone out of my comfort zone, even expanded my purchasing patterns. Not long ago I detected a look of respect in the eye of a young salesman with many piercings at the music store as he took in my heavy middle-aged girth and then the rap music CD featuring songs of murder and gangsterism that I had selflessly decided to buy. My life is usually devoid of great excitement or difficulty, knock wood and thank God, and I have nothing to cry about, but I've also noticed in the media recently a strong approval for uninhibited public crying. So now, along with the shopping, I've been crying a lot, too. Sometimes I cry and shop at the same time.

As I'm pushing my overfull shopping cart down the aisle, sobbing quietly, moving a bit more slowly because of the extra weight I've lately

> **But what if . . . the national crisis worsens, and more shopping is required?**

put on, a couple of troubling questions cross my mind. First, I start to worry about the real depth of my shopping capabilities. So far I have more or less been able to keep up with what the government expects of me. I'm at a level of shopping that I can stand. But what if, God forbid, events take a bad turn and the national crisis worsens, and more shopping is required? Can I shop with greater intensity than I am shopping now? I suppose I could eat even more than I've been eating, and order additional products in the mail, and go on costlier trips, and so on. But I'm not eager, frankly, to enter that "code red" shopping mode. I try to tell myself that I'd be equal to it, that in a real crisis I might be surprised by how much I could buy. But I don't know.

My other worry is a vague one, more in the area of atmospherics, intangibles. I feel kind of wrong even mentioning it in this time of trial. How can I admit that I am worried about my aura? I worry that my aura is not . . . well, that it's not what I had once hoped it would be. I can explain this only by comparison, obliquely. On the top shelf of my bookcase, among the works vital to me, is a book called *Trials and Triumphs: The Record of the Fifty-Fifth Ohio Volunteer Infantry*, by Captain Hartwell Osborn. I've read this book many times and studied it to the smallest detail, because I think the people in it are brave and cool and admirable in every way.

The Fifty-Fifth was a Union Army regiment, formed in the Ohio town of Norwalk, that fought throughout the Civil War. My great-great-grandfather served in the regiment, as did other relatives. The book lists every mile the regiment marched and every casualty it suffered. I like reading about the soldiering, but I can't really identify with it, having never been in the service myself. I identity more with the soldiers' wives and mothers and daughters, whose home-front struggles I can better imagine. *Trials and Triumphs* devotes a chapter to them, and to an organization they set up called the Soldiers' Aid society.

The ladies of the Soldiers' Aid Society worked for the regiment almost constantly from the day it began. They sewed uniforms, made pillows, held ice-cream sociables to raise money, scraped lint for bandages, emptied their wedding chests of their best linen and donated it all. To provide the men with antiscorbutics while on campaign, they pickled everything that would pickle, from onions to potatoes to artichokes. Every other day they were shipping out a new order of homemade supplies. Some of the women spent so much time stooped over while packing goods in barrels that they believed they had permanently affected their postures. When the war ended the ladies of the Soldiers' Aid said that for the first time in their lives they understood what united womanhood could accomplish. The movements for prohibition and women's suffrage that grew powerful in the early 1900s got their start among those who'd worked in similar home-front organizations during the war.

I don't envy my forebears, or wish I'd lived back then. I prefer the greater speed and uncertainty and complicatedness of now. But I can't help thinking that in terms of aura, the Norwalk ladies have it all over me. I study the pages with their photographs, and admire the plainness of their dresses, the set of their jaws, the expression in their eyes. Next to them my credit card and I seem a sorry spectacle indeed. Their sense of purpose shames me. What the country needed from those ladies it asked for, and they provided, straightforwardly; what it wants from me it somehow can't come out and ask. I'm asked to shop more, which really means to spend more, which eventually must mean to work more than I was working before. In previous wars, harder work was a civilian sacrifice that the government didn't hesitate to ask. Nowadays it's apparently unwilling to ask for any sacrifice that might appear to be too painful, too real.

But I want it to be real. I think a lot of us do. I feel like an idiot with my tears and shopping cart. I want to participate, to do something — and shopping isn't it. Many of the donors who contributed more than half a billion dollars to a Red Cross fund for the families of terror attack victims became angry when they learned that much of the money would end up not where they had intended but in the Red Cross bureaucracy. People want to express themselves with action. In New York City so many have been showing up recently for jury duty that the courts have had to turn hundreds away; officials said a new surplus of civic consciousness was responsible for the upsurge. I'd be glad if I were asked to — I don't know — drive less or turn the thermostat down or send in seldom-used items of clothing or collect rubber bands or plant a victory garden or join a civilian patrol or use fewer disposable paper products at children's birthday parties. I'd be willing, if asked, just to sit still for a day and meditate on the situation, much in the way that Lincoln used to call for national days of prayer.

A great, shared desire to do something is lying around mostly untapped. The best we can manage, it seems, is to show our U.S.A. brand loyalty by putting American flags on our houses and cars. Some businesses across the country even display in their windows a poster on which the American flag appears as a shopping bag, with two handles at the top. Above the flag-bag are the words "America: Open for Business." Money and the economy have gotten so tangled up in our politics that we forget we're citizens of our government, not its consumers. And the leaders we elect, who got where they are by selling themselves to us with television ads, and who often are only on short loan from the corporate world anyway, think of us as customers who must be kept happy. There's a scarcity of ideas about how to direct all this patriotic feeling because usually the market, not the country, occupies our minds. I'm sure it's possible to transform oneself from salesman to leader, just as it is to go from consumer to citizen. But the shift of identity is awkward, without many precedents, not easily done. In between the two — between selling and leading, between consuming and being citizens — is where our leaders and the rest of us are now.

We see the world beyond our immediate surroundings mostly through television, whose view is not much wider than that of a security peephole in a door. We hear over and over that our lives have forever changed, but the details right in front of us don't look very different, for all that. The forces fighting in Afghanistan are in more danger than we are back home, but perhaps not so much more; everybody knows that when catastrophe comes it could hit anywhere, most likely someplace it isn't expected. Strong patriotic feelings stir us, fill us, but have few means of expressing themselves. We want to be a country, but where do you go to do that? Surely not the mall. When Mayor Giuliani left office at the end of 2001, he said he was giving up the honorable title of mayor for the more honorable title of citizen. He got that right. Citizen is honorable; shopper is not.

DISCUSSION

1. Frazier's essay compares two distinct conceptions of what it means to perform one's "patriotic duty": a contemporary one stressing the need to consume and a nineteenth-century one emphasizing the virtues of sacrifice. On what basis does Frazier argue for the superiority of this older model? What does his discussion of this kind of sacrifice imply is missing from our current definition?

2. What, according to Frazier, does playing the role of shopper principally involve? And what supposedly makes doing so incompatible with being a patriotic citizen? How do you understand the relationship between these roles?

3. Part of the problem, according to Frazier, is that shopping comes to supplant other, more legitimate ways of performing our civic duty. What do you make of this claim? What are the kinds of duties you associate with shopping?

WRITING

4. Think of another activity that, in our day and age, is presented as something through which we are supposed to act out our patriotic feelings. Write a description of that activity. What ways of acting, talking, even thinking does it script for us? And more specifically, what conception of duty does it promote? What, in your view, are the benefits or advantages of putting this belief into action? What, conversely, are the limitations of such a performance?

5. When placed alongside the stories about "the ladies of the Soldiers' Aid Society," Frazier confesses, "my credit card and I seem a sorry spectacle indeed." What do you think Frazier means by this? According to this essay, what values, priorities, or ways of life does the credit card symbolize? And how do they compare to those he believes are modeled by the example of the Soldiers' Aid Society members? Are you inclined to draw the same conclusions about each that Frazier does? Why or why not?

6. How do you think James Twitchell (p. 28) would evaluate Frazier's experiences with the world of shopping and credit? Write a comparison between the ways these two writers assess the advantages and pitfalls of living according to consumerist ideals.

Then and Now: *Feeling (In)Secure*

To be sure, belief is partly about those things we've been taught to value and embrace, but it's also about those things we've been taught to fear. When it comes to the threats we are told are most dangerous, what exactly are we supposed to believe? How are we taught to define these threats? What instructions are we issued for how to deal with them? These days, no danger looms more ominously or ubiquitously in our lives than the threat of terrorism. From nightly news broadcasts to political speeches, color-coded government alerts to made-for-TV dramas, it is made clear to us in countless different ways that the world is full of shadowy enemies who despise "our way of life" and are therefore intent on doing us harm.

So ingrained has this belief in the omnipresent terrorist threat become, in fact, that we have reorganized major swaths of our public behavior to accommodate it. There is no more vivid illustration of this fact than in the changes that have reshaped modern air travel. For the millions of Americans who travel by plane, things like long lines at security checkpoints, constantly changing restrictions on what may and may not be brought on board, and random body searches have long since become established facts of life. Less clear, though, are the particular anxieties and fears that these new security rituals have simultaneously normalized. Indeed, it could well be argued that all of these precautions and prohibitions have served to make air travel itself into a kind of extended tutorial in how and what we are supposed to fear. Every time we remove our shoes at the security check-in or dispose of our contraband toothpaste before getting on board, we are acting on (and thereby reinforcing) a particular definition of who and what our enemies are.

When framed as an example of cultural instruction, our modern-day preoccupation with terrorist threats starts to look less new than it first appears.

The twentieth century in America was marked by a series of "scares" — from the Palmer raid fears about alien immigrants in the 1920s to the anti-communist "red menace" hysteria of the 1950s — which taught Americans to define and fear the threats to the nation in very specific ways. During the Cold War, for instance, which most historians believe started soon after the end of World War II, these fears revolved largely around the twin specters of Soviet Communism and nuclear weapons. Anticipating in many ways the media coverage we see today, television broadcasts and newspaper headlines of this era were replete with warnings about the "enemies" who might be lurking "in our midst"; politicians regularly enjoined audiences to remain vigilant against "sneak attacks," which, they cautioned, could happen at any time. As a result, countless Americans became convinced that their highest civic duty was to prepare against a Soviet missile attack, digging bomb shelters or stocking basements with canned goods. In contrast to the airport restrictions of today, the rituals through which people acted out these fears centered on the classroom. For elementary schoolchildren of the 1950s, air-raid alerts and "duck and cover" drills came to stand as the norm, the midcentury equivalent to the metal detectors and bomb-sniffing dogs of today.

When we place these two sets of security rituals side by side, what (if any) differences do we see? On the basis of the roles scripted for us in these respective eras, does it seem that we've learned to define and deal with the threats confronting us in new and different ways? Or does it seem instead that we've simply carried old attitudes and anxieties forward?

WRITING

1. Compare the ways that each image demonstrates the concept of safety. How are the rituals depicted in these photos designed to make us *feel* about our own safety?

2. While they may seem at first glance merely to be objective portraits, the images can also be read as depicting *public performances* in which people are shown acting out social scripts that have been written for them. It is from this perspective that such activities can start to seem like tutorials in security, scenarios designed to teach us what and how to fear. For each set of activities shown in the photographs, create instructions that lay out the steps for the safety rituals depicted and state why Americans should perform these steps.

REBECCA SAXE
Do the Right Thing:
Cognitive Science's Search for a Common Morality

Challenging a different set of culturally ingrained beliefs, Rebecca Saxe delves into the world of modern scientific research and invites us to draw some unorthodox conclusions about both the promises and the limits of technological innovation. Questioning much of the received wisdom, Saxe declines to script science and technology as the twin solutions to the world's social and ethical ills. Rather, she wonders whether we look to these domains for answers that cannot entirely be contained within them. Saxe is an assistant professor of brain and cognitive sciences at the Massachusetts Institute of Technology, where she received an Angus MacDonald Award for Excellence in Undergraduate Teaching. She has also been named a Kavli Foundation Fellow and received a grant from the Harvard Milton Foundation. She has published over a dozen articles in cognitive science journals. "Do the Right Thing" originally appeared in 2005 in *Boston Review*.

CONSIDER THE FOLLOWING DILEMMA: MIKE IS SUPPOSED TO BE THE best man at a friend's wedding in Maine this afternoon. He is carrying the wedding rings with him in New Hampshire, where he has been staying on business. One bus a day goes directly to the coast. Mike is on his way to the bus station with 15 minutes to spare when he realizes that his wallet has been stolen, and with it his bus tickets, his credit cards, and all his forms of ID.

At the bus station Mike tries to persuade the officials, and then a couple of fellow travelers, to lend him the money to buy a new ticket, but no one will do it. He's a stranger, and it's a significant sum. With five minutes to go before the bus's departure, he is sitting on a bench trying desperately to think of a plan. Just then, a well-dressed man gets up for a walk, leaves his jacket with a bus ticket to Maine in the pocket, lying unattended on the bench. In a flash, Mike realizes that the only way he will make it to the wedding on time is if he takes that ticket. The man is clearly well off and could easily buy himself another one.

Should Mike take the ticket?

My own judgment comes down narrowly, but firmly against stealing the ticket. And in studies of moral reasoning, the majority of American adults and children answer as I do: Mike should not take the ticket, even if it means missing the wedding. But this proportion varies dramatically across cultures. In Mysore, a city in the south of India, 85 percent of adults and 98 percent of children say Mike should steal the ticket and go to the wedding. Americans, and I, justify our choice in terms of justice and fairness: it is not right for me to harm this stranger — even in a minor way. We could not live in a world in which everyone stole whatever he or she needed. The Indian subjects focus instead on the importance of personal relationships and contractual obligations, and on the relatively small harm that will be done to the stranger in contrast to the much broader harm that will be done to the wedding.

An elder in a Maisin village in Papua New Guinea sees the situation from a third perspective, focused on collective responsibility. He rejects the dilemma: "If nobody [in the community] helped him and so he [stole], I would say *we* had caused that problem."

> ### Can we discern a common . . . "moral sense" in our human nature?

Examples of cross-cultural moral diversity such as this one may not seem surprising in the 21st century. In a world of religious wars, genocide, and terrorism, no one is naive enough to think that *all* moral beliefs are universal. But beneath such diversity, can we discern a common core — a distinct, universal, maybe even innate "moral sense" in our human nature?

In the early 1990s, when James Q. Wilson first published *The Moral Sense*, his critics and admirers alike agreed that the idea was an unfashionable one in moral psychology. Wilson, a professor of government and not psychology, was motivated by the problem of non-crime: how and why most of us, most of the time, restrain our basic appetites for food, status, and sex within legal limits, and expect others to do the same. The answer, Wilson proposed, lies in our universal "moralsense, one that emerges as naturally as [a] sense of beauty or ritual (with which morality has much in common) and that will affect [our] behavior, though not always, and in some cases not obviously."

But the fashion in moral psychology is changing.

A decade after Wilson's book was published, the psychological and neural basis of moral reasoning is a rapidly expanding topic of investigation within cognitive science. In the intervening years, new technologies have been invented, and new techniques developed, to probe ever deeper into the structure of human thought. We can now acquire vast numbers of subjects over the Internet, study previously inaccessible populations such as preverbal infants, and, using brain imaging, observe and measure brain activity non-invasively in large numbers of perfectly healthy adults. Inevitably, enthusiasts make sweeping claims about these new technologies and the old mysteries they will leave in their wake. ("The brain does not lie" is a common but odd marketing claim, since in an obvious sense, brains are the only things that ever do.)

The appeal of the new methods is clear: if an aspect of reasoning is genuinely universal, part of the human genetic endowment, then such reasoning might be manifest in massive cross-cultural samples, in subjects not yet exposed to any culture, such as very young infants, and perhaps even in the biological structure of our reasoning organ, the brain.

How far have these technologies come in teaching us new truths about our moral selves? How far could they go? And what will be the implications of a new biopsychological science of natural morality? "The truth, if it exists, is in the details," wrote Wilson, and therefore I will concentrate on the details of three sets of very recent experiments, each of which approaches the problem using a different method: an Internet survey, a cognitive study of infants, and a study of brain imaging. Each is at the cutting edge of moral psychology, each is promising but flawed, and each should be greeted with a mix of enthusiasm and interpretative caution.

Mike, the man we left sitting at the bus station, is in a particularly bad moral predicament: he must choose between two actions (stealing and breaking an obligation), both of which are wrong. Moral psychologists call cases like these "moral dilemmas." Over the last half century, batteries of moral dilemmas have been presented to men and women, adults and children, all over the world. The questions at the heart of these studies are these: How do people arrive at the moral judgment that an action, real or contemplated, is right or wrong? What are the rules governing these moral calculations, and from where do they come? Which, if any, of the fundamental components are universal?

All of them, answered the eminent psychologist Lawrence Kohlberg. In the 1970s and 1980s, Kohlberg argued that moral reasoning is based on explicit rules and concepts, like conscious logical problem-solving; over the course of an individual's development, the rules and concepts that he or she uses to solve moral problems unfold in a well-defined, universal sequence of stages. These stages are biologically determined but socially supported. In early stages, moral reasoning is strongly influenced by external authority; in later stages, moral reasoning appeals first to internalized convention, and then to general principles of neutrality, egalitarianism, and universal rights. It may be that what makes one culture, one sex, or one individual different from another is just how high and how fast it manages to climb the moral ladder.

To test this hypothesis, moral dilemmas were presented to people of varying ages and classes, both sexes, and many cultures (including people in India, Thailand, Iran, Turkey, Kenya, Nigeria, and Guatemala; communities of Alaskan Inuit; Tibetan Buddhist monks; and residents of an Israeli kibbutz). Kohlberg's key methodological insight was to focus not on the answers that people give to moral dilemmas but on how they justify their choice. A seven-year-old and a white-haired philosopher may agree that Mike should not steal the ticket, but they will differ in their explanations of why not. The seven-year-old may say that Mike shouldn't steal because he will get caught and punished, while the philosopher may appeal to an interpretation of Kant's categorical imperative: act only on a principle that you would wish everyone to follow in a similar situation.

Kohlberg's claims were deeply controversial, not least because the highest stage of moral development was accorded almost exclusively to Western adults, and among those, mostly to men. Critics attacked everything from the specific dilemmas to the coding criteria to the whole philosophy of monotonic universal moral development. The psychologist Carol Gilligan, for example, argued that women justify their moral choices differently from men, but with equal sophistication. Men, she claimed, tend to reason about morality in terms of justice, and women in terms of care: "While an ethic of justice proceeds from the premise of equality — that everyone should be treated the same — an ethic of care rests on the premise of non-violence — that no one should be hurt." Similar arguments were made for non-Western cultures — that they emphasize social roles and obligations rather than individual rights and justice. On the whole, this emphasis on group differences won the day. Kohlberg's vision was rejected, and the psychological study of moral universals reached an impasse.

Very recently, though, the use of moral dilemmas to study moral universals has reemerged. Marc Hauser of Harvard University and John Mikhail of Georgetown University are among the cognitive scientists leading the charge. The current theorists take as their model for moral reasoning not conscious problem-solving, as Kohlberg did, but the human language faculty. That is, rather than "moral reasoning," human beings are understood to be endowed with a "moral instinct" that enables them to categorize and judge actions as right or wrong the way native speakers intuitively recognize sentences as grammatical or ungrammatical.

We can draw three predictions from the theory that morality operates as language does. First, just as each speaker can produce and understand an infinite number of completely original sentences, every moral reasoner can make fluent, confident, and compelling moral judgments about an infinite number of unique cases, including ones that they have never imagined confronting. Second, cross-culturally, systems of moral reasoning can be as diverse as human languages are, without precluding that a universal system of rules, derived from our biological inheritance, underlies and governs all these surface-level differences. Finally, just as native speakers are often unable to articulate the rules of grammar that they obey when speaking, the practitioners of moral judgment may have great difficulty articulating the principles that inform their judgments. Hauser, Mikhail, and their colleagues have tested these predictions with a set of moral dilemmas originally introduced by the philosopher Phillipa Foot in 1967 and now known collectively as the Trolley Problems. To illustrate the category, let's begin with Anna, standing on the embankment above a train track, watching a track-maintenance team do its work. Suddenly, Anna hears the sound of a train barrelling down the tracks: the brakes have failed, and the train is heading straight for the six workers. Beside Anna is a lever; if she pulls it, the train will be forced onto a side track and will glide to a halt without killing anyone. Should she pull the lever?

No moral dilemma yet. But now let's complicate the story. In the second scenario, Bob finds himself in the same situation, except that one of the six maintenance people is working on the side track. Now the decision Bob faces is whether to pull the lever to save five lives, knowing that if he does, a man who would otherwise have lived will be killed.

In a third version of what is clearly a potentially infinite series, the sixth worker is standing beside Camilla on the embankment. The only way to stop the train, and save the lives of the five people on the track, is for Camilla to push the man beside her down onto the track. By pushing him in front of the train and so killing him, she would slow it down enough to save the others.

Finally, for anyone not yet convinced that there are cases in which it is wrong to sacrifice one person in order to save five, consider Dr. Dina, a surgeon who has five patients each dying from the failure of a different organ. Should she kill one healthy hospital visitor and distribute the organs to her patients in order to save five lives?

By putting scenarios like these on a Web site (moral.wjh.harvard.edu) and soliciting widely for participants, Hauser and his lab have collected judgments about Trolley Problems from thousands of people in more than a hundred countries, representing a broad range of ages and religious and educational backgrounds. The results reveal an impressive consensus. For example, 89 percent of subjects agree that it is permissible for Bob to pull the lever to save five lives at the cost of one but that it is not permissible for Camilla to make the same tradeoff by pushing the man onto the track.

More importantly, even in this enormous sample and even for complicated borderline cases, participants' responses could not be predicted by their age, sex, religion, or educational background. Women's choices in the scenarios overall were indistinguishable from men's, Jews' from Muslims' or Catholics', teenagers' from their parents' or grandparents'. Consistent with the analogy to language, these thousands of people make reliable and confident moral judgments for a whole series of (presumably) novel scenarios. Also interestingly, Hauser, Mikhail, and their colleagues found that while the "moral instinct" was apparently universal, people's subsequent justifications were not; instead, they were highly variable and often confused. Less than one in three participants could come up with a justification for the moral difference between Camilla's choice and Bob's, even though almost everyone shares the intuition that the two cases *are* different.

So what can we learn from this study? Has the Internet — this new technology — given us a way to reveal the human universals in moral judgments?

We must be cautious: Web-based experiments have some obvious weaknesses. While the participants may come from many countries and many backgrounds, they all have Internet access and computer skills, and therefore probably have significant exposure to Western culture. (In fact, although the first study included just over 6,000 people from more than a hundred countries, more than two thirds of them were from the United States.) Because the survey is voluntary, it includes a disproportionate number of people with a preexisting interest in moral reasoning. (More than two thirds had previously studied moral cognition or moral philosophy in some academic context, making it all the more surprising that they could not give clear verbal justifications of their intuitions.) And because subjects fill out the survey without supervision or compensation, sincerity and good faith cannot be ensured (although Hauser, Mikhail, and their colleagues did exclude the subjects who claimed to live in Antarctica or to have received a Ph.D. at 15).

Also, this is only one study, focused on only one kind of moral dilemma: the Trolley Problems. So far, we don't know whether the universality of intuitions observed in this study would generalize to other kinds of dilemmas. The results of the experiment with Mike and the bus ticket suggest it probably would not.

On the other hand, the survey participants did include a fairly even balance of sexes and ages. And the fact that sex in particular makes no difference to people's choices in the Trolley Problems, even in a sample of thousands (and growing), could be important. Remember, Carol Gilligan charged that Lawrence Kohlberg's theory of multi-stage moral development was biased toward men; she claimed that men and women reason about moral dilemmas with equal sophistication, but according to different principles. Hauser and Mikhail's Internet study lets us look at the controversy from a new angle. Gilligan's analysis was based on justifications: how men and women consciously reflect upon, explain, and justify the moral choices that they make. It is easy to imagine that the way we justify our choices depends a lot on the surrounding culture, on external influences and expectations. What Hauser and Mikhail's results suggest is that though the reflective, verbal aspects of moral reasoning (which Hauser and Mikhail found inarticulate and confused, in any case) may differ by sex, the moral intuition that tells us which choice is right and which wrong for Anna or Bob or Camilla is

> **The moral intuition that tells us which choice is right . . . is part of human nature.**

part of human nature, for women just as for men.

Still, the Internet's critical weakness is intransigent. As long as people must have Internet access in order to participate, the sample will remain culturally biased, and it will be hard to know for sure from where the moral consensus comes: from human nature or from exposure to Western values. The only way to solve this problem is to investigate moral reasoning in people with little or no exposure to Western values. And cognitive scientists are beginning to do just that.

One group of experimental participants that is relatively free of cultural taint is preverbal infants. Before they are a year old, while their vocabulary consists of only a few simple concrete nouns, infants have presumably not yet been acculturated into the specific moral theories of their adult caretakers. Infant studies therefore offer scientists the chance to measure innate moral principles in mint condition. With this opportunity, of course, comes a methodological challenge. How can we measure complex, abstract moral judgments made by infants who are just beginning to talk, point, and crawl?

To meet this challenge, developmental psychologists who study all areas of cognition have become adept — often ingenious — at teasing meaning out of one of the few behaviors that infants can do well: looking. Infants look longer at the things that interest them: objects or events that are attractive, unexpected, or new. Looking-time experiments therefore gauge which of two choices — two objects, people, or movies — infants prefer to watch.

From just this simple tool, a surprisingly rich picture of infant cognition has emerged. We have learned, for example, that infants only a few days old prefer to look at a human face than at other objects; that by the time they are four months old, infants know that one object cannot pass through the space occupied by another object; and that by seven months, they know that a billiard ball will move if and only if it is hit by something else.

Only recently, though, has this tool begun to be applied to the field of moral cognition. The questions these new studies seek to answer include the following: Where do we human beings get the notions of "right," "wrong," "permissible," "obligatory," and "forbidden?" What does it mean when we judge actions — our own or others' — in these terms? How and why do we judge some actions wrong (or forbidden) and not just silly, unfortunate, or unconventional?

Not all transgressions are created equal; some undesirable or inappropriate actions merely violate conventions, while others are genuinely morally wrong. Rainy weather can be undesirable, some amateur acting is very bad, and raising your hand before speaking at a romantic candlelit dinner is usually inappropriate, but none of these is morally wrong or forbidden. Even a tsunami or childhood cancer, though both awful, are not immoral unless we consider them the actions of an intentional agent.

The psychologist Elliott Turiel has proposed that the moral rules a person espouses have a special psychological status that distinguishes them from other rules — like local conventions — that guide behavior. One of the clearest indicators of this so-called moral–conventional distinction is the role of local authority.

We understand that the rules of etiquette — whether it is permissible to leave food on your plate, to belch at the table, or to speak without first raising your hand — are subject to context, convention, and authority. If a friend told you before your first dinner at her parents' house that in her family, belching at the table after dinner is a gesture of appreciation and gratitude, you would not think your friend's father was immoral or wrong or even rude when he leaned back after dinner and belched — whether or not you could bring yourself to join in.

Moral judgments, in contrast, are conceived (by hypothesis) as not subject to the control of local authority. If your friend told you that in her family a man beating his wife after dinner is a gesture of appreciation and gratitude, your assessment of that act would presumably not be swayed. Even three-year-old children already distinguish between moral and conventional transgressions. They allow that if the teacher said so, it might be okay to talk during nap, or to stand up during snack time, or to wear pajamas to school. But they also assert that a teacher couldn't make it okay to pull another child's hair or to steal her backpack. Similarly, children growing up in deeply religious Mennonite communities distinguish between rules that apply because they are written in the Bible (e.g., that Sunday is the day of Sabbath, or that a man must uncover his head to pray) and rules that would still apply even if they weren't actually written in the Bible (including rules against personal and material harm).

There is one exception, though. James Blair, of the National Institutes of Health, has found that children classified as psychopaths (partly because they exhibit persistent aggressive behavior toward others) do not make the normal moral–conventional distinction. These children know which behaviors are not allowed at school, and they can even rate the relative seriousness of different offenses; but they fail when asked which offenses would still be wrong to commit even if the teacher suspended the rules. For children with psychopathic tendencies (and for psychopathic adults, too, though not for those Blair calls "normal murderers"), rules are all a matter of local authority. In its absence, anything is permissible.

Turiel's thesis, then, is that healthy individuals in all cultures respect the distinction between conventional violations, which depend on local authorities, and moral violations, which do not.

This thesis remains intensely controversial. The chief voice of opposition may come not from psychologists but from anthropologists, who argue that the special status of moral rules cannot be part of human nature, but is rather just a historically and culturally specific conception, an artifact of Western values. "When I first began to do fieldwork among the Shona-speaking Manyika of Zimbabwe," writes Anita Jacobson-Widding, for example, "I tried to find a word that would correspond to the English concept 'morality.' I explained what I meant by asking my informants to describe the norms for good behavior toward other people. The answer was unanimous. The word for this was *tsika*. But when I asked my bilingual informants to translate *tsika* into English, they said that it was 'good manners.' And whenever I asked somebody to define *tsika* they would say 'Tsika is the proper way to greet people.'"

Jacobson-Widding argues that the Manyika do not separate moral behavior from good manners. Lying, farting, and stealing are all equal violations of *tsika*. And if manners and morals cannot be differentiated, the whole study of moral universals is in trouble, because how — as Jacobson-Widding herself asks — can we study the similarities and differences in moral reasoning across cultures "when the concept of morality does not exist?" From the perspective of cognitive science, this dispute over the origins of the moral–conventional distinction is an empirical question, and one that might be resolvable with the new techniques of infant developmental psychology.

One possibility is that children first distinguish "wrong" actions in their third year of life, as they begin to recognize the thoughts, feelings, and desires of other people. If this is true, the special status of moral reasoning would be tied to another special domain in human cognition: theory of mind, or our ability to make rich and specific inferences about the contents of other people's thoughts. Although this link is plausible, there is some evidence that distinguishing moral right from wrong is a more primitive part of cognition than theory of mind, and can exist independently. Unlike psychopathic children, who have impaired moral reasoning in the presence of intact theory of mind, autistic children who struggle to infer other people's thoughts are nevertheless able to make the normal moral–conventional distinction.

Another hypothesis is that children acquire the notion of "wrong" actions in their second year, once they are old enough to hurt others and experience firsthand the distress of the victim. Blair, for example, has proposed that human beings and social species like canines have developed a hard-wired "violence-inhibition mechanism" to restrain aggression against members of the same species. This mechanism is activated by a victim's signals of distress and submission (like a dog rolling over onto its back) and produces a withdrawal response. When this mechanism is activated in an attacker, withdrawal means that the violence stops. The class of "wrong" actions, those that cause the victim's distress, might be learned first for one's own actions and then extended derivatively to others' actions.

Both of these hypotheses suggest a very early onset for the moral–conventional distinction. But possibly the strongest evidence against the anthropologists' claim that this distinction is just a cultural construct would come from studies of even younger children: preverbal infants. To this end, developmental psychologists are currently using the new looking-time procedures to investigate this provocative third hypothesis: that before they can either walk or talk, young infants may already distinguish between hurting (morally wrong) and helping (morally right).

In one study, conducted by Valerie Kuhlmeier and her colleagues at Yale, infants watched a little animated ball apparently struggling to climb a steep hill. A triangle and a square stood nearby. When the ball got just beyond halfway up, one of two things happened: either the triangle came over and gave the ball a helpful nudge up the hill, or the square came over and pushed the ball back down the hill. Then the cycle repeated. Later, the same infants saw a new scene: across flat ground the little ball went to sit beside either the triangle or the square. Twelve-month-old infants tended to look longer when the ball went to sit beside the "mean" shape. Perhaps they found the ball's choice surprising. Would you choose to hang out with someone who had pushed you down a hill?

Another study, by Emmanuel Dupoux and his colleagues in France, used movies of live human actors. In one, the "nice" man pushes a backpack off a stool and helps a crying girl get up onto the stool, comforting her. In the second movie, the "mean" man pushes the girl off the stool, and picks up and consoles the backpack. The experiment is designed so that the amounts of crying, pushing, and comforting in the two movies are roughly equal. After the movies, the infants are given a choice to look at, or crawl to, either the "mean" man or the "nice" one. At 15 months, infants look more at the mean man but crawl more to the nice one.

These results are interesting, but each of these studies provides evidence for a fairly weak claim: by the time they are one year old, babies can distinguish between helpful actions and hurtful ones. That is, infants seem to be sensitive to a difference between actions that are nice, right, fortunate, or appropriate and ones that are mean, wrong, undesirable, or inappropriate — even for novel actions executed by unknown agents. On any interpretation, this is an impressive discovery. But the difference that infants detect need not be a moral difference.

These first infant studies of morality cannot answer the critical question, which is not about the origin of the distinction between nice and mean, but between right and wrong; that is, the idea that some conduct is unacceptable, whatever the local authorities say. Eventually, infant studies may provide evidence that the concepts of morality and convention can be distinguished, even among the Manyika — that is, that a special concept of morality is part of the way infants interpret the world, even when they are too young to be influenced by culture-specific constructions. So far, though, these infant studies are a long way off.

In the meantime, we will have to turn to other methods, traditional and modern, to adjudicate the debate between psychologists and anthropologists over the existence of moral universals. First, if Hauser and Mikhail's Internet-survey results really do generalize to a wider population, as the scientists hope, then we might predict that Manyika men and women would give the same answers that everyone else does to the Trolley Problems. If so, would that challenge our notions of how different from us they really are?

Second, if Elliott Turiel and his colleagues are right, then even Manyika children should distinguish between manners, which depend on local custom, and morals, which do not, when asked the right kinds of questions. For example, according to Manyika custom, "If you are a man greeting a woman, you should sit on a bench, keep your back straight and your neck stiff, while clapping your own flat hands in a steady rhythm." What if we told a four-year-old Manyika child about another place, very far away, where both men and women are supposed to sit on the ground when greeting each other? Or another place where one man is supposed to steal another man's yams? Would the children accept the first "other world" but not the second? I have never met a Manyika four-year-old, so I cannot guess, but if so, then we would have evidence that the Manyika do have a moral–conventional distinction after all, at the level of moral judgment, if not at the level of moral justification.

Finally, some modern cognitive scientists might reply, we scientists hold a trump card: we can now study moral reasoning in the brain.

In the last ten years, brain imaging (mostly functional magnetic resonance imaging, or fMRI) has probably exceeded all the other techniques in psychology combined in terms of growth rate, public visibility, and financial expense. The popularity of brain imaging is easy to understand: by studying the responses of live human brains, scientists seem to have a direct window into the operations of the mind.

A basic MRI provides an amazingly fine-grained three-dimensional picture of the anatomy of soft tissues such as the gray and white matter (cell bodies and axons) of the brain, which are entirely invisible to x-rays. An fMRI also gives the blood's oxygen content in each brain region, an indication of recent metabolic activity in the cells and therefore an indirect measure of recent cell firing. The images produced by fMRI analyses show the brain regions in which the blood's oxygen content was significantly higher while the subject performed one task — a moral-judgment task, for example — than while the subject performed a different task — a non-moral-judgment task.

Jorge Moll and his colleagues, for example, compared the blood-oxygen levels in the brain while subjects read different kinds of sentences: sentences describing moral violations ("They hung an innocent"), sentences describing unpleasant but not immoral actions ("He licked the dirty toilet"), and neutral sentences ("Stones are made of water"). They found that one brain region — the medial orbito-frontal cortex, the region just behind the space between the eyebrows — had a higher oxygenation level while subjects read the moral sentences than either of the other two kinds of sentences. Moll proposed that the medial orbito-frontal cortex must play some unique role in moral reasoning.

In fact, this is not a new idea. In 1848 Phineas Gage was the well-liked foreman of a railroad-construction gang until a dynamite accident destroyed his medial orbito-frontal cortex (along with a few neighboring brain regions). Although Gage survived the accident with his speech, motion, and even his intelligence unimpaired, he was, according to family and friends, "no longer Gage": obstinate, irresponsible, and capricious, he was unable to keep his job, and later he spent seven years as an exhibit in a traveling circus. Modern patients with similar brain damage show the same kinds of deficits: they are obscene, irreverent, and uninhibited, and they show disastrous judgment, both personally and professionally.

Still, the claim of a moral brain region remains controversial among cognitive scientists, who disagree both about whether such a brain region exists and what the implications would be if it did. Joshua Greene of Princeton University, for example, investigates brain activity while subjects solve Trolley Problems. He finds lots of different brain regions recruited — as one might imagine — including regions associated with reading and understanding stories, logical problem-solving, and emotional responsiveness. What Greene doesn't find is any clear evidence of a "special" region for moral reasoning per se.

More broadly, even if there were a specialized brain region that honored the moral–conventional distinction, what would this teach us about that distinction's source, or universality? Many people share the intuition that the existence of a specialized brain region would provide prima facie evidence of the biological reality of the moral–conventional distinction. The problem is that even finding a specialized neural region for a particular kind of thought does not tell us how that region got there. We know, for example, that there is a brain region that becomes specially attuned to the letters of the alphabet that a person is able to read, but not of other alphabets; this does not make any one alphabet a human universal. Similarly, if Western minds (the only ones who participate in brain-imaging experiments at the moment) distinguish moral from conventional violations, it is not surprising that Western brains do.

In sum, both enthusiasm and caution are in order. The discovery of a specialized brain region for moral reasoning will not simply resolve the venerable problem of moral universals, as proponents of imaging sometimes seem to claim. On the other hand, not every function a brain performs is assigned a specialized brain region. In visual cortex, there are specialized regions for seeing faces and human bodies, but there is no specialized region for recognizing chairs or shoes, just a general-purpose region for recognizing objects. Some distinctions are more important than others in the brain, whatever their importance in daily life. Cognitive neuroscience can tell us where on this scale the moral–conventional distinction falls.

> **The discovery of a specialized brain region for moral reasoning will not . . . resolve the . . . problem of moral universals.**

One thing these cutting-edge studies certainly cannot tell us is the right answer to a moral dilemma. Cognitive science can offer a descriptive theory of moral reasoning, but not a normative one. That is, by studying infants or brains or people around the world, we may be able to offer an account of how people *actually* make moral decisions — which concepts are necessary, how different principles are weighed, what contextual factors influence the final decision — but we will not be able to say how people *should* make moral decisions.

Cognitive scientists may eventually be able to prove that men and women reason about Trolley Problems with equal sophistication, that African infants distinguish moral rules that are independent of local authority from conventions that are not, and even that the infants are using a specialized brain region to do so. What they cannot tell us is whether personal and social obligations should triumph over the prohibition against stealing, whether Mike should steal the ticket, and whether in the end it would be a better world to live in if he did.

DISCUSSION

1. Take a moment to consider the title of this essay. How do you think Saxe would define "doing the right thing"? On what basis does she suggest we can decide this complicated question? How does her definition compare to yours?

2. What do you think Saxe means by the phrase "natural morality"? How does the essay define this concept? And how does her discussion of scientific thinking invite us to think about it?

3. What are some of your own assumptions about the world of science? Where do they come from? What kinds of problems are you encouraged to believe science can resolve?

WRITING

4. Choose one of the moral dilemmas Saxe describes here. In a short essay, formulate an answer that you think would resolve the ethical questions it poses. As you lay out the terms of your solution, make sure you address whether you think it affirms or challenges the conclusion that Saxe draws.

5. Saxe spends a good deal of time here talking about the "moral–conventional" distinction: the differences between our own ethical standards and those we have simply been taught to endorse by society. Write an essay in which you reflect on the ways you understand this distinction. Do you think it is possible to definitively distinguish between these two kinds of standards? If so, on what basis? If not, what factors keep us from being able to do so?

6. Saxe cites numerous examples of scientific research that seeks to learn more about the nature of morality. Write an essay in which you examine Saxe's essay with respect to what Sarah Igo (p. 10) believes about the influence scientific data has over our beliefs. Are these authors' points of view complementary or at odds? Why? What are the complications that arise from trying to scientifically determine where morality comes from? In your opinion, how important is such research in understanding how our society operates?

CATHERINE NEWMAN

I Do. Not.:
Why I Won't Marry

In this essay, Catherine Newman offers her views on both the allure and the pitfalls of monogamy. What does it mean, she asks, to choose a "lifelong partner"? In answering this question, she spends a good deal of time exploring the monogamy-marriage paradigm that stands as the norm in our culture. Along the way, Newman tells her personal story as well, describing her own efforts to situate her "unconventional" relationship within the parameters established by this norm. Newman is the author of the memoir *Waiting for Birdy* (2005) and writes a weekly online journal about parenting called *Bringing Up Ben and Birdy*. Her essays have appeared in the *New York Times* and have been collected in a number of anthologies, including *The Bitch in the House* (2002) where this essay comes from. She lives in Amherst, Massachusetts, with her partner and their two children.

O F COURSE NOBODY THINKS TO ASK ME AND MICHAEL — MY PART-ner of eleven years and the father of our two-year-old son — why we're not married until we're all at a *wedding,* which is kind of awkward, at best. "Um, maybe because marriage is a tool of the *patriarchy?*" I could say, and smile and take another bite of poached salmon and wink across the table at the bride and groom. But I don't, because I love weddings, and I'm in a borrowed stone-colored outfit, and I probably cried when the bride kissed her parents at the altar and I've just read my special passage from Rumi or Rainer Maria Rilke, and I'm buzzed and happy and eating the entrée I checked off on the reply card months ago. And Michael's terribly handsome in his blazer, and he's probably touching my linen-encased thigh under the table, moony and drunk off of other people's vows. But somebody's father or uncle always has to lean over, all shiny and loose with champagne, and ruin it. "So, how come you two aren't doing this?" he might ask, with a hand gesture that takes in the bride, the cake, the open bar. My best bet is to stall elaborately over a mouthful of fish. There are so many reasons, and they're all only partly true and shot through with contradiction, and I can't say any of them out loud — not here, anyway.

Because marriage is about handing the woman off, like a baton, from her father to her husband. Also known as "traffic in women," this is how men have historically solidified their economic connections to other men (think *empires;* think *in-laws*) and guaranteed the continuation of their Seed. The woman has always, of course, been deeply valued for her own sake, hence the *dowry* that required her family to bribe another family with lots of money and cattle and embroidered pillow shams to take her off their hands. Thank goodness we're so much more evolved now. Except, of course, for the embarrassing detail of the bride's family shelling out the ten or fifty thousand dollars for the wedding itself. And the awkward transfer of the veiled woman, father to son-in-law, at the altar. Wives can bear a disconcerting resemblance to objects. Back in the sixteenth century, adultery was a crime of theft (like making off with your neighbor's snowblower), since wives were no less, or more, than personal property. Thank goodness we're so much more evolved now. Except at a very Catholic wedding we attended recently where the bride was handed a lit candle, which she used to light a candle for her husband. She then had to blow out the first candle, which was supposed to represent her naughty old independent self — the same lucky self that had now been absorbed, and extinguished, by her husband. Hooray for modernity.

> **Wives can bear a disconcerting resemblance to objects.**

Because the Religious Right and their Defense of Marriage Act use marriage as a vehicle for homophobic legislation. Marriage is, of course, a supremely natural and God-given institution and a naturally and God-givenly straight one. But *just in case,* we'd better treat it like it's a fragile and gasping little injured bird, and we'll make it illegal for gay people to even visit a town where there's a bridal boutique. As long as they don't tell us they're gay, though, they can still serve as our Wedding Coordinators, because, let's face it, they really do understand fabrics and color. That's the political version. There's another, less noble version: *Because I'd feel like a real A-hole if I put on a beaded cream bodice and vowed myself away in front of all our gay friends — smiling and polite in their dark silk shirts or gossiping wickedly about our choice of canapés — who cannot themselves marry.* Not that they would all deign to get married, even if they could (see above). But what they're snubbing should certainly be a viable option.

Because I could, myself, have ended up with a woman. Into my mid-twenties, I spent some time in love and in bed with women — a handful of astonishing romances that left me with a lot of steamy memories and a crew cut. You can imagine my horror, then, when I surreptitiously bedded and fell in love with Michael, who played hockey (ice, roller, *and* video) and was relentlessly cheerful. A handsome, athletic, doting guy: not my ideal specimen for a life partner, but there it was. I persist in the knowledge that women are, way more often than not, sexier, funnier, kinder, and more interesting than men. All of my friends certainly are. Do I still think of myself as bisexual? If a tree falls in the forest but you're inside reading *Spotted Yellow Frogs* for the fourth time in five minutes, do you give a shit? If you have ever lived with a two-year-old, then you know that Grappling With Your Sexuality does not tend to make it onto the roster of daily activity goals, like brushing your teeth or not locking the baby in the car with your keys. My mind, it is not such a vibrant organ these days. I can squint past the clogging mass of words like "nasal aspirator" and "glycerin suppositories" and just barely make out the dim shape of a memory of sexual identity, but that's about it. Pulling the crispy skin off of a roast chicken and eating it right there in the kitchen, before the bird even makes it to the table — now *that's* a sensual act worth defending. Especially these days, when our bed is more like a museum of Cheerios artifacts than a place of sexual worship. But it does seem weaselly to participate in a privilege — specifically, marriage — that I would have been denied if I had ended up engaged in a different kind of relationship. Or, really, just a different configuration of wild-thing hydraulics, which is all we're actually talking about here. (I do love the idea that the Law has nothing better to do than referee the naked Hokey Pokey: "No, no — you put *that* in. No! No! Not in *there!* Yes, we know it happens to *fit* there, but that's not where it belongs.")

Because we don't believe in monogamy. At least in theory. Can it possibly be that climbing onto the same exact person for fifty years maximizes the erotic potential of our brief fling here on earth? Especially back in the early days, when I identified more physically and politically as bisexual (*Bisexual People Speak Out!* is a book I had, which makes me want to write, for kids, something more mundanely exuberant like *Bisexual People Buy Bananas!*), it seemed cruel and unusual that one should have to give up so much in order to commit to a man. Open, honest nonmonogamy seemed like the ideal solution. Abstractly, it sounded righteous and right. But in real life, nonmonogamy can sound more like your partner's lover revving a motorcycle right outside your bedroom window, which is just a total bummer. It can look, more or less, like a trampy, selfish bout of sleeping around, talking about it, and hurting everybody's feelings. Beliefs, even strongly held one's can be somewhat aloof from the world where people actually *feel* things. We are too well trained in the grammar of possession and jealousy, too mired in the blurring of sex and love, to simply turn our backs on convention; we are poorly insulated from the sharp pokes of heartsoreness and humiliation.

And, it turns out, that *third* person inevitably has feelings, too, of all things! Feelings you can't control, not even by chanting "I'll never leave my boyfriend" over and over like a mantra. That third person might even be likely, in fact, to have *extra* feelings, the kind that find expression only in phoning compulsively throughout the night or popping by after supper with an ice pick. Michael and I were ultimately so strained by a few rounds of nondomestic toad-in-the-hole that we gave it up. (A friend of mine who is a famously radical theorist of sexuality once said, tiredly, "Maybe sex just doesn't even *matter* that much.") But we still believe in honesty over the sticky lies of the motel room; we still believe in imagination over living by the available scripts; and we believe, I hope, in treating each other's desires with respect and compassion. We still believe in the *principle* of nonmonogamy, even if we don't have the energy to do it.

Because I will not be possessed. Michael holds everything that comes into his life — our son, a peeled orange, a bath towel, me — as if it is as fragile and fleeting as a soap bubble; he has the lightest, most beautiful touch. And yet — and this is the worst, brattiest king of contradiction — I wish sometimes that he would demand that I marry him, that he would despair so poetically and much about his great love for me that he would have to possess me entirely. (Sometimes, because we share a decade of inside jokes about ourselves, Michael slits his eyes at me over lunch and snarls, "I *must* have you this instant," with his bare foot pressing around in my lap and the baby grinning gamely from his high chair.) Michael is not, how shall I say it, the most passionate tool in the shed. We were recently leafing through our photo album, and there's this glorious picture of me, forty weeks pregnant, which he took himself, and I'm naked and radiant with the gold of the sunset illuminating my huge, ripe belly, two days before the harrowing and miraculous birth of our baby, and Michael says only, about a half-full plastic bottle in the foreground, "Oh, honey, remember how you made that fruit punch? Yum."

You know that kind of romance where your hair is always all matted in the back and you get rug burns on your elbows, and you stay awake all night chain-smoking and watching each other breathe? Everyone has at least one of these. ("Mmmm, the hot dog man," my friend Megan sighed over her passionate interlude with a snack vendor.) Michael's more likely to hop up after sex and say, amiably, "Want a bowl of Golden Grahams? I'm having one." So he would, for instance, never punch someone out over me, like my beautiful and spindly high school boyfriend who once, on the subway, shook his bony, lunatic fist in the face of an innocent bystander and growled, "You staring at my woman?"

But even though I catch myself longing for it sometimes, the truth is that extremes of passion have unnerved me. The people who write poems about your forearm hairs glistening in the moonlight are the same ones who, later, throw beer bottles through your kitchen window from the street and call drunk and weepy every New Year's Eve. They're the same ones who don't always seem to actually *know* you that well — who say baffling, wrong things like, "I just really love how *calm* you are," which send you reeling out to the bookstore to skim *The Complete Idiot's Guide to Zen Meditation.* The best life partner might, I think, be the one who sees you as you are and loves that person — the person who is boring and

The best life partner is exactly the sort of person who doesn't crave possession.

anxious or blotchy from a weekly scrub mask — not the imaginary one who is poetic and broodingly smart and sexy and ecstatic all the time. The best life partner is exactly the sort of person who doesn't crave possession.

Because not being married means we get to keep choosing each other. Can married people do this? Of course they can (although one married friend described this as the difference between, in our case, choosing to stay together and, in hers, choosing not to divorce). For us, there's something psychically liberating about that little bit of unmarried space that allows us to move forward, to come toward each other, over and over again. Michael knows me deeply — he sees me truly — and, astonishingly, keeps deciding to stay with me. He can walk into the bathroom while I'm tweezing the hairs on my chin, wrap his arms around my waist, and smile gently at me into the mirror, instead of shouting, "Step right up, folks! See the incredible Bearded Lady!" which is what I would surely do in his place. When I'm not completely infuriated over his occasional bouts of remoteness, or overwhelmed by the frantic dullness that can suck the life out of making a home together, I look at Michael and breathe a huge sigh of relief. I would choose him again this second: his strong shoulders from rocking our baby to sleep every afternoon; his utter lack of unkindness; the way he finds the things I've lost — keys, my cardigan — and then returns them to me as gifts, all wrapped up in fancy paper and ribbons. If you believe, and I do, that people are secretly their truest selves in the middle of the night, then my truest self might be, "Are you going to snore like that until I put a bullet in my head?" Michael's is, "Oh, sweetheart, can't you sleep?" whilst he pats the smooth, cool of his chest for me to crawl onto. I would choose that again in a heartbeat.

Because we have a kid together. So, um, scratch that last paragraph, because I am stuck with Michael forever. What more permanent soul binding can there be than the sharing of a child? This is the real till-death-do-us-part. We could still split up, of course, but only if the benefits seemed distinctly greater than, say, the awkwardness of showing up separately at all the same bar mitzvahs and eighth-grade performances of *Our Town*; and still, we would be ultimately connected. When we were in the hospital, with the baby just born and the three of us in love in our matching plastic ID bracelets like a little nuclear gang, a yearning flitted through me for all of us to have the same last name; I really got it, for a minute — that desire for a united front. (Instead, the baby has my last name. Don't try this unless you want to spend the rest of your life with everybody getting all panicked and sweaty and saying, "Oh, that's so *fascinating!*" about it, as if your kid has an extra limb sprouting from his forehead.) But we are that, anyway — a united front — with or without a shared name or the deed to our relationship. The difference between us and a married couple, apart from some nuances of tax paying and title wielding (Mrs. Michael J. Millner? Who could that possibly be, besides his drag-queen persona?), is slender indeed.

Because we already have rings, is what we always end up saying, and we hold up our hands as proof of commitment. "We got them on our seventh anniversary — seven years is common-law marriage in California." Common-law marriage? That and three-fifty will get you a latte at Starbucks. We don't even know what it means. But for somebody's father or uncle at a wedding, it tends to settle the issue more often than not. Nobody has to know that we fought like the dickens while we were *getting* the rings — that Michael, instead of gazing at me committedly, was humming a Coors Light jingle (he doesn't even *drink* beer), which enraged me inexplicably much. So much that, in the end, instead of the intimate, beachside vows we had planned, there was merely a "Take your stupid ring!" accompanied by the peevish flinging of velvet boxes.

But I do wear his ring. He is the father of my child. I take Michael in contradiction and in mayhem. In grief and in delight. To cherish, dismay, and split burritos with. For good company and daily comfort. For the tornado of rage and for love. I take him. I do.

DISCUSSION

1.   Newman begins by evoking a stereotypical wedding scene. Why do you think she decides to begin her essay this way? What kind of framework does this opening establish for her subsequent discussion of her own unconventional relationship?

2.   What are the specific roles that Newman worries the conventional marriage model scripts for her? What specifically does she think is wrong, dangerous, or problematic about following these scripts?

3.   What are your experiences with what Newman calls the "marriage paradigm"? Have you or people you know struggled with decisions over how or even whether to marry? How do these experiences compare with the problems and questions posed in this essay? Does Newman's discussion give you any different vantage on your experiences? How or how not?

WRITING

4.   Among other things, this essay asks us to look closely at the rituals that have come to define the conventional wedding ceremony. Write an essay in which you analyze the particular messages (for example, about marriage, relationships, gender, monogamy, economics, or the like) you think these conventional rituals are designed to convey.

5.   Newman structures her essay very deliberately as a string of *because* statements that all respond to the single question of why she doesn't want to get married. Write your own essay about some common rite of passage that you don't believe is for you (for example, getting an office job, having children, or joining a fraternity or sorority), styling your response after Newman. Then, write a short reflection on why you think Newman chose this particular style for her response and whether you believe it is effective.

6.   Newman devotes a good part of her discussion to tracing the unspoken assumptions that have served throughout history to legitimatize the conventional monogamous-marriage model. Write an essay in which you describe and analyze some of the assumptions and ideas that this traditional model has historically excluded. What makes them incompatible with those that have been elevated as the norm? How would our notions about and definitions of marriage change if these alternative assumptions were accorded wider acceptance?

DAVID BROOKS

People Like Us

What norms surround how we think about race? In this essay, David Brooks takes up some of the key terms that currently anchor our public discussions of race, prompting us to think about the assumptions we bring to bear on this question. Do we, he asks, really care about diversity? And even more provocatively, should we? Brooks, a prominent voice for conservative politics, has been a columnist at the *New York Times* since 2003. He has also worked at the *Weekly Standard, Newsweek,* and the *Atlantic Monthly* and is a regular commentator on NPR's *All Things Considered* and PBS's *NewsHour.* He has published two books of commentary on American culture, *Bobos in Paradise: The New Upper Class and How They Got There* (2000) and *On Paradise Drive: How We Live Now (and Always Have) in the Present Tense* (2004). The following essay first appeared in the September 2003 issue of the *Atlantic Monthly.*

MAYBE IT'S TIME TO ADMIT THE OBVIOUS. WE DON'T REALLY CARE about diversity all that much in America, even though we talk about it a great deal. Maybe somewhere in this country there is a truly diverse neighborhood in which a black Pentecostal minister lives next to a white anti-globalization activist, who lives next to an Asian short-order cook, who lives next to a professional golfer, who lives next to a postmodern-literature professor and a cardiovascular surgeon. But I have never been to or heard of that neighborhood. Instead, what I have seen all around the country is people making strenuous efforts to group themselves with people who are basically like themselves.

Human beings are capable of drawing amazingly subtle social distinctions and then shaping their lives around them. In the Washington, D.C., area Democratic lawyers tend to live in suburban Maryland, and Republican lawyers tend to live in suburban Virginia. If you asked a Democratic lawyer to move from her $750,000 house in Bethesda, Maryland, to a $750,000 house in Great Falls, Virginia, she'd look at you as if you had just asked her to buy a pickup truck with a gun rack and to shove chewing tobacco in her kid's mouth. In Manhattan the owner of a $3 million SoHo loft would feel out of place moving into a $3 million Fifth Avenue apartment. A West Hollywood interior decorator would feel dislocated if you asked him to move to Orange County. In Georgia a barista from Athens would probably not fit in serving coffee in Americus.

It is a common complaint that every place is starting to look the same. But in the information age, the late writer James Chapin once told me, every place becomes more like itself. People are less often tied down to factories and mills, and they can search for places to live on the basis of cultural affinity. Once they find a town in which people share their values, they flock there, and reinforce whatever was distinctive about the town in the first place. Once Boulder, Colorado, became known as congenial to politically progressive mountain bikers, half the politically progressive mountain bikers in the country (it seems) moved there; they made the place so culturally pure that it has become practically a parody of itself.

But people love it. Make no mistake — we are increasing our happiness by segmenting off so rigorously. We are finding places where we are comfortable and where we feel we can flourish. But the choices we make toward that end lead to the very opposite of diversity. The United States might be a diverse nation when considered as a whole, but block by block and institution by institution it is a relatively homogeneous nation.

> **We are increasing our happiness by segmenting off so rigorously.**

When we use the word "diversity" today we usually mean racial integration. But even here our good intentions seem to have run into the brick wall of human nature. Over the past generation reformers have tried heroically, and in many cases successfully, to end housing discrimination. But recent patterns aren't encouraging: according to an analysis of the 2000 census data, the 1990s saw only a slight increase in the racial integration of neighborhoods in the United States. The number of middle-class and upper-middle-class African-American families is rising, but for whatever reasons — racism, psychological comfort — these families tend to congregate in predominantly black neighborhoods.

In fact, evidence suggests that some neighborhoods become more segregated over time. New suburbs in Arizona and Nevada, for example, start out reasonably well integrated. These neighborhoods don't yet have reputations, so people choose their houses for other, mostly economic reasons. But as neighborhoods age, they develop personalities (that's where the Asians live, and that's where the Hispanics live), and segmentation occurs. It could be that in a few years the new suburbs in the Southwest will be nearly as segregated as the established ones in the Northeast and the Midwest.

Even though race and ethnicity run deep in American society, we should in theory be able to find areas that are at least culturally diverse. But here, too, people show few signs of being truly interested in building diverse communities. If you run a retail company and you're thinking of opening new stores, you can choose among dozens of consulting firms that are quite effective at locating your potential customers. They can do this because people with similar tastes and preferences tend to congregate by ZIP code.

The most famous of these precision marketing firms is Claritas, which breaks down the U.S population into sixty-two psycho-demographic clusters, based on such factors as how much money people make, what they like to read and watch, and what products they have bought in the past. For example, the "suburban sprawl" cluster is composed of young families making about $41,000 a year and living in fast-growing places such as Burnsville, Minnesota, and Bensalem, Pennsylvania. These people are almost twice as likely as other Americans to have three-way calling. They are two and a half times as likely to buy Light n' Lively Kid Yogurt. Members of the "towns & gowns" cluster are recent college graduates in places such as Berkeley, California, and Gainesville, Florida. They are big consumers of Dove Bars and *Saturday Night Live*. They tend to drive small foreign cars and to read *Rolling Stone* and *Scientific American*.

Looking through the market research, one can sometimes be amazed by how efficiently people cluster — and by how predictable we all are. If you wanted to sell imported wine, obviously you would have to find places where rich people live. But did you know that the sixteen counties with the greatest proportion of imported-wine drinkers are all in the same three metropolitan areas (New York, San Francisco, and Washington, D.C.)? If you tried to open a motor-home dealership in Montgomery County, Pennsylvania, you'd probably go broke, because people in this ring of the Philadelphia suburbs think RVs are kind of uncool. But if you traveled just a short way north, to Monroe County, Pennsylvania, you would find yourself in the fifth motor-home-friendliest county in America.

Geography is not the only way we find ourselves divided from people unlike us. Some of us watch Fox News, while others listen to NPR. Some like David Letterman, and others — typically in less urban neighborhoods — like Jay Leno. Some go to charismatic churches; some go to mainstream churches. Americans tend more and more often to marry people with education levels similar to their own, and to befriend people with backgrounds similar to their own.

My favorite illustration of this latter pattern comes from the first, noncontroversial chapter of *The Bell Curve*. Think of your twelve closest friends, Richard J. Herrnstein and Charles Murray write. If you had chosen them randomly from the American population, the odds that half of your twelve closest friends would be college graduates would be six in a thousand. The odds that half of the twelve would have advanced degrees would be less than one in a million. Have any of your twelve closest friends graduated from Harvard, Stanford, Yale, Princeton, Caltech, MIT, Duke, Dartmouth, Cornell, Columbia, Chicago, or Brown? If you chose your friends randomly from the American population, the odds against your having four or more friends from those schools would be more than a billion to one.

Many of us live in absurdly unlikely groupings, because we have organized our lives that way.

It's striking that the institutions that talk the most about diversity often practice it the least. For example, no group of people sings the diversity anthem more frequently and fervently than administrators at just such elite universities. But elite universities are amazingly undiverse in their values, politics, and mores. Professors in particular are drawn from a rather narrow segment of the population. If faculties reflected the general population, 32 percent of professors would be registered Democrats and 31 percent would be registered Republicans. Forty percent would be evangelical Christians. But a recent study of several universities by the conservative Center for the Study of Popular Culture and the American Enterprise Institute found that roughly 90 percent of those professors in the arts and sciences who had registered with a political party had registered Democratic. Fifty-seven professors at Brown were found on the voter-registration rolls. Of those, fifty-four were Democrats. Of the forty-two professors in the English, history, sociology, and political-science departments, all were Democrats. The results at Harvard, Penn State, Maryland and the University of California at Santa Barbara were similar to the results at Brown.

What we are looking at here is human nature. People want to be around others who are roughly like themselves. That's called community. It probably would be psychologically difficult for most Brown professors to share an office with someone who was pro-life, a member of the National Rifle Association, or an evangelical Christian. It's likely that hiring committees would subtly — even unconsciously — screen out any such people they encountered. Republicans and evangelical Christians have sensed that they are not welcome at places like Brown, so they don't even consider working there. In fact, any registered Republican who contemplates a career in academia these days is both a hero and a fool. So, in a semi-self-selective pattern, brainy people with generally liberal social mores flow to academia, and brainy people with generally conservative mores flow elsewhere.

> *People want to be around others who are roughly like themselves. That's called community.*

The dream of diversity is like the dream of equality. Both are based on ideals we celebrate even as we undermine them daily. (How many times have you seen someone renounce a high-paying job or pull his child from an elite college on the grounds that these things are bad for equality?) On the one hand, the situation is appalling. It is appalling that Americans know so little about one another. It is appalling that many of us are so narrow-minded that we can't tolerate a few people with ideas significantly different from our own. It's appalling that evangelical Christians are practically absent from entire professions, such as academia, the media, and filmmaking. It's appalling that people should be content to cut themselves off from everyone unlike themselves.

The segmentation of society means that often we don't even have arguments across the political divide. Within their little validating communities, liberals and conservatives circulate half-truths about the supposed awfulness of the other side. These distortions are believed because it feels good to believe them.

On the other hand, there are limits to how diverse any community can or should be. I've come to think that it is not useful to try to hammer diversity into every neighborhood and institution in the United States. Sure, Augusta National should probably admit women, and university sociology departments should probably hire a conservative or two. It would be nice if all neighborhoods had a good mixture of ethnicities. But human nature being what it is, most places and institutions are going to remain culturally homogeneous.

It's probably better to think about diverse lives, not diverse institutions. Human beings, if they are to live well, will have to move through a series of institutions and environments, which may be individually homogeneous but, taken together, will offer diverse experiences. It might also be a good idea to make national service a rite of passage for young people in this country: it would take them out of their narrow neighborhood segment and thrust them in with people unlike themselves. Finally, it's probably important for adults to get out of their own familiar circles. If you live in a coastal, socially liberal neighborhood, maybe you should take out a subscription to the *Door,* the evangelical humor magazine; or maybe you should visit Branson, Missouri. Maybe you should stop in at a megachurch. Sure, it would be superficial familiarity, but it beats the iron curtains that now separate the nation's various cultural zones.

Look around at your daily life. Are you really in touch with the broad diversity of American life? Do you care?

DISCUSSION

1. According to Brooks, our good intentions to create a more racially integrated society have failed because they "have run into the brick wall of human nature." Do you agree? Is segregation in America largely or exclusively a matter of human nature? And what kinds of solutions to this problem does such an understanding imply?

2. What do you make of the title of Brooks's essay? What, in his view, makes choosing "people like us" a preferable option to that of integration?

3. One of the main assumptions behind Brooks's argument is that issues like where we live and whom we associate with are fundamentally matters of personal choice. How accurately do you think his discussion treats the issue of choice? Do we all possess this kind of freedom to choose? And if not, what factors or circumstances undermine this possibility?

WRITING

4. Brooks ends his essay by challenging his readers: "Look around at your daily life. Are you really in touch with the broad diversity of American life? Do you care?" Write an essay in which you respond directly to Brooks's questions. How does the organization of your life (for example, by community, by living situation, by leisure activities) either support or refute Brooks's argument? In a hypothetical world that reflected an idealized portrait of diversity, what would need to change in the ways your life is structured to bring you in line with the ideal?

5. What kind of reader do you think would respond most favorably to Brooks's argument? Write an essay in which you sketch out a portrait of the ideal reader for this essay. What background, education, or political beliefs would this ideal reader have? What attitudes, values, or worldview? Make sure to explain, using quotes from Brooks's essay, why you define this reader in the ways you do. In what ways does defining this ideal reader strengthen or diminish Brooks's argument?

6. To what extent does Brooks's discussion of diversity intersect with Debra Dickerson's (p. 73) critique of what could be called "scientific racism," or the notion that race is permanently fixed in biology? Write an assessment of the differing ways these two authors seem to understand the issue of racial difference. What particular features of each author's argument accounts for the contrasting conclusions?

DEBRA J. DICKERSON

The Great White Way

In this book review, Debra Dickerson questions the status of "whiteness" as our culture's preeminent racial and social norm, the standard against which all other racial and ethnic identity is defined as "different." Challenging the hegemony this term has long exerted over American thought, she offers a succinct historical overview of the ways the boundaries dividing white from nonwhite have shifted in America. Dickerson's work has appeared in many publications, including the *New Republic, Slate,* and *Vibe*, and she writes a regular column for Salon.com. Her memoir, *An American Story* (2001), describes her move from the rough St. Louis neighborhood where she grew up to her success as a Harvard Law School-trained, award-winning journalist. Her most recent book is *The End of Blackness: Returning the Souls of Black Folk to Their Rightful Owners* (2005). The following book review discusses *Working Toward Whiteness: How America's Immigrants Became White* (2005), by David R. Roediger, and *When Affirmative Action Was White: An Untold History of Racial Inequality in Twentieth-Century America* (2005), by Ira Katznelson. It was originally published in the September/October 2005 issue of *Mother Jones.*

WHEN SPACE ALIENS ARRIVE TO COLONIZE US, RACE, ALONG WITH The Atkins diet and Paris Hilton, will be among the things they'll think we're kidding about. Oh, to be a fly on the wall when the president tries to explain to creatures with eight legs what blacks, whites, Asians, and Hispanics are. Race is America's central drama, but just try to define it in 25 words or less. Usually, race is skin color, but our visitors will likely want to know what a "black" person from Darfur and one from Detroit have in common beyond melanin. Sometimes race is language. Sometimes it's religion. Until recently, race was culture and law: Whites in the front, blacks in the back, Asians and Hispanics on the fringes. Race governed who could vote, who could murder or marry whom, what kind of work one could do and how much it could pay. The only thing we know for sure is that race is not biology: Decoding the human genome tells us there is more difference within races than between them.

Hopefully, with time, more Americans will come to accept that race is an arbitrary system for establishing hierarchy and privilege, good for little more than doling out the world's loot and

> **Race is an arbitrary system for establishing hierarchy and privilege.**

deciding who gets to kick whose butt and then write epic verse about it. A belief in the immutable nature of race is the only way one can still believe that socioeconomic outcomes in America are either fair or entirely determined by individual effort. [David Roediger's *Working Toward Whiteness* and Ira Katznelson's *When Affirmative Action Was White*] should put to rest any such claims.

If race is real and not just a method for the haves to decide who will be have-nots, then all European immigrants, from Ireland to Greece, would have been "white" the moment they arrived here. Instead, as documented in David Roediger's excellent *Working Toward Whiteness,* they were long considered inferior, nearly subhuman, and certainly not white. Southern and eastern European immigrants' language, dress, poverty, and willingness to do "nigger" work excited not pity or curiosity but fear and xenophobia. Teddy Roosevelt popularized the term "race suicide" while calling for Americans to have more babies to offset the mongrel hordes. Scientists tried to prove that Slavs and "dagoes" were incapable of normal adult intelligence. Africans and Asians were clearly less than human, but Hungarians and Sicilians ranked not far above.

It gives one cultural vertigo to learn that, until the 1920s, Americans from northern Europe called themselves "white men" so as not to be confused with their fellow laborers from southern Europe. Or that 11 Italians were lynched in Louisiana in 1891, and Greeks were targeted by whites during a 1909 Omaha race riot. And curiously, the only black family on the Titanic was almost lost to history because "Italian" was used to label the ship's darker-skinned, nonwhite passengers.

Yet it was this very bureaucratic impulse and political self-interest that eventually led America to "promote" southern and eastern Europeans to "whiteness." The discussion turned to how to fully assimilate these much-needed, newly white workers and how to get their votes. If you were neither black nor Asian nor Hispanic, eventually you could become white, invested with enforceable civil rights and the right to exploit — and hate — nonwhites. World War II finally made all European Americans white, as the "Americans All" banner was reduced to physiognomy alone: Patriotic Japanese Americans ended up in internment camps while fascist-leaning Italian Americans roamed free. While recent European immigrants had abstained from World War I-era race riots, racial violence in the 1940s was an equal-opportunity affair. One Italian American later recalled the time he and his friends "beat up some niggers" in Harlem as "wonderful. It was new. The Italo-American stopped being Italo and started becoming American."

While European immigrants got the racial stamp of approval, the federal government was engaged in a little-recognized piece of racial rigging that resulted in both FDR's New Deal and Truman's Fair Deal being set up largely for the benefit of whites. As Ira Katznelson explains in *When*

Affirmative Action Was White, these transformative public programs, from Social Security to the GI Bill, were deeply — and intentionally — discriminatory. Faced with a de facto veto by Southern Democrats, throughout the 1930s and 1940s Northern liberals acquiesced to calls for "states' rights" as they drafted the landmark laws that would create a new white middle class. As first-generation white immigrants cashed in on life-altering benefits, black families who had been here since Revolutionary times were left out in the cold.

Disbursement of federal Depression relief was left at the local level, so that Southern blacks were denied benefits and their labor kept at serf status. In parts of Georgia, no blacks received emergency relief; in Mississippi, less than 1 percent did. Agricultural and domestic workers were excluded from the new Social Security system, subjecting 60 percent of blacks (and 75 percent of Southern blacks) to what Katznelson calls "a form of policy apartheid" far from what FDR had envisioned. Until the 1950s, most blacks remained ineligible for Social Security. Even across the North, black veterans' mortgage, education, and housing benefits lagged behind whites'. Idealized as the capstone of progressive liberalism, such policies were as devastatingly racist as Jim Crow.

To remedy this unacknowledged injustice, Katznelson proposes that current discussions about affirmative action refer to events that took place seven, rather than four, decades ago, when it wasn't called affirmative action but business as usual. He's frustrated by the anemic arguments of his liberal allies, who rely on the most tenuous, least defensible of grounds — diversity — while their opponents invoke color blindness, merit, and the Constitution. In short, affirmative action can't be wrong now when it was right — and white — for so long.

Together, these two books indict the notion of race as, ultimately, a failure of the American imagination. We simply can't imagine a world in which skin color does not entitle us to think we know what people are capable of, what they deserve, or their character. We can't imagine what America might become if true affirmative action — not the kind aimed at the Huxtable kids but at poverty and substandard education — was enacted at anywhere near the level once bestowed on those fortunate enough to be seen as white.

DISCUSSION

1. Dickerson opens her essay with a hypothetical scenario in which space aliens are faced with the task of understanding how Americans have perceived and sought to deal with race. Why do you think she chooses to begin her discussion on race by focusing on it from an "alien" perspective? What kind of commentary on race does this particular strategy imply?

2. Dickerson refers to race as the "central drama" of American history. Why do you think she uses the term drama? Does her discussion of racial politics and racialist violence invite us in any way to think about this history in terms of role-playing, performance, or social and cultural scripts? If so, how?

3. According to Dickerson, race is best understood as a question of power. "Hopefully, with time," she writes, "more Americans will come to accept that race is an arbitrary system for establishing hierarchy and privilege." What do you make of this claim? To what extent do you share Dickerson's conviction about the arbitrariness of racial categories and racial difference?

WRITING

4. The dominant ways of thinking about race in America, argues Dickerson, are more the product of social fantasy than a reflection of objective reality. In a brief essay, evaluate the validity of this thesis. To what extent is it valid to think of the racial scripts that get taught in our culture as fantastic or fictional? Does this possibility diminish or accentuate the power they can wield?

5. One of the clear goals underlying this essay involves de-naturalizing the racial differences we've been taught to accept. Choose an example from our popular culture (for example, a television show, an advertisement, or a news story) that, in your view, encourages us to accept a view about race and racial difference that you consider artificial. Then, write an essay in which you explain how this product or image goes about promoting this view. How does it endeavor to represent this false view as right or normal? And what do you think are the specific consequences of adopting this view?

6. Dickerson and Rebecca Saxe (p. 46) share a common skepticism regarding scientific authority. Write an essay in which you compare the critiques against scientific methodology and scientific thinking that each of these essays levels. To what degree do they also identify and criticize social practices and norms?

Scenes and Un-Scenes: *Political Protest*

There is a long and storied tradition in America of social or political protest. From the Boston Tea Party to the women's suffrage movement, antisegregation campaigns to abortion rights rallies, our national history is replete with efforts to challenge the practices and beliefs that, at one time or another, have stood as unexamined norms. But how do these public demonstrations actually succeed — if indeed they do — in rewriting beliefs that, for any given era, have become so embedded, entrenched, assumed? The short answer, of course, is that these beliefs were never quite as universal as they may have appeared. Bringing together people who felt marginalized or oppressed by a given societal norm, these demonstrations were designed to challenge the beliefs on which such norms rested, to offer up for scrutiny the embedded practices and unspoken assumptions that justified the status quo. For each of the following examples, how fully would you say this objective is achieved? What particular beliefs does each put on display? What social scripts does each attempt to rewrite?

▲▲ *Even today, the civil rights movement led by Martin Luther King Jr. in the 1960s still stands as a model for how Americans think about social or political protest. The tradition of public, nonviolent protest that King pioneered persists within the public imagination as the blueprint for how "the people" can effect not only tangible changes in public policy, but also meaningful shifts in social attitude. His famous 1963 March on Washington, for example, marks a watershed both for efforts to create new civil rights legislation and for the struggle to challenge and undo long-standing public attitudes about race.*

The *Million Man March* sought to carry forward King's standard of public, nonviolent protest into the present day. At the same time, though, such spectacles make evident how much has changed over the last forty plus years. In updating King's messages for our contemporary "wired" age, for example, it reminds us how different the tactics of public protest have become. Availing itself of the same tools we might find at a sporting event or rock concert, this image shows how deeply shaped by our media culture political protest is these days.

◄◄ *Over the years, in fact, King's legacy has moved well beyond the realm of racial politics, coming to underlie and inform all manner of different causes. His tradition of public, nonviolent protest as well as his rhetoric of civil and social "rights" have long been adopted by a variety of other constituencies and used to advance a host of other interests. Not surprisingly, this tactic has led to the marriage of these tactics to a number of unlikely seeming causes. We might well wonder, for example, what particular "right" a celebrity-studded, Scientology-sponsored demonstration against the use of antidepressants is meant to advance. When you compare this spectacle to King's March on Washington, how much commonality do you discern?*

◀◀ *Another arena in which King's tradition of public demonstration and civil rights protest has been taken up in recent years is gay rights—in particular, the much publicized and highly contentious issue of gay marriage. In ways large and small, proponents of this movement have sought to model their efforts along the lines of the African American struggle for justice and equality before the law. Deploying some of the same rhetoric, many have framed the demand for legalized marriage as a natural extension of King's work. Do you agree with this analogy?*

▲▲ *We have even reached the point where technological changes now allow us to alter or fictionalize the historical record itself, a tactic that takes the whole idea of scripting to an entirely new level. In this still image from the film* Forrest Gump, *the title character, played by Tom Hanks, has been inserted into actual footage of a Vietnam War protest. How do you think such an image plays with the idea of social protest?*

DISCUSSION

1. Which of these protests raises an issue that most resonates with your personal experience? Which one touches on an issue or conflict that you feel a personal stake in? To what extent does its embedded or unspoken critique reflect your own views?

2. Choose one of the previous examples. What relationship between public spectacle and societal belief does it showcase? That is, in what ways does this protest seem designed to affect or alter a more fundamental and underlying social norm?

3. What political or social controversy does this collection leave out? What protest would you add to this list, and what in your view would make it worthy of inclusion?

WRITING

4. Choose something from our popular culture (for example, a television show, a commercial, a movie, or the like) that shows an example of a political or social protest that tells the story of how a particular societal rule gets challenged. Describe how this protest gets depicted. How are the protesters presented? What specific issues or ideas are offered up for critique? How do the symbols match or differ from the images you've viewed in this feature? How compelling or convincing do you find this depiction to be? Why?

5. Choose one of the images above that offers a blueprint for social protest that you would not follow yourself. Identify and evaluate the particular aspects of this protest that you find problematic, inadequate, or otherwise ineffective. Then, use this critique to create a model of the kind of protest you would endorse. What different sorts of tactics would this model utilize? What different objectives would it attempt to achieve? And finally, what, in your estimation, makes this alternative more preferable?

6. The role of social protest in our culture has gone a long way toward normalizing certain issues. In "Statistical Citizens" (p.10), Sarah Igo discusses how survey science has also influenced the beliefs of Americans. In your opinion, how effective is social protest as a tool for changing American minds? How does this tactic reach people in ways that polling doesn't?

Putting It into Practice: *Scripting Belief*

Now that you've read the chapter selections, try applying your conclusions to your own life by completing the following exercises.

SURVEYING OURSELVES   Sarah E. Igo discusses at length the ways the surveys have helped us characterize the idea of what "normal" Americans think. Visit the Gallup Poll website (www.galluppoll.com) and click the link "Poll Topics A to Z." Here, you will find a long list of survey topics and summaries of how Americans responded to different surveys on these topics. Choose two or three topics and decide how you would answer the survey questions posed. Write an essay in which you compare your beliefs to those of the American majority. Are you "normal" or are you "different"? How do you respond to being categorized in either of those groups?

MARKETING BELIEF   Choose some venue or organization that you think actively works to promote or market a set of beliefs to the general public (for example, a church, a military recruitment center, a campus activist group, or a similar group). Research the ways that this group advertises itself to the larger community. Write an essay in which you explore what tactics the group uses to court new members. What symbols does it use in its advertising? What language do these ads include that is designed to inspire new believers?

SELL IT   Try combining the two activities above. Choose one of the survey topics you wrote about in the first assignment and design an ad you think would be effective in appealing to nonbelievers. This ad could be anything from a speech to a commercial or billboard. What images or language do you believe are most important in convincing others to follow the particular belief you've chosen?

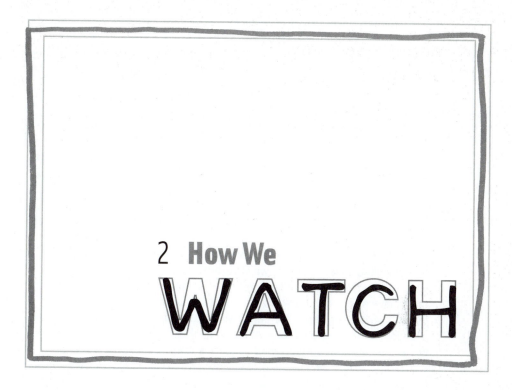

2 How We WATCH

Introduction

SEEING IS BELIEVING?

Do the names Carrie Underwood and Taylor Hicks mean anything to you? Do you let your answering machine pick up calls that come in during *America's Next Top Model*? Or do you find yourself regularly debating who should have been voted off the show in the latest episode of *Survivor*? If so, you are not alone. Reality TV draws millions of viewers like you who enjoy watching everyday people live out certain "realities" in front of the camera. And these viewers, also like you, accurately sense that few other television genres work as hard as reality TV to teach us how to play the *role* of viewer.

As anyone who has seen even an episode or two can attest, very clear but unspoken rules dictate the ways we are and are not supposed to watch reality television. Cardinal among these rules is the presumption that what we see on these shows truly is a snapshot of reality, a window through which we glimpse the personal, private details of real people in real situations feeling real emotions. At the same time, however, we are aware that within the boundaries established by these shows not everything counts equally as reality. If we want to properly perform our role as viewer, we know that our attention needs to remain focused on very specific aspects of what is on display. We must view *selectively.* These shows work only if we suspend disbelief and buy into the idea that what we're seeing is more or less real.

This unspoken message doesn't pertain only to reality television. Indeed, few things abound more plentifully in our world than the opportunity to play the role of watcher. Whether it is the candid photos that pop up on our cell phones, the billboards we drive past on the interstate, the clothing catalogues that litter our mailboxes, or the stories broadcast on the nightly news, we are called constantly to view things. So natural does the experience of watching become, however, that we may miss the larger implication: that at the same time we are being taught how to *watch*, we are also being taught how to *think* about the world around us.

Take, for example, the typical ad for a luxury car. Because we have grown so accustomed to seeing this sort of image in television commercials or magazine ads, we don't really need to be explicitly told how to look at it. Through countless encounters with examples just like it, we have in a sense internalized what the expected form of watching is. And because we have already been schooled about what role to play, we already know how we are supposed to think about this image: what associations we are supposed to make, what conclusions we are supposed to draw. We know, for example, that when we come across one of these glossy portraits, there is a very specific type of person we are allowed to imagine sitting behind the wheel, a person with a certain kind of look (young, fit, fashionable); a certain kind of lifestyle (yuppie professional but also rugged and outdoorsy); a particular circle of friends (similarly young, fit and fashionable); and a certain level of income (comfortably upper middle class). And we further know that our job as viewers is not only to accurately define this hypothetical driver, but also to admire him, to see him as a stand-in for ourselves. Once we have taken this step, we are well on our way to accepting and adopting the other

messages an image like this conveys (about, for instance, the desirability of wealth, the importance of status, or the proper definition of success).

To a very real degree, it is this same formula that underlies our visual encounters with virtually everything in our popular culture: rules of spectatorship that turn the ever-expanding universe of images, signs and messages surrounding us into a kind of classroom where we are taught the "true" difference between what matters and what doesn't, what we should aspire to or emulate and what we should spurn. And when this sort of thing happens in places other than our entertainment industry, the stakes involved can be even higher — as, for example, in our news industry. Whether it is a presidential press conference or combat footage from Iraq, a Fox news roundtable on immigration reform or CNN coverage of the photos released of prisoner abuse at Abu Ghraib, every depiction or discussion of current events is underwritten by the same basic requirement: to accept the assumptions and norms being presented as our own. When we catch the tail-end of a Fox news commentator attacking war protesters for burning the U.S. flag or a mock news story on the *Colbert Report* making fun of Vice President Cheney, we are no less intimately caught up

Everybody Knows That . . .

Tabloids like *US Weekly* tell us "stars are just like us!"

navigating our culture's ideals and expectations than when we catch a glimpse of A-list celebrities strolling down the red carpet.

To return one final time to the example of reality television, think for a moment about what these shows teach us about, say, the importance of not only watching, but also being watched and about the pleasures and payoffs

Everybody Knows That . . .

"The administration's initial response [to the leaking of photos from Abu Ghraib] was to say that the president was shocked and disgusted by the photographs — as if the fault or horror lay in the images, not in what they depict."

— *Susan Sontag, "Regarding the Torture of Others"*

that supposedly result from turning ourselves into an entertainment spectacle. Since we rarely see a cast member on one of these shows expressing annoyance or dismay over having their lives filmed twenty-four hours a day, is it really all that strange to consider that we might begin to feel the same way — that we might start regarding the prospect of being scrutinized by others as ordinary, unremarkable, just "the ways things are"?

To expand this inquiry, in fact, we might note how often this expectation gets reinforced elsewhere in our pop culture. We need only take stock of the growing ubiquity of personal webcam technology, the burgeoning popularity of online sites like Friendster and MySpace, for example, to get a sense of how widespread this norm has become. Is the emergence of popular Internet sites like YouTube an extension of a need to watch ourselves the way we have grown so accustomed to watching others? We certainly don't lack for images that encourage us to think about the private lives of other people as material fit for public consumption. As we've already seen, when we accept this premise — when we look at the websites, television shows, and magazines in the ways prescribed for us — we find ourselves confronting additional expectations as well: from the clothing brands we should wear to the body images we should cultivate to the reasonableness of being watched ourselves.

To sketch out this process does not by itself answer or resolve the thorny questions this introduction poses: Is seeing believing? In a world defined by personal webcams and Photoshop software, Pixar-animated movies and network television "docudramas," how do we know the difference between what is real and what is scripted? How does the role of watcher we're taught affect our assumptions about the world around us? And does this role eventually blur the boundaries between watching and being watched? Given the sheer volume and enormous variety of what we are shown day to day, it should not surprise us that answering these questions gets pretty complicated pretty quickly.

Nonetheless, this task is taken up by each of the following selection authors. The authors in this chapter fall into two basic categories: those exploring some aspect of how we are taught to look, and those addressing some dimension of how we are looked at. Within the first are writers like Ann-Marie Cusac, Naomi Klein, and Daniel Harris. Trying to make sense of the complicated and surprisingly intimate connection between fictional television and real-world events, Cusac's essay explores the degree to which the public debate in the United States about torture has been scripted by plotlines from the hit Fox show *24.* In her exploration of corporate branding,

Naomi Klein pursues a very similar line of inquiry — pondering how campus activism these days has been co-opted and largely driven by the logic of commercial advertising. Striking a more ironic tone, Daniel Harris takes aim at the popular enthusiasm for "cute kitsch," wondering aloud what our predilection for things like Hallmark cards and teddy bears tells us about not only our more deeply embedded ideals but our hidden fears as well. Within the second category are writers like Harriet McBryde Johnson, Ariel Levy, Brooke A. Knight, and Michael Eric Dyson. In recounting her debate with famed medical ethicist Peter Singer, Johnson, an American with disabilities, offers a startlingly blunt and thought-provoking meditation on what it means to be viewed — and stereotyped — as the "token cripple." Surveying the rise of

Everybody Knows That . . .

"raunch culture," Levy examines the phenomenon of stereotyping from a radically different perspective, documenting what she sees as a perplexing eagerness among young American women to make themselves into sexualized spectacles for predominantly male audiences. Levy's focus finds a useful complement in Knight's discussion of personal websites, yet another venue in our contemporary world dedicated to the purveying of women's bodies as visual spectacles. Focusing his attention on the same issues of image and representation raised by these other three, Dyson shifts our focus to the question of race and offers a searing analysis of the inaccurate and discriminatory double standards underlying the mainstream news coverage of Hurricane Katrina.

While they range widely across the landscape of our modern popular culture, these selections do remain linked in one fundamental way: By questioning some of the key visual roles that get scripted in our world, each in its own way inclines us to wonder whether what we *see* is truly what we *get*.

"EVERYBODY KNOWS THAT" EXERCISE

Choose one of the images or quotations featured in the margins on the previous pages and answer the following questions:

1. What does this image or quotation ask you to believe?

2. What are the particular ideas, values, or attitudes it invites us to accept as *normal*?

3. What would it feel like to act on or act out these norms in our personal lives?

Rule **Maker** > > > > > > > > Rule **Breaker**

❝ We thought if you trained cameras on people who were really interesting, and edited that in an interesting way and cut it to music, what do you have? Each person has a unique story and you have to care about them. . . . They are direct with each other about what they are feeling and that comes up clearly. . . . We watch this because it holds a mirror up to ourselves."

— MARY ELLIS-BUNIM, CREATOR OF
REALITY SERIES *THE REAL WORLD,*
ROAD RULES, AND *STARTING OVER,* ON
LARRY KING LIVE, JUNE 27, 2000

❝ I'm very honored to have been selected and it changed my life. However, there is a reality behind reality television, and that reality is not real. . . . I can tell you that what I've watched and what I've lived through are two different things. . . . If I taped you over three days and I had the discretion of choosing whatever I wanted, I could paint you in any light I wanted."

— OMAROSA MANIGAULT-STALLWORTH,
REALITY PARTICIPANT ON *THE APPRENTICE* AND
THE SURREAL LIFE, IN AN INTERVIEW WITH
THE MORNING NEWS, JANUARY 17, 2006

Taken together, these quotations capture what is perhaps the trickiest and most fundamental question about reality television: Is what we are shown, in fact, *real*? The answer, of course, depends on whom you ask. For those who create and produce these shows, the answer could quite easily be "yes." They might acknowledge that those who apply to become cast members are put through a rigorous screening process designed to find specific types of people who viewers will want to root for or revile, people who fit roles and possess character traits that audiences are accustomed to. They might also concede that specific storylines and dramatic conflicts are tailored and polished in the editing room to achieve a show with a more narrative arc. Reality television producers like the late Mary Ellis-Bunim have been pretty upfront that they use the conventional tricks of more traditional scripted television — lighting, music cues, reaction shots from other cast members — to increase dramatic tension. Despite all this, however, reality television producers likely would maintain that what gets broadcast is nonetheless authentic. After all, they might say, reality television still brings viewers into contact with people being *themselves.*

For those on the other side of the camera, however, the answer could be very different. From their vantage point, reality television might easily be less like an opportunity to showcase the "real you" than a job: one that requires you to conform to a role you had no direct hand in creating. It is hardly a secret that shows like these operate according to clear-cut, well-established rules. It doesn't take too many hours of watching before it becomes obvious that only certain character types, certain relationships, and certain kinds of conflict qualify as fit subject matter. Every reality show has its villain, its crybaby, its average Joe. As these shows become more and more popular, the scripts that underline the way they work become more obvious. And for those who aspire to be on these shows, who work to find themselves included in these finished portraits of "reality," are also more aware of how these shows are scripted. Does it follow, then, that these reality television participants may be acting a part well before they're even cast to increase their chances of being selected? Are they turning the reality television formula on its head and removing producers' last claim to authenticity?

GETTY IMAGES

FIND THE RULES: Spend an evening watching the reality television show of your choice and write a profile of this show. Begin by summarizing the goals of the show. Is there a prize for winning, or does the show instead present itself as an examination of human behavior with no prize in sight? Next, analyze the participants on the show. What roles do they seem to play, and what about their behavior leads you to this conclusion? Finally, which storylines in the show seem to get the most attention? How do the editors seem to script these storylines (pay attention to the music they use, whether prize situations or challenges have anything to do with creating conflict, and so forth)?

MAKE YOUR OWN RULES: Imagine that you are creating your own reality television show, with one catch: Your show must be 100 percent real. In a brief essay, describe what this show would look like. What would its format be? What setting would you choose? What types of characters? Explain how this show would rewrite the rules and norms by which reality television shows are conventionally created. To create your "100 percent real" show, what aspects of the reality format do you think you would have to change?

HARRIET McBRYDE JOHNSON
Unspeakable Conversations

What does it mean to be tokenized, to have the stereotypes based on how we look become the scripts by which others think about and define us? In recounting her two-day experience playing the role of what she calls the "token cripple" on a Princeton University visit, Harriet McBryde Johnson raises a series of provocative questions about the ways in which our physical appearance comes to stand as definitive proof of who and what we are. Johnson is a practicing lawyer in Charleston, South Carolina. She earned a BS in history from Charleston Southern University (1978), a master's in public administration from the College of Charleston (1981), and a JD from the University of South Carolina (1985). She has written about political and disability issues for a number of publications, such as *South Carolina Lawyer* and *Review of Public Personnel Administration.* She is also a writer of fiction and is at work on a novel, provisionally titled *Accidents of Nature.*

HE INSISTS HE DOESN'T WANT TO KILL ME. HE SIMPLY THINKS IT would have been better, all things considered, to have given my parents the option of killing the baby I once was, and to let other parents kill similar babies as they come along and thereby avoid the suffering that comes with lives like mine and satisfy the reasonable preferences of parents for a different kind of child. It has nothing to do with me. I should not feel threatened.

Whenever I try to wrap my head around his tight string of syllogisms, my brain gets so fried it's . . . almost fun. Mercy! It's like *Alice in Wonderland.*

It is a chilly Monday in late March, just less then a year ago. I am at Princeton University.

My host is Prof. Peter Singer, often called — and not just by his book publicist — the most influential philosopher of our time. He is the man who wants me dead. No, that's not at all fair. He wants to legalize the killing of certain babies who might come to be like me if allowed to live. He also says he believes that it should be lawful under some circumstances to kill, at any age, individuals with cognitive impairments

> *My host is Prof. Peter Singer . . . He is the man who wants me dead.*

so severe that he doesn't consider them "persons." What does it take to be a person? Awareness of your own existence in time. The capacity to harbor preferences as for the future, including the preference for continuing to live.

At this stage of my life, he says, I am a person. However, as an infant, I wasn't. I, like all humans, was born without self-awareness. And eventually, assuming my brain finally gets so fried that I fall into that wonderland where self and other and present and past and future blur into one boundless, formless all or nothing. Then I'll lose my personhood and therefore my right to life. Then, he says, my family and doctors might put me out of my misery, or out of my bliss or oblivion, and no one count it murder.

I have agreed to two speaking engagements. In the morning, I talk to 15 undergraduates on selective infanticide. In the evening, it is a convivial discussion, over dinner, of assisted suicide. I am the token cripple with an opposing view.

I had several reasons for accepting Singer's invitation, some grounded in my involvement in the disability rights movement, others entirely personal. For the movement it seemed an unusual opportunity to experiment with modes of discourse that might work with very tough audiences and bridge the divide between our perceptions and theirs. I didn't expect to straighten out Singer's head. But maybe I could reach a student or two. Among the personal reasons: I was sure it would make a great story, first for telling and then for writing down.

By now I've told it to family and friends and colleagues, over lunches and dinners, on long car trips, in scads of e-mail messages and a couple of formal speeches. But it seems to be a story that just won't settle down. After all these tellings, it still lacks a coherent structure; I'm miles away from a rational argument. I keep getting interrupted by questions like these:

Q: Was he totally grossed out by your physical appearance?

A: He gave no sign of it. None whatsoever.

Q: How did he handle having to interact with someone like you?

A: He behaved in every way appropriately and treated me as a respected professional acquaintance and was a gracious and accommodating host.

Q: Was it emotionally difficult for you to take part in a public discussion of whether your life should have happened?

A: It was very difficult. And horribly easy.

Q: Did he get that job at Princeton because they like his ideas on killing disabled babies?

A: It apparently didn't hurt. But he's most famous for animal rights. He's the author of *Animal Liberation*.

Q: How can he put so much value on animal life and so little value on human life?

That last question is the only one I avoid. I used to say I don't know, it doesn't make sense. But now I've read some of Singer's writing, and I admit it does make sense — within the conceptual world of Peter Singer. But I don't want to go there. Or at least, not for long.

So I will start from those other questions and see where the story goes this time.

That first question, about my physical appearance, needs some explaining.

It's not that I'm ugly. It's more that most people don't know how to look at me. The sight of me is routinely discombobulating. The power wheelchair is enough to inspire gawking, but that's the least of it. Much more impressive is the impact on my body of more than four decades of a muscle wasting disease. At this stage of my life, I'm Karen Carpenter thin, flesh mostly vanished, a jumble of bones in a floppy bag of skin. When, in childhood, my muscles got too weak to hold up my spine, I tried a brace for a while, but fortunately a skittish anesthesiologist said no to fusion, plates, and pins — all the apparatus that might have kept me straight. At 15, I threw away the back brace and let my spine reshape itself into a deep twisty S-curve. Now my right side is two deep canyons. To keep myself upright, I lean forward, rest my rib cage on my lap, plant my elbows beside my knees. Since my backbone found its own natural shape, I've been entirely comfortable in my skin.

> **It's not that I'm ugly. It's more that most people don't know how to look at me.**

I am in the first generation to survive to such decrepitude. Because antibiotics were available, we didn't die from the childhood pneumonias that often come with weakened respiratory systems. I guess it is natural enough that most people don't know what to make of us.

Two or three times in my life — I recall particularly one largely crip, largely lesbian cookout halfway across the continent — I have been looked at as a rare kind of beauty. There is also the bizarre fact that where I live, Charleston, S.C., some people call me Good Luck Lady: they consider it propitious to cross my path when a hurricane is coming and to kiss my head just before voting day. But most often, the reactions are decidedly negative. Strangers on the street are moved to comment:

I admire you for being out; most people would have given up.

God bless you! I'll pray for you. You don't let the pain hold you back, do you? If I had to live like you, I think I'd kill myself.

I used to try to explain that in fact I enjoy my life, that it's a great sensual pleasure to zoom by power chair on these delicious muggy streets, that I have no more reason to kill myself than most people. But it gets tedious. God didn't put me on this street to provide disability awareness training to the likes of them. In fact, no god put anyone anywhere for any reason, if you want to know.

But they don't want to know. They think they know everything there is to know, just by looking at me. That's how stereotypes work. They don't know that they're confused. That they're really expressing the discombobulation that comes in my wake.

So. What stands out when I recall first meeting Peter Singer in the spring of 2001 is his apparent immunity to my looks. His apparent lack of discombobulation, his immediate ability to deal with me as a person with a particular point of view.

Then, 2001, Singer has been invited to the College of Charleston not two blocks from my house. He is to lecture on "Rethinking Life and Death." I have been dispatched by Not Dead Yet, the national organization leading the disability-rights opposition to legalized assisted suicide and disability based killing. I am to put out a leaflet and do something during the Q and A.

On arriving almost an hour early to reconnoiter, I find the scene almost entirely peaceful; even the boisterous display of South Carolina spring is muted by gray wisps of Spanish moss and mottled oak bark.

I roll around the corner of the building and am confronted with the unnerving sight of two people I know sitting on a park bench eating veggie pitas with Singer. Sharon is a veteran activist for human rights. Herb is South Carolina's most famous atheist. Good people. I've always thought — now sharing veggie pitas and conversation with a proponent of genocide. I try to beat a retreat, but Herb and Sharon have seen me. Sharon tosses her trash and comes over. After we exchange the usual courtesies she asks, "Would you like to meet Professor Singer?" She doesn't have a clue. She probably likes his book on animal rights. "I'll just talk to him in the Q and A." But Herb, with Singer at his side, is fast approaching. They are looking at me and Herb is talking, no doubt saying nice things about me. He'll be saying that I'm a disability rights lawyer and that I gave a talk against assisted suicide at his secular humanist group a while back. He didn't agree with everything I said, he'll say, but I was brilliant. Singer appears interested, engaged. I sit where I'm parked. Herb makes an introduction.

Singer extends his hand.

I hesitate. I shouldn't shake hands with the Evil One. But he is Herb's guest, and I simply can't snub Herb's guest at the college where Herb teaches. Hereabouts, the rule is that if you're not prepared to shoot on sight, you have to be prepared to shake hands. I give Singer the three fingers on my right hand that still work. "Good afternoon, Mr. Singer. I'm here for Not Dead Yet." I want to think he flinches just a little. Not Dead Yet did everything possible to disrupt his first week at Princeton. I sent a check to the fund for the 14 arrestees, who included comrades in power chairs. But if Singer flinches, he instantly recovers. He answers my questions about the lecture format. When he says he looks forward to an interesting exchange, he seems entirely sincere.

It is an interesting exchange. In the lecture hall that afternoon, Singer lays it all out. The "illogic" of allowing abortion but not infanticide, of allowing withdrawal of life support but not active killing. Applying the basic assumptions of preference utilitarianism, he spins out his bone-chilling argument for letting parents kill disabled babies and replace them with nondisabled babies who have a greater chance at happiness. It is all about allowing as many individuals as possible to fulfill as many of their preferences as possible.

As soon as he's done, I get the microphone and say I'd like to discuss selective infanticide. I'm a lawyer. I disagree with his jurisprudential assumptions. Logical inconsistency is not a sufficient reason to change the law. As an atheist, I object to his using religious terms (the doctrine of the sanctity of human life) to characterize his critics. Singer takes a note pad out of his pocket and jots down my points, apparently eager to take them on, and I proceed to the heart of my argument: that the presence or absence of a disability doesn't predict quality of life. I question his replacement-baby theory, with its assumption of "other things equal," arguing that people are not fungible. I draw out a comparison of myself and my nondisabled brother Mac (the next-born after me), each of us with a combination of gifts and flaws so peculiar that we can't be measured on the same scale.

He responds to each point with clear and lucid counterarguments. He proceeds with the assumption that I am one of the people who might rightly have been killed at birth. He sticks to his guns, conceding just enough to show himself open-minded and flexible. We go back and forth for 10 long minutes. Even as I am horrified by what he says and by the fact that I have been sucked into a civil discussion of whether I ought to exist, I can't help being dazzled by his verbal facility. He is so respectful, so free of condescension, so focused on the argument, that by the time the show is over, I'm not exactly angry with him. Yes, I am shaking, furious, enraged — but it's for the big room, 200 of my fellow Charlestonians who have listened with polite interest, when in decency they should have run him out of town on a rail.

My encounter with Peter Singer merits a mention in my annual canned letter that December. I decide to send Singer a copy. In response, he sends me the nicest possible e-mail message. Dear Harriet (if he may) . . . Just back from Australia where he's from. Agrees with my comments on the world situation. Supports my work against institutionalization. And then some pointed questions to clarify my views on selective infanticide.

I reply. Fine, call me Harriet, and I'll reciprocate in the interest of equality, though I'm accustomed to more formality. Skipping agreeable preambles, I answer his questions on disability-based infanticide and pose some of my own. Answers and more questions come back. Back and forth over several weeks it proceeds, an engaging discussion of baby killing, disability prejudice, and related points of law and philosophy. Dear Harriet. Dear Peter.

Singer seems curious to learn how someone who is as good an atheist as he is could disagree with his entirely reasonable views. At the same time, I am trying to plumb his theories. What has him so convinced it would be best to allow parents to kill babies with severe disabilities, and not other kinds of babies if no infant is a "person" with a right to life? I learn it is partly that both biological and adoptive parents prefer healthy babies. But I have trouble with basing life-and death decisions on market considerations when the market is structured by prejudice. I offer a hypothetical comparison: "What about mixed-race babies, especially, when the combination is entirely nonwhite, who I believe are just about as unadoptable as babies with disabilities? Wouldn't a law allowing the killing of these undervalued babies validate race prejudice?" Singer agrees there is a problem. "It would be horrible," he says, "to see mixed-race babies being killed because they can't be adopted, whereas white ones could be." What's the difference? Preferences based on race are unreasonable. Preferences based on ability are not. Why? To Singer, it's pretty simple: disability makes a person "worse off."

Are we "worse off?" I don't think so. Not in any meaningful sense. There are too many variables. For those of us with congenital conditions, disability shapes all we are. Those disabled later in life adapt. We take constraints that no one could choose and build rich and satisfying lives within them. We enjoy pleasures other people enjoy, and pleasures peculiarly our own. We have something the world needs.

Pressing me to admit a negative correlation between disability and happiness, Singer presents a situation: imagine a disabled child on the beach, watching the other children play.

> *Imagine a disabled child on the beach, watching the other children play.*

It's right out of the telethon. I expected something more sophisticated from a professional thinker. I respond: "As a little girl playing on the beach, I was already aware that some people felt sorry for me, that I wasn't frolicking with the same level of frenzy as other children. This annoyed me, and still does. I take the time to write a detailed description of how I, in fact, had fun laying on the beach, without the need of standing, walking or running. But, really, I've had enough. I suggest to Singer that we have exhausted our topic, and I'll be back in touch when I get around to writing him.

He responds by inviting me to Princeton. I fire off an immediate maybe.

Of course, I'm flattered. Mama will be impressed. But there are things to consider. Not Dead Yet says — and I completely agree — that we should not legitimate Singer's views by giving them a forum. We should not make disabled lives subject to debate. Moreover, any spokesman chosen by the opposition is by definition a token. But even if I'm a token, I won't have to act like one. Anyway, I'm kind of stuck. If I decline, Singer can make some hay: "I offered them a platform, but they declined rational discussion." It's an old trick, and I've laid myself wide open.

My invitation is to have an exchange of views with Singer during his undergraduate course. He also proposes a second "exchange," open to the whole university later in the day. This sounds a lot like debating my life — and on my opponent's turf with my opponent moderating, to boot, I offer a counterproposal, to which Singer proves amenable. I will open the class with some comments on infanticide and related issues and then let Singer drill me as hard as he likes before we open it up for the students. Late in the day, I might take part in a discussion of some other disability issues in a neutral forum. Singer suggests a faculty-student discussion group sponsored by his department but with cross-departmental membership. The topic I select is "Assisted Suicide, Disability Discrimination and the Illusion of Choice. A Disability Rights Perspective." I inform a few movement colleagues of this turn of events, and advice starts rolling in. I decide to go with the advisers who counsel me to do the gig, lie low, and get out of Dodge.

I ask Singer to refer me to the person who arranges travel at Princeton. I imagine some capable and unflappable woman like my sister, Beth, whose varied job description at a North Carolina University includes handling visiting artists. Singer refers me to his own assistant, who certainly seems capable and unflappable enough. However, almost immediately Singer jumps back in via e-mail. It seems the nearest hotel has only one wheelchair-accessible suite available with two rooms for $600 per night. What to do? I know I shouldn't be so accommodating, but I say I can make do with an inaccessible room if it has certain features. Other logistical issues come up. We go back and forth. Questions and answers. Do I really need a lift-equipped vehicle at the airport? Can't my assistant assist me into a conventional car? How wide is my wheelchair?

By the time we're done, Singer knows that I am 28 inches wide. I have trouble controlling my wheelchair if my hand gets cold. I am accustomed to driving on rough, irregular surfaces, but I get nervous turning on steep slopes. Even one step is too many. I can swallow purees, soft bread and grapes. I use a bedpan, not a toilet. None of this is a secret: none of it cause for angst. But I do wonder whether Singer is jotting down my specs in his little note pad as evidence of how "bad off" people like me really are. I realize I must put one more issue on the table: etiquette. I was criticized within the movement when I confessed to shaking Singer's hand in Charleston, and some are appalled that I have agreed to break bread with him in Princeton. I think they have a very good point, but again, I'm stuck. I'm engaged for a day of discussion, not a picket line. It is not in my power to marginalize Singer at Princeton; nothing would be accomplished by displays of personal disrespect. However, chumminess is clearly inappropriate. I tell Singer that in the lecture hall it can't be Harriet and Peter, it must be Ms. Johnson and Mr. Singer.

He seems genuinely nettled. Shouldn't it be Ms. Johnson and Professor Singer, if I want to be formal? To counter, I invoke the ceremonial low country usage. Attorney Johnson and Professor Singer, but point out that Mr./Ms. is the custom in American political debates and might seem more normal in New Jersey. All right, he says. Ms./Mr. it will be.

I describe this awkward social situation to the lawyer in my office who has served as my default lunch partner for the past 14 years. He gives forth a full body shudder.

"That poor, sorry son of a bitch! He has no idea what he's in for."

Being a disability rights lawyer lecturing at Princeton does confer some cachet at the Newark airport. I need all the cachet I can get. Delta Airlines has torn my power chair. It is a fairly frequent occurrence for any air traveler on wheels.

When they inform me of the damage in Atlanta, I throw a monumental fit and tell them to have a repair person meet me in Newark with new batteries to replace the ones inexplicably destroyed. Then I am told no new batteries can be had until the morning. It's Sunday night. On arrival in Newark, I'm told of a plan to put me up there for the night and get me repaired and driven to Princeton by 10 A.M.

"That won't work. I'm lecturing at 10. I need to get there tonight, go to sleep and be in my right mind tomorrow."

"What? You're lecturing? They told us it was a conference. We need to get you fixed tonight!"

Carla, the gate agent, relieves me of the need to throw any further fits by undertaking on my behalf the fit of all fits.

Carmen, the personal assistant with whom I'm traveling, pushes me in my disabled chair around the airport in search of a place to use the bedpan. However, instead of diaper-changing tables, which are functional, though far from private, we find a flip-down plastic shelf that doesn't look like it would hold my 70 pounds of body weight. It's no big deal: I've restricted my fluids. But Carmen is a little freaked. It is her first adventure in power-chair air travel. I thought I prepared her for the trip, but I guess I neglected to warn her about the probability of wheelchair destruction. I keep forgetting that even people who know me well don't know much about my world.

> **I keep forgetting that even people who know me well don't know much about my world.**

We reach the hotel at 10:15 P.M., four hours late.

I wake up tired. I slept better than I would have slept in Newark with an unrepaired chair, but any hotel bed is a near guarantee of morning crankiness. I tell Carmen to leave the TV off. I don't want to hear the temperature.

I do the morning stretch. Medical people call it passive movement but it's not really passive. Carmen's hands move my limbs following my precise instructions, her strength giving effect to my will. Carmen knows the routine, so it is in near silence that we begin easing slowly into the day. I let myself be propped up to eat oatmeal and drink tea. Then there's the bedpan and then bathing and dressing, still in bed. As the caffeine kicks in, silence gives way to conversation about practical things. Carmen lifts me into my chair and straps a rolled towel under my ribs for comfort and stability. She tugs at my clothes to remove wrinkles that could cause pressure sores. She switches on my motors and gives me the means of moving without anyone's help. They don't call it a power chair for nothing.

I drive to the mirror. I do my hair in one long braid. Even this primal hairdo requires, at this stage of my life, joint effort. I undo yesterday's braid. Fix the part and comb the hair in front. Carmen combs where I can't reach. I divide the mass into three long hanks and start the braid just behind my left ear. Section by section, I hand it over to her — and her unimpaired young fingers pull tight. Crisscross, until the braid is fully formed.

A big polyester scarf completes my costume. Carmen lays it over my back. I tie it the way I want it. But Carmen starts fussing with it trying to tuck it down in the back. I tell her that it's fine, and she stops.

On top of the scarf, she wraps the two big shawls that I hope will substitute for an overcoat. I don't own any real winter clothes. I just stay out of the cold, such cold as we get in Charleston.

We review her instructions for the day. Keep me in view and earshot; be instantly available but not intrusive. Be polite, but don't answer any questions about me. I am glad that she has agreed to come. She's strong, smart, adaptable, and very loyal. But now she is digging under the shawl, fussing with that scarf again.

"Carmen. What are you doing?" "I thought I could hide this furry thing you sit on." "Leave it, Singer knows lots of people eat meat. Now he'll know some crips sit on sheepskin."

The walk in is cold but mercifully short. The hotel is just across the street from Princeton's wrought-iron gate and a few short blocks from the building where Singer's assistant shows us to the elevator. The elevator doubles as the janitor's closet — the cart with the big trashcan and all the accouterments is rolled aside so I can get in. Evidently, there aren't a lot of wheelchair people using this building.

We ride the broom closet down to the basement and are led down a long passageway to a big lecture hall. As the students drift in, I engage in light badinage with the sound technician. He is squeamish about touching me but I insist that the cordless lavaliere is my mike of choice. I invite him to clip it to the big polyester scarf.

The students enter from the rear door, way up at ground level and walk down stairs to their seats. I feel like an animal in the zoo. I hadn't reckoned on the architecture, those tiers of steps that separate me from a human wall of apparent physical and mental perfection, that keep me confined down here in my pit.

It is 5 before 10. Singer is loping down the stairs. I feel like signaling to Carmen to open the door, summon the broom closet, and get me out of here. But Singer greets me pleasantly and hands me Princeton's check for $500, the fee he offered with apologies for its inadequacy.

So. On with the show.

My talk to the students is pretty Southern. I've decided to pound them with heart, hammer them with narrative and say "y'all" and "folks," I play with the emotional tone, giving them little peaks and valleys, modulating three times in one 45 second patch. I talk about justice. Even beauty and love. I figure they haven't been getting much of that from Singer.

Of course, I give them some argument too. I mean to honor my contractual obligations. I lead with the hypothetical about mixed-race, nonwhite babies and build the ending around the question of who should have the burden of proof as to the quality of disabled lives. And woven through the talk is the presentation of myself as a representative of a minority group that has been rendered invisible by prejudice and oppression, a participant in a discussion that would not occur in a just world.

I let it go a little longer than I should. Their faces show they're going where I'm leading, and I don't look forward to letting them go. But the clock on the wall reminds me of promises I mean to keep, and I stop talking and submit myself to examination and inquiry.

Singer's response is surprisingly soft. Maybe after hearing that this discussion is insulting and painful to me, he doesn't want to exacerbate my discomfort. His refraining of the issues is almost pro forma, abstract, entirely impersonal. Likewise, the students' inquiries are abstract and fairly predictable: anencephaly permanent unconsciousness, eugenic abortion. I respond to some of them with stories, but mostly I give answers I could have e-mailed in.

I call on a young man near the top of the room.

"Do you eat meat?" "Yes, I do," "Then how do you justify —"

"I haven't made any study of animal rights, so anything I could say on the subject wouldn't be worth everyone's time." The next student wants to work the comparison of disability and race, and Singer joins the discussion until he elicits a comment from me that he can characterize as racist. He scores a point, but that's all right. I've never claimed to be free of prejudice, just struggling with it.

Singer proposes taking me on a walk around campus, unless I think it would be too cold. What the hell? "It's probably warmed up some. Let's go out and see how I do." He doesn't know how to get out of the building without using the stairs, so this time it is my assistant leading the way. Carmen has learned of another elevator, which arrives empty. When we get out of the building, she falls behind a couple of paces, like a respectful chaperone.

In the classroom, there was a question about keeping alive the unconscious. In response, I told a story about a family I knew as a child, which took loving care of a non-responsive teenage girl, acting out their unconditional commitment to each other, making all the other children and me as their visitor, feel safe. This doesn't satisfy Singer. "Let's assume we can prove, absolutely that the individual is totally unconscious and that we can know absolutely, that the individual will never regain consciousness." I see no need to state an objection with no stenographer present to record it; I'll play the game and let him continue.

"Assuming all that," he says, "don't you think continuing to take care of that individual would be a bit weird?" "No. Done right, it could be profoundly beautiful."

"But what about the caregiver, a woman typically, who is forced to provide all this service to a family member, unable to work, unable to have a life of her own?" "That's not the way it should be. Not the way it has to be. As a society, we should pay workers to provide that care, in the home. In some places, it's been done that way for years. That woman shouldn't be forced to do it, any more than my family should be forced to do my care."

Singer takes me around the architectural smorgasbord that is Princeton University by a route that includes not one step, unramped curb, or turn on a slope. Within the strange limits of this strange assignment, it seems Singer is doing all he can to make me comfortable.

He asks what I thought of the students' questions.

"They were fine, about what I expected. I was a little surprised by the question about meat eating." "I apologize for that. That was out of left field. But — I think what he wanted to know is how you can have such high respect for human life and so little respect for animal life."

"And what do you answer?"

"I say I don't know. It doesn't make a lot of sense to me."

"Well, in my view — "

"Look, I have lived in blissful ignorance all these years, and I'm not prepared to give that up today."

"Fair enough," he says and proceeds to recount bits of Princeton history. He stops, "this will be of particular interest to you, I think. This is where your colleagues with Not Dead Yet set up their blockade." I'm grateful for the reminder. My brothers and sisters were here before me and behaved far more appropriately than I am doing.

A van delivers Carmen and me early for the evening forum. Singer says he hopes I had a pleasant afternoon.

Yes, indeed. I report a pleasant lunch and a very pleasant nap, and I tell him about the Christopher Reeve Suite in the hotel which has been remodeled to accommodate Reeve, who has family in the area.

"Do you suppose that's the $600 accessible suite they told me about?" "Without doubt. And if I'd known it was the Christopher Reeve Suite, I would have held out for it." "Of course you would have!" Singer laughs. "And we'd have had no choice, would we?"

We talk about the disability rights critique of Reeve and various other topics. Singer is easy to talk to, good company. Too bad he sees lives like mine as avoidable mistakes.

I'm looking forward to the soft vegetarian meal that has been arranged; I'm hungry. Assisted suicide, as difficult as it is, doesn't cause the kind of agony I felt discussing disability-based infanticide. In this one, I understand, and to some degree can sympathize with the opposing point of view, misguided though it is.

My opening sticks to the five-minute time limit. I introduce the issue as framed by academic articles Not Dead Yet recommended for my use. Andrew Batavia argues for assisted suicide based on autonomy, a principle generally held high in the disability rights movement. In general, he says, the movement fights for our right to control our own lives; when we need assistance to effect our choices, assistance should be available to us as a matter of right. If the choice is to end our lives, he says, we should have assistance then as well. But Carol Gill says that it is differential treatment — disability discrimination — to try to prevent most suicides while facilitating the suicides of ill and disabled people. The social-science

The case for assisted suicide rests on stereotypes.

literature suggests that the public in general, and physicians in particular, tend to underestimate the quality of life of disabled people, compared with our own assessments of our lives. The case for assisted suicide rests on stereotypes that our lives are inherently so bad that it is entirely rational if we want to die.

I side with Gill. What worries me most about the proposals for legalized assisted suicide to their veneer of beneficence — the medical determination that, for a given individual suicide is reasonable or right. It is not about autonomy but about nondisabled people telling us what's good for us.

In the discussion that follows, I argue that choice is illusory in a context of pervasive inequality. Choices are structured by oppression. We shouldn't offer assistance with suicide until we all have the assistance we need to get out of bed in the morning and live a good life. Common causes of suicidality — dependence, institutional confinement, being a burden — are entirely curable. Singer, seated on my right, participates in the discussion but doesn't dominate it. During the meal, I occasionally ask him to put things within my reach and he competently complies.

I feel as if I'm getting to a few of them. When a student asks me a question, the words are all familiar, but they're strung together in a way so meaningless that I can't even retain them — it's like a long sentence in Tagalog. I can only admit my limitations. "That question's too abstract for me to deal with. Can you rephrase it?" He indicates that it is as clear as he can make it, so I move on.

A little while later my right elbow slips out from under me. This is awkward. Normally I get whoever is on my right to do this sort of thing. Why not now? I gesture to Singer. He leans over, and I whisper, "Grasp this wrist and pull forward one inch, without lifting." He follows my instructions to the letter. He sees that now I can again reach my food with my fork. And he may now understand what I was saying a minute ago, that most of the assistance disabled people need does not demand medical training.

A philosophy professor says, "It appears that your objections to assisted suicide are essentially tactical."

"Excuse me?"

"By that I mean they are grounded in current conditions of political, social, and economic inequality. What if we assume that such conditions do not exist?"

"Why would we want to do that?"

"I want to get to the real basis for the position you take."

I feel as if I'm losing caste. It is suddenly very clear that I'm not a philosopher. I'm like one of those old practitioners who used to visit my law school, full of bluster about life in the real world. Such a bore! A once-sharp mind gone muddy! And I'm only 44 — not all that old.

The forum is ended, and I've been able to eat very little of my pureed food. I ask Carmen to find the caterer and get me a container. Singer jumps up to take care of it. He returns with a box and obligingly packs my food to go.

When I get home, people are clamoring for the story. The lawyers want the blow-by-blow of my forensic triumph over the formidable foe; when I tell them it wasn't like that, they insist that it was. Within the disability rights community, there is less confidence. It is generally assumed that I handled the substantive discussion well, but people worry that my civility may have given Singer a new kind of legitimacy: I hear from Laura, a beloved movement sister. She is appalled that I let Singer provide even minor physical assistance at the dinner. "Where was your assistant?" she wants to know. How could I put myself in a relationship with Singer that made him appear so human, even kind?

I struggle to explain. I didn't feel disempowered; quite the contrary, it seemed a good thing to make him do some useful work. And then, the hard part: I've come to believe that Singer actually is human, even kind in his way. There ensues a discussion of good and evil and personal assistance and power and philosophy and tactics for which I'm profoundly grateful.

I e-mail Laura again. This time I inform her that I've changed my will. She will inherit a book that Singer gave me, a collection of his writings with a weirdly appropriate inscription: "To Harriet Johnson, So that you will have a better answer to questions about animals. And thanks for coming to Princeton. Peter Singer. March 25, 2002." She responds that she is changing her will, too. I'll get the autographed photo of Jerry Lewis she received as an M.D.A. poster child. We joke that each of us has given the other a "reason to live."

I have had a nice e-mail message from Singer, hoping Carmen and I and the chair got home without injury, relaying positive feedback from my audiences — and taking me to task for a statement that isn't supported by a relevant legal authority, which he looked up. I report that we got home exhausted but unharmed and concede that he has caught me in a generalization that should have been qualified. It's clear that the conversation will continue.

I am soon sucked into the daily demands of law practice, family, community, and politics. In the closing days of the state legislative session, I help get a bill passed that I hope will move us one small step toward a world in which killing won't be such an appealing solution to the "problem" of disability. It is good to focus on this kind of work. But the conversations with and about Singer continue. Unable to muster the appropriate moral judgments, I ask myself a tough question: am I in fact a silly, little lady whose head is easily turned by a man who gives her a kind of attention she enjoys? I hope not, but I confess that I've never been able to sustain righteous anger for more than about 30 minutes at a time. My view of life tends more toward tragedy.

The tragic view comes closest to describing how I now look at Peter Singer. He is a man of unusual gifts, reaching for the heights. He writes that he is trying to create a system of ethics derived from fact and reason, that largely throws off the perspectives of religion, place, family, tribe, community, and maybe even species — to "take the point of view of the universe." His is a grand, heroic undertaking.

But like the protagonist in a classical drama, Singer has his flaw. It is his unexamined assumption that disabled people are inherently "worse off," that we "suffer," that we have lesser "prospects of a happy life." Because of this all-too-common prejudice and his rare courage in taking it to its logical conclusion, catastrophe looms. Here in the midpoint "of the play, I can't look at him without fellow-feeling."

I am regularly confronted by people who tell me that Singer doesn't deserve my human sympathy. I should make him an object of implacable wrath, to be cut off, silenced, destroyed absolutely. And I find myself lacking an argument to the contrary.

I am talking to my sister Beth on the phone. "You kind of like the monster, don't you?" she says.

I find myself unable to evade, certainly unwilling to lie. "Yeah, in a way. And he's not exactly a monster." "You know Harriet, there were some very pleasant Nazis. They say the SS guards went home and played on the floor with their children every night."

She can tell that I'm chastened; she changes the topic, lets me off the hook. Her harshness has come as a surprise. She isn't inclined to moralizing; in our family, I'm the one who sets people straight.

When I put the phone down, my argumentative nature feels frustrated. In my mind, I replay the conversation but this time defend my position. "He's not exactly a monster. He just has some strange ways of looking at things." "He's advocating genocide." "That's the thing. In his mind, he isn't. He's only giving parents a choice. He thinks the humans he is talking about aren't people, aren't 'persons.'"

"But that's the way it always works, isn't it? They're always animals or vermin or chattel goods. Objects, not persons. He's repacking some old ideas. Making 'them acceptable.'" "I think his ideas are new, in a way. It's not old-fashioned hate. It's a twisted, misinformed, warped kind of beneficence. His motive is to do good."

"What do you care about motives?" she asks. "Doesn't this beneficent killing make disabled brothers and sisters just as dead?"

"But he isn't killing anyone. It's just talk."

"Just talk? It's talk with an agenda, talk aimed at forming policy. Talk that's getting a receptive audience. You of all people know the power of that kind of talk."

"Well, sure, but — "

"If talk didn't matter, would you make it your life's work?"

"But," I say, "his talk won't matter in the end. He won't succeed in reinventing morality. He stirs the pot, brings things out into the open. But ultimately, we'll make a world that's fit to live in, a society that has room for all its flawed creatures. History will remember Singer as a curious example of the bizarre things that can happen when paradigms collide."

"What if you are wrong? What if he convinces people that there's no morally significant difference between a fetus and a newborn, and just as disabled fetuses are routinely aborted now, so disabled babies are routinely killed: Might some future generation take it further than Singer wants to go? Might some say there's no morally significant line between a newborn and a 3-year-old child?"

"Sure. Singer concedes that a bright line cannot be drawn. But he doesn't propose killing anyone who prefers to live."

"That overarching respect for the individual's preference for life — might some say it's a fiction, a fetish, a quasi-religious belief."

"Yes," I say. "That's pretty close to what I think. As an atheist, I think all preferences are moot once you kill someone. The injury is entirely to the surviving community."

"So what if that view wins out, but you can't break disability prejudice? What if you wind up in a world where the disabled person's 'irrational' preference to live must yield to society's 'rational' interest in reducing the incidence of disability? Doesn't horror kick in somewhere? Maybe as you watch the door close behind whoever has wheeled you into the gas chamber?"

"That's not going to happen."

"Do you have empirical evidence?" she asks. "A logical argument?"

"Of course not. And I know it's happened before, in what was considered the most progressive medical community in the world. But it won't happen. I have to believe that."

Belief. Is that what it comes down to? Am I a person of faith after all? Or am I clinging to foolish hope that the tragic protagonist, this one time, will shift course before it's too late?

DISCUSSION

1.   Johnson devotes a good deal of time acquainting her readers with the facts about her disability, itemizing the various things that, as a result of her physical condition, she can and cannot do. Why do you think she does this? How does this tactic help her advance her argument about the ways disabled people are seen in our culture?

2.   Look again at the photograph of Johnson that begins the essay. What were your initial assumptions about her based on her picture? In what ways does our popular culture encourage us both to see and *not* see people with disabilities? That is to say, how do the images of and stories about disability that we typically see encourage us to think about people with disabilities?

3.   To what extent is it valid to think of Johnson's account here as expanding or enlarging the scope of the ways disabled people are conventionally seen? What quotes can you find from her essay to support your opinion?

WRITING

4.   Take a moment to look at the photo that Johnson includes of herself in this essay. What are your immediate reactions? What does it feel like to be shown this picture? In a short essay, describe the particular cultural or social norms you think the portrait is designed to challenge or violate. How does this image differ from those we typically see? What alternative messages (for example, about disabled experience itself, about how it gets represented) do you think it is intended to convey? What quotes from Johnson's essay support your reading of this image? Finally, argue either for or against the validity of showing this kind of image.

5.   Have you ever felt "tokenized" because of your physical or external appearance? When people first meet you, what assumptions do you think they make about you based on your appearance? Write a personal essay in which you recount what the experience of being seen in this particular way is like. What perceptions of you did people have? What conclusions did they draw? And in what ways were they inaccurate, unfair, or otherwise limiting? Use quotes from Johnson's essay to pinpoint both the parallels and the key differences between your own experience and what Johnson recounts in her essay.

6.   Johnson and Michael Eric Dyson (p. 123) both draw a clear connection between watching and stereotyping. Each of their essays points centrally to the ways that being "misread" by the public at large can lead to being marginalized, disenfranchised, and oppressed. Write an essay in which you compare and contrast the differences in the ways these two writers explore this connection. Despite their shared concern over stereotyping, how and where do their discussions diverge?

ANNE-MARIE CUSAC

Watching Torture in Prime Time

Foremost among our pop culture's signature features is its striking confluence of fiction and reality. To what extent, we could well ask, is our understanding of real-world events conditioned and mediated by the entertainment spectacles, shows, and images that we watch? For Anne-Marie Cusac, this very possibility poses a fundamental and troubling question: When it comes to the news and current events, how do we ever know the real story? Cusac is an investigative reporter for the *Progressive.* Her magazine articles have won several prizes, including the George Polk Award. She has also published poems in a number of journals, and her work has been nominated twice for the Pushcart Prize. Her book of poems, *The Mean Days,* was published in 2001. The following essay first appeared in the August 2005 issue of the *Progressive.*

I N THE SAME WEEK AS THE ONE-YEAR ANNIVERSARY OF ABU GHRAIB, an episode of the Fox hit show 24 opened with a scene of the Counter Terrorism Unit medical clinic. Lying in a hospital bed, attended to by physicians, was the terrorism suspect who, in the last seconds of the previous episode, had screamed as the show's hero, Jack Bauer, broke the bones in his hand.

As Fox pumped out advertisements for 24's season finale, the newspapers boiled over with revelations of more real torture by U.S. officers. Then the finale came, and Jack and company saved Los Angeles from a nuclear bomb thanks to a wild series of strategies that included brutal torture.

In the days that followed, Amnesty International issued what amounted to an all-points bulletin for Bush Administration officials: "The officials implicated in these crimes are . . . subject to investigation and possible arrest by other nations while traveling abroad." Like Jack Bauer, the 24 star who in the final scene of the last episode flees to Mexico, Donald Rumsfeld and George W. Bush were suddenly wanted men, accused of breaking international law.

Rarely in my days has fictional television seemed so entwined with our national political life.

Unlike most current cop shows, 24 is concerned with crime prevention. In 24, the would-be crimes are so huge and so imminent that the anti-terrorism team

> *Rarely in my days has fictional television seemed so entwined with our national political life.*

believes it does not have the luxury of playing by the rules. Anxiety — which the show manipulates with exaggerated plot twists — explains some of 24's appeal. Among other explanations is 24's proximity to real events and public fears. The shadow of 9/11 hangs over the show. And then there is torture itself, which has a unique power to horrify.

Kiefer Sutherland, an executive producer on the show as well as the star who plays Jack Bauer, seems driven to address the places where his show intersects with American guilt. "Do I personally believe that the police or any of these other legal agencies that are working for this government should be entitled to interrogate people and do the things that I do on the show? No, I do not," he said in an interview with Charlie Rose.

Joel Surnow, also an executive producer, has connected 24's realism with an appearance of conservatism. "Doing something with any sense of reality to it seems conservative," he told the rightwing paper the *Washington Times,* which praised the show. Surnow also told the paper that 24's writers are both liberal and conservative, that 24 doesn't "try to push an agenda," but is "committed to being non-PC." He also offered a defense of torture under extreme circumstances, the sort that characterize the world of 24. "If there's a bomb about to hit a major U.S. city and you have a person with information . . . if you don't torture that person, that would be one of the most immoral acts you could imagine," he told the *Washington Times*. Surnow doesn't admit this, but the continual regurgitation of situations involving imminent bombings and torture separates 24 from reality and renders it a fantasy show. Impending disaster has rarely, if ever, accompanied the real tortures that get into our newspapers.

Torture on 24 is as contradictory as the statements of its producers. In this past season, 24 depicted torture and terrorism as married. The show's logic ran like this: A nuclear bomb launched from Iowa was in the air on its way to . . . no one knew exactly where. The target was almost certainly a large coastal city. The hardworking counter-terrorism employees who never ate, used the toilet, or slept, whose cell phone batteries never died, needed to stop the explosion from killing millions of innocent people. They had no information on the bomb. They did, however, have a suspect in custody.

It's an unfair competition. If you place torture of a few people, innocent or not, next to an imminent nuclear holocaust, torture seems like a necessity.

But 24's voyeuristic interest in torture is an uncomfortable one. For one thing, and I count this as a detail in the show's favor, 24 differs from many cop shows in that it does not mince around pain. Physical hurt is audible and visible on this show and often difficult to watch. The pain is a harsh contrast to the "happy violence" (which avoids realistic depictions of suffering) that critics of TV have complained about for decades. That 24 insists on rendering pain with such clarity is disturbing in light of the fact that, in this past season, the torturers caused extreme hurt to the wrong people several times. The possibility of torturing an innocent is a hovering concern of the show.

On the other hand, 24 also depicts torture as a useful tool as long as the torturers manage to choose the correct victim. Both those who know a lot and those who know a little spill important information within seconds after the pain starts — which is not a common occurrence.

But efficacy doesn't have the only vote here. Some of those who disagree with Jack's action are straw men, but one voice of reason and goodness belongs to Audrey, who loves Jack and whose own personality and situation are compelling. When she starts to wonder about her love for him, Jack starts to seem monomaniacal and dangerous. After Audrey sees the man with broken fingers lying in the CTU hospital bed, for instance, she turns on the man she loves. "Jack, you cannot keep working outside the law and not expect consequences," she says.

One big consequence is that, by season's end, Jack has lost Audrey's love. After seeing Jack torture her estranged husband, Paul, using a lamp's electrical wires, Audrey also watches as he commands the medical personnel who are trying to save Paul's life to disconnect him from the machines. As Paul begins to die, Jack forces the doctor to save another man so that Jack can interrogate him. "You killed him," accuses Audrey. "I hate you."

But Audrey, who represents, among other things, an ineffectual President, U.S. law, and human love, is not the only indication that Jack's behavior has been criminal. Equally revealing is the post-torture scene, where the victim lies in a hospital bed getting torture aftercare — a physical position often occupied by victims of crime in police dramas.

Those humanistic messages bump up against others that depict Jack as a hero. When Audrey, who is the daughter of the Defense Secretary, tells her dad that she no longer sees the humane Jack, he responds, "We need men like that." And the season finale's very last scene shows Jack in sunglasses walking off into (really!) the sunset.

These multiple meanings suggest why both Amnesty International (which sees torture in the show as "educational") and the conservative magazine National Review (which compared the show's conflicts to Greek tragedy) have praised 24. But some critics read the torture scenes as advocating the practice rather than questioning it.

> **Some critics read the torture scenes as advocating the practice rather than questioning it.**

In a May 22 article in the New York Times, Adam Green asks: "Has 24 descended down a slippery slope in portraying acts of torture as normal and therefore justifiable?" His article bears the unsubtle title, "Normalizing

Torture, One Rollicking Hour at a Time." He wonders whether the audience of the show, "and the public more generally," is "reworking the rules of war to the point where the most expedient response to terrorism is to resort to terror." How that debate "plays out on 24 may say a great deal about what sort of society we are in the process of becoming," he writes.

But in certain parts of American society, torture is already normal. The cultural conditions and political decisions that created Abu Ghraib and widespread torture of detainees by American forces happened before 24. We are already a society that tortures — evidently we became that long ago. What is left to us now as a public is a decision we can make or avoid. We can deal with torture or ignore it. Television does not determine the outcome of that decision; we do.

The more our government sanctions torture, the more that high-level officials do not face censure, the more our democracy erodes. When our highest officials are not held to account, it is often tempting to feel apathetic about torture, as if we have nothing to do with its existence. Intentional disregard seems to be the way we are dealing with this, though few of us are saying so.

In bringing its loudmouthed depictions of extreme cruelty into a show as otherwise attractive and suspense-driven as 24, the show's writers are giving their often fervent fans something to trouble them.

DISCUSSION

1.   "Rarely in my days," writes Cusac, "has fictional television seemed so entwined with our national political life" as in the case of the popular television show *24*. Can you think of another example from our current pop culture that fictionalizes current events? Another show where the line between fact and fiction seems similarly blurred?

2.   In your view, is there a clear connection between the images of and stories about violence we see and our own personal behavior? What is the best way to understand the relationship between the things we look at and the things we do?

3.   *24*'s depiction of torture remains compelling, Cusac argues, in part because the show is able to instill in its viewers an almost palpable feeling of fear. "Anxiety," she writes, "which the show manipulates . . . explains some of *24*'s appeal." Do you agree with this argument? Do we live in a world where the pleasure of watching is tied in some way to the prospect of being frightened? How or how not?

WRITING

4.   Cusac contrasts the ways torture gets depicted on *24* to the countless examples elsewhere on television of what she calls "happy violence," violence where the terrible and tangible are largely erased. Choose one such example from our current pop culture and describe the particular ways this show works to expunge the consequences of violence from its presentation. And as you sketch out how this process works, make sure that you address what you think this process means, what the consequences are of rendering the effects of violence invisible and what this trend suggests about the ways we are taught to think about violence in our culture more generally. What attitude toward violence does this kind of portrayal seem designed to normalize?

5.   Under what conditions can something even as shocking and taboo as torture come to seem like an unremarkable norm? Make a list of all the things about torture that you think are wrong: all the aspects of this practice that render it outside the bounds of our conventional (social, political, ethical) norms. Then create a second list of the particular circumstances (political crisis, catastrophic event, and so on) under which somebody could argue for the validity, even the necessity, of torture. Write an essay in which you argue how Cusac sees the role of television as normalizing torture. Do you agree or disagree?

6.   Cusac shares with Naomi Klein (p. 114) a common concern over the ways our entertainment media can shape public attitudes regarding current events, especially the political. What aspects of Cusac's thinking do you think Klein would most likely endorse? Where might the two part ways? Offer a response to Cusac's argument that, in your view, Klein herself would write, using quotes from both writers to support your argument.

NAOMI KLEIN

Patriarchy Gets Funky:
The Triumph of Identity Marketing

To what extent do we turn to the world of commercial advertising for guidance about how to think through social and political questions? Tracking the growing phenomenon of identity marketing, Naomi Klein tells the story of how such companies as Benetton and MTV have learned to use mass-produced and mass-marketed models of racial and ethnic diversity as brand names for the products they sell. Wondering about and worrying over the growing indistinguishability between our political and commercial lives, Klein shows how intimately corporate iconography has insinuated itself into the ways we view not just the issue of social activism but the idea of social justice as well. Klein, a writer and activist, was born into a political family in Montreal, Quebec, and currently lives in Toronto. She has worked as the editor of *THIS Magazine* and as a weekly columnist for the *Toronto Star,* and she is currently a columnist for the *Nation* and the *Guardian.* Her books *No Logo,* where this selection comes from, (2000) and *Fences and Windows* (2002) discuss globalization and its countermovement. Her latest book is *The Shock Doctrine: The Rise of Disaster Capitalism* (2007).

A S AN UNDERGRADUATE IN THE LATE EIGHTIES AND EARLY NINETIES, I was one of those students who took a while to wake up to the slow branding of university life. And I can say from personal experience that it's not that we didn't notice the growing corporate presence on campus — we even complained about it sometimes. It's just that we couldn't get particularly worked up about it. We knew the fast-food chains were setting up their stalls in the library and that profs in the applied sciences were getting awfully cozy with pharmaceutical companies, but finding out exactly what was going on in the boardrooms and labs would have required a lot of legwork, and, frankly, we were busy. We were fighting about whether Jews would be allowed in the racial equality caucus at the campus women's center, and why the meeting to discuss it was scheduled at the same time as the lesbian and gay caucus — were the organizers implying that there were no Jewish lesbians? No black bisexuals?

   In the outside world, the politics of race, gender, and sexuality remained tied to more concrete, pressing issues, like pay equity, same-sex spousal rights, and police violence, and these serious movements

114

were — and continue to be — a genuine threat to the economic and social order. But somehow, they didn't seem terribly glamorous to students on many university campuses, for whom identity politics had evolved by the late eighties into something quite different. Many of the battles we fought were over issues of "representation" — a loosely defined set of grievances mostly lodged against the media, the curriculum, and the English language. From campus feminists arguing over "representation" of women on the reading lists to gays wanting better "representation" on television, to rap stars bragging about "representing" the ghettos, to the question that ends in a riot in Spike Lee's 1989 film *Do the Right Thing* — "Why are there no brothers on the wall?" — ours was a politics of mirrors and metaphors.

These issues have always been on the political agendas of both the civil-rights and the women's movements, and later, of the fight against AIDS. It was accepted from the start that part of what held back women and ethnic minorities was the absence of visible role models occupying powerful social positions, and that media-perpetuated stereotypes — embedded in the very fabric of the language — served to not so subtly reinforce the supremacy of white men. For real progress to take place, imaginations on both sides had to be decolonized.

But by the time my generation inherited these ideas, often two or three times removed, representation was no longer one tool among many, it was the key. In the absence of a clear legal or political strategy, we traced back almost all of society's problems to the media and the curriculum, either through their perpetuation of negative stereotypes or simply by omission. Asians and lesbians were made to feel "invisible," gays were stereotyped as deviants, blacks as criminals, and women as weak and inferior: a self-fulfilling prophecy responsible for almost all real-world inequalities. And so our battlefields were sitcoms with gay neighbors who never got laid, newspapers filled with pictures of old white men, magazines that advanced . . . "the beauty myth," reading lists that we expected to look like Benetton ads, Benetton ads that trivialized our reading-list demands. So outraged were we media children by the narrow and oppressive portrayals in magazines, in books, and on television that we convinced ourselves that if the typecast images and loaded language changed, so too would the reality. We thought we would find salvation in the reformation of MTV, CNN, and Calvin Klein. And why not? Since media seemed to be the source of so many of our problems, surely if we could only "subvert" them to better represent us, they could save us instead. With better collective mirrors, self-esteem would rise and prejudices would magically fall away, as society became suddenly inspired to live up to the beautiful and worthy reflection we had retouched in its image.

For a generation that grew up mediated, transforming the world through pop culture was second nature. The problem was that these

Transforming the world through pop culture was second nature.

fixations began to transform us in the process. Over time, campus identity politics became so consumed by personal politics that they all but eclipsed the rest of the world. The slogan "the personal is political" came to replace the economic as political and, in the end, the Political as political as well. The more importance we placed on representation issues, the more central a role they seemed to elbow for themselves in our lives — perhaps because, in the absence of more tangible political goals, any movement that is about fighting for better social mirrors is going to eventually fall victim to its own narcissism.

Soon "outing" wasn't about AIDS, but became a blanket demand for gay and lesbian "visibility" — all gays should be out, not just right-wing politicians but celebrities as well. By 1991, the radical group Queer Nation had broadened its media critique: it didn't just object to portrayals of homicidal madmen with AIDS, but any non-straight killer at all. The group's San Francisco and L.A. chapters held protests against *The Silence of the Lambs,* objecting to its transvestite serial-killer villain, and they disrupted filming on *Basic Instinct* because it featured ice-pick-wielding killer lesbians. GLAAD (Gay and Lesbian Alliance Against Defamation) had moved from lobbying the news media about its use of terms like "gay plague" to describe AIDS, and had begun actively pushing the networks for more gay and lesbian characters in TV shows. In 1993, Torie Osborn, a prominent U.S. lesbian rights activist, said that the single biggest political issue facing her constituency was not same-sex spousal benefits, the right to join the military, or even the right of two women to marry and adopt children. It was, she told a reporter, "Invisibility. Period, End of sentence."[1]

Much like a previous generation of anti-porn feminists who held their rallies outside peep shows, many of the political demonstrations of the early nineties had shifted from the steps of government buildings and courthouses to the steps of museums with African art exhibits that were deemed to celebrate the colonial mindset. They massed at the theater entrances showing megamusicals like *Showboat* and *Miss Saigon,* and they even crept right up to the edge of the red carpet at the 1992 Academy Awards.

These struggles may seem slight in retrospect, but you can hardly blame us media narcissists for believing that we were engaged in a crucial battle on behalf of oppressed people everywhere: every step we took sparked a new wave of apocalyptic panic from our conservative foes. If we were not revolutionaries, why, then, were our opponents saying that a revolution was under way, that we were in the midst of a "culture war"? "The transformation of American campuses is so sweeping that it is no exaggeration to call it a revolution," Dinesh D'Souza, author of *Illiberal Education*, informed his readers. "Its distinctive insignia can be witnessed on any major campus in America today, and in all aspects of university life."[2]

Despite their claims of living under Stalinist regimes where dissent was not tolerated, our professors and administrators put up an impressively vociferous counteroffensive: they fought tooth and nail for the right to offend us thin-skinned radicals; they lay down on the tracks in front of every new harassment policy, and generally acted as if they were fighting for the very future of Western civilization. An avalanche of look-alike magazine features bolstered the claim that ID politics constituted an international emergency: "Illiberal Education" (*Atlantic Monthly*), "Visigoths in Tweed" (*Fortune*), "The Silences" (*Maclean's*), "The Academy's New Ayatollahs" (*Outlook*), "Taking Offense" (*Newsweek*). In *New York* magazine, writer John Taylor compared my generation of campus activists with cult members, Hitler Youth, and Christian fundamentalists.[3] So great was the threat we allegedly posed that George Bush even took time out to warn the world that political correctness "replaces old prejudices with new ones."

The Marketing of ID

The backlash that identity politics inspired did a pretty good job of masking for us the fact that many of our demands for better representation were quickly accommodated by marketers, media makers, and pop-culture producers alike — though perhaps not for the reasons we had hoped. If I had to name a precise moment for this shift in attitude, I would say August of 1992: the thick of the "brand crisis" that peaked with Marlboro Friday. That's when we found out that our sworn enemies in the "mainstream" — to us a giant monolithic blob outside of our known university-affiliated enclaves — didn't fear and loathe us but actually thought we were sort of interesting. Once we'd embarked on a search for new wells of cutting-edge imagery, our insistence on extreme sexual and racial identities made for great brand-content and niche-marketing strategies. If diversity is what we wanted, the brands seemed to be saying, then diversity was exactly what we would get. And with that, the marketers and media makers swooped down, airbrushes in hand, to touch up the colors and images in our culture.

> **If diversity is what we wanted, the brands seemed to be saying, then diversity was exactly what we would get.**

The five years that followed were an orgy of red ribbons, Malcolm X baseball hats, and Silence = Death T-shirts. By 1993, the stories of academic Armageddon were replaced with new ones about the sexy wave of "Do-Me Feminism" in *Esquire* and "Lesbian Chic" in *New York* and

Newsweek. The shift in attitude was not the result of a mass political conversion but of some hard economic calculations. According to *Rocking the Ages,* a book produced in 1997 by leading U.S. consumer researchers Yankelovich Partners, "Diversity" was the "defining idea" for Gen-Xers, as opposed to "Individuality" for boomers and "Duty" for their parents.

> Xers are starting out today with pluralistic attitudes that are the strongest we have ever measured. As we look towards the next twenty-five years, it is clear that acceptance of alternative lifestyles will become even stronger and more widespread as Xers grow up and take over the reins of power, and become the dominant buying group in the consumer marketplace. . . . *Diversity is the key fact of life for Xers, the core of the perspective they bring to the marketplace.* Diversity in all of its forms — cultural, political, sexual, racial, social — is a hallmark of this generation [italics theirs] . . .[4]

The Sputnik cool-hunting agency, meanwhile, explained that "youth today are one big sample of diversity" and encouraged its clients to dive into the psychedelic "United Streets of Diversity" and not be afraid to taste the local fare. Dee Dee Gordon, author of *The L. Report,* urged her clients to get into Girl Power with a vengeance: "Teenage girls want to see someone who kicks butt back";[5] and, sounding suspiciously like me and my university friends, brand man Tom Peters took to berating his corporate audiences for being "OWMs — Old White Males."

As we have seen, this information was coming hot on the heels of two other related revelations. The first was that consumer companies would only survive if they built corporate empires around "brand identities." The second was that the ballooning youth demographic held the key to market success. So, of course, if the market researchers and cool hunters all reported that diversity was the key character trait of this lucrative demographic, there was only one thing to be done: every forward-thinking corporation would have to adopt variations on the theme of diversity as their brand identities.

Which is exactly what most brand-driven corporations have attempted to do. In an effort to understand how Starbucks became an overnight household name in 1996 without a single national ad campaign, *Advertising Age* speculated that it had something to do with its tie-dyed, Third World aura. "For devotees, Starbucks' 'experience' is about more than a daily espresso infusion; it is about immersion in a politically correct, cultured refuge. . . ."[6] Starbucks, however, was only a minor player in the P.C. marketing craze. Abercrombie & Fitch ads featured guys in their underwear making goo-goo eyes at each other; Diesel went further, showing two sailors kissing; and a U.S. television spot for Virgin Cola depicted "the first-ever gay wedding featured in a commercial," as the press release proudly announced. There were also gay-targeted brands like Pride Beer and Wave Water, whose slogan is

"We label bottles not people," and the gay community got its very own cool hunters — market researchers who scoured gay bars with hidden cameras.[7]

The Gap, meanwhile, filled its ads with racially mixed rainbows of skinny, childlike models. Diesel harnessed frustration at that unattainable beauty ideal with ironic ads that showed women being served up for dinner to a table of pigs. The Body Shop harnessed the backlash against both of them by refusing to advertise and instead filled its windows with red ribbons and posters condemning violence against women. The rush to diversity fitted in neatly with the embrace of African-American style and heroes that companies like Nike and Tommy Hilfiger had already pinpointed as a powerful marketing source. But Nike also realized that people who saw themselves as belonging to oppressed groups were ready-made market niches: throw a few liberal platitudes their way and, presto, you're not just a product but an ally in the struggle. So the walls of Nike Town were adorned with quotes from Tiger Woods declaring that "there are still courses in the U.S. where I am not allowed to play, because of the color of my skin." Women in Nike ads told us that "I believe 'babe' is a four-letter word" and "I believe high heels are a conspiracy against women."

And everyone, it seemed, was toying with the fluidity of gender, from the old-hat story of MAC makeup using drag queen RuPaul as its spokesmodel to tequila ads that inform viewers that the she in the bikini is really a he; from Calvin Klein's colognes that tell us that gender itself is a construct to Sure Ultra Dry deodorant that in turn urges all the gender benders to chill out: "Man? Woman? Does it matter?"

OPPRESSION NOSTALGIA

Fierce debates still rage about these campaigns. Are they entirely cynical or do they indicate that advertisers want to evolve and play more positive social roles? Benetton's mid-nineties ads careered wildly between witty and beautiful challenges to racial stereotypes on the one hand, and grotesque commercial exploitation of human suffering on the other. They were, however, indisputably part of a genuine attempt to use the company's vast cultural real estate to send a message that went beyond "Buy more sweaters"; and they played a central role in the fashion world's embrace of the struggle against AIDS. Similarly, there is no denying that the Body Shop broke ground by proving to the corporate sector that a multinational chain can be an outspoken and controversial political player, even while making millions on bubble bath and body lotion. The complicated motivations and stark inconsistencies inside many of these "ethical" businesses [are] explored [elsewhere]. But for many of the activists who had, at one point not so long ago, believed that better media representation would make for a more just world, one thing had become abundantly clear: identity politics weren't fighting the system, or even subverting it. When it came to the vast new industry of corporate branding, they were feeding it.

The crowning of sexual and racial diversity as the new superstars of advertising and pop culture has understandably created a sort of Identity Identity Crisis. Some ex-ID warriors are even getting nostalgic about the good old days, when they were oppressed, yes, but the symbols of their radicalism weren't for sale at Wal-Mart. As music writer Ann Powers observed of the much-vaunted ascendancy of Girl Power, "at this intersection between the conventional feminine and the evolving Girl, what's springing up is not a revolution but a mall . . . Thus, a genuine movement devolves into a giant shopping spree, where girls are encouraged to purchase whatever identity fits them best off the rack."[8] Similarly, Daniel Mendelsohn has written that gay identity has dwindled into "basically, a set of product choices . . . At least culturally speaking, oppression may have been the best thing that could have happened to gay culture. Without it, we're nothing."

The nostalgia, of course, is absurd. Even the most cynical ID warrior will admit, when pressed, that having Ellen Degeneres and other gay characters out on TV has some concrete advantages. Probably it is good for the kids, particularly those who live outside of larger urban settings — in rural or small-town environments, where being gay is more likely to confine them to a life of self-loathing. (The attempted suicide rate in 1998 among gay and bisexual male teens in America was 28.1 percent, compared with 4.2 percent among straight males of the same age group.)[9] Similarly, most feminists would concede that although the Spice Girls' crooning, "If you wanna be my lover, you have to get with my friends" isn't likely to shatter the beauty myth, it's still a step up from Snoop Dogg's 1993 ode to gang rape, "It ain't no fun if my homies can't have none."

And yet, while raising teenagers' self-esteem and making sure they have positive role models is valuable, it's a fairly narrow achievement, and from an activist perspective, one can't help asking: Is this it? Did all our protests and supposedly subversive theory only serve to provide great content for the culture industries, fresh new lifestyle imagery for Levi's new "What's True" ad campaign and girl-power-charged record sales for the music business? Why, in other words, were our ideas about political rebellion so deeply non-threatening to the smooth flow of business as usual?

The question, of course, is not Why, but Why on earth not? Just as they had embraced the "brands, not products" equation, the smart businesses quickly realized that short-term discomfort — whether it came from a requirement to hire more women or to more carefully vet the language in an ad campaign — was a small price to pay for the tremendous market share that diversity promised. So while it may be true that real gains have emerged from this process, it is also true that Dennis Rodman wears dresses and Disney World celebrates Gay Day less because of political progress than financial expediency. The market has seized upon multiculturalism and gender-bending in the same ways that it has seized upon youth culture in general — not just as a market niche but as a source of new carnivalesque imagery. As Robert Goldman and Stephen Papson note, "White-bread culture will simply no longer do."[10] The $200 billion culture industry — now America's biggest export — needs an ever-changing, uninterrupted supply of street styles, edgy music videos, and rainbows of colors. And the radical critics of the media clamoring to be "represented" in the early nineties virtually handed over their colorful identities to the brandmasters to be shrink-wrapped.

The need for greater diversity — the rallying cry of my university years — is now not only accepted by the culture industries, it is the mantra of global capital. And identity politics, as they were practiced in the nineties, weren't a threat, they were a gold mine. "This revolution," writes cultural critic Richard Goldstein in *The Village Voice*, "turned out to be the savior of late capitalism."[11] And just in time, too.

NOTES

[1]Jeanie Russell Kasindorf, "Lesbian Chic," *New York,* 10 May 1993, 35.

[2]Dinesh D'Souza, "Illiberal Education," *Atlantic Monthly,* March 1991, 51.

[3]John Taylor, "Are You Politically Correct?" *New York,* 21 January 1991.

[4]J. Walker Smith and Ann Clurman, *Rocking the Ages* (New York: HarperCollins, 1997), 88.

[5]*Vogue,* November 1997.

[6]"Starbucks Is Ground Zero in Today's Coffee Culture," *Advertising Age,* 9 December 1996.

[7]Jared Mitchell, "Out and About," *Report on Business Magazine,* December 1996, 90.

[8]Powers, "Everything and the Girl," 74.

[9]Gary Remafedi, Simone French, Mary Story, Michael D. Resnick and Robert Blum, "The Relationship between Suicide Risk and Sexual Orientation: Results of a Population-Based Study," *American Journal of Public Health,* January 1998, 88, no. 1, 57–60.

[10]Goldman and Papson, *Sign Wars,* v.

[11]Richard Goldstein, "The Culture War Is Over! We Won! (For Now)," *Village Voice,* 19 November 1996.

DISCUSSION

1. How do you respond to the term *identity marketing* as Klein defines it? What kinds of images or associations does it evoke? Is identity something you naturally think of as marketable? How or how not?

2. Among the many problems with commercial marketing, Klein argues, is its tendency to define ethnic and racial difference in very limited ways. Choose one of the ad campaigns Klein references in her essay. In what particular ways might you alter the portrait of diversity so that it offers a more accurate or realistic depiction? In your view, would doing so enhance or inhibit the marketability of the product being sold?

3. In our culture, is there any social or political issue that could never be marketed? What would this issue be? And what aspect of it would make it impervious to commercial or corporate uses?

WRITING

4. Choose a commercial image you've come across recently, one that you think attempts to sell a particular definition of diversity. First, describe what definition or model this image endeavors to convey. Next, analyze the ways this definition seems connected to the particular product this commercial is also trying to sell. How (if at all) does this image of diversity shape viewer attitudes toward the product itself?

5. Klein asks whether identity marketing campaigns are "entirely cynical or do they indicate that advertisers want to evolve and play more positive social roles?" Write an essay in which you take a position on this question, using examples from ad campaigns you remember or those Klein discusses in her writing. Make sure that you consider both sides of the question in your argument.

6. Klein and Michael Eric Dyson (p. 123) are concerned with the ways our contemporary media teaches us both to see and not to see racial and ethnic difference. Write an essay in which you analyze how each writer discusses the idea of diversity and how it is portrayed in popular culture. What aspects of diversity are of particular concern to Klein? How do you think Dyson would respond to her argument that diversity sells?

MICHAEL ERIC DYSON

Frames of Reference

How do media outlets shape, perhaps even create, our impressions of the news? Using the coverage of the Hurricane Katrina disaster as his case study, noted public intellectual Michael Eric Dyson explores some of the consequences of the contrasting ways in which the media "framed" white and black experiences of this event. Dyson is the Avalon Foundation Professor in the Humanities at the University of Pennsylvania as well as an ordained Baptist minister. He is the author of twelve nonfiction books, many of which address race in American society, including *Between God and Gangsta Rap: Bearing Witness to Black Culture* (1996), *Why I Love Black Women* (2003), and *Debating Race* (2007). A number of his essays, speeches, and interviews are collected in *The Michael Eric Dyson Reader* (2004). "Frames of Reference" is from Dyson's *Come Hell or High Water: Hurricane Katrina and the Color of Disaster* (2006).

I F THE MILITANT ADVOCATES HELPED TO FRAME FOR THEIR GENERA-tion the racial consequences of a natural and economic disaster, the media was critical in framing perceptions of people and events surrounding the catastrophe. This was painfully evident with a set of photos, and their accompanying captions (parts of which I will italicize for emphasis), that were widely circulated on the Internet the day after the storm struck. In the first photo, a young black man clasps items in each arm as he forges through the flood waters. The caption to the AP (Associated Press) photo of him reads: "A young man walks through chest deep flood water after *looting a grocery store* in New Orleans on Tuesday, Aug. 20, 2005. Flood waters continue to rise in New Orleans after Hurricane Katrina did extensive damage when it made landfall on Monday."[1] In the second photo, also from AP, a young white man and woman tote food items in their hands as they carry backpacks and slush through the flood waters. The caption accompanying their photograph reads: "Two residents wade through chest-deep water after *finding bread and soda from a local grocery store* after Hurricane Katrina came through the area in New Orleans, Louisiana."[2]

In this case, the captions say it all: the young black man *loots* his groceries, the white youth *find* theirs. With no stores open, the white youth clearly couldn't have found their groceries, and would have had to obtain them the same way the young black man did. It didn't appear in either photo that someone's charity was responsible for any of the people pictured receiving food, which probably means that the young black man and the white youth stormed a store to get groceries, a quite understandable move under the circumstances. While the white youth's move is rendered "quite understandable" by the language — what else were they to do, after all, and the language lessens the obvious means of their acquiring groceries — the black youth's move is rendered as legally and morally questionable. If he has "looted" then he has broken the legal and moral codes of society.

He is further alienated from his civic standing by simply being described as "a young man" while his white peers are cited as citizens — "two residents." The value judgment communicated by the photo and its caption is largely implicit, though strongly implied by the language. The captions help lend value, and a slant, to essentially neutral photographs, pictures that, on their own, suggest solidarity of circumstance between the black and white youth. But the identical character of their experience is shattered by the language, which casts their actions in contrasting lights: the white youth have been favored by serendipity and thus "naturally" exploit their luck in "finding" food, a gesture that relieves them of culpability; the black youth, by comparison, has interrupted the natural order of things to seize what didn't belong to him and thus remains responsible for his behavior.

> **The captions help lend value, and a slant, to essentially neutral photographs.**

To be sure, none of this is expressly articulated; the existing framework of racial reference suggests its meaning. Such a framework, one that weaves white innocence and black guilt into the fabric of cultural myths and racial narratives, is deeply embedded in society and affects every major American institution, including the media. How black folk are "framed" — how we are discussed, pictured, imagined, conjured to fit a negative idea of blackness, or called on to fill a slot reserved for the outlaw, thug, or savage — shapes how we are frowned on or favored in mainstream society. Words help to interpret images; language and pictures in combination reinforce ideas and stories about black identity. The words that accompany these photos, like the reams of words that accompany the images of black folk in society throughout history, help to underscore hidden bias and sleeping bigotry, often in the most innocent, gentle, and subtle form imaginable. Hence, plausible deniability is critical to such maneuvers, allowing invested parties to reply when called to act count: "I didn't mean it that way"; "You're too sensitive"; "You're exaggerating"; or "You're reading too much into things." Thus, the burden to explain or justify behavior is shifted from offender to victim.

The media's role in framing blacks as outlaws and savages achieved a rare blatancy when it endlessly looped on television the same few frames of stranded blacks "looting" food and other items, largely for survival. The repetition of the scenes of black "looting" contains its own indictment: there wasn't enough film of vandalizing behavior to feature several instances. By repeating the same few scenes the media helped to spread the notion that black folk were in a state of social anarchy and were tearing violently at the fabric of civility and order. The framework didn't allow for blacks to receive the benefit of the doubt extended to the white couple that "found" food. Neither was the compelling imagery often accompanied by commentary to suggest that people who had been abandoned by their government had a right to help themselves — a theme that surely ought to have pleased the bootstrapping Republicans at the helm of the federal government. Instead, many critics bitterly lamented the actions of people who did what they had to do to survive.

To be sure, besides taking food and items to survive — as did local officials and authorities, including aides to the mayor and the police, who were given the sort of pass that the masses would never receive — black folk took clothes and appliances, and a few took guns. These blacks were drowned in a second flood of media and social criticism that vilified them for their inexcusable behavior. Even those critics who were sympathetic to the urgent conditions of the abandoned blacks felt pressured to embrace the frame of reference of black criminality before otherwise defending poor blacks. Such critics had to acknowledge that yes, these were awful and heinous acts, but still, distinctions must be made between acts of survival and acts of greed, wanton cynicism, or reckless morality. In order to defend them, their supporters had to prove that they were willing to establish a hierarchy of the "good Negro" and the "bad Negro." They often failed to realize that such moral ordering is futile in a society where the inclination to misbehavior is viewed as true of black folk in general. Although separating "worthy" from "unworthy" blacks is supposed to strengthen the cause of the "good Negro," such distinctions ultimately make all blacks more vulnerable because they grant legitimacy to a distorted racial framework. Thus, the looting for looting's sake, versus the looting for survival's sake, may appear to be a legitimate ordering of black morality, but it is just as likely to obscure how black identity is seen though a muddy lens. The very act of black folk taking food, even when conditions are oppressive, generates the sort of suspicion that white folk will not as a rule be subject to — as in the case of "looting" versus "finding" food.

Thus, when a moral distinction is made between taking food and taking other items, it denies the stigma already attached to blacks who simply sought to survive. I am not arguing that because of the ethical distortion found in drawing faulty distinctions among black folk, one cannot thereby condemn immoral behavior. I am simply suggesting that what constitutes "immoral" black behavior conveniently shifts in reference to black folk to suit the social or racial purposes of a given moment, or crisis, in the culture. Katrina was one of those moments of crisis. By exaggerating the crisis, the media proved it was caught in a crisis of exaggeration.

Moreover, the hand wringing over poor black folk "looting" exposes the ugly reality that may explain the apparent glee with which some black folk "looted": that property matters more than poor and black people in many quarters of the culture. Some people took clothing items because they needed to change from their soiled clothing where they had to urinate or defecate on themselves. Some people took televisions to barter for food. Some saw luxury items as capital to purchase momentary relief from their misery, whether through exchanging those for food or for money that might, however illusorily, get them and their families free of their situation. Perhaps they could pay somebody with a car to drive them to safety on higher ground. And some of them must have learned their seemingly illogical behavior — that is, for those critics who suggest the black poor couldn't do anything practical or purposeful with the items they filched — from a culture of consumption from which they had been barred. The lesson of that culture seemed to be: have it because you want it.

Of course some were greedy, but that greed wasn't any different — in fact, was its naked face in miniature — than the greed that passed as normal and desirable when it showed up in the upper, richer, whiter classes. To begrudge poor people a gleeful moment of rebellion against property — by taking it, by possessing it, by hoarding it, and by having a taste of things they had been denied all their lives, nice things that they saw the people for whom they slaved routinely enjoy and treasure, even more than they did the poor black folk who stoked their leisure, is an act of arrogant and self-righteous indifference to the plight of the black poor, most of whom, mind you, would never in a million years take anything that didn't belong to them. But desperate people do in desperation what capitalist and political and cultural looters do daily — steal and give little thought to its moral consequence. In a comparative ethical framework, the black poor come out looking a lot more justified than do the disingenuous critics who lambaste them.

That is why New Orleans rapper Juvenile expressed compassion for the black poor and called into question the sanctification of property that would be washed away anyhow. "I don't call it looting," the rapper said. "They stole everything from out of my house, and I'm not mad at the person that stole out of my house. Because the hurricane was gonna hit and the house was gonna get hit with 25 feet of storm surging. It was gonna be damaging. I couldn't do nothing with it anyway. . . . And I think the looting in New Orleans, I don't call it looting, I call it survival."[3] Juvenile explains the logic of folk stealing televisions in order to better their chances of survival. "I might could get this TV and sell it to somebody and get some money. They talking about the TVs and VCRs, 'Why would you take that?' There's still people that got money that could buy where money was still useful. We don't know. The average person don't know. They wasn't down there in the waters. They had people who just wanted some herb to calm they damn nerves."[4]

As journalist Jordan Flaherty argues, the real criminal activity in Katrina can't be laid at the feet of the black *poor*, but at those who benefited from unjust economic and racial arrangements long before the storm struck. Moreover, the media framed black survivors as lawless thugs while ignoring the social conditions that made their lives hell.

> **The media framed black survivors as lawless thugs while ignoring the social conditions that made their lives hell.**

While the rich escaped New Orleans, those with nowhere to go and no way to get there were left behind. Adding salt to the wound, the local and national media have spent the last week demonizing those left behind. As someone that loves New Orleans and the people in it, this is the part of this tragedy that hurts me the most, and it hurts me deeply. No sane person should classify someone who takes food from indefinitely closed stores in a desperate, starving city as a "looter," but that's just what the media did over and over again. Sheriffs and politicians talked of having troops protect stores instead of perform rescue operations. Images of New Orleans' hurricane-ravaged population were transformed into black, out-of-control, criminals. As if taking a stereo from a store that will clearly be insured against loss is a greater crime than the governmental neglect and incompetence that did billions of dollars of damage and destroyed a city. This media focus is a tactic, just as the eighties focus on "welfare queens" and "super-predators" obscured the simultaneous and much larger crimes of the Savings and Loan scams and mass layoffs, the hyper-exploited people of New Orleans are being used as a scapegoat to cover up much larger crimes.[5]

The media also framed the black poor when it helped to spread rumors about violent and animalistic black behavior in the shelters to which they fled. Television reports and newspaper accounts brimmed with the unutterable horror of what black folk were doing to each other and their helpers in the Superdome and the convention center: the rape of women and babies, sniper attacks on military helicopters, folk killed for food and water, armed gang members assaulting the vulnerable, dozens of bodies being shoved into a freezer.[6] As the *Times-Picayune* reported, the "picture that emerged was one of the impoverished masses of flood victims resorting to utter depravity, randomly attacking each other, as well as the police trying to protect them and the rescue workers trying to save them."[7] Nearly every one of the allegations proved to be baseless rumor. Of course, the mayor and police commissioner of New Orleans helped spread the rumors as well in famous interviews on *Oprah*. Police commissioner Eddie Compass broke down crying while describing "the little babies getting raped," and Mayor Nagin spoke of the mayhem of people "in that frickin' Superdome for five days watching dead bodies, watching hooligans killing people, raping people."[8]

But hyperbole pervaded the media as well. A day before evacuations began at the Superdome, *Fox News* television issued an "alert" warning of "robberies, rapes, carjackings, riots, and murder. Violent gangs are roaming the streets at night, hidden by the cover of darkness." The *Los Angeles Times* featured a lead news story that dramatically reported National Guard troops taking "positions on rooftops, scanning for snipers and armed mobs as seething crowds of refugees milled below, desperate to flee. Gunfire crackled in the distance." Although the *New York Times* was more cautious in its reporting, noting that reports couldn't be verified, it still repeated stories and reports about widespread violence and unrest. And neither was the exaggeration quarantined to the states. The *Ottawa Sun*, a Canadian tabloid, reported unverified news of "a man seeking help gunned down by a National Guard Soldier" and "a young man run down and then shot by a New Orleans police officer." And the *Evening Standard*, a London newspaper, compared the carnage and chaos to the Mel Gibson futuristic film *Mad Max* and to the novel *Lord of the Flies*.[9]

Most of the information reported by the media proved to be urban legends and cultural myths that swirled in the toxic stew unleashed by Katrina. "It just morphed into this mythical place where the most unthinkable deeds were being done," said National Guard spokesman Major Ed Bush. As government help failed to arrive, a conceptual vacuum opened up that was filled with a powerful mix of lies and legends. There were reports that an infant's body was found in a trash can, that there were sharks unschooled from Lake Pontchartrain swimming through the city's business district, and that hundreds of bodies had been stashed in the basement of the Superdome.[10] A physician from FEMA arrived at the Superdome after international reports of the killings, rapes, murders, and gang violence, expecting a huge cache of bodies. "I've got a report of 200 bodies," National Guard Colonel Thomas Beron recalls the doctor saying to him. "The real total was six."[11] Four people had died of natural causes, one overdosed on drugs, and the other committed suicide by jumping to his death.

Eddie Jordan, the Orleans Parish District Attorney, was outraged by the media's glaring inaccuracies in framing the shelter survivors as

> "It just morphed into this mythical place where the most unthinkable deeds were being done."

animals. "I had the impression that at least 40 or 50 murders had occurred at the two sites," Jordan said. "It's unfortunate we saw these kinds of stories saying crime had taken place on a massive scale when that wasn't the case. And they [national media outlets] have done nothing to follow up on any of these cases, they just accepted what people [on the street] told them. . . . It's not consistent with the highest standards of journalism."[12]

Of course, given the nature of rape — a crime that is dramatically underreported under normal conditions — it is likely that such crimes indeed did occur, but, it seems, with nothing near the frequency as reported. Neither has there been any verification of widespread reports of murder — in fact, only one person in the convention center appears to have been a victim of homicide, by stabbing, but even that case is murky. It is likely that there were indeed some thugs present, but is seems clear that they were Antediluvian Thugs — thugs before the flood. But they didn't have much of an impact on the crowds at the Superdome and the convention center. Later, before he was asked to resign by Mayor Nagin, Compass admitted that he was wrong, adding, "The information I had at the time, I thought it was credible." Nagin, too, acknowledged that he didn't have, and probably never would have, an accurate picture of the alleged anarchy that prevailed. "I'm having a hard time getting a good body count."[13]

The *Times-Picayune* captured the remarkable dignity of the crowds and the grossly exaggerated nature of the reports of social disarray that occurred among the evacuees when it concluded that

> Few of the widely reported atrocities have been backed with evidence. The piles of bodies never materialized, and soldiers, police officers, and rescue personnel on the front lines say that although anarchy reigned at times and people suffered unimaginable indignities, most of the worst crimes reported at the time never happened. Military, law enforcement, and medical workers agree that the flood of evacuees — about 30,000 at the Dome and an estimated 10,000 to 20,000 at the Convention Center — overwhelmed their security personnel. The 400 to 500 soldiers in the Dome could have been easily overrun by increasingly agitated crowds, but that never happened, said Col. James Knotts, a midlevel commander there. Security was nonexistent at the Convention Center, which was never designated as a shelter. Authorities provided no food, water, or medical care until troops secured the building the Friday after the storm. While the Convention Center saw plenty of mischief, including massive looting and isolated gunfire, and many inside cowered in fear, the hordes of evacuees for the most part did not resort to violence, as legend has it.[14]

What fed the rumors? It seems that poor communications fostered by the breakdowns of telephones made it nearly impossible for reporters to get accurate information. But the major reason seems to be — as *Times-Picayune* editor Jim Amass admitted — a matter of race and class. "If the

> *Journalists outdid each other in the competitive urge to describe and remythologize the sheer horror of the huddled black masses.*

dome and Convention Center had harbored large numbers of middle class white people," Amoss said, "it would not have been a fertile ground for this kind of rumor-mongering."[15] It is safe to say that the media's framework was ready to receive and recycle rumors of vicious black behavior because such rumors seemed to confirm a widely held view about poor blacks. The more outrageous the reports, the juicier the alleged details, the more poetic and breathless the news reports became. Journalists outdid each other in the competitive urge to describe and remythologize the sheer horror of the huddled black masses. No adjective or metaphor seemed alien to reporters seeking to adequately conjure the chaos of blackness being unleashed on the world in all of its despotic wizardry and evil inventiveness. The cruelty, and crudity, of the poor black evacuees seemed to be a necessary analogue to the environmental misery they endured.

Besides, the media's framing of the black poor seemed to exonerate those who hadn't gotten there quickly enough to help them. The message seemed to be: "If this is how they act, if this is who they are, then their inhumanity is a justification for not rushing to their rescue." The government seemed to be let off the hook. Other folk may have argued that such negative actions among poor blacks could have been arrested had the government arrived on time. Still others thought that the government should have gotten there earlier to arrest the folk themselves. Law and order was a recurring motif of the criticism lobbed at the black evacuees: there was simply no excuse — not even one of the worst natural disasters in the nation's history — for them to misbehave in such fashion. It seems that the status quo and the powers that be needed precisely the sociological framework of the poor that the media presented.

How ironic, then, that the media should have gathered such kudos for locating again that part of their skeletal structure that threads down their backs. It is really doubly ironic. First, because it was at the expense of black suffering — which television reporters and cameras undoubtedly brought home to America in full color — that journalists got credit for regaining their voice. The edifying skepticism displayed by nearly the entire crew of frontline reporters, and on occasion those stationed at a safer distance at their home studios, was a lively and refreshing departure from the predictable banter that sadly passes for refined suspicion. It may have not been very refined, but the outright combativeness that frequently flared for a few days in the media was positively bracing. But the fact that it took such an utter tragedy for the media to stop pretending it was neutral — and to find a way between disingenuous claims of objectivity and crushing bias dressed up as fairness — is ultimately sad. That means that unless another crisis comes along — and already, despite protests to the contrary, America, and the media, have largely moved on past the tragic revelations of Katrina — the media will slink back into spineless endorsements of black pathology, especially for the poor, in one form or another.

The celebration of the media during Katrina is perhaps ultimately ironic since it is the media that has largely been responsible for communicating the culture's spleenful bigotry toward the black poor. To be championed as the defenders of the very population the media has harmed so much, whether intending to or not, should provide more than one occasion of intense discomfort and squirming for journalists. Unless the media reframe their very reference to blackness and poverty, which is not likely to occur without intense pressure, they will have not only failed to earn the encomiums they've received, but worse, they will have set back the quest to truly expose the problems the black poor face by pretending to have done so. As framers of black life, the media can either illumine for the world our complexity or shutter the dizzying dynamism of our identities behind stale stereotypes and callous clichés.

The media framed the evacuees at first as refugees, a term that caused denunciations by black leaders because it seemed to deny that black folk were citizens of the nation. A few critics responded by suggesting that, technically, the black poor could be considered refugees because they were fleeing a catastrophe and seeking refuge away from their homes. But what such clarifications missed is the spiritual truth of black identity that rested more in connotation than denotation, more in signification than grammar. Black folk felt that they had already, for so long, been treated as foreigners in their own land. We desperately sought to claim the rights and privileges that our bitterly fought-for membership in the society should provide.

I saw flashes of this when I visited one of the shelters in Houston for the black displaced, dislocated, and dispersed. When I stepped into the Reliant Center, where thousands of mostly black and poor folk from New Orleans, Mississippi, and Alabama had been chased by Hurricane Katrina's ugly force, I felt the hurt and desperation of a people whose middle name throughout history has been exile. A sea of green nylon cots was all that separated displaced bodies from pavement floors. Some of the folk needed medicine and healing talk. Their ailments of flesh and mind were indifferent to their current plight, as indifferent, it seems, as the government that miserably failed them in their hour of need. Grown men openly wept; resourceful women were emotionally depleted; younger folk had whatever innocence remained from childhoods already battered by poverty cruelly washed away. They were desperate for a glimpse of hope beyond the hell and high water into which they had been plunged. Instead, the richest nation in the world shuttled them to harsh makeshift quarters. But many of the evacuees called upon their faith to see them through. And some of them undoubtedly wondered where God was in all of this. Perhaps they even believed that this was God's will. Could it be that God caused Katrina?

NOTES

[1]"Black People Loot, White People Find?" *Boingboing: A Directory of Wonderful Things,* August 30, 2005, http://www.boingboing.net/2005/08/30/black_people_loot_wh.html.

[2]Ibid.

[3]Satten, "Still Lives Through," *XXL,* December 2005, pp. 112, 114.

[4]Ibid.

[5]Jordan Flaherty, "Notes from Inside New Orleans," *New Orleans Independent Media Center,* September 2, 2005, http://neworleans.indymedia.org/news/2005/09/4043.php.

[6]Susannah Rosenblatt and James Rainey, "Katrina Takes a Toll on Truth, News Accuracy," *Los Angeles Times,* September 27, 2005, p. A16; Brian Thevenot and Gordon Russell, "Rape. Murder. Gunfights. For Three Anguished Days the World's Headlines Blared that the Superdome and Convention Center Had Descended into Anarchy," *The Times-Picayune,* September 26, 2005, p. A01.

[7]Thevenot and Russell, "Rape. Murder. Gunfights."

[8]Rosenblatt and Rainey, "Katrina Takes a Toll."

[9]Ibid.

[10]Ibid.

[11]Thevenot and Russell, "Rape. Murder. Gunfights."

[12]Ibid.

[13]Ibid.

[14]Ibid.

[15]Rosenblatt and Rainey, "Katrina Takes a Toll."

DISCUSSION

1. According to Dyson, the tendency to associate African Americans with "lawlessness," "irresponsibility," "immorality," and "animalism" is one of our culture's most longstanding norms. Do you agree that this kind of thing reflects an ingrained cultural pattern? Can you think of another example where this same kind of association gets reinforced?

2. For Dyson, the term *media framing* has a double meaning, referring both to how an image can be selectively presented and to the ways such selection can lead viewers to form inaccurate or unfair opinions about what it is they see. To what extent do you see one or both of these meanings applying to the general depiction of African Americans in our contemporary culture?

3. In your opinion, how might the media coverage of the Katrina disaster have been different if the majority of the victims were not African American? Do you think Dyson would find himself swayed by your hypothesis?

WRITING

4. Dyson writes, "How black folk are 'framed' — how we are discussed, pictured, imagined, conjured to fit a negative idea of blackness, or called on to fill a slot reserved for the outlaw, thug, or savage — shapes how we are frowned on or favored in mainstream society." Write an essay that analyzes Dyson's argument. What are his main points, and what evidence or statements does he use to support his point of view? As a writer, how does Dyson use words to incite action in the reader?

5. In this essay, Dyson gives us examples of what he argues are the typical responses to the charge of race-specific media bias that he levels: "'You're too sensitive,'" "'You're exaggerating,'" "'You're reading too much into things.'" Indeed, these statements are often employed as a defense against thinking deemed too "politically correct," whether the topic is race, gender, sexuality, or politics. Pick a current event in the news where you see bias in the way a certain class of people has been characterized (illegal immigrants or gay marriage proponents, for example). Write an essay in which you summarize what characterizations of these people you see in the news stories about them. Pay careful attention to the words chosen to describe them or the debate. In what ways do these groups themselves address stories being written about them? Finally, argue whether you see media bias as existing in these cases, using quotes from Dyson's essay to support your argument.

6. Brooke A. Knight's essay, "Watch Me!" (p. 150) is another piece that attempts to understand what it means to have your personal travails played out as a media spectacle. The conclusions he draws about this, however, bear little resemblance to Dyson's thesis. Write an essay in which you analyze what accounts for the different ways each of these writers addresses this same larger topic. What are the differences in what each writer is trying to say, and how do they frame the topic of being watched differently in order to make their arguments?

DANIEL HARRIS

Cuteness

What sorts of things do we regard as cute, and where did we learn to draw these distinctions? Surveying the vast array of "cute kitsch" in our lives — from stuffed animals to greeting cards, children's books to cartoon calendars — Daniel Harris argues that our enthusiasm for looking at and displaying cuteness ultimately lays bare a deeper and darker preoccupation. Harris's first book, *Rise and Fall of Gay Culture* (1997), was an influential work of queer theory for a nonacademic audience. He followed it with *Cute, Quaint, Hungry, and Romantic: The Aesthetics of Consumerism* (2000), and his latest book, *Memoir of No One in Particular* (2002). He lives in Brooklyn, New York. The following piece is from *Cute, Quaint, Hungry, and Romantic*.

SHE STANDS IN MAROON BLOOMERS AND A PINK DRESS THAT FLARES tantalizingly above two acrylic legs that descend, unvaried in diameter, all the way down to her gout-stricken ankles crammed into booties. Her feet, crippled and pigeontoed, touch at their tips. A sassy tuft of a synthetic topknot sprays out of a helmet of auburn hair encircled by a polka dot bow that sits atop her head like a windmill, dwarfing the rest of her figure. Her nose is no bigger than a button, and her astonishingly candid eyes are two moist pools framed by eyebrows penciled like quizzical circumflexes on the vast dome of her forehead. Emptied of all internal life, these mesmerizing orbs, composing at least 25 percent of a face as wide as her shoulders, stare out directly at us with a reticence heightened by the hectic flush of her complexion. Her name is "So Shy Sherri," and she is one of toy manufacturer Galoob's nine new "Baby Faces," a set of "super posin'" dolls with names like "So Sweet Sandi," "So Sorry Sarah," and "So Delightful Dee Dee," each with an "adorable" expression and personality of her own.

Everywhere we turn we see cuteness, from cherubic figures batting their peepers on Charmin toilet paper to teddy bears frozen mid-embrace, the stubs of their pawless arms groping for hugs. In the eyes of most people, whose conditioned responses to this most rigid of styles prevent them from recognizing its artificiality, things like calendars with droopy-eyed puppies pleading for attention or greeting cards with kitty cats in raincoats are the very embodiment of innocence and as such represent an absence of the designed and manipulated qualities of what is in fact a heavily mannered aesthetic. For them, the foreshortened limbs and sad, saucer eyes of a doll like So Shy Sherri are part of a unique and readily identifiable iconography whose distortions trigger, with Pavlovian pre-dictability, maternal feelings for a mythical condition of endearing naivete. The chilling paradox of the fetishes over which we croon so irre-pressibly is that their cuteness suggests guilelessness, simplicity, and a refreshing lack of affectation, the very antithesis of what we would expect if we were to judge these toys on the basis of their extreme styliza-tion alone.

Cuteness is not an aesthetic in the ordinary sense of the word and must by no means be mistaken for the physically appealing, the attrac-tive. In fact, it is closely linked to the grotesque, the malformed. So Shy Sherri, for instance, is an anatomical disaster. Her legs are painfully swollen, her fingers useless pink stumps that seem to have been lopped off at the knuckles, and her rosy cheeks so bloated that her face is actually wider than it is long. Medieval or renaissance images of the Christ child, those obese monstrosities whose muscularity always strikes the modern viewer as bafflingly inaccurate, make an interesting compar-ison. In an era like our own, which prides itself on its ability to achieve effects of uncanny realism, the disfigured putti of the "Baby Face" series of dolls mark a decline rather than an advance in the representation of children, an eerie throwback to the slant-eyed sphinxes in Sienese icons: alien, carnivorous-looking creatures who are, in many ways, as pictorially inexact as So Shy Sherri.

> *Cuteness . . . must by no means be mistaken for the physically appealing, the attractive.*

Far from being an accident of bad craftsmanship, the element of the grotesque in cuteness is perfectly deliberate and must be viewed as the explicit intention of objects that elicit from us the complex emotions we feel when we encounter the fat faces and squat, ruddy bodies of creatures like the Trolls, with their pot bellies, pug noses, and teased-up mops of brightly colored hair. The grotesque is cute because the grotesque is pitiable, and pity is the primary emotion of this seductive and manipula-tive aesthetic that arouses our sympathies by creating anatomical pari-ahs, like the Cabbage Patch Dolls or even E.T., whose odd proportions and lack of symmetry diverge wildly from the relative balance and uniformity of ordinary bodies. The aesthetic of cuteness creates a class of outcasts and mutations, a ready-made race of lovable inferiors whom both chil-dren and adults collect, patronize, and enslave in the protective concubi-nage of vast harems of homely dolls and snugglesome misfits. Something becomes cute not necessarily because of a quality it has but because of a quality it lacks, a certain neediness and inability to stand alone, as if it were an indigent starveling, lonely and rejected because of a hideousness we find more touching than unsightly.

The koalas, pandas, and lambs of the stuffed animal series "Lost 'n Founds" directly allude to this state of homeless destitution. With their "adorable 'so-sad' eyes" that shed real tears, these shameless examples of the waif or pauper syndrome seem to be begging to be rescued from their defenseless state, so tellingly emphasized by paws as cumbersome as boxing gloves — absurd appendages that lie uselessly in their laps, totally free of any of the prehensile functions hands usually serve. Because it generates enticing images like these of ugliness and dejection, cuteness has become essential to the marketplace, in that advertisers have learned that consumers will "adopt" products that create, often in their packaging alone, an aura of motherlessness, ostracism, and melancholy, the silent desperation of the lost puppy dog clamoring to be befriended — namely, to be bought.

Cuteness, in short, is not something we find in our children but something we *do* to them. Because it aestheticizes unhappiness, helplessness, and deformity, it almost always involves an act of sadism on the part of its creator, who makes an unconscious attempt to maim, hobble, and embarrass the thing he seeks to idolize, as in the case of "Little Mutt," a teddy bear with a game leg that a British manufacturer has even fitted with an orthopedic boot. The process of conveying cuteness to the viewer disempowers its objects, forcing them into ridiculous situations and making them appear more ignorant and vulnerable than they really are. Adorable things are often most

> *Cuteness, in short, is not something we find in our children but something we do to them.*

adorable in the middle of a pratfall or a blunder: Winnie the Pooh, with his snout stuck in the hive; the 101 dalmatians of Disney's classic, collapsing in double splits and sprawling across the ice; Love-a-Lot Bear, in the movie *The Care Bears*, who stares disconsolately out at us with a paint bucket overturned on his head; or, the grimmest example of the cruelty of cuteness, the real fainting goat, which has acquired of late a perverse chic as a pet (bred with myatonia, a genetic heart defect, it coyly folds up and faints every time you scream at it). Although the gaze we turn on the cute thing seems maternal and solicitous, it is in actuality transformative and will stop at nothing to appease its hunger for expressing pity and big-heartedness, even at the cost of mutilating the object of its affections. The French-manufactured "Vet Set" takes the neediness of cuteness to macabre extremes: The kit is equipped with a wounded stuffed puppy whose imploring eyes seem to wince as it patiently awaits the physician, who can alleviate its suffering with a wide array of bandages, tourniquets, syringes, and even a stethoscope to monitor the irregular, fluttering thump of a mechanical heart that actually beats.

If cuteness is the aesthetic of deformity and dejection, it is also the aesthetic of sleep. Although adorable things can be bright eyed and bushy tailed, the pose we find cutest of all is not that of a rambunctious infant screaming at the top of his lungs but that of the docile sleepyhead, his chin nestled drunkenly in the crook of someone's neck, wearing the pjs in the FAO Schwarz catalog that consist of a full-length leopard suit made of spotted fur or a "sweet confection of lace" with fuzzy marabou touches of pristine white down sewn like a tutu around the waist. The world of cute things is transfixed by the spell of the sandman, full of napping lotus eaters whose chief attraction lies in their dormant and languorous postures, their defenseless immobility.

Turning its targets into statues and plush dolls, cuteness is ultimately dehumanizing, paralyzing its victims into comatose or semi-conscious things. In fact, the "thingness" of cute things is fixed firmly in our minds by means of the exaggerated textures and hues so characteristic of stuffed animals, with their shimmering satins and their luscious coats of fur, or dolls with their luxuriant profusion of hair, often of absurd length and body (as with the Cutie Kids of the "Cutie Club" series, a set of dolls whose psychedelic coiffures cascade down their sides in corkscrew curls longer than their own bodies). "Anxiously awaiting power snuggles," FAO Schwarz's huge grizzly bear is a slouching, seemingly invertebrate mammoth rippling with "serious spreads of soft spots" that are "just asking to be hauled and mauled," while their elephant, as large as a St. Bernard, is described as "big, plump, and deliciously soft with soulful brown eyes that encourage big-time hugging and smooching." Vacant and malleable, animals like these inhabit a world of soothing tactile immediacy in which there are no sharp cor-

> **Cuteness is ultimately dehumanizing, paralyzing its victims into comatose or semi-conscious things.**

ners or abrasive materials but in which everything has been conveniently soft-sculpturized to yield to our importunate squeezes and hugs. If such soulless insentience is any indication, cuteness is the most scrutable and externalized of aesthetics in that it creates a world of stationary objects and tempting exteriors that deliver themselves up to us, putting themselves at our disposal and allowing themselves to be apprehended entirely through the senses. In light of the intense physicality of our response to their helpless torpor, our compulsive gropings even constitute something one might call cute sex or, in point of fact, given that one of the partners lies there groggy and catatonic, a kind of necrophilia, a neutered coupling consummated in our smothering embrace of a serenely motionless object incapable of reciprocating. Far from being content with the helplessness of our young as we find them in their natural state, we take all kinds of artificial measures to dramatize this vulnerability even further by defacing them, embarrassing them, devitalizing them, depriving them of their selfhood, and converting them, with the help of all of the visual and sartorial tricks at our disposal, into disempowered objects, furry love balls quivering in soft fabrics as they lapse into withdrawal for their daily fix of TLC.

During the course of the twentieth century, the overwhelming urge to engage in cute sex profoundly affected the appearance of the teddy bear, whom toy manufacturers put on a rich diet, creating an irresistibly moon-faced dough boy whose corpulence invites caressing. The original designs for the teddy bear, produced during the 1880s, were modeled on actual taxidermic specimens and were relatively naturalistic in appearance, disfigured by scholiastic humps that jutted out of their backs, long, vulpine snouts, and slender, simian arms that hung all the way down to their feet. Over the last few decades, Pooh and Paddington have improved their posture, sprouted fat, dwarfish arms, and, moreover, submitted to a barrage of rhinoplastic amputations that has turned their crunching mandibles into harmless bulges that protrude only slightly from round, unthreatening faces. Casting melting glances from sad button eyes, today's winsome "critters" have also been redesigned as more serviceable cute sex toys, much like the gaping-mouthed dolls available in adult book stores: Their arms are now permanently sewn in an outstretched position, rather than dangling at their sides as they once did, simulating an embrace as lifeless as the latex clasp of our "fantasy playmates."

The strange consequence of the need to increase huggability is that all stuffed animals, from marsupials to pachyderms, are covered in fur, regardless of the fact that the real-life counterparts of Beatrice the Boa and Willy the Walrus have scales that are wet and slimy or hides that are bristly and tough. Behind the pleasure we take in the bodies of such cartoon heroes as Kermit and Snoopy is the fear of another sort of body altogether, the distasteful subtext of our plush toys: the excreting bodies of real live babies which, far from being clean and dry, are squalling factories of drool and snot. Our unenviable role as the hygienic custodians of children, whose dirty bottoms we must regularly wipe, noses we must blow, and soiled underwear we must launder, has led to a recurrent parental fantasy, that of the diaperless baby, the excretionless teddy bear, a low-maintenance infant whom we can kiss and fondle free of anxiety that it will throw up on our shoulder as we rock it to sleep or pee in our laps as we dandle it on our knees.

Exaggerating the vast discrepancies of power between the sturdy adult and the enfeebled and susceptible child, the narcissism of cuteness is evident in the way that the aesthetic ascribes human attributes to non-human things. Anthropomorphism is to a large extent *the* rhetorical strategy of children's books, which often generate their narratives from a kind of animal transvestism in which dogs, cats, bears, and pigs have the clothing and demeanor of human beings. Calendars, another rich source of cuteness, also employ animal transvestism as a major theme: mice as prima ballerinas in toe shoes and tutus, dogs in party hats and sunglasses, or swallow-tailed hamsters in tuxes and cummerbunds rearing up on their hind legs to give each other what appears to be an affectionate peck on the cheek. Even an artist as respected as William Wegman subtly refashions, in the appropriative style of post-modernism, the lowbrow aesthetic of cuteness by decking out his lugubrious mastiff, an irresistibly funereal pooch cheerlessly resigned to his fate, in everything from Christian Dior to Calvin Klein jeans. Examples like these reveal that the cute worldview is one of massive human chauvinism, which rewrites the universe according to an iconographic agenda dominated by the pathetic fallacy. Multiplying our image a thousand-fold and reverberating like an echo chamber with the familiar sounds of our own voices, the cute vision of the natural world is a world without nature, one that annihilates "otherness," ruthlessly suppresses the non-human, and allows nothing, including our own children, to be separate and distinct from us.

The imitative nature of cuteness can also be seen in the relation of the aesthetic to precocity. One of the things we find cutest in the behavior of our children is their persistence in mimicking us, not only in such time-honored traditions as dress-up (the anthropomorphic version of which is played out obsessively in children's literature) but in that most basic form of child's play, mothering, whether it be of a doll or of a family pet. The spectacle of toddlers rocking their babies, changing the diapers of the many incontinent toys on the market, placating anxious dolls, or thrashing disobedient teddy bears elicits some of our most gloating and unrestrained responses to cuteness. Nothing delights us more than the strange sight of a one-year-old in a stroller meeting a barely ambulatory two-year-old, who, rather than seeking to establish spontaneous esprit de corps with his peer, breaks rank and gibbers baby talk at the bewildered object of his curiously perfunctory affections. As co-conspirators in this game of make-believe maturity, we reward children who at once feign helplessness and assume adult authority in mothering others, reinforcing simultaneously both infantilism and precocity. The child is thus taught not only to be cute in himself but to recognize and enjoy cuteness in others, to play the dual roles of actor and audience, cootchy-cooing as much as he is cootchy-cooed. In this way, our culture actively inculcates the aesthetic doctrines of cuteness by giving our children what amounts to a thorough education in the subject, involving extensive and rigorous training in role-playing. By encouraging our children to imitate the way we ourselves fawn over their own preciousness, we give them the opportunity to know cuteness from both sides of the equation, not only from the standpoint of the object receiving the attention but from the standpoint of those giving it as well, from their appreciative audience-cum-artistic directors, whom they impersonate for brief and touching intervals in their own highly informative charades of child-rearing. We teach our children the nature and value of cuteness almost from the dawn of consciousness and initiate them into the esoteric rituals of its art, passing on to them the tribal legacy of its iconographic traditions, its strange, self-mutilating ceremonies, as alien in their way, at least to a culture unindoctrinated in cuteness, as the scarification customs of Africa or New Guinea. Because imitation allows children to observe their own behavior with the analytic detachment with which they in turn are observed by their admirers, cuteness is unique among aesthetics because it lays the foundations for its own survival by building into itself a form of proselytizing.

The association of cuteness with a delusional state of artlessness prevents us from realizing that the qualities of primitivism and droll savagery around which we have woven this all-consuming folk religion embody something we would like to see in children rather than something we actually do see there. The conventions of cuteness are the residue of unfulfilled wishes that crystallize in the gap between the daily realities of children and our quixotic and unobtainable notions of what they should, ideally, be like. Cuteness is every parent's portable utopia, the rose-colored lenses that color and blur the profound drudgery of child-rearing with soft-focused sentimentality. We use it to allay fears of our failures as parents and to numb us to the irritations of the vigilance we must maintain over creatures who are, despite the anesthetizing ideology of cuteness, often more in control of us than we are of them.

Although it is easy to sympathize with the disquieting frustrations that underlie this aesthetic, cuteness is in fact ultimately more a source of unhappiness than of comfort among parents. To superimpose the vast edifice of fetishized images and intricate rituals onto the shallow foundations of a reality that cannot withstand its weight is to invite disappointment, not only for us but for our children. Cuteness saturates the visual landscape of consumerism with utopian images that cause feelings of inadequacy among parents, who inevitably measure the rowdy and selfish behavior of their own children by exacting ideals of tractability, cuddliness, and quiescence. Just as the inundation of our culture with the glitzy images of recent video pornography has elevated our aesthetic standards in regard to our partners (and consequently interfered with our sexual enjoyment of ordinary bodies in all of their imperfections), so cuteness elevates our expectations in regard to our children. It prevents us from enjoying them in their natural, unindoctrinated state, oppressed as we are by our apparent failures as caregivers who strive unavailingly to discern in our headstrong offspring the lineaments of the model child.

The result of this psychological malaise is an entirely new aesthetic, an invention of the last few decades: the anti-cute. In an effort to counteract prevailing images of children, a culture like our own naturally produces as an antidote images of the exact opposite of cuteness: the perverse. Our belief that our children are harmless little cherubs who toss wreathes of posies hither and yon collides with their intransigence and generates in the process so much hostility that we are inclined to view them as corrupt, possessed, even satanic.

Cuteness thus coexists in a dynamic relation with the perverse. The failure of the hyperboles of one aesthetic gives rise to the hyperboles of the other, of the child as the vehicle of diabolical powers from the Great Beyond, which have appropriated the tiny, disobedient bodies of our elfish changelings as instruments for their assaults on the stability of family life. The spate of films about demonic possession shows just how assiduous we have become about building up the new iconography of the anti-cute. Catering to a deep need in the popular imagination, Hollywood has begun to manufacture images that function as outrageous travesties of cuteness, like those found in *Poltergeist*, in which a young girl becomes the conduit of tormented spirits of the damned who emerge from the throbbing blue light of the television set; or in *Child's Play*, in which the spirit of a dead serial killer inhabits the body of a doll named Chuckie, who, stalking down hallways with butcher knives tucked behind its back, murders Aunt Maggie, the baby-sitter, by giving her such a jolt that she staggers backwards out of the kitchen window and plummets ten floors to splatter on the hood of a parked car. Similarly, in David Cronenberg's *The Brood*, the protagonist's children, a pack of dwarfish gnomes, gestate in moldy embryonic sacks hanging outside of her belly and then, after birth, begin spontaneously to respond to her volatile moods, ultimately bludgeoning her mother to death with kitchen utensils in a fit of rage.

Although it is still the dominant mode of representing children, cuteness is an aesthetic under siege, the object of contempt, laughter, and skepticism. Its commercialized aura of greeting card naivete makes it so fragile, so vulnerable to ridicule, that it cannot withstand the frank realism with which matters of parenting, divorce, and sexuality are now being addressed by the public at large. In the last few decades, cuteness has been subjected to remorseless satire as we attempt to loosen the grip of its iconography on an imagination hungry for images closer to the harsh realities of the era of the latchkey kid, the two-career family, the single-parent household, the crack baby, and the less-than-innocent, drug-running sixth-grader with a beeper in one pocket and a .44 Magnum automatic pistol in the other. Loud and chaotic, *The Simpsons* is the anti-cute show of the 1990s, the "all-American dysfunctional family," as they have been nicknamed. Their household constitutes a direct subversion of the insipidity of cuteness, with its cartoon characters' harshly contoured shapes, gaping, lipless mouths, and enormous boiled-egg eyes goggling in such a way as to suggest the mindless somnambulism of compulsive TV viewers. The anti-cute launches a frontal assault on fuzzy-wuzziness with a blitz of images of the child as the petulant and demanding brat who disdains the sacrosanct laws of property ownership, gleefully annihilating Cuisinarts and microwaves as he mows a broad swathe of destruction through the household's inner sanctum.

With the rise of the anti-cute, we are witnessing what amounts to civil war in the contemporary aesthetic of the family, a battle in which the image of the child as the unnatural spawn of Satan, an impish spirit of pure malevolent mischievousness, has locked horns with that of the child as the inanimate stuffed animal. Generating their plots by pitting the cute against the anti-cute, Parts 1 and 2 of *Gremlins* provide a kind of allegory of this transformation. In Part 2, the adorable "Gizmo" (an appropriate name for this standard-bearer of cuteness, because it emphasizes the animal's status as an inert object) purrs with a contented coo, its droopy ears and sad eyes inviting the lubricious embraces of cute sex. After it is exposed to water, however, it begins to reproduce, laying eggs that enter a larval stage in repulsive cocoons covered by viscous membranes. Whereas Gizmo is soft, dry, and relatively well behaved, the ferocious aliens that quickly hatch from their water-induced hibernation are, as one character calls them, "ugly, slimy, mean-spirited, and gloppy." In them, both the behavior and appearance of cute objects are at once evoked and subverted. Gizmo's strokeable fur is transformed into a wet, scaly integument, while the vacant portholes of its eyes (the most important facial feature of the cute thing, giving us free access to its soul and ensuring its total scrutability, its incapacity to hold back anything) become diabolical slits hiding a lurking intelligence, just as its dainty paws metamorphose into talons and its pretty puckered lips into enormous Cheshire grimaces with full sets of sharp incisors. Whereas cute things have clean, sensuous surfaces that remain intact and unpenetrated (suggesting, in fact, that there is nothing at all inside, that what you see is what you get), the anti-cute Gremlins are constantly being squished and disemboweled, their entrails spilling out into the open, as they explode in microwaves and are run through paper shredders and blenders. With the help of food and water, they multiply exponentially and begin their devastating campaign — Hollywood's favorite plot device — against property ownership, destroying in Part 1 an entire town and, in Part 2, a skyscraper modeled on the Trump Tower. In this Manichean contrast between the precious Gizmo and its progeny, the hyperactive vandals who incarnate a new but equally stylized representation of youth and innocence, *Gremlins* neatly encapsulates the iconographic challenges to an aesthetic that is gradually relinquishing its hold on the popular imagination as we attempt to purge ourselves of the antiquated religion of infantilism.

DISCUSSION

1. Why do you think Harris begins his essay with such a detailed description of the So Shy Sherri doll? Choose one or two of the words he uses in this description, and evaluate what image or impression of this object they seem designed to convey.

2. Harris clearly implies that there is something wrong with accepting or embracing cuteness at face value. What problems does he suggest follow from accepting this image as a norm? What particular effects on how we live, how we view the world, does he suggest this kind of acceptance might entail?

3. Harris argues that our culturally widespread enthusiasm for cute things belies a more formative fascination with things that are malformed or grotesque. How valid do you think this hypothesis is? Can you think of an example of a cute object or product that has this kind of darker subtext?

WRITING

4. Choose some cute object that you have owned in the past, and write an essay in which you reflect on what it meant to you. First, describe this object: what it looked like, how you came to own it, when and where you played with it or looked at it. Next, identify and evaluate the specific things about it that made it feel significant or meaningful to you. Finally, use quotes to compare your experiences to what Harris has to say about "cute things" in this essay. Do your experiences confirm or confound the claims Harris makes?

5. Harris spends a great deal of his essay talking about an aesthetic he calls "anti-cute." What do you think he means by this? Write an essay in which you compare the quality of typically cute things, as Harris describes them, with his definition of what is anti-cute. For each type of object, what are its goals? What are the key qualities that distinguish the two aesthetics? Use examples and quotes from Harris's essay to make your distinctions clear.

6. Few topics would seem, at first glance, to differ more from what Harris discusses than Ariel Levy's (p. 144) examination of "raunch culture." Write an essay in which you identify and evaluate the key things that distinguish cute culture from raunch culture. Along the way, reflect on what the existence of both of these strands within our current popular culture says about the roles and norms that get scripted for us.

143

ARIEL LEVY

Women and the Rise of Raunch Culture

What does it feel like to be a consumer in the world of "raunch culture"? A world where, according to Ariel Levy, sexual self-exhibition has for women become not merely a norm but a perverse kind of social ideal? Focusing on the rise of such things as *Girls Gone Wild* and the Howard Stern radio show, Levy wonders about the new and troubling ways we have learned to think about gender equity, feminist politics, and the pursuit of civil rights. Levy studied literature at Wesleyan University and worked briefly at Planned Parenthood before starting her career as a journalist. Her articles have been published in the *New York Times,* the *Washington Post, Vogue,* and *Slate.* Her first book, published in 2005, is *Female Chauvinist Pigs: Women and the Rise of Raunch Culture.*

FIRST NOTICED IT SEVERAL YEARS AGO. I WOULD TURN ON THE TELE-vision and find strippers in pasties explaining how best to lap dance a man to orgasm. I would flip the channel and see babes in tight, tiny uniforms bouncing up and down on trampolines. Britney Spears was becoming increasingly popular and increasingly unclothed, and her undulating body ultimately became so familiar to me I felt like we used to go out.

Charlie's Angels, the film remake of the quintessential jiggle show, opened at number one in 2000 and made $125 million in theaters nationally, reinvigorating the interest of men and women alike in leggy crime fighting. Its stars, who kept talking about "strong women" and "empowerment," were dressed in alternating soft-porn styles — as massage parlor geishas, dominatrixes, yodeling Heidis in alpine bustiers. (The summer sequel in 2003 — in which the Angels' perilous mission required them to perform stripteases — pulled in another $100 million domestically.) In my own industry, magazines, a porny new genre called the Lad Mag, which included titles like *Maxim, FHM,* and *Stuff,* was hitting the stands and becoming a huge success by delivering what *Playboy* had only occasionally managed to capture: greased celebrities in little scraps of fabric humping the floor.

This didn't end when I switched off the radio or the television or closed the magazines. I'd walk down the street and see teens and young women — and the occasional wild fifty-year-old — wearing jeans cut so low they exposed what came to be known as butt cleavage paired with miniature tops that showed off breast implants and pierced navels alike.

Sometimes, in case the overall message of the outfit was too subtle, the shirts would be emblazoned with the Playboy bunny or say PORN STAR across the chest.

Some odd things were happening in my social life, too. People I knew (female people) liked going to strip clubs (female strippers). It was sexy and fun, they explained; it was liberating and rebellious. My best friend from college, who used to go to Take Back the Night marches on campus, had become captivated by porn stars. She would point them out to me in music videos and watch their (topless) interviews on *Howard Stern*. As for me, I wasn't going to strip clubs or buying *Hustler* T-shirts, but I was starting to show signs of impact all the same. It had only been a few years since I'd graduated from Wesleyan University, a place where you could pretty much get expelled for saying "girl" instead of "woman," but somewhere along the line I'd started saying "chick." And, like most chicks I knew, I'd taken to wearing thongs.

What was going on? My mother, a shiatsu masseuse who attended weekly women's consciousness-raising groups for twenty-four years, didn't own makeup. My father, whom she met as a student radical at the University of Wisconsin, Madison, in the sixties was a consultant for Planned Parenthood, NARAL, and NOW. Only thirty years (my lifetime) ago, our mothers were "burning their bras" and picketing Playboy, and suddenly we were getting implants and wearing the bunny logo as supposed symbols of our liberation. How had the culture shifted so drastically in such a short period of time?

> **Suddenly we were getting implants and wearing the bunny logo as supposed symbols of our liberation.**

What was almost more surprising than the change itself were the responses I got when I started interviewing the men and — often — women who edit magazines like *Maxim* and make programs like *The Man Show* and *Girls Gone Wild*. This new raunch culture didn't mark the death of feminism, they told me; it was evidence that the feminist project had already been achieved. We'd *earned* the right to look at *Playboy*; we were *empowered* enough to get Brazilian bikini waxes. Women had come so far, I learned, we no longer needed to worry about objectification or misogyny. Instead, it was time for us to join the frat party of pop culture, where men had been enjoying themselves all along. If Male Chauvinist Pigs were men who regarded women as pieces of meat, we would outdo them and be Female Chauvinist Pigs: women who make sex objects of other women and of ourselves.

When I asked female viewers and readers what they got out of raunch culture, I heard similar things about empowering miniskirts and feminist strippers, and so on, but I also heard something else. They wanted to be "one of the guys"; they hoped to be experienced "like a man." Going to strip clubs or talking about porn stars was a way of show-ing themselves and the men around them that they weren't "prissy little women" or "girly-girls." Besides, they told me, it was all in fun, all tongue-in-cheek, and for me to regard this bacchanal as problematic would be old-school and uncool.

I tried to get with the program, but I could never make the argument add up in my head. How is resurrecting every stereotype of female sexu-ality that feminism endeavored to banish *good* for women? Why is labor-ing to look like Pamela Anderson empowering? And how is imitating a stripper or a porn star — a woman whose *job* is to imitate arousal in the first place — going to render us sexually liberated?

Despite the rising power of Evangelical Christianity and the political right in the United States, this trend has only grown more extreme and more pervasive in the years that have passed since I first became aware of it. A tawdry, tarty, cartoonlike version of female sexuality has become so ubiquitous, it no longer seems particular. What we once regarded as a *kind* of sexual expression we now view *as* sexuality. As former adult film star Traci Lords put it to a reporter a few days before her memoir hit the bestseller list in 2003, "When I was in porn, it was like a back-alley thing. Now it's everywhere." Spectacles of naked ladies have moved from seedy side streets to center stage, where everyone — men and women — can watch them in broad daylight. *Playboy* and its ilk are being "embraced by young women in a curious way in a postfeminist world," to borrow the words of Hugh Hefner.

But just because we are post doesn't automatically mean we are fem-inists. There is a widespread assumption that simply because my genera-tion of women has the good fortune to live in a world touched by the feminist movement, that means everything we do is magically imbued with its agenda. It doesn't work that way. "Raunchy" and "liberated" are not synonyms. It is worth asking ourselves if this bawdy world of boobs and gams we have resurrected reflects how far we've come, or how far we have left to go.

> **Just because we are post doesn't automatically mean we are feminists.**

DISCUSSION

1. Levy's essay tries to pinpoint what she sees as a contradiction between the tactics of sexual or "porny" self-exhibition and the kind of liberation these acts of display supposedly enable. For Levy, there is something wrong with believing that miniskirts can be empowering or that stripping can be viewed as a feminist act. Do you agree? If so, what in your view makes this kind of association problematic? If not, why not?

2. For the women Levy interviews, there are clear rewards for displaying themselves in the ways they do — payoffs that, in their eyes, make putting on these particular acts well worth doing. How do you assess these so-called benefits? What, specifically, are they? And in your view are they adequate rewards for putting on this kind of role?

3. Choose one of the examples of so-called raunchy behavior described in this essay. Where else (either in the media or in your own experiences) have you seen this same kind of role acted out? What sort of statement about female empowerment do you think this performance made?

WRITING

4. Choose a product (for example, a show, an image, or an object) from our larger popular culture that, in your view, is designed to promote an empowering or liberating message for women. What role does it script, and how does this role compare to the examples cited by Levy? Write an analytical essay in which you argue the benefits and/or pitfalls of these two respective roles.

5. According to Levy, one of the signature aspects of raunch culture is the idea that women are encouraged to participate in it and, in many ways, to control it. Indeed, she writes, "What we once regarded as a *kind* of sexual expression we now view *as* sexuality." Write an essay in which you explore what you think Levy means by this statement. What are her criticisms of this conflation of sex and sexuality? In your opinion, what are some possible ways to address the problem as Levy sees it? How do you think she would respond to your suggestions?

6. Both Levy and Brooke A. Knight (p. 150) are interested in examining the motives behind self-exhibitionism, as well as pondering what it means for those who engage in this kind of practice. Write an essay in which you compare the ways each writer describes and evaluates the exhibitionist role itself: what behavior it involves, what audiences it addresses itself to, what objectives underlie it, what social scripts it seems to follow.

Then and Now:
Wearing Your Identity on Your Sleeve

Merchandisers have long sought to sell their goods by appealing to our sense of personal style: by flattering our desire to make an impression or cultivate an image that reflects our unique individuality. For years, this goal revolved around a strategy known as niche marketing, a tactic designed to associate a given product with the interests, hobbies, or "look" of a particular group. To wear a

specific brand of clothing, drive a certain model of car, drink a particular variety of soda was (according to this formulation) to demonstrate your membership within a cohort of people who wear, drive, and drink the same thing — in effect, to make a statement about the *type* of person you truly are. Niche marketing, in other words, encourages us to treat commercial marketing as a viable blueprint for *self-marketing*. In the 1980s Members Only jackets, similar in style to the jacket pictured at left, were one of many fashion trends designed to appeal to people's desire to identify with a certain group: It's right there in the name of the product. The irony, of course, is that this approach defines individuality exclusively in terms of group affiliation. It doesn't hold out the promise of cultivating our uniqueness so much as it sells us on the allure of belonging to a particular category.

These days, however, niche marketing is giving way to a new sales strategy, one that seems at first glance to resolve this contradiction. No longer content with associating their goods with a consumer type, many merchandisers nowadays promote products that they claim are tailored to non-conformist consumers. A website like Threadless.com, for example, allows artists to create designs that are then voted on by Threadless members, with the most popular designs being printed and sold by the company. For many, this change not only heralds the demise of niche marketing but also signals a movement beyond the outmoded ideas of self-marketing and image-creation. With the advent of customized marketing, we are told, it is now possible for shopping to serve as a truly legitimate means of self-expression, a vehicle for defining and displaying our true individuality.

But how much has *really* changed? Just because merchandisers now market customized products, after all, doesn't necessarily mean they've gotten out of the business of creating and marketing different images. No matter how personalized the messages on these design-your-own T-shirts are, they are still logos. We could well ask whether all of this so-called customized design is simply a different, admittedly more sophisticated, form of branding. At the end of the day, after all, customers who wear these products are still engaging in the same operation that customers always have, one in which they use brand images and logos to make statements about the types of people they are. Do we find ourselves drawn to these kinds of products because they really do help us showcase our genuine selves? Or do we respond to this come-on for the same old reasons — because these products promise to supply us with a genuine self that is made for us?

WRITING

1. In a brief essay, compare the different directions each image lays out for how and why we should shop. What role for the average consumer does each example seem to create? What parallels or similarities do you note? What differences? Which is a more effective way to market clothing? Why?

2. Naomi Klein (p. 114) and Daniel Harris (p. 134) each take up the issue of consumerism, exploring from different angles the ways that commercial culture influences some of our personal attitudes and beliefs. Put yourself in the position of one of these two authors for a moment and write out a description of the ways you think he or she would evaluate or respond to the notion of "personalized marketing." What aspects of this promotional campaign do you think Klein or Harris would focus most attention on? How would he or she evaluate the messages about shopping and identity these products encourage us to accept?

BROOKE A. KNIGHT

Watch Me! Webcams and the Public Exposure of Private Lives

In what ways has the Internet redrawn the boundaries between the public and the private? How typical is it nowadays for us to turn to the Web to learn more about each other's personal lives? Taking stock of the burgeoning popularity of personal webcam technology, Brooke A. Knight tries to make sense of this recent phenomenon, wondering aloud about the wisdom of a virtual world that we use to showcase our supposedly "true selves." Knight earned a BA in English from Davidson College in 1988 and an MFA in photography from CalArts in 1995. His work as a visual artist incorporates technology such as cell phones and webcams. He has also published articles about art and new media in *Words and Image* and *Art Journal.* He is an assistant professor in the Department of Visual and Media Arts at Emerson College. The following essay originally appeared in the Winter 2000 issue of *Art Journal.*

O N YOUR SCREEN, YOU SEE AN IMAGE OF A YOUNG WOMAN STARING intently to the right of the camera, presumably looking at her monitor. Behind her are a bookshelf and some computers. A minute later, she shifts her position slightly, and another image is captured and sent to you via her website. Jennicam, widely recognized as the progenitor of all personal webcams, often offers little more than this scene to the millions of hits her site receives each day.[1] While Jennifer Ringley sees her work as a diaristic documentary, I believe that this mode of communication creates a new kind of social space, in which the private is performed for the public, and interaction is initiated by the one who is being watched. Cams make manifest issues of surveillance, community, the cyborg, domestic space, intimacy, pornography, and self-image. They are a form of artistic practice, with an art historical context and correlatives in documentary production, self-portraiture, and performance.

Twenty-four hours a day, for over three years, Ringley has been living under the scrutiny of the cam's never-blinking eye. She observes, "For some reason, we think it's OK to watch PBS shows about bison and whales, but not about ourselves. . . . I think that's terrible, because we learn a lot by watching ourselves."[2] With the Internet, we are able to watch the daily habits of just about anyone who cares to share them. In many ways, this exposure of the self shifts the surveillance model. Those being seen control what is to be seen. As Ana Voog, one of the most popular and compelling "camgirls" says, "I can move the camera wherever I want, whenever I want. I'm in control."[3] This control goes beyond simply where to point the cam: unlike many other art forms, the artist has access to both the means of production and, through the Internet, the means of distribution.

Many cam producers choose to point their cameras at themselves while they are in their most vulnerable state — sleep. Voog started the Universal Sleep Station, a grid of images of sleeping cam people, because of the fan response to images of her in slumber. She writes, "When people are watching me sleeping and stuff, from all of the nice e-mails I get, I feel that everyone's sort of an angel, watching over me and protecting me."[4] Yet when I look at the Sleep Station, I feel like I'm a cross between the Tooth Fairy and a guard at a Supermax prison. The nearly panoptic view is disconcerting, perhaps because of the willingness of those on the screen to be seen. Jeremy Bentham's ideas for prison reform through constant surveillance have been applied here, but this time by way of the subjects' free will. Ironically, and fittingly, a wax figure of Bentham is the object of a proposed webcam as he "permanently sleeps."[5] While a graduate student at MIT, Steve Mann created a wearable cam that posted images to a website. Here, he has inverted the surveillance paradigm: the individual — rather than an unseen power — produces images of an event. Mann sees his projects as "Humanistic Intelligence," in which technology is used to safeguard individuals. He feels that if his human rights are abused, his documentation of the event will protect him, much like the "angels" in Voog's Sleep Station. There is no tape or disc to confiscate, and the dispersal of the image is nearly instantaneous.[6]

> **The nearly panoptic view is disconcerting, perhaps because of the willingness of those on the screen to be seen.**

Clearly, those involved in this type of production develop a sense of community. Voog states, "This is me. This is my life. I'm living on my cam. I've made friends through it. I've helped people through it."[7] Chip, a "veteran of online communities," says that Chipcam was a way of making himself accountable and "authenticated his online persona."[8] The Web problematizes our relationships: we feel dose to those with whom we communicate online, but are physically distanced from them through servers and wires. The critic Melita Zajc believes that all contemporary communication technologies isolate the individual by preventing physical proximity to others.[9] The homecam community, however, would say that they have generated friends through their shared experience of living online. "Holly Golightly" from www.iloveholly.com and Stephanie of www.stvlive.com consider themselves to be "twins" after having seen each other on cam.

Golightly traveled to Stephanie's home, and they are now each other's "best friend."[10] In October 1999, Voog attended Ringley's facetiously named "Jennicon," which produced one of the most unsettling things I have encountered: the two most celebrated camgirls on the same cam, at the same time. Each had been in her own "remote window" box on my monitor, and seeing them together forced me to regard them as more "real" than I had before.

Thomas Campanella, author of "Eden by Wire: Webcameras and the Telepresent Landscape," sees a role for the cam as the Internet allows for the creation of a new machine/body: "If the Internet and the World Wide Web represent [the] augmentation of collective memory, then webcameras are a set of wired eyes, a digital extension of the human faculty of vision."[11] Voog considers the Internet as a symbol for the collective unconscious, that it is "intimate in a different way."[12] While some critics envision the extension of the body into the corpus of the Net as a positive development, author Nell Tenhaaf cautions that there are "complications in proposing a language of technological media as a language of the body, in particular the female body." She feels that the declaration of the body in the technological apparatus is suspect, as the body becomes either idealized — and therefore a commodity — or fragmented in the form of the automaton and the cyborg, half metal/half flesh.[13]

Interestingly, women comprise the majority of webcam subjects and producers. These women understand, participate in, and profit from the specular economy. Many target male desire by highlighting the more prurient aspects of their cams, while also maintaining control over the image. The producers are the subjects of the images, and in this way challenge the to-be-looked-at-ness described in Laura Mulvey's work on narrative cinema.[14] Historically, some women artists have reclaimed their bodies with self-portraits in which they hold their drawing or painting tools;[15] in this way, they resemble the self-proclaimed geek girls, who proudly state that they have created the code for their webcam sites. The most successful personal webcams have several things in common: a young, attractive woman as the main focus who is able to spend most of her time at home, with significant computer skills and some exhibitionist tendencies. The fact that the production facility is the home is significant. The camgirls (or camboys) feel comfortable there; they can organize their time as they wish; and the space lends an air of "peeping tom" authenticity to fulfill the viewer/voyeur's desire. Marsha Meskimmon noted that the inclusion of the domestic in female self-portraiture is a feminist act — that the home has long been a place for artistic production, as typified by the work of Mary Cassatt.[16] The journalist Ben Greenman recounts his visit to Voog's house: "It is instantly recognizable to me in the same way as Rob and Laura Petrie's home or Seinfeld's apartment."[17] The home is transformed by the cam, from a cove of seclusion to the locus of projected desire. In a 1998 article, Simon Firth muses that "Perhaps home-cam fans are a new breed of *flâneur,* enabled by Internet technology to enter more intimate spaces and moments than their 19th Century fore-bears."[18] I believe this access to apparent intimacy marks our particular historical moment. As the media move from paparazzi and the stalking of celebrities to "reality" television, such as *Big Brother* and *Survivor,* the Web allows us the most secret of viewing experiences — ordinary people sleeping, taking baths, making love.

The computer screen — designed to be seen by one person at a time — creates an atmosphere of secrets among friends. Firth notes: "While people like Jenni and Ana are already celebrities and exist for most of us in a purely mediated, hyperreal space, they are the solitary surfer's own rather wonderfully disquieting discoveries."[19] The initial interaction is, at least on the surface, that between lurker/voyeur and object. However, the very structure of these sites indicates that the person on the cam wants to be known. Often included are a short biography, diaristic writings, archives, a section for their art, and a photo album. Most of the sites offer the possibility to chat, or at least to post to a bulletin board. Golightly alternately shows two distinct sides of herself on the cam — that as sex kitten or as Hello Kitty. Firth remarks that "[The fans'] postings betray a knowledge of, and often affection for, the objects of their gaze that suggest feelings entirely different from the quick, anonymous transactions of conventional porn. . . . The [delay between the refreshed images] forces the viewer into introspection and connection."[20]

> *The computer screen . . . creates an atmosphere of secrets among friends.*

Perhaps the act of watching cams is as different from other types of viewing as being the subject of the cam is from other types of exposure and disclosure. Erik Vidal, creator of "Here and Now," a multiroom, multi-person camsite, characterizes camwatching as "passive," as the viewer does not concentrate on the images, but rather chooses when she or he looks.[21] I would not term it as such; rather, it is up to the viewer to actively create the story as she or he watches. The action on the cam is always *in medias res,* as the narrative is really the person's life. One snapshot slice of their existence does not tell all that has gone on before. A minute later, another clue is sent to the site, and we are left to fill the interstice. Even in Vidal's own streaming audio and video world, there is action off camera. Maybe the key is what is unseen, rather than what is exposed. Detail by banal detail, the cam captures a small snippet from a life. What consti-tutes "the action" is usually unbearably boring: washing dishes, working on the computer, watching television. Content is created by living in front of the camera, without the quick cuts and distillation of events in MTV's

The Real World. There are no outside editors, directors, or producers to decide who gets how much airtime. Just like the Internet itself, there is no hierarchical order to the images we see. The sequence of pictures presented to us could either be the best or the worst day of the camgirl's life, and we might never know, as the cam captures everything in the same way.

Without editing and scripted action, cams test the limits of performance. In *Writing Performance: Poeticizing the Researcher's Body*, Ronald J. Pelias considers the defining factor in performance simply to be the cognizance of someone watching.[22] People on webcams are certainly aware that they are under the watch of many, but Ringley says, "Frankly, most of the time I forget that the camera is there. The camera is the least-intrusive thing in the world."[23] Vidal concurs: "After 20 minutes on the first day, we all totally forgot about it. . . . It's a lifestyle constraint, but it's not the psychologically intense experience you'd think it would be."[24] In many ways, the camera moves from a recording instrument to an integral aspect of the subjects' lives. Instead of an intruder intended to capture their culture as in the ethnographic films of the past, the cam occupies the same territory as a pair of glasses or a car or an incandescent light — transparent technology. So, if they forget the camera's eye, are they performing? Perhaps they are "non-matrixed" performers, in Michael Kirby's terms, where they do not pretend to be anyone other than who they are, nor do they act as if they are in any other space.[25] Webcams are creating a new theater. Firth writes: "What makes them troubling and captivating is that, instead of giving us something we already know, they are pioneering both a new erotics and a new kind of performance — one that could be called the art of the publicly lived private life."[26] Kirby also discusses John Cage's contention that duration is "the one dimension which exists in *all* performance."[27] What sets webcams apart from other varieties of performance is exactly the lack of a specified period of time. Golightly offers "lifetime" memberships, and Voog says, "The hope is that I'll want it to go on forever. I could be 50 and still doing it. Right now, I can't imagine wanting it to stop."[28]

Pat Quinn, the subject of "Cripplecam," feels that the constant eye of the cam is liberating and confidence-bolstering. He writes: "The first month or so I had the cam up, I'd make sure I coverd [sic] up when I got out of bed, and made sure my hair was brushed and what not. Any more, I couldn't care less. . . . I feel better about myself now that I've invited all to witness my quirks. . . . I feel that my online persona is an extension of who I really am, yes, but I don't bother to shave the rough edges. . . . I don't want people to think I am someone I am not."[29] Through the cam, Quinn has found a level of comfort with his body. The appellation "Cripplecam" directly addresses the fact that he has Friedrich's Ataxia and is willing to discuss it.[30] The Internet, in this case, is a form of empowerment. Tenhaaf also tackles issues of identity in the face of technology, seeing self-portraiture as a means to preserve a sense of humanity. She cites as an example Kate Craig's video piece *Delicate Issue,* in which an unseen assistant shoots Craig's entire body, lingering in certain intimate areas.[31] Craig takes control of the image by allowing this incursion into very private spaces, much as many camgirls do.

> *The webcam is remarkable because it presents the familiar, and . . . asks us to question what we find so fascinating.*

The webcam is remarkable because it presents the familiar, and in that presentation, asks us to question what we find so fascinating. Is it the obstinate consistency of it all; the predictable daily cycle; the endless refreshing of the image; the domesticity of the setting; or the candid, unmediated body? Privacy becomes publicity, and the performance is the never-ending nonevent. Technology allows for an obsessive documentation, which, in these cases, empowers the one under surveillance. It is a self-portrait of great importance because it is of seemingly nothing important at all.

NOTES

[1]Webcameras digitally capture images and distribute them via a website. Many sites include more than one camera, some allow the viewer to remotely control the angle of view, and a few stream full-motion video. There are thousands of active webcams right now, displaying everything from a fishbowl to the construction of a stadium.

[2]Su Avasthi. "Cam-Girls Aim to Please," *New York Post,* May 28, 1998; July 13, 2000 (www.anacam.com/analyze/980528nyp.html).

[3]Ben Greenman, "A Room Within a View," Yahoo Internet Life, October 1999, 173.

[4]Adam Pasick, "Living on Camera: Narcissism or New Wave?" Fox News Online (www.foxnews.com), October 28, 1999.

[5]Rory Hamilton, Jeremy Benthom On-Line (doric.bart.ucl.ac.uk/web/Nina/JBentham.html), July 13, 2000. Bentham proposed the Panopticon, a prison with a centralized guard tower and a ring of prisoner cells, in which total surveillance was linked to behavior modification.

[6]Steve Mann, "Humanistic Intelligence," in *Ars Electronica: Facing the Future,* ed. Timothy Druckery (Cambridge, Mass.: MIT Press, 1999), 420–21, 425–26.

[7]Greenman, 174.

[8]Simon Firth, "Live! From My Bedroom," Salon (www.salon.com/21st/feature/1998/01/cov_08feature.html/index.htm), January 18, 1998.

[9]Mann, 297.

[10]Holly Golightly, Twins page (www.iloveholly.com), February 10, 2000.

[11]Thomas J. Campanella, "Eden by Wire: Webcameras and the Telepresent Landscape," in *The Robot in the Garden: Telerobotics and Telepistemology in the Age of the Internet,* ed. Ken Goldberg (Cambridge, Mass.: MIT Press, 2000), 23.

[12]Marlee MacLeod, "TechnoSlice with Ana Voog," *Cake Magazine* (tt.net/macleod/other/anavoog.html), December 15, 1999.

[13]Nell Tenhaaf, "Of Monitors and Men and Other Unsolved Feminist Mysteries: Video Technology and the Feminine," in *Critical Issues in Electronic Media,* ed. Simon Penny (Albany: State University of New York Press, 1995), 230.

[14]Laura Mulvey, "Visual Pleasure and Narrative Cinema," in *Art After Modernism: Rethinking Representation,* ed. Brian Wallis (New York: New Museum of Contemporary Art, 1984), 361–73.

[15]Marsha Meskimmon, *The Art of Self-Reflection: Women Artists' Self-Portraiture in the Twentieth Century* (New York: Columbia University Press, 1996), 32.

[16]Ibid., 162–63.

[17]Greenman, 173.

[18]Firth.

[19]Ibid.

[20]Ibid.

[21]Erik Vidal, What's New page (www.hereandnow.net), February 9, 2000.

[22]Ronald J. Pelias, *Writing Performance: Poeticizing the Researcher's Body* (Carbondale: Southern Illinois University Press, 1999), 8.

[23]Avasthi.

[24]Pasick.

[25]Michael Kirby, *The Art of Time: Essays on the Avant-Garde* (New York: Dutton Press, 1969), 78.

[26]Firth.

[27]Kirby, 80.

[28]Greenman, 174.

[29]Pat Quinn, email to the author, December 3, 1999.

[30]Pat Quinn, Policy page (www.pquinn.com/cam/policy.html), December 2, 1999.

[31]Tenhaaf, 228.

DISCUSSION

1. Knight refers to personal webcam sites as an "artistic practice." What do you think he means? In your view, is this an accurate or helpful term to apply here? In what ways does or doesn't this technology involve choices or actions you would call "artful"?

2. One of the hallmarks of this technology is the striking absence of limits or boundaries. What do you think it would feel like to have your personal life broadcast twenty-four hours a day, seven days a week?

3. With the rise of sites like YouTube, personal video diaries have become easier and easier to post online for a wide audience. What do you think the appeal is in broadcasting personal lives over the Internet?

WRITING

4. In a free-write, sketch out a description of the person you think is the ideal type to be featured on one of these personal websites. Be as comprehensive as possible, not just in terms of how this person would or should look (for example, age, gender, body-type, and so on), but also in terms of his or her attitude or outlook. Next, write down some of the things you believe define the worst candidate for this kind of site. Write an essay in which you analyze the differences between these two portraits. What do the differences between the ideal and the anti-ideal tell us about the norms governing how we are supposed to watch in this particular case? Use quotes from Knight's essay to help you define the rules and norms.

5. One of the supposed appeals of watching someone's life unfold on a personal webcam involves the idea that what you are seeing is 100 percent real. Look back over the Rule Maker/Rule Breaker feature that begins this chapter and write an essay in which you argue whether personal webcams are truer depictions of reality than what you see on a reality television show. What are the key elements of each type of entertainment, and how are they supposed to appeal to us? Do they have any elements in common?

6. The "camgirls" profiled in this essay often draw a connection between the act of showing oneself on the Internet and the feeling of being in control. Does this connection seem to you to be a valid one? Write an essay in which you compare this argument to what Ariel Levy (p. 144) says about self-exhibition in her piece on raunch culture. How do you think Levy would respond to Knight's (p. 150) profile of these camgirls?

Scenes and Un-Scenes: *Picturing Disaster*

Whether it is a television commercial or a news broadcast, a web image or blockbuster movie, virtually everything we see has been selectively shaped for our inspection. While it may purport to show us "the way things are," the truth is that every image bears traces of some slant or bias, intentional or not. And yet while it may be inevitable, this doesn't mean it is automatically excusable – that such bias doesn't warrant our attention, doesn't deserve to be challenged, critiqued, or changed. Certainly when it comes to something as politically important and personally catastrophic as Hurricane Katrina, it is no small matter to know whether the images we are shown tell the true or whole story.

▼▼ *In the hours before it made landfall, media coverage tended to treat Hurricane Katrina as an entirely natural phenomenon. Tracking its movements from the supposedly objective vantage of outer space, for example, satellite photos like the one below reinforced an initial perception among many in the general public that no one was really to blame for this disaster.*

PRICE $3.95   THE   SEPT. 19, 2005

NEW YORKER

▲▲ *By contrast, this* New Yorker *cover demonstrates how drastically public opinion about Katrina had shifted a month later. Referencing the "flood" of criticism leveled against the Bush administration for its supposed indifference and inaction, this cartoon treats the issues of causation and responsibility quite differently — representing the Katrina disaster less as a natural event than a political and moral crime.*

▲ *The following caption originally accompanied this image: A young man walks through chest deep flood water after looting a grocery store in New Orleans on Tuesday, Aug. 30, 2005. Flood waters continue to rise in New Orleans after Hurricane Katrina did extensive damage when it made landfall on Monday.*

In the days immediately following the breach of the levees in New Orleans, news organizations ran countless images documenting local residents' struggles to survive. Despite their shared focus, however, not all such records invited viewers to think about this struggle in the same way. Take, for example, the two pictures featured above and on the facing page. Although taken on the same day and picturing virtually identical circumstances, the captions accompanying these images encouraged viewers to draw very different conclusions about what they were being shown. In the first, we are told, a "young man walks through chest deep flood water after looting a grocery store." In the second, we are told, "Two residents wade through chest deep water after finding bread and soda at a local grocery store." Bloggers across the Internet were quick to point out that the captions fed into possible racial biases, and although both photo agencies defended their methods for captioning the photos, the images were subsequently pulled from syndication.

▲▲ *The following caption originally accompanied this image: Two residents wade through chest-deep water after finding bread and soda from a local grocery store after Hurricane Katrina came through the area in New Orleans, Louisiana.*

▼▼ *Another hallmark of the Katrina coverage involved what we might call the
"sympathetic celebrity" story, in which a famous person toured the aftermath
of the flooding in New Orleans to showcase her or his "personal" anguish or outrage
at what was transpiring. What is the effect of casting Katrina as this type of human-
interest story? What kind of reaction does it seem designed to elicit from viewers?*

▶▶ **Unlike much of the media coverage nationally, headlines
such as the one on the facing page presented a view of the
disaster informed by a far more thorough and realistic understanding of the local conditions. Does this local perspective
seem different from that modeled in other examples?**

KATRINA: THE STORM WE'VE ALWAYS FEARED

The Times-Picayune

50 CENTS 169th year No. 221 | WEDNESDAY, AUGUST 31, 2005 | HURRICANE EDITION

UNDER WATER

LEVEE BREACH SWAMPS CITY FROM LAKE TO RIVER

Population urged to leave; years of cleanup ahead

STAFF PHOTO BY TED JACKSON

NEW ORLEANS: Graves at Greenwood and Metairie cemeteries mark the waterline of the sheet of water that covered the city from Lake Pontchartrain to nearly the French Quarter on Tuesday.

Daylong efforts to repair levee fail

By Dan Shea
Staff writer

New Orleans became an unimaginable scene of water, fear and suffering Tuesday after a levee breach sent billions of gallons of Lake Pontchartrain coursing through the city.

As the day wore on, the only dry land was a narrow band from the French Quarter and parts of Uptown, the same small strip that was settled by Bienville amid the swamps.

On Tuesday night, it appeared the city was returning to swamp when a daylong effort to shore the levee near the Hammond Highway failed. Mayor Ray Nagin said pumps were being overwhelmed and warned that a new deluge would bury the city in up to 15 feet of water.

With solid water from the lake to the French Quarter, the inundation and depopulation of an entire American city was at hand.

"Truth to tell, we're not so far from filling in the bowl," said Terry Ebbert, the city's director of homeland security. The waters were still rising at 3 inches per hour, and eventually could move close to the French Quarter levee.

Although the breach occurred on the Orleans side of the canal, it did not spare the Jefferson side. Water found its way into much of the east bank, meeting the flow that came in from the west from Hurricane Katrina's storm surge Monday.

An accurate tally of death was hard to determine. Five deaths related to Katrina have been confirmed in Jefferson Parish, officials said. There also are seven people missing who decided to ride out Katrina on Grand Isle.

Gov. Kathleen Blanco spoke of "many deaths," but there were only rumors and anecdotes of firefighters tying floating bodies to trees.

"We have some bodies floating," Ebbert said. "Not like thousands, but we have seen some."

As to the living, with the absence of cars and electric motors in the powerless city, a sad tableau played itself out in an eerie quiet.

All day, a weary army of storm victims trudged through waist-deep muddy water toward the Superdome, where more than 20,000 people took refuge. The next problem is what to do with them. Late Tuesday Gov. Blanco ordered them out, saying the facility was too damaged to house people and the atmosphere too dangerous. Officials said the National Guard soon would begin driving them out to dry ground, then airlift them out of southeast Louisiana.

In other areas, lawlessness took hold.

See **KATRINA,** *A-2*

STAFF PHOTO BY ALEX BRANDON

MID-CITY: A New Orleans Police officer ferries refugees out of the danger zone as floodwaters rose Tuesday.

Flooding will only get worse

By Mark Schleifstein
Staff writer

The catastrophic flooding that filled the bowl that is New Orleans on Monday and Tuesday will only get worse over the next few days because

rainfall from Hurricane Katrina continues to flow into Lake Pontchartrain from north shore rivers and streams, and east winds and a 17.5-foot storm crest on the Pearl River block the outflow water through the Rigolets and Chef Menteur Pass.

The lake is normally 1 foot above sea level, while the city of New Orleans is an average of 6 feet below sea level. But a combination of storm surge and rainfall from Katrina have raised the lake's surface to 6 feet above sea level, or more.

All of that water moving from the lake has found several holes in the lake's banks - all pouring into New Orleans. Water that crossed St. Charles Parish in an area where the lakefront levee has not yet been completed, and that backed up from the lake in Jefferson Parish canals, is funneling into Kenner and Metairie.

A 500-yard and growing breach in the eastern wall of the 17th Street Canal separating New Orleans from Metairie is pouring hundreds of thousands of gallons of lake water per second into the New Orleans

See **WATER,** *A-4*

DISCUSSION

1. Are we always fully aware of the ways an image's bias shapes the conclusions we draw? Does it really matter? Would anything change if we were? How or how not?

2. In your view, does the racial identity of the viewer make any difference in what these images show or say? How might a white viewer draw different conclusions than an African American viewer? Why?

3. Is the Katrina coverage an isolated or idiosyncratic example of media bias, or do you think it reflects a more wide-ranging pattern? Can you think of another news event or controversy that ended up being defined by such contrasting sorts of images?

WRITING

4. The above portfolio makes abundantly clear that bias is a question not only of (mis)representation, but also of omission. That is, bias reveals itself not simply in terms of what an image shows, but also by virtue of what it leaves out. Choose one of the images showcased above and write a one-page assessment of the things it does not show. What key aspects of its portrait are left out? How do these omissions influence the conclusions viewers are encouraged to draw?

5. As discussed throughout this chapter, our culture's visual rules teach us not only how to watch but also how to think. Choose one of the images shown on the preceding pages and write a one-page script for how the image is supposed to make us think about race. What sorts of ideas concerning racial difference and racial conflict does it encourage viewers to adopt? Is this script different based on what race the viewer belongs to?

6. As Michael Eric Dyson (p. 123) reports, media bias within the Hurricane Katrina coverage revealed itself in both subtle and explicit ways. Choose three of the images previously listed and in two or three sentences write the kind of caption you think Dyson would create for each. What aspect of each image would Dyson focus on? What specific sort of bias or slant would he identify? Then, write a second set of captions you think accurately describes what is happening in the photos you've chosen. How does your perspective compare to Dyson's?

Putting It into Practice: **Keep an Eye Out**

Now that you've read the chapter selections, try applying your conclusions to your own life by completing the following exercises.

WINDOW SHOPPING   Pay a visit to the retail store of your choice. Based on the décor and marketing images inside the store, what sort of customer do you think it is trying to attract? How does the store's layout, products, and signage stereotype this customer? Do your fellow patrons appear to fit the image of the store's ideal customer? How? Imagine that you are creating a store designed to attract a certain type of person, whether it is the soccer mom, macho guy, or urban hipster. Describe what your customer looks like, and then decide what sort of marketing images you would use to draw the customer into your store.

RATING THE HEADLINES   In television news, stories are typically covered in the order that news producers deem most important to least important. Watch a broadcast of the national evening news and keep a running record of the order in which the stories of the day are covered. What images stand out in your mind that characterize each story? Write a brief essay in which you discuss why you think certain stories are given more weight or are broadcast earlier than others, and be sure to include examples from the broadcast you've just watched. If you were a news producer, in what order would you broadcast the same stories? Why?

THE REAL YOU   Make a photo collage of images you think express facets of your identity, whether they are personal photos, advertisements for products you like, or pieces of art you find important. In class, swap collages with a peer and write a brief characterization of him or her based on the collage you've been given. Based on your collage, what do your classmates have to say about you? How closely does their description of you match what you had in mind? How might you have portrayed yourself differently to get them to describe you more accurately?

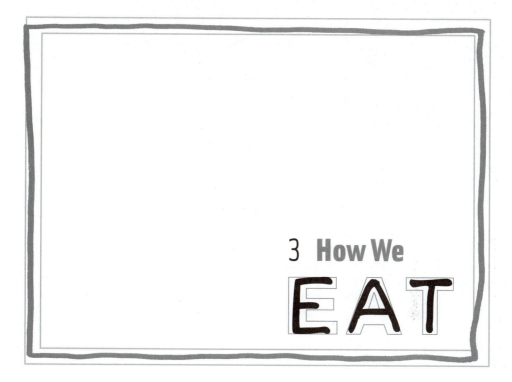

3 **How We**
EAT

Introduction

SCRIPTING THE PERFECT MEAL

Few activities seem as straightforward as eating. We do it so regularly and for such apparently obvious reasons, it's hard at first to take seriously the idea that there's all that much to it. We're hungry, we eat. What's so complicated about that? Because we tend to treat eating as such a given, such an essential and unexamined part of our lives, it's easy to believe that the choices we make about it are entirely our own. Some people like Chicken McNuggets while others prefer sushi; some of us are die-hard vegetarians while others fall into the meat-and-potatoes camp. Whichever way we slice it, however, the underlying assumption is the same: How and what we eat are, in every sense of the word, matters of personal taste.

We might want to pause, however, before too quickly accepting this premise. We do, after all, live in a world that presents us with an almost endless array of food-related choices. For starters, there's the question of *what* to eat. Meat or opt for vegetarian? Homemade or takeout? Organic or processed? High carb, low carb, or no carb? Following this, there is the question of *how* to eat. Alone or with friends? Driving in our cars or sitting in front of the TV? Fresh from a wok or out of a microwave? And then, there are those questions concerning the economics of eating: Do we shop at 7-11 or Whole Foods? Do we need to buy what's on sale, or can we splurge instead? When we really stop to think about it, how *do* we make up our minds?

In answering these questions, we would do well to start by acknowledging a basic (if often overlooked) fact about our modern food culture: No matter how instinctive our individual eating choices feel to us, they aren't, in the strictest sense, personal at all. We don't make our decisions about food all by ourselves; we get a lot of help. From diet books to FDA guidelines, fast-food commercials to gourmet magazines, we are surrounded by images and instructions, messages and advice — all of which aim to fix our "proper" relationship to food. Our culture has rules for what types of food we are supposed to eat, when we are supposed to eat them, and in what amounts. We have rules for how different meals should be prepared, and others for how they should be hosted. And rules dictate how much all of

Everybody Knows That . . .

❝ Atkins Diet: The Rules of Induction

Rule 4. Eat nothing that isn't on the Acceptable Foods list. And that means absolutely nothing. Your "just this one taste won't hurt" rationalization is the kiss of failure during this phase of Atkins."

— *Atkins Nutritional Approach, www.atkins.com*

168

these different things cost. Whether these rules take the form of government-issued regulations about growth hormones, diet fads proscribing our daily allowance of carbohydrates, fast-food commercials instructing us to supersize our selections, or websites extolling the benefits of going vegan, every one of these rules reminds us of the same inescapable truth: Our food choices are framed long before we ever set foot in the kitchen, the grocery store, or the restaurant.

Everybody Knows That . . .

— *U.S. Department of Agriculture,*
www.mypyramid.gov

FOOD FOR THOUGHT

Nor are these rules concerned solely with how we *act*. They play just as formative a role in shaping how we *think* as well. Whether this means following the 15 percent tipping rule or memorizing Dr. Phil's ten steps to a slimmer waistline, every time we live up to one of our culture's food-related instructions we simultaneously endorse the value or ideas that underlie it. To illustrate, let's compare two representative but quite distinct eating experiences: a Thanksgiving dinner and a McDonald's meal. Even if our own experiences sometimes deviate from the stereotype, few of us would argue that there aren't well-entrenched and universally recognized rules dictating how these two meals are supposed to unfold. In each of these settings, only a few select items may properly appear on the menu: We are far more likely to come across turkey and cranberry sauce at the Thanksgiving table than veggie kabobs or tuna salad, and burgers and fries at the fast-food counter rather than tofu stir-fry. Very different dress codes apply in each case too. Cut-off jeans are far more appropriate when we are sitting in a plastic booth at McDonald's than when we are sitting at a holiday dinner table. Very different social rituals prevail also: Napkins go on laps and pleases and thank-yous accompany requests for food at a Thanksgiving gathering, while at McDonald's it is OK to eat with your hands and to throw away plates, containers, and napkins once the meal is finished.

These sorts of differences, as we've already begun to see, are not terribly difficult to list. A bit trickier to discern, however, are the ways these instructions simultaneously function as social scripts. When we live up to the more formal edicts of a traditional Thanksgiving dinner, we are doing more than playing the role of a particular kind of diner. In donning this costume and adhering to this script, we are just as firmly giving our assent to a number of related notions: about the importance of tradition, about the special role that home and family should play in commemorating national holidays, even about which version of American history to accept as right. Similarly, when we assume the role of the typical fast-food consumer, our performance registers our tacit acceptance of a number of unspoken priorities: processed over "whole" foods, speed and efficiency over patience, convenience over nutrition.

This particular relationship — between the eating roles we take on and the eating rules we follow on the one hand and the social norms that underlie them on the other — links all of the readings in this chapter. Because our eating habits offer such a sensitive barometer of our current ideals and anxieties, each of the following selections uses its portrait of eating as a jumping-off point for investigating a larger issue or controversy to which food is connected. In several cases, writers focus their attention on the ways our contemporary system of food production and consumption is organized. Pursuing just this line of inquiry, Michael Pollan examines the complicated and increasingly influential role that organic food plays in our eating lives. Assessing our food economy from the other end of the spectrum, Loretta Schwartz-Nobel chronicles the struggles of several homeless Americans to survive in a world where basic access to food and shelter is far from guaranteed. Forgoing this explicit focus on economics, other selections conduct investigations into some of the different cultural attitudes embedded within our current eating practices. In what ways and for what reasons, these writers ponder, have we learned to differentiate ideal from taboo forms of eating? And what are the consequences of trying to live up to these distinctions? Surveying the cultural history of "gluttony," Francine Prose indicts our contemporary society for its long-standing demonization of overeating, a tradition that has led so many of us to stigmatize so-called fat people as benighted victims, social misfits, or pariahs. Addressing what we might call the flip side of this issue, Caroline Knapp chronicles her own decade-long struggle with

Everybody Knows That . . .

❝ How do I prepare my TOMBSTONE FOR ONE Pizza?

Toaster Oven/Conventional Oven Cooking Directions: Preheat the oven to 400 degrees Fahrenheit. Remove pizza from box and overwrap. Discard silver cooking circle. Place pizza directly on oven rack in Center Position (8 to 10 inches from bottom of oven). Bake according to the table below, or until the cheese is melted and edges are golden brown. Oven temperatures vary, so adjust baking time and oven temperature as necessary. Supreme: 12 to 16 minutes. Extra Cheese: 9 to 12 minutes. Pepperoni: 9 to 12 minutes. CAUTION: Do not use silver circle in toaster oven or conventional oven."

— *Frequently Asked Questions, www.kraftfoods.com*

anorexia, a struggle that revolved centrally around an effort to make sense of our culture's treacherous and contradictory food injunctions to be "slim" and "beautiful." In his journalistic account of "professional eating," Jason Fagone draws a different set of conclusions about our culture's imperatives regarding food, detecting within the surprising popularity of such events as the National Hot Dog Eating Contest the outlines of the classic American dream. And finally, Taras Grescoe rounds out this survey by evaluating the role our modern food attitudes play in underwriting our current "war on drugs."

"EVERYBODY KNOWS THAT" EXERCISE

Choose one of the images or quotations featured in the margins on the preceding pages and answer the following questions:

1. What does this image or quotation ask you to believe?

2. What are the particular ideas, values, or attitudes it invites us to accept as *normal*?

3. What would it feel like to act on or act out these norms in our personal lives?

Rule *Maker* > > > > > > > > Rule *Breaker*

❝ *I am not sure if merely because of our size and success Whole Foods Market deserves the pejorative label 'Big Organic' or 'Industrial Organic,' or even to be linked to those categories. I would argue instead that organic agriculture owes much of its growth and success over the past 20 years to Whole Foods Market's successful growth and commitment to organic. As an organization we continually challenge ourselves to be responsible and ethical tenants of the planet. Through our stores, large and small organic farmers, both local and international, can offer their products to an increasingly educated population that is more interested in organics every day. . . . Whole Foods Market is one of the "good guys" in this story about the "industrialization of agriculture."*

— JOHN MACKEY,
CEO WHOLE FOODS, 2006

❝ *[T]he trickiest contradiction Whole Foods attempts to reconcile is the one between the industrialization of organic food and the pastoral ideals on which that industry has been built. The organic movement, as it was once called, has come a remarkably long way in the last thirty years, to the point where it now looks considerably less like a movement than a big business. . . . So is an industrial organic food chain finally a contradiction in terms? It's hard to escape the conclusion it is. . . . As in so many other realms, nature's logic has proven no match for the logic of capitalism.*

— MICHAEL POLLAN,
THE OMNIVORE'S DILEMMA, 2006

Whole Foods vs. Michael Pollan

Since the 1960s and 1970s, the organic food industry has played a major role in reshaping how millions of Americans think about, shop for, and (of course) eat their food. Pioneered by a small cadre of local farmers, grocery co-op proprietors, and eco-conscious consumers, the organic movement cast itself in its early years as a revolutionary alternative to what was often termed the "corporate" or "industrial" food economy, a system typified by the giant, chain grocery store, with its row after row of frozen TV dinners, pesticide-coated oranges, canned vegetables, and potato chips. Organizing their efforts around the twin ideals of *naturalness* and *community,* these early proponents supported weaning the general public from its reliance on mass-produced, artificially preserved, chemically altered foodstuffs.

And yet, while organic grocery stores have seen both the public enthusiasm for their goals and their own market shares rise steadily over the years, this very success has also raised some uncomfortable questions about whether these ventures remain true to the movement's original "green" ideals. As enormously popular and profitable stores like Whole Foods and Trader Joe's have become national chains, and as wholesale distributors like Harmony Valley or Cascadian Farms have adopted corporate-style growing and distribution practices, many have begun to wonder whether any meaningful differences still exist between industrial and organic food. In a world where even Wal-Mart has begun marketing organic selections to its shoppers, does it still make sense to talk about this movement as a kind of anticorporate revolution? For observers like food critic Michael Pollan, the answer is "not really." For people like Whole Foods CEO John Mackey, on the other hand, such doubts are shortsighted and unfair, overlooking the ways that the organic industry has succeeded in rewriting the rules by which countless Americans eat.

FIND THE RULES: Next time you're at the grocery store (whether it is an organic chain like Whole Foods or another corporate chain with an organic section), takes notes on the way the store presents itself to you. In what ways is the décor designed to appeal to an organic foods shopper? What assumptions about the typical shopper does the store's design make? Pay attention to the types of products the store keeps in stock. How does the labeling of something like organic macaroni and cheese differ from a brand like Kraft's? How do the nutritional facts about each compare? What about their prices? If you are unable to visit a store in person, you can find information about Whole Foods products on its website (www.wholefoodsmarket.com). After you have collected your observations, write a one-page summary describing your trip.

MAKE YOUR OWN RULES: Proponents of organic farming and markets list many reasons for favoring these methods, including better nutrition, more responsible use of land, and reduced pollution from trucks that bring conventional products a long way to market. According to Michael Pollan, however, large organic grocery chains sometimes, to continue operating, resort to practices that are against their founding ideals. Write a one-page essay in which you propose a happy medium — that is, the type of shopping scenario that would preserve the organic ideals while allowing consumers to buy everything they needed. What complications might arise from the scenario you've proposed?

MICHAEL POLLAN
Big Organic

When you hear the word *natural*, what do you think of? How has this term come to carry such powerful and positive associations in our modern food culture? Are these associations always valid? Using the growth of the organic food industry as his case study, Michael Pollan asks some pointed questions about where our enthusiasm for natural foods comes from and whether this ideal always lives up to its billing. Pollan is a contributing writer for the *New York Times Magazine.* His most recent book, *The Omnivore's Dilemma* (2006), follows four different meals on their journey from the farm to the table. He has published three other nonfiction books, *Second Nature* (1991), *A Place of My Own* (1997), and *The Botany of Desire* (2001). He is the Knight Professor of Journalism at the University of California, Berkeley. The following selection is from *The Omnivore's Dilemma.*

SUPERMARKET PASTORAL

I ENJOY SHOPPING AT WHOLE FOODS NEARLY AS MUCH AS I ENJOY browsing a good bookstore, which, come to think of it, is probably no accident: Shopping at Whole Foods is a literary experience, too. That's not to take anything away from the food, which is generally of high quality, much of it "certified organic" or "humanely raised" or "free range." But right there, that's the point: It's the evocative prose as much as anything else that makes this food really special, elevating an egg or chicken breast or bag of arugula from the realm of ordinary protein and carbohydrates into a much headier experience, one with complex aesthetic, emotional, and even political dimensions. Take the "range-fed" sirloin steak I recently eyed in the meat case. According to the brochure on the counter, it was formerly part of a steer that spent its days "living in beautiful places" ranging from "plant-diverse, high-mountain meadows to thick aspen groves and miles of sagebrush-filled flats." Now a steak like that has got to taste better than one from Safeway, where the only accompanying information comes in the form of a number: the price, I mean, which you can bet will be considerably less. But I'm evidently not the only shopper willing to pay more for a good story.

With the growth of organics and mounting concerns about the wholesomeness of industrial food, storied food is showing up in supermarkets everywhere these days, but it is Whole Foods that consistently offers the most cutting-edge grocery lit. On a recent visit I filled my shopping cart with eggs "from cage-free vegetarian hens," milk from cows that live "free from unnecessary fear and distress," wild salmon caught by Native Americans in Yakutat, Alaska (population 833), and heirloom tomatoes from Capay Farm ($4.99 a pound), "one of the early pioneers of the organic movement." The organic broiler I picked up even had a name: Rosie, who turned out to be a "sustainably farmed" "free-range chicken" from Petaluma Poultry, a company whose "farming methods strive to create harmonious relationships in nature, sustaining the health of all creatures and the natural world." Okay, not the most mellifluous or even meaningful sentence, but at least their heart's in the right place.

In several corners of the store I was actually forced to choose between subtly competing stories. For example, some of the organic milk in the milk case was "ultrapasteurized," an extra processing step that was presented as a boon to the consumer, since it extends shelf life. But then another, more local dairy boasted about the fact they had said no to ultra-pasteurization, implying that their product was fresher, less processed, and therefore *more* organic. This was the dairy that talked about cows living free from distress, something I was beginning to feel a bit of myself by this point.

This particular dairy's label had a lot to say about the bovine lifestyle: Its Holsteins are provided with "an appropriate environment, including shelter and a comfortable resting area, . . . sufficient space, proper facilities and the company of their own kind." All this sounded pretty great, until I read the story of another dairy selling raw milk — *completely unprocessed* — whose "cows graze green pastures all year long" which made me wonder whether the first dairy's idea of an appropriate environment for a cow included, as I had simply presumed, a pasture. All of a sudden the absence from their story of that word seemed weirdly conspicuous. As the literary critics would say, the writer seemed to be eliding the whole notion of cows and grass. Indeed, the longer I shopped in Whole Foods, the more I thought that this is a place where the skills of a literary critic might come in handy — those, and perhaps also a journalist's.

Wordy labels, point-of-purchase brochures, and certification schemes are supposed to make an obscure and complicated food chain more legible to the consumer. In the industrial food economy, virtually the only information that travels along the food chain linking producer and consumer is price. Just look at the typical newspaper ad for a supermarket. The sole quality on display here is actually a quantity: tomatoes $0.69 a pound; ground chuck $1.09 a pound; eggs $0.99 a dozen — special this week. Is there any other category of product sold on such a reductive basis? The barebones information travels in both directions, of course, and farmers who get the message that consumers care only about price will themselves care only about yield. This is how a cheap food economy reinforces itself.

One of the key innovations of organic food was to allow some more information to pass along the food chain between the producer and the consumer — an implicit snatch of narrative along with the number. A certified organic label tells a little story about how a particular food was produced, giving the consumer a way to send a message back to the farmer that she values tomatoes produced without harmful pesticides, or prefers to feed her children milk from cows that haven't been injected with growth hormones. The word *organic* has proved to be one of the most powerful words in the supermarket: Without any help from government, farmers and consumers working together in this way have built an $11 billion industry that is now the fastest growing sector of the food economy.

> **A certified organic label tells a little story about how a particular food was produced.**

Yet the organic label itself — like every other such label in the supermarket — is really just an imperfect substitute for direct observation of how a food is produced, a concession to the reality that most people in an industrial society haven't the time or the inclination to follow their food back to the farm, a farm which today is apt to be, on average, fifteen hundred miles away. So to bridge that space we rely on certifiers and label writers and, to a considerable extent, our imagination of what the farms that are producing our food really look like. The organic label may conjure an image of a simpler agriculture, but its very existence is an industrial artifact. The question is, what about the farms themselves? How well do they match the stories told about them?

Taken as a whole, the story on offer in Whole Foods is a pastoral narrative in which farm animals live much as they did in the books we read as children, and our fruits and vegetables grow in well-composted soils on small farms much like Joel Salatin's. "Organic" on the label conjures up a rich narrative, even if it is the consumer who fills in most of the details, supplying the hero (American Family Farmer), the villain (Agribusinessman), and the literary genre, which I've come to think of as Supermarket Pastoral. By now we may know better than to believe this too simple story, but not *much* better, and the grocery store poets do everything they can to encourage us in our willing suspension of disbelief.

Supermarket Pastoral is a most seductive literary form, beguiling enough to survive in the face of a great many discomfiting facts. I suspect that's because it gratifies some of our deepest, oldest longings, not merely for safe food, but for a connection to the earth and to the handful of domesticated creatures we've long depended on. Whole Foods understands all this better than we do. One of the company's marketing consultants explained to me that the Whole Foods shopper feels that by buying organic he is "engaging in authentic experiences" and imaginatively enacting a "return to a utopian past with the positive aspects of modernity intact." This sounds a lot like Virgilian pastoral, which also tried to have it both ways. In *The Machine in the Garden* Leo Marx writes that Virgil's shepherd Tityrus, no primitive, "Enjoys the best of both worlds — the sophisticated order of art and the simple spontaneity of nature." In keeping with the pastoral tradition, Whole Foods offers what Marx terms "a landscape of reconciliation" between the realms of nature and culture, a place where, as the marketing consultant put it, "people will come together through organic foods to get back to the origin of things" — perhaps by sitting down to enjoy one of the microwaveable organic TV dinners (four words I never expected to see conjoined) stacked in the frozen food case. How's that for having it both ways?

Of course the trickiest contradiction Whole Foods attempts to reconcile is the one between the industrialization of the organic food industry of which it is a part and the pastoral ideals on which that industry has been built. The organic movement, as it was once called, has come a remarkably long way in the last thirty years, to the point where it now looks considerably less like a movement than a big business. Lining the walls above the sumptuously stocked produce section in my Whole Foods are full-color photographs of local organic farmers accompanied by text blocks setting forth their farming philosophies. A handful of these farms — Capay is one example — still sell their produce to Whole Foods, but most are long gone from the produce bins, if not yet the walls. That's because Whole Foods in recent years has adopted the grocery industry's standard regional distribution system, which makes supporting small farms impractical. Tremendous warehouses buy produce for dozens of stores at a time, which forces them to deal exclusively with tremendous farms. So while the posters still depict family farmers and their philosophies, the produce on sale below them comes primarily from the two big corporate organic growers in California, Earthbound Farm and Grimmway Farms,[1] which together dominate the market for organic fresh produce in America. (Earthbound alone grows 80 percent of the organic lettuce sold in America.)

As I tossed a plastic box of Earthbound prewashed spring mix salad into my Whole Foods cart, I realized that I was venturing deep into the belly of the industrial beast Joel Salatin had called "the organic empire." (Speaking of my salad mix, another small beyond organic farmer, a friend of Joel's, had told me he "wouldn't use that stuff to make compost" — the organic purist's stock insult.) But I'm not prepared to accept the premise that industrial organic is necessarily a bad thing, not if the goal is to reform a half-trillion-dollar food system based on chain supermarkets and the consumer's expectations that food be convenient and cheap.

And yet to the extent that the organic movement was conceived as a critique of industrial values, surely there comes a point when the process of industrialization will cost organic its soul (to use a word still uttered by organic types without irony), when Supermarket Pastoral becomes more fiction than fact: another lie told by marketers.

The question is, has that point been reached, as Joel Salatin suggests? Just how well does Supermarket Pastoral hold up under close reading and journalistic scrutiny?

About as well as you would expect anything genuinely pastoral to hold up in the belly of an $11 billion industry, which is to say not very well at all. At least that's what I discovered when I traced a few of the items in my Whole Foods cart back to the farms where they were grown. I learned, for example, that some (certainly not all) organic milk comes from factory farms, where thousands of Holsteins that never encounter a blade of grass spend their days confined to a fenced "dry lot," eating (certified organic) grain and tethered to milking machines three times a day. The reason much of this milk is ultrapasteurized (a high-heat process that damages its nutritional quality) is so that big companies like Horizon and Aurora can sell it over long distances. I discovered organic beef being raised in "organic feedlots" and organic high-fructose corn syrup — more words I never expected to see combined. And I learned about the making of the aforementioned organic TV dinner, a microwaveable bowl of "rice, vegetables, and grilled chicken breast with a savory herb sauce." Country Herb, as the entrée is called, turns out to be a highly industrialized organic product, involving a choreography of thirty-one ingredients assembled from far-flung farms, laboratories, and processing plants scattered over a half-dozen states and two countries, and containing such mysteries of modern food technology as high-oleic safflower oil, guar and xanthan gum, soy lecithin, carrageenan, and "natural grill flavor." Several of these ingredients are synthetic additives permitted under federal organic rules. So much for "whole" foods. The manufacturer of Country Herb is Cascadian Farm, a pioneering organic farm turned processor in Washington State that is now a wholly owned subsidiary of General Mills. (The Country Herb chicken entrée has since been discontinued.)

I also visited Rosie the organic chicken at her farm in Petaluma, which turns out to be more animal factory than farm. She lives in a shed with twenty thousand other Rosies, who, aside from their certified organic feed, live lives little different from that of any other industrial chicken. Ah, but what about the "free-range" lifestyle promised on the label? True, there's a little door in the shed leading out to a narrow grassy yard. But the free-range story seems a bit of a stretch when you discover that the door remains firmly shut until the birds are at least five or six weeks old — for fear they'll catch something outside — and the chickens are slaughtered only two weeks later.

FROM PEOPLE'S PARK TO PETALUMA POULTRY

If you walk five blocks north from the Whole Foods in Berkeley along Telegraph Avenue and then turn right at Dwight Street, you'll soon come to a trash-strewn patch of grass and trees dotted with the tattered camps of a few dozen homeless people. Mostly in their fifties and sixties, some still affecting hippie styles of hair and dress, these men and women pass much of their days sleeping and drinking, like so many of the destitute everywhere. Here, though, they also spend time tending scruffy little patches of flowers and vegetables — a few stalks of corn, some broccoli plants gone to seed. People's Park today is the saddest of places, a blasted monument to sixties' hopes that curdled a long time ago. And yet, while the economic and social distances separating the well-heeled shoppers cruising the aisles at Whole Poods from the unheeled homeless in People's Park could not be much greater, the two neighborhood institutions are branches of the same unlikely tree.

Indeed, were there any poetic justice in the world, the executives at Whole Foods would have long ago erected a commemorative plaque at People's Park and a booth to give away organic fruits and vegetables. The organic movement, much like environmentalism and feminism, has deep roots in the sixties' radicalism that briefly flourished on this site; organic is one of several tributaries of the counterculture that ended up disappearing into the American mainstream, but not before significantly altering its course. And if you trace that particular tributary all the way back to its spring, your journey will eventually pass through this park.

People's Park was born on April 20, 1969, when a group calling itself the Robin Hood Commission seized a vacant lot owned by the University of California and set to work rolling out sod, planting trees, and, perhaps most auspiciously, putting in a vegetable garden. Calling themselves "agrarian reformers," the radicals announced that they wanted to establish on the site the model of a new cooperative society built from the ground up; that included growing their own "uncontaminated" food. One of the inspirations for the commission's act of civil disobedience was the example of the Diggers in seventeenth-century England, who had also seized public land with the aim of growing food to give away to the poor. In People's Park that food would be organic, a word that at the time brimmed with meanings that went far beyond any particular agricultural method.

In *Appetite for Change*, his definitive account of how the sixties' counterculture changed the way we eat, historian Warren J. Belasco writes that the events in People's Park marked the "greening" of the counterculture, the pastoral turn that would lead to the commune movement in the countryside, to food co-ops and "guerilla capitalism," and, eventually, to the rise of organic agriculture and businesses like Whole Foods. The moment for such a turn to nature was ripe in 1969: DDT was in the news, an oil spill off Santa Barbara had blackened California's coastline, and Cleveland's Cuyahoga River had caught fire. Overnight, it seemed, "ecology" was on everybody's lips, and "organic" close behind.

As Belasco points out, the word *organic* had enjoyed a currency among nineteenth-century English social critics, who contrasted the social fragmentation and atomism wrought by the Industrial Revolution with the ideal of a lost organic society, one where the bonds of affection and cooperation still held. *Organic* stood for everything industrial was not. But applying the word *organic* to food and farming occurred much more recently: in the 1940s in the pages of *Organic Gardening and Farming*. Founded in 1940 by J. I. Rodale, a health-food fanatic from New York City's Lower East Side, the magazine devoted its pages to the agricultural methods and health benefits of growing food without synthetic chemicals — "organically." Joel Salatin's grandfather was a charter subscriber.

> **Organic stood for everything industrial was not.**

Organic Gardening and Farming struggled along in obscurity until 1969, when an ecstatic review in the *Whole Earth Catalog* brought it to the attention of hippies trying to figure out how to grow vegetables without patronizing the military-industrial complex. "If I were a dictator determined to control the national press," the *Whole Earth* correspondent wrote,

> *Organic Gardening* would be the first publication I'd squash, because it's the most subversive. I believe that organic gardeners are in the forefront of a serious effort to save the world by changing man's orientation to it, to move away from the collective, centrist, superindustrial state, toward a simpler, realer one-to-one relationship with the earth itself.

Within two years *Organic Gardening and Farming*'s circulation climbed from 400,000 to 700,000.

As the *Whole Earth* encomium suggests, the counterculture had married the broader and narrower definitions of the word *organic*. The organic garden planted in People's Park (soon imitated in urban lots across the country) was itself conceived of as a kind of scale model of a more cooperative society, a landscape of reconciliation that proposed to replace industrialism's attitude of conquest toward nature with a softer, more harmonious approach. A pastoral utopia in miniature, such a garden embraced not only the humans who tended and ate from it but "as many life kingdoms as possible," in the words of an early account of Berkeley's People's Gardens in an underground paper called *Good Times*. The vegetables harvested from these plots, which were sometimes called "conspiracies of soil," would supply, in addition to wholesome calories, an "edible dynamic" — a "new medium through which people can relate to one another and their nourishment." For example, organic's rejection of agricultural chemicals was also a rejection of the war machine, since the same corporations — Dow, Monsanto — that manufactured pesticides also made napalm and Agent Orange, the herbicide with which the U.S. military was waging war against nature in Southeast Asia. Eating organic thus married the personal to the political.

Which was why much more was at stake than a method of farming. Acting on the ecological premise that everything's connected to everything else, the early organic movement sought to establish not just an alternative mode of production (the chemical-free farms), but an alternative system of distribution (the anticapitalist food co-ops), and even an alternative mode of consumption (the "countercuisine").These were the three struts on which organic's revolutionary program stood; since ecology taught "you can never do only one thing," what you ate was inseparable from how it was grown and how it reached your table.

A countercuisine based on whole grains and unprocessed organic ingredients rose up to challenge conventional industrial "white bread food." ("Plastic food" was an epithet thrown around a lot.) For a host of reasons that seem ridiculous in retrospect, brown foods of all kinds — rice, bread, wheat, eggs, sugar, soy sauce, tamari — were deemed morally superior to white foods. Brown foods were less adulterated by industry, of course, but just as important, eating them allowed you to express your solidarity with the world's brown peoples. (Only later would the health benefits of these whole foods be recognized, not the first or last time an organic conceit would find scientific backing.) But perhaps best of all, brown foods was also precisely what your parents *didn't* eat.

How to grow this stuff without chemicals was a challenge, especially to city kids coming to the farm or garden with a head full of pastoral ideals and precisely no horticultural experience. The rural communes served as organic agriculture's ramshackle research stations, places where neophyte farmers could experiment with making compost and devising alternative methods of pest control. The steepness of their learning curve was on display in the food co-ops, where sorry-looking organic produce was the rule for many years. But the freak farmers stuck with it, following Rodale's step-by-step advice, and some of them went on to become excellent farmers.

One such notable success was Gene Kahn, the founder of Cascadian Farm, the company responsible for the organic TV dinner in my Whole Foods cart. Today Cascadian Farm is foremost a General Mills brand, but it began as a quasi-communal hippie farm, located on a narrow, gorgeous shelf of land wedged between the Skagit River and the North Cascades about seventy-five miles northeast of Seattle. (The idyllic little farmstead depicted on the package turns out to be a real place.) Originally called the New Cascadian Survival and Reclamation Project, the farm was started in 1971 by Gene Kahn with the idea of growing food for the collective of environmentally minded hippies he had hooked up with in nearby Bellingham. At the time Kahn was a twenty-four-year-old grad school dropout from the South Side of Chicago, who had been inspired by *Silent Spring* and *Diet for a Small Planet* to go back to the land — and from there to change the American food system. This particular dream was not so outrageous in 1971, but Kahn's success in actually realizing it surely is: He went on to become a pioneer of the organic movement and probably has done as much as anyone to move organic food into the mainstream, getting it out of the food co-op and into the supermarket. Today, the eponymous Cascadian Farm is a General Mills showcase — "a PR farm," as its founder freely acknowledges — and Kahn, erstwhile hippie farmer, is a General Mills vice president. Cascadian Farm is precisely what Joel Salatin has in mind when he talks about an organic empire.

Like most of the early organic farmers, Kahn had no idea what he was doing at first, and he suffered his share of crop failures. In 1971 organic agriculture was in its infancy — a few hundred scattered amateurs learning by trial and error how to grow food without chemicals, an ad hoc grassroots R & D effort for which there was no institutional support. (In fact, the USDA was actively hostile to organic agriculture until recently, viewing it — quite rightly — as a critique of the industrialized agriculture the USDA was promoting.) What the pioneer organic farmers had instead of the USDA's agricultural extension service was *Organic Gardening and Farming* (to which Kahn subscribed) and the model of various premodern agricultural systems, as described in books like *Farmers of Forty Centuries* by F. H. King and Sir Albert Howard's *The Soil and Health* and *An Agricultural Testament*. This last book may fairly be called the movement's bible.

Perhaps more than any other single writer, Sir Albert Howard (1873–1947), an English agronomist knighted after his thirty years of research in India, provided the philosophical foundations for organic agriculture. Even those who never read his 1940 *Testament* nevertheless absorbed his thinking through the pages of Rodale's *Organic Gardening and Farming*, where he was lionized, and in the essays of Wendell Berry, who wrote an influential piece about Howard in the *The Last Whole Earth Catalog* in 1971. Berry seized particularly on Howard's arresting — and prescient — idea that we needed to treat "the whole problem of health in soil, plant, animal, and man as one great subject."

For a book that devotes so many of its pages to the proper making of compost, *An Agricultural Testament* turns out to be an important work of philosophy as well as of agricultural science. Indeed, Howard's drawing of lines of connection between so many seemingly discrete realms — from soil fertility to "the national health"; from the supreme importance of animal urine to the limitations of the scientific method — is his signal contribution, his method as well as his message. Even though Howard never uses the term *organic*, it is possible to tease out all the many meanings of the word — as a program for not just agricultural but social renovation — from his writings. To measure the current definition of organic against his genuinely holistic conception is to appreciate just how much it has shrunk.

Like many works of social and environmental criticism, *An Agricultural Testament* is in broad outline the story of a Fall. In Howard's case, the serpent in question is a nineteenth-century German chemist by the name of Baron Justus von Liebig, his tempting fruit a set of initials: NPK. It was Liebig, in his 1840 monograph *Chemistry in its Application to Agriculture*, who set agriculture on its industrial path when he broke down the quasi-mystical concept of fertility in soil into a straightforward inventory of the chemical elements plants require for growth. At a stroke, soil biology gave way to soil chemistry, and specifically, to the three chemical nutrients Liebig highlighted as crucial to plant growth: nitrogen, phosphorus, and potassium, or to use these elements' initials from the periodic table, N-P-K. (The three letters correspond to the three-digit designation printed on every bag of fertilizer.) Much of Howard's work is an attempt to demolish what he called the "NPK mentality."

The NPK mentality embraces a good deal more than fertilizer, however. Indeed, to read Howard is to begin to wonder if it might not be one of the keys to everything wrong with modern civilization. In Howard's thinking, the NPK mentality serves as a shorthand for both the powers and limitations of reductionist science. For as followers of Liebig discovered, NPK "works": If you give plants these three elements, they will grow. From this success it was a short step to drawing the conclusion that the entire mystery of soil fertility had been solved. It fostered the wholesale reimagining of soil (and with it agriculture) from a living system to a kind of machine: Apply inputs of NPK at this end and you will get yields of wheat or corn on the other end. Since treating the soil as a machine seemed to work well enough, at least in the short term, there no longer seemed any need to worry about such quaint things as earthworms and humus.

Humus is the stuff in a handful of soil that gives it its blackish cast and characteristic smell. It's hard to say exactly what humus is because it is so many things. Humus is what's left of organic matter after it has been broken down by the billions of big and small organisms that inhabit a spoonful of earth — the bacteria, phages, fungi, and earthworms responsible for decomposition. (The psalmist who described life as a transit from "dust to dust" would have been more accurate to say "humus to humus.") But humus is not a final product of decomposition so much as a stage, since a whole other group of organisms slowly breaks humus down into the chemical elements plants need to grow, elements including, but not limited to, nitrogen, phosphorus, and potassium. This process is as much biological as chemical, involving the symbiosis of plants and the mycorrhizal fungi that live in and among their roots; the fungi offer soluble nutrients to the roots, receiving a drop of sucrose in return. Another critical symbiotic relationship links plants to the bacteria in a humus-rich soil that fix atmospheric nitrogen, putting it into a form the plants can use. But providing a buffet of nutrients to plants is not the only thing humus does: It also serves as the glue that binds the minute mineral particles in soil together into airy crumbs and holds water in suspension so that rainfall remains available to plant roots instead of instantly seeping away.

To reduce such a vast biological complexity to NPK represented the scientific method at its reductionist worst. Complex qualities are reduced to simple quantities; biology gives way to chemistry. As Howard was not the first to point out, that method can only deal with one or two variables at a time. The problem is that once science has reduced a complex phenomenon to a couple of variables, however important they may be, the natural tendency is to overlook everything else, to assume that what you can measure is all there is, or at least all that really matters. When we mistake what we can know for all there is to know, a healthy appreciation of one's ignorance in the face of a mystery like soil fertility gives way to the hubris that we can treat nature as a machine. Once that leap has been made, one input follows another, so that when the synthetic nitrogen fed to plants makes them more attractive to insects and vulnerable to disease, as we have discovered, the farmer turns to chemical pesticides to fix his broken machine.

In the case of artificial manures — the original term for synthetic fertilizers — Howard contended that our hubris threatened to damage the health not only of the soil (since the harsh chemicals kill off biological activity in humus) but of "the national health" as well. He linked the health of the soil to the health of all the creatures that depended on it, an idea that, once upon a time before the advent of industrial agriculture, was in fact commonplace, discussed by Plato and Thomas Jefferson, among many others. Howard put it this way: "Artificial manures lead inevitably to artificial nutrition, artificial food, artificial animals, and finally to artificial men and women."

Howard's flight of rhetoric might strike our ears as a bit over the top (we are talking about fertilizer, after all), but it was written in the heat of the pitched battle that accompanied the introduction of chemical agriculture to England in the 1930s and 1940s. "The great humus controversy," as it was called, actually reached the floor of the House of Lords in 1943, a year when one might have thought there were more pressing matters on the agenda. But England's agriculture ministry was promoting the new fertilizers, and many farmers complained their pastures and animals had become less robust as a result. Howard and his allies were convinced that "history will condemn [chemical fertilizer] as one of the greatest misfortunes to have befallen agriculture and mankind." He claimed that the wholesale adoption of artificial manures would destroy the fertility of the soil, leave plants vulnerable to pests and disease, and damage the health of the animals and peoples eating those plants, for how could such plants be any more nutritious than the soil in which they grew? Moreover, the short-term boosts in yield that fertilizers delivered could not be sustained; since the chemicals would eventually destroy the soil's fertility, today's high yields were robbing the future.

Needless to say, the great humus controversy of the 1940s was settled in favor of the NPK mentality.

Howard pointed down another path. "We now have to retrace our steps," he wrote, which meant jettisoning the legacy of Liebig and industrial agriculture. "We have to go back to nature and to copy the methods to be seen in the forest and prairie." Howard's call to redesign the farm as an imitation of nature wasn't merely rhetorical; he had specific practices and processes in mind, which he outlined in a paragraph at the beginning of *An Agricultural Testament* that stands as a fair summary of the whole organic ideal:

> Mother earth never attempts to farm without live stock; she always raises mixed crops; great pains are taken to preserve the soil and to prevent erosion; the mixed vegetable and animal wastes are converted into humus; there is no waste; the processes of growth and the processes of decay balance one another; the greatest care is taken to store the rainfall; both plants and animals are left to protect themselves against disease.

Each of the biological processes at work in a forest or prairie could have its analog on a farm: Animals could feed on plant wastes as they do in the wild; in turn their wastes could feed the soil; mulches could protect bare soil in the same way leaf litter in a forest does; the compost pile, acting like the lively layer of decomposition beneath the leaf litter, could create humus. Even the diseases and insects would perform the salutary function they do in nature: to eliminate the weakest plants and animals, which he predicted would be far fewer in number once the system was operating properly. For Howard, insects and diseases — the bane of industrial agriculture — are simply "nature's censors," useful to the farmer for "pointing out unsuitable varieties and methods of farming inappropriate to the locality." On a healthy farm pests would be no more prevalent than in a healthy wood or pasture, which should be agriculture's standard. Howard was thus bidding farmers to regard their farms less like machines than living organisms.

The notion of imitating whole natural systems stands in stark opposition to reductionist science, which works by breaking such systems down into their component parts in order to understand how they work and then manipulating them — one variable at a time. In this sense, Howard's concept of organic agriculture is premodern, arguably even antiscientific: He's telling us we don't need to understand how humus works or what compost does in order to make good use of it. Our ignorance of the teeming wilderness that is the soil (even the act of regarding it as a wilderness) is no impediment to nurturing it. To the contrary, a healthy sense of all we don't know — even a sense of mystery — keeps us from reaching for oversimplifications and technological silver bullets.

A charge often leveled against organic agriculture is that it is more philosophy than science. There's some truth to this indictment, if that is what it is, though why organic farmers should feel defensive about it is itself a mystery, a relic, perhaps, of our fetishism of science as the only credible tool with which to approach nature. In Howard's conception, the philosophy of mimicking natural processes precedes the science of understanding them. The peasant rice farmer who introduces ducks and fish to his paddy may not understand all the symbiotic relationships he's put in play — that the ducks and fishes are feeding nitrogen to the rice and at the same time eating the pests. But the high yields of food from this ingenious polyculture are his to harvest even so.

> **A charge often leveled against organic agriculture is that it is more philosophy than science.**

The philosophy underlying Howard's conception of organic agriculture is a variety of pragmatism, of course, the school of thought that is willing to call "true" whatever works. Charles Darwin taught us that a kind of pragmatism — he called it natural selection — is at the very heart of nature, guiding evolution: What works is what survives. This is why Howard spent so much time studying peasant agricultural systems in India and elsewhere: The best ones survived as long as they did because they brought food forth from the same ground year after year without depleting the soil.

In Howard's agronomy, science is mostly a tool for describing what works and explaining why it does. As it happens, in the years since Howard wrote, science has provided support for a great many of his unscientific claims: Plants grown in synthetically fertilized soils *are* less nourishing than ones grown in composted soils;[2] such plants *are* more vulnerable to diseases and insect pests;[3] polycultures *are* more productive and less prone to disease than monocultures;[4] and that in fact the health of the soil, plant, animal, human, and even nation are, as Howard claimed, connected along lines we can now begin to draw with empirical confidence. We may not be prepared to act on this knowldge, but we know that civilizations that abuse their soil eventually collapse.[5]

If farms modeled on natural systems work as well as Howard suggests, then why don't we see more of them? The sad fact is that the organic ideal as set forth by Howard and others has been honored mainly in the breach. Especially as organic agriculture has grown more sucessful, finding its way into the supermarket and the embrace of agribusiness, organic farming has increasingly come to resemble the industrial system it originally set out to replace. The logic of that system has so far proven more ineluctable than the logic of natural systems.

The journey of Cascadian Farm from the New Cascadian Survival and Reclamation Project to General Mills subsidiary stands as a parable of this process. On an overcast morning a few winters ago, Kahn drove me out to see the original farm, following the twists of the Skagit River east in a new forest-green Lexus with vanity plates that say ORGANIC. Kahn is a strikingly boyish-looking man in his midfifties, and after you factor in a shave and twenty pounds, it's not hard to pick his face out from the beards-beads-and-tractors photos on display in his office. Walking me through the history of his company as we drove out to the farm, Gene Kahn spoke candidly and without defensiveness about the compromises made along his path from organic farmer to agribusinessman, and about "how everything eventually morphs into the way the world is."

By the late seventies, Kahn had become a pretty good organic farmer and an even better businessman. He had discovered the economic virtues of adding value to his produce by processing it (freezing blueberries and strawberries, making jam), and once Cascadian Farm started processing food, Kahn discovered he could make more money buying produce from other farmers than by growing it himself — the same discovery conventional agribusiness companies had made a long time before.

"The whole notion of a 'cooperative community' we started with gradually began to mimic the system," Kahn told me. "We were shipping food around the country, using diesel fuel — we were industrial organic farmers. I was bit by bit becoming more of this world, and there was a lot of pressure on the business to become more privatized."

> **"The whole notion of a 'cooperative community' we started with gradually began to mimic the system."**

That pressure became irresistible in 1990, when in the aftermath of the "Alar scare" Kahn nearly lost everything — and control of Cascadian Farm wound up in corporate hands. In the history of the organic movement the Alar episode is a watershed, marking the birth pangs of the modern organic industry. Throughout its history, the sharpest growth of organic has closely followed spikes in public concern over the industrial food supply. Some critics condemn organic for profiting time and again from "food scares," and while there is certainly some truth to this charge, whether it represents a more serious indictment of organic or industrial food is open to question. Organic farmers reply that episodes focusing public attention on pesticides, food poisoning, genetically modified crops, and mad cow disease serve as "teachable moments" about the industrial food system and its alternatives. Alar was one of the first.

After a somewhat overheated *60 Minutes* exposé on apple growers' use of Alar, a growth-regulating chemical widely used in conventional orchards that the Environmental Protection Agency had declared a carcinogen, Middle America suddenly discovered organic. "Panic for Organic" was the cover line on one newsweekly, and overnight, demand from the supermarket chains soared. The ragtag industry was not quite ready for prime time, however. Like a lot of organic producers, Gene Kahn borrowed heavily to finance an ambitious expansion, contracted with farmers to grow an awful lot of organic produce — and then watched in horror as the bubble of demand subsided along with the headlines about Alar. Badly overextended, Kahn was forced to sell a majority stake in his company — to Welch's — and the onetime hippie farmer set out on what he calls his "corporate adventure."

"We were part of the food industry now," he told me. "But I wanted to leverage that position to redefine the way we grow food — not what people want to eat or how we distribute it. That sure as hell isn't going to change." Becoming part of the food industry meant jettisoning two of the three original legs on which the organic movement had stood: the countercuisine — what people want to eat — and the food co-ops and other alternative modes of distribution. Kahn's bet was that agribusiness could accommodate itself most easily to the first leg — the new way to grow food — by treating organic essentially as a niche product that could be distributed and marketed through the existing channels. The original organic ideal held that you could not divorce these three elements, since (as ecology taught) everything was connected. But Gene Kahn, for one (and he was by no means the only one), was a realist, a businessman with a payroll to meet. And he wasn't looking back.

"You have a choice of getting sad about all that or moving on. We tried hard to build a cooperative community and a local food system, but at the end of the day it wasn't successful. This is just lunch for most people. *Just lunch*. We can call it sacred, we can talk about communion, but it's just lunch." . . .

To serve such a scrupulously organic meal begs an unavoidable question: Is organic food better? Is it worth the extra cost? My Whole Foods dinner certainly wasn't cheap, considering I made it from scratch: Rosie cost $15 ($2.99 a pound), the vegetables another $12 (thanks to that six-buck bunch of asparagus), and the dessert $7 (including $3 for a six-ounce box of blackberries). Thirty-four dollars to feed a family of three at home. (Though we did make a second meal from the leftovers.) Whether organic is better and worth it are certainly fair, straightforward questions, but the answers, I've discovered, are anything but simple.

Better for what? is the all-important corollary to that question. If the answer is "taste," then the answer is, as I've suggested, very likely, at least in the case of produce — but not necessarily. Freshly picked conventional produce is bound to taste better than organic produce that's been riding the interstates in a truck for three days. Meat is a harder call. Rosie was a tasty bird, yet, truth be told, not quite as tasty as Rocky, her bigger non-organic brother. That's probably because Rocky is an older chicken, and older chickens generally have more flavor. The fact that the corn and soybeans in Rosie's diet were grown without chemicals probably doesn't change the taste of her meat. Though it should be said that Rocky and Rosie both taste more like chicken than mass-market birds fed on a diet of antibiotics and animal by-products; which makes for mushier and blander meat. What's in an animal's feed naturally affects how it will taste, though whether that feed is organic or not probably makes no difference.

Better for what? If the answer is "for my health" the answer, again, is probably — but not automatically. I happen to believe the organic dinner I served my family is healthier than a meal of the same foods conventionally produced, but I'd be hard-pressed to prove it scientifically. What I could prove, with the help of a mass spectrometer, is that it contained little or no pesticide residue — the traces of the carcinogens, neurotoxins, and endocrine disruptors now routinely found in conventional produce and meat. What I probably can't prove is that the low levels of these toxins present in these foods will make us sick — give us cancer, say, or interfere with my son's neurological or sexual development. But that does not mean those poisons are *not* making us sick: Remarkably little research has been done to assess the effects of regular exposure to the levels of organophosphate pesticide or growth hormone that the government deems "tolerable" in our foods. (One problem with these official tolerances is that they don't adequately account for children's exposure to pesticides, which, because of childrens' size and eating habits, is much greater than adults'.) Given what we do know about exposure to endocrine disruptors, the biological impact of which depends less on dose than timing, minimizing a child's exposure to these chemicals seems like a prudent idea. I very much like the fact that the milk in the ice cream I served came from cows that did not receive injections of growth hormone to boost their productivity, or that the corn those cows are fed, like the corn that feeds Rosie, contains no residues of atrazine, the herbicide commonly sprayed on American cornfields. Exposure to vanishingly small amounts (0.1 part per billion) of this herbicide has been shown to turn normal male frogs into hermaphrodites. Frogs are not boys, of course. So I can wait for that science to be done, or for our government to ban atrazine (as European governments have done), or I can act now on the presumption that food from which this chemical is absent is better for my son's health than food that contains it.

Of course, the healthfulness of a food is not simply a question of its toxicity; we have also to consider its nutritional quality. Is there any reason to think my Whole Foods meal is any more nutritious than the same meal prepared with conventionally grown ingredients?

Over the years there have been sporadic efforts to demonstrate the nutritional superiority of organic produce, but most have foundered on the difficulty of isolating the great many variables that can affect the nutritional quality of a carrot or a potato — climate, soils, geography, freshness, farming practices, genetics, and so on. Back in the fifties, when the USDA routinely compared the nutritional quality of produce from region to region, it found striking differences: Carrots grown in the deep soils of Michigan, for example, commonly had more vitamins than carrots grown in the thin, sandy soils of Florida. Naturally this information discomfited the carrot growers of Florida, which probably explains why the USDA no longer conducts this sort of research. Nowadays U.S. agricultural policy, like the Declaration of Independence, is founded on the principle that all carrots are created equal, even though there's good reason to believe this isn't really true. But in an agricultural system dedicated to quantity rather than quality, the fiction that all foods are created equal is essential. This is why, in inaugurating the federal organic program in 2000, the secretary of agriculture went out of his way to say that organic food is no better than conventional food. "The organic label is a marketing tool," Secretary Glickman said. "It is not a statement about food safety. Nor is 'organic' a value judgment about nutrition or quality."

Some intriguing recent research suggests otherwise. A study by University of California–Davis researchers published in the *Journal of Agriculture and Food Chemistry* in 2003 described an experiment in which identical varieties of corn, strawberries, and blackberries grown in neighboring plots using different methods (including organically and conventionally) were compared for levels of vitamins and polyphenols. Polyphenols are a group of secondary metabolites manufactured by plants that we've recently learned play an important role in human health and nutrition. Many are potent antioxidants; some play a role in preventing or fighting cancer; others exhibit antimicrobial properties. The Davis researchers found that organic and otherwise sustainably grown fruits and vegetables contained significantly higher levels of both ascorbic acid (vitamin C) and a wide range of polyphenols.

The recent discovery of these secondary metabolites in plants has brought our understanding of the biological and chemical complexity of foods to a deeper level of refinement; history suggests we haven't gotten anywhere near the bottom of this question, either. The first level was reached early in the nineteenth century with the identification of the macronutrients — protein, carbohydrate, and fat. Having isolated these compounds, chemists thought they'd unlocked the key to human nutrition. Yet some people (such as sailors) living on diets rich in macronutrients nevertheless got sick. The mystery was solved when scientists discovered the major vitamins — a second key to human nutrition. Now it's the polyphenols in plants that we're learning play a critical role in keeping us healthy. (And which might explain why diets heavy in processed food fortified with vitamins still aren't as nutritious as fresh foods.) You wonder what else is going on in these plants, what other undiscovered qualities in them we've evolved to depend on.

In many ways the mysteries of nutrition at the eating end of the food chain closely mirror the mysteries of fertility at the growing end: The two realms are like wildernesses that we keep convincing ourselves our chemistry has mapped, at least until the next level of complexity comes into view. Curiously, Justus von Liebig, the nineteenth-century German chemist with the spectacularly ironic surname, bears responsibility for science's overly reductive understanding of both ends of the food chain. It was Liebig, you'll recall, who thought he had found the chemical key to soil fertility with the discovery of NPK, and it was the same Liebig who thought he had found the key to human nutrition when he identified the macronutrients in food. Liebig wasn't wrong on either count, yet in both instances he made the fatal mistake of thinking that what we knew about nourishing plants and people was all we needed to know to keep them healthy. It's a mistake we'll probably keep repeating until we develop a deeper respect for the complexity of food and soil and, perhaps, the links between the two.

But back to the polyphenols, which may hint at the nature of that link. Why in the world should organically grown blackberries or corn contain significantly more of these compounds? The authors of the Davis study haven't settled the question, but they offer two suggestive theories. The reason plants produce these compounds in the first place is to defend themselves against pests and diseases; the more pressure from pathogens, the more polyphenols a plant will produce. These compounds, then, are the products of natural selection and, more specifically, the coevolutionary relationship between plants and the species that prey on them. Who would have guessed that humans evolved to profit from a diet of these plant pesticides? Or that we would invent an agriculture that then deprived us of them? The Davis authors hypothesize that plants being defended by man-made pesticides don't need to work as hard to make their own polyphenol pesticides. Coddled by us and our chemicals, the plants see no reason to invest their resources in mounting a strong defense. (Sort of like European nations during the Cold War.)

A second explanation (one that subsequent research seems to support) may be that the radically simplified soils in which chemically fertilized plants grow don't supply all the raw ingredients needed to synthesize these compounds, leaving the plants more vulnerable to attack, as we know conventionally grown plants tend to be. NPK might be sufficient for plant growth yet still might not give a plant everything it needs to manufacture ascorbic acid or lycopene or resveratrol in quantity. As it happens, many of the polyphenols (and especially a subset called the flavonols) contribute to the characteristic taste of a fruit or vegetable. Qualities we can't yet identify in soil may contribute qualities we've only just begun to identify in our foods and our bodies.

Reading the Davis study I couldn't help thinking about the early proponents of organic agriculture, people like Sir Albert Howard and J. I. Rodale, who would have been cheered, if unsurprised, by the findings. Both men were ridiculed for their unscientific conviction that a reductive approach to soil fertility — the NPK mentality — would diminish the nutritional quality of the food grown in it and, in turn, the health of the people who lived on that food. All carrots are *not* created equal, they believed; how we grow it, the soil we grow it in, what we feed that soil all contribute qualities to a carrot, qualities that may yet escape the explanatory net of our chemistry. Sooner or later the soil scientists and nutritionists will catch up to Sir Howard, heed his admonition that we begin "treating the whole problem of health in soil, plant, animal, and man as one great subject."

So it happens that these organic blackberries perched on this mound of vanilla ice cream, having been grown in a complexly fertile soil and forced to fight their own fights against pests and disease, are in some quantifiable way more nutritious than conventional blackberries. This would probably not come as earthshaking news to Albert Howard or J. I. Rodale or any number of organic farmers, but at least now it is a claim for which we can supply a scientific citation: *J. Agric. Food. Chem.* vol. 51, no. 5, 2003. . . .

Obviously there is much more to be learned about the relationship of soil to plant, animals, and health, and it would be a mistake to lean too heavily on any one study. It would also be a mistake to assume that the word *organic* on a label automatically signifies healthfulness, especially when that label appears on heavily processed and long-distance foods that have probably had much of their nutritional value, not to mention flavor, beaten out of them long before they arrive on our tables.

The better for what? question about my organic meal can of course be answered in a much less selfish way: Is it better for the evironment?

Better for the farmers who grew it? Better for the public health? For the taxpayer? The answer to all three questions is an (almost) unqualified yes. To grow the plants and animals that made up my meal, no pesticides found their way into any farmworker's bloodstream, no nitrogen runoff or growth hormones seeped into the watershed, no soils were poisoned, no antibiotics were squandered, no subsidy checks were written. If the high price of my all-organic meal is weighed against the comparatively low price it exacted from the larger world, as it should be, it begins to look, at least in karmic terms, like a real bargain.

And yet, and yet . . . an industrial organic meal such as mine does leave deep footprints on our world. The lot of the workers who harvested the vegetables and gathered up Rosie for slaughter is not appreciably different from that of those on nonorganic factory farms. The chickens lived only marginally better lives than their conventional counterparts; in the end a CAFO is a CAFO [Confined Animal Feeding Operation], whether the food served in it is organic or not. As for the cows that produced the milk in our ice cream, they may well have spent time outdoors in an actual pasture (Stonyfield Farm buys most — though not all — of its milk from small dairy farmers), but the organic label guarantees no such thing. And while the organic farms I visited don't receive direct government payments, they do receive other subsidies from taxpayers, notably subsidized water and electricity in California. The two-hundred-thousand-square-foot refrigerated processing plant where my salad was washed pays half as much for its electricity as it would were Earthbound not classified as a "farm enterprise."

> *An industrial organic meal such as mine does leave deep footprints on our world.*

But perhaps most discouraging of all, my industrial organic meal is nearly as drenched in fossil fuel as its conventional counterpart. Asparagus traveling in a 747 from Argentina; blackberries trucked up from Mexico; a salad chilled to thirty-six degrees from the moment it was picked in Arizona (where Earthbound moves its entire operation every winter) to the moment I walk it out the doors of my Whole Foods. The food industry burns nearly a fifth of all the petroleum consumed in the United States (about as much as automobiles do). Today it takes between seven and ten calories of fossil fuel energy to deliver one calorie of food energy to an American plate. And while it is true that organic farmers don't spread fertilizers made from natural gas or spray pesticides made from petroleum, industrial organic farmers often wind up burning more diesel fuel than their conventional counterparts: in trucking bulky loads of compost across the countryside and weeding their fields, a particularly energy-intensive process involving extra irrigation (to germinate the weeds before planting) and extra cultivation. All told, growing food organically uses about a third less fossil fuel than growing it conventionally, . . . though that savings disappears if the compost is not produced on site or nearby.

Yet growing the food is the least of it: only a fifth of the total energy used to feed us is consumed on the farm; the rest is spent processing the food and moving it around. At least in terms of the fuel burned to get it from the farm to my table, there's little reason to think my Cascadian Farm TV dinner or Earthbound Farm spring mix salad is any more sustainable than a conventional TV dinner or salad would have been.

Well, at least we didn't eat it in the car.

So is an industrial organic food chain finally a contradiction in terms? It's hard to escape the conclusion that it is. Of course it is possible to live with contradictions, at least for a time, and sometimes it is necessary or worthwhile. But we ought at least face up to the cost of our compromises. The inspiration for organic was to find a way to feed ourselves more in keeping with the logic of nature, to build a food system that looked more like an ecosystem that would draw its fertility and energy from the sun. To feed ourselves otherwise was "unsustainable," a word that's been so abused we're apt to forget what it very specifically means: *Sooner or later it must collapse.* To a remarkable extent, farmers succeeded in creating the new food chain on their farms; the trouble began when they encountered the expectations of the supermarket. As in so many other realms, nature's logic has proven no match for the logic of capitalism, one in which cheap energy has always been a given. And so, today, the organic food industry finds itself in a most unexpected, uncomfortable, and, yes, unsustainable position: floating on a sinking sea of petroleum.

NOTES

[1]Grimmway Farms owns Cal-Organic, one of the most ubiquitous organic brands in the supermarket.

[2]Asami, et al. (2003); Benbrook (2005); Carbonaro and Mattera (2001); Davis, et al. (2004).

[3]Altieri (1995); Tilman (1998).

[4]Altieri (1995, 1999); Tilman (1998); Wolfe (2000).

[5]Diamond (2005).

WORK CITED

Altieri, Miguel. *Agroecology: The Science of Sustainable Agriculture* (Boulder, CO: Westview Press, 1995).

———. "The Ecological Role of Biodiversity in Agroecosystems," *Agric. Ecosyst. and Env.* 74 (1999), 19–31.

Asami, Danny K., et al. "Comparison of the Total Phenolic and Ascorbic Acid Content of Free-Dried and Air-Dried Marionberry, Strawberry, and Corn Using

Conventional, Organic, and Sustainable Agricultural Practices," *Journal of Agricultural and Food Chemistry* 51 (2003), 1237–41. This is the study I discuss at some length.

Benbrook, Charles M. *Elevating Antioxidant Levels in Food Through Organic Farming and Food Processing: An Organic Center State of Science Review* (Foster, RI: Organic Center, 2005).

Carbonaro, Marina, and Maria Mattera. "Polyphenoloxidase Activity and Polyphenol Levels in Organically and Conventionally Grown Peaches," *Food Chemistry 72* (2001), 419–24.

Davis, Donald R., et al. "Changes in USDA Food Composition Data for 43 Garden Crops, 1950 to 1999," *Journal of the American College of Nutrition* 23, no. 6 (2004), 669–82.

Diamond, Jared. *Collapse: How Societies Choose to Fail or Succeed* (New York: Viking, 2005).

Tilman, David. "The Greening of the Green Revolution," *Nature,* 396 (November 19, 1998).

Wolfe, M. S. "Crop Strength Through Diversity," *Nature* 406, no. 17 (August 2000).

DISCUSSION

1. In Pollan's eyes, there is something odd, even abnormal, about thinking of the organic food movement as an industry. In your view, is there anything wrong or contradictory about putting these two terms together? What sorts of ideas or images does each of these words conjure in your mind?

2. Pollan spends a good deal of this essay dissecting the "pastoral narrative" that he claims is central to the ways Whole Foods markets its organic products. Where else in our popular or commercial culture do we see this kind of narrative perpetuated? What other product is this type of story used to sell? In what particular ways does it contribute to this product's appeal? In thinking about your example, do you find yourself agreeing with Pollan that the "pastoral narrative" is more myth than truth?

3. For Pollan, the experience of shopping at an organic grocery store is most akin to reading: "I enjoy shopping at Whole Foods nearly as much as I enjoy browsing a good bookstore." In your experience as a food shopper, how valid is this parallel? To what extent does your shopping require you to make your way through different stories about the foods displayed? How much influence do these sorts of images and texts have over what you buy?

WRITING

4. Choose a food that you think fits our culture's current definition of *natural.* Write an essay in which you analyze what attitudes about food this product promotes. In your opinion, how is such a product designed to appeal to consumers? That is, how does this food fit the script that Pollan analyzes about whom the organic movement is designed to appeal to?

5. "The word *organic,*" says Pollan, "has proved to be one of the most powerful words in the supermarket." Make a list of all the different words that come to mind when you hear the word *organic.* What do these words have in common? Write an essay in which you reflect on the ways these words seem to script a particular way to think about eating organic foods. On the basis of this list, who would you say is the ideal organic consumer? How does Pollan's essay support or contradict your argument?

6. Compare what Pollan has to say about the power of the term *natural* to the ways Taras Grescoe (p. 235) addresses this question in his discussion of contemporary drug use. Do you think Pollan's analysis would help or hinder Grescoe's effort to argue in favor of certain "natural" intoxicants and hallucinogens? In what ways do their understandings of this term seem to overlap?

FRANCINE PROSE
The Wages of Sin

When it comes to eating, how much is too much? And where do we learn to draw this line? Taking aim at our current fixation on food, dieting, and body image, Francine Prose contemplates whether ours has become a culture in which overeating now stands as the preeminent sign of our moral and physical failure. Prose graduated from Radcliffe College in 1968 and currently lives and writes in New York City. She is the author of nine novels, including *The Blue Angel* (2001), a finalist for the National Book Award, and *A Changed Man* (2005), which won the Dayton Literary Peace Prize. She has also published several nonfiction books, including *Gluttony* (2003), from which the following is excerpted, and *Reading Like a Writer* (2006).

MORE AND MORE OFTEN, WE READ ARTICLES AND HEAR TV COMMEN- tators advocating government intervention to protect us from the greed of a corporate culture that profits from our unhealthy attraction to sugary and fatty foods. Legal experts discuss the feasibility of mounting class action suits — on the model of the recent and ongoing litigation against so-called big tobacco companies — against fast-food restaurants, junk-food manufacturers, and advertisers who target children with ads for salty fried snacks and brightly colored candy masquerading as break-fast cereal.

What's slightly more disturbing is the notion that not only do fat people need to be monitored, controlled, and saved from their gluttonous impulses, but that we need to be saved from them — that certain forms of social control might be required to help the overweight resist temptation. Writing in the *San Francisco Chronicle,* essayist Ruth Rosen has suggested that such actions might be motivated by compassion for such innocent victims as the parents of a child whose overweight helped lead to dia-betes, or the child of a parent who died from weight-related causes. Of course the bottom line is concern for our pocketbooks, for the cost — shared by the wider population — of treating those who suffer from obesity-related ailments. As a partial remedy, Rosen proposes that schools and employers might forbid the sale of junk food on campus and in offices. Finally, she suggests that, in a more glorious future, the host who serves his guests greasy potato chips and doughnuts will incur the same horrified disapproval as the smoker who lights up — and blows smoke in our faces.

Rosen is not alone in her belief that legislation may be required to regulate the social costs of overeating. A recent item on CBS worriedly considered the alarming growth in the number of overweight and obese young people — a group that now comprises 14 percent of American children. According to the news clip, overweight was soon expected to surpass cigarette smoking as the major preventable cause of death: each year, 350,000 people die of obesity-related causes. Thirteen billion dollars is spent annually on food ads directed at children, and four out of five ads are for some excessively sugary or fatty product. The problem is undeniable, but once more the projected solution gives one pause; several interviewees raised the possibility of suing the purveyors of potato chips and candy bars. How far we have come from Saint Augustine and John Cassian and Chrysostom, taking it for granted that the struggle against temptation would be waged in the glutton's heart and mind — and not, presumably, in the law courts.

> You're so fat when they pierced your ears, they had to use a harpoon.
> You're so fat you've got to put on lipstick with a paint roller.

In studies that have examined the causes and motives behind the stigmatization of the overweight, such prejudice has been found to derive from the widely accepted notion that fat people are at fault, responsible for their weight and appearance, that they are self-indulgent, sloppy, lazy, morally lax, lacking in the qualities of self-denial and impulse control that our society (still so heavily influenced by the legacy of Puritanism) values and rewards. In a 1978 book, *The Seven Deadly Sins: Society and Evil,* sociologist Stanford M. Lyman takes a sociocultural approach to the reasons why we are so harsh in our condemnation of the so-called glutton.

> The apparently voluntary character of food gluttony serves to point up why it is more likely to seem "criminal" than sick, an act of moral defalcation rather than medical pathology. Although gluttony is not proscribed by the criminal law, it partakes of some of the social sanctions and moral understandings that govern orientations toward those who commit crimes. . . . Gluttony is an excessive *self*-indulgence. Even in its disrespect for the body it overvalues the ego that it slavishly satisfies.[1]

Most of us would no doubt claim that we are too sensible, compassionate, and enlightened to feel prejudice against the obese. We would never tell the sorts of cruel jokes scattered throughout this chapter. But let's consider how we feel when we've taken our already cramped seat in coach class on the airplane and suddenly our seatmate appears — a man or woman whose excessive weight promises to make our journey even more uncomfortable than we'd anticipated. Perhaps, contemplating a trip of this sort, we might find ourselves inclined to support Southwest

Airline's discriminatory two-seats-per-large-passenger rule. Meanwhile, as we try not to stare at our sizable traveling companion, we might as well be the medieval monks glaring at the friar who's helped himself to an extra portion. For what's involved in both cases is our notion of one's proper share, of surfeit and shortage — not enough food in one case, not enough space in the other.

"The glutton is also noticeable as a defiler of his own body space. His appetite threatens to engulf the spaces of others as he spreads out to take more than one person's ordinary allotment of territory. If he grows too large, he may no longer fit into ordinary chairs . . . and require special arrangements in advance of his coming."[2] The glutton's "crime" is crossing boundaries that we jealously guard and that are defined by our most primitive instincts: hunger, territoriality — that is to say, survival.

> *The glutton's "crime" is crossing boundaries that we jealously guard and that are defined by our most primitive instincts: hunger, territoriality — that is to say, survival.*

So we come full circle back to the language of crime and innocence, sin and penance, guilt and punishment — a view of overweight frequently adopted and internalized by the obese themselves. "Many groups of dieters whom I studied," writes Natalie Allon, "believed that fatness was the outcome of immoral self-indulgence. Group dieters used much religious language in considering themselves bad or good dieters — words such as sinner, saint, devil, angel, guilt, transgression, confession, absolution, diet Bible — as they partook of the rituals of group dieting."[3] Nor does the association between gluttony and the language of religion exist solely in the minds of dieters, the obese, and the food-obsessed. In fact it's extremely common to speak of having overeaten as having "been bad"; rich, fattening foods are advertised as being "sinfully delicious"; and probably most of us have thought or confessed the fact that we've felt "guilty" for having eaten more than we should have.

Like the members of other Twelve-Step programs, and not unlike the medieval gluttons who must have felt inspired to repent and pray for divine assistance in resisting temptation, the members of Overeaters Anonymous employ the terminology of religion. *Lifeline,* the magazine of Overeaters Anonymous, is filled with stories of healing and recovery, first-person accounts in which God was asked to intercede, to provide a spiritual awakening, and to remove the dangerous and destructive flaws from the recovering overeater's character.

Routinely, the capacity to achieve sobriety and abstinence — which for OA members means the ability to restrict one's self to three healthy and sensible meals a day — is credited to divine mercy and love, and to the good effects of an intimate and sustaining relationship with God. In one testimonial, a woman reports that coming to her first meeting and identifying herself as a recovering compulsive eater was more difficult for her than to say that she was a shoplifter, a serial killer, or a prostitute. Only after admitting that she was powerless over food and asking for the help of a higher power was she at last able to end her unhappy career as a "grazer and a binger."

For perhaps obvious reasons, the term "gluttony" is now rarely used as a synonym for compulsive eating. Yet Stanford Lyman conflates the two to make the point that our culture's attitude toward the obese is not unlike an older society's view of the gluttonous sinner:

> Societal opposition to gluttony manifests itself in a variety of social control devices and institutional arrangements. Although rarely organized as a group, very fat individuals at times seem to form a much beset minority, objects of calculating discrimination and bitter prejudice. Stigmatized because their addiction to food is so visible in its consequences, the obese find themselves ridiculed, rejected, and repulsed by many of those who do not overindulge. Children revile them on the streets, persons of average size refuse to date, dance, or dine with them, and many businesses, government, and professional associations refuse to employ them. So great is the pressure to conform to the dictates of the slimness culture in America that occasionally an overweight person speaks out, pointing to the similarities of his condition to that of racial and national minorities.[4]

Indeed, the overweight have found a forum in which to speak out, at the meetings, conventions, and in the bimonthly newsletter sponsored by NAAFA — the National Association to Advance Fat Acceptance. A recent issue of the newsletter, available on the internet, calls for readers to write to the government to protest the National Institute of Health's ongoing studies of normal-sized children to find out if obesity might have a metabolic basis. There are directions for giving money and establishing a living trust to benefit NAAFA, reviews of relevant new books, a report on the Trunk Sale at a NAAFA gathering in San Francisco, an update on the struggle to force auto manufacturers to provide seat belts that can save the lives of passengers who weigh over 215 pounds, and an article on the problems — the fear of appearing in public in a bathing suit, the narrow ladders that often provide the only access to swimming pools — that make it more difficult for the overweight to get the exercise that they need. There is a brief discussion of how obesity should be defined, and another about the effectiveness of behavioral psychotherapy in helping patients lose weight. Finally, there are grateful letters from readers whose lives have been improved by the support and sustenance they gain from belonging to NAAFA.

Equally fervent — if somewhat less affirmative and forgiving — are the gospel tracts, also available on-line. One of the most heartfelt and persuasive is the work of a preacher identified only as George Clark:

> After conducting healing campaigns and mailing out thousands of anointed handkerchiefs — since 1930 — I have learned that the greatest physical cause of sickness among the people of God is coming from this lust for overindulgence in eating. . . . Tens of thousands of truly converted people are sick and are suffering with heart trouble coming from high blood pressure and other ailments which result from overeating. . . . Did you ever wonder why artists have never depicted any of Jesus' disciples as being overweight or of the fleshy type? No one could have followed Jesus very long and remained overweight. . . . If eating too much has brought on high blood pressure, heart trouble, or many of the other diseases which come from being overweight, then God requires a reduction in your eating.

Given our perhaps misguided sense of living in a secular society, it's startling to find that our relationship with food is still so commonly translated directly into the language of God and the devil, of sin and repentance. But why should we be surprised, when we are constantly being reminded that our feelings about our diet and our body can be irrational, passionate, and closer to the province of faith and superstition than that of reason and science?

NOTES

[1]Stanford M. Lyman, *The Seven Deadly Sins: Society and Evil* (New York: St. Martin's Press, 1978), 220.

[2]Ibid., 223.

[3]Benjamin Wolman, ed., *Psychological Aspects of Obesity: A Handbook* (New York: Van Nostrand Reinhold, 1982), 148.

[4]Lyman, *Seven Deadly Sins,* 218.

BIBLIOGRAPHY

Albala, Ken. *Eating Right in the Renaissance.* Berkeley: University of California Press, 2002.

Augustine, Saint. *The Confessions of Saint Augustine,* trans. Edward B. Pusey, D. D. New York: The Modern Library, 1949.

Bell, Rudoph M. *Holy Anorexia.* Chicago: University of Chicago Press, 1985.

Chaucer, Geoffrey. *The Works of Geoffrey Chaucer,* ed. F. N. Robinson. Boston: Houghton Mifflin, 1957.

Chernin, Kim. *The Obsession.* New York: Harper Perennial, 1981.

Chesterton, G. K. *Saint Thomas Aquinas.* New York: Image Books, Doubleday, 2001.

Fielding, Henry. *Tom Jones.* New York: The Modern Library, 1994.

Fisher, M. F. K. *The Art of Eating.* New York: Vintage, 1976.

Lyman, Stanford M. *The Seven Deadly Sins: Society and Evil.* New York: St. Martin's Press, 1978.

Petronius. *The Satyricon,* trans. William Arrowsmith. New York: Meridian, 1994.

Pleij, Herman. *Dreaming of Cockaigne,* trans. Diane Webb. New York: Columbia University Press, 2001.

Rabelais, François. *Gargantua and Pantagruel,* trans. Burton Raffel. New York: W. W. Norton, 1991.

Roth, Geneen. *When Food Is Love.* New York: Plume, 1991.

Schwartz, Hillel. *Never Satisfied: A Cultural History of Fantasies and Fat.* New York: The Free Press, 1986.

Shaw, Teresa M. *The Burden of the Flesh: Fasting and Sexuality in Early Christianity.* Minneapolis: Fortress Press, 1996.

Spenser, Edmund. *The Faerie Queene.* New York: E. P. Dutton & Company, 1964.

Wolman, Benjamin, ed., with Stephen DeBerry, editorial associate. *Psychological Aspects of Obesity: A Handbook.* New York: Van Nostrand Reinhold, 1982.

DISCUSSION

1. Elsewhere in this essay Prose writes, "The so-called glutton is a walking rebuke to our self-control, our self-denial, and to our shaky faith that if we watch ourselves, then surely death cannot touch us." What exactly does she mean by this? Do you think she is right? In what ways do we use the images and examples of those body types that are regarded in our culture as deficient or abnormal as role models for what *not* to be ourselves?

2. From diet books to exercise videos, there is no shortage of material that scripts the ways we are and are not supposed to eat. Choose one such example from our current culture and describe the specific steps it itemizes. What does this list imply is the right attitude we should have toward food? How does it endeavor to get readers to adopt this view? What incentives does it offer? What punishments does it threaten?

3. There is, according to Prose, a close and complex connection between gluttony and guilt. Whether in the form of FDA warnings or ad copy for "sinfully delicious desserts," overeating is regularly associated in our culture with some kind of misbehavior or even moral failing. What do you make of this connection? Choose an example from our pop culture that you think is designed to teach this kind of guilt.

WRITING

4. Choose some venue (for example, a fast-food restaurant, health club, doctor's office, or similar place) that in your view endeavors to teach us specific attitudes about overeating. Spend a couple of hours there. First, write out as comprehensive a description of this place as you can. What kind of people do you observe? What sorts of equipment or décor? Next, write a short essay in which you speculate about the rules for eating that this venue attempts to instill. What relationship to food are people here encouraged to form? How does this relationship get presented or packaged as the norm?

5. One of the hallmarks of our contemporary culture, according to Prose, is that overeating is no longer viewed as a vice or sin but as an illness. Do you agree? What are some of the ways this change in thinking is communicated in popular culture or in the media? Write an essay in which you argue for or against gluttony as a moral issue.

6. Prose and Jason Fagone (p. 204) address the issue of gluttony in different ways. Write an essay in which you compare how each writer uses the idea of overeating to talk about larger cultural issues. How does each piece use food and appetite as a metaphor to comment on other social rules? Do you think this metaphor is effective? Why or why not?

JASON FAGONE
In Gorging, Truth

There is nothing within our media culture, it would seem, that can't be made into a competition — even eating. Recounting his experiences following the "competitive eating" circuit, Jason Fagone wonders about what our newfound enthusiasm for events like the National Hot Dog Eating Contest say not only about the current state of popular culture, but also about the American dream. Fagone is a journalist who has written for the city magazines *Cincinnati* and *Philadelphia*. In 2002, *Columbia Journalism Review* named him one of "Ten Young Writers on the Rise." His first book, *Horsemen of the Esophagus: Competitive Eating and the Big Fat American Dream,* from which "In Gorging, Truth" was taken, was published in 2006.

THE DAY AFTER GEORGE W. BUSH WON HIS SECOND TERM, A FRIEND OF mine e-mailed me, "How about this as a possible theme for your book?"

> americans are big, fat, infantile, stupid assholes who love to shovel shit down their throats, and so to shovel more shit down one's throat than any other is to be truly king of america.

At that point I had been covering eating contests for three months. In the thick of a nasty presidential election and a dumb bloody war fueled by certain American appetites, I had been humping around the country on Southwest Airlines, taking notes on the exploits of professional gluttons. It was hard not to make the connection. One Saturday in October, I flew to Jackson, Mississippi, for a Krystal-brand hamburger contest. When I woke up the next morning in my Red Roof Inn in an asphalt no-man's-land next to a Whataburger franchise (TRY OUR TRIPLE MEAT AND TRIPLE CHEESE), an anonymous Bush adviser informed me, via the online *New York Times,* "We're an empire now," and anyone who didn't agree was "in what we call the reality-based community." The adviser said that "when we act, we create our own reality. . . . We're history's actors . . . and you, all of you, will be left to just study what we do." Pass the gravy, suckers. I walked fifty yards to the Waffle House and ate my reality-based eggs along with fifteen or twenty other Jacksonians, all of them non-historical actors like me. Somebody had left a *Clarion-Ledger* on the counter, with headlines like N. KOREAN NUKES LIKELY POWELL TOPIC and UTAH BIOWEAPONS TEST SITE TO GROW. I walked to the fair, where the Federation's gurgitators[1] visited terrible indignities upon their hamburgers under a sweltering sun. In the bleachers, I talked to a man with one tooth who said he eats all day and never gets full. I met two men from Texas who'd driven eleven hours to compete here. "I think it's sort of a celebration," said one. "A celebration of our prosperity. We're able to do this, so we might as well do it, I guess." After the contest, the TV cameras descended upon Nick Blackburn, a roly-poly local who had placed third. I interviewed his loudest supporter, a youngish guy with black spiky hair, who said he was Nick's pastor. If Christ happened upon an eating contest, I asked, what would Jesus do? "God knows our heart," the pastor said. "He judges what's in our hearts, not the stupid things we do." He laughed. "If he did that, we'd *all* be in trouble."

The Federation's critics are easy to find, having left a trail of acerbic, disapproving quotes in thousands of newspaper and wire stories about competitive eating. Food historians like Barbara Haber ("It's the fall of Rome, my dear") and physicians like the Harvard Medical School's George Blackburn ("This is sick, abnormal behavior") have lined up to take a whack, as have foreign critics such as the *Guardian*, which in the same 2002 article that quoted Blackburn called competitive eating "a sport for our degraded times" and connected its rise to "an unprecedented boom in the American economy fuelled by rampant consumption." In 2003, consumer advocate Ralph Nader sounded the alarm about four "signs of societal decay": three involved corporate greed and congressional gerrymandering, and the fourth was competitive eating. The Federation's chairman, George Shea, responded to Nader by talking up his Turducken contest. A Turducken is a chicken stuffed into a duck stuffed into a turkey. Shea called his contest "the first real advancement in Thanksgiving since the Indians sat down with the Pilgrims." Shea's counterattacks tend to mix deadpan charm and gentle mockery: "There are those who object to our sport," Shea told me when I asked if it was wise to promote gluttony in the fattest nation on earth,[2] "and for the moment I'd like to refer to them as," and Shea's voice sped up and dropped a half-octave to let me in on the joke, "knee-jerk reactionaries and philistines." He continued, normal-voiced, "A lot of people have had trouble separating this superficial visual of people stuffing their faces with large quantities of food with the stereotype of the Ugly American. That is not where I am. I see beauty. I see physical poetry."

Poetry, exactly. Shea's eating contests were poetic in their blatancy, their brazen mixture of every American trait that seemed to terrify the rest of the planet: our hunger for natural resources that may melt the ice caps and flood Europe, our hunger for cheap thrills that turns Muslim swing voters into car bombers.[3] If anti-American zealots anywhere in the world wanted to perform a minstrel show of our culture, this is what they'd come up with. Competitive eating was a symbolic hairball coughed up by the American id. It was

> **Competitive eating was a symbolic hairball coughed up by the American id.**

meaningful like a tumor was meaningful. It seemed to have a purpose, a message, and its message was this: Look upon our gurgitators, ye Mighty, and despair. Behold these new supergluttons, these ambassadors of the American appetite, these horsemen of the esophagus.

There was a time, of course — a year and fifteen pounds ago — when I didn't watch people gorge themselves in public and try to figure out what it meant, or if it meant anything at all. I was a serious journalist with a good job. I wrote for a magazine in Philadelphia. I wrote about doctors, developers, politicians, and the occasional eccentric who wanted to change the world. I had never heard of the Belt of Fat Theory. I couldn't tell the difference between "Hungry" Charles Hardy and Hungry Hungry Hippo. I couldn't rap a single verse of competitive-eating-themed hip-hop. The only thing I knew about competitive eating was what everybody else knows: that every year, some skinny Japanese guy kicks all of our American asses in hot dogs.

I was okay with all of that.

Then, one day in the summer of 2004, while using my magazine's Internet connection to distract myself from thinking about my doctors and developers and politicians and eccentrics who wanted to change the world, I came across the Federation's website, ifoce.com.

The outer rim of the donut hole.

Across the top of the page, a banner spelled out INTERNATIONAL FEDERATION OF COMPETITIVE EATING. The site's design was unremarkable except for an illustration on the page's upper left: a heraldic seal with two facing lions. Upon closer inspection, the lions were eating a hot dog from both ends while pawing tubes of mustard and ketchup that crossed, like swords, to form an X. A Latin inscription read IN VORO VERITAS.

In Gorging, Truth.

I clicked "Media Inquiries."

Within a day or two I got a call back from Rich Shea, younger brother of George Shea. In the meantime I had done some more reading. I had discovered that my hometown, Philly, hosted an annual chicken-wing contest called Wing Bowl. A couple of times since I had moved to Philly, friends and strangers had tried to tell me about Wing Bowl, but I must have blown them off. On the phone, Rich Shea explained the significance of Wing Bowl's greatest champion, a truck driver named Bill "El Wingador" Simmons. "Wingador's done a lot for competitive eating, certainly in Philly," Rich said. "So, you know, he could be the Moses Malone — did Moses Malone play for the Sixers? He could be the Doctor J" — he paused, thought of something better — "the G. Love and Special Wing Sauce of competitive eating." He laughed.

Rich talked quickly and thought quickly. He explained that he and his brother maintained a public relations firm in New York — Shea

Communications — and their bread-and-butter clients were legitimate types like detectives and commercial real estate managers. The Federation was a separate track of the business, run from the same loft office in Chelsea. The Sheas got into the eating game in the late eighties, when both of them graduated from college, one after the other, and went to work in New York City for two old-school PR guys from the era when PR guys were called "press agents." The two old-school PR guys were the ones who invented the biggest eating contest in the world, the Nathan's Famous Hot Dog contest, back in the 1970s. The brothers eventually took over the Nathan's account and formed the Federation in 1997 with the goal of extruding that single hot dog contest into a gluttonous empire.

And they were getting close. The Federation claimed to have 300 active eater-members. Rich said that by the end of 2004, the Federation would have sanctioned about seventy-five contests that year, anywhere from three to ten per month. This was in addition to a handful of non-Federation contests that came in two flavors: indie and bootleg. The indie contests — one or two per month — were organized under the umbrella of an offshoot league called the Association of Independent Competitive Eaters, or AICE. Because AICE was newer, its contests were far smaller than the Federation's. As for the bootleg contests, they were harder to characterize: dozens, maybe hundreds, of minor spectacles at low-rent venues, at America's crummy bars, small-town carnivals, drive-time radio stations.

Eaters had options, but there was a catch. They couldn't mix and match. The Federation required its top talent to sign exclusive eighteen-month management contracts, and it had not been reluctant to shoot off cease-and-desist letters to wayward eaters it suspected of breaching the contract. Ambitious eaters — those who desired the imprimatur of a league — were therefore forced to pick either AICE or the Federation. Most eaters went with the Federation because it was bigger in every way: bigger stage, bigger money, bigger media. The Federation contests were sponsored by food companies, mostly, but also by municipal festivals and casinos on Indian reservations. The Sheas earned a per-contest fee from each sponsor, usually in the mid-four to low-five figures. The sponsors also put up the prize money, which Rich described as "a thousand dollars here, a thousand dollars there." In 2004, the total cash prize money was more than $60,000, of which the top American eater, Sonya Thomas, took home at least $17,000, plus a car — but the prizes, the number of contests, and the fan base were all growing; in 2005, sponsors would dole out more than $160,000, and Sonya would double her cash winnings. "It appeals to our competitive nature," Rich told me, adding, "You could also argue it's packaging and promotion and marketing. We've been very careful with how we've presented it." The Shea brothers had targeted "that guy demo," landing the horny eighteen-to-thirty-four set that loved

Maxim and *FHM*. Capturing the guy demo allowed them to pitch eating specials to the Travel Channel, the Food Network, the Discovery Channel, and even such bigger fish as Fox. In 2004, ESPN scored 765,000 household viewers for its first live broadcast of the Nathan's contest.

Eventually, said Rich, he and his brother hoped to convert eating from a hobby into a professional sport, like bass fishing. "That's sort of the curve we're looking at," Rich said.

He didn't mention it, but in 2001, the B.A.S.S. league sold to ESPN for a purported $35 million.

Eating contests weren't invented by the Shea brothers or their mentors, or even by Americans. Anthropological studies and old copies of scurrilous newspapers suggest that the will to gorge is universal. Speed and volume competitions pop up in Greek myth, in the *Eddas* of Norse myth,[4] and even in what may be mankind's first novel, Apuleius's *Golden Ass*, written in the second century A.D.: "Last night at supper, I was challenged to an eating race by some people at my table and tried to swallow too large a mouthful of polenta cheese." (Choking ensued.) Ethnographies show that eating contests were regular events at lavish Native American potlatch feasts, and there's historical evidence of rice contests in Japan, beefsteak contests in Britain, mango contests in India. Even in France, that supposed bastion of foody sanity, *les goinfres* (pigs) compete to pound *le fromage* at seasonal festivals.

We're different because we have more of it, more types of contests in more places. We do it broader and bigger, and unlike the British, the French, and the Germans — whose health ministry explicitly condemned the German variation of eating contests, called *Wettessen*, in a letter to a researcher of mine — we make no apologies. We unabashedly marry the public-gorging impulse to our most sacred American rituals (the catching of the greased pig followed by the pie contest followed by the reading of the Declaration of Independence on the Fourth of July) and give organized gluttony an iconic role in our most iconic movies. One of the feel-good pinnacles of *Cool Hand Luke*, Paul Newman's epic prison flick, is the scene in which Luke wins over his fellow prisoners by declaring, casually, that he can eat fifty hardboiled eggs — "Yeah, well, it'll be somethin' to do," says Luke — commencing days of fevered speculation, betting, logistical preparation, training meals, and exercise leading up to the eventual eating performance itself. Luke eats the fifty eggs, winning his buddy Dragline a ton of cash and triumphing existentially over his captors by making prison seem like fun. Also uplifting, though in a different sense, is the infamous blueberry-pie-eating scene in *Stand by Me*. A young boy in a small town, cruelly nicknamed "Lardass" and taunted by classmates and adults alike, gets revenge by entering a pie contest and vomiting on one of his competitors. Lardass ignites a chain reaction: "Girlfriends barfed on boyfriends. Kids barfed on their parents. A fat lady barfed in her purse. The Donnelly twins barfed on each other. And the Women's Auxiliary barfed all over the Benevolent Order of Antelopes . . ."

I never found a newspaper clipping that described a "total barf-o-rama" like the one in *Stand by Me*, but minus the barf-o-rama, it could be any contest in any small town. Prison masculinity tests like the one in *Cool Hand Luke* also have a basis in reality, if my interview with a Baltimore gurgitator nicknamed Tony Hustle, formerly incarcerated in the state of Maryland for armed robbery, is any indication. When it comes to contest lore, fact trumps fiction. The great Damon Runyon, the bard of 1920s Broadway, staged a fictional eating contest for his short story "A Piece of Pie," but for my money, his nonfiction account of an eating contest in the March 5, 1920, *New York American* is more pleasurable. Runyon, reporting from the Yankees training camp in Florida, describes preparations for a "gustatory grapple" between the sportswriters (especially a top eater-scribe named Irwin Cobb) and the ballplayers (primarily Babe Ruth, for obvious reasons):

> It was decided that Mr. Cobb should start from scratch with Ruth, and that they shall spot their competitors one Virginia ham each, and a double porterhouse. George Mogridge, who is managing Ruth, insisted on a rule that Mr. Cobb shall not be permitted to tell any stories during the encounter, as George says his man cannot do a menu justice if he has to stop and laugh, while Mr. Cobb's ability to laugh and eat at the same time is well known. He can emit a raucous guffaw and chamber a Dill pickle simultaneously.

Maybe because of the nature of the subject, it's impossible to find a boring account of an eating contest, even if you go all the way back to the beginning — back as far as 1793, when a newspaper in York, Pennsylvania, noted that "two young men of this County, an hour after dining, undertook to eat twenty-four ginger Cakes each, to have them gratis provided they accomplished it." In sclerotic nineteenth-century New York City, fat mayors and even fatter aldermen settled bets with their jaws while corrupt Tammany Hall racketeers treated their armies of tenement dwellers to pie-eating contests at lavish picnics. On the ambrosial frontier of pre-smog Los Angeles, a gold-rusher's daughter challenged her friends to "an eating race" of peaches, while on the mean, fallen frontier, in the mining town of Galena, Montana, the Fourth of July "was ushered in by the booming of giant powder which shook the buildings from roof to basement," followed by "the soup eating contest between Sperindo Perrcri, superintendent of the Savage mine, and Defenbaugh, watchman at the Red Cloud, for the championship of the Hills and a silver-striking hammer." The contests belched out the fierce impulses of a new country. By the turn of the century, every town from Rolla, Missouri, to Bountiful, Utah, speed-ate pies on the Fourth. Contests attracted chowhounds from the most dignified institutions (academia, the church, the military[5]) and lifted nobodies to mythic heights.[6] An eating contest was a natural icebreaker for picnics, summer camps, and county fairs because it swallowed people's differences in its broad, low humor — though there was a certain breed of contest that did the exact opposite, that heightened differences, and cruelly so. From the late nineteenth century through the Great Depression, whites recruited blacks — often little kids — to eat watermelons. The supposed voracity of the black appetite had its roots in the minstrel-show tradition. NO MINSTREL SHOW, IF YOU PLEASE, protested one conservative[7] black newspaper in 1922: "The comic supplement Negro, the water melon eating Negro, is the one which our enemies would have us resemble."

> **An eating contest . . . swallowed people's differences in its broad, low humor.**

As America grew more body-conscious, the stigma of public gluttony spread to whites. In 1946, the wife of the Army's top eater, PFC Chester Salvatori, divorced him "on grounds of cruelty" because she was "humiliated by the publicity that came from her husband's feats in eating," according to a wire story. Once the occasion for manly pride, eating contests now faded into the hidden recesses of personal biography, to be trotted out later for laughs should the person become famous, as in the case of Colonel Parker (whose biographer notes that he promoted a contest, once, before he met Elvis), and the segregationist George Wallace (who is shown at a pie contest in an old college snapshot, gazing "pensively at the floor," according to a biographer), and even Al Gore Jr., whose eventual political profilers couldn't resist noting that a young Al Gore, working as a cub reporter in Tennessee, once reported on a Whopper-eating contest at Burger King.[8]

Eating contests lost their swagger. Adults ceded the competition table to little kids and frat boys. Contests grew stunty and tame.

And then the Federation came along, and eating contests became big and dangerous and wild again. Into the delicate ecosystem of American gurgitation, the Federation introduced several new elements: first, a full-time promoter — the Shea brothers — and second, a core group of pioneering gurgitators, the first people in history to self-identify as professional eaters. "We did all the footwork years ago," as "Hungry" Charles Hardy told me. "Traveling here, traveling there. We didn't really make no kinda money. We pretty much took it to where it was today."

I started calling eaters in September 2004, starting with the veterans like Hardy and Ed "Cookie" Jarvis and Don "Moses" Lerman. They all said they were amazed by eating's trajectory, its quick-rising legitimacy: "The life has been a lot better, eating on the circuit," Hardy said, owing to the uptick in prize pots. Ed Jarvis said, "Let's face it. We're on ESPN. If that's not professional sports, I don't know what is." Don Lerman said, "I think in three years it'll be as big as PGA golf. In five years it may be in the Olympics."[9] The one eater to offer me a reality check was Arnie "Chowhound" Chapman, the renegade with the league of his own. He told me he wanted eating to be chilled-out and shticky, not corporate. Arnie was the bizarro-world version of the Federation guys, believing them all delusional and the Federation morally depraved. "The elite eaters," Arnie said, "they're addicted to adulation, they're addicted to publicity."

Arnie was half right. There were definite hints of pride and obsession in those early calls, not least in Arnie's own anti-Federation spiel. Ed said he maintained a trophy room. "It's like a shrine," Ed said. "I mean, people look in and they're like, 'God.'" Don had a trophy room, too. And a weight problem. "Since I'm thirty, I've been fighting obesity," Don said. Ed was pushing four hundred and also trying to lose weight.[10] The day I talked to him, he was pondering an upcoming cannoli contest. Ed was the cannoli champ, but was thinking about not defending his title. "It's rough on the body," he said. "One, you're eating 11,000 calories. Two, there's no money. Three, all that said, the bottom line is 'What am I doing this for?' I'm basically putting 11,000 calories into my body with the chance I could get hurt. What for? There's gotta be a cause." Even Arnie admitted, "I'm even a little concerned about myself. I'm now 245 pounds. I've never been that heavy before."

Slander, rivalry, hubris, recklessness: that was half of the Shakespearean palette, the exact half you'd expect to find in a group of pro gluttons. But the more eaters I called, and the more I pushed past their immediate need to impress upon me that they weren't a bunch of freaks, the more I saw that they really weren't. I got a sense of the other half of the palette, the subtler shades. With a few conspicuous exceptions, the eaters didn't seem to be lifelong publicity hounds or career eccentrics. They had wives and kids. They had jobs as construction workers, social workers, bankers, engineers, lawyers. I would come to know them as genuinely sweet and generous guys, most of them. Except for their collective waist size, they were as averagely American as the Americans in campaign commercials. They had to know that competitive eating was a marketing ploy, and yet — out of some psychic contortion it was too soon for me to guess at — rarely spoke of it that way. Eating, to them, wasn't a ploy. It was fun. It was a chance to compete, to travel the country and make a little money, or at least break even. It was a chance to be on ESPN.

How many people get to be on ESPN?

And beyond the obvious rewards were the intangibles, borne of the fact that eating was a community, one with its own distinct interior culture, its own goals and sacred controversies. (The controversies, if anything, legitimize the community, as sociologist Gary Alan Fine told me: "It means . . . there are some things that matter.") Charles Hardy, who in a few months would tattoo the letters "IFOCE" on his right bicep, said, "We're like one big family." Ed Jarvis said, "I'm with a group, not by myself . . . It's nice to have a group." They readily talked trash and bestowed compliments, too. He's fast (said Don of Ed), he's got capacity, he's got technique, "he believes in what he does." Belief/believes/believer. The eaters kept conjugating that word. I talked to another eater, twenty-seven-year-old Tim "Eater X" Janus, who told me the story of the first time George Shea offered to pay for his hotel room at an out-of-state contest. "I was pretty flattered, actually," Tim said. "I knew it could lead to big things . . . I don't know, it's just neat to see people believe in you, for anything, really."

It didn't seem that it could be so welcoming, this weird little corner of the culture, but there it was, warm and cozy, teeming with improbably hopeful activity, In *The Control of Nature*, John McPhee writes that the founders of New Orleans built a city "where almost any camper would be loath to pitch a tent." Here on the pro gluttony circuit, atop the same cultural terrain that made me feel, in my bitterest moments, ashamed to be an American, the eaters were planting their dearest desires — for fair and honest competition, for a pat on the back, to get noticed, to prove themselves, to make their kids and spouses proud.

Life/liberty/pursuit of happiness by way of eating/shitting/vomiting/shilling.

In Gorging, Truth.

Could it work?

Could the eaters really draw blood from this stone? Could they extract, from this grotesque spectacle, meaning? And if they could, did that mean the spectacle wasn't as grotesque as it seemed to someone like me, looking in from the outside? Was there something nourishing hidden within American trash culture?

Look, to be clear: these were my own existential questions. Not the eaters'. The eaters weren't staying up nights wondering if they could extract meaning from the grotesque. Eating wasn't grotesque, it was cool, and if the eaters did stay up nights, it was to trade stomach-stretching techniques on the phone or check the latest eating gossip on beautiful brian.com.

This is where we converged. Seriousness. The eaters took eating seriously — they trained, they spent their money and time, risked their health and their relationships — and I felt like I should take eating as seriously as they did. That didn't mean adopting a persona and joining the circuit as a gurgitator, although once, at a pastrami contest at New York's Second Avenue Deli, I did step up to the competition table myself, about which the less said the better.[11]

No: serious, to me, meant, on a basic level, going to a ton of contests. Starting with a Krystal hamburger qualifier in Knoxville, Tennessee, on September 19, 2004, and ending with a blueberry pie contest in Machias, Maine, on August 20, 2005, I would eventually attend twenty-seven eating contests in thirteen states and two continents, including seventeen Federation contests, five AICE contests, two local TV contests, one sports radio contest, one contest sponsored by a United Church of Christ congregation, and one contest organized by a Japanese weatherman. I would attend, for instance, four Krystal hamburger events and five Nathan's hot-dog events. I would attend the Gameworks World Tex Mex Roll-Eating Championship Presented by Great Lakes Crossing at the Great Lakes Crossing Mall in Auburn Hills, Michigan. The World's Greatest Shoo-Fly Pie-Eating Championship at the Rockvale Outlets in Lancaster, Pennsylvania. The ACME World Oyster Eating Championship in Metairie, Louisiana. The World Cheesecake-Eating Championship in Brooklyn. The Entenmann's Pies Thanksgiving Invitational in the Chelsea district of New York City. The Ball Park Fiesta Bowl National Hot Dog Eating Championship in Tempe, Arizona. The Third Annual International Chili Society's World Championship Chili Eating Contest at Mandalay Bay Hotel and Casino in Las Vegas. And after enough contests, after filling enough notebooks with columns of numbers signifying quantities of meats and sweets, I would become akin to an actual serious beat reporter covering an actual serious beat — which was my goal starting out. I wanted the coverage *itself*, not just the effort, to be serious. I wanted to cover eating as if it were important. Not mock-important.[12] Truly important.

It was possible, of course, that it wasn't important — that it was all just empty calories, signifying nothing. It was possible that the eaters weren't harbingers of the coming apocalypse, just an excuse for headline writers to make bad puns. Appetite for Destruction. Cool Hand Puke. Lord of the Wings.[13] Wing Eaters Peck for Position. Frankly Speaking. Great Balls of Matzo. Getting Stuffed.[14] A Competitor With Guts. Big Eater Can Stomach the Competition. Man Bites Dogs, Over and Over. She Meats Expectations. This isn't a knock on reporters — I am one — but, for most of us, an eating piece isn't a project, it's a blessed break from *other* projects, which is why eating always gets shoehorned into a few standard and easy-to-pull-off formats: (1) the shlocky thirty-second "brite" segment at the end of a local newscast; (2) the half-playful, half-serious newspaper feature; (3) the puffy, sprawling alt-weekly profile of the alt-weekly's town's most prominent eater; or (4) the stripped-down News of the Weird brief sandwiched contextless between other, wildly unrelated briefs.[15]

And they fail. They all fail to capture the mad galumphing experience of an eating contest, a really good one, when the crowd's into it, gawking, screaming, and the food's detonated on contact with a merciless line of teeth and jaws, and Shea's on his game — *we cannot SEE, we cannot HEAR, we need something MORE!* — and when, scanning the crowd's faces, I can tell that we're all feeling something, something intense, maybe revulsion, maybe joy, maybe just a deep curiosity, but it's more than can be expressed in a thirty-second brite or a fifty-word brief. Whatever's happening doesn't feel

> **A cross-section of the promise and the threat we represent to the world and to ourselves.**

shabby or small, but instead — I swear to the Virgin Mary Grilled Cheese — broad and big and consequential, as though America has vomited up its deepest hope and deepest dread in one place and now something worthwhile having to do with this *big, fat, infantile, stupid* country can be learned, or accomplished. The whole goopy range of it, everything that makes America so undeniably great and infuriating, loved and hated, everything that makes me want to buy a ranch in Montana one day and move to Scandinavia the next: a cross-section of the promise and the threat we represent to the world and to ourselves.

I wanted to capture that range. And I wanted to do it by writing about the eaters, who were living it. That meant I needed eaters of a certain type. Eaters who embodied eating's risks (meaning they competed often enough to strain their bodies) and also its rewards (meaning they were talented and high-ranked). I needed eaters with a good chance of transcending the pro circuit's intrinsic comedy, tragedy, slander, and bad food to achieve true athletic grace, maybe even redemption.

I found three of the lucky ones, and latched on.

I'm talking about Bill "El Wingador" Simmons, chicken-wing champion of the world. I'm talking about Tim "Eater X" Janus, tiramisu-eating champion of the world.

I'm talking, especially, about David "Coondog" O'Karma, tag-team bratwurst champion of Canton, Ohio.

NOTES

[1]The word "gurgitator" is actually a registered trademark of the Federation, but, perhaps owing to its dull-edged awkwardness, the competitors preferred to call themselves "eaters." The fan site trencherwomen.com later made the term gendered, separating "gurgitators" (men) from "gurgitrices" (women), though the proper word probably should have been "gurgitatrices."

[2]Now that residents of several E.U. countries have been found to be more obese than Americans, and obesity panics have taken hold in Britain and France, any Europeans who mock the girth of our nation are merely throwing stones at fat houses. Luckily for them, American-style eating contests are still totally mockable.

[3]Not to mention the contests' wankish indifference to the 800 million global hungry and also the 12 percent of American households our own Department of Agriculture considers "food-insecure."

[4]The god Loki loses to a giant. Both eat all of their meat, but the giant eats his plate, too, proving that competitive eating really does have a strategic component.

[5]U.S. troops have battled with food on navy battleships and inside Trident nuclear submarines; they have staged eating contests while stationed in Paris in 1918 (pie), Italy in 1945 (pie), Vietnam in 1968 (eggs), and Beirut in 1984 (dog biscuits).

[6]The eating prowess of "Honest Red" Dugan, a poor Lower Manhattan cabdriver who died in 1911, scored him a *Times* obituary longer than that of most congressmen.

[7]So conservative, in fact, that it had refused to criticize the governor of Missouri when he vetoed an anti-lynching bill.

[8]Gore's fastidious coverage of the event ("one of the contestants regurgitated his first three Whoppers on the table and dampened the morale of his competitors") was later interpreted by one profiler as proof of Gore's resolve not to skate by on merely his "pedigree" and his "cum laude Ivy League diploma," and to get his hands dirty by taking on what the profiler called "stories like that." It was seen to be revealing of his inner character which is probably why it was so much fun to learn, from the *Los Angeles Times* in early 2006, that the disgraced lobbyist Jack Abramoff, who elevated mere conflict of interest to a lucrative criminal art, once organized "a Quarter Pounder–eating contest at a McDonald's, with some proceeds going to the American Cancer Society" — a fundraising effort that the Wonkette weblog called "uniquely ironic."

[9]As a publicity stunt for a Spam-eating contest, George Shea once arranged an Olympic-style "torch run" using a can of Spam mounted on a chair leg. He later told the *Washington Post* it was "the first-ever meat-based torch run in the United States, if not the world." He also claimed to have lobbied unsuccessfully for eating's inclusion in the Olympics: "I strongly believe that we have overtaken curling in the overall pantheon of sports," he told the *McGill Daily* (whose interviewer, by the way, had decided to call Shea after "musing about what could be accomplished in the world if all the money spent on eating contests in the U.S. per year were to be diverted toward, say, treating preventable disease in sub-Saharan Africa," only to be wooed by Shea's deadpan savvy into publishing a full Q&A of their exchange), "and I think tennis is next."

[10]Caveat: pinning down an eater's poundage is more difficult than it may seem. One reason is that the eaters' weights fluctuate significantly; Don "Moses" Lerman has weighed as much as 250 pounds and as little as 142. Also, the official "weigh-in" ceremonies have been known to produce odd numbers, and the IFOCE's "bib sheets," which list eaters' weights and heights, are rarely updated. Absent any canonical source, I tend to trust what the eaters tell me. Still, all weights in this book should be considered estimates.

[11]Okay, I'll say this: prior to the contest, I agonized about how far I should push myself — i.e., whether it was the better part of valor to stop if I felt like I was about to vomit, or to keep going, so as to more fully empathize with the discomfort my subjects often endure. As it turned out, owing to the chewiness of the meat and also my inability to resist the urge, every ten seconds or so, to pick up a napkin and wipe my face, I ended up eating one sandwich in ten minutes. One.

[12]The *New York Post*'s Gersh Kuntzman, writing in the IFOCE's newsletter *The Gurgitator* ("Life on the Circuit"): ". . . the Land of the Rising Bun is the one remaining breeding ground for the next generation of gustatory gladiators. Whether it's in their elementary schools, where kids learn about the legendary eaters like Nakajima, Shirota, and Arai, or in the buffet academies, where potential stars are groomed for eating greatness, Japan prepares while the rest of the world errs . . . "

[13]The title, I'm sad to say, of my own article about the Philadelphia Wing Bowl.

[14]There's a definite and creepy sexual subtext to some of the headlines, a gleeful, violative aggression; somebody once told a friend of mine that he hated this book's title because it seemed like someone was "getting orally raped."

[15]Page 6 news briefs, *Ottawa Sun*, November 27, 2005: (1) Toronto boy falls off a building and dies; (2) Colorado teen faces a year in prison for hitting and killing a bicyclist "while text-messaging"; (3) Sonya Thomas eats a Thanksgiving turkey in twelve minutes; (4) tribal leaders in South Africa oppose government's outlawing of virginity tests for young girls.

DISCUSSION

1.   What do you make of the title "professional eater"? What kind of person does it conjure in your mind? Is there anything surprising or odd (that is, against the norm) about joining these two terms? Does it make sense to think of eating as a professional undertaking?

2.   Fagone reports one eating contest mogul as saying that competitive eating "'appeals to our competitive nature.'" In your view, is this true? Does it make more sense to think of competition as something natural or as something we are trained or taught to regard as a norm? To what extent would you describe the types of competition featured in these eating contests to be natural?

3.   How does competitive eating compare to the forms of eating we regard as the norm? Are there any similarities between the eating showcased in events like the World Oyster Eating Championship or the National Hot Dog Eating Championship and the ways you typically eat? And if so, what do these parallels tell us about the messages or scripts around eating purveyed by our larger culture?

WRITING

4.   One of this essay's underlying premises is that our individual eating practices are a kind of societal mirror, reflecting the values, ideals, and norms purveyed within our larger culture. Write an essay in which you analyze this argument. How does Fagone use evidence to support it? Can you find additional evidence from your own experience that confirms what Fagone is proposing? Evidence against it?

5.   Fagone concludes his essay with the coda: "In gorging, truth." What do you think he means by this? Write an essay in which you discuss the explicit ways that Fagone connects the metaphor of competitive eating with larger American culture. Do you agree with his conclusion? Why or why not?

6.   Fagone and Caroline Knapp (p. 217), in many ways write about eating from opposite ends of a spectrum. Yet both writers connect the topic of eating to larger cultural phenomena. Write an essay in which you compare the ways both writers look at eating as a symptom of or reaction to larger cultural influences. How is it possible for these two very different perspectives to coexist?

CAROLINE KNAPP

Add Cake, Subtract Self-Esteem

When are our appetites about more than just food? Detailing her own struggle with anorexia, Caroline Knapp offers some pointed observations about the ways our contemporary culture fosters "disorders of the appetite" in women, creating an environment in which it has become normal to define questions of female self-worth and female power in relation to what one does (or does not) eat. Knapp was a columnist for the *Boston Phoenix.* Some of the pieces she wrote as the anonymous "Alice K." are collected in *Alice K.'s Guide to Life* (1994). Her other books include *Drinking: A Love Story* (1996) and *Pack of Two: The Intricate Bond Between People and Dogs* (1998). She died in 2002 from complications of lung cancer, just after completing her last book, *Appetites: Why Women Want* (2003), the book in which the following essay appears.

T HE LURE OF STARVING — THE BAFFLING, SEDUCTIVE HOOK — WAS that it soothed, a balm of safety and containment that seemed to remove me from the ordinary, fraught world of human hunger and place me high above it, in a private kingdom of calm.

This didn't happen immediately, this sense of transcendent solace, and there certainly wasn't anything blissful or even long-lived about the state; starving is a painful, relentless experience, and also a throbbingly dull one, an entire life boiled down to a singular sensation (physical hunger) and a singular obsession (food). But when I think back on those years, which lasted through my mid-twenties, and when I try to get underneath the myriad meanings and purposes of such a bizarre fixation, that's what I remember most pointedly — the calm, the relief from an anxiety that felt both oceanic and nameless. For years, I ate the same foods everyday, in exactly the same manner, at exactly the same times. I devoted a monumental amount of energy to this endeavor — thinking about food, resisting food, observing other people's relationships with food, anticipating my own paltry indulgences in food — and this narrowed, specific, driven rigidity made me feel supremely safe: one concern, one feeling, everything else just background noise.

Disorders of appetite — food addictions, compulsive shopping, promiscuous sex — have a kind of semiotic brilliance, expressing in symbol and metaphor what women themselves may not be able to express in words, and I can deconstruct anorexia with the best of them. Anorexia is a response to cultural images of the female body — waiflike, angular — that both capitulates to the ideal and also mocks it, strips away all the ancillary signs of sexuality, strips away breasts and hips and butt and leaves in their place a garish caricature, a cruel cartoon of flesh and bone. It is a form of silent protest, a hunger strike that expresses some deep discomfort with the experience of inhabiting an adult female body. It is a way of co-opting the traditional female preoccupation with food and weight by turning the obsession upside down, directing the energy not toward the preparation and provision and ingestion of food but toward the shunning of it, and all that it represents: abundance, plenitude, caretaking. Anorexia is this, anorexia is that. Volumes have been written about such symbolic expressions, and there's truth to all of them, and they are oddly comforting truths: They help to decipher this puzzle; they help to explain why eating disorders are the third most common chronic illness among females in the United States, and why fifteen percent of young women have substantially disordered attitudes and behaviors toward food and eating, and why the incidence of eating disorders has increased by thirty-six percent every five years since the 1950s. They offer some hope — if we can understand this particularly devastating form of self-inflicted cruelty, maybe we can find a way to stop it.

I, too, am tempted to comfort and explain, to look back with the cool detachment of twenty years and offer a crisp critique: a little cultural commentary here, a little metaphorical analysis there. But what recedes into the background amid such explanations — and what's harder to talk about because it's intangible and stubborn and vast — is the core, the underlying drive, the sensation that not only made anorexia feel so seductively viable for me some two decades ago but that also informs the central experience of appetite for so many women, the first feeling we bring to the table of hunger: anxiety, a sense of being overwhelmed.

There is a particular whir of agitation about female hunger, a low-level thrumming of shoulds and shouldn'ts and can'ts and wants that can be so chronic and familiar it becomes a kind of feminine Muzak, easy to dismiss, or to tune out altogether, even if you're actively participating in it. Last spring, a group of women gathered in my living room to talk about appetite, all of them teachers and administrators at a local school and all of them adamant that this whole business — weight, food, managing hunger — troubles them not at all. "Weight," said one, "is not really an issue for me." "No," said another, "not for me, either." And a third: "I don't really think about what I'm going to eat from day to day. Basically, I just eat what I want."

This was a cheerful and attractive group, ages twenty-two to forty-one, and they were all so insistent about their normalcy around food that, were it not for the subtle strain of caveat that ran beneath their descriptions, I might have believed them.

The caveats had to do with rules, with attitudes as ingrained as reflexes, and with a particularly female sense of justified reward: They are at the center of this whir, an anxious jingle of mandate and restraint. The woman who insisted that weight is "not really an issue," for instance, also noted that she only allows herself to eat dessert, or second helpings at dinner, if she's gone to the gym that day. No workout, no dessert. The woman who agreed with her (no, not an issue for her, either) echoed that sentiment. "Yeah," she nodded, "if I don't work out, I start to feel really gross about food and I'll try to cut back." A third said she eats "normally" but noted that she always makes a point of leaving at least one bite of food on her plate, every meal, no exceptions. And the woman who said she "basically just eats what she wants" added, "I mean, if someone brings a cake into the office, I'll have a tiny slice, and I might not eat the frosting, but it's not like a big deal or anything. I just scrape the frosting off."

Tiny slices, no frosting, forty-five minutes on the StairMaster: These are the conditions, variations on a theme of vigilance and self-restraint that I've watched women dance to all my life, that I've danced to myself instinctively and still have to work to resist. I walk into a health club locker room and feel an immediate impulse toward scrutiny, the kneejerk measuring of self against other: *That one has great thighs, this one's gained weight, who's thin, who's fat, how do I compare?* I overhear snippets of conversation, constraints unwittingly articulated and upheld in a dollop of lavish praise here *(You look fabulous, have you lost weight?)*, a whisper of recriminating judgment there *(She looks awful, has she gained weight?)*, and I automatically turn

> **That one has great thighs, this one's gained weight, who's thin, who's fat, how do I compare?**

to look: Who looks fabulous, who looks awful? I go to a restaurant with a group of women and pray that we can order lunch without falling into the semi-covert business of collective monitoring, in which levels of intake and restraint are aired, compared, noticed: *What are you getting? Is that all you're having? A salad? Oh, please.* There's a persistent awareness of self in relation to other behind this kind of behavior, and also a tacit nod to the idea that there are codes to adhere to, and self-effacing apologies to be made if those codes are broken. *I'm such a hog,* says the woman who breaks rank, ordering a cheeseburger when everyone else has salad.

Can't, shouldn't, I'm a moose. So much of this is waved away as female vanity — this tedious nattering about calories and fat, this whining, shallow preoccupation with surfaces — but I find it poignant, and painful in a low-level but chronic way, and also quite revealing. One of the lingering cultural myths about gender is that women are bad at math — they lack confidence for it, they have poor visual-spatial skills, they simply don't excel at numbers the way boys do. This theory has been widely challenged over the years, and there's scant evidence to suggest that girls are in any way neurologically ill-equipped to deal with algebra or calculus. But I'd challenge the myth on different grounds: Women are actually superb at math; they just happen to engage in their own variety of it, an intricate personal math in which desires are split off from one another, weighed, balanced, traded, assessed. These are the mathematics of desire, a system of self-limitation and monitoring based on the fundamental premise that appetites are at best risky, at worst impermissible, that indulgence must be bought and paid for. Hence the rules and caveats: Before you open the lunch menu or order that cheeseburger or consider eating the cake with the frosting intact, haul out the psychic calculator and start tinkering with the budget.

Why shouldn't you? I asked a woman that question not long ago while she was demurring about whether to order dessert at a restaurant.

Immediate answer: "Because I'll feel gross."

Why gross?

"Because I'll feel fat."

And what would happen if you felt fat?

"I hate myself when I feel fat. I feel ugly and out of control. I feel really un-sexy. I feel unlovable."

And if you deny yourself the dessert?

"I may feel a little deprived, but I'll also feel pious," she said.

So it's worth the cost?

"Yes."

These are big trade-offs for a simple piece of cake — add five hundred calories, subtract well-being, allure, and self-esteem — and the feelings behind them are anything but vain or shallow. Hidden within that thirty-second exchange is an entire set of mathematical principles, equations that can dictate a woman's most fundamental approach to hunger. Mastery over the body — its impulses, its needs, its size — is paramount; to lose control is to risk beauty, and to risk beauty is to risk desirability, and to risk desirability is to risk entitlement to sexuality and love and self-esteem. Desires collide, the wish to eat bumping up against the wish to be thin, the desire to indulge conflicting with the injunction to restrain. Small wonder food makes a woman nervous. The experience of appetite in this equation is an experience of anxiety, a burden and a risk; yielding to hunger may be permissible under certain conditions, but mostly it's something to be Earned or Monitored and Controlled. $E = mc^2$.

During the acute phases of my starving years, I took a perverse kind of pleasure in these exhibitions of personal calculus, the anxious little jigs that women would do around food. Every day at lunchtime, I'd stand in line at a café in downtown Providence clutching my 200-calorie yogurt, and while I waited, I'd watch the other women deliberate. I'd see a woman mince edgily around the glass case that held muffins and cookies, and I'd recognize the look in her eye, the longing for something sweet or gooey, the sudden flicker of *No*. I'd overhear fragments of conversation: debates between women (*I can't eat that, I'll feel huge*), and cajolings (*Oh, c'mon, have the fries*), and collaborations in surrender (*I will if you will*). I listened for these, I paid attention, and I always felt a little stab of superiority when someone yielded (*Okay, fuck it, fries, onion rings, PIE*). I would not yield — to do so, I understood, would imply lack of restraint, an unseemly, indulgent female greed — and in my stern resistance I got to feel coolly superior while they felt, or so it seemed to me, anxious.

But I knew that anxiety. I know it still, and I know how stubbornly pressing it can feel, the niggling worry about food and calories and size and heft cutting to the quick somehow, as though to fully surrender to hunger might lead to mayhem, the appetite proven unstoppable. If you plotted my food intake on a graph from that initial cottage cheese purchase onward, you wouldn't see anything very dramatic at first: a slight decline in consumption over my junior and senior years, and an increasing though not yet excessive pattern of rigidity, that edgy whir about food and weight at only the edges of consciousness at first. I lived off campus my senior year with a boyfriend, studied enormously hard, ate normal dinners at home with him, but permitted myself only a single plain donut in the morning, coffee all day, not a calorie more. The concept of "permission" was new to me — it heralded the introduction of rules and by-laws, a nascent internal tyrant issuing commands — but I didn't question it. I just ate the donut, drank the coffee, obeyed the rules, aware on some level that the rigidity and restraint served a purpose, reinforced those first heady feelings of will and determination, a proud sensation that I was somehow beyond ordinary need. I wrote a prize-winning honors thesis on two hundred calories a day.

The following year, my first out of college, the line on the graph would begin to waver, slowly at first, then peaking and dipping more erratically: five pounds up, five pounds down, six hundred calories here, six thousand there, the dieting female's private NASDAQ, a personal index of self-torture.

This was not a happy time. I'd taken a job in a university news bureau, an ostensible entree into writing and a fairly hefty disappointment (I was an editorial assistant in title, a glorified secretary in fact, bored nearly senseless from day one). The boyfriend had left for graduate school in California, and I was living alone for the first time, missing him with the particularly consuming brand of desperation afforded by long-distance love. I was restless and lonely and full of self-doubt, and the low-level tampering I'd been doing with my appetite began to intensify, my relationship with food thrown increasingly out of whack. This is familiar territory to anyone with a long history of dieting: a fundamental severing between need and want begins to take place, eating gradually loses its basic associations with nourishment and physical satisfaction and veers onto a more complex emotional plane in which the whole notion of hunger grows loaded and confusing. Sometimes I was very rigid with my diet during this period, resolving to consume nothing but coffee all day, only cheese and crackers at night. Other times I ate for comfort, or because I was bored, or because I felt empty, all reasons that frightened and confused me. I'd make huge salads at night, filled with nuts and cubes of cheese and slathered in creamy dressings; I'd eat big bowls of salty soups, enormous tuna melts, hideously sweet oversized chocolate chip cookies, purchased in little frenzies of preservation (should I? shouldn't I?) from a local bakery. I started drinking heavily during this period, too, which weakened my restraint; I'd wake up feeling bloated and hungover and I'd try to compensate by eating nothing, or next to nothing, during the day.

For a year, I gained weight, lost weight, gained the weight back, and I found this deeply unnerving, as though some critical sense of bodily integrity were at risk, my sense of limits and proportion eroding. I'd feel my belly protrude against the waistband of my skirt, or one thigh chafing against another, and I'd be aware of a potent stab of alarm: *Shit*, the vigilance has been insufficiently upheld, the body is growing soft and doughy, something central and dark about me — a lazy, gluttonous, insatiable second self — is poised to emerge. Women often brought pastries into the office where I worked. Sometimes I'd steadfastly avoid them, resolve not even to look; other times I'd eye the pastry box warily from across the room, get up periodically and circle the table, conscious of a new sensation of self-mistrust, questions beginning to flitter and nag. *Could I eat one pastry, or would one lead to three, or four, or six? Was I actually hungry for a Danish or a croissant, or was I trying to satisfy some other appetite? How hungry — how rapacious, greedy, selfish, needy — was I?* The dance of the hungry woman — two steps toward the refrigerator, one step back, that endless loop of hunger and indulgence and guilt — had ceased to be a game; some key middle ground between gluttony and restraint, a place that used to be easily accessible to me, had grown elusive and I didn't know how to get back there.

This, of course, is one of appetite's insidious golden rules: The more you meddle with a hunger, the more taboo and confusing it will become. Feed the body too little and then too much, feed it erratically, launch that maddening cycle of deprivation and overcompensation, and the sensation of physical hunger itself becomes divorced from the

> **The more you meddle with a hunger, the more taboo and confusing it will become.**

body, food loaded with alternative meanings: symbol of longing, symbol of constraint, form of torture, form of reward, source of anxiety, source of succor, measure of self-worth. And thus the simple experience of hunger — of wanting something to eat — becomes frightening and fraught. What does it mean this time? Where will it lead? Will you eat *everything* if you let yourself go? Will you prove unstoppable, a famished dog at a garbage bin? Young and unsure of myself and groping for direction, I was scared of many things that year — leaving the structure of college was scary, entering the work world was scary, living on my own was scary, the future loomed like a monumental question mark — but I suspect I was scared above all of hunger itself, which felt increasingly boundless and insatiable, its limits and possible ravages unknown.

I suspect, too, that this feeling went well beyond the specific issue of food, that anxiety about caloric intake and body size were merely threads in a much larger tapestry of feeling that had to do with female self-worth and power and identity — for me and for legions of other women. This time period — late 1970s, early 1980s — coincided with the early stages of the well-documented shift in the culture's collective definition of beauty, its sudden and dramatically unambiguous pairing with slenderness. There is nothing new about this today; the pressure (internal and external) to be thin is so familiar and so widespread by now that most of us take it for granted, breathe it in like air, can't remember a time when we weren't aware of it, can't remember how different the average model or actress or beauty pageant contestant looked before her weight began to plummet (in the last twenty-five years, it's dropped to twenty-five percent below that of the average woman), can't remember a world in which grocery store shelves didn't brim with low-cal and "lite" products, in which mannequins wore size eight clothes instead of size two, in which images of beauty were less wildly out of reach.

But it's worth recalling that all of this — the ratcheted-up emphasis on thinness, the aesthetic shift from Marilyn Monroe to Kate Moss, the concomitant rise in eating disorders — is relatively recent, that the emphasis on diminishing one's size, on miniaturizing the very self, didn't really heat up until women began making gains in other areas of their lives. By the time I started to flirt with anorexia, in the late 1970s, women had gained access to education, birth control, and abortion, as well as widespread protection from discrimination in most areas of their lives. At the same time, doctors were handing out some ten billion appetite-suppressing amphetamines per year, Weight Watchers had spread to forty-nine states, its membership three million strong, and the diet-food business was about to eclipse all other categories as the fastest-growing segment of the food industry.

This parallel has been widely, and sensibly, described as the aesthetic expression of the backlash against feminist strength that Susan Faludi would document in 1992. At a time when increasing numbers of women were demanding the right to take up more space in the world, it is no surprise that they'd be hit with the opposite message from a culture that was (and still is) both male-dominated and deeply committed to its traditional power structures. Women get psychically larger, and they're told to grow physically smaller. Women begin to play active roles in realms once dominated by men (schools, universities, athletic fields, the workplace, the bedroom), and they're countered with images of femininity that infantilize them, render them passive and frail and non-threatening. "The female body is the place where this society writes its messages," writes Rosalind Coward in *Female-Desires*, and its response to feminism was etched with increasing clarity on the whittled-down silhouette of the average American model: Don't get too hungry, don't overstep your bounds.

The whispers of this mandate, audible in the 1970s and 1980s, have grown far louder today; they are roars, howls, screams. The average American, bombarded with advertisements on a daily basis, will spend approximately three years of his or her lifetime watching television commercials, and you don't have to look too closely to see what that deluge of imagery has to say about the female body and its hungers. A controlled appetite, prerequisite for slenderness, connotes beauty, desirability, worthiness. An uncontrolled appetite — a fat woman — connotes the opposite, she is ugly, repulsive, and so fundamentally unworthy that, according to a *New York Times* report on cultural attitudes toward fat, sixteen percent of adults would choose to abort a child if they knew he or she would be untreatably obese.

Hatred of fat, inextricably linked to fear of fat, is so deeply embedded in the collective consciousness it can arouse a surprising depth of discomfort and mean-spiritedness, even among people who consider themselves to be otherwise tolerant and sensitive to women. Gail Dines, director of women's studies and professor of sociology at Wheelock College in Boston and one of the nation's foremost advocates of media literacy, travels around the country giving a slide show/lecture called "Sexy or Sexist: Images of Women in the Media." The first half of the presentation consists of images, one after the other, of svelte perfection: a sultry Brooke Shields clad in a blue bikini on a *Cosmo* cover, an achingly slender leg in an ad for Givenchy pantyhose, a whisper-thin Kate Moss. Then, about halfway into the presentation, a slide of a postcard flashes onto the screen, a picture of a woman on a beach in Hawaii. The woman is clad in a bright blue two-piece bathing suit, and she is very fat; she's shown from the rear, her buttocks enormous, her thighs pocked with fleshy folds, and the words on the postcard read: HAVING A WHALE OF A TIME IN HAWAII. The first time I saw this, I felt a jolt of something critical and mean — part pity, part judgment, an impulse to recoil — and I felt immediately embarrassed by this, which is precisely the sensation Dines intends to flush out. At another showing before a crowd at Northeastern University, the image appears on the screen and several people begin to guffaw, nervous titters echo across the room. Dines stops and turns to the audience. "Now why is this considered funny?" she demands. "Explain that to me. Does she not have the right to the dignity that you and I have a right to? Does having extra pounds on your body deny you that right?" The crowd falls silent, and Dines sighs. There it is: This obese woman, this object of hoots and jeers, is a tangible focus of female anxiety, a 350-pound picture of the shame and humiliation that will be visited upon a woman if her hunger is allowed to go unchecked.

Dines, among many others, might identify culture as the primary protagonist in this narrative, a sneering villain cleverly disguised as Beauty who skulks around injecting women with a irrational but morbid fear of fat. There is certainly some truth to that — a woman who isn't affected to some degree by the images and injunctions of fat-and-thin is about as rare as a black orchid. But I also think the intensity of the struggle around appetite that began to plague me twenty years ago, that continues to plague so many women today, speaks not just to cultural anxiety about female hunger, profound though it may be, but also to deep reservoirs of personal anxiety, Fear of fat merely exists on the rippled surface of that reservoir; mass-market images are mere reflections upon it. Underneath, the real story — each woman in her own sea of experience — is more individual and private; it's about what happens when hunger is not quite paired with power, when the license to hunger is new and unfamiliar, when a woman is teased with freedom — to define herself as she sees fit, to attend to her own needs and wishes, to fully explore her own desires — but may not quite feel that freedom in her bones or believe that it will last.

> *Fear of fat merely exists on the rippled surface of that reservoir; mass-market images are mere reflections upon it.*

Once, several months into that first year of weight gain and weight loss, I met some friends for Sunday brunch, an all-you-can-eat buffet at a local hotel restaurant. All-you-can-eat buffets terrify me to this day — I find them sadistic and grotesque in a particularly American way, the emphasis on quantity and excess reflecting something insatiably greedy and short-sighted about the culture's ethos — and I date the onset of my terror to that very morning. Such horrifying abundance! Such potential for unleashed gluttony! The buffet table seemed to stretch out for a mile: at one station, made-to-order omelets and bacon and sausage; at another, waffles and pancakes and crêpes; at another, bagels and muffins and croissants and pastries; at yet another, an entire array of desserts, cakes and pies and individual soufflés. If you're confused about hunger, if the internal mechanisms that signal physical satiety have gone haywire, if food has become symbolically loaded, or a stand-in for other longings, this kind of array can topple you. I couldn't choose. More to the point, I couldn't trust myself to choose moderately or responsibly, or to stop when I was full, or even to know what I wanted to begin with, what would satisfy and how much. And so I ate everything. The suppressed appetite always rages just beneath the surface of will, and as often happened during that period, it simmered, then bubbled up, then boiled over. I ate. I ate eggs and bacon and waffles and slabs of cake, I ate knowing full well that I'd feel bloated and flooded with disgust later on and that I'd have to make restitution — I'd starve the next day, or go for a six-mile run, or both. I ate without pleasure, I ate until I hurt.

Years later, I'd see that brunch in metaphorical terms, a high-calorie, high-carbohydrate testament to the ambiguous blessings of abundance, its promise and its agonizing terror. As a rule, women of my generation were brought up without knowing a great deal about how to understand hunger, with very little discussion about how to assess and respond adequately to our own appetites, and with precious few examples of how to negotiate a buffet of possibility, much less embrace one. Eating too much — then as now — was a standard taboo, a mother's concern with her own body and weight handed down to her daughter in a mantle of admonishments: *Always take the smallest portion; always eat a meal before you go on a date lest you eat too much in front of him; don't eat that, it'll go straight to your hips.* Sexual hunger was at best undiscussed, at worst presented as a bubbling cauldron of danger and sin, potentially ruinous; the memory banks of women my age are riddled with images of scowling mothers, echoes of recriminating hisses (*Take that off, you look like a slut!*), fragments of threat-laden lectures about the predatory hunger of boys. And the world of ambition was in many ways uncharted territory, one that required qualities and skills — ego strength, competitiveness, intellectual confidence — that were sometimes actively discouraged in girls (*Don't brag, don't get a swelled head, don't be so smart*), rarely modeled.

This is a complicated legacy to bring to a world of blasted-open options, each *yes* in potential collision with an old *no*, and it makes for a great deal of confusion. The underlying questions of appetite, after all, are formidable — What *would* satisfy? How much *do* you need, and of what? What *are* the true passions, the real hungers behind the ostensible goals of beauty or slenderness? — and until relatively recently, a lot of women haven't been encouraged to explore them, at least not in a deep, concerted, uniform, socially supported way. We have what might be called post-feminist appetites, whetted and encouraged by a generation of opened doors and collapsed social structures, but not always granted unequivocal support or license, not always stripped of their traditional alarm bells and warnings, and not yet bolstered by a deeper sense of entitlement.

Freedom, it is important to note, is not the same as power; the ability to make choices can feel unsettling and impermanent and thin if it's not girded somehow with the heft of real economic and political strength. Women certainly have more of that heft than they did a generation ago; we are far less formally constrained, far more autonomous, and far more politically powerful, at least potentially so. Forty-three million women — forty percent of all adult women — live independently today, without traditional supports. Women make the vast majority of consumer purchases in this country — eighty-three percent — and buy one fifth of all homes. We have an unprecedented amount of legal protection, with equality on the basis of sex required by law in virtually every area of American life. We are better educated than the women of any preceding generation, with women representing more than half of full-time college enrollments. By all accounts, we ought to feel powerful, competent, and strong — and many women no doubt do, at least in some areas and at some times.

But it's also true that an overwhelming majority of women — estimates range from eighty to eighty-nine percent — wake up every morning aware of an anxious stirring of self-disgust, fixated on the feel of our thighs as we pull on our stockings, the feel of our bellies and hips as we zip up our pants and skirts. Women are three times as likely as men to feel negatively about their bodies. Eighty percent of women have been on a diet, half are actively dieting at any given time, and half report feeling dissatisfied with their bodies all the time. There is no doubt that this negativity is a culturally mediated phenomenon, that culture gives the female preoccupation with appearance (which in itself is nothing new) its particular cast, its particularly relentless focus on slenderness. But the sheer numbers, which indicate an unprecedented depth and breadth of anxiety about appearance in general and weight in particular, suggest that something more complex than imagery is at work, that our collective sense of power and competence and strength hasn't quite made it to a visceral level.

To be felt at that level, as visceral and permanent and real, entitlement must exist beyond the self; it must be known and acknowledged on a wider plane. And this is where women still get the short end of the stick; for all the gains of the last forty years, we are hardly ruling the world out there. Congress is still ninety percent male, as are ninety-eight percent of America's top corporate officers. Ninety-five percent of all venture capital today flows into men's bank accounts. The two hundred highest-paid CEOs in America are all men. Only three women head Fortune 500 companies, a number that hasn't budged in twenty years. We also have less visibility than men; women — our lives, issues, concerns — are still featured in only fifteen percent of page-one stories, and when we do make front-page news, it is usually only as victims or perpetrators of crime. And we still have less earning power: Women continue to make eighty-four cents for every dollar a man makes; women who take time off from work to have children make seventeen percent less than those who don't even six years after they return; men with children earn the most money while women with children earn the least.

This gap, I think — this persistent imbalance between personal freedom on the one hand and political power on the other — amps up the anxiety factor behind desire; it can leave a woman with a sense that something does not quite compute; it can give choices a partial, qualified feel. A woman, today, can be a neurosurgeon, or an astrophysicist; she can marry or not marry, leave her spouse, pack up, and move across the country at will. But can she take such choices a step further, or two or ten? Can a woman be not just an astrophysicist, but a big, powerful, lusty astrophysicist who feels unequivocally entitled to food and sex and pleasure and acclaim? Can she move across the country and also leave behind all her deeply ingrained feelings about what women are really supposed to look and act and be like? External freedoms may still bump up against a lot of ancient and durable internal taboos; they may still collide with the awareness, however vague, that women still represent the least empowered portion of the population, and these collisions help explain why appetites are so particularly problematic today; they exist in a very murky context, and an inherently unstable one, consistently pulled between the opposing poles of possibility and constraint, power and powerlessness.

The world mobilizes in the service of male appetite; it did during my upbringing and it does still. Whether or not this represents the actual experience of contemporary boys and men, our cultural stereotypes of male desire (and stereotypes exist precisely because they contain grains of truth) are all about facilitation and support: Mothers feed (Eat! Eat!), fathers model assertion and unabashed competitiveness, teachers encourage outspoken bravado. At home and at work, men have helpers, usually female, who clean and cook and shop and type and file and assist. And at every turn — on billboards, magazine covers, in ads — men are surrounded by images of offering, of breasts and parted lips and the sultry gazes of constant availability: Take me, you are entitled, I exist to please you. For all the expansion of opportunity in women's lives, there is no such effort on behalf of female appetite, there are no comparable images of service and availability, there is no baseline expectation that a legion of others will rush forward to meet our needs or satisfy our hungers. The striving, self-oriented man is adapted to, cut slack, his transgressions and inadequacies explained and forgiven. *Oh, well, you wouldn't expect him to cook or take care of his kids, who cares if he's put on a few pounds, so what if he's controlling or narcissistic, he's busy, he gets things done, he's running the show, he's running the company, he's running the COUNTRY.* That litany of understanding does not apply to women; it sounds discordant and artificial if you switch the genders, and if you need a single example of the double standard at work here, think about Bill and Hillary Clinton. Bill's pudginess and fondness for McDonald's was seen as endearing; his sexual appetite criticized but ultimately forgiven by most Americans, or at least considered irrelevant to his abilities on the job; Hillary got no such latitude, the focus on her appearance (hairstyle, wardrobe, legs) was relentless, the hostility released toward her ambition venomous.

The one exception to this rule, the one area where a legion of others might, in fact, rush forward in service to a woman's needs, is shopping, particularly high-end retail shopping, but in itself, that merely underscores how lacking the phenomenon is in other areas, and how constricted the realm of appetite is for women in general: We can want, and even expect, the world to mobilize on our behalf when we're equipped with an American Express gold card and an appetite for Armani. But beyond the world of appearances and consumer goods, expressions of physical hunger and selfish strivings rarely meet with such consistent support. Instead, the possibility of risk can hang in the air like a mildly poisonous mist; for every appetite, there may be a possible backlash, or a slap or a reprimand or a door that opens but has caveats stamped all over the welcome mat. A novelist tells me in a whisper about a glowing review she's received; she can barely get the words out, so strong are the chastising echoes of her family: *Now, don't you let it go to your head*, her mother used to say, and it took her decades to realize how truly defeating that phrase was. ("Where's it supposed to go," she asks today, "someone else's head?") A scientist, brilliant and respected, secures a major grant for a project she's dreamed of taking on for years and later describes what an emotional hurdle it was to fully take pride in the accomplishment, to really revel in it: "I couldn't say it aloud, I just couldn't get the words out," she says. "I don't think a man would *get* that." An educator, who's taught high school for thirteen years and is now pursuing a PhD in education, tells me, "For years, I've carried around the feeling that if I really allow myself to follow my passions, something bad will happen." She can't follow that line of thought to any logical conclusion; rather, it expresses an amalgam of worries, some specific (she's apprehensive about being consumed by work, and about making sacrifices in her personal life), but more of them generic, as though the admission of hunger and ambition is in itself a dangerous thing, quite likely a punishable offense.

This quiet, dogged anxiety, this internalized mosquito whine of caveat, may explain why the memory of that hotel brunch would stick with me for so long; the experience seemed to capture something about the times, about the onset of a complicated set of conflicts between an expansive array of options on the one hand and a sense of deep uncertainty on the other, a feeling that this freedom was both incomplete and highly qualified, full of risks. Certainly that's how I felt in those early unformed twentysomething years, as though I were standing before an enormous table of possibilities with no utensils, no serving spoons, no real sense that I was truly entitled to sample the goods, to experiment or indulge or design my own menu.

DISCUSSION

1. Knapp begins her personal account of anorexia by referring to the "lure of starving." How do you react to this provocative phrase? In your view, is it possible for something as harrowing and harmful as self-starvation to feel so compelling or desirable? If so, how?

2. For Knapp, anorexia is both a personal and a societal disease, starkly registering the ways women can be taught to internalize and act on destructive gender stereotypes. How valid does this hypothesis seem to you? Does it make sense to think about this illness as a blueprint for the scripts that get written out and imposed on women?

3. As Knapp relates, denying herself food felt for so long like the right thing to do in part because it gave her an enhanced sense of "being in control." Choose one of the diets Knapp describes having followed during her anorexic years and evaluate it as a recipe for achieving a particular form of control. In your view, does the diet achieve this objective?

WRITING

4. Much of Knapp's writing of her own hunger centers around imaginary conversations or internal dialogue that express common embedded attitudes about eating and appetite. Write an essay in which you analyze how effective this approach to writing about appetite is. Who is Knapp talking to in these conversations, and how does she use this dialogue to highlight her own attitudes toward eating?

5. Here is a partial list of the words Knapp tells us she learned to associate with her own hunger: *rapacious*, *greedy*, *selfish*, *needy*, *unsexy*, *bad*. Write an essay in which you propose what scripts about food and eating have given rise to these kinds of associations. What scripts in food advertising, nutritional guidelines, or the popular media do you think reinforce this type of thinking? In your opinion, are these scripts intentional? How might you approach communicating messages about health or beauty without triggering the negative associations that Knapp discusses?

6. For Knapp, cultural attitudes about food formed "a low-level thrumming of shoulds and shouldn'ts, and can'ts and wants," or what the author calls a kind of "feminine Musak." In your view, does this analogy do a good or bad job of capturing the ways we learn to absorb or internalize cultural norms around eating? Write an essay in which you compare these messages and this process of internalization to what Francine Prose (p. 197) has to say in her piece on gluttony. Does Prose seem to share Knapp's view of where our norms vis-à-vis food typically come from and the ways they come to feel so normal? How or how not?

Then and Now: *How to Make Meatloaf*

Far more than a list of ingredients and steps, each of these recipes offers a quick snapshot of the sorts of attitudes toward eating that, at two different moments in our food culture's recent history, passed for the norm. Meatloaf is a classic American dish that first became popular on family dinner tables during the Great Depression. It's a dish families could make on a budget because the recipe relied on cheaper cuts of meat and included bread or cracker crumbs as a way to create more servings. The first recipe is a classic meatloaf recipe from the Heinz ketchup company. Looking at it we may learn more about what the prevailing food attitudes were by focusing on what the recipe does *not* say — that is, on the things it simply takes for granted. The instructions are much less explicit than what we're used to today: no temperature setting for the oven, no specifications for the size of baking dish, and no order for the ingredients added. The recipe also omits nutritional information — no discussion of calories or cholesterol here, or references to recommended daily allowances of fiber or calcium. These omissions stem in part from ingrained assumptions about eating that people of this era simply regarded as *common sense.* To put it mildly, any dish whose list of ingredients goes no further than pepper, ground beef, and bologna didn't achieve popularity at a historical moment that placed a terribly high premium on physical health. The point of eating, this recipe all but says out loud, is not to make us live longer; it is to put things into our bodies that conform to a particular standard of good taste or smart spending — a standard that in this case appears to have revolved primarily around adding flavor using the least expensive ingredients possible.

Contrast the second recipe, which transforms the all-American dish. The tofu meatloaf recipe carefully acquaints its readers with the particular facts

Circa 1956

HEINZ KETCHUP MEATLOAF RECIPE

   2 lbs. ground beef
   ½ lb. bologna
   1 tablespoon grated onion
   1 cup moist cracker crumbs
   1 egg
   1 teaspoon salt
   ½ cup Heinz Tomato Ketchup
   Pepper

Chop bologna finely and add to the meat. Add other ingredients, adding Tomato Ketchup last, and bake in a moderate oven, basting frequently.

about the ingredients it assembles, a tactic exemplified in its references to "light miso," "tahini," and "dried dill." This difference underscores how much more diversified our culture's prevailing definitions of American cuisine have grown since the Depression era. But perhaps even more important, it suggests how much more worried we are about what we put into our bodies. This recipe is meat-free and includes all-natural ingredients and exotic flavors. Indeed, if this Moosewood Restaurant recipe is a reliable guide, we could well argue that ours has become a food culture in which concerns over physical health (as well as its corollary, physical appearance) and ideology now supplant expense as the primary standard by which we judge the quality of our food.

These recipes may represent night and day in terms of what goes in them, but both represent a certain anxiety over eating. The first recipe includes just a few inexpensive ingredients (and relies on ketchup to provide the zing), while the second includes numerous fresh and healthy ingredients that are tough to find in some areas and cost considerably more than a bottle of ketchup. While the first recipe's author is conscious of the cook's pocketbook, the second is conscious of his or her health and lifestyle. Each recipe provides a revealing glimpse into how meatloaf can reflect our cultural concerns.

2001

TOFU MEATLOAF

Serves 8
Prep time: 30 minutes
Baking time: 25–30 minutes

> 2 cakes firm tofu (16 ounces each)
> 2 tablespoons vegetable oil
> 2 cups diced onions
> 1 cup peeled and grated carrots
> 1 cup diced bell peppers
> 1 teaspoon dried oregano
> 1 teaspoon dried basil
> 1 teaspoon dried dill
> ⅔ cups chopped walnuts
> 1 cup bread crumbs
> 2 tablespoons tahini
> 2 tablespoons light miso
> 2 tablespoons soy sauce
> 1-2 tablespoons Dijon mustard

Press the tofu between two plates and rest a heavy weight on the top plate. Press for 15 minutes, then drain the liquid.

Meanwhile, heat the oil in a frying pan and sauté the onions, carrots, peppers, oregano, basil, and dill for about 7 minutes, until the vegetables are just tender. Crumble the pressed tofu into a large bowl, or grind it through a food processor. Stir in the walnuts, bread crumbs, tahini, miso, soy sauce, and mustard. Add the sautéed vegetables and mix well.

Preheat the oven to 350° or 375° degrees. Press the mix into an oiled casserole dish, and bake for about 30 minutes, until lightly browned.

—Reprinted from **Moosewood Restaurant New Classics,** *Copyright © 2001 by the Moosewood Collective, Clarkson N. Potter, New York, publishers.*

WRITING

1. How does each recipe seem to define "good" eating? What is supposed to make each dish worth eating? What does each recipe seem to define its standards of good eating against? Why? Write a one-page essay in which you analyze and evaluate the key differences between these two scripts. In what ways have the norms around eating changed since the first recipe was popular?

2. Both Michael Pollan (p. 174) and Loretta Schwartz-Nobel (p. 249) write at length about food and economics. What do you think each author would have to say about these meatloaf recipes? Use quotations and examples from their essays to write a brief essay comparing and contrasting how each author might respond to these recipes in terms of what they say about economics and health.

TARAS GRESCOE

Maté de Coca:
Never Say No

Our airwaves and news publications are filled with warnings and prohibitions about drug use. But what happens to our preconceptions about this issue when we reexamine them in a context in which the norms are entirely different, say one in which drugs are treated less like illicit substances and more like food? Seeking to unlock what he calls "the mystery of coca leaves," Taras Grescoe travels to Bolivia, a trip that not only affords him firsthand experience of this intoxicating herb, but more provocatively still, presents him with an entirely different way to think about American society's "war on drugs." Grescoe lives in Montreal and writes about travel for publications that include *National Geographic Traveler* and the *New York Times.* His first book, *Sacre Blues: An Unsentimental Journey through Quebec* (2000) won the Mavis Gallant Prize for Nonfiction. He has also published *The End of Elsewhere: Travels Among the Tourists* (2003) and, most recently, *Devil's Picnic: Around the World in Pursuit of Forbidden Fruit* (2005), which includes the following selection.

I N LA PAZ, THE FIRST THING THAT HITS YOU IS THAT YOU ARE HIGH. Too high. As high, probably, as you have ever been before; higher, certainly, than is proper for any human body to come in the course of a single day. Your plane curves in over the low-wattage slumscape of the highest shantytown in the world, you touch down at the highest international airport in the world, and you go through passport control fifteen hundred feet above the highest capital city in the world. Waiting at the luggage carousel for your backpack to drop onto the rubber, you are thirteen thousand feet above sea level, at the same altitude as the mountaineers who summit Eiger after two days of hard climbing.

Heaped atop the other violent dislocations of intercontinental jet travel — latitudinal, cultural, temporal — the change in altitude elicits groans of protest from your body. *Soroche,* or mountain sickness, is a kind of intoxication that afflicts those who come too high, too fast: the Andean bends, if you will. For most people, *soroche* involves a couple of days of tingling fingers, fatigue, faintness, and mild headaches, though in extreme cases fluid can collect in the brain and lead to cerebral edema, coma, and death. The day I flew south, my father called to tell me about the son of a friend, a man younger than I was, who was found dead in his La Paz hotel after retiring to his room complaining of a migraine and shortness of breath. Changing planes in the low-lying eastern Bolivian city of Santa

Cruz, I'd met a young woman from the American embassy in Uruguay, who'd offered me a blister pack of acetazolamide pills, which she said would help me metabolize oxygen better. The drug's side effects seemed almost as severe as *soroche* itself: the box recommended you call a doctor if you experienced unusual bleeding or bruising, tremors in your hands, a pain in your groin, fever, or rash. It sounded like a typically technocratic treatment; I decided to hold out for a more natural remedy.

The Bolivians, not surprisingly, have long since mastered their *soroche*. In the cab from the airport, I watched awestruck from the bubble of my fatigue as barrel-chested men in long-sleeved dress shirts jogged *up* the switchbacks we were driving down, bearing heavy backpacks. The people of the Andes owe their endurance to generations and lifetimes spent adapting to these mountains, but they also have a secret weapon in their folk armamentarium. After dropping my backpack in my hotel room, I went to a lounge in the lobby, picked a tea bag from the basket of chamomile, tutti-frutti, and anise-flavored infusions, and poured hot water over the sachet labeled "maté de coca." After letting the bag steep for five minutes, I had my first sip of coca-leaf tea.

It was mildly herbal, more reminiscent of Sleepytime than grassy-tasting yerba maté, the bitter national infusion of Argentina. More interesting than its flavor was its effect: after my second cup, the tingling in my fingers stopped and a tightness that had been flickering around my temples relaxed; after my third, I was suffused with a perceptible, if subtle, sense of relaxation and clearheadedness. Coca leaves contain fourteen different alkaloids, one of which is cocaine; a single cup of maté contains a little over four milligrams, enough to make a midsize house cat slightly more skittish than usual, though it's no more stimulating than a regular cup of coffee. There is just enough cocaine, however — as there is just enough morphine in two poppy-seed bagels — to produce a positive result on a drug test. Bolivian soccer player Luis Cristaldo got caught in a urine test after a World Cup qualifier, as did a Chicago woman who drank some coca tea she'd brought back after a vacation in Peru in 2001. Cristaldo was subsequently exonerated, but the woman lost her job at the Cook County sheriff's office.

In Bolivia, visiting dignitaries are typically offered a cup of maté de coca when they step off the plane; John Paul II accepted one, as did the king and queen of Spain, and Princess Anne, who reportedly enjoyed Bolivia's leading brand, Windsor. (Perhaps less surprisingly, Fidel Castro pointedly requested a cup on a 1993 visit, provoking cheers across the nation.) In a poor continent's poorest country, where the average income is $72 a month, coca provides a living for tens of thousands of peasant farmers. You can buy coca tea in the duty-free shop at the airport; local markets sell coca biscuits and toothpaste; and the next president of Bolivia may well be a coca grower. Eradicating coca in South America, an anthropologist told me, would be akin to ridding the northern hemisphere of coffee, tobacco, and Communion wafers.

I took my cup of maté de coca to my room, had a few sips as I watched the children in the street below dueling with discarded cardboard tubes, and wondered if the son of my father's friend would have survived his stay in La Paz if he'd drunk enough coca tea. Thanks to decades of American pressure on the United Nations, Bolivia, Argentina, and Peru are now the only places on earth where you can legally enjoy this beverage. Meanwhile, the Drug Enforcement Agency is sworn to a war whose tools include Black Hawk helicopters, chemical defoliants, and biological arms, and whose goal seems to be the utter elimination of the coca plant from the face of the earth. If there was any way out of the international prohibition of drugs, that nine-decade-long sinkhole of corruption, constantly eroding civil liberties, and wasted lives, I suspected it might lie in the contents of the soggy tea bag at the bottom of my cup.

I turned off the light and fell into a deep and dreamless sleep. Unlike a café au lait or an Earl Grey tea, maté de coca is one stimulant that doesn't keep you awake at night.

"In Bolivia, coca is part of what maintains connections between people," anthropologist Andrew Orta told me, as he soothed his *soroche* with a big bowl of vegetable soup. "It's a part of daily sociability."

We were sitting in a restaurant on Calle Linares; I was working on a llama steak — thinly sliced, none too fatty, delicious. Orta, a soft-spoken man with round glasses and thinning red hair, was an associate professor at the University of Illinois, and he'd agreed to meet me before I'd flown down to Bolivia. By coincidence, we were neighbors in the same hotel; I'd caught him reading a paperback in a patch of sunlight on the landing outside my room. South America, apparently, can be a small continent — especially for gringos carrying the Lonely Planet guide.

Orta's fieldwork involved living with Aymara peasants in Jesús de Machaqa, a town one hundred kilometers west of La Paz. About 60 percent of Bolivians are of indigenous, rather than European, descent. The two leading groups are the Aymara and the Quechua; the latter are directly descended from the Incas, whose empire of twelve million subjects once ran from Ecuador to central Chile. Though coca didn't grow in the high plains where Orta did his research, it was an essential part of daily life, brought to the altiplano through trade with other communities.

"The leadership of these communities is something all adults are expected to participate in," explained Orta, "and the highest level they achieve in this area is called *mallku*, which is a kind of community leadership that married couples undertake. During the time they serve, they're expected to carry coca around with them in a *chuspa*, or coca purse, at all times. People come to them to resolve family problems, and the way they start talking honestly and openly about something is by sharing coca. Typically, during their *mallku*, these extended patrilineal families will build an additional room around the patio, and this is where they'll receive guests. People would be kind of horrified if there was no coca."

In the traditional context, coca was offered freely, with no expectation of payment. Like tobacco, peyote, or Communion wine in other settings, it was a commodity that was excluded from the regular economy — a gift both valueless and invaluable — and meant to be consumed with other members of the community. Apart from its role in divination, coca had been used for its powerful anesthetic qualities well before the Spanish conquered the Incas in 1532.

I asked Orta whether he'd ever accepted coca from his hosts.

"Oh, sure! You know, it's pretty mild. It has a numbing effect on your mouth, but in terms of a buzz, I would say a couple of espressos would do more for you. Even the Catholic Church acknowledges the ritual use of coca now, which is a turnaround from their position in the 1950s." (And an even more radical departure from their stance of 1552, when the First Council of Lima called for a total prohibition. King Philip II of Spain called coca's stimulating effects an "*ilusión del demonjo*," only changing his tune, and overturning the ban when it was pointed out that the Indians wouldn't go down and slave in the Spanish mines without first stuffing a good wad of coca in their cheeks.) "The only people who preach against coca these days are evangelical Protestant groups, like the Mormons or Seventh-Day Adventists. But then again, they don't chew gum or smoke cigarettes."

The waitress cleared away our plates and brought two cups of coca tea, which we accompanied with puffs of another New World psychoactive, tobacco.

"You know, if you were to grow a cash crop," mused Orta, exhaling a plume of Camel smoke, "you would be foolish not to grow coca. It's perfectly suited for the Bolivian market. You never have to worry about your crop rotting; lack of demand is never a problem. And your clients actually come to you to get it."

In La Paz, the newcomer's gaze is torn between the allures of a prodigious distance and the demands of a teeming proximity. If you allow your eyes to skip up the tiers of cubical terra-cotta-toned homes on the sun-bleached hills that enfold the skyscrapers of the city center, you risk being run over by a packed microbus trolling the curb for one last passenger. Should you become obsessed with the lone toddlers holding up boxes of Q-tips and toothpicks and bars of Lux soap, you find yourself sideswiped, at the turn of the corner, by a view of the five peaks of snow-shawled Illimani, as imposingly pyramidal as the fringe-mantled women who squat behind endless piles of mousetraps, alpaca sweaters, and Windows 98 software.

So, as I entered the food market that rambles up Calle Rodriguez, I was glad that I had settled on a single desideratum — if only to shield my already overloaded senses from the surfeit of *chuño, oca, tunto,* and the two hundred or so other varieties of spotted, elongated, yellow, truffle-shaped, or dehydrated potatoes that are the mainstay of the Andean diet. The task wasn't as easy as it looked: there are many things, it turns out, that the uninitiated shopper could mistake for coca in a Bolivian market. I paused at a metal cart, with its own hand-operated mill, piled with cacao beans and dried leaves, until I realized I was dealing with a spice merchant. Beyond a wheelbarrow of puffed quinoa, I asked a juice seller behind a stack of glasses what the little green blob sunk in clear liquid was.

"*Quisa!*" she said. "It's sweet."

As the stalls crept ever higher up the hillside, I finally went into a butcher's and asked if she knew where I could find coca leaves. She came out from behind the counter and gave me a firm nudge — I was leaning against the dripping cadaver of a cow hanging from a hook.

"Coca, for chewing?" she asked, wiping her hands on a blood-stained smock.

I nodded. She tugged at my sleeve, pulled me into the street, and pointed toward the hills, directing me in the inimitable South American manner. "Go up one block, turn right, then go down one block, then down again one more half block."

Her directions led me to two fifty-kilogram burlap bags slumped on a street corner, overflowing with leaves. The stallkeeper, seated beneath a parasol, eyed me suspiciously. She was a *chola,* the term for the La Paz-born Indian women who follow a strict dress code: a bowler hat straight out of Edwardian London, and fringed shawls draped over pleated, floral-patterned skirts (a hot look, apparently, in seventeenth-century Toledo). The full *chola* is a bizarre confluence of anachronisms; it was Carmen goes to the City, in the Tibet of the Americas.

All business, she was obviously having none of my exoticizing gaze.

"How much do you want?" she asked brusquely. "One boliviano? Two? Five?"

I opted for five bolivianos' worth — the equivalent of sixty-three U.S. cents — and she scooped the leaves into a green plastic bag, which completely filled my shoulder bag.

"Would you like *lejía?*"

Lejía, which means "bleach," is actually a highly alkaline combination of burnt roots and cane sugar that facilitates the extraction of alkaloids from the leaves. The sweet variety, sold between two pieces of plastic wrap, looks like a squashed chunk of very black hashish.

I pulled out some change, among which were some Chilean pesos and Canadian quarters.

"I don't want any of your foreign money!" she said with a grimace.

Her younger colleague leaned over and said, with a giggle. "But I would like to come to your country!"

The *chola* in the bowler showed me how to nip off a piece of *lejía* with a thumbnail and fold it into the leaf. She took the opportunity to stuff her cheek with leaves.

Sizing me up, she said, "You should start with ten leaves." There had been at least three times as many in the handful she'd taken.

I told her I had high hopes they'd help with my altitude sickness. In the noontime heat, I was feeling the edges of a migraine looming every time I started walking uphill.

"They're also good for the digestion," she said, patting her round belly. "Very nutritious!"

I thanked her and found a shaded bench outside a shop where I could take the time to properly prepare my quid. The leaves were oval, dark on one side, lighter on the other, and tapered at both ends, but no more remarkable in appearance than the bay leaves that float in a pot of spaghetti sauce. I nipped a nugget of *lejía*, folded the leaf over it, and tucked it between my gums and cheek. Nip, fold, tuck: once I realized the few passersby who noticed me didn't give a rat's ass about what I was doing, I started to enjoy the rhythm of the slow-paced ritual. My fingers were soon stained black and green, my cheeks bulged — I stuffed in twenty, then thirty leaves — until I noticed the tip of my tongue was going numb. Reduced to a pulpy wad by my saliva, the leaves combined with the alkaline *lejía*, raising the pH in my mouth, which in turn broke down the coca's cell walls, finally releasing tiny amounts of cocaine. Though it was time for lunch, my hunger had disappeared. So had the throb in my temples, as the sweaty malaise of mingled jet lag and *soroche* released its grip.

Suddenly, as the coca took hold, there was no better place on earth to be in than La Paz, and I had all the time in the world, and a seemingly bottomless reserve of energy, to explore it. The precipitous sidewalks were no longer to be slogged up, step by step, but taken at a trot. On the Prado I chatted with the shoeshine boys in black Zapatista-style balaclavas, paused with a group of children who stood rapt before a sidewalk black-and-white television on which Jackie Chan's feet flew, and was anointed with holy water by a nun in the portico of the San Francisco Church. Everywhere I marked my path with globs of fluorescent green spit. It was a lot more satisfying than pan, the gum-staining, betel-nut stimulant I'd chewed in India, and a lot less disgusting than chewing tobacco, with which I'd briefly flirted as a teenager. Coca induced a subtle euphoria, longer lasting than the crystalline buzz of eternal dissatisfaction that comes with cocaine. If chemicals are all about the rush, then the plants from which they are derived offer a softer, more salutary version of the same sensation. Chewing coca, which takes a serious investment of time, is akin to pipe or cigar smoking: a habit from before the industrial revolution, ideal for days of contemplation and outdoor activity.

Perhaps too it was the context. In La Paz, there was nothing covert or shameful about chewing coca; on the contrary, it was an expression of solidarity with the people. Graffiti daubed on peeling walls called for the LIBRE CULTIVO DE COCA, the "free cultivation of coca," and T-shirts in the tourist ghettos proclaimed LA HOJA DE COCA NO ES DROGA — "the coca leaf isn't a drug." My happy, afternoon-long buzz didn't seem to corroborate this last assertion: if the coca leaf wasn't a drug, than neither was the coffee bean, *cannabis sativa*, the tobacco plant, or the opium poppy.

But if agreeing meant I could enjoy my coca with impunity, I was willing to play along. . . .

The War on Drugs is a war on plants by another name. Name a major drug of abuse, no matter how artificial or synthetic it may sound, and ultimately you can trace its existence back to a plant. OxyContin, or "hillbilly heroin," the painkiller that got conservative commentator Rush Limbaugh strung out, comes from the poppies that grow in World War I cemeteries and the highlands of Afghanistan. Crystal meth, or speed, is a synthetic modification of ephedrine, derived from the ephedra plant that grows wild throughout Asia and the American West. Nature is the great biochemical genius. In contrast, man is a dogged lab technician, shamelessly plagiarizing the complex molecules that took millions of years to evolve in rain forests and mountain meadows.

> **The War on Drugs is a war on plants by another name.**

Why do plants synthesize substances that induce euphoria, hyperactivity, or even hallucinations in animals? Simple: they can't move, and they are afflicted by mobile pests — insects and herbivores — that bore through their trunks and chew up their leaves. Unable to flee, they have resorted to chemical warfare, relying on mutation and natural selection to innovate bitter alkaloids that repel parasites by killing their appetite or sex drive, disorienting and temporarily paralyzing them. I'd already encountered a few examples in my travels: the poppy, whose seeds go into Marks & Spencer's narcotic crackers, produces morphine and thebaine, which can poison horses, cattle, and other herbivores that browse on them. The tobacco plant makes nicotine, which paralyzes its predators or sends them into convulsions. Wormwood, which is so bitter that even goats won't touch it, produces thujone, a convulsant neurotoxin that, like camphor and other terpenes, repels moths. The coffee bush makes caffeine, which prevents insects from reproducing. More interestingly, plants such as jimsonweed, or datura, produce scopolamine; which stops larger animals from grazing by sending them on a three-day-long dissociative trip of dry mouth and hallucination — overkill indeed.

Drugs, then, are poisons. In large doses, they can kill; in small doses, they intoxicate, a sensation that can be pleasurable, confusing, enlightening, and, in some cases, addictive. Early man probably observed animals — from cats lolling and mewing after gorging on catnip, to cattle overdosing on inebriating locoweed — for tip-offs about which plants to investigate. Elephants like to get drunk on the juice of fallen, fermenting berries, actually ramming the trunks of the marula tree to hasten the process. (In South Africa, the same berries are used to make a cream liqueur called amarula.) Pigeons get uncoordinated and listless when they eat cannabis seeds, which might be how the ancient Scythians figured out hemp was good for more than just rope-making. The urge to alter one's consciousness is so universal that psychopharmacologist Ronald K. Siegel has called it the fourth drive, after hunger, thirst, and sexual desire. Even when drugs aren't available, people find ways to get out of their heads, which explains such diverse phenomena as the self-flagellation of Capuchin monks, the whirling of Sufi dervishes, the meditation of Hindu sadhus, hyperventilation among children, and bungee jumping.

Every known human society has used some kind of plant intoxicant. Tongan fishermen drink endless bowls of relaxing kava kava, Somalian tribesmen while away afternoons in inspired conversation between mouthfuls of the stimulant shrub khat, and even nomads in the bleak tundra of Siberia trip out on hallucinogenic toadstool called fly agaric. (The only historical exception were the Inuit of North America, who had no greenery to speak of.) "That humanity at large will ever be able to dispense with Artificial Paradises seems very unlikely," wrote Aldous Huxley in *The Doors of Perception*. "Most men and women lead lives at the worst so painful, at the best so monotonous, poor and limited that the urge to escape, the longing to transcend themselves if only for a few moments, is and always has been one of the principal appetites of the soul."

As Huxley intuited, drugs are not just a poor, material substitute for religious transcendence, but probably the source of religion itself. Psychoactive substances are nestled too close to the heart of too many faiths for this to be mere coincidence. The Indo-Aryans, whose Rig Veda is the earliest known religious scripture, worshiped soma, the inducer of "bliss-bringing Rightness," which may have been the fly agaric or the harmel plant, a weed that has the same vision-inducing alkaloids as the Amazonian jungle vine yajé. The likes of Plato, Socrates, and Aristotle attended the Mysteries of Eleusis, a harvest festival that involved the consumption of a hallucinogenic potion, probably the ergot fungus that colonizes barley and rye and is also the source of LSD. Anthropologists have theorized that humanity's encounters with intoxicants — particularly magic mushrooms, those chemical inducers of waking dreams and transcendent visions — were the seeds that crystalized early man's capacity for religious senti-ment. Name any plant intoxicant, and you will find, even today, a group of humans who use it to worship. Peyote is a sacrament in the Native American church, marijuana is a holy herb for Rastafarians, opium candy and bhang (the pollen of cannabis) are sold in gov-ernment shops in Varanasi to induce trances in Hindu temples. And during

> **Drugs are not just a poor, material substitute for religious transcendence, but probably the source of religion itself.**

Mass, Catholics line up to consume wine (an appropriation of the Dionysian and bacchic rites of antiquity), which they believe is trans-formed into the blood of Jesus Christ as they drink it from the chalice.

Clues to the original role of drugs, as agents of pleasure, transcen-dence, and strengtheners of community (rather than addiction, impover-ishment, and alienation), lie in the way they were used in traditional societies. Even tobacco, now the most banalized of commodities, was once the object of respectful ritual. Before the arrival of Europeans, the Karuk Indians, who lived in what is now California, consumed tobacco in tribal gatherings that were limited to adult males. In large doses, nicotine provokes hallucinations, and Karuk shamans ingested so much that they vomited and went into convulsions and a deathlike trance that they believed put them into direct contact with the spirit world. European traders taught the Karuk to smoke "white man's tobacco," which was less potent, but consumed far more frequently. From occasional communal use, during which treaties were made and the pipe was passed from hand to hand, the Karuk fell into the contemporary pattern of casual private abuse and addiction. An anthropologist who lived with the Karuk noted that, as late as the 1920s, "the old-time Indians never smoked but the merest fraction of the day, disapproved even of the smoking of men as old as in their twenties, and regarded the modern boy and girl cigarette fiend with disgust."

Typically, sacramental use of drugs is also use outside of commerce. There is no charge for Communion wine, nor for the peyote consumed in the Native American church; and in traditional Rastafarian belief, mari-juana is a sacred herb that can be given as a gift but not bought or sold. (That's not to say that early civilizations — particularly the more orga-nized kleptocracies — didn't equate psychoactive plants with currency. The Aztec ruler Montezuma I, whose empire was a vast military machine for exacting tribute from subjugated peasants, limited chocolate use to warriors and kept a treasury of a billion cacao beans in his palace.) Traditional use also tended to be occasional use: hunter-gatherer Siberi-ans, for example, had to compete with reindeer foraging for psychedelic mushrooms, and — as I learned in Norway — the Vikings could afford to squander only a little of their precious grain on communal alcoholic binges. I'd seen how coca was offered to guests in traditional contexts in Bolivia. Only with the rise of modern commerce were plant drugs snatched from their sacred roles and turned into items of trade.

The first step was medicalization: in Europe, plant knowledge, once the domain of pagans, was taken over by the doctors. The pharmacopoeia of Paracelsus, considered the Father of Medicine, was a wholesale pilfering of the belladonna, cannabis, mandrake, opium, henbane, and other plants that went into the hallucinogenic flying potions of witches. The second step was industrialization: opium, for example, was refined into morphine, used to spike cheap and widely available patent medicines, and finally synthesized into heroin, which could instantly be administered through the hypodermic syringe. The hour-long tobacco pipe was supplanted by the half-hour cigar, then the five-minute cigarette. The slow, subtle high of coca leaves gave way to the instant rush of cocaine, and eventually the ten-minute buzz of crack. From one perspective, the industrialization of plant drugs was also their democratization: where a fifty-cent Havana had been the indulgence of plutocrats, nickel-a-pack Camels were well within working-class budgets. From another, it was their final debasement. There was wisdom, after all, in the religious instinct that such powerful substances should not be banal items of commerce; once you deliver them to the ingenuity of industry, you give quacks and amoral entrepreneurs a license to profit from the potentially limitless market in addiction.

These days, it is plants — atavistic, smelly, pagan — that stir modern legislators into a frenzy. Opium was probably the first drug systematically cultivated by early man; deposits of poppy seeds have been found in Neolithic Swiss lake villages dating to 6000 B.C. For most of human history, it was regarded as a panacea and served as one of the most useful painkillers and anxiety relievers in the pharmacopoeia of medical men and women. Throughout the nineteenth century, when opiate nostrums could be purchased at drugstores and soda counters in the form of Mrs. Winslow's Soothing Syrup or Battley's Sedative Solution, the typical dope fiend was a middle-aged woman, troubled by nothing more than constipation, drowsiness, and shame. (Doctors too were quiet users. Dr. William Halsted, the father of American surgery and founder of Johns Hopkins Medical Center, took morphine all his adult life and died at the age of seventy, after having performed some of his most brilliant operations as a junkie.)

Opium was first banned in 1875 in San Francisco — the first modern law criminalizing drug users — on the ground that it was a Chinese conspiracy to addict the white youth of California. Cocaine had to be proscribed because it turned the Southern Negro into a crazed rapist.

Marijuana presented more of a challenge; it was hard, after all, to demonize a weed that tended to make people giggle and eat too many potato chips. In the absence of any demonstrable nefariousness, the prohibitionists decided to toss every possible accusation at cannabis to see what would stick. When smoking marijuana was nothing more than an obscure habit of Mexicans who came to the Southwest looking for work, scare stories about dope-crazed psychotic killers led to the El Paso ordinance of 1914 that gave local police the perfect pretext for arbitrary body searches of immigrants. Headlines about Negro jazz musicians in Harlem smoking "muggles" gave additional impetus to the passing of the Marijuana Tax Act of 1937, which required anybody growing marijuana to apply for a tax stamp. (It was the prototypical catch-22, well before Joseph Heller: the Treasury Department *didn't give* stamps to hemp farmers.) In the 1950s, the emphasis switched to the fifth column: pot raids netted entertainment types like Robert Mitchum and Gene Krupa, and drug peddlers were accused of being Communists trying to dope up the youth of America.

Eventually, though, the official propaganda about marijuana — that it caused murderous rampages, that it was a steep, slippery slope to heroin — started to backfire as tens of millions tried it without turning into bank-robbing Bolshevik junkies. By the 1960s, the "enemy within" — once a minority of beatniks and Reds — turned out to be anybody curious enough to take a toke at a party, and an unofficial civil war, between turned-on baby boomers and the so-called silent majority, was declared. Richard Nixon abrogated fundamental constitutional principles by empowering the newly created Drug Enforcement Agency to tap phones and spy on private citizens; Ronald Reagan launched the War on Drugs, overturning a law dating to the Civil War that prevented the U.S. military from interfering in civil affairs; and George Bush Sr. built more jails to house the casualties of the Zero Tolerance Program. (The only retreats came during Jimmy Carter's presidency, in which marijuana was actually decriminalized in Oregon, and Bill Clinton's tenure, when some drug war money was diverted into research on addiction.)

Too much has been written about the absurdity of marijuana prohibition for me to dwell on it for long here. The immeasure of the penalties has become a kind of cliché — even conservative legislators sense there's something disproportionate about the fact that a citizen of Oklahoma can be jailed for life for growing a single marijuana plant in his yard. By 2000, the American prison population reached two million — the highest of any nation in the world, including China — and a quarter of them were serving time for drug offenses, mostly possession. Fortunately for the government, the War on Drugs is rather good for the budget. Since the Zero Tolerance Policy was introduced under Ronald Reagan in 1988, the feds have been allowed to seize all assets associated with drug arrest; including, in one incident, a $2.5 million yacht on which a tenth of an ounce of marijuana was found. The U.S. Customs Service is the only government department that regularly turns a profit.

Was there a way to end this institutionalized insanity? Frankly, I wasn't optimistic. The notion of resacralizing traditional drugs, like Delachaux's absinthe and Rivera's coca leaves, struck me as romantic but disingenuous: most users, certainly in North America and Europe, are too removed from traditional communities for this to be anything but a New Age affectation, a kind of bogus Timothy Leary trip. Besides, the genie has been out of the bottle far too long: it would be impossible to unlearn the knowledge of extracting cocaine from the coca shrub or of synthesizing heroin from the poppy. As Ronald K. Siegel has written, "Once the alkaloids are freed from the plant, it is difficult to put them back." His technological solution was to campaign for the invention of new drugs. "The ideal intoxicants," he wrote in an article in the *Washington Post*, "would balance optimal positive effects, such as stimulation or pleasure, with minimal or nonexistent toxic consequences. The drugs would be ingested as fast-acting pills or liquids or breathed in the form of gases. They would have fixed durations of action and built-in antagonists to prevent excessive use or overdoses." Wishful thinking: given the current political climate in the United States, there was no way the National Research Council would in the near future be funding university labs to devise more pleasurable highs for the population.

The solution was perhaps not to go forward, in the hopes of brewing brave, new, and nonaddictive forms of soma, but to stick with the plants that have accompanied humanity since before humans could stand upright. Khat, coca, poppies, kratom, iboga, ergot, psilocybin, ayahuasca, kava, salvia: there are enough substances in the natural world to keep humanity busy for a long time. And, as the growers of Purple Thai and Sweet Skunk (not to mention herbicide-resistant "super-cocas") have shown, a lot can be achieved through traditional plant-breeding techniques. Legislators could start by acknowledging the absurdity of outlawing plants and stop incarcerating people for planting seeds on their own land. Making milder alternatives to addictive drugs available might bring about a slow but subtle change. Under Prohibition, the popularity of hard liquor soared; but given the easy availability and social acceptance that followed repeal, people reverted to milder forms of alcohol, so that most drinkers now get their ethanol in the form of beer and wine. Just as not everybody prefers hashish to marijuana, it's likely that, if plant-derived alternatives to hard drugs were available, many users would opt for the milder forms. (Interestingly, marijuana use by teenagers actually decreased in the decade that followed the introduction of cannabis "coffee shops" in Holland in 1976; to this day, only 8 percent of Dutch teenagers between the age of sixteen and nineteen are users, versus 16 percent in the same age group in the United States, where full prohibition is in effect.) It's a move that could start in the industrialized nations of the developed world — the ones that suffer most from drug addiction. It would keep Bolivian farmers, like Alberto Chura, in business, growing a mild, pleasant stimulant. Meanwhile, the United States could devote some of the up to $40 billion it spends annually on the War on Drugs to supporting treatment programs for addicts, rather than buying new helicopters.

The only thing that encouraged me was my certainty that the War on Drugs was ultimately doomed to failure. Short of defoliating the entire planet and napalming all of the earth's arable land, the total eradication of drug crops is an unattainable goal: the yearly needs of every heroin addict in the United States could be supplied with the poppies grown on a single twenty-square-mile patch of land. An entire year's supply of cocaine for every user in the United State could be stashed in thirteen truck trailers; and all of the thirty tons of heroin consumed in Britain would fit in a single midsize truck. If Armageddon reduced civilization to a handful of farmers, I was positive that one of the first crops they'd harvest would include some kind of psychoactive: coffee or coca bushes, cannabis or tobacco plants, or the grain and grapes to make alcohol. The human drive to intoxication, self-transcendence, or temporary escape — whatever you want to call it — is too strong to be denied.

The people of Bolivia didn't have to be reminded. They had the statues with bulging cheeks, dating back millennia before the arrival of the Spaniards, to prove that they had always coexisted with mama coca. And they had reason to be optimistic: in South America at least, the tide was turning on the war against plants. Xavier too was convinced that former coca grower Evo Morales, or another coca-friendly indigenous leader, was going to be the next president of the nation.

I lifted the soggy tea bag out of my cup and had a sip of maté de coca, anticipating its subtly revivifying lift. Maybe after dinner, I'd treat myself to another quid of coca leaves and spend some time writing in my journal. One thing was pretty certain: I'd better enjoy it while I could, while I was still in the heartland of legal coca production. There would be no smuggling a backpack full of dried coca leaves back home. If there's one thing that customs officers hate — and that their dogs love to sniff out — it's plants.

Besides, my next destination wasn't exactly a haven for narcotourists. And though there was a forbidden substance waiting for me, it wasn't one I was looking forward to trying.

DISCUSSION

1. For people in Bolivia, Grescoe reports, chewing coca leaves is a commonplace and universally accepted activity. What particular rules governing how coca may be consumed does Grescoe outline? How, in your view, do these rules help explain why chewing coca stands as such an unremarkable and innocuous norm?

2. Like coca, Grescoe tells us, virtually every other recreational drug has its origin in the natural world. In your opinion, what difference (if any) does this fact make? What happens to your assumptions about drugs and drug-taking when you start thinking of them as "natural" activities?

3. Take a moment to ponder the title of Grescoe's essay. How does it compare to that well-known prohibition in our culture to "just say no" to drugs? In what ways does Grescoe's discussion seem to critique the particular attitudes toward drugs promoted by the "just say no" campaign?

WRITING

4. Grescoe devotes much of his essay to describing the manifold pleasures and payoffs of chewing coca leaves: additional energy, enhanced focus, vanishing headaches, even intensified feelings of happiness. Write a persuasive or argumentative essay in which you seek to discredit the benefits Grescoe itemizes and persuade your readers of the downsides or costs of chewing coca. Make sure to use quotes from Grescoe's essay in your counterargument.

5. At first glance, it might seem odd to talk about consuming drugs in the same way we talk about consuming food. What ways that Grescoe writes about the consumption of coca leaves mirror the rules or norms about food consumption? Write an essay in which you discuss how these rules are similar and how they diverge. You may want to consider eating norms as they are addressed by writers such as Francine Prose (p. 197), Jason Fagone (p. 204), or Caroline Knapp (p. 217) in your argument.

6. Grescoe and Michael Pollan (p. 174) both devote considerable attention to the role the idea of "naturalness" plays in our contemporary eating habits. In an essay, compare, contrast, and evaluate the similarities and differences in how each writer depicts this *idea* of naturalness as a powerful cultural *ideal.*

LORETTA SCHWARTZ-NOBEL

America's Wandering Families

There is a widespread, and false, conviction among many Americans that in the United States "nobody starves." Seeking to explode this myth, Loretta Schwartz-Nobel takes her readers on a tour of one of our nation's many homeless shelters, relating her encounters with a handful of the thousands of Americans who depend on these places for their very survival. Schwartz-Nobel's first article on hunger appeared in 1974 in *Philadelphia* magazine. In 1981 she published a book on the issue called *Starving in the Shadow of Plenty.* Her nonfiction works include *Engaged to Murder: The Inside Story of the Main Line Murders* (1987) and *Baby Swap Conspiracy: The Shocking Truth behind the Florida Case of Two Babies Switched at Birth* (1993). In her most recent book, *Growing Up Empty* (2002), she returns to the issue of hunger in America. The following excerpt is from that book.

EACH NIGHT, WHEN DARKNESS FALLS, MORE THAN 100,000 AMERICAN children have no home of their own to go back to. Some of them sleep in cars or abandoned buildings and eat whatever they can find. Some stay in overcrowded houses with friends or relatives. Others sleep in cheap run-down motels or overpriced residential hotels. The rest lay their heads down on the streets or in crowded, often dangerous shelters. Most move from place to place as they search for food and shelter. Every year their numbers increase.

These children and their parents signal the rise of a new, more desperate level of poverty and hunger in America. Twenty-five years ago, the homeless population was composed primarily of the mentally ill, the alcoholic, or the drug addicted. Now that underclass has increased from single people who were lost long before homelessness ruled their lives, to families who are lost because it does. "Today homeless families account for between 38 percent and 77 percent of the homeless population, depending on the area. Two-thirds of the people in these families are children."

In the year 2000, unemployment was lower than it had been in thirty years but hunger, poverty, and the number of children without homes was higher than it had been since the Depression of the 1930s.

Part of this was due to the increasing gap between the incomes of the working poor and the cost of living. More and more families who lived in wealthy cities like San Diego simply couldn't afford the rent and ended up on the street. Today, their children create an underclass of hungry street urchins who sometimes wander among the wealthy. Their need for emergency food assistance is often as urgent as their need for housing.

> ## Like many cities, . . . the well educated and highly skilled prosper while one in three children live in poverty.

Like many cities, San Diego is a place where the well educated and highly skilled prosper while one in three children live in poverty.

St. Vincent de Paul Village, one of the largest and best-known shelters in the country, is only minutes from San Diego's upscale Gas Light District, where well-dressed tourists and residents eat expensive meals at lovely restaurants, but it is also a world away.

St. Vincent's rises like a giant hacienda out of the grim industrial section of town. The perimeter of the huge yellow brick building takes up an entire city block. The main two-door entrance is topped by a bell tower reminiscent of the old California missions. In the year 2000, St. Vincent de Paul Village had an annual budget of $9.5 million. It employed 180 people and had more than 500 volunteers. Each night, about 850 men, women and children slept at St. Vincent's and, each day, more than 2,000 hungry people were fed there. All this is relatively recent.

The Village began as a small breakfast feeding program for the homeless in 1982, when the late Bishop Maher of the Diocese of San Diego decided to respond to the growing needs of the homeless. A short time later, he asked Father Joe Carroll, a native of New York, to spearhead the new project. Father Joe had worked at jobs that ranged from bookstore manager to teacher before becoming an ordained Roman Catholic priest at the age of thirty-three. During his first eight years in the priesthood, he had developed a reputation for being a man who made things happen. Between 1982 and 1987, true to his reputation, Father Joe raised $11.5 million for St. Vincent's.

When he began fund-raising, he had three major objectives: the first was to create a facility that would last forever; the second was to make it a beautiful building that would enhance the self-esteem of the people it served, and the third was to provide comprehensive services. Father Joe designed what he called a campus or a "one stop shopping center" so that the homeless could get the food, shelter, health care, child care, education, counseling, public assistance, jobs, and permanent housing they needed. His unique concept became an internationally recognized model, but Father Joe still wasn't satisfied. He said he would not rest until all the homeless in downtown San Diego who wanted a bed had one. At that time there were over four thousand homeless people in San Diego. So, even feeding two thousand people a day and providing beds for eight hundred left him with a long way to go.

"The lunch line at St. Vincent's begins forming at nine A.M. each morning and stretches around the block by ten. We feed five hundred to six hundred people an hour, every day, seven days a week," explained John Moore, the heavyset, cheerful retired military officer who serves as the director of volunteers. "Families always come first, and then the disabled, but the mass of people waiting for food includes the homeless and the working poor and the military families. Some come only occasionally but we can usually pick out a hundred or a hundred fifty regulars, people who come every day. We ask no questions because we don't want to make them feel uncomfortable about being here. We know that many of them are not homeless, at least not yet. So I always tell them, 'Save your money to pay your rent and your other bills and come here to eat with us. That way you won't become homeless.'

"We also provide medical help to anyone without insurance," Moore explained as we walked through the mission's kitchen, filled with gleaming pots, cooks learning their trade, and volunteers practicing their skills. It was noon now and the dining room was rapidly filling up. Hundreds of women and children were already sitting at long, narrow tables, so close together that they were almost elbow to elbow.

About two hundred more people with trays in their hands were walking along the rapidly moving line. A dozen or so of those had the dazed look in their eyes that comes with having been at the bottom too long. It was like nothing I had ever seen before but a lot like what I imagined a Red Cross relief effort might look like in a third world country during a famine or after a natural disaster. It seemed almost impossible to believe that this was actually San Diego. The hall was filled with a loud but indecipherable hum. There were so many people eating and talking at once that it was impossible to hear what anyone was saying.

A pretty, young blonde girl in a pink T-shirt and black shorts caught my eye. She was holding a baby and had been led to the front of the line. Both the mother and baby were stuffing food into their mouths as if they were starving.

"We'd rather be overcrowded like this than turn away someone who needs us in their moment of crisis," John said, speaking loudly and leaning close enough for me to hear. "Our determining factor is whether they are at risk. If there is a child involved like that one over there on the line, we always immediately assume that they are at risk."

As we watched the young woman and the baby, I couldn't help wondering where her own mother and father were, what had gone wrong at home and how she and her little daughter had fallen through all the cracks in all the programs and wound up here.

"People are often starving when they first arrive at our door because they have waited too long to come to us," John said, as if he were reading my thoughts. "They have resisted us too hard. They are also often sick for the same reason. We have four volunteer doctors and nurses who see thirteen hundred to fifteen hundred patients every month. There is no charge to them. The only requirement is that they have no health insurance. We've had the American Medical Association visit us here to see how we do it. That's how amazed they are.

"Our biggest concern," John added as my eyes moved away from the baby and her mother out over the huge crowd, "is how we can help people get back on their feet. It starts with the simple gift of a meal. It's usually the hunger that brings them in, but the urgency of hunger provides us with the opportunity to address the deeper, longer-term series of needs. People usually want help, and after their second or third time eating here, they feel safe enough to start asking questions about our other services.

"Meeting their needs is a huge challenge. We know we can't do it all but we just keep trying. There were five or six thousand people on our streets last winter. They come because it's warm here. They often just don't realize how difficult it is to find work or affordable housing in San Diego. They also don't know how tough it can be to live without shelter even in a warm climate. We respect the fact that it's hard for them to come to us. A lot of people are very proud and they're afraid that if they show up here they will be considered incompetent. Some of them think that they might lose their kids. They are scared to death of that.

> *A lot of people are . . . afraid . . . they will be considered incompetent.*

"One woman came here for lunch when her baby was only a few days old. She was living out on the street but she didn't tell us that, she just said she wanted food. We accepted that and sent her to the lunchroom. We deliberately don't have any caseworkers in the lunchroom because we don't want to frighten people like her away. We want them to feel comfortable coming here. We want them to know that they can eat with no questions asked and no downstream repercussions. Only when they ask do we tell them that we are a resource center in the fullest sense, a helping hand, not just a handout."

As John talked, the line of hungry people just kept coming and coming in what seemed to be an almost endless procession.

"Do you ever run out of food?" I asked, glancing at the mother and baby again. They were finally about to sit down but a lot of the food on their tray had already disappeared. Some, I noticed, had been stuffed directly into the mother's pockets.

"Yes," John said. "We run out all the time. It's a constant turnover. The food comes in and it goes back out. We never know exactly how much we'll need or even how much we'll get. Even with our regular suppliers like Food Chain, it's hard to predict. Both the supply and the demand are always uncertain. The only thing we know is that we always need more. There is really never enough.

"But then sometimes, just when we're feeling most concerned, something amazing happens. Like last year, Bill Gates was planning a big party for two or three thousand people, and then the weather got bad. When the party was canceled, he donated the food to us. Bill Gates was personally out there along with Father Joe helping to unload the food. Can you imagine that? Bill Gates himself unloading all those crates of food for the hungry." John grinned broadly. "It renewed my faith.

"Father Joe doesn't run the Village like a priest," he explained, turning serious again. "He runs it like a businessman, like Gates himself might. He has to because, just to keep things going, he needs to raise $43,000 every day. We are on a $24-million-a-year non-profit budget. But at the same time, we're independent, at least in our thinking. We've turned down grants, big grants from the government, because Father Joe doesn't want them to control him. We could have grown bigger, quicker, but he wants to remain true to his vision and true to his dream. He's an organized man but he's also a man with a vision. To do what he's done, you need both. If you're not organized, you will simply be overwhelmed by the need that's out there. It would be like taking a bag of bread crumbs and throwing it up in the sky and all of a sudden there would be one hundred birds. You can't just say, 'Come and eat,' without a plan and without resources because you will be overwhelmed. They will want more than you have to give.

"Father Joe's a bubbly guy who gives parties and does a lot of entertaining to raise money so we can keep on expanding. His entire job now is fund-raising. He signs one hundred fifty letters a day. He's turned over the daily operations to others. Some people think that's a shame, but after all, he's just one man, one man who doesn't know the word stop. Folks like me are here because we believe in Father Joe and we believe in his dream. His belief empowers us. Because of it, there is nothing we can't do. We can make the rules, we can bend the rules and we can break the rules. Our vision is to do what we can for everyone who is in need. It is a huge vision but it is also as individual as each person we serve."

I was still thinking about St. Vincent's the next day at lunchtime as I sat in my car in front of the Presbyterian Crisis Center. The modest, yellow clapboard house on Market Street was about as different from St. Vincent's in appearance as anything I could imagine. The clientele, however, were very similar. There were several mothers with small children, an elderly couple, and a father with two teenage daughters sitting on the porch eating oranges.

The place had the look of a cozy cottage that had been misplaced on a busy street in a poor neighborhood. The front porch was filled with white chairs and the low green fence was covered by creeping vines and bounded by a small city lot. The Crisis Center, which began in the late '80s, provides emergency food, clothing, transportation tokens and whatever other emergency assistance they can.

"We sit down with people," explained director Bill Radatz, the warm, articulate pastor who heads the Presbyterian Ministry, "and we say, 'Have you thought things through and figured out why you are in crisis?' We've got some folks who have been coming here every month for years and others who are in an acute state for the first time in their lives. We try not to enable them but, at the same time, we want to meet their needs. Sometimes, it's a delicate balance."

Then Bill stopped talking and leaned back in his chair. "On second thought, I'm not sure I really meant what I just said about it being a delicate balance. I think most of the people we see here really do want to be self-sufficient. We've moved more toward advocacy recently because so many people are just trapped in an economic situation where they can't earn enough to make it no matter what they do. Housing availability in San Diego is down to two percent and some people are spending between fifty and seventy percent of their income on a place to live. We know that they will never work their way out of poverty when that much of their income is spent on shelter.

"To barely get by, and I mean barely, a family of four needs to have someone who earns eleven dollars an hour, forty hours a week plus benefits. So if it's five dollars and seventy-five cents an hour and there are no benefits, no matter how hard they are working, we know they are doomed. Our politicians don't have the political will to help these people by changing the system or even the minimum wage, at least not nearly enough. They'd rather pretend that the people had problems instead of admit that the system did."

Bill stood up, walked to his office door, and closed it for privacy. "The political will is to eliminate welfare, not to eliminate poverty," he said. "It's a very important distinction. They want to cover up the problem, not solve it. On the other hand, it is also true that a few of our clients are not highly motivated enough. I've had people come to me and say that they don't have time to work because getting food takes all day. After breakfast, they have to wait on the lunch line, then after lunch they have to get on the dinner line." He smiled. "I know it sounds like a joke and I personally don't accept it as a reason to give up on working, and yet I also know that there's more than a grain of truth to it."

> *"The political will is to eliminate welfare, not to eliminate poverty."*

"Yes," I said, as the memory of two thousand people stretched around several blocks came back. "The lunch line at St. Vincent's starts forming at nine A.M. and it's halfway around the block by ten. It takes three hours just to get lunch."

"You think that's difficult? Take a look at this free-meal announcement," Bill said as he handed me a sheet that listed other free-meal centers in the San Diego area.

I glanced down at the page:

- Breakfast — Lutheran Church, Third and Ash — 9:00 A.M. *Fridays only*

- Lunch — Neil Good Day Center, 299 17th Street — 1:30 P.M. *Wednesdays only*

- Dinner — Vacant lot, 13th and Broadway — 4:30 P.M. *Thursdays only*

There were a half dozen more meal sites on the list that were scattered throughout the city but many served one meal only, one day a week. I thought about how tough it would be to get to the right place at the right time on the right day for the right meal without any money or transportation, and how difficult the logistics might get if you were also working part- or full-time but didn't earn enough for food. To make it even more complicated there was a note at the bottom of the page that said you must attend church services to receive certain meals at certain sites. In some cases you also had to attend services at one specific address or on one specific day to get a ticket to eat your meal at another site on another day. When I pointed this out to Bill, he nodded and said, "Yes, I know, and some people have to figure out how to get over here to the crisis center first to get a free bus token to take them over there."

When I turned the sheet over, I saw that in order to get a free token, a client had to remember to bring valid identification or a birth certificate. In some cases, they also needed a social security card and appropriate clothing. Even then, the tokens were strictly limited to six per month.

As we talked, Bill led me into the small client waiting room. I immediately spotted the same mother and baby I had seen eating so quickly the day before on the lunch line at St. Vincent's. I smiled at the mother and thought I saw a flash of recognition in her eyes.

"I saw you yesterday at St. Vincent's," I ventured, stooping down to greet the baby, who was sitting in a small, portable plaid stroller with red plastic wheels.

"Yes. I remember you," she said shyly. Her smile was beautiful. Her eyes were pale blue and shining.

Everything about her, even her voice, her pink T-shirt, her short, blonde hair, and her perfect teeth made her seem more like a midwestern high school cheerleader than a hungry, homeless mother.

"Do you live around here?" I asked while the baby squeezed my index finger. She laughed, nervously.

"I don't know where I live right now," she said, seeming to take my question literally. "It's like I really don't live anywhere. I mean I don't have a place. That's why I'm here."

"I'm sorry," I said, hoping I hadn't embarrassed her.

"That's OK," she answered, sweetly. "I just said that, I don't know why. I know what you meant. I grew up in Michigan then one of my brothers invited me to move to Arizona. While I was there, I met an ex-Marine. We're still best friends but we got divorced when he moved back to New York to finish college. Things have been pretty bad ever since."

I settled down in the chair next to her, told her about the book I was writing, and asked if she'd like to be part of it.

"Wow, me in a book? Sure, that's cool. But why would anyone care about me?" She tilted her head and smiled her beautiful smile again. "My father never did. My stepfather never did. I thought my husband was different till he started hitting me and messing around with other girls, but I think that's because we were too young for a committed relationship."

"Were you abused?" I asked, thinking of Bertha and the statistics on poverty and homelessness.

First, she shrugged and said, "No, not really," then the story poured out. "He beat me up a couple of times but he was always sorry. Now he's gone back to his old girlfriend but I don't think it will work out for the two of them. My mother always said an X is an X for some reason and I believe that. My mom's still in Michigan with my stepfather. I really miss her a lot. I came out here with my mother-in-law. It's kind of a screwed-up situation. See, she's HIV positive because her husband was on drugs. She needed care and she couldn't get it in Arizona, so we came out here together with a hundred fifty dollars after bus fare. We got a room at the Y but then she got real sick and went into the hospital. I ran out of money. My real mom always said I was impulsive and I guess I didn't think this thing through very well.

"I get three hundred fifty dollars a month from my husband whenever he remembers. It goes directly into my checking account. I think it will come soon but it's not here yet. I only had twenty-nine cents left yesterday and we were really hungry. I mean like really hungry. We hadn't eaten in two days. That's when you saw me. Right after lunch, I applied for welfare. I hate the idea of getting welfare and if I didn't have a baby, I'd rather live on the beach. But the baby needs food and shelter and stuff."

As Tina spoke, I was struck again by the fluctuations in her tone, which wavered between childishness and maturity, depression and cheerfulness, hope and fear.

She picked her baby up. "You can't live on the beach," she cooed. "No. No. It's too hot and you're too little." She kissed the baby then put her back in the stroller.

"So, I told the caseworker that we were homeless and we needed help right away and she gave us this hotel voucher for one night. But what good is a one-night voucher when another night's coming in just a few hours?"

Then Jean, an attractive, well-dressed, middle-aged caseworker, came over to us. "Tina," she said softly, "I've pulled some strings and gotten you and April into St. Vincent's. Be there at the front desk at 4:30. No later." She stroked the baby's hair and continued without waiting for an answer. "They're strict, and if you're late you can lose your place. They'll keep you there for ninety days and then you can apply for transitional housing."

Tina's eyes widened. Her face turned crimson. "Wow. Ninety days, ninety whole days," she said. "That's ninety days I don't have to worry."

She started to laugh with childlike delight then suddenly she was crying.

"I knew something good was going to happen when I walked in here today," she said, hugging Jean. "I could just feel it. Thank you sooo much. How did you do it? How'd you ever get me in?"

"I pulled all the strings," Jean answered gently. "We're small and they're big but they owe us, and every once in a while when I really need a favor, I remind them of that."

Tina was still laughing and crying. "I just know we're gonna be safe there. We were at their food line yesterday. I was so hungry that I was about to faint. The place was jam-packed. It was the longest food line I've ever seen in my whole life and I thought, how am I ever gonna stand here on this line and wait my turn, but guess what? They saw me holding my baby and they came right over and led us to the front of the line, I mean the very front, and then they gave us all this food. They didn't just give us a little. They gave us a lot, a whole lot. I'm not used to eating very much anymore 'cause for a long time I've just been eating a little here and there and giving the rest to my baby, but at St. Vincent's there was so much that I filled up both of my pockets and we ate some for dinner last night and some for breakfast this morning."

She sniffed then laughed again. "Boy, I still can't believe it. No more going hungry for ninety whole days. I've been hungry a lot lately. Even when I got my child support, it was only three hundred fifty dollars, and my rent was two hundred ninety-five dollars including utilities, so that left just fifty-five dollars a month for food and everything else. We haven't had a phone for two years. But I sure learned how to shop. I bought a lot of rice and beans and Bisquick mix. I bought big bags of cereal for two dollars and powdered milk because it is cheaper and it lasts longer. I almost never bought meat." She shook her head incredulously again. "I still can't get over this. I feel like I've just been rescued. I thought about asking the people yesterday at St. Vincent's if we could stay there, but when I saw how many people they had on that line, I said to myself, 'No way. Never. There's no room for us here.'"

Another flood of tears poured down Tina's cheeks. "I'm not sure why I can't stop crying," she said, laughing again. "I'm just so happy. I think it's because this is the start of something good. I think my luck is finally going to change. I can just sort of like feel it."

She wiped her eyes with the bottom of her pink T-shirt then tucked the shirt into her shorts. "I want to go back to college so much." She sniffled. "And I want to major in business and then someday, I want to own a chain of hotels." Tina was talking quickly now and her flawless young face was a brighter pink than her shirt. She looked pretty and buoyant. She raised her shoulders, let them drop again and wrinkled her nose. "Well, maybe it won't be a chain exactly," she said, making the compromise with herself out loud. "But it has to be at least two hotels. If you're rich and you're mean, you will go to the expensive hotel. If you're nice, you can go to the free hotel even if you have money.

"You know," she added reflectively. "In a weird way, it's a funny thing that I'm homeless, me of all people, because ever since I was a little girl and I saw this huge farmhouse one day, my whole focus has been on housing. I couldn't have been more than four but I can still remember exactly how that farmhouse looked. It had three stories and it had to have at least ten bedrooms. I told my momma that I wanted to buy it and paint it blue, not just any blue but cobalt blue with a fluorescent pink door. Then I wanted my whole broken-up family to come and live there all together in that one farmhouse. See, my stepbrothers lived with their mother and I only got to see them once in a while. My stepdad had five kids from before and one little girl with my mom. That's my little sister. I'd kill for her. She was two and a half years younger than me and I always protected her. If she was bad, which was pretty often, my stepdad would whip out his big black belt with the brass buckle, but, I'd always run in front of her and say, 'I did it, Dad. I did it. It was me.' So I'd get hit, of course.

"My husband said I was abused. I never thought of it that way. I thought it was just another whopping. Anyhow, it was my idea, my dream that we'd all come together in this one big house and my stepfather would have to leave because there would be no whopping allowed. Then we'd be a real family and live happily ever after.

"My real father died when I was very little. I don't remember him. My stepfather works for General Motors. My mom's a school cook."

Some more tears leaked out of Tina's eyes and landed on her shorts.

"I'm sorry I'm so emotional today and I know I'm talking too fast and too much. I'm just so relieved. See, I would never ask my mom to send me any money because I know she would do it and then she'd get in trouble with my stepdad and he'd wop her. I've always taken the fall for her too, for her and for my little sister. I never want her to ask him for anything that will bring a whopping down on her. That's why I never want her to have to send money."

"Why'd you always take the fall, honey?" a very thin, sallow-skinned woman who introduced herself as Melissa asked. "Why do you think it's your place to get punished?"

I had noticed the woman watching and listening to us a few minutes before but I had been too captivated by Tina's breathless speech to think much about it. I looked at her more carefully now. She had a sad face. Her forehead was high and deeply creased. She was much thinner than she was meant to be and her teeth were brown and rotted.

Tina shrugged. "I don't know why I took the fall," she answered, look-ing confused and a little uncomfortable. "I guess it's just the way I am. But I better get going now so I won't be late for the shelter." She hugged me and invited me to stop by and see her once she was settled.

"My son Shad's a bright boy," Melissa said even before Tina was out the door, "but he was failing in school because he was always hungry. Now, he gets As and Bs because I go to the store almost every day and steal food for him so he can concentrate. We've talked about it together, my son and me. I'm not proud of it but I'm not ashamed either. It's just something I have to do to take care of my boy. I tried all the other options first and they didn't work."

She leaned closer. There was an odor I recognized but couldn't name. I'd smelled it before in urban tenements and in rural shacks but I had never known if it was the smell of illness, of hunger, or of simply being unwashed. A wave of nausea swept over me and I felt myself moving back a little.

"I always tell my boy never to steal. If there is anyone getting caught and getting in trouble, I want it to be me."

I looked up and nodded to indicate that I understood the fierce pro-tective instinct.

"I go in with my purse and my backpack, then I get a shopping cart," Melissa explained. "I put the things I'm going to buy into the big part and, in the little part where the baby's supposed to sit, I put the things that I'm going to steal. I keep my purse open and I put some small things in there. I also put some flat items like cheese and lunch meat under my sweat-shirt, which has a tight band at the bottom. I wait till I get to an aisle where there are no cameras or people before I take the things from the top part of the cart and put them into my backpack."

Melissa looked at me again to check my reaction.

"There are two tricks to not getting caught," she said, solemnly. "The first is to make sure everyone there thinks you're a regular customer. The second is to always buy a couple of items."

She paused again. "Food is the only thing I have ever stolen. I still steal it because I have no choice. I have to do it or my son and I will both go without eating. There is nothing and nobody that's going to tear us apart. Over the past year, I've done it a lot. This month, we got thirty-seven dollars in food stamps. Thirty-seven dollars spread over four weeks. You know how far that goes? Usually, for me personally, I only take what I consider to be the necessities, but last week I stole some coffee for myself and a candy bar to go with it. I knew I shouldn't

> ## *I have to do it or my son and I will both go without eating.*

have done it because they were luxuries that I didn't have to have. I think I just needed to pamper myself and I gave in to it." Her face colored. "For Shad, it's a different story. He's a growing boy. He has to eat. Last week, I stole meat and a lot of other things he enjoys. When I got home, I dumped out the backpack and the purse I was carrying and I compared everything I bought with everything I had stolen. It was fifty-eight dollars that I stole and ten dollars that I bought. There's just no other way. Fruit is too expensive, even milk. Meat is way too high.

"Yesterday, I bought a couple of potatoes and some macaroni and cheese, the cheap things to go with dinner, but all the rest I stole."

Melissa straightened up and folded her arms defensively across her chest.

"What the hell else am I supposed to do with thirty-seven dollars in food stamps, a growing teenage boy and a boss who doesn't pay me? Whenever I go to the store, I take a little something. Lately, I almost feel like it's our right because I work hard. I've worked hard ever since I was a young girl and it never got me anywhere."

She slumped down in her chair again.

"I prefer to be honest," she said. "I'm really trying to make it without stealing. Today I got three bags of food from the Salvation Army but we get so tired of eating that stuff. I know the poor aren't supposed to care what they eat, but they do just like everyone else, especially the kids. You don't get any fresh meat or even sandwich meat. I've tried everything else and I've resigned myself to the fact that the only way to eat right when you are poor is to take what you can't afford to buy.

"My welfare check was five hundred forty dollars a month. Then, Welfare to Work came along. They hooked me up with a job and my stamps were cut. My job was cleaning empty apartments so they could be rented. It was hard work with mops and brooms, vacuums and scrub buckets, bending over half the day with a bad back. I was supposed to be paid six dollars and twenty-five cents an hour once a month, but that's not how it went. I worked for one month, then on payday my boss told me that I had to work another month. I said, 'Wait a minute. I started May thirteenth and now it's June seventeenth. In my book that's more than a month.' He said, 'No, love. That's not how it works. One month is always withheld.' Meanwhile, welfare thought I'd been paid and they cut all my benefits.

"I brought my boss a paper saying he hadn't paid me and I asked him to sign it so I could keep getting my welfare. 'Not now, love,' he said. 'But they're cutting me off welfare,' I told him. He didn't care. He didn't give a damn. He wasn't signing anything. I couldn't pay my rent so I lost my apartment. I was still working full-time but now I was homeless and hungry. I was desperate and panicked. I was half out of my mind when I finally came to the crisis center with my son. They put us up in a cheap motel, and that's where we are now.

"A month later my boss finally gave me a hundred dollars just to get me off his back because he knew it was illegal. He said, 'This is all I have now. Call me in a couple of days, love, and I'll have some more.' I called his cell phone, his pager, his home phone. He had caller ID, and when he saw it was me, he wouldn't answer.

"I had no choice but to steal food," she said, sighing deeply. "If I waited for him to pay me, hell would freeze over and my son would starve. Five or six days later, I called from a pay phone. He didn't recognize it and he answered, saying, 'Hello. How can I help you?' I said, 'This is Melissa.' He said, 'Who?' Then the phone clicked dead, so I went to the supermarket and took our dinner. I'm trying to get our benefits back but in the meantime . . ." Melissa shrugged, then said a little nervously, "There's only one thing worrying me. I've heard that stealing is a felony and that in California if you have three felony convictions you can get a life sentence. It's called the three-strikes law. Can you imagine that, a life sentence for feeding your kids? Thank God I've never been caught, because if you get caught stealing food even once, you're no longer eligible for food stamps or any kind of aid.

"It's ironic, isn't it? You steal food because your children are hungry and you don't have enough food stamps to feed them. You get caught and you lose the few food stamps you had, so naturally you need to steal again. Pretty soon, you've eaten it all up, you're hungry. After all, people have to eat. Then what happens? It's your third offense, so they can put you in jail for life where they have to feed you and house you until you die. They put your kid in foster care where they have to pay a stranger to house him and feed him. They break up your family. They take away your freedom. They spend a fortune punishing you, so why not just give you and your kid the food you need to stay alive in the first place?"

DISCUSSION

1. What are some of the typical ways we are encouraged to think about homelessness? And where in our larger culture do we most often get these views reinforced?

2. Here is a partial list of the requirements that, according to Schwartz-Nobel, homeless people in search of food and shelter often have to adhere to: attending church services, bringing a birth certificate, and moving daily from one shelter site to another. What do you think is the overarching rationale behind these rules? What larger objective does it seem designed to accomplish? Is this objective, in your view, valid?

3. One of the most long-standing and ingrained scripts in our culture has to do with what is often called the "myth of self-reliance": the expectation that, no matter what obstacles are put in our way, we are all ultimately and personally responsible for whatever befalls us (good or bad). How do you think Schwartz-Nobel would respond to this claim? Do you think she would find this script a viable one for the people she interviews?

WRITING

4. Schwartz-Nobel writes, "St. Vincent de Paul Village, one of the largest and best-known shelters in the country, is only minutes from San Diego's upscale Gas Light District, where well-dressed tourists and residents eat expensive meals at lovely restaurants, but it is also a world away." Write an essay in which you discuss the differences between the ways we are accustomed to thinking of food and eating and what the homeless in Schwartz-Nobel's essay encounter. How do these people break the rules and norms that most of us take for granted? What are some ways that Schwartz-Nobel encourages us to modify our understanding of hunger?

5. Reread the portraits of Tina and Melissa, the two homeless mothers who are profiled in this essay. Choose one and then write a description of the ways you think she is characterized. What traits stand out? What words best describe the person who emerges in this portrayal? Next, assess whether this portrait conforms to the most common stereotypes about homeless people. What aspects of this stereotype get challenged or rewritten? Which aspects get reinforced?

6. From very different perspectives, Schwartz-Nobel and Caroline Knapp (p. 217) both write essays exploring what we might call the phenomenon of undereating. How do their respective treatments of this issue compare? Assess the key differences in what each has to say about where this phenomenon comes from, what its significance and effects are, and what should be done to address it.

Scenes and Un-Scenes: *Giving Thanks*

Thanksgiving stands out as one of our few genuinely American holidays. Its rituals are rooted in American myth, one that is separate from religious doctrine. Regardless of who we are, where we come from, or what we do, virtually all Americans celebrate this holiday in one way or another. Of course, what makes things tricky is the fact that we don't all share a single view of how this meal should go or what it means. We may all be familiar with the classic Thanksgiving stereotype (the harmonious and homogeneous nuclear family gathered around the well-stocked dinner table), but this doesn't mean our own holiday experiences conform to this standard. It is precisely this question of difference, in fact, that the portraits assembled here highlight. Representing Thanksgiving dinner from a range of vantage points, the following images underscore various ways Americans observe and think about this national holiday. In each case, we can pose two related sets of questions. First, what vision of the typical holiday meal does it present? What typical ways of eating? What typical American family? What typical American values? And second, how does this depiction serve to either challenge or reinforce those traditional ideals this meal is supposed to symbolize?

▶▶ *Painted at the height of World War II, Norman Rockwell's "Freedom from Want" remains arguably the most well-known and influential depiction of Thanksgiving dinner ever created. For decades, its old-fashioned, homespun portrait has succeeded in setting the boundaries around how we are supposed to think about this particular holiday. Connecting this meal to one of the nation's core freedoms, it has encouraged countless Americans over the years to regard Thanksgiving as a celebration of the values (such as comfort, security, and abundance) universally available to all Americans. Given how this picture defines the typical American family and the typical American meal, however, do these values seem as universal as they are intended? (See next page.)*

▼▼ *Created over a half century later, John Currin's* Thanksgiving *rewrites*
Rockwell's portrait in dramatic ways. Replacing Freedom's *vision of comfort
and plenitude with a darker and more anxiety-ridden image of thwarted desire and
unfulfilled appetite, Currin makes this holiday meal into an occasion for critiquing
our long-standing emphasis on excessive consumption. As one reviewer puts it,
"We've come a long way from Norman Rockwell."*

For artists of color, the effort to revise the Rockwell Thanksgiving vision has frequently revolved around challenging its assumptions about who gets to count as a typical American — a definition that treats being white as an unexamined given. Seeking to enlarge the boundaries of this definition, John Holyfield's Blessing II does more than merely recapitulate the basic terms of the Thanksgiving myth; it also subtly alters them. What sort of messages (about comfort and security, about family and tradition) would you say this image conveys? And to what extent do they either resemble or rework the messages discernible in the Rockwell portrait?

The stereotypical Thanksgiving scene is so familiar to most Americans that is has become shorthand for visual artists seeking to comment on current events. This cartoon by Oliphant adopts the traditional Thanksgiving scene in order to make a satirical point about paranoia surrounding recent news reports about possible bird flu outbreaks in the United States.

▲▲ Not every modern portrayal of Thanksgiving, of course, adopts such an ironic, skeptical, or dismissive perspective. It could be argued, for example, that this image from the 1990s sitcom *Friends* presents us with simply an updated version of the same ideals promoted by Rockwell. What do you think of this proposition? Does this portrait define the typical American family in the same ways? The typical American meal?

▶▶ Many of these old-fashioned Thanksgiving ideals have proved so enduring, in fact, that they have become woven into the fabric of our political life as well. No politician these days passes up an opportunity to be pictured celebrating this holiday meal with one or another group of "regular" Americans — a ritual designed to promote the same vision of America that we see in Norman Rockwell's painting. How well would you say this photo-op does this? Does it offer a similarly convincing portrait of community?

DISCUSSION

1. Which of these portraits most closely resembles your typical Thanksgiving experience? Which least resembles your experience? Why?

2. What does each of these images define its portrait of Thanksgiving against? In your view, which of these visions (ideal or anti-ideal) strikes you as more legitimate? How so?

3. As these pictures make clear, our eating attitudes and habits can serve as a revealing metaphor for the other kinds of things we think and care about. Based on the above portfolio, which cultural issues and debates would you say eating gets connected to most often in our culture?

WRITING

4. First, focus on how eating is being represented in one of the images you've just reviewed. What stands out? What seems most important or noteworthy? And what, by contrast, seems noticeably absent? Then, analyze the ways you think this image uses its dining portrait to define the typical or ideal American family. What behaviors and attitudes does it seem to present as normal? And what values, beliefs, or ideas does this portrait seem to endorse as right?

5. Taken together, the images assembled here make clear what boundaries exist around how we are and are not allowed to think about eating. On the basis of what this portfolio includes, where do these boundaries seem to get drawn? Write an essay in which you speculate about the kinds of activities, attitudes, assumptions, and values that this collection of images implies lies outside the norm. Make sure you argue either in favor of or against drawing the boundary in these particular ways, using details from these images and your own experience to reinforce your point of view.

6. Choose one of the examples above. How does its depiction of the typical meal compare to the eating practices by Jason Fagone (p. 204) or Caroline Knapp (p. 217)? In a page, evaluate how the norms promoted by this image compare to those profiled in one of these two essays. What similarities? What differences? To what extent do you think either Fagone or Knapp would subscribe to or choose to emulate them? Why or why not?

Putting It into Practice: *Consumer Profiling*

Now that you've read the chapter selections, try applying your conclusions to your own life by completing the following exercises.

FOOD JOURNAL   For one week, keep a written account of all your meals, including what you eat, what time, where you ate, how healthy you felt your meal was, and how much it cost. At the end of the week, write a brief essay in which you reflect on the reasons or motives behind *why* you made these particular choices. Identify and evaluate the different scripts, rules, and norms you think may have played a part in your eating habits. How many of your choices were simply prompted by cravings and how many by nutritional concerns? How much did your physical appearance influence your choices? How much was determined by nonfood-related factors (such as your time schedule or financial budget)? Do any of your decisions line up with the topics discussed by the authors in this chapter? How?

CONSUMING OTHER CULTURES   Taras Grescoe (p. 235) writes at length about the intrinsic links between food and culture. Indeed, as you have seen, what and how we eat are greatly influenced by the cultures in which we're raised. Pick a region of the world that you are unfamiliar with and research its eating customs: what foods are most popular, how they are eaten, the settings in which meals take place, and the significance of food within the larger culture (for example, in religious rituals or festivals). Pick one dish of particular significance from that culture and make a list of the ways it parallels a familiar American dish. Write a brief essay in which you discuss how learning about the foods of another culture has shed light on the way you view eating as a cultural exercise in your own culture. Be sure to cite your research in your discussion.

WHOLESALE MESSAGES   For this exercise, find some examples of the ways that food and eating are advertised: how restaurants, food brands, or diet gurus try to sell you on their products and the experiences of consuming them as positive ones. What elements of these products seem to have the most weight in terms of marketing? Taste? Fitness? Fun? Family? Write an essay in which you discuss which key elements seem to occur most often. Why do you think that is? Do you feel like food and eating are sold as part of a larger package? That is, when you are being sold the idea of eating, what other norms are you also buying, according to these advertisers?

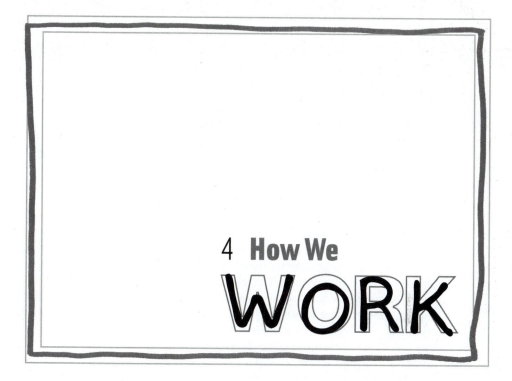

4 **How We**

WORK

Introduction

RULES AND ROLES/REWARDS AND PUNISHMENTS

Think back to your last job. Was it waiting tables? Making cold calls as a telemarketer? Perhaps you gave guided tours at a museum or worked construction. Or maybe you delivered pizzas, sold insurance, or interned at a nonprofit. Whatever type of job it was, chances are it didn't take you very long to discover that it had some basic and nonnegotiable rules in place — rules laying out in fairly specific detail the things you were and were not permitted to do. Whether white-collar, blue-collar, or no-collar, every job is defined by certain regulations and instructions, some of which are spelled out explicitly and others of which remain unspoken. Usually, for example, we are told up front what tasks we have to perform and how much we're going to get paid to complete them. Other expectations are laid out less overtly: the norms, for instance, about how employees interact with bosses or dress appropriately for their jobs. Whether formal or informal, overt or implied, however, all of these rules share one thing: They are set in stone long before we ever step behind the counter, sit down at a desk, pick up a shovel, or type our first word on the computer.

Why do so many of us adhere to rules like these written by some-body else? Is this the normal cost of "doing business"? The short answer, of course, is because we *have* to. Adhering to the rules governing a given job, common sense tells us, is required to keep it. And yet while undoubtedly true, this explanation is incomplete. The rules of work are more than just marching orders, commands we have no choice but to obey simply because we can't think of any alternative. It is more accurate, in fact, to think of these rules as *propositions* or *bargains* in which we choose to adopt a particular role or conform to a particular script in exchange for a payoff that we've decided makes doing so worth it. From the perks or promotions dangled in front of us to the threats of reprimand or dismissal we face, the truth is that our day-to-day lives on the job are shaped less by a set of abstract rules per se than by a set of very tangible rewards and punishments. When we go along with the office mandate to wear "standard business attire" or accede to our supervisor's reminder to "always wear a smile," we're doing so not because we are mindless robots or powerless pawns, but rather because we have made the calculation that such compliance is in our better interest. When reframed in these kinds of cost/benefit terms, we confront a slightly

Everybody Knows That . . .

"The second verse is for my dogs working 9 to 5
That still hustle cause a nigga can't shine off $6.55
And everybody selling make-up, Jacobs
And bootleg tapes just to get they cake up"

— *Kanye West, "We Don't Care"*

different set of questions: On what basis do we decide to make these choices? Where do we learn which standards are the right ones to employ?

SELLING SUCCESS, SCRIPTING FAILURE

It is tempting to answer this last question by saying simply "ourselves." However, as with so many other aspects of our daily lives, it is far more likely that the standards and priorities we use as we navigate our work lives have their origins at least partly in the popular culture that surrounds us. And if you doubt this contention, just think back to all the different television shows, movies, and commercials you've seen in the last few months that convey one message or another about work. Even if we sample this kind of material only sporadically, it's difficult not to come away with a clear sense of the attitudes toward work that it's our "job" to adopt. We quickly learn, for example, that we should covet certain jobs and spurn others. We become adept at identifying, almost instinctively, the things that make one career choice advantageous and another altruistic. We learn that being, say, a corporate CEO is a more "legitimate" undertaking than being a nurse, a social worker, or a high school teacher. The work it involves, the contribution it makes, and therefore the rewards it garners are supposedly far superior. Whether we embrace these lessons or resist them, whether they accurately reflect our personal views and experiences or drastically misrepresent them, one thing seems indisputable: Our culture's tutorial vis-à-vis work goes on constantly.

To be sure, our world abounds with messages and markers that tell us how to measure not only a job's desirability but also its fundamental worthiness as well as our worthiness in taking it. Perhaps the most obvious of these has to do with money. If we are looking for the quickest way to see where certain jobs rank within the official hierarchy of American employment, we need look no further than at the disparity in salary between them. And this difference is closely related to other, non-monetary kinds of distinctions we are encouraged to draw between these two jobs — between, for instance, the relative respectability or social status accorded to each. All of this thinking gets reinforced and elaborated by the ways these jobs get depicted in our popular media as well — by the clichés and stereotypes that typically attach themselves to each. We all know we're more likely to come across a flattering portrait of Wall Street finance in a television commercial or nightly news broadcast than we are a sympathetic portrayal of custodial work.

And the more familiar this instruction becomes, the easier it is to believe that we really do know the difference between worthy and unworthy work. What makes all this more than a little dangerous, of course, is that the

> *Everybody Knows That ...*
>
> **❝ I'm not a doctor, but I play one on TV"**
>
> *— Aspirin commercial from the 1970s featuring Robert Young, who played the title character on the popular show* **Marcus Welby, M.D.**

Everybody Knows That . . .

❝ Today's the day.❞

— Monster.com slogan

conclusions we are encouraged to draw are often wildly off the mark. Put simply, they are cultural stereotypes rather than objective facts. Pointing this out, however, doesn't necessarily diminish their influence. Indeed, we may be drawn to these generalizations precisely *because* they're stereotypes — because they take a situation that otherwise would feel complicated and messy, and render it disarmingly simple. It's no easy task to figure out what really makes work meaningful, to decide what is valid about certain jobs and not valid about others. While commercials depict corporate boardrooms filled with zany pranksters and free-thinking individuals, construction sites populated by truck-driving he-men, and insurance offices staffed with empathetic, dedicated salespeople, we know on some level that these images don't supply us with scripts that adequately explain the true meaning or value of work.

It is precisely this question of valuation that the selections in this chapter invite you to ponder. How is it, their authors ask, that work has come to stand as our culture's preeminent marker of self-worth? What does it mean that we so often turn to our jobs as definitive expressions of who and what we are? To delve into the assumptions and norms around work is to confront one of the key places in our world where we learn to draw distinctions between success and failure, to differentiate being a "winner" from being a "loser." Our job, of course, is hardly to take such distinctions for granted. Rather, it is to make sense of what these instructions mean and what they do: whether these scripts are helpful or harmful, whether they crowd out other, more valid ways to measure our personal value. In doing so, we will devote our energy not only to examining some of the different jobs available in our world, but also to expanding our understanding of what exactly work is.

One of the most versatile, encompassing terms in our modern vocabulary, work really describes any activity or undertaking — from doing algebra homework to taking out the garbage — that involves a degree of effort. Because of its very capaciousness, in fact, work offers us an especially resonant metaphor for understanding our relationship to popular culture in general. The term *work* underscores the degree to which the cultural messages conveyed to us, the standards mapped for us, the scripts written for us are presented not as optional things but as requirements. Like a job, our pop culture calls on us to take up particular tasks and perform particular roles. And as with a job, these expectations or rules get enforced in terms of the rewards and punishments facing us for following along or rebelling against. And finally, there is the double meaning of using this term in a cultural context, referring not only to the work our pop culture assigns to us, but also to the ways we respond to these expectations, the ways, that is, we "work out" our individual relationship to these scripts. The term reminds us that pop culture, like the jobs we hold, is not just a task master, but also a testing ground. It is the place where we assess whether these rules and roles really "work" for us.

Despite their differences, each of the essays collected here is informed by this particular understanding. Each selection author invites us to look more closely at the places where work and culture most powerfully intersect. Some pieces accomplish this goal by chronicling the ways different kinds of work gets done day to day, detailing the real-world pressures and rules that dictate how different jobs unfold. Anthony DePalma, for example, tells the story of Mexican restaurant workers in New York City, whose struggles to remain gainfully employed in a volatile job market underscore how factors like race and class can drastically skew the sorts of opportunities available. Training his attention on a very different segment of the American labor market, Christopher Byron's exposé of CEO misbehavior offers readers both satiric and sobering lessons about the workplace norms that currently prevail in corporate America. Barbara Ehrenreich, meanwhile, explores what might be called the flip side of this subject, acquainting us with the world of white-collar unemployment — a world filled with empowerment seminars, self-help books, and "life coaches." Other essays in this chapter focus instead on the cultural dimensions of work, foregrounding the myths, stereotypes, and scripts by which our work ideals are often defined. In his analytical discussion of national unemployment, for instance, Louis Uchitelle, uses his analysis of under- and unemployment trends in contemporary America to critique some of our most deeply embedded and psychically harmful unfair assumptions about success and self-worth. Addressing the contradictions of our culture's success myths from a decidedly ironic perspective, Robert Sullivan's essay lays out instructions for how "not to become rich and famous" — a satiric how-to-list that gleefully skewers the work-related values and priorities we are so often encouraged to embrace. And finally, Judith Warner directs our attention to the world of parenting, posing hard questions about what it means that modern motherhood has now come to be largely defined as its own kind of job.

Everybody Knows That . . .

"About 24 million more people are on payrolls today than in 1993. In fact, more Americans (143.6 million) are working today than ever before. This robust jobs growth is a testament to the strength, flexibility and dynamism of our nation's work-force and economy, and to the President's pro-growth policies."

— Elaine Chao, Secretary of Labor, April 7, 2006

"EVERYBODY KNOWS THAT" EXERCISE

Choose one of the quotations featured in the margins and answer the following questions:

1. What does this quotation ask you to believe?

2. What are the particular ideas, values, or attitudes it invites us to accept as *normal*?

3. What would it feel like to act on or act out these norms in our personal lives?

Rule *Maker* > > > > > > > > Rule *Breaker*

❝ Give me a W!
Give me an A!
Give me an L!
Give me a squiggly!
Give me an M!
Give me an A!
Give me an R!
Give me a T!

What's that spell?
Wal-Mart!

Whose Wal-Mart is it?
It's my Wal-Mart!

Who's number one?
The customer! Always!"

— THE WAL-MART CHEER

❝ Wal-Mart, the recidivist criminal, is back in trouble with the law. Jesse James, Bonnie & Clyde, and Al Capone had nothing on this notorious violator of our nation's laws and moral code of behavior. It routinely robs its nearly one million workers, depriving them of a fair wage and a fair chance. For example: Wal-Mart illegally compels employees to work an extra hour or so without pay after their shift is over. More than 30 states have filed class-action suits against the company for requiring this 'off the clock' work."

— JIM HIGHTOWER,
"WAL-MART RIDES AGAIN,"
NOVEMBER 11, 2003

WAL-MART VS. JIM HIGHTOWER

How does the promise of work compare to the reality? How often do the jobs we take actually live up to the ways they've been promoted? Whether in television commercials or magazine spreads, Internet job sites or help-wanted ads, it is hardly a secret that virtually every job gets hyped in ways calculated to cast it in the best possible light. No matter what the position being offered, we can pretty much rest assured we'll be told it offers "stimulating challenges" and "opportunities for advancement," that employees are fairly compensated for the work they perform, and that relations between management and labor are entirely harmonious. As many of us know from personal experience, however, sooner or later most such rosy predictions bump up against the kinds of pressures and limitations that these promotions rarely mention. We know, for example, that in the "real world" discrepancies in economic and educational background or barriers of race and class can drastically restrict the opportunities available to people looking for work.

Or that when we actually find ourselves in a given job, the interests of employers and rights of employees are not always in sync. Take, for instance, the current controversy surrounding Wal-Mart's employment practices. While it may be commonplace for corporate boosters to describe their workforce as one big, happy family, it is also true that such feel-good language can serve to direct attention away from more serious and pressing discussions: about things like fair wages, hiring discrimination, or unionization. In this case, the gap between the promise and the reality suggests that we may need to rethink the ways we talk about work. Should we rewrite the scripts that teach us what to expect from our jobs? And if so, what would these new scripts look like?

FIND THE RULES: What attitudes about working for Wal-Mart does the "Wal-Mart Cheer" seemed designed to promote? Make a list of these attitudes and write a one-page essay in which you discuss how this cheer helps script the idea of working for Wal-Mart in a certain light.

MAKE YOUR OWN RULES: How do you think Jim Hightower or others critical of Wal-Mart's employment practices would respond to the "Wal-Mart Cheer"? Rewrite the cheer to reflect such criticism of Wal-Mart, and write a brief response explaining why you rewrote the cheer the way you did.

Finding a Coach in the Land of Oz

Which would you say involves more work: having a job or looking for one? So competitive and scarce have meaningful jobs become, writes Barbara Ehrenreich, that the process of job searching has become a veritable industry unto itself. Surveying the vast landscape of unemployment self-help — from personality tests to motivational books to career networking websites — Ehrenreich tells the story of going "undercover" as a white-collar job seeker. Recounting her experiences with "career coaches" and job search "experts," she tries to make sense of this new, and often baffling, unemployment industry. Ehrenreich is a writer and political activist who has written for a wide variety of magazines and newspapers including the *Nation,* the *Atlantic Monthly, Ms.,* and the *Progressive.* She has published over a dozen books of journalism and social commentary. *Nickel and Dimed: On Not Getting By in America* (2002) is an undercover investigation of low-wage jobs, and a chapter of it won Ehrenreich a Sydney Hillman Award for Journalism. Among her other books are *Blood Rites: Origins and History of the Passions of War* (1997), *Bait and Switch: The (Futile) Pursuit of the American Dream* (2005) where this selection appears, and, most recently, *Dancing in the Streets: A History of Collective Joy* (2007).

W HERE TO BEGIN? MY FIRST FORAY INTO THE WORLD OF JOB SEARCHing, undertaken at my computer on a gloomy December afternoon, is distinctly intimidating. These days, I have gathered from a quick tour of relevant web sites, you don't just pore over the help-wanted ads, send off some résumés, and wait for the calls. Job searching has become, if not a science, a technology so complex that no mere job seeker can expect to master it alone. The Internet offers a bewildering variety of sites where you can post a résumé in the hope that a potential employer will notice it. Alternatively, you can use the net to apply directly to thousands of companies. But is the résumé eye-catching enough? Or would it be better to attempt face-to-face encounters at the proliferating number of "networking events" that hold out the promise of meaningful contacts?

Fortunately, there are about 10,000 people eager to assist me — "career coaches" — who, according to the coaching web sites, can help you discover your true occupational "passion," retool your résumé, and hold your hand at every step along the way. The coaches, whose numbers have been doubling every three years, are the core of the "transition industry" that has grown up just since the midnineties, in a perhaps inevitable response to white-collar unemployment.[1] Unlike blue-collar people, the white-collar unemployed are likely to have some assets to invest in their job search; they are, in addition, often lonely and depressed — a perfect market, in other words, for any service promising prosperity and renewed self-esteem. Some coaches have formal training through programs like the Career Coach Academy's fifteen-week course; others are entirely self-anointed. You can declare yourself a coach without any credentials, nor are there any regulatory agencies looking over your shoulder — which means that, for the job seeker, it's the luck of the draw.[2]

I find Morton on the web, listed as a local career coach, although — as I will soon learn — most coaching is done by phone so there is no need for geographic proximity. Morton has been there, is my thought. The background material that he sends me shows a history of what appear to be high-level, defense-related jobs, including, somewhat datedly, "Senior Intelligence Analyst and Branch Chief Responsible for Analyzing Soviet Military Research." He has given seminars at Carnegie Mellon University and spoken frequently at Kiwanis and Rotary clubs. Surely he can guide my transformation into the marketable middle-level professional I aspire to be. Besides, he assures me, I will not have to pay for our first, trial session.

I have no trouble recognizing him at Starbucks in Charlottesville's Barracks Road Mall; he's the one wearing the "JMU" baseball cap, as promised, a description that encouraged me to come in rumpled gray slacks and sneakers. The top is better, though — black turtleneck, tweed blazer, and pearl earrings — which I am hoping will pass as "business casual." Flustered by being five minutes late because my normal route to the mall was blocked by construction, I stumble over my new name in the handshake phase. He appears not to notice. In fact, he doesn't seem to be much into the noticing business or perhaps already regards me as a disappointment.

After exchanging some observations on the pre-Christmas parking situation at the mall, I lay out my situation for him: I do public relations and event planning, I tell him, but I've been doing it on a freelance basis and am now seeking a stable corporate position with regular benefits, location flexible. How to present myself? Where to begin? I pull out the résumé that I completed over the weekend and slide it across the table toward him. In the worst-case scenario, he will grab it and quiz me on it while holding it in such a way that I will be unable to refresh my memory with an occasional glance. But he regards the stapled papers with only somewhat more enthusiasm than if a fly were advancing across the table toward his arm. Maybe he can tell without reading it, by the very format of the pages — the lack, as I now see it, of bullets and bolding — that it isn't worth a serious coach's attention.

But he is bringing something out of his briefcase — an 8½ × 11 inch transparency — which he places methodically over a sheet of white paper so that I can read: "Core Competencies and Skills," or "the four competencies," as he refers to them. These are Mobilizing Innovation, Managing People and Tasks, Communicating, and Managing Self. This must be what I need — an introduction to the crisp, linear concepts that shape the corporate mind. I am taking notes as fast as I can, but he assures me that he will leave me with copies, so I am free to focus on the content.

The next transparency features a picture of a harness racer and horse, and reads:

> Clear mind, skillful driver
> Sound spirit, strong horse.
> Strong body, sound carriage.
> Mind, body, spirit work as one . . .
> Path to victory is clear.

The syntax is a bit disturbing, particularly the absence of articles, which gives it a kind of ESL feel, but if modern-day executives can derive management principles from Buddhism or Genghis Khan, as the business sections of bookstores suggest, surely they can imagine themselves as harness racers. The horse, driver, and carriage, Morton is telling me, symbolize Head, Heart, and Gut, but I miss which one is which. This is going to be a lot harder than I anticipated. Already, the four competencies are leaking away from memory, or maybe it should be self-evident that Mobilizing Innovation equals Head or possibly Gut.

With the next transparency, things take a seriously goofy turn. It's titled "Three Centers of Intelligence" and illustrated with characters from *The Wizard of Oz*: the scarecrow, representing "Mental," the tin man, representing "Emotional," and the lion, representing "Instinctual." When he teaches his course on "Spirituality and Business," Morton is explaining, he does this with dolls. That was his wife's idea. She said, "You should have dolls!" and you know what? She went out and found them for him. I profess to being a little sketchy about my *Wizard of Oz*, and Morton digresses into the back story on the tin man, trying to recall how he got such a hard "shell." All I can think is that I'm glad he didn't bring the dolls with him, because Starbucks has gotten crowded now and I wouldn't want it to look like I'm being subjected to some peculiar doll-based form of therapy.

But while I am still struggling to associate the tin man with Emotional and so forth, we move away from Oz to the Enneagram, which is defined in a transparency as:

- A description of personality types

- Based on ancient learning about motivation

- A diagram easily learned and applied

- Provides clues about moving toward balance

The visuals here feature a figure composed of a number of connected triangles enclosed in a circle. I feel a dizziness that cannot be explained by the growing distance from breakfast, and not a single question occurs to me that might shed some light on the ever-deepening complexity before me. Somehow, the Enneagram leads to "The Nine Types," which are also the "nine basic desires or passions." Perhaps sensing my confusion, Morton tells me that, in his course, the Enneagram takes a lot of time to get across. "It's more or less a data dump."

I furrow my brow and nod. All around us, money is being exchanged for muffins in mutually agreeable amounts, and the corporate world continues to function in its usual mindlessly busy, rational way. But the continuance of the corporate enterprise is not something, I realize for the first time, that you can necessarily take for granted. Not if its underlying principles emanate from Oz.

It's a great relief when the higher math of the Enneagram gives way, in the sequence of transparencies, to the familiar *Wizard of Oz* creatures, now seen decorating a series of grids labeled "Emotional Centered Types," "Mentally Centered Types," and "Instinctual Centered Types." On the left side of each grid are five entries, the most intriguing of which is "distorted passion," described by Morton as a "bad passion," or one that you have to recognize and overcome. For example, the lion has as one of its distorted passions "Lust for life. I want to experience and control the entire world," while the scarecrow is potentially burdened with "Avarice — I keep knowledge to myself to avoid being seen as incompetent." I interrupt to ask why keeping knowledge to oneself is called avarice, and he replies evenly, "Because it's keeping something to yourself." Then I notice among the distorted passions, "Gluttony — I can never get enough experience." In among the wanderings of Dorothy in Oz and the "ancient learning" of the Enneagram, Morton — or the inventor of the Enneagram — has managed to weave the Seven Deadly Sins.

What all this leads up to is that I have to take a test, the Wagner Enneagram Personality Style Scales (WEPSS), which will reveal my personality type and hence what kind of job I should be looking for. I already told Morton what kind of job I'm looking for, but obviously not in a language that fits into his elaborate personal metaphysics. I'll take the test at home, send it to him, and then meet for an evaluation. The whole thing will cost $60.

So the search for a career coach who can actually help me with the mechanics of job searching continues. I register at the CoachLink web site, which nets me three e-mails offering coaching services and one phone call. I go with the phone caller, Kimberly, whose web site describes her as "a career and outplacement consultant, trainer and writer" — for showing initiative — and agree to a weekly half-hour session by phone at $400 a month, or $200 an hour. My "homework," due on our first session, is to "fantasize" about my ideal job. What would my day be like at this ideal job?

My "homework" . . . is to "fantasize" about my ideal job.

It's not a bad assignment. Everyone should take some time for utopian thinking, and what better occasion than when you have nothing else to do? So I fantasize about a small- to medium-size company with offices in a wooded area, mine looking out on a valley and rolling green hills. An espresso cart rolls around every morning and afternoon; there's an on-site gym to which we're encouraged to retreat at least once a day, and the cafeteria features affordable nouvelle cuisine. None of that goes into my written fantasy, however, which focuses on finding a balance between the intense camaraderie of my "team" and periods of creative solitude in my office, which of course has a door — no cubicles for me. I put myself in charge of my team, over which I wield a collegial, "empowering" form of leadership. I am utterly fascinated by my work, whatever it is, and frequently carry on till late at night.

Kimberly, when our first session rolls around, is "excited" by my résumé, "excited" by my fantasy, and generally "excited" to be working with me. I get high marks for the fantasy job: "You're very clear about what you want! Many clients don't get to this stage for months. I think you're going to be a quick study." Already, the excitement level is beginning to exhaust me. In my irritation, I picture her as a short-haired platinum blonde, probably wearing a holiday-themed sweater and looking out from her ranch home on a lawn full of reindeer or gnomes.

As for how she sees herself: "I've gone through some branding processes, and I realize the brand you're getting from me is wildly optimistic, fiercely compassionate, and totally improvisational." I am to think of myself in the same way — as a "brand," or at least a product.

"What do you do in PR?"

I let a beat go by, not sure if this is a test of whether I am actually what I claim to be. But this turns out to be her MO — the teasing question, followed by the dazzlingly insightful answer: "You *sell* things, and now you're going to *sell* yourself!"

Looking down at my sweatpants and unshod feet, all of which is of course invisible to Kimberly, I mumble about lacking confidence, the tight job market, and the obvious black mark of my age. This last defect elicits a forceful "Be really aware of the negative self-talk you give yourself. Step into the take-charge person you are!"

Now comes the theoretical part. She asks me to think of two overlapping circles. One circle is me, the other is "the world of work," and the overlapping area is "the ideal position for you." "What you need is confidence," Kimberly is saying. "You have to see the glass as half-full, not half-empty." I draw the overlapping circles as she speaks, then redraw them so that they are almost entirely overlapping, thus vastly expanding my employment prospects.

Our half an hour is drawing to a close, I note with relief. She thinks I will need three months of coaching, meaning she will need $1,200. This will be a lot of work for me, she says, because she practices "co-active coaching," which is "very collaborative." "I want you to design me as your best coach," she says, perhaps forgetting that she has already been not only designed but "branded." If I were "designing" her, I'd throw in a major serotonin antagonist to damp down the perkiness, and maybe at some point I will find a tactful way to suggest that she chill. The session has left me drained and her more excited than ever: "We'll dance together here!" is her final promise.

I feel that I'm not finished with Morton. I should at least take the test so he'll get his $60 and I will perhaps redeem the hour already spent with him. There are 200 questions on the WEPSS test, each in the form of a word or phrase which I am to rate from A to E in terms of its applicability to me; for example: *dry, pleasure seeking, strength, peacemaker,* and *vengeful.* I sit down at the dining room table with the intention of zipping through the test in ten minutes or less, but it's not as easy as it looks. Am I *special?* From whose vantage point? What about *looking good,* which certainly depends on how much effort has gone into the project? Or *what's the difference* — how can that describe anyone? Most of the terms are adjectives like *judgmental,* but there are plenty of nouns like *fantasy* and even a scattering of verbs like *move against.* Could I describe myself as almost never, occasionally, or almost always *move against?* Am I sometimes, never, or always *wow* or *no big deal?*

> **Am I sometimes, never, or always wow or no big deal?**

Even where the syntax fails to offend me as a writer — or, as I should now put it, a "communications" professional[3] — the answers are by no means obvious. *Harmonious,* for example: sometimes, but it depends on who or what's around to harmonize with. *Avoid conflict?* If possible, but there are times when I seek it out, and in fact enjoy nothing better than a good table-thumping debate. How about *powerful* or *happy?* I am, I realize, not the kind of person who, well, ever speaks of herself as "not the kind of person who . . ."

The very notion of personality, which is what we are trying to get at here, seems to have very limited application to me and quite possibly everyone else. *Self* is another dodgy concept, since I am, when I subject this "I" to careful inspection, not much more than a swarm of flickering affinities, habits, memories, and predilections that could go either way — toward neediness or independence, for example, courage or cowardice. The best strategy, I decide, is to overcome *hesitant, worrying,* and *correctness seeking* and give what seem like the right, or most admirable, answers. I check "almost always" for *disciplined, high ideals, independent,* and *principled,* while firmly rejecting *lazy, abrasive, procrastinate,* and *laid-back.*

A week later, after Morton has had time to "grade" my personality, we meet at his home to go over the results. It's a modest ranch house in a residential area I have never visited, decorated in a style I recognize as middle-class Catholic, circa 1970 — prints of nineteenth-century pastoral scenes, a teddy bear on a child-size rocking chair, a Madonna overlooking the armoire. In other words, perfectly normal — at least until we arrive at the dining room table, on which three foot-high dolls are perched — a scarecrow, a tin man, a lion, and — what movie is this? — a plastic Elvis.

I decided in advance to lead off with my criticisms of the test, because if I give them after the results he may think I'm using them to deflect any criticisms of me that have emerged in his analysis. How in the world, I ask him, could I say whether *marketing* (that's one of the test terms) applies to me? It's a noun, for heaven's sake, and while I may be "good at marketing," I am not, by any stretch of the imagination, "marketing." I tell him there's no excuse for such sloppiness, and that I realize that in saying so I may well be revealing something about my personality: something rigid and unforgiving.

Completely unfazed, Morton picks up the Elvis doll, whose legs are sticking out at a right angle to his trunk in some hideous form of rigor mortis, and tells me that he uses it to make the point that "there is about as much similarity between the doll and the real Elvis as there is between you and your personality type." I want to object that the doll does resemble the real Elvis, in his youth anyway and before his unfortunate weight gain; at least anyone could see that it is not a Barbara doll. But that misses the larger questions of what I am doing here if the test is meaningless and what it has to do with finding a job anyway. Besides, he's putting Elvis down on a side table now, leaving us alone with the Oz crew.

We move on to the results. It turns out that my scores "could fit almost any personality type." I'm highest in Original and Effective, and when you plot that out on an Enneagram, the diagonal lines connect me to Good and Loving. This makes me a tin man with a little lion thrown in, he says, fingering the appropriate dolls. Next, he brings out the baffling transparencies, which have been sitting here all along in a file folder. This time I resolve to get to the bottom of things, but when he flashes the transparency labeled

"The Enneagram Symbol," with its nested triangles, all I can come up with is, "What is the circle doing here?" It's there, he explains, "for graphic unity" — meaning that he just likes the look of it? — and also to show that "we are talking about a whole person." And the big triangle? I continue, losing heart. "Those are the three centers of intelligence."

It turns out, though, that my Original, Effective, Good, and Loving traits are not the point. The point is to understand my "nonresourceful" side, which seems to be my bad side, because this is what I need to do something about. Some people, Morton says, addressing the brown and wintry lawn outside the dining room window, resist hearing about this side. One woman, a schoolteacher, broke into tears when she learned about hers. In my case, the nonresourceful side includes being overly sensitive and prone to melancholy and envy, not to mention the bad traits that come up when you draw diagonals from Loving and Effective. What this comes down to, in a practical sense, is that, given my highly emotional and artistic personality (where did *that* come from?), I probably "don't write very well." The "suggested activity," in my case, would be "intensive journaling workshops" to polish my writing skills.

There is nothing to do but mumble my thanks, write out the check, and leave. I think of my father, whose personality traits included brash, cynical, bombastic, obnoxious, charming, kindly, and falling-down drunk, yet who managed to rise from the copper mines of Butte to the corporate stratosphere, ending up as vice president of research for a multinational firm. Did he ever take a personality test or submit to executive coaching? Or were things different in the fifties and sixties, with a greater emphasis on what you could actually *do*? What would he have made of Morton, the dolls, and the ancient wisdom of the Enneagram? I drive home with his deep guffaws echoing in my head. . . .

> **Were things different in the fifties and sixties, with a greater emphasis on what you could actually do?**

Career coaches can perhaps be forgiven for using baseless personality tests to add a veneer of scientific respectability to the coaching process. But the tests enjoy wide credibility, not just among coaches but among corporate decision makers. In 1993, the Myers-Briggs test was administered to three million Americans; eighty-nine of the Fortune top 100 companies use it to help slot their white-collar employees into the appropriate places in the hierarchy.[4] On its web site, the Enneagram Institute lists, among the companies supposedly using the Enneagram test to sort out their employees, Amoco, AT&T, Avon, Boeing, DuPont, eBay, General Mills, General Motors, Alitalia Airlines, KLM Airlines, Hewlett-Packard,

Toyota, Procter & Gamble, International Weight Watchers, Reebok Health Clubs, Motorola, Prudential Insurance, and Sony. Amazon offers a score of books on the Enneagram, none of them apparently critical, including *The Enneagram in Love and Work, The Spiritual Dimension of the Enneagram,* and *The Enneagram for Managers.*

It is true that I encountered the Enneagram in the particularly wacky company of *The Wizard of Oz.* But the test I took was the real thing, which, a web search reveals, is variously said to be derived from Sufism, Buddhism, Jesuit philosophy, and Celtic lore — with a generous undergirding of numerology. The early twentieth-century Russian mystic G.I. Gurdjieff seems to have been a fount of inspiration, but the actual development of the Enneagram theory is usually credited to two men — Oscar Ichazo, a Bolivian-born mystic, and Claudio Naranjo, a psychiatrist who made his mark in the nineteen sixties by employing hallucinogenic drugs in psychotherapy. Whatever "ancient learning" the Enneagram test purports to represent, it is nothing more than a pastiche of wispy New Age yearnings for some mystic unity underlying the disorder of human experience.

Even the more superficially rational of these tests, the Myers-Briggs Type Indicator, possesses not a shred of scientific respectability according to Annie Murphy Paul's 2004 book, *The Cult of Personality*. It was devised, in the early forties, by a layperson — a homemaker in fact — who had become fascinated by her son-in-law's practical, detailed-oriented personality, which was so different from her own, more intuitive, approach. Inspired by the psychoanalyst Carl Jung's notion of "types" — which were by no means meant to be innate or immutable — Katharine Briggs devised a test to sort humanity into sixteen distinct types, all of them fortunately benign. (There were no psychopaths, of the kind who might show up at work one day with an automatic weapon, in Briggs's universe.) To her eternal frustration, the test never won respect from the academic psychology profession, and not only because of her outsider status. Serious psychologists have never been convinced that people can be so readily sorted into "types."

Leaving aside the validity of "types," the Myers-Briggs Type Indicator has zero predictive value even in its own terms. In one study, undertaken by proponents of Myers-Briggs, only 47 percent of people tested fell into the same category on a second administration of the test. Another study found 39 to 76 percent of those tested assigned to a different "type" upon retesting weeks or years later. Some people's "types" have been found to vary according to the time of day. Paul concludes that "there is no evidence that [Briggs's] sixteen distinct types have any more validity than the twelve signs of the zodiac."[5]

So why is the corporate world, which we think of as so fixated on empirical, in fact, quantifiable, measures of achievement like the "bottom line," so attached to these meaningless personality tests? One attraction must be that the tests lend a superficial rationality to the matching of people with jobs. No one, after all, wants a sadistic personnel director or a morbidly shy publicist; and if you failed at one job, it is probably comforting to be told that it was simply not a good "fit" for your inner nature. As Paul writes:

> The administration of personality tests is frequently presented as a gesture of corporate goodwill, a generous acknowledgement of employees' uniqueness. Under this banner of respect for individuality, organizations are able to shift responsibility for employee satisfaction onto that obligatory culprit, "fit." There's no bad worker and no bad workplace, only a bad fit between the two.[6]

Of course, if the function of the tests is really ideological — to promote the peg-in-hole theory of employment — they do not have to be in any way accurate as predictors of performance or satisfaction. They serve more as underpinnings of corporate etiquette, allowing employers to rationalize rejection or dismissal in terms of an inadequate "fit." We believe that there is a unique slot for each person, the tests announce — even though we may fail to find it in your particular case.

My job, though, is to find a "fit," however wobbly, in any institutional structure that will have me. And with this simple task in mind, the personality tests seem even more mysterious. If I am a public relations person by training and experience, what good will it do me to discover that my personality is better suited to a career as an embalmer? Presumably there are extroverted engineers and introverted realtors, who nevertheless manage to get the job done. The peculiar emphasis on "personality," as opposed to experience and skills, looms like a red flag, but I have no way of knowing yet what the warning's about.

> **Why is the corporate world . . . so attached to these meaningless personality tests?**

NOTES

[1]See Daniel C. Feldman, "Career Coaching: What HR Professionals Need to Know," *Human Resources Planning* 24:2 (2001), p. 26. Even an improving economy poses no threat to the coaching industry, representatives of the Career Coach Academy and the Career Coach Institute assured me, since companies often hire the same coaches to rev up their executives and employed individuals often seek them out when they see "the handwriting on the wall" — a subject common enough to be the topic of Internet and conference call seminars. Some coaches work as individuals; others are in firms offering, for a fee, office space and equipment for the job seeker.

[2]See Stratford Sherman and Alyssa Freas, "The Wild West of Executive Coaching," *Harvard Business Review,* November 2004. Although this article is about executive, as opposed to career, coaching, many individuals do both, and the same lack of credentialing and regulations applies to career coaching generally.

[3]The corporate disability with language is now an acknowledged problem, with some companies paying for writing courses for their executives. See Sam Dillon, "What Corporate America Cannot Build: A Sentence," *New York Times*, December 7, 2004.

[4]Annie Murphy Paul, *The Cult of Personality: How Personality Tests Are Leading Us to Miseducate Our Children, Mismanage Our Companies, and Misunderstand Ourselves* (New York: Free Press, 2004), p. 125.

[5]Paul, *Cult of Personality*, pp. 133–34.

[6]Ibid., p. 130.

DISCUSSION

1. According to Ehrenreich, looking for a job has become so complicated, structured, and time-intensive that it now qualifies as a job unto itself. What do you make of this proposition? What kind of job description would you write for this hypothetical position of job seeker?

2. If, as Ehrenreich strongly implies, the personality tests so widely employed by businesses these days have no empirical validity, what other purpose might they serve? Why else might companies make these tests such a prominent part of their application process?

3. A hallmark of the standardized tests typically administered to job applicants, writes Ehrenreich, is their tendency to divide people into different types. How valid a system is this? If you had to, what type would you categorize yourself as? And how relevant or useful to a job search do you think doing so would be?

WRITING

4. "Job searching," writes Ehrenreich, "has become, if not a science, a technology so complex that no mere job seeker can expect to master it alone." Choose one such technology that Ehrenreich describes and write an essay in which you identify and evaluate the particular script you think it outlines for a potential job seeker. What sorts of instruction or advice does it offer? What does it suggest is the proper role for the prospective employee to play? What attitude toward work, to potential jobs, does it establish as normal? How useful or helpful do you think it would be to act out this script in your life?

5. Among other things, Ehrenreich contends, the corporate world's reliance on standardized personality tests exposes what she calls the "corporate disability with language." Choose language from one of these tests excerpted in this essay. What you think this particular word, phrase, or sentence actually means? How can this "business-speak" be translated into more accessible terminology that a layperson might use? Evaluate the purpose you think this kind of language actually serves. What (if anything) makes it useful? Necessary? What would change if this example were rewritten using a more accessible, everyday formulation?

6. How useful do you think the workers profiled by Anthony DePalma (p. 312) or Louis Uchitelle (p. 299) would find the career advice offered to Ehrenreich in this essay? Choose one of these two essays and write an essay in which you assess the advantages and/or limitations of the job advice Ehrenreich describes receiving, from the point of view of either DePalma or Uchitelle. Do you think DePalma or Uchitelle would have views similar to Ehrenreich's regarding the usefulness of this material? How or how not?

CHRISTOPHER BYRON
Let's Party Like It's 1999

Our newspaper headlines seem dominated these days by accounts of corporate scandal. So ubiquitous have these tales of power-mad executives, gullible investors, and cooked books become, in fact, that they have come to stand as our culture's preeminent cautionary tale about the dangers of unchecked ambition. But do we really take these lessons to heart? In a world where the average CEO still makes a hundred times the salary of the average worker, where the autobiographies of corporate titans like Jack Welch and Donald Trump continue to top the bestseller list, are we really all that troubled by the lessons about "success" these scandals teach? Presenting a salacious smorgasbord of corporate malfeasance, Christopher Byron answers "perhaps not." Byron has written about business and finance for over thirty years. A contributing editor and feature financial columnist for *Playboy*, the *New York Observer*, and *MSNBC*, his writing has also appeared in *Esquire, Worth, Men's Health* and *Travel Holiday.* He has also been a weekly columnist for the *New York Daily News* and *New York* magazine and has served as the managing editor of *Forbes* and an editor and correspondent for *Time.* His books include *Skin Tight: The Bizarre Story of Guess vs. Jordache* (1992) and *Martha, Inc: The Incredible Story of Martha Stewart Living Omnimedia* (2002). A graduate of Columbia University School of Law, Byron is also a United States Navy veteran. He lives with his family in Connecticut. The following piece is from *Testosterone Inc.: Tales of CEOs Gone Wild* (2004).

E XTRAVAGANT BIRTHDAY PARTIES ARE A GREAT TRADITION OF THE moneyed classes, especially among those whose capacity for consumption has developed faster than the sensitivity of their palates.[1] Yet it is not often that one encounters a more vivid example of what the collective failure of taste and decorum can lead to than the weeklong festivities hosted by Dennis and Karen [Kozlowski] at the Hotel Cala di Volpe in Sardinia.

The great bull market of the 1980s and 1990s produced many grand genuflections before the altar of one's aging. In the summer of 1989, when financier Saul Steinberg turned fifty, his recently acquired trophy wife, Gayfryd, spent $1 million of her husband's money to throw a birthday party for 250 of their closest friends at the couple's Long Island estate.

Among the intimates were Saul's fellow Wharton alumnus and junk-bond grandee, Ron Perelman, accompanied by his wife of the moment, Claudia. And panning the crowd for familiar faces — or at least recognizable names — one could as well have spotted diminutive leveraged buyout biggie Henry Kravis along with his trophy wife of the period, Carolyne Roehm. Ditto for U.S. Secretary of Commerce Robert Mosbacher, and *his* trophy wife, Georgette.

The party itself, incorporating a theme of seventeenth-century Holland and the world of the Old Masters, featured a custom-built replica of a Flemish farmhouse, complete with ten separate Old Masters "paintings" in which live models moved about inside what looked to be dioramas based on the original paintings. One diorama included a female model posing naked as Rembrandt's *Dana*. Outside, vast stretches of Oriental carpeting covered the lawns, while two nubile twins frolicked as mermaids in the pool. Waiters served beluga whole grain caviar by the bucketful. Dinner was served under an air-conditioned tent the size of a tennis court — the table settings featured treasure chests with pearls spilling out of them.[2]

Three weeks later, this same group of people, plus at least five hundred more, headed for Morocco — now in new roles as among the 750 "closest friends" of publishing magnate Malcolm Forbes. Their mission: to provide trim to Malcolm's efforts to throw a seventieth birthday party for himself that not even Saul Steinberg would be able to match if and when *he* turned seventy.

Like the Steinberg affair, Malcolm's three-day desert do came wrapped in the garb of "entertainment" for the guests, though its real purpose was to burnish the *Forbes* brand-name while helping the proprietor move up another rung or two on the ladder of renown. Understanding that the more money he spent, the more attention he'd get, Malcolm *doubled* the Steinberg outlay, thereby instantly raising the price of a ticket to the world of the hyper-party to a full $2 million. In doing so, Malcolm cleverly managed to turn Steinberg's $1 million in effect into part of the promotional budget for Malcolm's own party, reducing the entire Steinberg affair, and all its attendant publicity, to little more than a warm-up act for the Forbes celebration.

And of course, Malcolm also knew that the more big-name people he could get to accept invitations, the more the press would want to cover the party, creating yet more buzz about the event, which would bring in yet more big-name acceptances. In this way, he succeeded in turning the party into an actual news event, with the Associated Press distributing a list of "accepted invitations" on the AP national wire on the eve of the party.[3]

The celebrations featured fireworks, bus rides to various sights, 250 galloping Moroccan horsemen, 830 roasted chickens, 150 cooks — and under the starry, starry night, Metropolitan Opera star Beverly Sills singing *Happy Birthday Dear Malcolm*. It was a setting that was certainly more exotic, though in other respects not very much different, from the circumstances under which Al Dunlap had arranged things to receive similar sentiments from his own group of snickering "best friends" nearly fifteen years earlier at Nitec Paper Company in Niagara Falls, New York.

What distinguished Dennis and Karen's efforts from the foregoing — aside from the fact that the Kozlowski effort was paid for with shareholder money and the other extravaganzas were private affairs — was certainly not the scale of the undertaking, which as these things go was almost intimate, with barely seventy-five revelers finally making an appearance. Nor was the cost of the affair especially notable one way or the other. At a total price of $2 million, the party was not much more expensive, when adjusted for inflation, than the cost of Steinberg's $1 million bash twelve years earlier. And it certainly looked like a bargain when compared with the Forbes party.

What distinguished Dennis and Karen's effort — in fact, what set it apart from almost any arriviste lunge for social acceptance one might think of — was the utter earnestness of the effort . . . and the unalloyed completeness of the resulting failure. One thinks of the little boy called Alfalfa in the old *Our Gang* comedies, singing desperately to his true love, Darla.

There he stands (or sits, or sometimes kneels) before her, his hands clutched together and pressed against his bosom. The hands might be holding a wilted flower, a token of his love. The coat is four sizes too small, and the pants are ready for high-water wading. From the top of his head sticks his lard-slicked cowlick. He is a mess. Yet all he knows is his desperation and his need and his hunger for Darla's love. So he cannot even begin to imagine what he sounds like as he sings of his love for her — more shrill and off-key with each note — nor understanding the grimaced and pained expression that begins to spread across her face as he continues. And knowing nothing else to do, he sings louder, and the pained look in Darla's eyes grows more intense and even frightened. Finally, the dog at her feet, Pete, puts a paw over one ear and begins to howl . . . at which point she clasps her hands to her ears and shrieks "Alfalfa, Alfalfa, will you please shut up!"

> **What distinguished Dennis and Karen's effort . . . was the utter earnestness of the effort.**

That is what set Dennis and Karen's Sardinian soireé apart from all the others: the painful earnestness of the entire off-key experience, inflicted on the rest of humankind because a videotape of the affair managed two years later to come into the possession of New York prosecutors in the Kozlowski case. From their outstretched hands, it next moved smoothly and swiftly onto the evening news at nearly every television station in America.

Some of the scenes on the tape were pronounced by the judge in the case, New York State Supreme Court Judge Michael Obus, to be so prejudicial to a fair trial for Kozlowski that they were edited out and never seen by the jury or the public.[4] Among other attractions, for example, the party featured a life-size copy, rendered in ice, of Michelangelo's marble statute of David. A videotaped scene of giggling women at the party filling their glasses with chilled vodka that poured in a stream from the ice sculpture's penis was one such moment that the judge ordered snipped.

Another involved Karen's birthday cake, which had been baked in the shape of a nude female. When the cake was brought out to be cut and served — with Fourth of July sparklers twinkling from its nipples — the breasts themselves exploded. That too was excised from the videotape by the judge, as was a scene of an apparently intoxicated reveler dropping his pants and mooning the camera. Yet another scene, in which Karen was shown being carried around overhead by two Italian male models in Speedo bathing suits, also hit the cutting-room floor.

Learning all this, we are struck not so much by the shock value of such moments, which is minimal, as by the banality of the whole affair. Having transported themselves to the frontiers of licentiousness, clutching $2 million in mad money and a license to blaze, the resulting failure of the imagination seems astounding. Was this the best they could do — exploding tits and a statue that peed booze out the whizzer? They could have stayed home and watched Tom Cruise have a better party all by himself in *Risky Business* — in particular the part where his parents go away for the weekend and he strips down to his skivvies and socks, pours himself a glass of gin, and starts dancing around the living room to an old Bob Seger tune. For isn't that what this $2 million effort at a week's worth of full-bore karaoke was all about? Today's music don't have the same soul? Then give 'em some old time rock and roll.

We are struck as well by the marked absence of recognizable names on the guest list, which followed the route of the videotape from the prosecutors to the public. On this list, we find no celebrities. No actors, no sports figures, not even anyone from cable television. Nor are there recognizable names from the worlds of business or Wall Street.

Who's on the list? Well, there's a fellow named James Bartle. He's Tyco's corporate chef. And a fellow named Nelson Cantave. He's the company's personal trainer. And a man named Peter Carrie (a personal friend of the happy couple). And Joel and Paula Curcio (ditto). There's Bob and Debbie DeCostas (more personal friends) and Gary Fagin (the company physician). There's Sparky Kania (a member of the *Endeavor* sailboat's crew) and Nancy Maley (an employee of Tyco's travel agency). And, of course, Woody and Hal Mayo (they would be Karen's parents).

It just went on and on like that until one reached the bottom of the list. Save for a couple of directors, and Tyco's corporate treasurer, and one or two others, that was it. For Dennis's parade into business world immortality, he had lined the boulevard with . . . Debbie and Sparky and Gary and Paula and Nelson and Pete . . . with the company doc and the company cook and the company gym coach and the crew of the boat. The guests arrived for the most part on the afternoon of Sunday, June 10.[5] A reception buffet was waiting, followed by a dinner at 8 o'clock. The next day, Monday, featured . . . well, basically, nothing. It was sort of like free period at camp. You could eat, or swim, or sleep . . . or sleep, or eat, or swim. Tuesday was the same, except that dinner featured the presentation to Dennis and Karen of a large ceramic platter, signed by everyone and thanking them for such a nice time. On Wednesday, there was a scavenger hunt, followed by another eat-swim-sleep cycle, with Thursday blocked out to rest up from Wednesday and prepare for Thursday evening, which was the main event — namely Karen's birthday party. On Friday everybody rested up from Thursday, and on Saturday they all went home.

The birthday party on Thursday evening was held at the resort's golf course clubhouse where — Sardinia being part of Italy, which, of course, was once part of ancient Rome — the clubhouse had been decorated in what Barbara Jacques described during her trial testimony as "a Roman theme."

To that end, some local models — both male and female — had been hired and dressed up in toga-type affairs. The males — mostly dressed in Speedo bathing suits and nothing else — walked around flexing their shaved and oiled pecs at the ladies. The females — dressed in more, but not a whole lot — tried to look demure while going as much as possible for arched-back poses that helped with the front cleavage.

After this came "the music." But it brought with it such a jolting hiccup in the theme of Roman bacchanalia as to make one grab the arm-rails of one's chair, as if watching George Washington lead his men across the Delaware not in the bow of the first boat, but from a speeding Windsurfer.

That is because, on this Night of a Thousand Muscles, the music invited no thoughts of gladiatorial combat, nor even the distant encores of La Scala. There were to be no arias from Puccini on this birthday to end all birthdays, nor even a soundtrack from Fellini.

No, for the finale to end all finales in this grand opera of the imagination, the revelers were to get what really turned on Dennis and Karen more than anything else — right there onstage, live before their eyes in exotic Hotel Cala di Volpe Sardinia — forty-five minutes of the master himself . . . the man who'd gone double-platinum more times than Dolly Parton's hair . . . who'd blown through more flip-flops, and stepped on more pop-tops . . . Unhuh, that's right . . . it's him . . . (Hey, are you still lookin' for that shaker of salt, James? . . . Jimmy [the music is coming up now] Buffett!

From Barbara Jacques' testimony at the trial one may begin to tease forth how all this happened — how the secret, and apparently conflicting fantasies that Dennis and Karen held as to what adulthood would be like, got resolved into this monstrosity of a birthday party.

The picture is incomplete, but it is a start. And without at least something, we are lost. How else do we get from "birthday-bash-as-Roman-orgy," to its accompanying musical subtext of Jimmy Buffett on his six-string?[6] The answer is, we don't.

We begin as we must, with the models, watching with our host's intended sense of awe as they walk around in Hollywood versions of Roman togas, circa 1960. The togas are cut high on the thigh and slit becomingly on the side, and one of the models even looks a bit like Victor Mature. Cue the chariots out by the putting green and it would not be surprising to see Judah Ben Hur gallop past, whipping his steed and looking strangely like Charlton Heston.

But what is it with the music! On one level we're watching a Russ Meyer remake of *Spartacus*, and we can go with that. But below the soft porn visuals we hear this, live through the Dolby speakers, from the man himself:[7]

> Nibblin' on sponge cake
> Watchin' the sun bake

This is like a question in the Stanford-Binet IQ test, in which the sixth-grade student is shown the series of three frames — one containing a drawing of a hammer, the next a drawing of a nail, and the third a drawing of something that looks like it might be a slice of chocolate cake. The student is then asked, "Okay, Skip, which of these doesn't belong?"

That's the problem: We can have ourselves a Roman orgy. And we can also have a bender in Margaritaville. But we cannot have half-naked Roman slaves blowing out their flip-flops, stepping on poptops, then shaking their booties at the tourists and hurrying home.

Where was this coming from? The Roman orgy bit was a slam dunk, as any of the guests who arrived on the morning of the first day could see readily enough. There to greet them at the hotel entrance stood Dennis, beaming ear to ear with a female toga-babe draped on each arm.

But what about the jarring sense of time-travel from the visuals to the music? How does one get from Pliny the Elder all the way to six strings and porch swings? Where did *that* come from?

How does one get from Pliny the Elder all the way to six strings and porch swings?

From the trial testimony of Barbara Jacques, who actually organized a lot of what transpired, it would appear that it came from the birthday girl herself. Karen, it seems, had been kind of hoping for a "beach party" sort of theme . . . so much so, that Barbara went out and found a group of boys who "sounded like the Beach Boys" and sent them down to the beach to play during the noon hour on Tuesday. Meanwhile, explained Barbara,

Dennis had long since told her to book Jimmy Buffett for the party and keep it as a surprise for Karen because, apparently, she adored him too, just like Dennis did.

A day later and it was over; the $2 million was gone; and by Saturday morning, Sardinia was but a memory. Karen and a dozen of her friends left on the Tyco jet for Florence and some cooking classes at Cucina al Focolare, and by the end of the month, she and Dennis were back in New York, stocking up on Monets, Renoirs, Cézannes, and whatnot — all on the Tyco tab — to distribute around the apartment on Fifth Avenue and in the house in Palm Beach.

But one senses an unreality about all this: the $1.2 million gift to the Christopher Reeve Paralysis Foundation . . . the photo ops with Karen and her million-dollar Palm Beach tan . . . the speeches at the Waldorf. There was something wrong with it all.

For one thing, the CIT group acquisition hadn't turned out to be another Dennis Kozlowski masterstroke at all. The deal was actually proving to be an out-and-out fiasco, and it was starting to drag down the stock. Then came a problem with the board member who had promoted it to him: Frank Walsh. Dennis had paid him that $20 million finder's fee but, yikes, he'd never cleared it with the board.

Then came something even worse: Some paintings that Tyco had bought for the Fifth Avenue apartment had been invoiced as if they had been shipped instead to Tyco's offices in New Hampshire. Before anyone knew it, prosecutors in the office of Manhattan District Attorney Robert Morgenthau had opened a tax fraud investigation. In May 2002, Kozlowski was charged with evading more than $1 million worth of New York State sales taxes, and it was only the beginning — though for Dennis Kozlowski, it was already the end.

In September 2002, Kozlowski was charged with having looted more than $600 million from Tyco and its shareholders since 1995 alone. In October 2003, his trial on the charges began in a New York State court, and lasted six months before being sent to the jury in March 2004. No verdict had been reached by the time this book went to press.

Meanwhile, new management had been installed at Tyco, the board of directors had been replaced, and the company had closed its New York office and moved to New Jersey. From there, Tyco filed its own $600 million civil fraud suit against their one-time boss, thus ending, in the twilight of his career, any hope that Dennis may have had for dislodging Jack Welch from his throne as the King of American business.

— Editor's Note: *Dennis Kozlowski was sentenced to 8 to 25 years in prison in 2005. He was also ordered to repay Tyco $134 million.*

NOTES

[1] Flamboyant weddings are part of many cultures and are characteristic of celebrity-world marriages in Hollywood. The 2000 wedding of Jennifer Aniston and Brad Pitt was reported to cost $1 million, with much of it spent on flowers. The wedding in 2000 of Madonna and film director Guy Ritchie at a rented castle in Scotland was reported to have cost $2.1 million. The November 2000 wedding of actors Michael Douglas and Catherine Zeta-Jones in New York cost a reported $1.5 million.

[2] See E. Sporkin, "Marriage with a Midas Touch," *People* (May 7, 1990), p. 150.

[3] Among those who showed up: Betsy Bloomingdale, William F. Buckley Jr., Walter Cronkite, Oscar de la Renta, Doris Duke, James Goldsmith, Katherine Graham, John Gutfreund, Lee Iacocca, Henry Kissinger, Calvin Klein, John Kluge, Rupert Murdoch, Regis Philbin, Joan Rivers, Elizabeth Taylor, Barbara Walters, and of course Ron Perelman.

[4] See B. Ross and B. Hutchinson, "Tyco Jurors View Video," *New York Daily News* (October 29, 2003), p. 5.

[5] The details of the festivities, including the itinerary, are drawn from the court testimony of participants, in the case of the *People of the State of New York v. L. Dennis Kozlowski and Mark H. Swartz* (September 2003).

[6] Buffett was flown to Sardinia and brought to the hotel under the pseudonym of "Elvis Smith," ostensibly to prevent throngs of autograph seekers. It seems just as likely that the real reason was his reluctance to be publicly identified with the affair, which simply did not have a quality caché, even from the start.

[7] Buffett was popular with other CEO rock and rollers besides the guitar-playing Kozlowski, and was a particular favorite of Ron Perelman, who fancied himself a drummer. In March 1995, Patricia Duff organized a dinner at the Perelman home in Palm Beach for President Bill Clinton, and Buffett attended, leading the group after dinner in a chorus of *Margaritaville*. See E. Bumiller, "700 Days in Society and Politics: Fundraiser Wed to Billionaire Finds Roles Clash," *New York Times* (November 3, 1996), p. 41. For his appearance at Kozlowski's Sardinian bash, Buffett received $250,000 for performing a single, forty-five-minute set of Jimmy Buffett favorites. Buffett's imputed fee of $5,555.00 per minute was cheap compared with what the parents of Perelman's second wife, Claudia Cohen, paid for ten minutes worth of singing by the Pointer Sisters at the couple's wedding reception: $8,000.00 per minute. See G. Grig, "Lipstick on His Dollars," *New York Times* (September 26, 1993). For the fact that Claudia Cohen's parents picked up the tab, see Richard Hack, *When Money Is King* (Los Angeles, CA: Dove Books, 1996), p. 43.

DISCUSSION

1. Do you think it's possible to turn Byron's description of corporate abuse and CEO criminal irresponsibility on its head? Can his accounts be read as a blueprint of behavior and values that are actually our cultural ideals?

2. For Byron, the corporate critique he presents is a gendered one. The misbehaviors he catalogs and the attitudes he skewers are all expressions of the underlying machismo that Byron sees at the center of today's business culture. How valid do you think this view is? Are there any counterexamples from the world of business that you think would complicate or contradict this thesis?

3. One of the core questions underlying Byron's exposé has to do with the relationship between ambition and greed. Where, in your view, does being ambitious stop and being greedy begin? Is it even valid to think of them as related concepts?

WRITING

4. Make a list of all the offenses committed by corporate CEOs that this essay lists. Choose one of them and write a one-page essay in which you explain and evaluate work-related norms or rules it supposedly violates. What is it about this behavior that makes it criminal? Do you share this same view? Or is it possible that this behavior has itself become a norm in the corporate world?

5. Our airwaves are replete these days with shows — from *Mad Money* to *The Apprentice* — that present us with the flip side of Byron's portrayal: shows, that is, that celebrate the achievements and acumen of America's business elite. Choose one such example and write an essay in which you contrast the central differences between its depiction and Byron's.

6. How do you think Barbara Ehrenreich (p. 278) would respond to Byron's portrait of white-collar misbehavior? Is there anything she identifies in the culture of white-collar work that would account for or lead to the sorts of crimes recorded in "Let's Party Like It's 1999"? Write out the kind of review of Byron's piece you think Ehrenreich would present. How much sympathy for Byron's depiction of and explanation for CEO crime do you think she would have?

LOUIS UCHITELLE
The Consequences — Undoing Sanity

Perhaps the most glaring counterpoint to the corporate environment just detailed by Christopher Byron is the world of unemployment evoked in this next essay. Chronicling what he calls the "psychiatric aspects of layoffs," Louis Uchitelle uses a focus on joblessness to better understand the social messages and cultural values that teach Americans to connect their work to their self-worth. In a world ever more frequently marked by downsizing and layoffs, Uchitelle asks whether it's still possible to treat such cherished notions as job security and the dignity of work as indisputable facts of life. Uchitelle writes about business and economics for the *New York Times*, and he won a George Polk Award for the *Times* series "The Downsizing of America," an investigation of layoffs that ran in 1996. He addressed the subject again in his book *The Disposable American: Layoffs and Their Consequences* (2006), from which the following selection is taken. Before moving to the *Times*, he worked at the Associated Press as a foreign correspondent, reporter, and editor. He has taught at Columbia University and in 2002–2003 was a visiting scholar at the Russell Sage Foundation in New York.

HARD AS SHE TRIED, STACY BROWN COULD NOT REKINDLE IN HER husband, Erin, the passion for work that he lost when United Airlines laid him off as a mechanic at its giant aircraft maintenance center in Indianapolis. She loved Erin; that is, she loved the engaged and energetic young man she had married three years earlier. "He was just going a million miles a minute before this all happened," she said. She wanted that Erin back, and soon. Not for the income. If need be, she could support the family quite handsomely herself, as a litigator at a white-shoe Indianapolis law firm. But as we talked in late 2004, she was six months pregnant with their second child, and it was time to embrace the roles they had planned for themselves when they married: she as the mother and care-giver, he as the really skilled engineer, mechanic, and craftsman rising adventurously in the corporate world, or going out on his own as an entrepreneur. The layoff had destroyed all this and her distress was unrestrained.[1]

"I think the layoff destroyed his self-esteem," Stacy said, her words coming rapidly and intensely. "I don't think he will ever admit that but I think it has. That is a hard thing to overcome and I don't

> **"I think the layoff destroyed his self-esteem."**

know how you overcome it to get back into the working world, which is what I think he is going to have to do. When he fills out résumés and applies for jobs, you can see it is not with the extreme belief that he is going to get one. He waits until the last minute and gets the résumé in, but maybe doesn't get it in completely. I think that is because he is probably depressed."

Two years after Erin Brown lost his job at United Airlines, his wife was attempting, in a drastic, risky way, to jump-start her husband's self-confidence — to puncture his inertia and bring him quickly to the point that he would once again want to step into a career and take on the risks involved in pursuing uncertain goals. She had insisted on the purchase of a rundown three-bedroom house half a block from their own home in their once splendid Victorian-era neighborhood, which was now coming back as a downtown enclave for young professionals and executives. Erin had balked at the purchase, as he had balked at earlier opportunities to acquire and renovate rundown houses in the neighborhood, then flip them at a profit. Too risky, he insisted. This time, ignoring her husband's reluctance, Stacy put in a bid anyway, winning the house for a rock-bottom $95,000 at a mortgage foreclosure sale. She closed the deal by doing all the paperwork herself, moving forward decisively once Erin assured her that the eighty-four-year-old dwelling with its spacious front veranda was structurally sound.

They paid cash, drawing on their savings, and immediately put the house up for sale at $165,000, untouched. They were ready in their own minds, or at least Stacy was, to accept a counteroffer of $140,000 for this handyman special. Gentrification alone would bring them a sufficient profit, she reasoned, and that success would rebuild in Erin some of the self-esteem and energy that the layoff had destroyed. Or, faced with ownership — having been pushed by his wife into a gamble — Erin would renovate the house and they would then resell it for at least $195,000, an even greater success for him. Mainly, however, Stacy hoped for the quick resale. She doubted that Erin possessed the self-confidence to carry out the renovation. "He's going to want to start this and then he's not going to be able to finish it in a very timely manner," she said, "so we will end up hanging on to two houses, which is okay, but what it doesn't do is give him that sense of accomplishment and purpose and financial reward, which is what he needs to function effectively again."

In the cataloging of damage that results from layoffs, incapacitating emotional illness almost never appears on the lists that economists, politicians, sociologists, union leaders, business school professors, management consultants, and journalists compile. There is much discussion of income loss, downward mobility, a decrease in family cohesion, a rise in the divorce rate, the unwinding of communities, the impact on children, the impact on survivors who dodge a layoff but are left feeling insecure and guilty that they kept their jobs while colleagues did not.[2]

Extended periods of unemployment bring a cascade of damages, including depression, and these too are documented. One study, for example, found that for every percentage point change in the unemployment rate, up or down, the national suicide rate rose or fell in tandem, and so did the frequency of strokes, heart attacks, crime, and accidents.[3]

The layoff, however, is seldom singled out as damaging in itself, quite apart from the unemployment that follows. But the trauma of dismissal — the "acuteness of the blow," as Dr. Theodore Jacobs, the New York psychoanalyst, put it — unwinds lives in its own right, damaging self-esteem, undoing normal adaptive mechanisms, and erecting the sort of emotional barriers that have prevented Erin Brown and thousands of others, perhaps millions of others, from returning energetically to the workforce in jobs that draw productively on their education and skills. "There are many people who do not want to face that trauma again and to some degree they lose a sense of reality," Dr. Jacobs said. "They give themselves a lot of conscious reasons why they cannot accept this job or that job, but deeper down they don't want to face the rigors and anxieties of work and the fears they won't be up to it and they will be dropped again."[4]

I did not think in the early stages of the reporting for this book that I would be drawn so persistently into the psychiatric aspect of layoffs. But a surprisingly high number of the laid-off people with whom I talked described from every angle and over and over again what, in their minds, had been done to them, the mistakes they had made, their bad luck in being caught in the particular situation that cost them their jobs, the shortsightedness or outright evil of the bosses who failed to protect them or did not want to do so, how cut adrift they felt, or, hiding their loss and hurt in elaborate rationalizations, how comfortable they insisted they were in some new way of life, safely separated from challenging work.

The emotional damage was too palpable to ignore. Whenever I insisted that layoffs were a phenomenon in America beyond their control, they agreed perfunctorily and then went right back to describing their own devaluing experiences, and why it was somehow their fault or their particular bad luck. When I turned to psychiatrists and psychologists for an explanation of what I was finding, they offered similar observations of their own. "Chipping away at human capital," Dr. Jacobs called it. "Even when a person accurately realizes that he has done a good job, that the company is in a bad way, that it has to lay off a lot of people and it is not about me, there is always some sense of diminishment. Others at the company are not laid off, so why me? And that sense of having been judged and found wanting dovetails with older feelings of inadequacy about one's self that were acquired growing up."

Dr. Kim Cameron, an organizational psychologist at the University of Michigan's business school, focuses in his work on developing ways for

Layoffs are destructive psychologically for the individuals who lose their jobs.

corporate managers to carry out layoffs benignly, the goal being to limit the damage to the victims and in doing so soften the blow to morale among the survivors. In the same vein, management consultants and business school professors write endlessly about the various techniques for finessing layoffs. Dr. Cameron has concluded, however, that no matter how sophisticated the technique, there is not much balm: layoffs are destructive psychologically for the individuals who lose their jobs.

I told him Brown's story, including the conflicts with his manager at United Airlines over his inspection reports and the related setback in his application to advance to the engineering department at United's maintenance center, and Dr. Cameron replied that Brown seemed to be an example of a "fundamental in-the-bones blow to ego and self-worth.[5]

"You can have all kinds of people like spouses and friends say you are terrific, you are wonderful, you are great," Dr. Cameron said, "but in the core you say, I am not, and I have big evidence that I am not. Layoffs diminish the ability to restart. They are the opposite of life giving; they literally deplete life." In Brown's case and in many others, Dr. Cameron said, the damage is hard to observe. "It is subversive in that it limits all kinds of other activities — for example, the ability to form emotional bonds with people, the ability to be energized and aggressive in pursuing a new job or position, and the ability to try new things. Trial-and-error learning is diminished. If I am feeling awful about myself, I don't want one more failure. If you try new things, the probability seems higher that you will fail, so you don't try them."[6]

Psychiatrists and psychologists uncover these hidden linkages in therapy. Living with Erin, Stacy also gradually saw them, although her husband tried to hide what he was feeling from her, and from himself. The emotional damage from layoffs varies, of course, from case to case. Brown had to contend with his wife's success as a lawyer and her earning power. His parents' divorce when he was a boy may have also undermined his sense of himself as an effective worker. But who among us does not have contributing factors embedded in our lives waiting for a catalyst, like a layoff, to set them off? At age thirty, Erin was frozen, unable to act, not just in home renovation but in elbowing his way back into a job that would draw on his considerable skills. Denial and anger justified his inaction and hid its deeper causes.

A year after her husband's layoff, Stacy prodded him into applying for a job at a Rolls-Royce engine plant in Indianapolis. The opening was for a technical specialist in the engineering department, a job involving research on jet engines that Erin later said he wanted. But his description of his encounter with the human resources manager who interviewed him was laced with resentment and insult, and the manager must have noticed. "I was well-qualified and I went through a lot of effort to get that one," Erin said, "and it turns out the guy who was doing the hiring had not bothered to understand the nature of the job he was in charge of filling."

In Brown's view, the candidate finally selected was inferior to him in education and know-how. "He had no bachelor's degree in engineering and he lacked the analytical skill that the job required," Erin asserted, berating the interviewer for bureaucratically placing too much importance on a relatively insignificant aspect of the job description: shop-floor experience in machining. The winning candidate had that experience and that made the difference, Erin said, despite his plea to the interviewer that he could come up to speed as a machinist in two weeks. "I said to this guy, 'Hey, look, I have the training, I just don't have the experience in the field, but I'll do whatever you want me to do on my own time to get it.' No interest on his part. They want everything exactly according to the specifications. . . . And then, even if you are among the top applicants, they don't have the decency to get back to you and say, 'Thanks, but no thanks.' I mean you have to call them and hound them to see what happened with the position."

His account of the purchase of the house down the street from their home differed alarmingly from his wife's subsequent explanation. He did not mention her decisive role in making the purchase or that she was trying to prod him out of what she described as a mild but incapacitating depression. Instead, he left the impression that he had taken the initiative in making the purchase. If the house did not resell quickly — and it was already on the market — then he would remodel the kitchen and add a garage to increase the resale value. None of Stacy's anguish came through in the optimistic plans that Erin described. Before doing any of the remodeling, he said, sounding sure of himself, he just might move his family into the new dwelling while he completed the long-drawn-out renovation of his own home. The Rolls-Royce debacle, he said, he had put behind him. He had made no further attempt to apply for challenging jobs in big corporations. Henceforth, he said, he would go the entrepreneurial route, relying on himself. As evidence of his determination and effectiveness, he declared that he had finally completed construction of the two-story carriage house behind his and Stacy's home. It was ready to be sold or rented as office space, he said.

This was the project that Erin had started while Stacy was on maternity leave in the winter and spring of 2003, shortly after he lost his job at United. Birth, layoff, and maternity leave melded. During Stacy's leave, Erin did 60 percent of the construction work and then, when she went back to her job, he stopped, not touching the carriage house again for more than a year; caring for Kyle took up too much of his time, he said. Now, after all those months of inactivity, Erin told me by phone that he had completed the project, the work carried out in what appeared to be a spurt of energy and activity despite the time consumed in child care. He e-mailed me a photo of the exterior, freshly painted green and white. But he had not finished the interior. Inside that cozy two-story house, wiring and electricity were yet to be installed and studs were still exposed.

Stacy set me straight on the status of the carriage house. Her husband had indeed completed the exterior, she said. "He did beautiful work." But he had acted because he had no choice: either he used the materials he had purchased or they would "sit there and rot." As for the interior, Erin found reasons to put off doing that essential work, and Stacy saw the postponements as a signal from her husband — a signal whose true meaning he suppressed — that he did not want to take the risk of actually finishing the carriage house and then somehow having that achievement, too, taken from him.

She had finally concluded that Erin's emotional damage had become a barrier to the family life they both seemed to want. "Our hope is that . . . there will be a time for me to stay home with our children for a while," Stacy told me. "But at the same time, just this morning, we were talking that it was time to make elections next year for my work and my contributions to the medical savings account and things like that, and he says, 'What happens if you have to go back to work?' And I thought, What do you mean what happens if I have to go back to work? I thought the plan was that *you* were going to go to work. So I think at the same time he's just such an optimistic soul, but I think in the back of his mind, I think he is doubting. I mean, I think he is doubting his ability to get gainful employment and employment that supports our family. I mean, all along, even though he wanted to be laid off in the sense that he thought he was ready to leave United, I firmly believe the layoff impacted him very much. To think back to the person he was when I met him — he enjoyed his job, he really thought he had a career going. And to watch the person that he is today, so averse to employment and so averse to being a worker."

Stacy asked me for help. She had appealed to Erin's father, but father and son did not communicate easily, and Erin resisted taking advice from members of her family. "He talks to you," she said. So I waited a couple of weeks and called Erin. I said that he had misled me at times, without meaning to, and that Stacy and I were concerned about his inaction. I suggested that he see a therapist, that therapy might help him get through this crisis. He did not respond directly to my suggestion, nor did he veer from amiability. "What worries Stacy and you is that I am not really concerned about working to my potential," he replied.

That did worry us, but Erin would not be swayed. He had just completed a two-evening-a-week course in air-conditioner repair, learning very little that he did not already know, to get the necessary certification for a $13- or $14-an-hour dead-end job. Driving about in a panel truck making repairs to air-conditioning units would give him health insurance and some income for the family, once Stacy left her law firm, he explained to me. Most important, he would have a nondemanding, unthreatening platform from which to branch out and ample spare time for truly challenging work: renovating and reselling rundown homes, for example. "I know that I will be overqualified for the next position that I take," he said.

Not everyone has as much difficulty as Erin Brown in shaking off the emotional setback that layoffs produce. Some of those whose stories have been told earlier managed to move on to a next stage in their lives with their mental health more or less intact. But the majority did not. Psychiatrists and psychoanalysts view layoffs as catalysts for emotional damage. There is no mechanism, however, for collecting and disseminating what they know so that the consequences of corporate layoffs can be publicly flagged. The Centers for Disease Control and Prevention in Atlanta track the number of cases of flu, AIDS, measles, polio, Lyme disease, and other physical illnesses, and when the number spikes for one of these ailments, the center alerts us that an epidemic may be brewing, one that requires stepped-up medical treatment and a concerted public effort to shrink the number of cases. While doctors and hospitals funnel data about physical illness to the Centers for Disease Control, psychiatrists and psychologists do not similarly report the incidence among their patients of disabling neuroses connected to layoffs. Nor do the organizations that represent them adopt resolutions that declare layoffs to be a source of mental illness and therefore a menace to public health.

The American Psychiatric Association, whose 35,000 members are likely to treat mental illness related to layoffs, has never formally declared that the modern American layoff is hazardous to health. The president of the association, Dr. Steven S. Sharfstein, readily acknowledges the linkage as do other leaders of the organization.[7] Divorce, however, also damages mental health, Dr. Sharfstein said. So does the death of a spouse or a parent, not to mention the trauma of war. For psychiatry to oppose these events on public health grounds would be futile, he argued, and in the case of layoffs very possibly counterproductive. "If a company refrains from a layoff and then, as a result, is forced out of business, everyone would end up laid off," he said. So the American Psychiatric Association acquiesces in the practice and pushes instead to expand treatment of the victims. It lobbies business, for example, to expand coverage for mental illness. "We do see there are major shortcomings with employer health insurance in terms of access to mental health care," Dr. Sharfstein said, "and that is how we go at this issue."

Only one group of psychiatrists that I could find had singled out the layoff, the act in which a worker is sent away, as damaging in itself to mental health. The alert had come from the three hundred members of the Group for the Advancement of Psychiatry, or more specifically from the dozen or so in the group's Committee on Psychiatry in Industry. These were psychiatrists whose practices focused on working with companies as consultants. Their client companies engaged in layoffs and they had first-hand knowledge of what people went through. In 1982, when the modern layoff was still a raw American experience, they published a monograph, *Job Loss — a Psychiatric Perspective,* in which they declared: "Our experience in industry and with patients suggests that those who lose their functional role as workers may behave as if their society no longer values them. Because they accept that as true, they suffer a consequent loss in the perception of their value in their families and to themselves."[8]

They distributed that study, with its straightforward, unpleasant observation, and eight years later, three psychiatrists on the committee expanded their findings into a book, *The Psychosocial Impact of Job Loss.*[9] Neither drew any attention. "Company managers were more interested in talking about the coping skills of those who remained on the job than they were about the damage to those they had laid off," Dr. Stephen Heidel, a consultant to businesses and a clinical professor of psychiatry at the University of California, San Diego, told me. I asked the doctors why, in their opinion, they had had so little success in publicizing the message in their monograph and book.[10] Various possibilities were mentioned, but all seemed to agree with Dr. Heidel's observation that managers don't want to be told about damage to mental health that results from a layoff they initiated. "If a psychiatrist goes out and says, I am an expert in job loss, the manager does not want to hear that and the psychiatrist won't be consulted about other services he can provide to a corporation," Dr. Heidel said. "If you lead with that, the door will be shut. You need to put a positive spin on things."

> **Company managers were more interested in talking about the coping skills of those who remained on the job.**

While the nation's psychiatrists remain all but silent as a group, psychologists and sociologists in academic research seldom spot the sorts of debilitating neuroses that are evident in one-on-one therapy. Academics place much more faith in what they can document through empirical studies. They seek quantifiable evidence and shun the diagnostic judgment that is unavoidable in psychotherapy, whose raw material is narrative and free association. Their work, in consequence, relies heavily on surveys that blend together layoffs and unemployment and correlate the undifferentiated experience with measurable reactions: elevated blood pressure; an increased incidence of stomach problems, headaches, and insomnia; noticeably greater anxiety; a tendency to drink and smoke more; an increase in hospital admissions for ostensibly physical ailments. No survey of observable symptoms would pick up Brown's malady.

Psychoanalysts like Dr. Jacobs are also reluctant to single out layoffs publicly as damaging to mental health. By way of explanation, Dr. Jacobs said that people who seek psychoanalysis do so because of "long-standing character problems and in the course of analysis they mention a layoff, which has magnified what is already there or latently there." As a result, the layoff is not a central issue for the 2,500 members of the American Psychoanalytic Association. None of the numerous sessions at the association's four-day semiannual conferences have focused on layoffs and mental health. When I posted a request at the winter meeting in January 2005 to interview psychoanalysts concerned about the linkage, the only response came from Dr. Alexandra K. Rolde, a psychiatrist and psychoanalyst in private practice in Boston and a clinical instructor in psychiatry at Harvard Medical School.[11] For some of her patients, layoffs were indeed a central theme.

Dr. Rolde, a Czech immigrant in her late sixties, lived through the German occupation of Prague during World War II, in "semihiding" with her mother, as she puts it, to escape deportation and death as Jews. It was an experience that familiarized her with trauma, which is now her specialty in psychiatry. After the war she moved to Canada with her mother and stepfather, and the parents thrived in the jewelry business, first in Montreal and then in Toronto. When they moved the business from one city to the other, acting out of concern that Quebec's separatist movement might isolate the province from the rest of Canada, all fifty of the employees moved, too. No one was laid off, Dr. Rolde said, proud of the loyalties that kept her parents and their workers together. She has treated roughly thirty patients over the past twenty years for layoff-related ailments, she said, and she considers the layoffs to have been life-changing for them. Like Dr. Jacobs, she sees children as well as adults, and they, too, are often damaged.

"It is a trauma to the entire family," she said. "You have a parent working at a prestigious full-time job. All of a sudden the parent sits at home and can't find a job and is depressed. And suddenly the child's role model sort of crumbles. Instead of feeling admiration for the parent, the child eventually begins to feel disrespect. Because the children identify with their parents, they begin to doubt that they can accomplish anything. They feel they won't be successful in life and their self-esteem plummets. This of course is a long-term thing. We call it transgenerational trauma; it is similar to what we used to see with Holocaust survivors and their children. The children feel as damaged as their parents, even though they did not experience the trauma directly themselves."

She told me about a woman she had treated for years after the woman was laid off from an executive job at General Electric. "She got back into the workforce quickly enough, but in a job she did not like, yet she clung to it anyway," Dr. Rolde said. "She was so traumatized by the layoff that she did not have the self-confidence to risk moving on to more suitable work."

NOTES

[1] Interview with Stacy Brown, December 27, 2004.

[2] Concerning children, some studies show that children in two-parent families react differently to a father's job loss than to a mother's. In a study of 4,500 school-age children, for example, Ariel Kalil and Kathleen M. Ziol-Guest of the University of Chicago found that "mothers' employment is never significantly associated with children's academic progress. In contrast, we found significant adverse associations between fathers' job losses [and] children's probability of grade repetition and school suspension/expulsion."

[3] M. Merva and R. Fowles, "Effects of Diminished Economic Opportunities on Social Stress: Heart Attacks, Strokes and Crime," Salt Lake City Economic Policy Institute, University of Utah, 1992. The study covered fifteen metropolises over a twenty-year period. For other studies of the effects of unemployment on health, see "Links in the Chain of Adversity Following Job Loss: How Financial Strain and Loss of Personal Control Lead to Depression, Impaired Functioning and Poor Health," by Richard H. Price, Jin Nam Choi, and Amiram D. Vinokur, *Journal of Occupational Health Psychology* 7 (2002).

[4] Interview with Dr. Theodore Jacobs, August 5, 2004. In addition to his posts as a clinical professor of psychiatry at New York University School of Medicine and at the Albert Einstein College of Medicine, Dr. Jacobs is also the supervising analyst at the Psychoanalytic Institute at New York University and at the New York Psychoanalytic Institute.

[5] Interviews with Kim Cameron, January 17, 2005, and February 2, 2005.

[6] Interview with Kim Cameron, February 2, 2005.

[7] Interview with Dr. Steven Sharfstein, January 17, 2005. Dr. Sharfstein's one-year term as president of the APA began in May 2005. He is president and chief executive of Sheppard Pratt Health Care System, a nonprofit organization in Baltimore that provides mental health care for drug addicts and education for mentally disturbed children, among other services. He has a private psychiatric practice in Baltimore and has been a clinical professor of psychiatry at the University of Maryland.

[8] *Job Loss — a Psychiatric Perspective*, published by Mental Health Materials Center, New York, 1982.

[9] Nick Kates, Barrie S. Grieff, and Duane Hagen, *The Psychosocial Impact of Job Loss* (American Psychiatric Press, 1990).

[10] The conversation took place on April 8, 2005, during and after a session of the Committee on Psychiatry and Industry at the spring meeting of the Group for the Advancement of Psychiatry.

[11] The request was posted at the winter meeting, January 2005, at the Waldorf-Astoria. Dr. Rolde is also on the faculty of the Psychoanalytic Institute of New England East (PINE) and is a member of the Psychoanalytic Society of New England East (PSNE) as well as the Boston Psychoanalytic Society and Institute (BPSI).

DISCUSSION

1. It is far more conventional to speak about layoffs in economic rather than emotional terms. How does Uchitelle challenge this convention? In what ways does his examination of the psychiatric aspects of joblessness rewrite the scripts by which we are taught to think about unemployment?

2. "'You can have all kinds of people like spouses and friends say you are terrific, you are wonderful, you are great,'" Uchitelle quotes one medical expert as saying, "'but in the core you say, I am not, and I have big evidence that I am not. Layoffs diminish the ability to restart.'" Why are layoffs so often considered such convincing evidence of our self-worth? What does it tell us about the kind of importance we are taught to place on the work we do?

3. "In the cataloging of damage that results from layoffs," writes Uchitelle, "incapacitating emotional illness almost never appears on the lists that economists, politicians, sociologists, union leaders, business school professors, management consultants, and journalists compile." Why doesn't it? What would you say are the assumptions or norms that keep us from viewing emotional illness as a legitimate consequence of unemployment?

WRITING

4. One of the costs of layoffs, according to Uchitelle, is that they deprive people of a primary way to define their self-worth. Write an essay in which you reflect on the role that work plays in anchoring and validating your views of yourself. Can you think of a job you've held or a career path you've pursued (or one you would like to) that you've used to define your self-worth? What would the effect be of having this particular work outlet taken away?

5. Some of the psychological or emotional effects of being laid off that Uchitelle lists are low self-esteem, nervousness, inability to form close bonds, and fear of trying new things. Do you think it is reasonable for employers to consider the emotional costs of layoffs in determining whether to let workers go? How might an employer address the criticisms that Uchitelle is making? Ultimately, is an employer responsible for the emotional well-being of its employees? Why or why not?

6. Cast yourself in the role of the career coach that Barbara Ehrenreich (p. 278) describes in her essay. Write an essay in which you lay out the advice you might offer to one of the unemployed workers profiled by Uchitelle. What problems or shortcomings would you identify? What specifically would you recommend that this person do differently and why? How effective do you think this advice would actually be?

Then and Now: *Dressing for Success*

The rules establishing proper workplace attire have changed markedly over the years. But are these changes merely cosmetic? Or do they tell us something about the ways our attitudes toward work, or perhaps even our social or cultural attitudes, have changed? To be sure, there is a long and storied history in America of treating workplace wardrobe as a kind of societal barometer. In the case of the 1950s office worker, for example, the "gray flannel suit" came to be widely viewed as a metaphor for the corporate standardization, political conformity, and social conservatism that for many defined American life during this period. For countless commentators, this unadorned and anonymous business uniform not only captured the supposedly faceless, robotic nature of 1950s office work, but it also symbolized a pervasive hostility in midcentury America toward individuality, creativity, and dissent.

Designed for modern living

Plateau—smooth 100% worsted—the suit with the "weightless feel"

It's a PACIFIC Worsted BY PACIFIC MILLS ... WEAVERS OF FINE WOOLENS, WORSTEDS, COTTONS, RAYON

When compared to the corporate dress codes that prevail today, it's hard not to feel we've come a long way from this buttoned-down, bygone era. Nowadays the drab uniformity of gray flannel has given way to the more flexible and informal wardrobe norms of so-called business casual — a shift, we are told, that proves how much more liberated, freewheeling, and creative office work has become. No longer the faceless drone of yore, the corporate employee of the twenty-first century (at least according to what we see in countless commercials) plies his or her trade in an environment where individuality and diversity are prized, a world in which employees are members of teams, professional colleagues are also personal friends, and creativity rather than conformity is the rule of thumb.

But is this actually true? Does this shift in dress code really prove how much more liberated office life — or life in general — has become? In answering this question, we might begin by pointing out a paradox: Despite its emphasis on nonconformity and individual choice, business casual is nonetheless still a *style*, a wardrobe standard established for and marketed to us. Just because we get to wear khakis and sandals to the office these days doesn't automatically mean we're now using clothes to express our individuality — particularly when we may well have gotten the idea for this outfit by paging through a clothing catalog. Even when an office wardrobe is informal, it isn't necessarily any less of an office uniform. What the rise of business casual may well demonstrate, in fact, is not how nonconformist modern American culture has become, but rather how the terms defining such conformity have simply changed. It certainly seems a stretch to claim that white-collar work is no longer hier-archical or rigidly organized, or that the contemporary busi-ness landscape has grown any less "corporate." Perhaps this shift toward casualness is best understood not as a move-ment beyond conformity than as a compensation for con-formity: a style change designed to add a gloss of informality and autonomy to a work world still largely dictated by scripts we ourselves do not write.

WRITING

1. Write an essay in which you analyze what sorts of norms about work are conveyed by the style of dress in these two examples. What, if anything, seems to have changed between the depictions of work dress in the 1950s versus today? In your opinion, which example seems more typical of the concepts of work and career? Why?

2. One of the biggest differences between white-collar and blue-collar work is the difference in dress. How do you think Anthony DePalma (p. 312) would respond to the idea of business casual dress? In your opinion, does the idea of business casual highlight or diminish the differences between white- and blue-collar work? Why?

ANTHONY DePALMA

Fifteen Years on the Bottom Rung

America, it is said, is the "land of opportunity." Depending on where you're born, what pressures you face, or what circumstances you find yourself in, however, this myth can play itself out in radically different ways. Anthony DePalma focuses on one group of workers for whom the supposedly universal promise of opportunity bumps up against the hard realities that often confront those on the lower rungs of the socioeconomic ladder. DePalma is the author of The *Man Who Invented Fidel* (2006), a study of the *New York Times* reporter who help to create the myth surrounding Castro. He has also published *Here: A Biography of the New American Continent* (2001). DePalma is a staff writer for the *New York Times*, and as bureau chief for Mexico and Canada, he covered political events such as the Zapatista uprising, economic news such as the crisis of the peso, and natural disasters such as the Quebec ice storm. He has also worked as a business correspondent in both the Metropolitan and National divisions. He now reports on environmental issues for the *Times*. The following essay is from *Class Matters* (2005), by correspondents of the *New York Times*.

IN THE DARK BEFORE DAWN, WHEN MADISON AVENUE WAS ALL BUT deserted and its pricey boutiques were still locked up tight, several Mexicans slipped quietly into 3 Guys, a restaurant that the Zagat guide once called "the most expensive coffee shop in New York."

For the next ten hours they would fry eggs, grill burgers, pour coffee, and wash dishes for a stream of customers from the Upper East Side of Manhattan. By 7:35 A.M., Eliot Spitzer, attorney general of New York, was holding a power breakfast back near the polished granite counter. In the same burgundy booth a few hours later, Michael A. Wiener, cofounder of the multibillion-dollar Infinity Broadcasting, grabbed a bite with his wife, Zena. Just the day before, Uma Thurman slipped in for a quiet lunch with her children, but the paparazzi found her and she left.

More Mexicans filed in to begin their shifts throughout the morning, and by the time John Zannikos, one of the restaurant's three Greek owners, drove in from the north Jersey suburbs to work the lunch crowd, Madison Avenue was buzzing. So was 3 Guys.

"You got to wait a little bit," Zannikos said to a pride of elegant women who had spent the morning at the Whitney Museum of American

Art, across Madison Avenue at 75th Street. For an illiterate immigrant who came to New York years ago with nothing but $100 in his pocket and a willingness to work etched on his heart, could any words have been sweeter to say?

With its wealthy clientele, middle-class owners, and low-income workforce, 3 Guys is a template of the class divisions in America. But it is also the setting for two starkly different tales about breaching those divides.

The familiar story is Zannikos's. For him, the restaurant — don't dare call it a diner — with its twenty-dollar salads and elegant décor represents the American promise of upward mobility, one that has been fulfilled countless times for generations of hardworking immigrants.

But for Juan Manuel Peralta, a thirty-four-year-old illegal immigrant who worked there for five years until he was fired in May 2004, and for many of the other illegal Mexican immigrants in the back, restaurant work today is more like a dead end. They are finding the American dream of moving up far more elusive than it was for Zannikos. Despite his efforts to help them, they risk becoming stuck in a permanent underclass of the poor, the unskilled, and the uneducated.

That is not to suggest that the nearly five million Mexicans who, like Peralta, are living in the United States illegally will never emerge from the shadows. Many have, and undoubtedly many more will. But the sheer size of the influx — over 400,000 a year, with no end in sight — creates a problem all its own. It means there is an ever-growing pool of interchangeable workers, many of them shunting from one low-paying job to another. If one moves on, another one — or maybe two or three — is there to take his place.

> **There is an ever-growing pool of interchangeable workers, many of them shunting from one low-paying job to another.**

Although Peralta arrived in New York almost forty years after Zannikos, the two share a remarkably similar beginning. They came at the same age to the same section of New York City, without legal papers or more than a few words of English. Each dreamed of a better life. But monumental changes in the economy and in attitudes toward immigrants have made it far less likely that Peralta and his children will experience the same upward mobility as Zannikos and his family.

Of course, there is a chance that Peralta may yet take his place among the Mexican-Americans who have succeeded here. He realizes that he will probably not do as well as the few who have risen to high office or who were able to buy the vineyards where their grandfathers once picked grapes. But he still dreams that his children will someday join the millions who have lost their accents, gotten good educations, and firmly achieved the American dream.

Political scientists are divided over whether the twenty-five million people of Mexican ancestry in the United States represent an exception to the classic immigrant success story. Some, like John H. Mollenkopf at the City University of New York, are convinced that Mexicans will eventually do as well as the Greeks, Italians, and other Europeans of the last century who were usually well assimilated after two or three generations. Others, including Mexican-Americans like Rodolfo O. de la Garza, a professor at Columbia, have done studies showing that Mexican-Americans face so many obstacles that even the fourth generation trails other Americans in education, home ownership, and household income.

The situation is even worse for the millions more who have illegally entered the United States since 1990. Spread out in scores of cities far beyond the Southwest, they find jobs plentiful but advancement difficult. President Vicente Fox of Mexico was forced to apologize in the spring of 2005 for declaring publicly what many Mexicans say they feel, that the illegal immigrants "are doing the work that not even blacks want to do in the United States." Resentment and race subtly stand in their way, as does a lingering attachment to Mexico, which is so close that many immigrants do not put down deep roots here. They say they plan to stay only long enough to make some money and then go back home. Few ever do.

But the biggest obstacle is their illegal status. With few routes open to become legal, they remain, like Peralta, without rights, without security, and without a clear path to a better future.

"It's worrisome," said Richard Alba, a sociologist at the State University of New York, Albany, who studies the assimilation and class mobility of contemporary immigrants, "and I don't see much reason to believe this will change."

Little has changed for Peralta, a cook who has worked at menial jobs in the United States for fifteen years. Though he makes more than he ever dreamed of in Mexico, his life is anything but middle class and setbacks are routine. Still, he has not given up hope. "*Querer es poder,*" he sometimes says — want something badly enough and you will get it.

But desire may not be enough anymore. That is what concerns Arturo Sarukhan, Mexico's consul general in New York. In early 2005, Sarukhan took an urgent call from New York's police commissioner about an increase in gang activity among young Mexican men, a sign that they were moving into the underside of American life. Of all immigrants in New York City, officials say, Mexicans are the poorest, least educated, and least likely to speak English.

The failure or success of this generation of Mexicans in the United States will determine the place that Mexicans will hold here in years to come, Sarukhan said, and the outlook is not encouraging.

"They will be better off than they could ever have been in Mexico," he said, "but I don't think that's going to be enough to prevent them from becoming an underclass in New York."

DIFFERENT RESULTS

There is a break in the middle of the day at 3 Guys, after the lunchtime limousines leave and before the private schools let out. That was when Zannikos asked the Mexican cook who replaced Peralta to prepare some lunch for him. Then Zannikos carried the chicken breast on pita to the last table in the restaurant.

"My life story is a good story, a lot of success," he said, his accent still heavy. He was just a teenager when he left the Greek island of Chios, a few miles off the coast of Turkey. World War II had just ended, and Greece was in ruins. "There was only rich and poor, that's it," Zannikos said. "There was no middle class like you have here." He is seventy now, with short gray hair and soft eyes that can water at a mention of the past.

Because of the war, he said, he never got past the second grade, never learned to read or write. He signed on as a merchant seaman, and in 1953, when he was nineteen, his ship docked at Norfolk, Virginia. He went ashore one Saturday with no intention of ever returning to Greece. He left behind everything, including his travel documents. All he had in his pockets was $100 and the address of his mother's cousin in the Jackson Heights–Corona section of Queens.

Almost four decades later, Juan Manuel Peralta underwent a similar rite of passage out of Mexico. He had finished the eighth grade in the poor southern state of Guerrero and saw nothing in his future there but fixing flat tires. His father, Inocencio, had once dreamed of going to the United States, but never had the money. In 1990, he borrowed enough to give his firstborn son a chance.

Peralta was nineteen when he boarded a smoky bus that carried him through the deserted hills of Guerrero and kept going until it reached the edge of Mexico. With eight other Mexicans he did not know, he crawled through a sewer tunnel that started in Tijuana and ended on the other side of the border, in what Mexicans call El Norte.

He had carried no documents, no photographs, and no money except what his father gave him to pay his shifty guide and to buy an airline ticket to New York. Deep in a pocket was the address of an uncle in the same section of Queens where John Zannikos had gotten his start. By 1990, the area had gone from largely Greek to mostly Latino.

Starting over in the same working-class neighborhood, Peralta and Zannikos quickly learned that New York was full of opportunities and obstacles, often in equal measure. On his first day there, Zannikos, scared and feeling lost, found the building he was looking for, but his mother's cousin had moved. He had no idea what to do until a Greek man passed by. Walk five blocks to the Deluxe Diner, the man said. He did.

The diner was full of Greek housepainters, including one who knew Zannikos's father. On the spot, they offered him a job painting closets, where his mistakes would be hidden. He painted until the weather turned cold. Another Greek hired him as a dishwasher at his coffee shop in the Bronx.

It was not easy, but Zannikos worked his way up to short-order cook, learning English as he went along. In 1956, immigration officials raided the coffee shop. He was deported, but after a short while he managed to sneak back into the country. Three years later he married a Puerto Rican from the Bronx. The marriage lasted only a year, but it put him on the road to becoming a citizen. Now he could buy his own restaurant, a greasy spoon in the South Bronx that catered to a late-night clientele of prostitutes and undercover police officers.

Since then, he has bought and sold more than a dozen New York diners, but none have been more successful than the original 3 Guys, which opened in 1978. He and his partners own two other restaurants with the same name farther up Madison Avenue, but they have never replicated the high-end appeal of the original.

"When employees come in, I teach them, 'Hey, this is a different neighborhood,'" Zannikos said. What may be standard in some other diners is not tolerated here. There are no Greek flags or tourism posters. There is no television or twirling tower of cakes with cream pompadours. Waiters are forbidden to chew gum. No customer is ever called "Honey."

"They know their place and I know my place," Zannikos said of his customers. "It's as simple as that."

His place in society now is a far cry from his days in the Bronx. He and his second wife, June, live in Wyckoff, a New Jersey suburb where he pampers fig trees and dutifully looks after a bird feeder shaped like the Parthenon. They own a condominium in Florida. His three children all went far beyond his second-grade education, finishing high school or attending college.

They have all done well, as has Zannikos, who says he makes about $130,000 a year. He says he is not sensitive to class distinctions, but he admits he was bothered when some people mistook him for the caterer at fund-raising dinners for the local Greek church he helped build.

All in all, he thinks immigrants today have a better chance of moving up the class ladder than he did fifty years ago.

"I'm in the middle and I'm happy."

"At that time, no bank would give us any money, but today they give you credit cards in the mail," he said. "New York still gives you more opportunity than any other place. If you want to do things, you will."

He says he has done well, and he is content with his station in life. "I'm in the middle and I'm happy."

A DIVISIVE ISSUE

Juan Manuel Peralta cannot guess what class John Zannikos belongs to. But he is certain that it is much tougher for an immigrant to get ahead today than fifty years ago. And he has no doubt about his own class.

"La pobreza," he says. "Poverty."

It was not what he expected when he boarded the bus to the border, but it did not take long for him to realize that success in the United States required more than hard work. "A lot of it has to do with luck," he said during a lunch break on a stoop around the corner from the Queens diner where he went to work after 3 Guys.

"People come here, and in no more than a year or two they can buy their own house and have a car," Peralta said. "Me, I've been here fifteen years, and if I die tomorrow, there wouldn't even be enough money to bury me."

In 1990, Peralta was in the vanguard of Mexican immigrants who bypassed the traditional barrios in border states to work in far-flung cities like Denver and New York. The 2000 census counted 186,872 Mexicans in New York, triple the 1990 figure, and there are undoubtedly many more today. The Mexican consulate, which serves the metropolitan region, has issued more than 500,000 ID cards just since 2001.

Fifty years ago, illegal immigration was a minor problem. Now it is a divisive national issue, pitting those who welcome cheap labor against those with concerns about border security and the cost of providing social services. Though newly arrived Mexicans often work in industries that rely on cheap labor, like restaurants and construction, they rarely organize. Most are desperate to stay out of sight.

Peralta hooked up with his uncle the morning he arrived in New York. He did not work for weeks until the bakery where the uncle worked had an opening, a part-time job making muffins. He took it, though he didn't know muffins from crumb cake. When he saw that he would not make enough to repay his father, he took a second job making night deliveries for a Manhattan diner. By the end of his first day he was so lost he had to spend all his tip money on a cab ride home.

He quit the diner, but working there even briefly opened his eyes to how easy it could be to make money in New York. Diners were everywhere, and so were jobs making deliveries, washing dishes, or busing tables. In six months, Peralta had paid back the money his father gave him. He bounced from job to job and in 1995, eager to show off his newfound success, went back to Mexico with his pockets full of money, and married. He was twenty-five then, the same age at which Zannikos married. But the similarities end there.

When Zannikos jumped ship, he left Greece behind for good. Though he himself had no documents, the compatriots he encountered on his first days were here legally, like most other Greek immigrants, and could help him. Greeks had never come to the United States in large numbers — the 2000 census counted only 29,805 New Yorkers born in Greece — but they tended to settle in just a few areas, like the Astoria section of Queens, which became cohesive communities ready to help new arrivals.

Peralta, like many other Mexicans, is trying to make it on his own and has never severed his emotional or financial ties to home. After five years in New York's Latino community, he spoke little English and owned little more than the clothes on his back. He decided to return to Huamuxtitlán, the dusty village beneath a flat-topped mountain where he was born.

"People thought that since I was coming back from El Norte, I would be so rich that I could spread money around," he said. Still, he felt privileged: his New York wages dwarfed the $1,000 a year he might have made in Mexico.

He met a shy, pretty girl named Matilde in Huamuxtitlán, married her, and returned with her to New York, again illegally, all in a matter of weeks. Their first child was born in 1996. Peralta soon found that supporting a family made it harder to save money. Then, in 1999, he got the job at 3 Guys.

"Barba Yanni helped me learn how to prepare things the way customers like them," Peralta said, referring to Zannikos with a Greek title of respect that means Uncle John.

The restaurant became his school. He learned how to sauté a fish so that it looked like a work of art. The three partners lent him money and said they would help him get immigration documents. The pay was good.

But there were tensions with the other workers. Instead of hanging their orders on a rack, the waiters shouted them out, in Greek, Spanish, and a kind of fractured English. Sometimes Peralta did not understand, and they argued. Soon he was known as a hothead.

Still, he worked hard, and every night he returned to his growing family. Matilde, now twenty-seven, cleaned houses until their second child, Heidi, was born in 2002. Now Matilde tries to sell Mary Kay products to other mothers at Public School 12, which their son Antony, who is eight, attends.

Most weeks, Peralta could make as much as $600. Over the course of a year that could come to over $30,000, enough to approach the lower middle class. But the life he leads is far from that and uncertainty hovers over everything about his life, starting with his paycheck.

To earn $600, he has to work at least ten hours a day, six days a week, and that does not happen every week. Sometimes he is paid overtime for the extra hours, sometimes not. And, as he found out, he can be fired at any time and bring in nothing, not even unemployment, until he lands another job. In 2004, he made about $24,000.

Because he is here illegally, Peralta can easily be exploited. He cannot file a complaint against his landlord for charging him $500 a month for a nine- by nine-foot room in a Queens apartment that he shares with nine other Mexicans in three families who pay the remainder of the $2,000-a-month rent. All thirteen share one bathroom, and the established pecking order means the Peraltas rarely get to use the kitchen. Eating out can be expensive.

Because they were born in New York, Peralta's children are United States citizens, and their health care is generally covered by Medicaid. But he has to pay out of his pocket whenever he or his wife sees a doctor. And forget about going to the dentist.

As many other Mexicans do, he wires money home, and it costs him $7 for every $100 he sends. When his uncle, his nephew, and his sister asked him for money, he was expected to lend it. No one has paid him back. He has middle-class ornaments, like a cellphone and a DVD player, but no driver's license or Social Security card.

He is the first to admit that he has vices that have held him back; nothing criminal, but he tends to lose his temper and there are nights when he likes to have a drink or two. His greatest weakness is instant lottery tickets, what he calls "los scratch," and he sheepishly confesses that he can squander as much as $75 a week on them. It is a way of preserving hope, he said. Once he won $100. He bought a blender.

Years ago, he and Matilde were so confident they would make it in America that when their son was born they used the American spelling of his name, Anthony, figuring it would help pave his passage into the mainstream. But even that effort failed.

"Look at this," his wife said one afternoon as she sat on the floor of their room near a picture of the Virgin of Guadalupe. Peralta sat on a small plastic stool in the doorway, listening. His mattress was stacked against the wall. A roll of toilet paper was stashed nearby because they dared not leave it in the shared bathroom for someone else to use.

She took her pocketbook and pulled out a clear plastic case holding her son's baptismal certificate, on which his name is spelled with an H. But then she unfolded his birth certificate, where the H is missing.

"The teachers won't teach him to spell his name the right way until the certificate is legally changed," she said. "But how can we do that if we're not legal?"

PROGRESS, BUT NOT SUCCESS

An elevated subway train thundered overhead, making the afternoon light along Roosevelt Avenue blink like a failing fluorescent bulb. Peralta's daughter and son grabbed his fat hands as they ran some errands. He had just finished a ten-hour shift, eggs over easy and cheeseburgers since 5:00 A.M. It had been especially hard to stand the monotony that day. He kept thinking about what was going on in Mexico, where it was the feast day of Our Lady of the Rosary. And, oh, what a feast there was — sweets and handmade tamales, a parade, even a bullfight. At night, fireworks, bursting loud and bright against the green folds of the mountains. Paid for, in part, by the money he sends home.

But instead of partying, he was walking his children to the Arab supermarket on Roosevelt Avenue to buy packages of chicken and spare ribs, and hoping to get to use the kitchen. And though he knew better, he grabbed a package of pink and white marshmallows for the children. He needed to buy tortillas, too, but not there. A Korean convenience store a few blocks away sells La Maizteca tortillas, made in New York.

> *In 1953, . . . most immigrants . . . were Europeans, and . . . their Caucasian features helped them blend into New York's middle class.*

The swirl of immigrants in Peralta's neighborhood is part of the fabric of New York, just as it was in 1953, when John Zannikos arrived. But most immigrants then were Europeans, and though they spoke different languages, their Caucasian features helped them blend into New York's middle class.

Experts remain divided over whether Mexicans can follow the same route. Samuel P. Huntington, a Harvard professor of government, takes the extreme view that Mexicans will not assimilate and that the separate culture they are developing threatens the United States.

Most others believe that recent Mexican immigrants will eventually take their place in society, and perhaps someday muster political clout commensurate with their numbers, though significant impediments are slowing their progress. Francisco Rivera-Batiz, a Columbia University economics professor, says that prejudice remains a problem, that factory jobs have all but disappeared, and that there is a growing gap between the educational demands of the economy and the limited schooling that the newest Mexicans have when they arrive.

But the biggest obstacle by far, and the one that separates newly arrived Mexicans from Greeks, Italians, and most other immigrants — including earlier generations of Mexicans — is their illegal status. Rivera-Batiz studied what happened to illegal Mexican immigrants who became legal after the last national amnesty in 1986. Within a few years, their incomes rose 20 percent and their English improved greatly.

"Legalization," he said, "helped them tremendously."

Although the Bush administration talks about legalizing some Mexicans with a guest worker program, there is opposition to another amnesty, and the number of Mexicans illegally living in the United States continues to soar. Desperate to get their papers any way they can, many turn to shady storefront legal offices. Like Peralta, they sign on to illusory schemes that cost hundreds of dollars but almost never produce the promised green cards.

Until the 1980s, Mexican immigration was largely seasonal and mostly limited to agricultural workers. But then economic chaos in Mexico sent a flood of immigrants northward, many of them poorly educated farmers from the impoverished countryside. Tighter security on the border made it harder for Mexicans to move back and forth in the traditional way, so they tended to stay here, searching for low-paying unskilled jobs and concentrating in barrios where Spanish, constantly replenished, never loses its immediacy.

"*Cuidado!*" Peralta shouted when Antony carelessly stepped into Roosevelt Avenue without looking. Although the boy is taught in English at school, he rarely uses anything but Spanish at home.

Even now, after fifteen years in New York, Peralta speaks little English. He tried English classes once, but could not get his mind to accept the new sounds. So he dropped it, and has stuck with Spanish, which he concedes is "the language of busboys" in New York. But as long as he stays in his neighborhood, it is all he needs.

It was late afternoon by the time Peralta and his children headed home. The run-down house, the overheated room, the stacked mattress, and the hoarded toilet paper — all remind him how far he would have to go to achieve a success like John Zannikos's.

Still, he says, he has done far better than he could ever have done in Mexico. He realizes that the money he sends to his family there is not enough to satisfy his father, who built stairs for a second floor of his house made of concrete blocks in Huamuxtitlán, even though there is no second floor. He believes Juan Manuel has made it big in New York and he is waiting for money from America to complete the upstairs.

His son has never told him the truth about his life up north. He said his father's images of America came from another era. The older man does not know how tough it is to be a Mexican immigrant in the United States now, tougher than any young man who ever left Huamuxtitlán would admit. Everything built up over fifteen years here can come apart as easily as an adobe house in an earthquake. And then it is time to start over, again.

A CONFLICT ERUPTS

It was the end of another busy lunch at 3 Guys in the late spring of 2003. Peralta made himself a turkey sandwich and took a seat at a rear table. The Mexican countermen, dishwashers, and busboys also started their breaks, while the Greek waiters took care of the last few diners.

It is not clear how the argument started. But a cross word passed between a Greek waiter and a Mexican busboy. Voices were raised. The waiter swung at the busboy, catching him behind the ear. Peralta froze. So did the other Mexicans.

Even from the front of the restaurant, where he was watching the cash register, Zannikos realized something was wrong and rushed back to break it up. "I stood between them, held one and pushed the other away," he said. "I told them: 'You don't do that here. Never do that here.'"

Zannikos said he did not care who started it. He ordered both the busboy and the waiter, a partner's nephew, to get out.

But several Mexicans, including Peralta, said that they saw Zannikos grab the busboy by the head and that they believed he would have hit him if another Mexican had not stepped between them. That infuriated them because they felt he had sided with the Greek without knowing who was at fault.

Zannikos said that was not true, but in the end it did not matter. The easygoing atmosphere at the restaurant changed. "Everybody was a little cool," Zannikos recalled.

What he did not know then was that the Mexicans had reached out to the Restaurant Opportunities Center, a workers' rights group. Eventually six of them, including Peralta, cooperated with the group. He did so reluctantly, he said, because he was afraid that if the owners found out, they would no longer help him get his immigration papers. The labor group promised that the owners would never know.

The owners saw it as an effort to shake them down, but for the Mexicans it became a class struggle pitting powerless workers against hard-hearted owners.

Their grievances went beyond the scuffle. They complained that with just one exception, only Greeks became waiters at 3 Guys. They challenged the sole Mexican waiter, Salomon Paniagua, a former Mexican army officer who, everyone agreed, looked Greek, to stand with them.

But on the day the labor group picketed the restaurant, Paniagua refused to put down his order pad. A handful of demonstrators carried signs on Madison Avenue for a short while before Zannikos and his partners reluctantly agreed to settle.

Zannikos said he felt betrayed. "When I see these guys, I see myself when I started, and I always try to help them," he said. "I didn't do anything wrong."

The busboy and the Mexican who intervened were paid several thousand dollars and the owners promised to promote a current Mexican employee to waiter within a month. But that did not end the turmoil.

Fearing that the other Mexicans might try to get back at him, Paniagua decided to strike out on his own. After asking Zannikos for advice, he bought a one-third share of a Greek diner in Jamaica, Queens. He said he put it in his father's name because the older man had become a legal resident after the 1986 amnesty.

After Paniagua left, 3 Guys went without a single Mexican waiter for ten months, despite the terms of the settlement. In March, an eager Mexican busboy with a heavy accent who had worked there for four years got a chance to wear a waiter's tie.

Peralta ended up having to leave 3 Guys around the same time as Paniagua. Zannikos's partners suspected he had sided with the labor group, he said, and started to criticize his work unfairly. Then they cut back his schedule to five days a week. After he hurt his ankle playing soccer, they told him to go home until he was better. When Peralta came back to work about two weeks later, he was fired.

Zannikos confirms part of the account but says the firing had nothing to do with the scuffle or the ensuing dispute. "If he was good, believe me, he wouldn't get fired," he said of Peralta.

Peralta shrugged when told what Zannikos said. "I know my own work and I know what I can do," he said. "There are a lot of restaurants in New York, and a lot of workers."

When 3 Guys fired Peralta, another Mexican replaced him, just as Peralta replaced a Mexican at the Greek diner in Queens where he went to work next.

This time, though, there was no Madison Avenue address, no elaborate menu of New Zealand mussels or designer mushrooms. In the Queens diner a bowl of soup with a buttered roll cost two dollars, all day. If he fried burgers and scraped fat off the big grill for ten hours a day, six days a week, he might earn about as much as he did on Madison Avenue, at least for a week.

His schedule kept changing. Sometimes he worked the lunch and dinner shift, and by the end of the night he was worn out, especially since he often found himself arguing with the Greek owner. But he did not look forward to going home. So after the night manager lowered the security gate, Peralta would wander the streets.

One of those nights he stopped at a phone center off Roosevelt Avenue to call his mother. "Everything's okay," he told her. He asked how she had spent the last $100 he sent, and whether she needed anything else. There is always need in Huamuxtitlán.

Still restless, he went to the Scorpion, a shot-and-beer joint open till 4 A.M. He sat at the long bar nursing vodkas with cranberry juice, glancing at the soccer match on TV and the busty Brazilian bartender who spoke only a little Spanish. When it was nearly eleven, he called it a night.

Back home, he quietly opened the door to his room. The lights were off, the television murmuring. His family was asleep in the bunk bed that the store had now threatened to repossess. Antony was curled up on the top, Matilde and Heidi cuddled in the bottom. Peralta moved the plastic stool out of the way and dropped his mattress to the floor.

The children did not stir. His wife's eyes fluttered, but she said nothing. Peralta looked over his family, his home.

"This," he said, "is my life in New York."

Not the life he imagined, but his life. In early March 2005, just after Heidi's third birthday, he quit his job at the Queens diner after yet another heated argument with the owner. In his mind, preserving his dignity is one of the few liberties he has left.

"I'll get another job," he said while babysitting Heidi at home a few days after he quit. The rent is already paid till the end of the month and he has friends, he said. People know him. To him, jobs are interchangeable — just as he is to the jobs. If he cannot find work as a grillman, he will bus tables. Or wash dishes. If not at one diner, then at another.

"It's all the same," he said.

It took about three weeks, but Peralta did find a new job as a grillman at another Greek diner in a different part of New York. His salary is roughly the same, the menu is roughly the same (one new item, Greek burritos, was a natural), and he sees his chance for a better future as being roughly the same as it has been since he got to America.

A LONG DAY CLOSES

It was now dark again outside 3 Guys. About 9:00 P.M. John Zannikos asked his Mexican cook for a small salmon steak, a little rare. It had been another busy ten-hour day for him, but a good one. Receipts from the morning alone exceeded what he needed to take in every day just to cover the $23,000 a month rent.

He finished the salmon quickly, left final instructions with the lone Greek waiter still on duty, and said good night to everyone else. He put on his light tan corduroy jacket and the baseball cap he picked up in Florida.

"'Night," he said to the lone table of diners.

Outside, as Zannikos walked slowly down Madison Avenue, a self-made man comfortable with his own hard-won success, the bulkhead doors in front of 3 Guys clanked open. Faint voices speaking Spanish came from below. A young Mexican who started his shift ten hours earlier climbed out with a bag of garbage and heaved it onto the sidewalk. New Zealand mussel shells. Uneaten bits of portobello mushrooms. The fine grounds of decaf cappuccino.

One black plastic bag after another came out until Madison Avenue in front of 3 Guys was piled high with trash.

"Hurry up!" the young man shouted to the other Mexicans. "I want to go home, too."

DISCUSSION

1. DePalma begins his essay by presenting a list of the powerful or famous people who frequent the 3 Guys café. Why do you think he does this? What sort of framework does this introduction provide for the experiences of the Mexican workers whom the essay goes on to profile?

2. According to DePalma, the workplace portrait sketched here is a "template of the class divisions in America." How accurate does this claim seem to you? In what ways does the essay's depiction of work also function as a commentary on the ideals of class mobility?

3. How would you define the ideal working environment? What kinds of jobs or roles? How does this hypothetical world compare to or differ from the one depicted in this essay?

WRITING

4. This essay draws a clear connection between work and immigration, exploring the ways that the contemporary landscape for temporary workers threatens to rewrite what DePalma calls the "classic immigrant success story." Write an essay in which you assess the validity of this claim. What is the "classic immigrant success story"? What is its typical plot line, its traditional roles? How does this conventional script compare to the immigrant story DePalma relates about either Juan Manuel Peralta or John Zannikos? How closely does this example resemble the ideal?

5. Make a list of the different jobs Peralta performs during his years in the United States. Write an essay in which you describe the particular role you think these jobs script for the workers who undertake them. What is the profile of the typical person who performs these jobs? How accurate and fair do you think these descriptions are? Why?

6. How much of DePalma's discussion here reminds you of what Louis Uchitelle (p. 299) says about the kinds of psychic harm job-related struggles can inflict? Write a review of DePalma's essay that you think Uchitelle might offer. To what extent would Uchitelle's review find parallels in the social and economic hardships profiled here and his argument regarding the emotional costs of unemployment?

ROBERT SULLIVAN

How to Choose a Career That Will Not Get You Rich No Matter What Anyone Tells You

When it comes right down to it, what really is the best way to define a worthwhile job? And how do our personal standards compare to those we are taught by our larger culture? In this satiric piece, Robert Sullivan turns our conventional thinking on its head. Compiling a list of "non-Big-Buck-making careers," he skewers the long-standing norm in our culture that pegs the worthiness of a job solely to its profitability. Sullivan is a contributing editor to *Vogue* and a frequent contributor to the *New York Times.* His work has appeared in publications such as *Condé Nast Traveler* and the *New York Times Magazine.* He has sometimes been called a nature writer, but Sullivan has said, "If you're from New York or New Jersey, I didn't think you were allowed to be a nature writer." He lives in Hastings-on-Hudson, New York, but his book *Rats* (2004) examines the history of a New York City pest. Among his other books are *How Not to Get Rich, or Why Being Bad Off Isn't So Bad* (2005), from which this selection comes, and *Cross Country* (2006).

CHOOSING A CAREER PATH IS ESSENTIAL TO IMPLEMENTING A SPOT that is not in the top 2 percent of American incomes or anywhere near it, and an essential part of choosing the right career is choosing the right kind of education. These days, a good education is a must if you are planning on working your entire life and ending up with little or nothing. History tells us that at one time only the wealthiest Americans had a college education, and the people who did not go to college made money working in factory jobs that today no longer exist. Now you need a college education to work on the line in one of the few remaining auto plants, if you can afford a college education, that is. If you do manage to wrangle the absurdly large loans necessary to fund a trip to college, then, to not succeed financially, you will want to choose a field of study that will be

> You will want to choose a field of study that will be personally rewarding but have no apparent application in the real world.

personally rewarding but have no apparent application in the real world. Here are just a few possibilities:

Medieval literature. This is a wonderful area of essentially not-for-profit study, and, indeed, a study of just medieval poetry will only reinforce the improbability of retiring on what you will earn, even though you may see the world as a more beautiful place, and, through the sight of such beauty, you will be stock-poor but soul-enhanced. In addition to translating wonderful but sensationally obscure poems that could never be valued in accordance with their aesthetic worth, other areas of unprofitable expertise would include the study of medieval literary figures themselves, such as Alcuin, the once world-renowned and now not-so-well-known tutor to Charlemagne, who, excitingly, had a school of scholars translating and copying ancient texts in medieval France, and who reignited interest in Greek and Roman classics in Europe, giving us a glimpse back into a time when the world was smaller and you could retire to your kids' villa, rather than be forced to begin to apply to assisted-living places when you are in your forties in hopes of getting a spot that you probably won't be able to afford one day. Alcuin, who also tutored Pippin, the son of Charlemagne, rediscovered Socratic dialogue as a teaching method, so that the following questions might be offered to the following responses in the eighth century A.D.:

PIPPIN: What is a letter?

ALCUIN: The guardian of history.

PIPPIN: What is a word?

ALCUIN: The expositor of the mind.

PIPPIN: What produces a word?

ALCUIN: The tongue.

PIPPIN: What is the tongue?

ALCUIN: The whip of the air.

PIPPIN: What is the air?

ALCUIN: The guardian of life.

PIPPIN: What is life?

ALCUIN: The joy of the blessed, the sorrow of the miserable, the expectation of death.

PIPPIN: What is death?

ALCUIN: The inevitable issue, an uncertain pilgrimage, the tears of the living, the thief of man.

PIPPIN: What is man?

ALCUIN: The possession of death, a transient wayfarer, a guest.

PIPPIN: How is man situated?

ALCUIN: Like a lantern in the wind.

Magnificent, and it notably does not end the way a financial investment company's commercials typically end. You know the financial investment company commercials I'm referring to. They feature a long, sentimental, and joyful montage of images that portray the imaginary life you would have if you had nothing to worry about money-wise: sailing, croquet on the lawn of the beach house, sentimental gazes between well-dressed family members. Then, the ad ends with the logo of the financial investment company, the message being something along the lines of this: *Don't you want to have a really amazing life, as far as material goods go, or do you have some kind of a problem?*

If you should actually go into medieval studies, then your only real worry is that a huge movie star — say he has his car parked by the guy you sat next to in the waiting room of the downtown health clinic — hears about your obscure area of expertise, becomes enamored with Alcuin while on location in France, gets a kind of over-glamorized view of what it was like to run a medieval school of classical scholarship during the Holy Roman Empire, shows up with his entourage at your library cubicle one afternoon, lunches you, hires you as a consultant, makes a film in which the scene that you worked hardest on (where rows of robed scholars sat quietly copying ancient texts) is cut, after which you appear on a public television talk show to praise the movie's accuracy, after which you are offered your own television show on cable, which subsequently spawns best-selling books and CD-ROMs and a Wednesday spot on the *Today* show that features you translating French medieval lyrics for the viewers at home. Granted, that scenario is not incredibly likely, but it's a possibility, and to live the not-rich life completely, you have to stay on your toes.

Wildlife biologist. As far as not making it big goes, studies of flora and fauna are especially unlucrative, despite that flora and fauna are seemingly the most related to the world, or at least the living, breathing world. Why? Because they investigate an area that the economic system considers unprofitable — i.e., natural life. If you played your cards "right," you could spend years in graduate school studying biology and then finally manage to cobble together grant money to pursue your area of interest — Pacific-coast sea otters *(Enhydra lutris)*, let's say, hunted into near extinction in the eighteen hundreds for their pelts despite being, as can unprofitably be noted, one of the few mammals besides humans to use tools.[1] You will live in a tent in the cold watching a small radar screen indicating the location of the sea otter that you have forcibly but lovingly tagged, and you will make important discoveries about the animal's migratory patterns, and then your studies will be discounted by cruise ship and real estate interests. (Caution: Oil companies sometimes hire wildlife biologists, decorating oil-interested company reports with otter-friendly statistics that are subsequently ignored when drilling time comes.)

Traditional music. This is an excellent area of unprofitable possibilities, especially in light of today's popular music, which can, in many instances, be explained as multimillion-dollar marketing set to a computer-generated sound track — which is to say the sound track of a corporation raking it in. In some ways, someone choosing to become a professional hammer dulcimer player is the opposite of someone choosing a career that statistics indicate will manage to keep him or her alive — careers such as health care, education, and engineering, all of which are recommended by career planners and require advanced degrees that you will be paying for over many, many years.[2] Have you ever seen a mandolin player with a yacht? Do you know many full-time jug-band members with 401(k) plans? Is there in America today a professional pennywhistle player who has two homes and a condo on Central Park West in Manhattan? Do people who make their living as accordionists fly first-class out of LAX? No, in fact people with accordions are the butt of jokes even from other traditional musicians, implying a lowest-man-on-the-lowest-totem-pole status that can be applauded in the area of not getting fantastically rich. Some gratuitous accordion joke examples are as follows:

> **Have you ever seen a mandolin player with a yacht?**

Q: What's the difference between an onion and an accordion?

A: People cry when they chop up onions.

Q: What do you call ten accordions at the bottom of the ocean?

A: A good start.

Q: If you drop an accordion, a set of bagpipes, and a viola off a twenty-story building, which one lands first?

A: Who cares?[3]

There are, of course, an infinite number of non-wealth-producing careers to choose from. There's public broadcasting, wherein the person involved attempts to create radio and television programs that will attract viewers interested in a broad range of subjects that may not titillate advertisers, the core audience, it sometimes seems, for non-public broadcasting. There are more obvious examples, such as teaching, which has to do with the joy of learning and with the education of the next generation of adults, as well as the future of the economy and of the world. There is art that has no wide commercial appeal. There is commerce that has no wide commercial appeal but works on a limited basis in a limited area for a limited number of people until a chain store hears about it and comes in and takes over, putting everyone else out of business. In other words, the options for non-Big-Buck-making careers are wide-ranging. The one universally important thing to keep in mind when choosing a career that will not be making you loaded is to choose a field of study and expertise that interests you, to follow your passions — and unless your passion is making lots of money, you will be fairly assured of not getting rich. Ralph Waldo Emerson said, "The reward of doing a thing well is to have done it," and he had a point, though he is not factoring in the cost of child care, studio space, and gas, or even parking, all of which really add up.

NOTES

[1]Sea otters smash abalone shells on their chest using a small rock, and they tie themselves to the seafloor with kelp to sleep securely through the night, not that it matters to the stock market. I find sea otters fascinating: their hands, their apparent jocularity even in the face of tremendous waves and storms and currents. Sea otters also faced great dangers from hunters who wanted their valuable coats; they were hunted so heavily in the eighteenth and nineteenth centuries that they had to be placed on the U.S. government endangered species list. Today, the populations have come back to a large extent, but conservationists would like to continue to protect them. Fishermen would like them off the endangered species list to protect the abalone harvest, but not me. I could watch a sea otter all day and not get bored — or rich, for that matter.

[2]According the U.S. Department of Labor, two of the fastest-growing occupations between 2002 and 2012 are expected to be physician's assistants and network

systems and data communications analysts. Both of these jobs require bachelor's degrees and both are expected to pay in the highest anticipated wage category, which is $41,820 and up. As bad luck would have it, many of the fastest-growing occupations that do not require college are also in the lowest-earning category. Home health aide is an example of the latter category, and the demand for home health aides is expected to grow by 50 percent. Other examples of jobs that will be in the highest demand in the lowest wage-earning category are maids and personal aides, categories that are expected to grow by 40 percent. The lowest expected earnings category is up to $19,600 a year — nobody seems to want to pay maids a lot of money.

[3]A traditional joke regarding the moneymaking abilities of traditional musicians is as follows:

Q: How do you make a million dollars as a traditional musician?

A: Start with two million.

I heard this joke at a traditional-music festival. I heard it told by David Jones, an exquisite singer of old folk songs, ballads, and sea shanties, who sings regularly at the South Street Seaport in New York City, and at various folk festivals along the East Coast.

As far as I know, David Jones is not raking it in singing folk songs. I should also note, with reference to the idea of mandolin players owning a yacht, that the late Johnny Carson, who was a drummer, once asked, rhetorically, "Is that the banjo player's Porsche?"

DISCUSSION

1. Take a moment to evaluate the title of this essay. What is your immediate reaction? In what ways does the advice it proffers seem odd, even abnormal?

2. "To not succeed financially," writes Sullivan, "you will want to choose a field of study that will be personally rewarding but have no apparent application in the real world." How do you understand the distinction between personal reward and real-world applicability? To what extent in our culture are we taught to use this distinction in making our career choices? Is it valid to do so?

3. These days, notes Sullivan, the idea that one would choose a "non-lucrative" career over a financially profitable one has become close to unthinkable. According to the standards of our culture, what is it exactly that supposedly makes "Big-Buck-making" jobs so much more preferable than the alternatives? Can you think of advantages or benefits to a "non-lucrative" job that this kind of cultural logic overlooks?

WRITING

4. Sullivan concludes his essay by quoting Ralph Waldo Emerson's well-known dictum: " 'The reward of doing a thing well is to have done it.' " Write an essay in which you assess the particular ways Emerson's statement challenges the norms by which we are taught to measure the value of work. To what extent does this statement encourage us to use a different set of values or priorities when it comes to making our own career choices? What might a job modeled along these different lines look like? What sorts of tasks would it involve? What large goal or purpose would it be dedicated to? What rewards or benefits would it bring?

5. Sullivan uses satire to comment on the monetary value of work. Write your own satirical response to Sullivan in which you espouse the merits of *not* choosing a career that will leave you poor.

6. Perhaps the most glaring counterpoint to Sullivan's satiric portrait of work is the description of corporate culture Christopher Byron (p. 290) offers. Identify the different ways success gets defined in these two pieces. To what extent does Byron's depiction of CEOs lay out the script that Sullivan attempts to rewrite?

JUDITH WARNER
This Mess

We often hear that we now live in an era in which all of the old restrictions and prejudices around work — especially those regarding gender — have fallen away. But how much of this conceit is truth and how much is fantasy? Taking up this question, Judith Warner examines how motherhood — long idealized as a refuge from the world of work — has grown into one of the most intensively regulated, micromanaged, and anxiety-ridden "jobs" in our entire culture. Sharing insights culled from hundreds of interviews of working moms, she offers a sobering assessment of the expectations that frame the parenting choices available today. Warner is the author of the bestselling biography *Hillary Clinton: The Inside Story* (1993), and she collaborated with Howard Dean to write *You Have the Power: How to Take Back Our Country and Restore Democracy in America* (2004). A former special correspondent for *Newsweek* in Paris, she has also published articles on politics and women's issues for the *New Republic* and *Elle*. "This Mess" is an excerpt from her most recent book, *Perfect Madness: Motherhood in the Age of Anxiety* (2005).

I LISTENED TO MY FRIENDS, LISTENED TO TALK RADIO, TO THE MOTHERS on the playground, and to my daughter's nursery school teachers, and I found it all — the general culture of motherhood in America — oppressive. The pressure to perform, to attain levels of perfect selflessness was insane. And it was, I thought, as I listened to one more anguished friend wringing her hands over the work-family "balance," and another expressing her guilt at not having "succeeded" at breast-feeding, driving American mothers crazy.

Myself along with them.

It took very little time on the ground in America before I found myself becoming unrecognizable. I bought an SUV. I signed my unathletic elder daughter up for soccer. Other three-year-olds in her class were taking gymnastics, too, and art, and swimming and music. I signed her up for ballet. I bought a small library of pre-K skill books. I went around in a state of quiet panic.

The financial burden of trying to set up a life similar to the one I'd had in France was overwhelming. The calculation was grim: the way things were going, if I wanted to keep on writing, working at home, and seeing my children, I would have to take out a home-equity loan to pay my babysitter. Was is worth it? Was I really a good enough writer to justify the sacrifice? Or should I, at long last, just hang it up? The problem was, I wasn't all that good at being a stay-at-home mom.

I started to drink Calvados in the evenings.

At social events, the men and women separated out into two groups, the men discussing sports and stock prices and the women talking about their children. On vacation, the fathers took advantage of "their time" away from work to disappear for whole afternoons of fishing. The mothers continued their daily grind in a new locale.

This reversion to what I would once have termed 1950s-style sex roles wasn't necessarily so different from what I had witnessed among couples with young children in France. Yet there was one significant difference: in America, when couples found themselves sliding back into traditional "masculine" and "feminine" roles, a new power dynamic tended to fall into place as well, with the men distinctly coming out ahead. This was much less true in France — partly, I think, because many more mothers did work full-time and partly because, even in families where the husband was the sole wage earner, the cultural context that was leading American husbands to lord it over their wives was largely missing. Workaholism was frowned upon. Vacation was sacred, as were weekends and holidays. And no matter how hard they worked, no matter how much they tended to distance themselves from the drudgery of diapers and laundry, French men (unless they were the kinds of uncultured boors routinely mocked in movies and TV ads) did not permit themselves to retreat from domestic concerns altogether. They weighed in, as a matter of course, on areas that affected their quality of life: like food and home décor. "We are more 'feminine' than American men," a French diplomat in Washington mused to me. Whether or not that's so, it is true that the "feminine" realm in France is not routinely denigrated, as it is in the United States. And perhaps that's why, for French women my age, inhabiting a traditional "feminine" role as a mother doesn't feel like a tragedy.

Doing so in the States came as a shock to me. Ozzie and Harriet sex roles just weren't what I had expected to find back in America. I was a child of the 1970s, a feminist formed by the 1980s, a product of the girls-can-be-anything school of socialization, which rested on the idea that not only was biology not destiny, it was largely irrelevant. And I had truly believed, gazing back at my country from France, that American feminists had managed to secure for American women a sex-free public space in which they could operate with dignity as people first and women second. I remembered American women as smiling, sympathetic souls, self-possessed and forward-striding. Their prospects, I'd thought, were as unlimited as the blue sky that thrilled my eyes each time I came home and touched down at Kennedy Airport. American women, I'd thought, didn't have to fit into the gray landscape of Old World–style categories like wives or mothers. They were free to be themselves.

Ozzie and Harriet sex roles just weren't what I had expected to find back in America.

Some of this rosy view had been, no doubt, the symptom of a more general nostalgia for home. Some of it was fed by the only images of American women I had access to then: visions derived from CNN, where every woman, from Christian Amanpour to Janet Reno, looked, from a distance, like an action hero. Women politicians and TV personalities in France all too often were the wives or mistresses of more powerful men, and French movies were filled with sultry consumptives and tooth-baring madwomen. The American movies I saw on the Champs-Élysées in those years were full of virile female stars: Demi Moore as G.I. Jane and a kickboxing Ashley Judd and a blackbelt René Russo breaking heads while pregnant and a whole slew of new women warriors looking fabulous as they ran around with walkie-talkies and guns. I'd leave the theater after watching these American Amazons, see the French women lighting their cigarettes, tugging on their male companions' arms, and pouting their way off into the night, and I'd think: God Bless America. We're doing something right.

Now, back in the United States, I was belatedly realizing that there was a big difference between my memory of young womanhood, my faith in the far-reaching changes wrought by feminism, and the reality of motherhood in America. There was also a big gap between the virility projected by actresses on-screen and the vulnerability felt by the women who watched them. Indeed, I had a new take now on why there had been such a spate of hard-fighting comic book heroines on the American screen during the years I'd been away, the years in which my generation of women had fully come of age professionally and embarked upon motherhood. It wasn't for a sense of identification, not at all. It was to escape — from the feeling of powerlessness brought on by a society that made superhuman demands. To escape the impossible demands of motherhood in particular, just as men had always escaped via superhero movies from impossible demands for power and productivity.

I wondered: How did two generations of feminism bring us here? Why did life feel so difficult? Why, with all our rights and privileges, with all our opportunities and, for some, riches, hadn't we achieved a decent quality of life — that is to say, a life that included time for ourselves and some sense of satisfaction?

In the Spring of 2001, an editor at the *Washington Post's* "Outlook" section asked me to write a first-person piece comparing ideals of women's equality in France and America. After turning the topic around in my head for a number of weeks, I ended up writing about how my own ideas on the nature of real-life equality had changed: whereas once I'd mocked the French culture of "*différence*" and seduction and had believed that American women were more politically and socially evolved, since moving back to America as a mother I'd come to agree with many European observers that American women, despite their surface equality, lived "dogs' lives." It was time, I suggested, to shift the focus of our political debates away from parochial notions of equality and concentrate more on working to guarantee us all — men, women, and children alike — a decent quality of life.

In the days following the article's publication, I received dozens and dozens of e-mails from readers. Some women wrote me to protest the depiction of their mothering styles as "dogs' lives." But they were surprisingly few. Many more wrote to agree with me — and to ask for more. Why wasn't anybody else writing about this? they asked. Why wasn't anyone else focusing on the issue of quality of life? Could they tell me their stories? Could we keep in touch? Meet for coffee? Did I plan to write a book?

Over and over again, I heard the same refrain: You're right. There's a problem. Life doesn't have to be this way. It's time to take a step back and figure out how to make things better.

Over the course of the next year, I interviewed close to 150 women about their experience of motherhood in America. I talked to equal numbers of working and stay-at-home moms. About half the women were from Washington and its suburbs and the rest were from all around the United States. The majority were white. Many were African-American. Most were American, although a fair number either had grown up overseas or were from families that had only recently settled in the U.S. Almost all were college-educated. Some were well off, others struggled to make ends meet, and most were somewhere in the middle. Their children ranged in age from babies to young teenagers.

I tried not to interview women who were super-superwealthy — the social X-ray types ridiculed in *The Nanny Diaries* or the "New Economy Parents," with their $60,000-a-year nannies, kiddie limo services, and "family chaos consultants" featured in *Business Week*. I also did not interview working-class or poor women — not because I wasn't interested in them, but because I quickly saw that giving sufficient attention and understanding to their experiences was beyond the scope of what I could do with this book.

My goal was to write about the middle class. I soon realized, however, that it is very hard to write about the middle class in America *without* excessively focusing on the upper middle class. (Every other book on "American" motherhood that I have read, from *The Feminine Mystique* to Jessie Bernard's *The Future of Motherhood* to Naomi Wolf's *Misconceptions,* suffers the same fate.) And that is because the influence of the upper middle class is disproportionate in American culture. It is upper-middle-class homes that we see in movies, upper-middle-class lifestyles that are detailed in our magazines, upper-middle-class images of desirability that grace the advertising destined for us all. The upper middle class is our reference point for what the American good life is supposed to look like and contain. This has always been true in America, but became more so in the late 1990s, when the "luxury fever" of the boom years pushed everyone — rich and not-so-rich — to mimic the spending patterns, the ambitions, and the competitive keeping-up-with-the-Joneses of the wealthy. It is because of our overidentification with the upper middle class that so many of us came out of the boom years of the late 1990s so terribly in debt. It is also why so many of us turn ourselves inside out trying to parent to perfection, so that our children will be "winners."

The ways of the upper-middle-class affect everyone — including, to their detriment, the working class and the poor. And this is because our politicians hail, almost exclusively, from the upper-income reaches of our society. Thus to understand the conflicts and, I would say, the *pathologies* of upper-middle-class thinking is to understand the often perplexing state of family politics in America. As a woman who worked with Hillary Rodham Clinton on child care put it to me, "The whole problem of the upper class making policy is that they have choices and they're conflicted about their choices. The women have the conflict about whether they want to stay home or go to work and the men have the conflict of wanting women to have choices but also wanting their wives to stay home. The people making the policy are not the people enjoying the policy, so they're just conflicted for themselves and making policy for people who don't have the choice."

The middle-class and upper-middle-class women I interviewed for this book were strikingly similar in their attitudes toward motherhood, whatever their race, cultural background, or geographic location in America may have been. On the big issues there were no real differences between working and nonworking mothers, either — a fact that, though it flies in the face of received wisdom about the Mommy Wars — didn't surprise me, given my own experience of having moved between the worlds of working and stay-at-home motherhood.

It wasn't just that the working mothers and stay-at-home moms I interviewed felt similarly about motherhood. It was that they *went about it in much the same ways*. The "stay-at-home" moms very often worked part-time, either from their homes or in an office. Like the working mothers, they were dependent on child care. Indeed, one study I read about actually showed that *one-third* of "nonworking" mothers were *putting their kids in day care for an average of eighteen hours a week by the time they were twelve months old*. And the "working mothers," very often, worked only part-time. Meaning that if their kids were of school age, they saw them for about the same number of hours each day as did the stay-at-home moms.

Many studies have borne these similarities out. At the turn of the millennium, for example, we commonly heard that 64 percent of American mothers worked. In reality, though, just a minority of those mothers were working full-time. Only a third of married mothers with children under six were working full-time year-round, and fully two-thirds of mothers were working less than forty hours a week during their key career years. Indeed, the definition of "working" used to derive the Department of

Labor percentages for "working mothers" in America is so all-embracing that it catches many women who would probably consider themselves stay-at-home moms. It includes mothers who work part-time (sometimes as little as one hour a week), mothers who work only seasonally (as little as one week out of the year), mothers who work from home part-time, or mothers who work part-time without pay for a family business.

Clearly, the mothers we see represented in the media replays of the Mommy Wars — the militant stay-at-home moms and the round-the-clock workaholics — are very much the exception to the rule. Yet their images — and their alleged conflicts — tend to dominate our notions of contemporary motherhood. And the pressure to live up to their extreme examples inspires much of the sense of inadequacy that plagues us all. One of my most treasured goals for this book is to put the notion that mothers are profoundly divided — in calling, "values," and style of life — to rest.

> **The mothers we see represented in the media replays of the Mommy Wars . . . are very much the exception to the rule.**

Race, geographic location, self-identification as a working or stay-at-home mother — none of this made a real difference in the attitudes and mothering styles of the women I interviewed. What did matter, however, was something more intangible: a kind of personal philosophy. The more women bought into the crazy competitiveness of our time, the more they tended to suffer as mothers. Those who, in one way or another, managed to step outside of the parenting pressure cooker tended to have a greater degree of peace of mind and to mother with a greater level of sanity. They did not push themselves or their children to be "winners" — and so seemed to me to be winning out in terms of happiness and quality of life.

I "spoke" with about half of the women I interviewed for this book via the Internet — sending out questionnaires that they answered in essay form. I interviewed the other half in person. We would meet in the evenings, in groups of eight or ten, everyone "playing hooky" from their families, grinning complicitously and chortling pleasantly at the sound of the on-duty dad putting our hostess's kids to bed upstairs. (Meetings in my own home were the exception; my husband worked nights.)

The enthusiasm and excitement were incredible. Total strangers opened their homes to me, invited friends, and put out food for conversations that stretched as late into the night as the next morning's wakeup time allowed. Friends passed the word on to their friends, who spoke to their friends, until, by the end, I had to stop interviewing for sheer lack of time and the mental and physical resources necessary to transcribe and digest all the material.

When our conversations took off, it was exhilarating. It was exhausting. It felt, I imagined, like the consciousness-raising groups of the early days of the second-wave feminist movement (groups that, as a four- or five-year-old, I would not have attended and which took place, in any case, in universes far from my home). The women came to my groups with a sense of mission. They were going to get at the roots of the problems that plague mothers today. (Which some of them called "guilt," some of them called the Mommy Wars, and one of them, a working-mom-turned-stay-at-home, called "feeling like Alice down the rabbit hole.") They were going to find a way out. I always started off the sessions by telling the women about my move from France to America, and about how my shock at how difficult motherhood was here had grown into my book. Sometimes, toward the end of the evening, the tables turned, and they would ask me for some answers. What was the solution? they'd ask. How could we all calm down, feel better, and parent with the relative ease and insouciance that I'd felt as a mother in France?

I heard the questions with a kind of shame. I knew there were some mothers who managed to rise above the excessive nonsense of our times and work out ways to parent with reason and balance. Some of them came to my groups: the successful working mother with the stay-at-home husband, the stay-at-home mother of four who braved universal disdain to put her youngest children (twins) in part-time day care, the mother who stood out on her front lawn with bubbles and toys until the neighborhood kids stopped, and stayed, and enough trust was built among the parents that they started letting their kids run house to house. But I was not one of them.

In fact, as my time back in America lengthened from months into years, I became more and more bound up in all the aspects of motherhood I'd once found strange. The more I reconnected to the world I'd known as a young adult before leaving for France, the more I grew back into the person I'd always been here — a relatively typical, if quirky, would-be overachiever — and the worse I felt about myself as a mother.

In Paris, I'd felt very good about myself just for mothering according to my inclinations. Since I was an American, those inclinations were far more hands-on than those of the women around me, and so I'd easily enjoyed a somewhat smug sense of superiority. Simply by doing things I *enjoyed* — reading to my daughter for hours on end, taking her out to lunch and telling her stories, sitting on the edge of the sandbox in my sneakers, rather than perching peevishly on a park bench and smoking — *just by smiling* — I felt I was earning a perpetual merit badge for Good Motherhood. I had no qualms about eliminating those activities I found needlessly boring or stupid — like the lap-sit story hour at the nearby American Library, with the fish-out-of-water mommies clutching little plastic bags of Cheerios. If it wasn't fun, I figured, what was the point? If my daughter and I were doing some kind of added-value activity together and it wasn't a pleasure, then why bother?

In ever-smiling America, I was learning, it was actually a lot harder to maintain my sense of fun in motherhood. This was in part, for me, because the things I'd considered the simple pleasures of motherhood were harder and harder to come by. Things like pushing the stroller somewhere pretty for a walk — alone or with a friend. There was too much suburban sprawl and our lives were too atomized. Or things like spending lazy weekend days in the park or with another family. Everyone was too busy with "activities." It was hard to spend time just sort of vegetating in the sun because our kids, overstimulated by daily story hours and Gymboree, couldn't just play in the sandbox, or run around the flagpole, or climb without running to us every five minutes. Without our having constantly to explain, interpret, *facilitate* the world for them. (*"What that lady is saying is, she would really prefer you not empty your bucket of sand over her little boy's head. Is that okay with you, honey?"*)

Maybe our children could have run off and played. If we'd let them. But we didn't. There was so much pressure to always be *doing* something with or for them. And doing it right. And I was increasingly feeling that I was doing everything wrong. As a mother. As a woman. As a human being.

> **Maybe our children could have run off and played. If we'd let them. But we didn't. There was so much pressure to always be doing something with or for them.**

A year went by and I could not find a reliable babysitter. I put my elder daughter in a D.C. public school and watched the light in her eyes go dim. (Her kindergarten teacher there told me he'd put all his kids in private school.) I did not have a pediatrician available for human contact in an emergency (being given the "opinion of the practice" by one of his nameless nurses when my younger daughter cut her face open just didn't do the trick). I felt like all responsibility for my daughters' care, health, and education resided within our family. Often enough, it seemed to rest on my shoulders alone.

Sometimes now, when I berated myself for any one of my many shortcomings as a mother (I did not do enough ball-playing; I did not have a sufficient variety of arts-and-crafts supplies; I had not [yet] converted my basement into the requisite playroom), I was reminded of the way a friend in Paris — an American married to a Frenchman — had laughed at me when I'd once expressed guilt about sending my toddler daughter off to six hours a week of preschool. "Do you have a mini arts studio in your home?" she'd asked. "Do you have a playhouse and a variety of tricycles? Can you provide new sources of fun and stimulation every day?" The answers were, obviously, no on all counts. The mere idea of having all that equipment at home had seemed absurd. In fact, when she put things that way, it began to seem absurd to keep a child at home when so many wonderful opportunities existed on the outside.

But in Washington, everything was different. The homes around me *were* equipped like mini arts studios. Many people had backyard equipment that rivaled public parks. And there was a sense that whatever was done at home was best. Anything "institutional," as people put it, was far lesser — a sad replacement for the at-home loving care a good mother could provide by herself.

I tried to do it all myself: be mommy and camp counselor and art teacher and prereading specialist (and somehow, in my off-hours, to do my own work). I tried my absolute best. And like so many of the moms around me, I started to go a little crazy.

I spent night after night arranging toys by color and type in the basement and lining up children's books in size order on the bookshelves.

I spent hours on the phone with other mothers, arranging play dates and negotiating birthday party days.

People said I was "organized."

Sometimes, for no apparent reason, I broke out into hives.

Everything was spinning out of control.

DISCUSSION

1. What do you make of the conventional distinction in our culture that divides work and family into two entirely separate categories? To what extent does it make sense to think of each as its own form of work? And how might doing so challenge or rewrite the dominant scripts by which women's roles are currently defined?

2. "Ozzie and Harriet sex roles just weren't what I had expected to find back in America. I was a child of the 1970s, a feminist formed by the 1980s, a product of the girls-can-be-anything school of socialization, which rested on the idea that not only was biology not destiny, it was largely irrelevant." In your experience, how much of this promise seems to have been fulfilled? Does it seem to you that we now live in a world where biology is no longer destiny?

3. How does the work of motherhood, which Warner itemizes, compare to the tasks that — according to the myths or ideals of our culture — are supposed to more typically define this role? How the two sets of tasks compare? Which seems more accurate?

WRITING

4. Warner spends much of this essay critiquing what she calls the "culture of total motherhood": entrenched attitudes and expectations that, even in this day and age, continue to demand that women commit themselves first and foremost to the needs of their children. Write an essay in which you assess the kind of "work" you think the "culture of total motherhood" does in our culture. What specific roles does it script for women? How does it frame the choices mothers confront when pursuing careers outside the home?

5. According to Warner, there is a plethora of material — from parenting advice books to ballet lessons for three-year-olds — that encourages us to view motherhood as a structured and formalized type of job. Choose an example that Warner lists and write an assessment of the ways it defines the job of being a "proper" mother. What kind of work does it assign? What expectations and attitudes does it proscribe as mandatory? And what sort of payoff or reward does it suggest makes this work worthwhile?

6. Choose one of the interviews Warner excerpts in this essay. What story does it relate? What problem does it identify? Then, cast yourself in the role of one of the writers featured in this chapter. What kind of suggestions would he or she offer for solving the challenges or dilemmas of work that Warner describes? What solution would you recommend? And what, in your view, makes it most preferable?

Scenes and Un-Scenes: *A Woman's Work*

For decades, if not centuries, Americans have been encouraged not only to draw firm boundaries between men's work and women's work, but also to *value* these kinds of work in radically different ways. As many of us know firsthand, gender stereotypes continue to play a prominent role in scripting the ways we are taught to think about and evaluate life on the job. Whether measured in terms of annual income, social prestige, or professional clout, we know, for example, that we are supposed to view being a kindergarten teacher and being a corporate CEO very differently. We know how to assess and rank these respective occupations because our culture has supplied us with a set of ready-made and highly gendered assumptions (for example, about the kind of person who is the most natural fit for the job, about the rewards and respect such a jobholder is allowed to expect, and so on). But do these assumptions really offer us an accurate guide? Do they frame choices or script norms that actually "work" for us? And if they don't, to what extent can they be challenged or revised? Each of the following images presents us with an image that rewrites stereotypical scripts by which we have been taught to segregate men's work from women's work. What do these acts of revision involve? What particular norms do their portraits of women and work seem to parody or critique? And what new norms do they posit in their place?

>> *An image initially created as part of a government-led effort during World War II to recruit women into industries that had lost their all-male workforces to overseas fighting, Rosie the Riveter was originally intended to represent the country's short-term employment crisis. One of the most iconic work images of the twentieth century, Rosie the Riveter stands as a pointed rebuke to the ways Americans have traditionally been taught to think about "women's work."* (See next page.)

What do you make of an iconic image like Rosie the Riveter refashioned into an action figure? Toys, after all, are designed for fun and meant to entertain, not to educate. Does a figure like action-figure Rosie run the risk of undermining, even trivializing, this symbol's transgressive punch? Or does it make more sense to think of this figure as less a toy than a tool, an instrument offering kids the chance to imaginatively act out gender scripts or roles that deviate from the stereotypical norm? Indeed, if GI Joes or Barbie Dolls can be thought of as (either helpful or dangerous) role models for children, why can't Rosie? Can you imagine a scenario in which a child might use the Rosie action figure as a positive role model? What do you think this sort of play would look like?

>> *Other cultural texts have built on Rosie's legacy in different ways. Unlike its preceding counterparts, this image works much more clearly to redirect traditional gender stereotypes toward nontraditional ends. Rather than a sexist shorthand used to marginalize the contributions of working women, the phrase girltalk — uttered here by a female executive — gets transformed into a sly joke, one that inverts conventional gender hierarchies by making men the object of humor.*

▲ *In the 1980 film 9 to 5, three women office workers end up running their company when, through a series of comic misunderstandings, they end up holding their boss hostage. Over the last few decades, our airwaves have been filled with movies and television shows that attempt the very Rosie-like feat of placing women within positions of workplace authority traditionally occupied by men. However, this sort of role reversal has often been undertaken for comic effect: a way of poking fun at conventional gender norms and gender hierarchies by turning them upside down. In the end, though, how much of the film's comedy rests on the assumption that a woman running a company is inherently funny?*

"What do you say, gentlemen—ready for some girltalk?"

▲▲ *In 2007, Representative Nancy Pelosi (D-Calif.) became the first woman Speaker of the U.S. House of Representatives. Is there anything about the composition of this news photo that could be said to be reminiscent of the depiction of Rosie the Riveter from the 1940s? In what ways does it differ?*

DISCUSSION

1. How does the Rosie the Riveter image seem to define the ideal job? What kinds of work? What particular roles? And to what extent does this definition challenge or rewrite conventional gender stereotypes?

2. How accurately do the work portraits presented above capture or comment on your experiences on the job? Do they convey messages or model norms that would be considered acceptable within the work environments you know personally? How or how not?

3. How valid do you think the distinction between men's work and women's work is in this day and age? Is it a distinction that continues to exert influence in our culture? Does it present a script we are still encouraged to use?

WRITING

4. Choose the image above that you think most directly reinforces the connection between work and self-worth. Write an essay in which you assess the merits and/or flaws of this depiction. In what ways does this image encourage viewers to forge a connection between their work and their self-worth? What, in your view, are the implications of embracing this message? Of using it as the basis for living one's own life?

5. In addition to the distinction between men's and women's work, the examples above also underscore certain differences between white-collar and blue-collar jobs. What are the scripts in our culture by which we are taught to differentiate these two types of employment? Choose one of the images above and write an essay in which you analyze how particular gender stereotypes influence the depiction of white- or blue-collar work. What gender roles or gender scripts get associated with this kind of work? How does the photo convey them? Does this portrayal seem accurate? Fair? How or how not?

6. In "This Mess," Judith Warner (p. 333) writes about motherhood as a full-time job. How do you think she would respond to the images you have just seen, all of which depict women in stereotypically male-dominated types of work? What images can you think of from popular culture that might be added to the preceding set that would corroborate Warner's view of motherhood as a type of career?

Putting It into Practice: *Working Hard or Hardly Working?*

Now that you've read the chapter selections, try applying your conclusions to your own life by completing the following exercises.

BUILDING THE PERFECT WORK ENVIRONMENT   The selections in this chapter cover many different types of jobs, but they also describe, sometimes indirectly, different work *environments*. Write an essay in which you describe the different environments in two or three of these selections. What are the standards of dress or behavior you think these environments condone? What isn't allowed? What type of work environment do you believe is most suited to your personality? Why? What does your ideal "office" (whether it's a traditional workspace) look like? What are the standards of conduct you would implement?

EVALUATING SALARIES   The U.S. Department of Labor Bureau and Labor Statistics has compiled a list of mean salaries for 800 jobs (www.bls.gov/oes/current/oes_nat.htm). Select several different occupations and see how each one compares in terms of its related salary. Write an essay in which you discuss what salary tells us about the "value" of work. What sort of skills or training seem to lead to larger salaries? In your opinion, do the higher-earning jobs truly merit their larger salaries? Why or why not? If you could reassign rank to the jobs you've chosen, how would your list compare with the real salaries for the jobs you've chosen?

PUT YOUR BEST FOOT FORWARD   Bedford/St. Martin's *Re: Writing* website (bedfordstmartins.com/rewriting) has several models of effective résumés, which you can access by clicking the "Model Documents Gallery" link on the front page and then clicking "Business and Technical Writing." Think about a job or career path that you are interested in pursuing, and use these resources to write a resume for an entry-level job (or one commensurate with your experience) in this field.

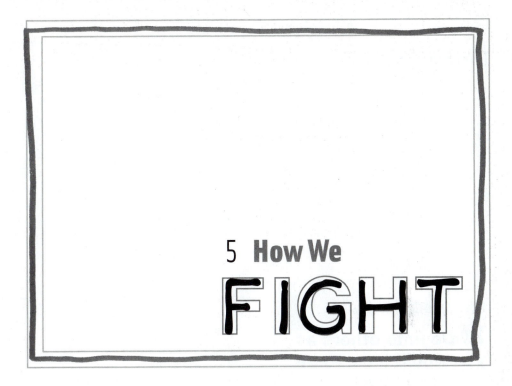

5 **How We**
FIGHT

Introduction

TEMPER TEMPER . . .

When you hear the word *fight*, what three images first pop into your head? A World Wrestling Entertainment match? U.S. combat soldiers patrolling Baghdad? A group of kindergarteners on the playground? That it requires so little effort to compile such a diverse list is itself proof that this issue may be a bit more complicated than it first appears. When it comes to fighting, in fact, it is safe to say we live in a fairly schizophrenic culture. On the one hand, nothing sounds more familiar to our ears than the admonition that "fighting is wrong." As children, we are told over and over that "fighting doesn't solve anything," are warned against the dangers of "losing our temper," and enjoined to "use our words, not our hands" or "count to ten." How often, after all, do we hear about the elementary schoolteacher who advises students to "go ahead and slug it out" or come across a parenting guide that lists "violence as your first option"? Never, right?

On the other hand, we shouldn't forget that we also live in a world where fighting is not only often showcased but downright celebrated as well. From the record audiences who tune in watch the Super Bowl to the enduring popularity of *The Sopranos*, it seems as if ours has become a culture where the line separating fighting from entertainment is entirely blurred. If it takes little effort to recount the sorts of prohibitions against fighting we've heard over the years, it surely doesn't take much more to catalog the television shows and movies, commercials and websites, gadgets and toys that seem bent on teaching us how to fight. From video games like Grand Theft Auto to reality shows like *Fear Factor*, Power Rangers toys to *Guns and Ammo* magazine, our airwaves and store shelves couldn't be more crammed with material that treats fighting as a completely acceptable pastime and as a kind of cultural ideal. Despite all the "nos" and "don'ts" we have been taught to internalize, we still have to deal with the confounding fact that fighting is a social taboo on one hand and a social norm on the other. Cast in these terms, the question confronting us changes somewhat: not *whether* fighting gets promoted in our culture (we know it does), but *when* and *why*. At what moments and under what conditions are we told it's OK to fight? What are the rules by which some forms of conflict get deemed acceptable and others get designated as wrong?

> *Everybody Knows That . . .*
>
> **❝Do unto others as you would have them do unto you."**
>
> — *Jesus in Gospels, Matthew 7:12, Luke 6:31, Luke 10:27*

PICKING FIGHTS AND CHOOSING SIDES

In answering these questions, we might start by taking stock of the myriad forms fighting takes in our culture. From combat missions overseas to domestic violence crimes at home, antiglobalization rallies to abortion clinic protests, mudslinging political campaigns to hostile corporate takeovers, we hardly lack for venues in which we see one kind of conflict or another unfold. Of course, how we think about these conflicts — whether they prompt outrage or interest, condemnation or celebration — depends in part on the lessons we glean from our larger popular culture. When we find ourselves caught up in personal conflicts, to what extent are we acting on messages and playing out roles scripted for us? Whether it be e-mail "flames," relationship breakups, or episodes of road rage, our own behavior may well afford the clearest glimpse of the fight-related rules that prevail in our culture.

However these rules change from one setting to the next, they all share one fundamental thing: Every one is connected to the question of *difference.* When we focus on the cultural rules that establish the norms around fighting, we confront the ways we are taught to think about and define the "other": those people whose ideas, beliefs, backgrounds, or "look" are not the same as our own. Lamentably, in our world it doesn't take very long to start viewing someone or something different as someone or something threatening. The distance between being an "other" and being an enemy can be quite short. And more often than not, it is our culture's messages about fighting that teach us how to navigate this path. When we survey the movies, television shows, and news programs we watch or the toys and games we buy, what sorts of messages about "otherness" do we discern? How valid is it to think of this vast collection of material as a kind of training ground that teaches us how to draw the boundaries dividing friends from enemies, us and them? To answer this, try the following experiment: Much of the rhetoric about combat recently centers on the term *terrorist.* What sort of person does this term conjure in your mind? How do you think we are taught to use this model enemy as a counterpoint for defining

> ### *Everybody Knows That . . .*
>
> ## ❝pwn (verb) An act of dominating an opponent [usually in an Internet game].
>
> **Originally dates back to the days of WarCraft, when a map designer mispelled 'Own' as 'Pwn.' What was originally supposed to be 'player has been owned' was 'player has been pwned.'**
>
> **Example: "Looks like you're about to get pwned. Yeah!!!" — Eric Cartman, *South Park* episode "Make Love, Not Warcraft," 2006**
>
> *— urbandictionary.com*

ourselves? What ideals and norms are we supposed to define this figure against?

To be sure, this exercise is meant to be more than a simple self-inventory. Rather, it is meant to capture in concrete terms the ways we learn to internalize and act on our culture's various fight-related scripts. Indeed, it's not really possible to conduct this kind of work without also wondering where it is exactly that these definitions come from. To illustrate further, let's consider the messages embedded in some combat video games (see the Rule Maker/Rule Breaker feature on page 356 for further discussion).

Everybody Knows That . . .

❝You're either with us or you are with the terrorists.❞

— *President George W. Bush,*
State of the Union Address, 2002

Games like Spec Ops 2: US Army Green Berets set very firm boundaries around the ways we are allowed to fight. Less immediately apparent, though, is how such instructions offer pointed (if implicit) lessons in "otherness." To win this game, players have to know the correct way to define and spot the enemy. In this world of virtual combat, only vaguely Middle Eastern locales get defined as enemy territory, combatants are exclusively composed of nonwhite "terrorists" (lurking behind doors sniping, shooting from rooftops), and consequently all the violence players perpetrate is automatically "self-defense." These kinds of instructions not only define the proper way to fight, but they also go a long way toward shaping our assumptions about who is and who is not "like us."

What makes this sort of investigation both so important and so tricky is that "otherness" — the ways we're taught to draw distinctions between friends and enemies, us and them — is far from a stand-alone question. It lies, in fact, at the heart of some of the most fundamental and contentious debates in our culture. In the above example, it's clear once we begin to look more closely that the fight scripts mapped out for us are designed to do more than teach us how to play the role of a combat soldier. They also supply us with the tools for thinking our way through and drawing conclusions about such pressing public issues as militarism and patriotism, race and ethnic difference. As one of our culture's most enduring and contested preoccupations, it probably should not surprise us that this is so. It does remind us, though, that we'd be well advised to treat the question of fighting in as inclusive and broad-ranging manner as possible. Rather than approaching fighting simply as an activity to be defended or deplored, a problem to be solved, we would be better off thinking of this phenomenon as a kind of cultural lens: a framework through which to better apprehend the ways we attempt to work through our differences. Where are the places where we most visibly and stridently disagree? What are the issues or questions most immediately at issue? And where do we learn the proper protocols and scripts for working them out?

Toward this end, the selections in this chapter profile some of the more representative forms that conflict can take in our culture these days. Kathy Dobie, for instance, offers a different perspective on what is perhaps the most emblematic fight of our era: the war in Iraq. Chronicling the decision of several soldiers to go AWOL, her essay raises difficult and disturbing questions about the ways we are trained to think about combat and killing. Presenting his own vantage on combat experience, war correspondent Chris Hedges offers his

Everybody Knows That . . .

"Make Love Not War"

— Popular slogan of the 1960s antiwar movement

reflections on two decades spent living in different war zones. In recounting these years, his essay works to revise some of our most entrenched conceits about war: particularly those that cast the battlefield as a proving ground for bravery and moral character. In contrast to Hedge's visceral account of the battlefield, Katy Vine turns our attention to a world where fights are waged on a far more abstract plane: cyberspace. Tracking the evolution of an online community from its early optimistic inception to its contentious and messy unraveling, her discussion highlights both the forms that "virtual conflict" can take as well as the consequences it can bring. Like Vine, Gerard Jones is interested in probing where traditional models of conflict intersect with new forms of technology — in this case, so-called violent video games. Challenging the perceived wisdom on this subject, Jones makes a powerful case that these games are best viewed not as tutorials in antisocial behavior but as useful outlets for channeling and resolving adolescent anxiety. In his damning portrait of the nation's supermax prison system, Sasha Abramsky offers what we might call the inverted, nightmarish version of Jones's view: a world in which violence, sadism, and punishment are the only operative norms. And finally, Bob Moser presents a bracing critique of the common use of the war metaphor in sports writing, arguing that its effects may be far more damaging that simply perpetuating clichés.

"EVERYBODY KNOWS THAT" EXERCISE

Choose one of the quotations featured in the margins on the preceding pages and answer the following questions:

1. What does this image or quotation ask you to believe?

2. What are the particular ideas, values, or attitudes it invites us to accept as *normal*?

3. What would it feel like to act on or act out these norms in our personal lives?

Rule *Maker* > > > > > > > Rule *Breaker*

❝ *You are now entering the world of Spec Ops 2: US Army Green Berets. And as in the previous version you will once again be able to control a choice US Army Special Operations group. You will be assigned missions that will take you around the world where the scenarios are based on real events plucked right out of today's headlines. . . .Rather than just the stereo-typical killing aliens/monsters from another dimension/planet/gate of hell, Spec Ops sets itself apart from the rest of the shooter genre by incorporating real world military combat, in actual hot-spot, real world locations, with the actual weapons and tactics used by the US armed services."*

— INTRODUCTION TO THE IGN STRATEGY GUIDE
FOR SPEC OPS 2: U.S. ARMY GREEN BERETS
(WWW.IGN.COM), 2006

❝ *Video game addiction is, without a doubt, becoming this century's most increasingly worrisome epidemic, comparable even to* **drug** *and* **alcohol abuse**. *All the while, the video game industry continues to market and promote* **hatred**, **racism**, **sexism**, *and the most disturbing trend:* clans *and* guilds, *an underground video game phenomenon which closely resembles* **gangs**.*"*

— MOTHERS AGAINST VIDEOGAME ADDICTION
AND VIOLENCE, WWW.MAVAV.ORG, 2007

VIDEO GAME DEVELOPERS VERSUS MOTHERS AGAINST VIDEOGAME ADDICTION AND VIOLENCE

There are countless examples of products, images, and shows in which fighting gets both packaged and promoted as a form of entertainment. Tempting players with the prospect of "firsthand" soldiering experience, video games like Special Ops 2: US Army Green Berets, for example, offer detailed instructions in how to play our proper "combat" role. But is it possible for these sorts of opportunities to become *too* real? Do video games such as these, with their breathless promotion of conflict and killing, their numerous directions and rules, ultimately write out scripts for us that are simply too violent? Read in this light, the invitation to enter "right into the heart of the action" might easily start to feel like more than just innocent fun. Certainly, as the Rule Breaker quote makes clear, some people think the violence in video games goes too far, promoting aggression and desensitizing children to violence. When it comes to the many varieties of violence and conflict we encounter day to day, what exactly is the proper attitude we are supposed to

strike with each? Which examples are we supposed to deplore as cruel, barbaric, self-defeating, or wrong? And which are we encouraged to celebrate, emulate, or idealize?

FIND THE RULES: In your opinion, what boundaries in our culture pertain to how we are supposed to react to violence? How do these boundaries change when the violence is imaginary (for example, in cartoons, films, or video games)?

MAKE YOUR OWN RULES: Do you believe that video games are too violent? Why or why not? How would you change popular video games like Spec Ops 2: US Army Green Berets to appease critics like Mothers against Video Addiction and Violence? Do you think it's possible?

KATHY DOBIE

AWOL in America: When Desertion Is the Only Option

Is it possible to be taught how to kill? Focusing on the tactics the military uses to trains new soldiers, Kathy Dobie recounts the experiences of several recruits for whom this kind of instruction becomes too much to bear. In the process, she offers a powerful meditation on what it means to teach violence, as well as the roles that such lessons ultimately script out. Dobie is a journalist and the author of a memoir, *The Only Girl in the Car* (2003). Her work has appeared in *Harper's, Salon, Vibe,* and the *Village Voice*. This selection appeared in the March 2005 edition of *Harper's*.

An AWOL Navy man was arrested . . . as he brought his pregnant wife to the hospital. . . . Roberto Carlos Navarro, 20, of Polk City [Florida] was charged as a deserter from the U.S. Navy. . . . Navarro became disenchanted with the constant painting and scraping of ships after two years in the Navy. — The Ledger, April 2, 2004

A 17-year-old was turned over to the Department of Defense last week after Bellingham police discovered the teenager, involved in a traffic accident, was allegedly a deserter from Army basic training. — The Boston Globe, August 12, 2004

I am seriously considering becoming a deserter. I am sorry if there are other military moms . . . that look poorly on me for thinking this way but . . . I WILL NOT LEAVE MY LITTLE BABY. — Online post to BabyCenter.com, November 21, 2004

AWOL, FRENCH LEAVE, THE GRAND BOUNCE, JUMPING SHIP, GOING over the hill — in every country, in every age, whenever and wherever there has been a military, there have been soldiers discharging themselves from the ranks. The Pentagon has estimated that since the start of the current conflict in Iraq, more than 5,500 U.S. military personnel have deserted, and yet we know the stories of only a unique handful, all whom have publicly stated their opposition to the war in Iraq, and some of whom have fled to Canada. The Vietnam war casts a long shadow, distorting our image of the deserter; four soldiers have gone over the Canadian border, looking for the safe haven of the Vietnam years, which no longer exists: there are no open arms for such refugees and almost no possibility of obtaining legal status. We imagine 5,500 conscientious objectors to a bloody quagmire, soldiers like Staff Sergeant Camilo Mejia, who strongly and eloquently protested the Iraq war, having actually served there and witnessed civilians killed and prisoners abused, and who was subsequently court martialed, found guilty of desertion, and given a year in prison. But deserters rarely leave for purely political reasons. They usually just quietly return home and hope no one notices.

Last summer, I read a news account of a twenty-one-year-old man caught by the police climbing through the window of a house. It turned out to be *his* house, but the cops found out he was AWOL from the Army and arrested him. That story, in all its recognizable, bungling humanity, intrigued me. It brought the truth of governments waging war home to me in a way that stories of combat had not — in particular, how the ambitions and desires of powerful men and women are borne by ordinary people: restless scrappers and tomboys from West Virginia, teenage immigrants from Mexico, and juvenile delinquents from Indiana; randy boys and girls, and callous ones; the stoic, the idealist, the aimless, the boastful and the bewildered; the highly adventurous and the deeply conformist. They carry the weight.

> *The ambitions and desires of powerful men and women are borne by ordinary people.*

After reading the story of the AWOL soldier sneaking into his own house, I contacted the G.I. Rights hot line, a national referral and counseling service for military personnel, and on August 23, 2004, I interviewed Robert Dove, a burly, bearded Quaker, in the Boston offices of the American Friends Service Committee, one of the groups involved with the hot line. Dove told me of getting frantic calls from the parents of recruits, and of recruits who are so appalled by basic training that they "can't eat, they literally vomit every time they put a spoon to their mouths, they're having nightmares and wetting their beds." Down in Chatham County, North Carolina, Steve and Lenore Woolford answer calls from the hot line in their home. Steve was most haunted by the soldiers who want out badly but who he can tell are not smart or self-assured enough to accomplish it; the ones who ask the same questions over and over again and want to know *exactly* what to say to their commanding officer. The G.I. Rights hot line introduced me to deserters willing to talk, and those soldiers put me in contact with others.

I met my first deserters in early September and over the next four months followed some of them through the process of turning themselves in and getting released from the military. They came from Indiana, Oregon, Washington, California, Georgia, Connecticut, New York, and Massachusetts. I met with the mother and sister of a Marine who was UA (Unauthorized Absence, the Navy and Marine term for AWOL) in the mother's home in Alto, Georgia, and at the Quantico base in Virginia one

Sunday afternoon I met with eight deserters returned to military custody, members of the Casualty Platoon, as the Marines refer to them, since they are "lost combatants." One of the AWOL soldiers, Jeremiah Adler, offered to show me the letters he had written home from boot camp; a Marine called with weekly reports from Quantico where he awaited his court-martial or administrative release. Through these soldiers, and the counselors at the G.I. Rights hot line, I discovered that the recruiting process and the training were keys to understanding why soldiers desert, as is an overextended Army's increasingly strong grip on them.

Since the mid-1990s, the Army has been quietly struggling with a manpower crisis, as the number of desertions steadily climbed from 1,509 in 1995 to 4,739 in 2001. During this time, deserters rarely faced court-martial or punishment. The vast majority — 94 percent of the 12,000 soldiers who deserted between 1997 and 2001 — were simply released from the Army with other-than-honorable discharges. Then, in the fall of 2001, shortly after 9/11, the U.S. Army issued a new policy regarding deserters, hoping to staunch the flow. Under the new rules, which were given little media attention, deserters were to be returned to their original military units to be evaluated and, when possible, integrated back into the ranks. It was not a policy that made the hearts of Army officers sing. As one company commander told DefenseWatch, an online newsletter for the grassroots organization Soldiers For The Truth, "I can't afford to baby-sit problem children every day."

According to DefenseWatch, in the first few months after the policy went into effect, 190 deserters were returned to military control, 89 of those were returned to the ranks, and 101 were discharged. Statistics at the end of the military fiscal year showed the desertion numbers dropping slightly, due, at least in part, to the new policy, which reintegrated almost half the runaways back into their units. It wasn't that fewer people were leaving the military, just that fewer people were able to stay gone.

Then we invaded Iraq, and as the war there rages on, the military has had to evacuate an estimated 50,000 troops: the dead and the wounded, combat- and non-combat-related casualties. Those soldiers must be replaced — and we're committed to sending in even more. The pressure to hold on to as many troops as possible has only increased, as is painfully evident in internal memos such as this one from Major General Claude A. Williams of the Army National Guard, dated May 2004: "Effective immediately, I am holding commanders at all levels accountable for controlling manageable losses." The memo goes on to say that commanders must retain at least 85 percent of soldiers who are scheduled to end their active duty, 90 percent of soldiers scheduled to ship for Initial Entry Training, and "execute the AWOL recovery procedures for every AWOL soldier." The military has issued stop-loss orders, dug deep into the ranks of reservists and guardsmen, extended tours of duty, and made it harder for recruits and active-duty personnel to get out through administrative means. According to the military's own research, this will result in more people going AWOL.

In the summer of 2002, the U.S. Army Research Institute for the Behavioral and Social Sciences released a study titled "What We Know About AWOL and Desertion." "Although the problem of AWOL/desertion is fairly constant, it tends to increase in magnitude during wartime — when the Army tends to increase its demands for troops and to lower its enlistment standards to meet that need. It can also increase during times, such as now, when the Army is attempting to restrict the ways that soldiers can exit service through administrative channels." In other words, close the door, and they will leave by the window.

> *Close the door, and they will leave by the window.*

At the G.I. Rights hot line, the desperation is obvious; the number of people calling in for help has almost doubled from 17,000 in 2001 to 33,000 in the last year. The majority of the calls are from people who want out of the military — soldiers with untreated injuries or urgent family problems, combat veterans who have developed a deep revulsion to war, National Guardsmen primed to deal with hurricanes, blizzards, and floods but not fighting overseas, and inactive reservists who have already served, started families and careers, and never expected to be called up again. And there are recruits — many, many recruits — who have decided, in a sentiment heard hundreds of times by the people manning the phones, "The Army's just not for me." Some of these callers were thinking about going AWOL; others had already left and wanted to know what could happen to them and what they should do next.

Soldiers who go AWOL have either panicked and see no other way out of their difficulties or are well-informed and know that deserting is sometimes the quickest, surest route out of the military. A soldier may not be eligible for a hardship or medical discharge, for instance, but he knows he wants out. He may not even be aware of the discharges available to him. Young, raw recruits, in particular, know only what their drill sergeants tell them. Counselors at the G.I. Rights hot line describe cases in which a recruit will ask about applying for a discharge and be told flatly by his drill sergeant, "Forget about it. Don't even think of applying. You're not getting out." Conscientious-objector applications have more than tripled since operations began in Iraq, but they take on average a year and a half to process, and then, quite often, are denied.

In the Army study, which examined data from World War II, Korea, Vietnam, and the years 1997–2001, it was found that deserters are more likely to be younger when they enlist, less educated, to come from "broken homes," and to have "engaged in delinquent behavior" prior to enlisting. In other words, they are both vulnerable and rebellious. During the Vietnam war, enlisted men were far more likely to desert than those who were drafted. Perhaps they had higher expectations of Army life, or perhaps a man who volunteers for service feels like he has some sense of control over his fate, a feeling a draftee could hardly share. Only 12 percent of the Vietnam-era deserters left specifically because of the war, according to the same study. Then, as now, most soldiers take off because of family problems, financial difficulties, and what the Army obliquely calls "failure to adapt" to military life and "issues with chain of command."

Almost all of the deserters I spoke to described the kind of person they thought succeeded in the military as "an alpha male type who can take orders real well," as one Marine put it. "If you can't do both? *Don't Join.*" Physical aggression and mental docility might seem an unlikely pairing, but as the military historian Gwynne Dyer wrote in his book titled, simply, *War,* "Basic training has been essentially the same in every army in every age, because it works with the same raw material that's always there in teenage boys: a fair amount of aggression, a strong tendency to hang around in groups, and an absolute desperate desire to fit in."

It's hard for me to be myself here. There's no room for dissent among the guys. Everywhere you listen you hear an abundant amount of B.S., a few beds over an obnoxious redneck has a crowd around him as he details a 3 some that he recently had. The vocabulary is much different here. The bathroom is called the latrine, food is called chow, women are bitches, sex is ass. . . . These people want to go to war and kill. It is that simple." — From a letter home, Jeremiah Adler

Jeremiah Adler arrives at my door in Brooklyn in late September, four days after he escaped Fort Benning, Georgia, with another Army recruit. At ten at night, while a friend on guard duty looked the other way, the boys took off out of the barracks, making a thirty-yard dash into the surrounding forest. They had no clue as to where they were. After an hour they heard sirens blasting, and then the baying of dogs. They spent five hours in the woods, following a bright patch in the sky that they rightly assumed to be the city of Columbus. When they finally reached the road, they saw cop cars zipping past them, lights flashing in the dark. It was terribly exciting, though the morning he arrives at my house he seems spent. Jeremiah and I had spoken for the first time the day before. He was hiding out at a friend's house in Atlanta, ready to hop the next plane home to Portland, Oregon, but he agreed to meet with me in New York first.

Jeremiah is slight, and his blue-green eyes seem unusually large, though that could be the effect of his shorn head. He has full lips and a fine-boned face that could easily become gaunt. He's eighteen, a deeply earnest eighteen, with a dry sense of humor. He has an odd habit for someone so young of sighing often, and wearily. He's also very hungry. We order a cheese pizza because he does not eat meat.

When Jeremiah announced his intention to join the military he took everyone who knew him in Portland by surprise. "He was raised in a pacifist, macrobiotic house," his mother exclaims. "He went to Waldorf schools. Here is a kid who's never even had a bite of animal flesh in his life!" Jeremiah had protested the Iraq war, in fact. He spent most of his senior year in high school convincing his family and what he and his mother call his "community" — a tightly knit group of families connected by the Portland Waldorf School and Rudolf Steiner's nontraditional philosophy of education — that joining the military was the right thing for him to do.

In the spring of his senior year, Jeremiah went on a "vision quest," hiking into an area called Eagle Creek, which was still covered in snow. There he made a video explaining his reasons for joining the Army. He sits on the ground facing the camera but looking off into the woods as he talks. He starts by making a case for the military being a tool for change, a possible force for good. But, "if you have a bunch of bloodthirsty young men with an I.Q. of twenty-three in the military, that's what the military's gonna be — until other people, other intelligent people with morals and values and convictions and ideals [join up]. Most people hate the military. Is the answer to distance yourself as far as you can and just protest all the time? What am I doing? I don't know anyone in the military. Neither do any of you. It takes a lot more balls for me to join the military than it does for one of you guys to go to a forty-grand liberal-arts school. Is that a huge step? You're gonna be around more open-minded people like yourself. You're not gonna experience any diversity there."

In this taped explanation he leaves out one reason for joining the Army, a reason that perhaps was too amorphous to put into words, or too personal, not something he felt the folks at Waldorf would understand. "My mom was single until I was eight years old," he tells me. "My entire life I was raised sensitive and compassionate. I have a craving for a sense of macho-ness, honestly. A sense of toughness." He remembers, the first time he thought the military

> *It's an ingenious marketing campaign. It goes straight to an eighteen-year-old male's testosterone.*

was "cool" — watching *Top Gun* at ten years old. Then in his senior year of high school, the recruiting commercials became a siren call. "I mean, it's an ingenious marketing campaign. It goes straight to an eighteen-year-old male's testosterone. You see them and you're almost sexually aroused," he says. He wanted to kick past the cocoon of family and community, to know how other people thought and lived. He wanted a coming-of-age ritual — his vision quest, which had ended with the insight "solitude sucks," didn't quite fill the bill. He wanted to become a man. Jeremiah took a year convincing his friends, family, and community, and yet within seventy-two hours of arriving at Fort Benning he was writing a letter home that began, "Hello All, You have got to get me out of here."

The recruits arrived at Reception Battalion at Fort Benning on September 16 close to midnight, completely disoriented. During the next seven days they were introduced to military life: First, their heads were shaved, a ritual that signifies the loss of one's individual identity, and was historically used to control lice and identify deserters. Then the recruits were issued boots, gear, and military I.D. They were taught how to march and stand at attention, made to recite the Soldier's Creed again and again, yelled at, incited, insulted, and then shipped to basic training; that is, put on a bus and sent to a training barracks at another location in Fort Benning.

The first day of Reception, the recruits should have been so busy and harassed that they wouldn't have had time for second thoughts or regrets, but Hurricane Ivan was sweeping through Georgia, and they were confined to their barracks — 104 young men, all keyed up, all on edge, about to embark on some mysterious journey, some awesome transformation that involved uniforms, mud, and guns. There was a constant jockeying for power, fights narrowly averted, a lot of enthusiasm for battle, for killing, or at least the pretense of enthusiasm. When Jeremiah suggested it might be better to wound someone than to kill him, he was quickly put in his place. "Fuck that. I'm putting two in the chest, one in the head just like I'm going to be trained to do."

The men in the barracks were whiter, poorer, and less educated than Jeremiah had expected. Guys who could barely read were astonished that Jeremiah had enlisted even though he'd been accepted at the University of Oregon. Skinheads, ex-skinheads perhaps (since active participation by soldiers in extremist groups is prohibited), showed off their tattoos — one had been told by his recruiter to say that his swastika tattoo was a "force directional signal." There were guys who had done jail time, though Jeremiah quickly adds, "Not that they're bad people by any means, but it kind of shows you the type of person they're recruiting."

The next day, a sergeant addressed the recruits with a speech that Jeremiah says he'll never forget. "You know, when I joined the Army nine years ago people would always ask me why I joined. Did I do it for college money? Did I do it for women? People never understood. I wanted to join the Army because I wanted to go shoot motherfuckers." The room erupted in hoots and hollers. A drill sergeant said something about an Iraqi coming up to them screaming, "Ah-la-la-la-la!" in a high-pitched voice, and how he would have to be killed. After that, all Arabs were referred to by this battle cry — the ah-la-la-la-las. In the barracks, they played war. One recruit would come out of the shower wearing a towel on his head, screaming, "Ah-la-la-la-la!" and the other recruits would pretend to shoot him dead. Jeremiah thought, "Oh my God, what am I doing here?"

That evening he wrote his first letter home, beginning with the word "Wow."

"I'm horrified by some of the things that they talk about. If you were in the civilian world and openly talked about killing people you would be an outcast, but here people openly talk about it, like it's going to be fun." In his second letter, written while he was doing guard duty, he tells his parents how sad the barracks are at night. "You can hear people trying to make sure no one hears them cry under their covers."

On his third day, Jeremiah went to one of the drill sergeants and told him, "I'm sorry, the military's not for me. For whatever reason, I'm not willing to kill. I had the idealistic view that it was more than that, and I realize, since coming here, that it's not." The sergeant stared at him. "Do you know what would happen if you came in here and talked to me fifty, a hundred years ago?"

"Yeah, but we're not living back then," Jeremiah replied. The sergeant said that was a shame, because if he had a 9-millimeter pistol, he'd shoot Jeremiah right then and there. The sergeant dared Jeremiah to refuse to ship, saying he would be sent to jail, that he, personally, would make an example of him.

So Jeremiah cooked up a plan with another unhappy recruit to pretend they were gay. That plan went about as badly as it could have — five drill sergeants questioned them, called them disgusting perverts, but refused to discharge either Jeremiah or his friend. Jeremiah was now stuck in one of the most macho and homophobic environments as a gay man, or, more bewilderingly, as a fake gay man. He had tried to get help from the military chaplain, who cited Bible passages proving that God was against murder, not killing, and told Jeremiah that Iraqis were running up to American troops requesting Bibles.

In his last letter home, written on his sixth day, Jeremiah's handwriting disintegrates; "HELP ME" is scrawled across one page. He was due to ship to basic training in the morning. He had decided to refuse. "I've heard that they try to intimidate you, ganging up on you, threatening you. I heard that they will throw your bags on the bus, and almost force you on. See what I am up against? I have nothing on my side. . . . I am so fucked up right now. . . . I feel that if I stay here much longer I am not going to be the same person anymore. I have to GO. Please help. . . . Every minute you sit at home I am stuck in a shithole, stripped of self-respect, pride, will, hope, love, faith, worth, everything. Everything I have ever held dear has been taken away. This fucks with your head. . . . This makes you believe you ARE worthless shit. Please help. By the time you get this, things will be worse."

After getting some information from his mother on a secretive call home, Jeremiah wrote a letter requesting Entry Level Separation from the

Army, citing his aversion to killing. Entry Level Separation, which exists for the convenience of the Army, allows for the discharge of soldiers who are obviously not cut out for military service. The Army has to provide an exit route for inept, unhealthy, depressed, even suicidal soldiers, but at the same time it doesn't want to open what might turn out to be flood-gates, so soldiers cannot themselves apply for ELS, and rarely even know about its existence. The Reception Battalion commander told Jeremiah that if he refused to ship, he would do everything in his power to court-martial him. Then the drill sergeants had their turn. One in particular was apoplectic. "He started *screaming* at me about how killing is the ultimate thrill in life and every single man wants to kill. Regardless of what you think you believe, it's every man's job to kill, it's the greatest high, it's our animal instinct, our animal desire."

When he refused to ship (he locked his duffel bag to his bed so it couldn't be thrown on the bus), Jeremiah was sent to Excess Barracks. About twenty other recruits were there, each of them trying to get out. It was at Excess Barracks that Jeremiah first got the idea to go AWOL, because there were people there who had done it already. On his ninth day at Fort Benning, he and another recruit, Ryan Gibson, decided to leave. They got all suited up — "a Rambo-like moment" is how Jeremiah describes it. "I'm not gonna lie, we were really excited," he says. "We were finally going to be able to go out into the woods and do something. Even if the only commando stuff we ever did in our entire Army career was escaping from the Army, we were still excited about it."

When Ryan arrived home in Indiana, his mother threatened to report him to the police unless he returned to Fort Benning. So Ryan did return, but he left again two days later, this time taking two other recruits with him. When Jeremiah arrived home in Portland, he told his mother, "Well, Mom, I guess I'm going to have to find a different way to become a man besides learning to kill."

DISCUSSION

1. What typical image do you have of a deserter? What words and images do you associate with this term? Does Dobie's account challenge or rewrite this vision in any way? And if so, does her alternative definition affect or alter your own?

2. Why do you think Dobie chooses to interview actual deserters for this essay? What perspective of the issue do you think these first-person stories add that simply discussing the facts and statistics about desertion could not? How do these interviews contribute to your understanding of the issue?

3. Evaluate the title of this essay. Do you share Dobie's view that, for these soldiers, desertion truly is the only option? If so, what is it about the circum-stances these soldiers find themselves in, the choices they face, that leave them with no other alternatives? If not, what alternatives do the soldiers profiled here overlook? And what, in your opinion, makes them preferable to desertion?

WRITING

4. Think about how our modern military markets itself. What sorts of arguments does it make in favor of service? What kinds of enticements or rewards does it proffer? How does it represent the mission, the role, of soldiering? Write an essay in which you evaluate how convincing you find this effort to be. Compare your own assessment of recruitment to the one offered by Dobie. How much overlap do you see between the two? What factors, in your view, account for the differences you see?

5. Dobie's essay offers some very harsh criticisms of the military's policies regarding soldiers who no longer wish to serve. Write a response to Dobie in which you defend the position of the military, making sure to directly address the points she makes in her essay.

6. According to Dobie, the experience of basic training for new recruits essentially unfolds as an extended exercise in role-playing and instruction — a process, she argues, that aims centrally to desensitize recruits to the act of killing. Write an essay in which you speculate about the ways you think Gerard Jones (p. 400) would evaluate this program. Would he draw the same conclusions regarding the fundamentally dehumanizing nature of this instruction? Or, based on what he says about violence in video games, would he offer an alternative way to understand such lessons?

CHRIS HEDGES

War Is a Force That Gives Us Meaning

How do our most familiar images of and stories about war compare to the real thing? Is it possible to retain a belief in the romantic ideals of fighting when you find yourself living in an actual war zone? To this second question, war correspondent Chris Hedges offers a resounding "no," cataloging instead all the comforting preconceptions that the actual experience of war throws into doubt. Hedges worked as a foreign correspondent for the *New York Times* from 1990 to 2005, serving as bureau chief in the Middle East and in the Balkans. He was part of the team that won a 2002 Pulitzer Prize for Explanatory Reporting for coverage of global terrorism. He also won the 2002 Amnesty International Global Award for Human Rights Journalism. He has a BA in English from Colgate University and a master of divinity from Harvard Divinity School, and has taught at Columbia University, New York University, and Princeton University. Hedges has published three nonfiction books, the introduction from *War Is a Force That Gives Us Meaning* (2002), from which this piece is excerpted; *What Every Person Should Know about War* (2003); and *Losing Moses on the Freeway: The 10 Commandments in America* (2003).

Only the dead have seen the end of war. — PLATO

SARAJEVO IN THE SUMMER OF 1995 CAME CLOSE TO DANTE'S INNER circle of hell. The city, surrounded by Serb gunners on the heights above, was subjected to hundreds of shells a day, all crashing into an area twice the size of Central Park. Ninety-millimeter tank rounds and blasts fired from huge 155-millimeter howitzers set up a deadly rhythm of detonations. Multiple Katyusha rockets — whooshing overhead — burst in rapid succession; they could take down a four- or five-story apartment building in seconds, killing or wounding everyone inside. There was no running water or electricity and little to eat; most people were subsisting on a bowl of soup a day. It was possible to enter the besieged city only by driving down a dirt track on Mount Igman, one stretch directly in the line of Serb fire. The vehicles that had failed to make it lay twisted and upended in the ravine below, at times with the charred remains of their human cargo inside.

Families lived huddled in basements, and mothers, who had to make a mad dash to the common water taps set up by the United Nations, faced an excruciating choice — whether to run through the streets with their children or leave them in a building that might be rubble when they returned.

The hurling bits of iron fragmentation from exploding shells left bodies mangled, dismembered, decapitated. The other reporters and I slipped and slid in the blood and entrails thrown out by the shell blasts, heard the groans of anguish, and were, for our pains, in the sights of Serb snipers, often just a few hundred yards away. The latest victims lay with gaping wounds untended in the corridors of the hospitals that lacked antibiotics and painkillers.

When the cease-fires broke down, there would be four to five dead a day, and a dozen wounded. It was a roulette wheel of death, a wheel of fire that knew no distinctions of rank or nationality. By that summer, after nearly four years of fighting, forty-five foreign reporters had been killed, scores wounded. I lived — sheltered in a side room in the Holiday Inn, its front smashed and battered by shellfire — in a world bent on self-destruction, a world where lives were snuffed out at random.

War and conflict have marked most of my adult life. I began covering insurgencies in El Salvador, where I spent five years, then went on to Guatemala and Nicaragua and Colombia, through the first *intifada* in the West Bank and Gaza, the civil war in the Sudan and Yemen, the uprisings in Algeria and the Punjab, the fall of the Romanian dictator Nicolae Ceauşescu, the Gulf War, the Kurdish rebellion in southeast Turkey and northern Iraq, the war in Bosnia, and finally to Kosova. I have been in ambushes on desolate stretches of Central American roads, shot at in the marshes of southern Iraq, imprisoned in the Sudan, beaten by Saudi military police, deported from Libya and Iran, captured and held for a week by Iraqi Republican Guard during the Shiite rebellion following the Gulf War, strafed by Russian Mig–21s in Bosnia, fired upon by Serb snipers, and shelled for days in Sarajevo with deafening rounds of heavy artillery that threw out thousands of deadly bits of iron fragments. I have seen too much of violent death. I have tasted too much of my own fear. I have painful memories that lie buried and untouched most of the time. It is never easy when they surface.

I learned early on that war forms its own culture. The rush of battle is a potent and often lethal addiction, for war is a drug, one I ingested for many years. It is peddled by mythmakers — historians, war correspondents, filmmakers, novelists, and the state — all of whom endow it with qualities it often does possess: excitement, exoticism, power, chances to rise above our small stations in life, and a bizarre and fantastic universe that has a grotesque and dark beauty. It dominates culture, distorts memory, corrupts language, and infects everything around it, even humor, which becomes preoccupied with the grim perversities of smut and death. Fundamental questions about the meaning, or meaninglessness, of our place on the planet are laid bare when we watch those around us sink to the lowest depths. War exposes the capacity for evil that lurks not far below the surface within all of us. And this is why for many war is so hard to discuss once it is over.

The enduring attraction of war is this: Even with its destruction and carnage it can give us what we long for in life. It can give us purpose, meaning, a reason for living. Only when we are in the midst of conflict does the shallowness and vapidness of much of our lives become apparent. Trivia dominates our conversations and increasingly our airwaves. And war is an enticing elixir. It gives us resolve, a cause. It allows us to be noble. And those who have the least meaning in their lives, the impoverished refugees in Gaza, the disenfranchised North African immigrants in France, even the legions of young who live in the splendid indolence and safety of the industrialized world, are all susceptible to war's appeal.

> *Only when we are in the midst of conflict does the shallowness and vapidness of much of our lives become apparent.*

Those who make war do so for many reasons, although many of these motives are never acknowledged publicly.

The Palestinian uprising was not just about throwing the Israelis out of Gaza and the West Bank, but also about crushing the urban elite, the shop owners and businessmen, in East Jerusalem and Gaza City. The "strikes" organized by the *shabab*, the young men who fueled the uprising from the refugee camps, hurt the Palestinian community far more than they hurt the Israelis. In Bosnia it was the same, the anger turned against a Communist hierarchy that kept for itself the privileges and perks of power even as power slipped from their hands in the decaying state. There is little that angers the disenfranchised more than those who fail to exercise power yet reap powerful rewards. Despots can be understood, even tolerated, but parasites rarely last long.

War is a crusade. President George W. Bush is not shy about warning other nations that they stand with the United States in the war on terrorism or will be counted with those that defy us. This too is a *jihad*. Yet we Americans find ourselves in the dangerous position of going to war not against a state but against a phantom. The *jihad* we have embarked upon is targeting an elusive and protean enemy. The battle we have begun is never-ending. But it may be too late to wind back the heady rhetoric. We have embarked on a campaign as quixotic as the one mounted to destroy us.

"We go forward," President Bush assures us, "to defend freedom and all that is good and just in the world."

The patriotic bunting and American flags that proliferated in the wake of the attacks on the World Trade Center and the Pentagon were our support for the war mounted against the "axis of evil." Elected officials, celebrities, and news anchors lined up to be counted. On Friday, September 14, three days after the attacks, Congress granted the President the right to "use all necessary and appropriate force against those nations, organizations, or persons he determines planned, authorized, committed, or aided the terrorist attacks." The resolution was passed unanimously by the Senate. There was in the House only one dissenting vote, from Barbara J. Lee, a Democrat from California, who warned that military action could not guarantee the safety of the country and that "as we act, let us not become the evil we deplore."

When we ingest the anodyne of war we feel what those we strive to destroy feel, including the Islamic fundamentalists who are painted as alien, barbaric, and uncivilized. It is the same narcotic. I partook of it for many years. And like every recovering addict there is a part of me that remains nostalgic for war's simplicity and high, even as I cope with the scars it has left behind, mourn the deaths of those I worked with, and struggle with the bestiality I would have been better off not witnessing. There is a part of me — maybe it is a part of many of us — that decided at certain moments that I would rather die like this than go back to the routine of life. The chance to exist for an intense and overpowering moment, even if it meant certain oblivion, seemed worth it in the midst of war — and very stupid once the war ended.

I covered the war in El Salvador from 1983 to 1988. By the end I had a nervous twitch in my face. I was evacuated three times by the U.S. embassy because of tips that the death squads planned to kill me. Yet each time I came back. I accepted with a grim fatalism that I would be killed in El Salvador. I could not articulate why I should accept my own destruction and cannot now. When I finally did leave, my last act was, in a frenzy of rage and anguish, to leap over the KLM counter in the airport in Costa Rica because of a perceived slight by a hapless airline clerk. I beat him to the floor as his bewildered colleagues locked themselves in the room behind the counter. Blood streamed down his face and mine. I refused to wipe the dried stains off my cheeks on the flight to Madrid, and I carry a scar on my face from where he thrust his pen into my cheek. War's sickness had become mine.

In the fall of 1995, a few weeks after the war in Bosnia ended, I sat with friends who had suffered horribly. A young woman, Ljiljana, had lost her father, a Serb who refused to join the besieging Serb forces around the city. She had been forced a few days earlier to identify his corpse. The body was lifted, the water running out of the sides of a rotting coffin, from a small park for reburial in the central cemetery. She was emigrating to Australia soon — where, she told me, "I will marry a man who has never heard of this war and raise children who will be told nothing about it, nothing about the country I am from."

Ljiljana was beautiful and young, but the war had exacted a toll. Her cheeks were hollow, her hair dry and brittle. Her teeth were decayed and some had broken into jagged bits. She had no money for a dentist. She hoped to fix them in Australia.

Yet all she and her friends did that afternoon was lament the days when they lived in fear and hunger, emaciated, targeted by Serbian gunners on the heights above. They did not wish back the suffering, and yet, they admitted, those days may have been the fullest of their lives. They looked at me in despair. I knew them when they were being stonked by hundreds of shells a day, when they had no water to bathe in or to wash their clothes, when they huddled in unheated, darkened apartments with plastic sheeting for windows. But what they expressed was real. It was the disillusionment with a sterile, futile, empty present. Peace had again exposed the void that the rush of war, of battle, had filled. Once again they were, as perhaps we all are, alone, no longer bound by that common sense of struggle, no longer given the opportunity to be noble, heroic, no longer sure what life was about or what it meant.

> *Peace had again exposed the void that the rush of war, of battle, had filled.*

The old comradeship, however false, that allowed them to love men and women they hardly knew, indeed, whom they may not have liked before the war, had vanished. Moreover, they had seen that all the sacrifice had been for naught. They had been betrayed. The corrupt old Communist Party bosses, who became nationalists overnight and got my friends into the mess in the first place, those who had grown rich off their suffering, were still in power. There was a 70 percent unemployment rate. They depended on handouts from the international community. They knew the lie of war, the mockery of their idealism and struggled with their shattered illusions. They had seen the grinning skull of death that speaks in the end for war. They understood that their cause, once as fashionable in certain intellectual circles as they were themselves, lay forgotten. No longer did actors, politicians, and artists scramble to visit, acts that were almost always ones of gross self-promotion. And yet they wished it all back. I did too.

A year later I received a Christmas card. It was signed "Ljiljana from Australia." It had no return address. I never heard from her again.

Many of us, restless and unfulfilled, see no supreme worth in our lives. We want more out of life. And war, at least, gives a sense that we can rise above our smallness and divisiveness.

The weeks after the September 11 attacks saw New York City, with some reluctance, slip back to normal. One felt the same nostalgia.

The attacks on the World Trade Center illustrate that those who oppose us, rather than coming from another moral universe, have been schooled well in modern warfare. The dramatic explosions, the fireballs, the victims plummeting to their deaths, the collapse of the towers in Manhattan, were straight out of Hollywood. Where else, but from the industrialized world, did the suicide hijackers learn that huge explosions and death above a city skyline are a peculiar and effective form of communication? They have mastered the language. They understand that the use of disproportionate violence against innocents is a way to make a statement. We leave the same calling cards.

Corpses in wartime often deliver messages. The death squads in El Salvador dumped three bodies in the parking lot of the Camino Real Hotel in San Salvador, where the journalists were based, early one morning. Death threats against us were stuffed in the mouths of the bodies. And, on a larger scale, Washington uses murder and corpses to transmit its wrath. We delivered such incendiary messages in Vietnam, Iraq, Serbia, and Afghanistan. Osama bin Laden has learned to speak the language of modern industrial warfare. It was Robert McNamara, the American Secretary of Defense in the summer of 1965, who defined the bombing raids that would eventually leave hundreds of thousands of civilians north of Saigon dead as a means of communication to the Communist regime in Hanoi.

It is part of war's perversity that we lionize those who make great warriors and excuse their excesses in the name of self-defense. We have built or bolstered alliances with Israel and Russia, forming a dubious global troika against terrorism, a troika that taints us in the eyes of much of the rest of the world, especially among Muslims. Suddenly all who oppose our allies and us — Palestinians, Chechens, and Afghans — are lumped into one indistinguishable mass. They are as faceless as we are for our enemies.

As the battle against terrorism continues, as terrorist attacks intrude on our lives, as we feel less and less secure, the acceptance of all methods to lash out at real and perceived enemies will distort and deform our democracy. For even as war gives meaning to sterile lives, it also promotes killers and racists.

Organized killing is done best by a disciplined, professional army. But war also empowers those with a predilection for murder. Petty gangsters, reviled in pre-war Sarajevo, were transformed overnight at the start of the conflict into war heroes. What they did was no different. They still pillaged, looted, tortured, raped, and killed; only then they did it to Serbs, and with an ideological veneer. Slobodan Milošević went one further. He opened up the country's prisons and armed his criminal class to fight in Bosnia. Once we sign on for war's crusade, once we see ourselves on the side of the angels, once we embrace a theological or ideological belief system that defines itself as the embodiment of goodness and light, it is only a matter of how we will carry out murder.

The eruption of conflict instantly reduces the headache and trivia of daily life. The communal march against an enemy generates a warm, unfamiliar bond with our neighbors, our community, our nation, wiping out unsettling undercurrents of alienation and dislocation. War, in times of malaise and desperation, is a potent distraction.

George Orwell in 1984 wrote of the necessity of constant wars against the Other to forge a false unity among the proles: "War had been literally continuous, though strictly speaking it had not always been the same war. . . . The enemy of the moment always represented absolute evil."[1]

Patriotism, often a thinly veiled form of collective self-worship, celebrates our goodness, our ideals, our mercy and bemoans the perfidiousness of those who hate us. Never mind the murder and repression done in our name by bloody surrogates from the Shah of Iran to the Congolese dictator Joseph-Désiré Mobutu, who received from Washington well over a billion dollars in civilian and military aid during the three decades of his rule. And European states — especially France — gave Mobutu even more as he bled dry one of the richest countries in Africa. We define ourselves. All other definitions do not count.

War makes the world understandable, a black and white tableau of them and us. It suspends thought, especially self-critical thought. All bow before the supreme effort. We are one. Most of us willingly accept war as long as we can fold it into a belief system that paints the ensuing suffering as necessary for a higher good, for human beings seek not only happiness but also meaning. And tragically war is sometimes the most powerful way in human society to achieve meaning.

But war is a god, as the ancient Greeks and Romans knew, and its worship demands human sacrifice. We urge young men to war, making the slaughter they are asked to carry out a rite of passage. And this rite has changed little over the centuries, centuries in which there has almost continuously been a war raging somewhere on the planet. The historian Will Durant calculated that there have only been twenty-nine years in all of human history during which a war was not underway somewhere. We call on the warrior to exemplify the qualities necessary to prosecute war — courage, loyalty, and self-sacrifice. The soldier, neglected and even shunned during peacetime, is suddenly held up as the exemplar of our highest ideals, the savior of the state. The soldier is often whom we want to become, although secretly many of us, including most soldiers, know that we can never match the

> *The tension between those who know combat . . . and those who propagate the myth, usually ends with the mythmakers working to silence the witnesses of war.*

ideal held out before us. And we all become like Nestor in *The Iliad*, reciting the litany of fallen heroes that went before to spur on a new generation. That the myths are lies, that those who went before us were no more able to match the ideal than we are, is carefully hidden from public view. The tension between those who know combat, and thus know the public lie, and those who propagate the myth, usually ends with the mythmakers working to silence the witnesses of war.

John Wheeler, who graduated from West Point in 1966, went to Vietnam, where he watched his class take the highest number of dead and wounded of all the classes that fought there. "I was a witness in Vietnam," he told me. "I spent half my time in a helicopter traveling around the country. I was a witness to the decimation of my West Point class. And I knew we were decimated for a lie." He left the army as a captain in 1971, went to Yale Law School, and became an activist. He was the driving force behind the Vietnam Veterans Memorial wall in Washington. "When I left law school the full impact of the lies hit me," he said. "I have been thinking about these lies, meditating on them and acting on them ever since. The honor system at West Point failed grotesquely within the chain of command. The most senior officers went along with McNamara and Johnson and were guilty. It was an abomination. If in order to do your duty as an Admiral or a General you have to lie, West Point should tell the new plebes."

The Iliad is about power and force. Those who inhabit its space abide by the warrior's code. Its heroes are vain, brave, and consumed by the heady elixir of violence and the bitterness of bereavement. The story is primarily that of one man, Achilles, who returns to the battlefield at Troy to attain *kleos*, the everlasting fame that will be denied to him without heroic death. *The Iliad* could have been written about Bosnia, with its competing warlords and its commanders willing to sacrifice men and villages to their egos and ambition.

The Odyssey is different. It is also built around one character, Odysseus. In *The Odyssey* the hubris and inflexibility of the warrior fail to ward off the capriciousness of fate, the indifference of nature. Odysseus has trouble coping with the conventions of civilized life. When he takes umbrage at more powerful forces and cannot resist revealing his name to the Cyclops, he condemns his men to death and himself to prolonged suffering. As the sailors beat the sea to white froth with their oars, Odysseus calls out to Cyclops: "With my men / hanging all over me and begging me not to," but they "didn't persuade my hero's heart."[2]

It is his hero's heart that Odysseus must learn to curb before he can return to the domestic life he left twenty years earlier. The very qualities that served him in battle defeat him in peace. These dual codes have existed, perhaps, since human societies were formed, and every recruit headed into war would be well advised to read *The Iliad*, just as every soldier returning home would be served by reading *The Odyssey*. No two works have come closer to chronicling the rage and consumption of war and the struggle to recover. The name Odysseus is tied to the Greek verb *odussomai*, which means "to suffer pain."

War exposes a side of human nature that is usually masked by the unacknowledged coercion and social constraints that glue us together. Our cultivated conventions and little lies of civility lull us into a refined and idealistic view of ourselves. But modern industrial warfare may well be leading us, with each technological advance, a step closer to our own annihilation. We too are strapping explosives around our waists. Do we also have a suicide pact?

Look just at the 1990s: 2 million dead in Afghanistan; 1.5 million dead in the Sudan; some 800,000 butchered in ninety days in Rwanda; a half-million dead in Angola; a quarter of a million dead in Bosnia; 200,000 dead in Guatemala; 150,000 dead in Liberia; a quarter of a million dead in Burundi; 75,000 dead in Algeria; and untold tens of thousands lost in the border conflict between Ethiopia and Eritrea, the fighting in Colombia, the Israeli-Palestinian conflict, Chechnya, Sri Lanka, southeastern Turkey, Sierra Leone, Northern Ireland, Kosova, and the Persian Gulf War (where perhaps as many as 35,000 Iraqi citizens were killed). In the wars of the twentieth century not less than 62 million civilians have perished, nearly 20 million more than the 43 million military personnel killed.

Civil war, brutality, ideological intolerance, conspiracy, and murderous repression are part of the human condition — indeed almost the daily fare for many but a privileged minority.

War is not a uniform experience or event. My time in the insurgencies in Central America, the Persian Gulf War — where two large armies clashed in the desert — and the Balkans, where warlords and gangsters tried to pass themselves off as professional soldiers, illustrated the wide differences that make up modern warfare. But war usually demands, by its very logic, the disabling of the enemy, often broadly defined to include civilians who may have little love for the Taliban or Saddam Hussein or Somali warlords. While we venerate and mourn our own dead we are curiously indifferent about those we kill. Thus killing is done in our name, killing that concerns us little, while those who kill our own are seen as having crawled out of the deepest recesses of the earth, lacking our own humanity and goodness. Our dead. Their dead. They are not the same. Our dead matter, theirs do not. Many Israelis defend the killing of Palestinian children whose only crime was to throw rocks at armored patrols, while many Palestinians applaud the murder of Israeli children by suicide bombers.

> *Our dead. Their dead.*
> *They are not the same.*
> *Our dead matter,*
> *theirs do not.*

Armed movements seek divine sanction and the messianic certitude of absolute truth. They do not need to get this from religions, as we usually think of religion, but a type of religion: Patriotism provides the blessing. Soldiers want at least the consolation of knowing that they risk being blown up by land mines for a greater glory, for a New World. Dissension, questioning of purpose, the exposure of war crimes carried out by those fighting on our behalf are dangerous to such beliefs. Dissidents who challenge the goodness of our cause, who question the gods of war, who pull back the curtains to expose the lie are usually silenced or ignored.

We speak of those we fight only in the abstract; we strip them of their human qualities. It is a familiar linguistic corruption. During the war in Bosnia, many Muslims called the Serbs "Chetniks," the Serbian irregulars in

World War II, who slaughtered many Muslims. Muslims, for many Serbs in Bosnia, were painted as Islamic fundamentalists. The Croats, to the Serbs and Muslims, were branded "Ustashe," the fascist quislings who ruled Croatia during World War II. And there were times when, in interviews, it was hard to know if people were talking about what happened a few months ago or a few decades ago. It all merged into one huge mythic campaign. It was as if Josip Broz Tito, who had held Yugoslavia together for most of the Cold War era, had put the conflicted country into a deep freeze in 1945.

The goal of such nationalist rhetoric is to invoke pity for one's own. The goal is to show the community that what they hold sacred is under threat. The enemy, we are told, seeks to destroy religious and cultural life, the very identity of the group or state. Nationalist songs, epic poems, twisted accounts of history take the place of scholarship and art.

America is not immune. We mourn the victims of the World Trade Center attack. Their pictures cover subway walls. We mourn the firefighters, as well we should. But we are blind to those whom we and our allies in the Middle East have crushed or whose rights have been ignored for decades. They seem not to count.

"The principle of the movement is whoever is not included is excluded, whoever is not with me is against me, so the world loses all the nuances and pluralistic aspects that have become too confusing for the masses," wrote Hannah Arendt in *The Origins of Totalitarianism*.[3]

Before conflicts begin, the first people silenced — often with violence — are not the nationalist leaders of the opposing ethnic or religious group, who are useful in that they serve to dump gasoline on the evolving conflict. Those voices within the ethnic group or the nation that question the state's lust and need for war are targeted. These dissidents are the most dangerous. They give us an alternative language, one that refuses to define the other as "barbarian" or "evil," one that recognizes the humanity of the enemy, one that does not condone violence as a form of communication. Such voices are rarely heeded. And until we learn once again to speak in our own voice and reject that handed to us by the state in times of war, we flirt with our own destruction.

And yet, despite all this, I am not a pacifist. I respect and admire the qualities of professional soldiers. Without the determination and leadership of soldiers like General Wesley K. Clark we might not have intervened in Kosova or Bosnia. It was, in the end, a general, Ulysses S. Grant who saved the union. Even as I detest the pestilence that is war and fear its deadly addiction, even as I see it lead states and groups towards self-immolation, even as I concede that it is war that has left millions of dead and maimed across the planet, I, like most reporters in Sarajevo and Kosova, desperately hoped for armed intervention. The poison that is war does not free us from the ethics of responsibility. There are times when we must take this poison — just as a person with cancer accepts chemotherapy to live. We can not succumb to despair. Force is and I suspect always will be part of the human condition. There are times when the force wielded by one immoral faction must be countered by a faction that, while never moral, is perhaps less immoral.

We in the industrialized world bear responsibility for the world's genocides because we had the power to intervene and did not. We stood by and watched the slaughter in Chechnya, Sri Lanka, Sierra Leone, Liberia, and Rwanda where a million people died. The blood of the victims of Srebrenica — a designated U.N. safe area in Bosnia — is on our hands. The generation before mine watched, with much the same passivity, the genocides of Germany, Poland, Hungary, Greece, and the Ukraine. These slaughters were, as in Gabriel García Márquez's book *Chronicle of a Death Foretold*, often announced in advance.[4] Hutu radio broadcasts from Kigali called on the Interahamwe in Rwanda to carry out genocide. The U.N. Belgian detachment, however, like the Dutch peacekeepers in Srebrenica, stood by and watched. The radio in Kigali was never shut down. The rampages began. There was never any secret about Milošević's plans for a greater Serbia or his intent to use force and ethnic cleansing to create it.

I wrote this book not to dissuade us from war but to understand it. It is especially important that we, who wield such massive force across the globe, see within ourselves the seeds of our own obliteration. We must guard against the myth of war and the drug of war that can, together, render us as blind and callous as some of those we battle.

We were humbled in Vietnam, purged, for a while, of a dangerous hubris, offered in our understanding and reflection about the war, a moment of grace. We became a better country. But once again the message is slipping away from us, even as we confront the possibility of devastating biological or nuclear terrorist attacks in Washington or New York. If the humility we gained from our defeat in Vietnam is not the engine that drives our response to future terrorist strikes, even those that are cataclysmic, we are lost.

The only antidote to ward off self-destruction and the indiscriminate use of force is humility and, ultimately, compassion. Reinhold Niebuhr aptly reminded us that we must all act and then ask for forgiveness. This book is not a call for inaction. It is a call for repentance.

NOTES

[1] Orwell, George, *1984* (San Diego: Harcourt Brace Jovanovich, 1949), p. 35.

[2] Homer, *The Odyssey*, translated by Stanley Lombardo (Indianapolis: Hackett, 2000), p. 138.

[3] Atendt, Hannah, *The Origins of Totalitarianism* (San Diego: Harcourt Brace Jovanovich, 1979), pp. 380–381.

[4] García Márquez, Gabriel, *Chronicle of a Death Foretold* (New York: Knopf, 1983).

DISCUSSION

1. Reread Hedges' opening account of his experiences in wartime Sarajevo. What are your reactions to the portrait of combat he presents? How does this description compare to the kinds of combat scenes you've seen depicted in the movies or on TV?

2. At the heart of his war experiences, Hedges acknowledges, is a surprising paradox, writing, "The enduring attraction of war is this: Even with its destruction and carnage it can give us what we long for in life. It can give us purpose, meaning, a reason for living." In your view, is it possible to resolve this seeming contradiction? Is it possible for war to be both heinously destructive and somehow attractive at the same time?

3. Hedges writes, "While we venerate and mourn our own dead we are curiously indifferent about those we kill. Thus killing is done in our name, killing that concerns us little, while those who kill our own are seen as having crawled out of the deepest recesses of the earth, lacking our own humanity and goodness. Our dead. Their dead. They are not the same." What do you make of the thinking Hedges exposes and critiques here? Is it really possible to draw moral distinctions between "our dead" and "theirs"?

WRITING

4. Hedges writes: "The attacks on the World Trade Center illustrate that those who oppose us, rather than coming from another moral universe, have been schooled well in modern warfare. The dramatic explosions, the fireballs, the victims plummeting to their deaths, the collapse of the towers in Manhattan, were straight out of Hollywood. Where else, but from the industrialized world, did the suicide hijackers learn that huge explosions and death above a city skyline are a peculiar and effective form of communication? They have mastered the language." Write an essay in which you take up this idea and create an argument in which you either affirm or challenge Hedges' claims here. Is it valid to think of warfare as a form of "communication," a kind of "language"? If so, what kind of script does it seem to write? Where does this language come from? What ideas or values does it convey? Do the messages conveyed by our own acts of warfare differ from those of others? How or how not?

5. According to Hedges, war gives us a black and white understanding of the world we live in. Write an essay in which you analyze and/or critique this proposition. Does it makes sense to think of war as a kind of map or blueprint for how we should view ourselves and those around us? Does it truly "simplify" our sense of the world, and if so, what would you say the risks or consequences of this are?

6. Both Hedges and Kathy Dobie (p. 358) analyze the ways that we are taught to make sense of war. Do you think these writers' arguments are complementary or at odds? Write an essay in which you analyze how each writer feels about the psychological effects of war. Based on your own feelings about war, which writer do you believe makes a stronger argument? Why? Where do your feelings come from?

KATY VINE

Love and War in Cyberspace

Familiar to most of us is the cliché, "sticks and stones may break my bones, but words will never hurt me." Of course, the person who wrote these lines never spent time on the Internet. For, as Katy Vine reveals in her account of one online community, cyberchat has evolved into one of the most common-place and destructive vehicles for fighting. Vine's work has appeared in the *Oxford American, Texas Monthly*, and on the radio show *This American Life.* Her articles have also been anthologized in *Best American Sports Writing 2005* and *2006.* She has bachelor's degrees in English and classical humanities from the University of Wisconsin–Madison. The following essay first appeared in the February 2001 issue of *Texas Monthly.*

BRANDON LANGLEY AND DENISE HEWITT MET IN AN ONLINE BAR.

He was living in Houston at the time, a nervous, six-four, big-boned twenty-year-old who wore a polo shirt and shorts, white tennies, and wire-rimmed glasses that rested on top of his dimpled cheeks as if he were an adult-size Harry Potter. He had learned the basics of computer programming at the age of seven. He was a brainy introvert, a software whiz, and a fanatical game player on the Internet. One of his legs would twitch and bounce when he talked. You would recognize the type: techie, nerd, geek. The guys who populate the tech companies of the so-called New Economy.

Twenty-three-year-old Denise, who lived in Connecticut, was his spiritual twin, a female version of the same type: a bright person who saw the glow of a computer screen as a necessary and important liberation from actual interaction with other human beings. Because of the sort of people they were, they both played a type of text-based Internet game in a domain called a Multi-User Dungeon. That's MUD for short, although Denise joked that it should stand for "Multi-Undergraduate Destroyer" because it was more responsible for her friends' failure to graduate from college than anything else she could name. (A gamer's ethos was some-thing akin to "tune in, turn on, drop right out of the outside world.") Denise and Brandon played the same game so often they began to recog-nize each other by name. They sidled up to a MUD chat area called "the bar" and typed back and forth while tossing back virtual alcoholic drinks. They eventually got to know each other well enough to swap outdated photos via snail mail. He saw Denise's long, red hair, her sweet, round face, and a big smile that showed the tiny space between her front teeth.

One night Brandon was electronically quieter than usual, and Denise made a move that was the equivalent to sitting down next to somebody on a bar stool, typing, "Usually you're pretty chatty. What's the deal?" This question led to $500-a-month phone bills and a meeting in the Hartford, Connecticut airport and love with a capital L. Denise moved to Houston, and in November 1997 they got married. She went to work as an assistant manager for a mortgage company while Brandon worked as a customer-help phone operator for software companies, in technical support at the University of Houston, and as a junior programmer at Schlumberger. Their lives consisted of little more than work. They loved each other, and they loved their computers and their gaming on the Web. But they were bored. They needed something to make it perfect. That was Walden.

Seen from the outside, Walden was a complex of fairly ordinary looking apartment units on the west side of Houston. On the inside it was a techno-commune, a utopian foster home for folks like Brandon and Denise — outsiders, loners, virtual gamers, fanatical users, and other alienated types who were more deeply affected by the personal computer and by the vast new worlds of the Internet than the rest of us. Almost all of them were in their twenties and thirties; all were trying to map a course in an adult world.

Walden was the brainchild of a multimillionaire Houston commercial real estate honcho named James Birney, who came up with the idea of creating a New Age community around what he advertised as the world's fastest residential Internet connection. That connection was the T-3, a fiber-optic data line so powerful that it could handle the telecommunications needs of a small country. Birney's idea was to sell the technology but also something intangible: a sense of belonging. He wanted to create a sort of Woodstock for the digitally obsessed — a place that would make a bridge for these new, uncomfortable grown-ups between the virtual world and the real world.

So in 1997 he fixed up a run-down two-hundred-unit Houston apartment complex and landscaped it with rustling palm trees and Hawaiian volcanic rocks and bubbling fountains that cascaded into a clear pool. Then he named it after Henry David Thoreau's essay celebrating the natural world, installed the T-3 — the big, fat pipe, as it was called — and moved himself and his wife into one of the apartments. The pipe cost him $6,500 a

> ## Come for the Bandwidth, Stay for the Community.

month, but he figured that with enough rental income from the apartments, the T-3 would pay for itself. Then he advertised with the slogan "Come for the Bandwidth, Stay for the Community."

The idea worked. Birney had courted Houston's information-technology workers, the hordes of people like Brandon and Denise who were the underbelly of Texas' New Economy, and Walden soon filled up with all sorts of computer types — techno-outsiders, hacker anarchists, ponytailed Web designers, and right-wing code analysts — who operated on the bleeding edge of technology. The new residents didn't sleep; they napped. They used terms like "grep" and "mobo" and proclaimed things like "Today, when I was just north of Freeport Southern Desert, I raised my intelligence by three points." They had nicknames like KilGrinch and WebGirlie. Most of them had worker-bee jobs in the computer industry, doing things like customer support or motherboard design or software consulting, but in some respects they were not like other people. They were smarter. They were more introverted. They owned awesomely powerful computers, which when hooked up to the T-3 delivered information to them like nerve impulses across a synapse. Click. Tick.

Within a few months, more than one hundred people had moved into Walden. Birney welcomed them. "We are committed to maintaining a cutting-edge environment for cutting-edge people," he e-mailed the residents. "So keep on cutting. That's how the Ganges and Brahmaputra maintained their ancient southerly course and cut through the Himalayas."

Like the others, newlyweds Brandon and Denise heard the siren song of the T-3. For them, it happened in February 1999, when they saw Birney's sign boasting "Fastest Internet Connection in the United States." They toured the landscaped paradise with Walden's tall, easygoing technology specialist, Alan LeFort. LeFort showed them the ten-ton volcanic rocks and bubbling fountains and clean, if slightly austere apartments. He also told them a remarkable story about Birney's T-3: The pipe was so much faster and more powerful than anything remotely accessible to ordinary humankind that in 1998, when Lebanese-Palestinian terrorists wanted to knock out Internet service providers in Israel, they hacked Birney's T-3. This story moved Denise and Brandon: Certainly, if it was good enough for terrorists, they thought, it was good enough for them. They signed the lease.

What amazed all of them was how quickly — with nothing more than vague communal ideals and a wickedly fast Internet hookup — Birney not only created a real community but also facilitated a breathtaking social transformation for his normally withdrawn residents. What he had wrought was in many ways the opposite of Thoreau's Walden; these were loners who had ventured out of solitude to discover their adult identities among their peers. Still, the residents of Birney's spontaneous, organic laboratory were fleeing the same things Thoreau was escaping 145 years ago. "Society is commonly too cheap," wrote Thoreau. "We meet at very short intervals, not having had time to acquire any new value for each other. We meet at meals three times a day, and give each other a new taste of that musty old cheese that we are. We have to agree on a certain set of rules, called etiquette and politeness, to make this frequent meeting tolerable. . . ."

For a while, the complex supplied the sense of belonging that its introverted, data-juiced denizens had been seeking. But two and a half years after its creation, the community at Walden imploded in ways that only a society constructed around an ultra high-speed data pipe could. It would destroy Denise and Brandon's marriage too. The introverts had blossomed, just as Birney had foreseen. What he had not predicted was that these emerging, intensifying personalities would soon be bickering and separating like the boys in *Lord of the Flies*.

Walden. The name conjures images of Thoreau's simple world of meandering streams and forest glades and sunlight diffused through rustling trees. That was nothing like Birney's Walden. Birney's Walden, like the tall, perfectly postured, gray-haired Birney himself, was as painstakingly manicured as a bonsai tree. Thoreau's paradise was centered at Walden Pond; Birney's had an oval concrete pool (which he called a "lagoon") with poolside Internet connections. Thoreau made his chair by hand; Brandon bought his main chair, an office model with wheels, from Ikea for around $100. Thoreau's Walden was a place to get away from social commerce; Brandon and Denise went to Birney's Walden because they were having trouble socializing in a world filled with people so different from themselves. Brandon explained, "Denise moved here from another state, and we never really created a social structure around us." Denise agreed. When she first moved to Texas, she says, "I was very introverted." Introverted? She said the magic word.

Because even though they lived a few feet apart, it was online that the shy Waldenites first got to know each other. And as they peeked out into the courtyard in Houston, they observed that despite their cohabitants' varying origins, which included Venezuela, India, Australia, Mexico, China, Canada, South Africa, Vietnam, Nigeria, Italy, and Europe, they looked alike. They were 20 to 28 years old. More than 95 percent of them were male. They wore polo shirts or beat-up black T-shirts. Many of them had goatees and either half-inch-long hair or lengthy locks tied back in wavy ponytails. A lot of them had irregular body shapes that they held either in a cowering slouch or in a near-military uprightness, as if to correct previous bad posture.

When making new social contacts, the Waldenites performed what might be best described as a stand-around shuffle: They'd walk up to a group of tenants, hover a short distance away, stare at the ground, and wait to be recognized. When someone from the group nodded in the new guy's direction and said, "Hey," the new guy would shuffle in closer and reply, "Hey!" as if to say, "Oh! I didn't see you over there!"

Then, when they began nodding and talking, they noticed that they all had nicknames — user names, really, from the virtual world. Strolling through the courtyard, they started calling out to each other.

"Little B!"

"Trip!"

These handles had been an important part of their identities since childhood when they started playing computer games. Brandon was Violent Bob (from a grisly therapeutic toy in Terry Pratchett's fantasy series, Discworld). Denise was Wrenling (taken from Charles de Lint's fantasy book *Riddle of the Wren*). Some of the residents even received junk mail and magazine subscriptions addressed to their fictional selves. ("Violent Bob, You May Have Just Won a Million Dollars!") Birth names disappeared at Walden.

Online, they became armed with two modes of communication: ICQ ("I seek you," an instant-messaging chat software) and an e-mail system for residents known as the mailing list. On the latter, the more personal exchanges took place on something called a misc list. They started out doing simple things like bartering: "I'll trade you my car for a decent motherboard and processor." Or about how much they liked Walden:

BOOMDUDE: I had a great time at the BBQ, great way for the new kid on the block to get acclimated to the hard drinkin', cpu abusin' culture that is the Walden.

CHE: Hey, I just moved here and let me say I am dizzy with the raw power of having such an internet connection for personal use.

GRIMHIPPI: I suspect that there will come a time when a need becomes evident [for an even faster connection]. My favorite T-shirt design for [Walden] is "Until then — Walden" with the picture of a port on the back of someone's neck.

Gradually, as people started to come out of their shells, the messages became more social:

EYEBURN: Howdy, "neighbors" — We're planning a small get together . . .

GREG: Anyone big on crawfish?

TERESA: Very big on crawfish!

MICHAEL: CRAWWWWWWWW-FISSHHHINNNNN . . .

Then they got a little more intimate:

STONER: Hey folks — I had this really kewl idea, and was gonna share it with ya. But this chick came on TV and I lost my train of thought.

ERIC: women, huh. (no offense to you women, we all love you just that you have strange effects on men such as memory loss.)

PAUL K: yeah? try marrying one — if only it was just memory loss . . .

LADYFIRE: Gotta luv that whole distraction thing. It CAN be fun.

DENNY: Distraction? I'm too busy working for a GOOD distraction any more.

The intimacy extended to discussions of the protocols that governed their electronic communications:

QARTMAN: Please don't think I am being rude, but I must urge this wild idea upon you — Paul, you should resist temptation more often when considering sending an email or not — or, maybe just save up all of your thoughts until the end of the day and send out one thorough email which addresses every temptation you encountered during the day . . .

CAMERON: I personally like seeing give and take of the emails and watch the windings of the conversations. So what if Paul is a bit prolific with what he has to say? I'm glad that we have forums in which we can communicate with each other. It helps the community-feel . . . I know I have gained some useful information from everyone's ramblings, rants, and raves.

And rant and rave they did. Once, Brandon came back from work, turned on his computer, tapped into the big, fat pipe, and found more than one hundred new posts on the misc list in which a Wiccan, a Muslim, and a Baptist — all Walden residents — were ferociously arguing the nature of God. Other discussions included guns, drugs, evolution, abortion, and politics; the opinions, especially on religion, were often sharp-edged:

CURT: Though a Christian will never say "I, as a Christian, firmly believe in bringing a halt to progress, science, knowledge, and understanding in the name of our lord and savior, Christ the Luddite," the zealous tenacity with which they cling to their literal interpretation of an ancient collection of parables amounts to pretty much the same thing . . .

It got nasty sometimes (Qartman: "[Y]ou deserve to be flamed dude — not via email, but with gasoline and a lighter"). But as far as the Waldenites were concerned, it could have said, "Hot Sexxx, free! No — wait! I'll pay YOU!" Brandon loved it. Almost all of them loved it. Brandon found himself spending up to a third of his waking hours poring over the misc list. It was a democratic space with no strictures, no dominant value system.

> *"Anyone posting spoilers to [revealing the details of] the Phantom Menace will be shot, beaten, stabbed, emasculated, raped, caned, eviscerated, car bombed, roach bombed, have their doors egged, find their pets are 'missing', etc, etc, etc."*

One of Brandon's first postings was: "Anyone posting spoilers to [revealing the details of] the Phantom Menace will be shot, beaten, stabbed, emasculated, raped, caned, eviscerated, car bombed, roach bombed, have their doors egged, find their pets are 'missing', etc, etc, etc." It was the way Brandon spoke on the list: imaginative, extreme, and occasionally bombastic.

"There were times I would do twenty-five posts going through the whole thing," Brandon said. "Horrible! But fun. It would just erupt! And then it was just deserted. Then a couple of days later, a new thread would start up." For people who had felt isolated or alone, it meant company all the time, a sort of nonstop, free-form conversation.

Brandon joined a team for a game called Tribes that was played at a LAN (local area network) party.

At a LAN party, ten to sixty gamers would either hook up to the game from their apartments or haul their computers into a bare room above the front office called the Nexus Cafe where they'd all plug into the T-3 and wage virtual war from ten in the evening to eleven the next morning.

"Get the flag!" would be followed with sounds of amplified gunfire.

"Taking fire — oh, no — they got me!" was accompanied by the clicking racket of 120 typing hands.

"Aarrgggh!"

The scene in the morning looked like a slumber party: Those who had stuck it out through the night lay slumped under the card tables, in deep sleep.

The more they got to know each other, the more oddities they found in common. They all lived like Trappist monks, for one thing. Their residences were, in the words of a baby-faced, ponytailed graphics designer named Christian, little more than "containers." Walking into an apartment, all you'd see were bare white walls, a sleeping bag, and an alarm clock on a plastic crate. A prisoner has as much. But smack in the center of these barren quarters, an average of four computers would dominate each Waldenite's den — the altar to the big, fat pipe. Some residents even boasted up to $600,000 of tech equipment — floor-to-ceiling towers requiring additional fans to cool the motors — to take advantage of the T-3's speed for role-playing and shoot-'em-up games.

The T-3 attracted some real oddballs too. One, a young man who had heard about the pipe from a resident named Nathan, flew from Arizona, parked himself on Nathan's floor, and started playing a game called EverQuest. It was so much cleaner, so much faster at Walden with the enormous pipe. The man is known around Walden to this day as Dude on the Floor because for two months, from the day he walked though Nathan's door, he didn't talk, he didn't move, he didn't work, he didn't bathe, he only played the game. At least that's the way it seemed to the others. Nathan's cat started using Dude on the Floor as a scratching post. But Dude was unmoved; he became werewolf-like, growing out his toe-nails and his fingernails and his hair. One day the Waldenites were hanging out in the hot tub when the repellent creature ventured out to bathe in the pool. "Who is that?" one of them asked. "It's Dude on the Floor!" another exclaimed. "Scatter!" After Nathan finally sent the Dude back to Arizona on a bus, he had to bleach the area where the Dude had sat, but the stain wouldn't come out. "We like games," the Waldenites thought, "but at least we're not as bad as the Dude."

Little by little, through these bonding experiences, the community began to gel. They started to understand that they needed to be brought together, proving that Birney's vision had large-scale possibilities. Maybe this — Walden — was the way the new American techie was going to live in the adult world. "In American society, the way it's made up right now, there is no tendency for people to seek out friendships," said Alan LeFort, the young man who had shown Brandon and Denise around. "How many neighbors do you know where you live? There's no common reference. Potential residents don't even know that they want community. They're suspicious. 'Why are people intruding in my space?' they think. And once they live here, it makes perfect sense. You can have all the components necessary to create life, yet you put it in a petri dish and nothing happens. Then one day — it happens!"

This is how it worked for Brandon.

One day a guy is doing the stand-around shuffle ("Hey," he says as his leg twitches) and the next thing he knows, the magnetic impulse takes hold of him and he's hanging out with the Waldenites in the pool, in the courtyard, across the street at Whataburger, and in their apartments.

Around the spring of 1999, after Brandon and Denise had settled in, Brandon had a daily schedule that was typical of a Waldenite. He got up at seven-fifty in the morning, drove down Westheimer, on the west side of Houston, stopped at Starbucks, got to work by eight-fifteen, and spent most of his day fixing problems for, as he puts it, either "intelligent people who [were] just having problems" or "the criminally obtuse." The monotony of work was broken up by ICQing upward of sixty Walden residents. Brandon would get home around eight, game with his Tribes team, and go to bed around midnight. Others with more important business stayed awake and chatted with each other through ICQ and the misc list all night long.

JOHNNYBRAVO: Anybody up this late?

LADY FIRE: hell — i am STILL up!

PAUL K: ok — it's 6:35am and I am still up, surely everyone else is sleeping by now?

LITTLE B: Hope you all get sleep.

EYE BURN: Note to ppl that don't know — quite a few of us gather by the hot tub . . . pretty much every evening (anywhere from 9pm to 3am on weeknights, 5pm to 8am on weekends). For myself and fellow gamers — it's where we take breaks from Tribes. Come out and meet your neighbors, most are nocturnal like you . . .

BOSCH: here here — even gamers find the time to move away from their puters to "hang" out so should everyone else. So come out you T3 addicted people and enjoy life!!

It never occurred to Denise that the T-3 could upset her whole grown-up world. She was making up the rules as she went along — like the other Waldenites — trying to adjust to social expectations, and she thought that maybe she would find some friends there, like Brandon had. But when she first got to Walden, the opposite occurred: She withdrew from everybody, including Brandon. She stayed home and nuzzled one-on-one with the T-3. In the first few months after she and Brandon had moved in, Denise was unemployed, and she knew exactly what to do with all that free time. Like Dude on the Floor, she played EverQuest twelve hours a day, every day. After Brandon left the apartment in the morning, she would roll out of bed, go online, and become her EverQuest character, "a little 31 enchanter." (The enchanter, she bragged, was the hardest class on EverQuest.)

"I'd use it as a chat function just to talk to people," she recalled, giggling. "So I'd start EverQuest, shower, get dressed, play EverQuest, go out and run errands, play EverQuest." She would chatter on about her EverQuest character to the few Waldenites she bumped into. She even tried to drag them back to her apartment to see for themselves just how great her "enchanter" was. She lived EverQuest.

She breathed it. It was better than the real world. She met more people, for one thing. There were chat rooms in the game that allowed people to get to know each other — in the same way Brandon and Denise had first met years before. Her obsession became infamous at Walden; residents told stories of the girl who was so obsessed with the game that it destroyed her marriage. See, before long, Denise met a special friend while playing the game.

Like the last time, her meeting in cyberspace led to a series of long-distance phone calls. Brandon noticed unfamiliar phone numbers on their phone bill and he thought, "She's playing one game all the time . . . this rings a bell. . . ." Their marriage, by this time, had already started to fall apart. They agreed that they would see other people. One weekend, when Brandon went out of town, Denise's new friend flew from California to visit her.

And, in short, it was O-V-E-R. Slam door, press hands over face, end of sentence. The virtual and the real worlds were colliding and turning against them. Click, tick.

> **The virtual and the real worlds were colliding and turning against them.**

But that's not the strangest part of their story. The strangest part is that neither one of them could bear to abandon Walden. Rather than leave their beloved T-3, they shook hands and went back to their respective corners. Denise moved into a two-bedroom Walden apartment with a male friend who played EverQuest (only friends, she insisted) and Brandon moved into a single poolside apartment.

News of the breakup was quickly disseminated both online and around the pool, which functioned like a giant barbershop. Brandon started dating his next-door neighbor, Melba, a Walden rarity: a quiet woman who was more interested in art movies than computers. Some of the tenants sat in the pool and watched them go into her apartment and close the door, then into his apartment and close the door. People talked. People wondered what was going on with Brandon. Rumors flew.

"The stories were just incredible," he said. "I was always going, 'They said what?!'" Walden was becoming a small town in the middle of America's fourth-largest city.

After Brandon and Denise broke up, they swapped roles. As Brandon got closer to Melba and withdrew from the group, Denise plunged head-first into the social life at Walden. She began dating Che, a programmer who was in the core group, and she started going out with crowds of up to twenty to dance clubs. They would stuff themselves into a few cars, then they'd speed down Houston's highways, accompanied by the deafeningly loud thump-thump-thump of dance music. Denise and a couple of others bought walkie-talkies so they could talk from their cars:

"Hey there, Little B — whoo! Hold on. [Sound of car accelerating.] Heyyy you there?"

[Laughing] "What are you doing?"

"Passing — would you get a load of this guy over here?"

"Hold on, Pata wants to talk."

"Hey there, Little B!"

Then they'd race back home and slip into the hot tub. Sometimes they'd stay in the fizzy water until sunrise. Even when they were stinking drunk and hunched over in the illuminated blue tub, the talk was computers and gadgets and gaming.

Walden was changing. Wallflowers like Denise were blossoming. Partying accelerated. "Someone brings a minilaser," Denise said, waving her hands as she talked, "then somebody brings in black lights, then somebody brings better speakers and a better mixer, and all of a sudden you've got this insane party." Parties at the complex became no-holds-barred events where beer and Ecstasy were consumed in large quantities. Thump-thump-thump.

By the fall of 1999, Walden had achieved its potential to become a mini-civilization, just as Birney had hoped. Birney, who still lived at the complex and had observed the results of his handiwork, was pleased. "In many cases," he said, "our residents feel like in the past they've been isolated pioneers running around doing their own thing, but even those who were seriously isolated — even positively rejected — come here and find a peer group that is stimulating and challenging." Ask any of the residents and they'd agree. "These people are rejects," said WebGirlie, with tears in her eyes. "We were the ones made fun of at the back of the class in high school, and this is a triumph: We are our own clique now." Another tenant, a bony Louisianan who went by the name Pitre, laughed eagerly when he recalled his life before Walden: "I had two friends, but they were mentally disturbed."

Waldenites internalized Birney's old ad slogan, "Come for the Bandwidth, Stay for the Community." To outsiders, they gushed about how utterly fan-tas-tic, how totally bliss-ful they were. "The level and the ability to communicate is unlike anywhere else," said Walter, one of the older Waldenites. "It's like a giant co-op at times."

Like Brandon and Denise, many found it hard, even impossible to leave. Bosch, a lean, constantly smiling resident, left Walden after he bought a house. But he moved back, he says with a shrug, because he got too lonely and wanted to "hang out with the guys."

Says WebGirlie, dryly: "This is a cult. You've heard of Jonestown? This is Jimstown, except . . . without the poisonous drinks. People go in and out, but when a guest comes you can smell 'em."

With the cult came a sense of belonging, of togetherness. One night, EyeBurn and eight other residents saw a burglar on the grounds. They hauled after the thief, tackled him, and sat on him until the police arrived. "If something happened to your neighbor, you'd help out because you knew them," Little B earnestly explained. If a tenant couldn't pay rent, others would pitch in to cover it. When somebody lost a job, the group would pay for his meals. Waldenites received birthday cards with at least fifty signatures. Frequently they'd ICQ each other in the middle of the night to say "I have beer; will be in hot tub" or "Anybody want to grab a bite at House of Pies?" and eleven people would meet out in the parking lot. They were making up for a whole lot of sheltered years; they were as excited as prison escapees reunited on a Hawaiian cruise ship.

Maybe they were enthusiastic too soon. While Walden's denizens were busy melding into the technocommune of Birney's dreams, the man himself had been busy thinking of his next move. Though he was basically a real estate man who owned and managed commercial complexes like Walden, he still had a pocketful of big ideas, most of which started with real estate and then spun up into something more spiritual. He believed that Walden itself, for example, "might develop into multi-use communities incorporating office structures and retail and residential and the whole works, built around the premise that it was the lifestyle of the future." But, ultimately, he was still a real estate man. He and his wife had been running properties in Houston and New Jersey for years. He knew his way around the Internet, sure, but — he wasn't one of the Waldenites. He waved and made small talk with them, but for the most part, he watched Walden develop from the other side of the office glass.

Birney had decided that if Walden "is a bold step forward, it must look like a bold step forward." It had been his idea, after all; it had worked splendidly. Now he had an idea for how to spruce the place up, make it even cozier and more inviting. In September 1999 he hired a crew who proceeded to paint Walden's eleven apartment buildings in a variety of blindingly bright colors that included Aztec blood red, marigold yellow, jade green, and Majorelle blue. The idea sounds harmless enough. But in the tiny, cloistered, intensely communal world Birney had created, the new paint was taken as nothing less than an invasion of privacy.

"There was no announcement," Denise said. "There was no saying, 'We're going to paint the building.' All that happened one day was the front building turned — I kid you not — coral pink. And we're talking about ninety-five percent guys in their twenties. They don't want to live in a pink apartment complex." Birney, waxing spiritual, explained to the tenants that it was "derived from primary color states, archetypal origins, primal states of nature, and cycles of life." But, of course, that made it worse. So, as dutiful members of their community, Waldenites made their opinions known on the misc list. Tap, tap, tap, double exclamation point. Tappity-tap, triple exclamation point. Many demanded that it be painted back to "a nice gray." Brandon wrote, sarcastically, "Dammit, when I own my own apt. complex with an OC-3 internet connection, I'm going to paint the buildings a nice camouflage color!" They felt cheated. This was their place. Why were they not consulted? Birney ruled that it was his building complex and he was keeping the colors. Period.

For reasons no one can quite explain, Birney's paint job coincided with a subtle but noticeable attitudinal shift at Walden. A handful of residents, like a Waldenite we'll call Kane, became increasingly notorious for their abusive comments on the misc list. In the real world Kane was cautious with strangers and didn't talk much. Many Waldenites had seen the stocky, Wrangler-jeans-wearing man sitting at the Nexus Cafe reading fantasy books, but figured that the Kane they knew online had to be somebody else, somebody with huge claws and sharp teeth, because when he got on the misc list he spouted off. Besides calling WebGirlie "fatso," "hag," and "Miss Piggy," he'd write things like "[R]elax, Miss Pompous, Holier-Than-Thou — nobody takes this too seriously, why should you?" Which she responded to with, "Well if that isn't the pot calling the kettle black."

KANE: Guess I can't stand religion so much that I can't even mention the word. These postings sure make you want to spew out your thoughts faster then you can type them in. Oh, yeah, and I can't stand that mythical "god" creature either. It didn't create me and I stick my middle finger at it. And I don't believe in Santa Claus either . . . Anyone offended by my beliefs? Too bad. Well I'm offended by yours that "God" is "watching over me" and that I should worship your "god." That really offends me.

WALTER: SHUT UP Already — I'm personally tired of reading your spew of SHIT! And more than a little embarrassed to find out just how F–ED UP one of my neighbors is!

KANE: Mr. Walter Fascist Meyer. So one of your neighbors is "F–ED UP" because they don't believe in God or don't like religion. You want me to "SHUT UP" don't you'? Just because I don't believe the same way you do. Censor. Fascist. Here's a little secret, Mr. Meyer: You sounded pretty "F–ED UP" with that last E-Mail. And I wonder how tough you talk in person instead of hiding behind your computer screen. You talk about this in person? Name the place.

[Another] WALTER: Somebody PLEASE tell me this is a bad joke I am awaking to, PLEASE?

Obviously they were messing with the karma. When the conflict got intense at Walden, it became increasingly difficult to keep a distance between neighbors. Once, Kane and Walter got into a fight on the misc list and ended the exchange with, "Meet me in the mailroom!" Residents who had been watching the post raced down to the mailroom to watch the fight, which was immediately halted when they snapped out of the virtual landscape back into the real world. Click, tick.

Brandon got drawn in too. "Once, I was in a hotel room in Chicago on business with nothing better to do than take out my frustrations on people who were being silly on the misc list," he says. "I always go for people who are being a little silly or off. Don't beat on the innocents. They don't deserve it." But it was so easy to go too far when you didn't see the readers' faces twist up with frustration or humiliation. He and Kane threw insults back and forth with all the style and tact of World Wrestling Federation wrestlers.

> *It was so easy to go too far when you didn't see the readers' faces twist up with frustration or humiliation.*

BRANDON: Funny — I didn't see a tiny little mustache on you when I saw you in the Nexus the other night — Sieg Heil!

KANE: Funny, I don't know who you are at the Nexus — why don't you introduce yourself to me?

BRANDON: If I had thought you were worth introducing myself to . . .

KANE: If you have a comment to say to me, then E-Mail at my personal address . . . so other people don't have to read your vicious garbage.

BRANDON: "sticks and stones might break my bones, but blah blah blah . . ." LAF! Oh my GOD that was SO funny! I'm dyin . . .

"My problem with him," said Bran, "is he doesn't know when to shut up when he's mailing. In person he's not that type of guy. E-mail does change you. When you don't have to look someone in the eye and say, 'You're a fat whore!' where's the restriction from it?" It came to them impulsively, like adolescent competition. A few tenants, like Brandon's new girlfriend, Melba, grew weary of the gossip and online sparring wars and moved out.

More and more of the formerly blissful Waldenites began behaving like Kane. By March 2000 the bickering got out of control. Paul K posted a message on the misc list saying that the connection wasn't actually as fast or powerful as promised, to which Birney himself took offense. Birney was unhappy in part because he had been taking some financial hits with his technocommune. The deal he had struck for his T-3 allowed full use of the pipe at night but only partial use during the day. He had never anticipated that Waldenites would be using the same huge amounts of bandwidth at two in the afternoon as they did at two in the morning. So it was costing him extra. Fed up, he cast Paul K out of the garden. A bitter Paul K wrote a farewell letter to the misc list: "By now the rumours I am sure are flying thick and furious. If you heard that my family and I are leaving Walden, then you have heard a half-truth, for we are being forced out against our will."

NEUBAUER: I'm sorry to see you go — It's always been my opinion that this community shit has not, and will not, ever work out the way the planners envisioned. It's just a bit too much to ask of the peanut gallery. It's been fun.

MELODIC: huh? I'm very new here, what is going on?!

KERNEL CRASH: Nothing much. Now take your "ignorance is bliss" pill and be a good lil AOL user.

And suddenly the rules changed. Birney, who had kept a sort of paternalistic distance and did not participate in hot tub parties or any of the usual socializing and rarely spoke online, suddenly came alive. He dispatched an e-mail to the group:

> A Policy of Civility & Etiquette — A Rebirth of an Inspirational Community Discussion Forum: . . . our efforts to provide a *totally* unfettered and unrestrained environment have run into (severe and chronic) problems and now must be "shaped." This is not an option, it is a requirement, if the positive experience at w@lden is to continue to develop, grow and attract broader and more diverse groups of residents . . . on an increasing basis, the lists have become a non-stop forum for flame-wars, rants, bitches, moans, and vicious attacks against fellow residents, ourselves, and, sometime, simply "anything that moves." Increasingly, we have found that persons who have much to contribute to our community are being (utterly) turned off by the present experience. This direction is *diametrically* opposed to the original intent and goal of the lists — to foster inspiration, pleasure, challenge, creativity and broaden the horizons and viewpoints of our residents . . . Consequently, henceforth, all lists will have basic policies of etiquette and civility that will be rigorously enforced.

The ultimatum was put forth: Be nice or get out. Order is being imposed. Leases will not necessarily be renewed. The landlord giveth, and the landlord can taketh away.

Brandon and some others who had used the pipe as their main way to vent felt this was censorship, pure and simple. The misc list had become a testament to their independence, and by this time they were used to acting abrasively. Adding the regulations now, Denise remembered thinking at the time, would be "like herding cats." She was right. Many of the residents had a juvenile stubbornness and naivete; they got paranoid and started murmuring that there was an Armageddon for Walden, a "hit list" of people who were going to be forced out. In fact, Birney began to realize that in addition to behavior problems, drugs were being used more openly and more frequently, and the time had come to clean house. A resident who wished to remain anonymous whispered, "I'll tell you something if you don't use my name . . . no, no. I'd better not. I have a nice office here, and I don't want to have to move."

For a resident who went by the name Dr. J, the imminent banishment was more than he could handle. He thought he was going to be fired from his job. He was so broke that he even sold his main computer, though his girlfriend screamed at him not to because she knew how important it was to him. He had plenty of reasons to be depressed. Then his eviction notice came. That night, when he got back from work, his girlfriend was sitting on the living room futon, dozing off. He went into the kitchen and she heard him say, "Oh, you made some tea." As she fell asleep, he went into his closet, loosened his multicolored tie, unbuttoned the top of his blue long-sleeved shirt, put a brown leather belt around his neck, and hanged himself from a clothes rod. His girlfriend found him the next day.

After more residents were expelled, the gang grew still more resentful of the rules. One weekend in May, Denise joined the others in the core Walden group who had decided to move. "Walden is a state of mind — it is!" said one Waldenite named Joel. "We're not leaving Walden behind. We're taking it with us."

So they unplugged themselves from the big, fat pipe. In a matter of three months, the entire core group was gone. Most of them moved to Milano Apartments and City West Luxury Apartments, where they planned to stay in touch with each other, searching for the next step.

Brandon, too, found that he could not live with Birney's new rules. In June he found an apartment in City West Luxury Apartments and quietly moved a month before his lease was up. Birney, meanwhile, had taken the opposite lesson from Walden. By the time Brandon had moved out, Birney had already opened new Walden complexes — now called Walden Internet Villages — including one near the medical center and one near the Galleria, all equipped with the T-3, though the residents who moved into those complexes were generally clean-cut young professionals, harmless users who liked to surf the 'Net but didn't write code or get too heavily into the pipe's technical aspects. Birney explained that "the Internet technology field is changing and broadening substantially. We're getting family people in now. They've got a mother club going."

"I think they're trying to discourage elements that are disruptive," Brandon contended, "but they're also going after the intelligent thinkers and independent people. They're happy with the people who are quiet and don't want to talk to anybody, and I think that's unfortunate for Walden because that will turn them into any other complex. As an apartment complex, Walden will be there for a long time, but I don't think it's going to be the same as it was for me."

Brandon doesn't ICQ anywhere near as often as he used to. His divorce from Denise is about to be finalized. They still get along and chat but — like Walden — it's not like it once was. On moving weekend he turned his back on the rustling palm trees and Hawaiian volcanic rocks and bubbling fountains that cascade into a clear pool with the poolside Internet connection and chirping mockingbirds that search for grubs in the thick, green turf and the Aztec blood red, marigold yellow, jade green, and Majorelle blue buildings and the pipe and the Waldenites. Back to reality — or, as Thoreau wrote of his return from the woods, "At present I am a sojourner in civilized life again."

DISCUSSION

1. What do you make of the term *online community*? Does it present a contradiction in terms? Does the technology of virtual communication seem to make possible the kinds of connection and interaction you would define as communal?

2. How do you understand the phenomenon of virtual relationships? Do connections or friendships forged online seem to you less legitimate, less "real" than those developed elsewhere? In your opinion, can you achieve genuine or meaningful connections within a medium that (in Vine's terms) "drops you right out of the real world"?

3. The apartment building within which the drama of these online conflicts unfolds is named Walden: an homage to the pastoral refuge famously extolled by nineteenth-century writer Henry David Thoreau. Does this term seem appropriate for this setting? Is there any way in which this wired environment can legitimately be viewed as a refuge? If so, from what?

WRITING

4. One of the rituals Vine details most extensively is the practice of online naming: the ways people shed their "real-world selves" by embracing and redefining themselves according to their online "handles." Create a portrait of an online character you could see yourself adopting. What name would you give your new self? What traits and characteristics do you think this new identity would enable you to adopt? Analyze why you chose this particular role. What did this role allow you to do, feel, or say that in your everyday life you may not have been able to?

5. Think about the e-mail "flame wars" featured in this piece. Based on the attacks and insults that get exchanged, write an essay in which you outline what rules seem to be used as this kind of online fighting unfolds. What kinds of rhetorical tactics seem to comprise the norm? What limitations (if any) seem to operate?

6. How would you characterize Vine's view about the benefits of this new online technology? Compare her views on technology to those advanced by Gerard Jones (p. 400). How does each define the relative advantages and pitfalls of the innovations she or he describes? Which view do you find more convincing? Why?

Then and Now: *From Gangster to Gangsta*

Depending on when you were born, you're likely to have very different images spring to mind when you hear the word *gangster*. In the early twentieth century, few people personified the term better than Al "Scarface" Capone, the Chicago gangster and boss of the Chicago Outfit who made a name for himself in the illegal trafficking of alcohol during Prohibition. The public has always been interested in the lure of mob stories, with movies and television shows like *The Godfather* and *The Sopranos* ranking among the most popular ever produced.

Today, however, the media seems more inclined to discuss *gangsta*, the genre of rap that fans argue is the sincere art of people raised in poverty and violence. Gangsta rap became especially popular in the early 1990s, with artists like Dr. Dre earning mainstream success with songs about guns, sex, and drugs that resonated both with inner-city and suburban kids. Since then, the gangsta image and vocabulary perseveres with groups like Three 6 Mafia, who won an Academy Award in 2005 for the song, "It's Hard Out Here for a Pimp," from the film *Hustle & Flow.* In fact, much of the way hip-hop is marketed or covered in the news presents many parallels with the coverage and image of organized crime of one hundred years ago.

While gangsta is now most prominent as a source of entertainment, discussion of it as a threat to morality and the rule of law is as prevalent now as this same discussion was in the days of Al Capone. Likewise, a parallel exists in the anxieties critics feel about the prominence some European immigrants achieved through organized crime and the mainstream success that African Americans have achieved in the entertainment industry. As one group of disenfranchised Americans has adopted some of the imagery made popular by other groups of disenfranchised Americans, how much of the adoption of the mythos of the gangster has to do with crime and how much has to do with identity and success?

WRITING

1. Write an essay in which you compare the stereotypes of the gangster with those of the gangsta. What features do they have in common? Where do the characteristics diverge?

2. Write an essay in which you discuss why books, films, and music about criminals seem to fascinate so many of us. Do you think the reasons people enjoy mob stories so much has anything in common with why people enjoy rap music?

Being Strong

Many critics argue that violent video games are harmful to kids. But how much evidence exists to support this claim? Wondering aloud about the validity of this long-held belief, Gerard Jones challenges the presumed connection between video violence and actual violence. Jones is the author of *Green Lantern: The Road Back* (1992), *Honey I'm Home! Sitcoms Selling the American Dream* (1993), *Killing Monsters: Why Children Need Fantasy, Superheroes, and Make-Believe Violence* (2002), and *Men of Tomorrow: Geeks, Gangsters, and the Birth of the Comic Book* (2004). From 1989 to 2001, he also wrote many comic books for Marvel Comics, DC Comics, and other publishers. The essay that follows is from *Killing Monsters*.

M Y FIRST MEMORY IS OF TEARING THE MONSTER'S ARM OFF.

I had crossed the sea to the hall of these warriors who were being terrorized by a nocturnal beast, boasted over mead that only I could slay it, pretended to sleep until the monster crept in to devour a warrior — and when it came to seize me I leapt up, seized its massive arm in my grip of steel, and held on as we battled through the hall, smashing the wooden walls with our fury, until at last in desperation it tore itself loose of its own limb and fled, bleeding and screaming, mortally wounded to its lair in the fens.

Quite a feat for a five-year-old.

When I was old enough to go to kindergarten, my mother went back to college to get her teaching credential. She hadn't had a lot of high culture in her own upbringing and she made sure that I was more fortunate: she tacked prints from the Metropolitan Museum to all the walls in the house and read classic literature to me at bedtime. She tried Stevenson's poems, *Gulliver's Travels*, Chaucer's *Reynard*. It all rolled off me. If I hadn't asked her about all this decades later, I'd never have known. The only one I remembered was *Beowulf*, with its pagan, barbarian monster-slayer of a hero.

He was a terrible role model. He didn't do any of the things we want our children's heroes to teach: didn't discuss solutions with the group, didn't think first of the safety of others, didn't try to catch the monster without harming it. He bragged, he bullied, he killed, and he even let his allies be devoured to further his plan. Yet, it was Beowulf I wanted to be, and Beowulf I became. I made my mom read it to me over and over, and I caught her when she tried to glide past the most gruesome parts ("The demon clutched a sleeping thane in his swift assault, tore him in pieces,

bit through the bones, gulped the blood, and gobbled the flesh . . . "[1]).
I carved scenes from his battles into my Playskool blocks with a ballpoint
pen and rearranged them in every possible narrative order. Running
naked from the bath across the polyester carpet I thumped my skinny
chest and roared, "Foe against foe, I'll fight the death!"

I was no warrior in real life. I was a mama's boy. I liked to play in the
house and the backyard, liked kids who were my age but not when they
got too wild. The prospect of kindergarten terrified me, and so did knowing that my mom was going to be away from home much of every day. But
at home, in my own world, I could tear a pillow off the bed with a
"*rrrrrrarrr!*" and see the monster Grendel fleeing in terror.

"You were an adorable barbarian," my mom said, helping me dig
through a box of my childhood artwork. I found a yellowing pad covered
with stick-figure warriors grimacing and flexing their muscles — loaf-like
bubbles protruding from line-thin arms — at toothy monsters. I remembered striking that pose — and how strong I felt. Then, with a mock sigh,
my mother added, "But I did so want you to be cultured."

As it turned out, I did grow up fairly cultured — or civilized, at least.
I was as cooperative, bookish, and conscientious as my parents could
have wanted. But I carried that monster-slaying hero inside me the whole
time. First as fantasy: Beowulf gave way to King Kong, then Batman, then
James Bond. As I outgrew fantasies, he became a scholarly interest. At one
point, I quit college for a series of intensive workshops and study tours
with Joseph Campbell, author of *The Hero with a Thousand Faces*. By my
thirties, I was building a reputation as a historian and analyst of popular
culture, and among my books was *The Comic Book Heroes*. That book
excited comic book editors enough that they invited me to try writing
superhero stories myself. I did, and I turned out to be good at it. Soon
I was writing for heroes like Batman, Spider-Man, and the Hulk, creating
new heroes and helping adapt them into video games, cartoon series, and
action figures, writing action screenplays for Warner Brothers and Fox.
Apparently that hero was still alive in me.

Even in becoming a superhero writer, however, I consciously resisted
what I saw as the crassness and violence of cheap entertainment. I down-
played fight scenes and stressed intellectual content. My comic books
earned citations from parent councils and anti-defamation societies.
I mentored kids who wanted to write and draw comics, and I worked hard
to meet my readers and learn what they were getting out of my stories.
That's what led me to a comics convention in Chicago in 1994 and to a
conversation that turned my relationship with action heroes in a whole
new direction.

The line of autograph seekers, mostly teenage boys, had finally
moved through. I was leaning back for some shoptalk with the other writers

at the table when I saw her. She looked about thirteen, bespectacled, plainly dressed, grimly shy, a girl I'd have expected to be reading an English fantasy novel or diving precociously into *Jane Eyre*. She was standing about thirty feet away. Staring at me.

"Can I help you?" I asked. She lurched over to me as though some invisible parent had a hand on her back. "Are you Gerard Jones?" she asked. I looked at the name tag on my chest and feigned surprise: "Well yeah — I am!" An old convention trick meant to make the kids laugh, but she kept her eyes fixed on me without a glimmer of emotion and said, "I just want to tell you that *Freex* is, in my opinion, the best comic book ever."

Freex was a writer's nightmare. Readers liked my subtle characters and challenging ideas but complained that my stories were too mild. They wanted extremes of emotion and wild fight scenes like those in *X-Men*. *Freex* was my effort to give them that without lowering my standards. I loved my idea: teenage runaways, cut off from the world by their deforming superpowers, who form a sort of street gang for mutual protection. I cared about teenage runaways, knew people who worked with them, wanted to capture their struggles in superheroic form. I was excited about trying to mix naturalistic teen dialogue with ferocious battles on the city streets. But my scripts just wouldn't *work*. I couldn't get the character scenes to flow smoothly into the fights. The heroes' rage felt forced. The violence felt gratuitous. I'd never devoted much thought to what makes fantasy combat work or why it spoke to me in my own youth. I was too uncomfortable with rage and violence. I couldn't feel what my Freex should feel. I began to make peace with the thought that this just wasn't a story I should have been writing. The readers seemed to agree with me: sales were dropping, and not one fan had mentioned it at the convention — until this girl said it was the best comic ever.

I asked her why, and as she talked about *Freex*, her shyness dissolved. Her name was Sharon. She lived in a small Wisconsin town with her parents, whom she loved, and she had friends, but there was no one who really shared her interests. She read a lot, both comics and real books. She insisted that her life was perfect, but I thought that she protested too much. I sensed constraint, timidity, a depressed quality, a tensely contained anger — feelings that resonated with my memories of my own thirteenth year. She loved the Freex for the variety of their personalities and their clashing emotions. I expected her favorite to be the shy Angelica, but she preferred Lewis, the charismatic jock-leader whose anger made his body lose form. I said, "It sounds like the character development scenes must be your favorites."

"No!" she said. It was the most animated I'd seen her. "It's the *fights*!"

"The *fights*?" I asked. "That's where you can see the feelings they have for each other," she said. "The way Michael goes crazy when he thinks

Angela's in danger. Or Val's angry at Ray, but then she instantly turns her anger against the villain instead, so you know she really cares about him." She paused to find a word. "That's when you see their *passion*. And their passion is what really makes them powerful!"

> **"The fights?" I asked. "That's where you can see the feelings they have for each other," she said.**

I asked her what she felt in those scenes. "Well," she said awkwardly. "I'm *them* when I'm reading about them, right? So . . . I'm powerful." And that, apparently, was as deep as she wanted to go into her own feelings. She thanked me again for *Freex*, and she left.

Sharon made me take a hard look at my own biases. I'd seen fight scenes as a necessary evil to induce kids to read the more valuable contents of my stories — but now I'd made the most meaningful contact with a reader of my career *through* the fights. The characters, plots, and themes mattered, but the truly affecting, truly transformative element of the story was the violence itself. The violence had helped a timid adolescent tap into her own bottled-up emotionality and discover a feeling of personal power.

I felt uneasy with that: what message was I sending kids like Sharon? I ran the question by my friend Anne, an English professor and a widely published authority on changing images of gender and the body in mass culture.

"Look," she said. "You touched that girl's life. You gave her something that means something to her. And that's as valuable as anything you can do."

Then Anne told me about her own adolescence in the 1980s: painful home life, estranged from her parents, drinking and jail at thirteen, a suicide attempt, out on her own at fifteen, fistfights, petty crime, crashing with friends in tough inner-city neighborhoods. What spoke to her at the very worst of it was pop culture: angry punk, death metal, Goth style, violent horror movies. "Not much I'd defend now as 'good,'" she said. "But when things felt absolutely black I discovered this stuff, and it showed me I wasn't alone with these feelings. I had words, or at last images, for what I was feeling. And I found other people who were into them. When I was in a club or a movie or listening to a tape with my friends, I didn't want to kill myself anymore." Some of the others in her group drifted to dead ends, but she was one of several who formed punk bands, played with Goth-inspired art and stories, and found their way to college.

"The main thing that drew me to college was the community I hoped I could find of people with similar interests," she said "It was partly the music and the rest of the 'junk culture' that showed me there could be communities like that. I don't know where your comic book might take that girl at the convention. But that 'passion' she mentioned is part of her life now. It's in her memory. It'll always be there, and somehow it'll keep coming back, and it'll give her something."

Sharon gave me something, too: a new career. I returned to my studies of American culture, but now with a focus on what aggressive fantasies mean to young people and what roles they play in personal development. I found that shockingly little had been written about it. For all the decades of psychological research attempting to prove that entertainment violence makes children more aggressive, or desensitizes them, or distorts their views of reality, very few studies have asked why they love it or what good it might do them. Hardly any, in fact, have even asked when or why it has a negative effect or how potential negative effects might be ameliorated. Bruno Bettelheim had summed up a great deal of psychiatric research on the benefits of violent fairy tales in his *Uses of Enchantment*,[2] but even he had dismissed mass entertainment out of hand — even though the fantasies, the themes, and the violence of that entertainment often echoed fairy tales and even though it obviously resonated powerfully with millions of modern children.

> **For all the decades of psychological research attempting to prove that entertainment violence makes children more aggressive . . . very few studies have asked why they love it or what good it might do them.**

So I interviewed psychiatrists, pediatricians, family therapists, teachers, screenwriters, game designers, and parents. I read the research. I asked children and teenagers what stories, movies, songs, and games they loved and what they meant to them. I dug back through my own growing up. I watched my son as he tackled the challenges of toddlerhood, preschool, and elementary school, choosing fantasies and entertainment to help him along the way. I gathered hundreds of stories of young people who had benefited from superhero comics, action movies, cartoons, shoot-'em-up video games, and angry rap and rock songs. I found stories of kids who'd used them badly, too, and others who'd needed adult help to use them well. But mostly I found young people using fantasies of combat in order to feel stronger, to access their emotions, to take control of their anxieties, to calm themselves down in the face of real violence, to fight their way through emotional challenges and lift themselves to new developmental levels.

During those same years, however, criticisms of entertainment violence became steadily more intense. The news was replete with stories of teenage violence (even though juvenile crime rates were dropping rapidly), and many of those stories drew connections between the crimes and movies, songs, or video games. The boys who killed their classmates and themselves at Columbine High School were discovered to have loved the video game *Doom*, and its influence soon dominated speculation on what might have influenced them. Congressional committees excoriated the entertainment industry. Prominent psychologists testified that video violence had been proven harmful to children. In March 2000, the American Academy of Pediatrics urged doctors to monitor their young patients' exposure to media violence and warn parents of its dangers.[3]

That same month, I found myself addressing a roomful of psychiatrists about *Pokémon*. I wasn't expecting to come out of it very well liked.

As adults were debating the dangers of the media, the schoolyards of America were being swept by the most intense and most universal kid craze I'd ever seen. And it was a true product of kid culture. I began hearing about this strange universe of battling pet monsters from preschoolers and middle schoolers, boys and girls, computer nerds and blossoming jocks, months before the Nintendo marketing machine caught on to what it had. I was fascinated. This new world was noisy and combative, but it was also warm and fuzzy and funny and infernally complex, and kids were weaving it into every sort of fantasy and game. When Viz Communications asked me to help adapt the Japanese *Pokémon* comic book and comic strip franchise to the American market, I jumped at the chance.

My unusual position as a creator of superheroes, an analyst of children's entertainment, and an American interpreter of that global fantasy fad landed me on NPR's *Fresh Air*, explaining the Poké-phenomenon to puzzled parents nationwide. On the basis of that interview, the Southern California Psychiatric Society invited me to deliver the keynote address at its 2000 conference on "Violence and Society." Although I'd been supported in my research by enthusiastic psychologists and psychiatrists, I was still under the impression that the mental health establishment as a whole condemned entertainment violence. Now I was about to tell a roomful of veteran mental health professionals stories illustrating the positive effects of cartoon mayhem. I braced myself for a rough question-and-answer period at the end.

One of the powers of stories, however, is to remind us that people rarely obey generalizations. We may view an abstraction — "psychiatric opinion" or "media violence" — as threatening, but stories of people wrestling with the fears, pains, and challenges of life bring us back to our own realities. Anxiety gives way to empathy, and suddenly we're not speaking in recycled newspaper headlines; we're discussing the endless individuality and unpredictability of human beings. The people at that conference, having spent their careers listening to stories, understood that well, and when my speech ended I found myself launched upon one of the most exhilarating conversations I'd ever known.

One child therapist related his own rewarding uses of Pokémon action figures with young patients. Another said that his concern was for children who didn't have the chance to talk through what they'd experienced in the media and that "what you've demonstrated here is how beneficial *any* media experience can be in the context of constructive adult attention." An especially enthusiastic psychoanalyst said, "We're so afraid of aggression in this society that we haven't been able to talk intelligently about it. You're doing for aggression what Papa Freud did for sexuality!" "You've made one little boy very happy," said a psychiatrist who'd come with her husband, another doctor. "We haven't let our son watch shows like *Pokémon*, but I think we will now."

Then Elizabeth Thoman raised her hand. President of the Center for Media Literacy in Los Angeles and a longtime critic of media violence, she, I assumed, was going to express some objections. She did have questions about whether lurid games like *Duke Nukem* could be beneficial in the same way as *Pokémon*, and I explained how they could be, depending on the young person and his reason for choosing the game. Then she said, "This way of discussing media violence in terms of individual experience could be really valuable, not just to groups like this, but to the kids themselves. You should take this into the schools."

I told her I was glad she thought so, because I already had. Beginning with my son's kindergarten class, then expanding into the higher grades at his school, I had been leading workshops in comic-strip creation in which I encouraged kids to put down their own stories and fantasies through words and pictures. As simple as they were, those workshops were sources of an astonishing wealth of juvenile imaginings and experiences. So, drawing upon the wisdom of educators, psychologists, and media literacy experts, I used those as the foundation for what I've come to call the Art and Story Workshops: programs adaptable to every level from preschool to high school that help kids pull together the images, thoughts, and emotions in their minds through individual storytelling in a comic strip-like form. I'd take over a classroom for a day or a week, get the kids talking about their ideas and passions, and challenge them to put them down on paper — in both words and pictures.

Children are usually taught to compartmentalize their communication into either linear narrative or static portraits, but storytelling that is both visual and verbal leads them to transcend the compartments, to experience their thoughts and feelings more completely. Comics also have an inherent funkiness that frees kids to express fantasies that the more adult-approved media inhibit. Visual storytelling unlocks the images they've stored up from cartoons, movies, and video games and helps them make more sense of the media-transmitted stories that fill their environments. The process gives young people a sense of authorship, of *authority* over their own emotions and the world's influences. It also reveals the way that children use fantasies, stories, and media images in building their sense of self.

What I've learned in the Art and Story Workshops has consistently reinforced my belief that the vast array of fantasies and stories that we tend to dismiss with such labels as "media violence" are used well by children. I've seen young people turn every form of imaginary aggression into sources of emotional nourishment and developmental support. But I'm startled sometimes, too. I bring in my own biases about what's beneficial and what's not. And sometimes a boy like Philip will smash them.

> **I've seen young people turn every form of imaginary aggression into sources of emotional nourishment and developmental support.**

The theme that day was "power." When I'm working with eighth and ninth graders, I find it useful to have the class agree on an overall theme as a starting point (usually after a very boisterous discussion). After that, every kid is responsible for telling the story that excites him or her most, however silly or sentimental or horrific or tasteless others might find it. I move around the room to help unstick ideas and bolster confidence, but I make it clear that because they're doing it for *themselves*, not for the school, the teacher, or a grade, there are no grown-up restraints or expectations to observe. Philip needed no help; he dove instantly into a humorous comic strip about a wily prostitute who tricks a corrupt police officer.

"Why that?" I asked. "Because I hate hypocrisy," he said, "especially when it acts like it's supposed to be morality." "Like what else?" I asked. That's when one of the girls sitting next to him asked Philip, "Can I tell him?" He nodded, and she told me that Philip had come out as gay a month before. The boys in the class had mostly avoided him since, and his friends now all came from one clique of sensitive, politically minded girls.

As she talked, I noticed Philip and a second girl writing lines of poetry on each other's pages. I asked if they were song lyrics. "Rap lyrics," said Philip proudly, and he and the girls told me about the hip-hop tastes they shared: Dr. Dre, DMX, Snoop Dogg. But, said Philip with obvious passion, his favorite was Eminem. That was what startled me. Eminem was then at the peak of his notoriety for rageful, homophobic epithets: *"My words are like a dagger with a jagged edge that'll stab you in the head whether you're a fag or lez."*[4] Philip noticed my reaction and forced a grin. "Don't say what my mom always says."

I asked him what that was. He nursed his thoughts for a moment, and then he poured it out: "She's being really cool about all this. Not like my dad. My dad's really making it hard, telling me it's just a phase, not letting me go to any support groups, blah blah blah. My mom's being really supportive, being there for me no matter what. But she just won't get Eminem. She calls his lyrics 'hate-mongering.' She keeps saying, 'How can

407

you listen to that if you're gay? Why don't you listen to something that makes you feel good about yourself?' And I try to tell her why it *does*."

"Why does it?" I asked.

"Because Eminem has the courage to say who he *is*."

It's easy to fall into the trap of thinking that young people emulate literally what they see in entertainment. That if they like a rapper who insults gays, then they must be learning hostility to gays, and if they love a movie hero who defeats villainy with a gun, then they must he learning to solve problems with violence. There is some truth in that. One of the functions of stories and games is to help children rehearse for what they'll be in later life. Anthropologists and psychologists who study play, however, have shown that there are many other functions as well — one of which is to enable children to pretend to be just what they know they'll *never* be.[5] Exploring, in a safe and controlled context, what is impossible or too dangerous or forbidden to them is a crucial tool in accepting the limits of reality. Playing with rage is a valuable way to reduce its power. Being evil and destructive in imagination is a vital compensation for the wildness we all have to surrender on our way to being good people.

In focusing so intently on the literal, we overlook the *emotional* meaning of stories and images. The most peaceful, empathetic, conscientious children are often excited by the most aggressive entertainment. Young people who reject violence, guns, and bigotry in every form can sift through the literal contents of a movie, game, or song and still embrace the emotional power at its heart. Children need to feel strong. They need to feel powerful in the face of a scary, uncontrollable world. Superheroes, video-game warriors, rappers, and movie gunmen are symbols of strength. By pretending to be them, young people are being strong.

Adults, however, often react to violent images very differently — and in the gap between juvenile and adult reactions, some of our greatest misunderstandings and most damaging disputes are born. Soon after the terrorist attacks of September 11, 2001, many toy retailers reported sharp increases in sales of G.I. Joe and other militaristic toys.[6] But some of those same retailers also began pulling such toys from the shelves, largely in response to parents' requests. Newspaper stories reported that many parents were forbidding violent toys and entertainment in their homes as a reaction to the tragedy. One mother said she'd hidden her sons' toy soldiers because "It's bad enough that they see the Army in the airport."

Many of us worried about how we would help children deal with the terror of September 11, but when I went into the classrooms, I found that the children were far less shaken than their parents and teachers.[7] Most of them talked about the horrific images they'd seen with a mixture of anger and excitement — and a lot of them wanted to draw pictures, tell stories, or play games involving planes destroying buildings or soldiers fighting terrorists. This isn't a failure to react appropriately to tragedy: this is how children deal with it. When something troubles them, they have to play with it until it feels safer. Rick Fitzgerald, a veteran director of the Little Red School House, the Branson School, and Live Oak School, told me that my workshops had become more important than ever: "They need to tell the violent stories that are in them now."

> **When something troubles them, they have to play with it until it feels safer.**

Adults are generally more empathetic, more attuned to the greater world, and more literalistic than children. We are more likely to feel the pain and anxiety caused by real violence when we see it in make-believe. It troubles us to see our kids having fun with something that we deplore. We fear that they are celebrating or affirming a horror that we desperately want to banish from reality. We want them to mirror our adult restraint, seriousness, compassion, and pacifism. But they can't — and shouldn't — mimic adult reactions. Play, fantasy, and emotional imagination are essential tools of the work of childhood and adolescence.

Anxiety about how our kids will turn out is an inescapable aspect of adulthood. That anxiety is always heightened in times of sudden change or general insecurity about the future. It can be a useful emotion when it helps us notice the ways in which children are using their aggressive fantasies, and when it energizes us to teach them nonviolent solutions to life's problems. It can be destructive, however, if it only heightens our children's own anxieties, or drives them away from us and deeper into a media-based reality, or keeps them from finding the fantasies they need.

In working with children, I've come up against my adult anxieties again and again. But I've also been brought back in memory to their kid's place in life, a place in which they may need precisely the images that their daily life doesn't provide, precisely the stories from which their parents have tried to protect them. For a long time, I resisted looking closely at my own adolescence. I dismissed it as simply too sheltered and assumed that superhero comics had been just a source of excitement for me. It was only when I began seriously exploring the function of aggressive fantasy in children's development that I let myself look fully at what I'd gone through in those years and began to understand why the figure of the hero kept fighting his way to such a central place in my psyche.

When I was thirteen I started cutting school. I didn't have the words to say why. We didn't talk about scary feelings in my house. My parents desperately wanted a polite and civilized home, unlike the ones they'd grown up in. My mother always seemed to be suppressing anger, my father always dodging a confrontation. They let me know in a thousand ways that they wanted a sweet little boy who didn't get angry or greedy or rebellious, and I badly wanted to be that.

They were going through a hard time; I can see that now, but then I didn't know what was happening. My mother would sit in front of the evening news drinking glass after glass of wine ("my anesthetic," she called it, although she wouldn't name the pain), telling me bitterly of a world that had mutilated her liberal ideals with assassinations, riots, war, rising crime, and racial violence, telling me as she drank how disillusioned she was as a high school teacher, how appalled she was at the new youth culture. My father would retreat into the back room with the newspaper. They barely spoke to each other and never told me why, and I could never make out their muted arguments behind closed doors.

I didn't know what to do. I hated junior high, felt threatened by what my peers were turning into. I didn't want adolescence, didn't want to have to go into that world my mother talked about. I hung out less and less with my friends, and I wouldn't tell them why. Pretty soon they stopped asking. I started faking headaches so I could stay home from school, even though home was cold and empty. My mother blamed the public school system and put me in a tiny experimental school full of misfits. I didn't protest; somehow it felt like the survival of my fragile world depended on being the nice boy who would fulfill all his parents' expectations. But by eighth grade I was cutting school to stay home all day and watch TV with the shades drawn. There was nothing on that wasteland of game shows and soap operas that spoke to me, but I kept watching, hoping for something to excite me, Sometimes late at night I would slip out of the house and take long walks alone, looking for I didn't know what.

My parents knew something was wrong, but they were lost, too. My mother tried to encourage my interests, hoping she could reignite some spark of my younger days, when I'd been so excited about everything I did. She gave me great books, and I read a lot of them. History was a pleasant place to escape to. But nothing I read moved me enough to change the way I was behaving — until a kid named Jack Baty turned in an independent study report for one of my mother's classes.

Jack was the kind of kid I think my mom wished I could be: nerdy but bright, a couple of steps off the mainstream but upbeat about his interests, always doing something creative with his gang of oddball friends. My mother probably thought that anything that excited Jack might have a positive influence on me. She must have had some doubts, though, when she saw that his report was on Marvel comic books.

I'd never really read comic books. My mom remembered the news stories in the 1950s about how experts had linked them to juvenile delinquency. By the late 1960s the news was full of expert opinion that violent TV, toys, and other pop culture was contributing to the violence in our society, and she let me know that such stuff was off-limits. But here was Jack Baty, telling her with passionate conviction that comic books, long reviled for their juvenility and violence, had matured into thought-provoking modern mythologies full of lofty messages of peace and understanding. She asked Jack to lend her a few; maybe this was something her son could get excited about. He brought them in the next day. The covers showed nothing but big guys punching each other, but she took Jack's word on the lofty messages, and she brought them home to me.

I was riveted. They spoke to me. They thrilled me more deeply than anything I'd seen in years; but not because of their lofty messages. The messages were there, dressing up the occasional plot, but I barely noticed them. The heart of the plots, what the stories were about, was *power*.

The character who entranced me, and freed me, was the Incredible Hulk: overgendered and undersocialized, half-naked and half-witted, raging against a frightened world that misunderstood and persecuted him. In normal life he was a government scientist who had to struggle desperately to maintain his altruistic self-restraint — because his own anger set off a reaction in his body that transformed him, uncontrollably, into a brute of raw, destructive power. "Mustn't . . . let myself . . . feel it!" he'd roar, and suddenly his body would explode with muscles that ripped through his clothes, and he'd hurl himself bare-chested and free through the walls around him and thoom into the sky with a mighty leap. The Hulk smashed through the walls of fear I'd been carrying inside me and freed me to feel everything I had been repressing: rage and pride and the hunger for power over my own life.

Suddenly I had a fantasy self who could show me what it felt like to be unafraid of my own desires and the world's disapproval, to be bold enough to destroy what had to be destroyed. I had my Beowulf back. And when he and I came down from the heights with an earth-shattering boom, I saw that we were on open desert beyond the narrow streets I'd been walking. "Puny boy follow Hulk!" roared my fantasy self, and I followed.

The Hulk led me on a passionate hunt for more comic books. When that wasn't enough to satisfy me, he led me to meet Jack Baty and his friends, then to call up my old friend Brian to convert him to my new devotion, then to seek out new friends, other young geeks whose inner superheroes gave meaning to their private fears, rages, and wishes. Pretty soon I was founding my own comic book club. I wrote letters to comics editors and got letters back. I went to comics conventions and met the former teenage geeks whose fantasies impelled them to write and draw the stories that gave form to my own. And when their fantasies weren't enough, I began to write my own.

After a few years I was done with comics, or so I thought. I moved on to more grown-up heroes and more sophisticated stories, established a career in writing, and resisted looking back at the painful cradle of it all. But once I began talking to kids, I could no longer ignore the Hulk standing there in the middle of my growing up. He hadn't smashed all my problems, but he'd led me to a new sense of myself. He'd helped me play through some of my deepest fears. He'd led me to the arrogant, self-exposing, self-assertive, superheroic decision to become a writer, to start writing the script of my own life.

He also gave me a new way of talking to my parents. Gerry the super-hero fan wasn't the same kid as Gerry the nice boy of my mother's imagination. I began to develop fantasies and tastes that she didn't understand and didn't wholly approve of. But she trusted that anything that excited me so much must be doing me some good, and she wanted me to share it with her. My father compared my superheroes with mock disdain to the Shadow and other violent heroes of the pulp magazines he'd grown up with. They would both listen to me prattle about my favorite characters, writers, and artists. We still didn't talk openly about my angers and frustrations, but at least we talked about my fantasies of being powerful and destructive. I felt that the darker side of myself was being seen and accepted for the first time.

> *I felt that the darker side of myself was being seen and accepted for the first time.*

My mother told me years later that her anxieties had eased when she saw my love of superheroes as coming from within me, not as something that had been imposed upon me by the entertainment industry. The comic books were made by others and sold to me as a commodity, but the desire to read them was *mine*. A lot of us stumble over that as parents, blaming what our children see for making them want things, forgetting that it's our children themselves who are doing the wanting. Each child's fantasies and emotional needs are very much his own, even if he shares them with millions of other kids. When we burden those needs with our own anxieties, we can confuse and frighten children about their own feelings. Adult anxieties about the effects of entertainment are sometimes the real causes of the very effects that we fear most.

As my articles on this subject began to appear in newspapers and magazines, I heard from parents and children on the front lines of the battle between entertainment violence and its critics. A woman named Leila living in a small town in Pennsylvania contacted me about the struggles of her eighth-grade grandson. Leila's daughter was a drug addict, and her daughter's son, Jimmy, had been taken from his mother by court order at the age of five and assigned to his grandparents' care. Leila and her husband found that they had quite a job on their hands. Jimmy had intense abandonment tears and separation anxiety. He had asthma, poor eyesight, and, as they discovered after three years of struggle in grade school, dyslexia. He responded to it all with disruptive behavior, becoming a class clown. The school district assigned a paraprofessional child worker to look after him during the school day, but her duties devolved into reporting on his conduct violations.

"He's a great kid," said Leila, "but he has a lot of fears. He works those fears out through humor — a lot of it not in very good taste, and sometimes provocative, but just humor. But because he's been labeled a 'problem,' everything he does becomes a crisis." Once another kid spilled some pizza on the floor, and Jimmy said, "It looks like roadkill!" That was entered into his record as "violence" and earned him one of many confrontations with school authorities.

In junior high, Jimmy fell in love with first-person shooter games, those video games like *Doom* and *Quake* in which the player has to explore a fantasy environment and gun down the bizarre opponents who attack him. Leila supported him in his enthusiasm. "Having been responsible for raising five younger siblings my whole childhood," she said, "I grew up with a lot of stress and anger. I still remember what a huge release it was to play war and shoot up not only my siblings but the other kids in the neighborhood who had it so much easier than me. Jimmy doesn't have that, because nobody plays war in our neighborhood, and they probably wouldn't play it with him anyway. But I could see him achieving the same release in his video games. He was always calmer and more confident after spending a while with his games."

When Jimmy began talking about his hobby at school, however, the official reaction wasn't so supportive. Two teachers and the principal, on separate occasions, sat him down and told him that the games he loved would desensitize him to violence, make him believe he could kill without consequence, give him a false sense of power, make him associate bloodshed with fun. With each encounter, Leila said, he came home frightened, agitated, and more inclined to act up than before. "The poor kid has enough real fears of his own without having adults dumping their fears on him," she said. "Instead of helping him deal with the fears he has, they send the message that they're afraid of *him* — and so they make him even more afraid of *himself.*"

Leila encouraged Jimmy to talk openly about what he liked, seeing that it helped him feel stronger and more in control of his life. Then a teacher called Leila into her office and told her that, under the school's "zero tolerance" policy, Jimmy was in danger of suspension for "promoting violence." She asked Leila to forbid Jimmy to play the games before that — or "something far worse" — happened.

Leila asked me whether I could provide any research on the value of shooter games that she could show the school authorities. I sent her what I'd compiled from my experiences and those of the psychologists, doctors, and educators I'd worked with and recommended that she ask school authorities to look past generalizations and do what she was doing: ask Jimmy why he loves the games he loves, show some empathy for his fantasies and feelings, trust that he's doing his best to meet his complex emotional needs, and offer help, not fear.

It made a difference, she said. The teachers didn't change their minds completely, but they listened. Tensions began to ease. Jimmy felt better about himself, if only because it seemed as though his teachers were finally thinking about who he *was* instead of what he might *do*.

When we consider children in relation to mass media and pop culture, we tend to define them as consumers, watchers, recipients, victims. But they are also *users* of that media and culture: they are choosers, interpreters, shapers, fellow players, participants, and storytellers. Viewing children as passive recipients of the media's power puts us at odds with the fantasies they've chosen, and thus with the children themselves. Viewing them as active users enables us to work with their entertainment — any entertainment — to help them grow. Shooter games, gangsta rap, *Pokémon* all become tools for parents and teachers to help young people feel stronger, calm their fears, and learn more about themselves.

In our anxiety to understand and control real-life violence, we've tried to reduce our children's relationships with their fantasies of combat and destruction to vast generalizations that we would never dream of applying to their fantasies about love and family and discovery and adventure. We don't usually ask whether game shows predispose our children to greed, or whether love songs increase the likelihood of getting stuck in bad relationships. But when aggression is the topic, we try to purée a million games and dreams and life stories into statistical studies. We ask absurdly sweeping questions like, What is the effect of media violence on children? as if violence were a single, simple phenomenon of which sandbox play-fights and mass murder were mere variations, as if the evening news and *Reservoir Dogs* and Daffy Duck were indistinguishable, as if children were like trees in an orchard who could all be raised to identical form by the same externalities. Many forces have been shown to contribute to aggression: religious fervor, patriotic fervor, sports rivalry, romantic rivalry, hot summer nights.[8] Entertainment has inspired some people to violence, but so have the Bible, the Constitution, the Beatles, books about Hitler, and obsessions with TV actresses. We don't usually condemn those influences as harmful, because we understand them better, we understand why people like them and the benefits most of us draw from them. What's lacking is an understanding of aggressive fantasies and the entertainment that speaks to them.

> We don't usually ask whether game shows predispose our children to greed, or whether love songs increase the likelihood of getting stuck in bad relationships.

"Narrative deals with the vicissitudes of human intentions," writes the great psychologist Jerome Bruner in *Actual Minds, Possible Worlds*.[9] "And since there are myriad intentions and endless ways for them to run into trouble — or so it would seem — there should be endless kinds of stories." My work with kids and entertainment has been a discovery of stories. Every story of a superhero or a monster or an angry rapper — even the video game that looks so simplistic at first glance — resonates with the personal stories of its audience. And every one becomes a different story depending on the listener, the viewer, the player. A child chooses a particular movie or game because his unique story has led him there, and he weaves a new, personal narrative out of the fantasy and play it inspires.

No one has taught me more about this than my son. When Nicky was five and anxious about the end of preschool and the beginning of kindergarten, I brought him *Beowulf*. He didn't like it. So I brought him the Greek myths, and the Grimms' fairy tales, and the Dr. Dolittle novels, and Superman and King Kong and all the other stories, violent and nonviolent, that had thrilled me as a child. He didn't want any of them. He wanted *Mighty Morphin' Power Rangers*.

I don't think I enjoyed watching *Power Rangers* episodes with Nicky quite as much as my mother enjoyed reading *Beowulf* to me. I liked the goofy rubber monsters, but the road to their scenes led through the most agonizing stretches of Saturday morning teen banter. Nicky, however, loved every minute of them, and I loved watching him love them. Every commercial break he'd be running, morphing, punching, kicking, knocking fearsome monsters (usually me) to the ground — with a confidence in his body and a decisiveness in his movements that I'd rarely seen in him. I could see his excitement driving the anxiety out of him.

Then he found a new fantasy: *Teletubbies*. That show was just then invading America and finding an audience not only among toddlers and ironic adults but among countless five- and six-year-olds discovering the regressive comforts of cute baby talk and cuddly hijinks in an underground burrow. Suddenly Nicky and his friends were waddling into group hugs and squealing, "Eh-oh, LaLa" and "Where Po 'cootah?"

This, I thought, must surely be the end of the Power Rangers. But not for Nicky. When he wasn't turning into Po and asking for a hug, he'd be morphing into the Red Ranger and blasting a monster. His mom noticed that he seemed to become a Ranger when he felt more sure of himself, a Tubby when he felt a little shaky and needed more nurturing. As the end of preschool drew near, those two contradictory fantasies grew to fill more and more of his play time.

One morning I woke him up, and as we walked to the bathroom he said, "I want to see more of the Battle Show." "What's the Battle Show?" I asked. He looked at me confusedly. "We were just watching it!" he said.

Then he realized: "It was a dream!" I asked him what it was like, and he laughed and told me: "The Teletubbies were playing on the grass in Tub-byland with their toys. Then these monsters were getting into Tubbyland. They looked kind of like Tyrannosauruses but they were destroying the flowers and windmill things and they were going to destroy the Tubbies' house. So Po touched something on his wrist and suddenly he morphed into the Red Ranger! Then the other Tubbies turned into Power Rangers. Only they were their own colors, so there was a Purple Ranger because of Tinky-Winky instead of a Blue Ranger or Pink Ranger. They fought the monsters and knocked them all the way out of Tubbyland, and then they morphed back into the Teletubbies!"

I asked him to draw pictures of it, but he wanted to playact it instead, and Tubby Rangers quickly became his favorite game. He took it to pre-school, where he and his friends added new details: the Tubbies' under-ground home could rocket into space; the Nu-Nu, their vacuum cleaner with eyeballs, could morph into a Battle-Zord; the televisions on their tummies would alert them to approaching danger.

Nicky had chosen stories that embraced the extremes of his fantasy life, the most aggressive and the gentlest. Then he'd remade them into what he needed them to be. Now he could be as powerful and fearless as he wanted but not sacrifice his need to be comforted and protected. Red Ranger Po united the most destructive and most nurturing powers in one happy self.

Children want to be strong, secure, and happy. Their fantasies will tell us what they feel they need to attain that, if we pay attention. But we need to look beyond our adult expectations and interpretations and see them through our children's eyes. First, we need to begin disentangling the fears and preconceptions that have prevented us from doing so.

NOTES

[1]From the edition my mother used to read to me which I found years later on her shelf: Charles W. Kennedy, trans., Beowulf, in The Literature of England, ed. George B. Woods, Homer A. Watt, and George K. Anderson (Chicago: Scott, Foresman, 1953), p. 34.

[2]Bruno Bettelheim, The Use of Enchantment: The Meaning and Importance of Fairy Tales (New York: Random House, 1976).

[3]Advice included in "The Role of the Pediatrician in Youth Violence Prevention in Clinical Practice and at the Community Level," a policy statement published in Pediatrics (January 1999); it was reiterated in an AAP press release (March 7, 2000) that received considerably more media attention.

[4]Lyrics by Eminem, The Marshall Mothers LP (2000), Uni/Interscope Records.

[5]The richest and most insightful of the resources on this topic are the works of Brian Sutton-Smith, the most recent and comprehensive being The Ambiguity of Play (Cambridge: Harvard University Press, 1997). See also his The Psychology of Play (North Stratford, N.H: Ayer, 1976) and Play and Learning (New York: John Wiley, 1979).

[6]Anne D'Innocenzio, "Toy Firms Downplay Violence," *San Francisco Chronicle*, September 28, 2001.

[7]This was supported by a Rand study that found that during the week after the attacks, 90 percent of people over eighteen years old suffered stress reactions while only 35 percent of those five through seventeen years old did so. Mark A. Schuster et al., "A National Survey of Stress Reactions after the September 11, 2001, Terrorist Attacks," *New England Journal of Medicine* (November 2001).

[8]Russell G. Green, *Human Aggression* (Pacific Grove, Calif.: McGraw-Hill, 1990); David H. Crowell, Ian M. Evans, and Clifford R. O'Donnell, eds., *Childhood Aggression and Violence* (New York: Plenum, 1987); and Leonard Berkowitz, *Aggression: Its Causes, Consequences, and Control* (New York: McGraw-Hill, 1993). See also Craig A. Anderson et. al., "Hot Temperatures, Hostile Affect, Hostile Cognition, and Arousal: Tests of a General Model of Affective Aggression," *Personality and Social Psychology Bulletin* 21 (1995).

[9]Jerome Bruner, *Actual Minds, Possible Worlds* (Cambridge: Harvard University Press. 1986), p. 16.

DISCUSSION

1. "When we consider children in relation to mass media and pop culture," Jones observes, "we tend to define them as consumers, watchers, recipients, victims. But they are also *users* of that media and culture." Do you agree with this claim? How would a more activist or user-based definition of play change the ways we debate the issue of pop culture violence?

2. To understand what's at stake in our debate over media violence, Jones argues, "we need to look beyond our adult expectations and interpretations and see [this violent material] through our children's eyes." What do you think Jones means by this? What particular expectations and interpretations does he seem to have in mind? And what makes a child's eye view of them different?

3. Underlying Jones's discussion is the notion that so-called fantasy games are less a retreat or escape from reality than a valuable means of dealing with and resolving the real-life challenges confronting children. Do you agree with this proposition? How or how not?

WRITING

4. One of the most dominant and commonplace worry among parents and educators is that violence in popular culture leads kids to emulate the behavior they see on display. Jones offers a different way to understand this relationship: one in which the child uses these depictions of violence to fulfill other needs. Choose a pop culture product that you think holds this possibility, and write an essay in which you argue how it offers users, viewers, or readers opportunities to redirect the violence depicted to other ends.

5. According to Jones, "Playing with rage is a valuable way to reduce its power." What do you think he means by this? Write an essay in which you argue either in support of or in opposition to this statement. Would you place any limits on the truth of this statement?

6. Both Jones and Katy Vine (p. 380) focus their attention on make-believe worlds. Write an essay in which you compare and contrast the way their two portrayals characterize these artificial worlds. In what ways do these "virtual" environments seem to foster similar attitudes toward violence? Does the cyber community Vine sketches afford its users the same opportunities for working through their feelings and fears as Jones's depiction of video games, movies, and books? If not, what makes the difference?

SASHA ABRAMSKY

Return of the Madhouse:
Supermax Prisons Are Becoming the High-Tech Equivalent of the Nineteenth-Century Snakepit

What typical images do we have of people in prison? And how do these stereotypes shape the ways we think about punishment and rehabilitation? Offering a firsthand account of prison life at a supermax facility, journalist Sasha Abramsky hazards some provisional answers to just such questions — inviting his readers to rethink some of our most entrenched assumptions regarding the ways those we deem criminal "deserve" to be treated. Abramsky was born in England; studied politics, philosophy, and economics at Balliol College, Oxford; and moved to the United States to pursue a master's in journalism at Columbia University. In 2000, he received a Soros Society, Crime and Communities Media Fellowship. He has published articles in the *Nation, Mother Jones*, and the *American Prospect*. He is also the author of four books about the U.S. prison system, including *Conned: How Millions Went to Prison, Lost the Vote, and Helped Send George W. Bush to the White House* (2006) and *American Furies: Crime, Punishment, and Vengeance in the Age of Mass Imprisonment* (2007). The selection that follows was first published in the February 11, 2002, issue of *American Prospect.*

LAST SUMMER, SOME 600 INMATES IN THE NOTORIOUS SUPER-maximum-security unit at California's Pelican Bay State Prison stopped eating. They were protesting the conditions in which the state says it must hold its most difficult prisoners: locked up for 23 hours out of every 24 in a barren concrete cell measuring 7½ by 11 feet. One wall of these cells is perforated steel; inmates can squint out through the holes, but there's nothing to see outside either. In Pelican Bay's supermax unit, as in most supermax prisons around the country, the cells are arranged in lines radiating out like spokes from a control hub, so that no prisoner can see another human being — except for those who are double-bunked. Last year, the average population of the Pelican Bay supermax unit was 1,200 inmates, and on average, 288 men shared their tiny space with a "cellie." Since 1995, 12 double-bunked prisoners in the Pelican Bay supermax unit have been murdered by their cell mates. But near-total isolation is the more typical condition.

Meals are slid to the inmates through a slot in the steel wall. Some prisoners are kept in isolation even for the one hour per day that they're allowed out to exercise; all are shackled whenever they are taken out of their cells. And many are forced to live this way for years on end.

Such extreme deprivation, the food strikers said, literally drives people crazy. Many experts agree. But the protest died out after two weeks, according to the jailhouse lawyer who organized it; and though a state senator promised that he would look into the strikers' complaints, so far conditions at Pelican Bay remain unchanged.

All told, more than 8,000 prisoners in California and at least 42,000 around the country, by the conservative estimate of the *Corrections Yearbook*, are currently held in similar conditions of extreme confinement. As of 2000, Texas alone boasted 16 supermax prisons and supermax units, housing some 10,000 inmates. In Florida, more than 7,000 inmates were double-bunked in such facilities and the corrections department was lobbying to build another one (at an estimated cost of nearly $50 million) to house an additional 1,000 offenders.

Seven years ago, in January 1995, inmates at Pelican Bay won a class-action lawsuit, *Madrid v. Gomez*, against the California Department of Corrections. Among other constitutional violations, U.S. District Court Judge Thelton Henderson found that the staff had systematically brutalized inmates, particularly mentally ill inmates. "The Eighth Amendment's restraint on using excessive force has been repeatedly violated at Pelican Bay, leading to a conspicuous pattern of excessive force," Henderson wrote in describing the severe beatings then common at the facility, the third-degree burns inflicted on one mentally ill inmate who was thrown into boiling water after he smeared himself with feces, and the routine use of painful restraining weapons against others. The judge ordered California to remove any seriously mentally ill or retarded inmates from the supermax unit, and he appointed a special master to overhaul the prison.

What Henderson didn't rule, however, was that the supermax model, per se, amounted to cruel and unusual punishment in violation of the Eighth Amendment. And so, while a new warden and new rules were brought to Pelican Bay, the basic conditions of sensory deprivation in its supermax unit have remained intact. Extremely mentally ill inmates are now held elsewhere; but critics say that less severe cases are still sent to the unit, where they often deteriorate drastically, for the same reasons that Judge Henderson originally identified: "The physical environment reinforces a sense of isolation and detachment from the outside world, and helps create a palpable distance from ordinary compunctions, inhibitions and community norms."

Meanwhile, the prescribed method for dealing with uncooperative inmates who "act out" in a supermax is still to send a team of guards into the cell with batons, stun guns, Mace, and tear gas. Thus, say critics, the chances for guard-inmate violence remain high at Pelican Bay, just as at other supermaxes around the country.

The supermax models emerged out of the prison violence of the 1970s and the early 1980s, when dozens of guards around the country, including two at the maximum-security federal prison at Marion, Illinois, were murdered by prisoners. First, prison authorities developed procedures to minimize inmate-staff contact; then they took to "locking down" entire prisons for indefinite periods, keeping inmates in their cells all day and closing down communal dining rooms and exercise yards. Eventually, they began to explore the idea of making the general prison population safer by creating entirely separate high-tech, supermax prisons in which "the worst of the worst" gang leaders and sociopaths would be incarcerated in permanent lockdown conditions. In the late 1980s, several states and the federal government began constructing supermax units. California — which had seen guards murdered by inmates between 1970 and 1973, and a staggering 32 prisoners killed by other inmates in 1972 alone — opened Corcoran State Prison and its supermax unit in 1988 and Pelican Bay the year following. In 1994 the first federal supermax opened, in Florence, Colorado. Soon, dozens of correctional systems across the country were embracing this model.

Indeed, throughout the 1990s, despite year-by-year declines in crime, one state after another pumped tens of millions of dollars into building supermax prisons and supermax facilities within existing prisons — sections that are usually called "secure housing units," or SHUs. Defenders of supermaxes, like Todd Ishee, warden of Ohio State Penitentiary (OSP), a supermax in Youngstown, argue that their restrictions provide a way to establish control in what is still — and inherently — an extremely dangerous environment. "In 1993," he says, "our maximum security prison at Southern Ohio Correctional Facility was host to a riot. One correctional officer was killed. A number of inmates were killed and several injured. Following the riot, the department made a decision that a 500-bed facility of this nature was needed to control the most dangerous inmates."

But while it may be necessary to maintain such restricted facilities as prisons of last resort for some inmates, critics point out that far less troublesome inmates end up being sent to them. In Ohio, for example, a special legislative committee appointed to inspect the state's prisons in 1999 concluded that fewer than half of the inmates at OSP met the state's own supermax guidelines. State correctional-department data indicate that of the more than 350 inmates currently incarcerated at OSP, 20 were ringleaders of the 1993 riot and 31 had killed either an inmate or a correctional officer while living among the general prison population; but the rest had been sent there for much less serious offenses (often little more than a fist fight with another inmate).

And Ohio isn't alone in this practice. According to a study issued by the state of Florida, fully one-third of the correctional departments across the country that operate supermax prisons report placing inmates in them simply because they don't have enough short-term disciplinary housing in lower-security prisons. Given that the supermaxes' average cost to taxpayers is about $50,000 per inmate per year — compared with $20,000 to $30,000 for lower-security prisons — this is hardly an economically efficient arrangement

Yet the available numbers suggest that casual overuse of these facilities is common. For in tough-on-crime America, imposing grim conditions on prisoners is all too often seen as a good in itself, regardless of the long-term costs. The U.S. Department of Justice's 1997 report on supermax housing (the most recent available) found Mississippi officials insisting that they needed to house fully 20 percent of their prison inmates in separate supermax-type prisons and another 35 percent in similar units within existing prisons. Arizona claimed that it needed to house 8 percent of its inmates in supermax prisons and another 20 percent in SHUs. In Virginia, after Jim Austin, the state's nationally renowned consultant on prisoner classification, told officials that they needed to put more of their inmates into medium security prisons, the state instead spent approximately $150 million to build Red Onion and Wallens Ridge, two supermax prisons with a combined capacity to house 2,400 prisoners.

> **For in tough-on-crime America, imposing grim conditions on prisoners is all too often seen as a good in itself.**

Proponents of the supermax system claim that its introduction has reduced violence in the general prison population — both by removing the most hard-core miscreants and also by introducing a fearsome deterrent to misbehavior. But the data on this are, at best, mixed. Among Ohio's total prison population, for example, there were more inmate-on-inmate assaults serious enough to be written up by officials in 2000 than there were in 1997, the year before the OSP supermax opened for business (8 assaults for every 1,000 prisoners in 1997 compared with 10 for every 1,000 in 2000). And even where lower-security prisons have been made somewhat safer, that safety has been purchased at a staggering financial and, ultimately, social cost.

Even the best-run of the supermax facilities seem to see high rates of mental illness among their inmates. For example, a study carried out by the Washington State Department of Corrections, which is known as one of the more humane, rehabilitation-focused prison systems in the country, found that approximately 30 percent of inmates in its supermax units show evidence of serious psychiatric disorders — at least twice the rate in the overall prison population.

In Connecticut's Northern Correctional Institution (NCI), Warden Larry Myers presides over an inmate population just shy of 500 and a staff of just over 300. With six mental-health professionals, a gradated three-phase program offering inmates the possibility of returning to the general prison population within one year, and relatively calm inmate-staff relations, Myers prides himself on running a tight ship. Unlike staffers at many other supermaxes, once those at NCI identify an inmate as psychotic, they remove him to an institution that caters to mentally ill prisoners. Myers says that to avoid a "ping-pong effect," with inmates bouncing back and forth between NCI and mental-health institutions, the prison has not accepted severely disturbed inmates since 1999.

Yet even in Myers's prison, psychiatrist Paul Chaplin estimates that 10 percent of the inmates are on antidepressants or antipsychotic drugs, and several times a month an inmate gets violent enough to be placed in four-point restraints. Last September, guards had to subdue prisoners with Mace on 12 occasions. As I toured the pink-painted steel tiers of level one, dozens of inmates began screaming out their often incoherent complaints in a bone-jarring cacophony of despair.

"This is shitty," shouted one of the more intelligible of them. "We ain't got no recreations, no space. If I try to sit back and motivate, you got people yelling." He said he sleeps for more than 10 hours a day, does push-ups, and sits around. "I have trouble concentrating," he yelled. Through the narrow Plexiglas window in the door of his cell, a 21-year-old shouted: "I'm in jail for behavior problems. My cellie has behavior problems. Why put two people with behavior problems in the same cell?"

The greatly disputed chicken-and-egg-question is: Do previously healthy inmates go mad under these extreme conditions of confinement, or do inmates who are already mentally unstable and impulsive commit disciplinary infractions that get them shipped off to SHUs or supermax prisons, where they are then likely to further decompensate?

Some psychiatrists, including Harvard University professor Stuart Grassian, have testified in court that the sensory deprivation in a supermax frequently leads otherwise healthy individuals to develop extreme manifestations of psychosis, such as hallucinations, uncontrollable rage, paranoia, and nearly catatonic depressions. Grassian and others have also documented examples of extreme self-mutilation: supermax inmates gouging out their eyes or cutting off their genitals. Using the tools of the supermax prison, writes James Gilligan in his book *Violence*, "does not protect the public; it only sends a human time bomb into the community" when the inmate is eventually released.

Other psychiatrists are more cautious, arguing that while some perfectly healthy people are driven insane by these dehumanizing prison settings, the more common problem is that mildly mentally ill inmates are often precisely the ones who find it hardest to control their behavior while in the general prison population and who therefore get sent to the supermax or SHU. Fudge Henderson acknowledged this in his Pelican Bay ruling; and in *Ruiz v. Johnson*, a 1999 case involving Texas's use of long-term inmate-segregation facilities in its prisons, another federal court likewise found that "inmates, obviously in need of medical help, are instead inappropriately managed merely as miscreants."

In the large supermaxes of Texas, correctional bureaucrats have devised a systematically humiliating and, indeed, dehumanizing regimen of punishments for prisoners who elsewhere would more likely be considered disturbed: no real meals, only a "food loaf" of all the day's food ground together, for prisoners who don't return their food trays; paper gowns forced on those who won't wear their clothes. I myself have heard guards joking about "the mutilators" who slash their own veins to get attention. According to Thomas Conklin, a psychiatrist and medical director at the Hampden County Jail in Massachusetts who was called on to evaluate mental-health care in one Texas supermax, "All suicide gestures by inmates [were] seen as manipulating the correctional system with the conscious intent of secondary gain. In not one case was the inmate's behavior seen as reflecting mental pathology that could be treated." In most supermaxes, this kind of thinking still seems to be the norm.

Although prison authorities say that they provide mental health care to their supermax inmates, prisoner advocates tend to dismiss these claims. Documentary-film maker Jim Lipscomb, who has interviewed scores of inmates in Ohio's most secure prisons, reports that mental-health programs there often consist of little more than in-cell videos offering such platitudes as "If you feel angry at one of the guards, try not to curse and shout at him."

"That's called mental health!" Lipscomb says in amazement.

"The forceful rushes of this isolational perversion has pulled my essence into a cesspool," wrote one inmate from a supermax in Pennsylvania to Bonnie Kerness of the American Friends Service Committee (ASFC). "This just ain't life, pathologized in a subsumed litany of steel and cement codes preoccupied with the disturbing thrust of death." Accompanying the florid words was a penciled image of a grown man curled into a fetal position against a brick wall.

The American Civil Liberties Union's National Prison Project is currently spearheading three class action lawsuits against supermaxes in Illinois, Ohio, and Wisconsin. In the Wisconsin case, U.S. District Court Judge Barbara Crabb issued a preliminary ruling in October against the Supermax Correctional Institute in Boscobel after hearing the testimony of various health experts, including Dr. Terry Kupers, a Berkeley psychiatrist and author of the book *Prison Madness*. Kupers, who had been to Boscobel, told me that "there're a lot of crazy people in here, and they need to be removed on an emergency basis because it's not safe." In court, he testified that he had interviewed inmates who had been diagnosed with paranoid schizophrenia and who continued to hallucinate despite being given high doses of Thorazine.

Judge Crabb ordered prison authorities to remove five mentally ill inmates from the facility immediately and to provide an independent mental-health assessment to any inmate with symptoms of mental illness. "The conditions at Supermax are so severe and restrictive," Crabb wrote, "that they exacerbate the symptoms that mentally ill inmates exhibit. Many of the severe conditions serve no legitimate penological interest; they can only be considered punishment for punishment's sake." She also set a trial date in July 2002 to hear evidence on the lawsuit's larger claim that the stringent conditions of confinement at the supermax — the extreme isolation, extraordinary levels of surveillance, and tight restrictions on personal property — constitute cruel and unusual punishment.

For advocates of prisoners' rights, this is the Holy Grail: a broad new reading of the Eighth Amendment that would prohibit supermax-style incarceration. And a broad reading is warranted, they say, by the international conventions that the United States has signed — such as the International Covenant on Civil and Political Rights and the United Nations' Standard Minimum Rules for Treatment of Prisoners, which prohibit torture and regulate prison conditions much more stringently than does U.S. case law. It's also a matter of human decency, says attorney Jamie Fellner of Human Rights Watch. "The moral critique is this: Secure-housing units have been designed, at the best, with utter disregard for human misery. At the worst, it's a deliberate use of human misery for deterrence and punishment."

> "The moral critique is this: Secure-housing units have been designed, at the best, with utter disregard for human misery. At the worst, it's a deliberate use of human misery for deterrence and punishment."

Pending such a ruling, however, the filing of lawsuits provides virtually the only public accountability for what goes on in the supermaxes. With the exception of the New York Correctional Association, there is no legislatively mandated oversight agency watching the prisons — no civilian review board or independent ombudsman — in any state with supermax facilities. And over the past few years, in response to a rash of critical media coverage and unfavorable reports by human-rights organizations, many prison authorities have stopped allowing outside observers to visit these prisons or interview their inmates. (In the past, I have visited supermax sites in California, Texas, and Illinois to report on them. For this article, only Connecticut opened its supermax doors to me; Arizona, New Jersey, Pennsylvania, Texas, and Virginia all refused to do so.) Says Human Rights Watch's Fellner: "It is incredible that it's sometimes easier to get access to prisons in closed regimes in third-world countries than it is in the U.S."

If nothing else, the lawsuits are keeping the human-rights questions on the table. Supermax critics are also trying to call attention to the public costs, which are not just financial. Tens of thousands of inmates are now being held in supermax facilities, and almost all of them will be released one day. Indeed, many states are releasing such inmates directly from the SHUs to the streets after their sentence is up, without even reacclimatizing them to a social environment.

Although no national tracking surveys of ex-supermax and ex-SHU inmates have been carried out, anecdotal evidence suggests that many prisoners have been made more violent by their long-term spells of extreme deprivation and isolation. Bonnie Kerness of the AFSC talks about a whole new generation of cons coming out of supermax prisons with hair-trigger tempers. One former inmate at Rikers Island jail in New York City, who now participates in a rehabilitation program run by the Manhattan-based Fortune Society, recalls that prisoners routinely referred to "Bing monsters." (The Bing is the nickname for the Rikers Island version of the SHU.)

"The impact on society could be devastating," says Steve Rigg, a former correctional officer who worked at California's supermax prison in Corcoran during the mid-1990s and blew the whistle on his fellow officers for organizing fights between rival prison-gang members. Corcoran's administration was overhauled after this, but Rigg warns that the underlying dangers in undermonitored supermaxes remain. "There's more [inmate] recidivism," he says of SHUs. "They breed the worst."

DISCUSSION

1. When you hear the word *supermax*, what are the first ideas or images that come to mind? What is the profile of the typical inmate in such a facility? Do these assumptions or stereotypes get reinforced or challenged in Abramsky's essay?

2. As Abramsky notes, the primary rationale for the supermax is punishment. Facilities like this are not intended to rehabilitate inmates, but rather designed simply to house those offenders considered "the worst of the worst." To what extent do you think this same rationale underlies the more general view of criminals in our culture? And is it valid?

3. In our culture, which offenses get labeled the "worst of the worst"? Are there gaps or omissions in what does and does not fall into this category? What standard or norm do you think should be used to make this designation?

WRITING

4. The most typical punishments at the supermax, Abramsky writes, involve isolation and sensory deprivation. Write an essay in which you argue either in favor of or against forms of punishment that use these two techniques. What goals or objectives does it seem designed to achieve? And in your view, are they valid? How or how not?

5. As Abramsky notes, one of the most common ways that prisoners rebel against the restrictions at the supermax is by "acting out": that is, by deliberately flouting the prison policy governing what they are allowed to do or say. In an essay, take up the idea that this form of resistance is, as Abramsky's term for it implies, a strategy that revolves primarily around "acting," or playing a role. To what extent does it make sense to view these deliberate acts of misbehavior as attempts to challenge the conventional roles for how guards and prisoners are supposed to interact? What particular norms or scripts of prison life does this kind of resistance seem to rewrite?

6. How does Abramsky's description of prison punishment compare to Kathy Dobie's (p. 358) description of military basic training tactics? What do these two forms of "training" seem to share in common? What practices are parallel? Where do they diverge? What larger goals or objectives stand behind them?

BOB MOSER

Make Metaphor No More?

Sportspeople Rethink Their Words of War

Have we learned to talk about sports as if it were war, and vice versa? Has the language of combat come to saturate our sports talk so thoroughly that we now no longer draw any meaningful distinctions between war and games? Contemplating precisely this possibility, Bob Moser explores some of the ways our sports clichés have come to function as one of our culture's most powerful social scripts, teaching us how to view violence itself as a natural, inevitable, even enjoyable aspect of our everyday lives. Moser is a contributing writer for the *Nation* and editorial director of the Nation Institute's Investigative Fund; his writing has also appeared in *Rolling Stone*. He is also a senior writer for *Intelligence Report,* a publication of the Southern Poverty Law Center (SPLC), a civil rights group based in Birmingham, Alabama, that tracks hate groups and white supremacists and develops tolerance education programs. The following essay first appeared on the Web at tolerance.org, a project of the SPLC.

"SPORTSCASTERS AND SPORTSWRITERS CARRY AROUND A MENTAL thesaurus that seems to have been compiled at the Pentagon," *Sports Illustrated* columnist Jack McCallum noted two weeks after the September 11 terrorist attacks. As if to prove his point, McCallum's magazine had positively brimmed with supporting evidence on the week of the attacks.

A story headlined "American Revolution" described a "battle for supremacy" in women's tennis. The golf section featured "Famous Flameouts," about once-prominent players who lost their luster. A pro football quarterback was deemed the "Baltimore Bullet," while a running back was praised as "the most dangerous weapon in the offense." A baseball article marveled at the success of a pitcher with "a less-than-overpowering arsenal."

This was par for the course before September 11. The sports-as-war metaphor has been folded into American culture for more than a century. Sportswriters, broadcasters, coaches, athletes, and fans are accustomed to borrowing liberally from the battlefield when they talk about their games — and the more bellicose, it seems, the better. American football, designed from the start to "simulate" war with offenses and defenses grappling for ground, is especially drenched in martial jargon: Coaches are field generals, if not commanders. Players are foot soldiers organized into platoons. Special teams are suicide squads. Long passes are bombs, often thrown from shotgun formations as part of an aerial attack mapped out in a war room.

Normally, sportspeople do not bat an eye at such terms. But when the United States declared a literal war, many began to reconsider the metaphors they use to talk about the games. And in the process, some went a step further, reconsidering the nature of the games themselves.

While they waited for regular sports schedules to resume after September 11, sportswriters and broadcasters — and even some athletes — solemnly vowed to find themselves a new thesaurus. "In the wake of the terrorist attacks," wrote USA Today's Christine Brennan, "our hyperbolic, self-serving, and often militaristic vernacular must change." The Rocky Mountain News pledged, "We shall never again refer to a long touchdown pass as a bomb."

Sunday Night Football producer Jay Rothman instructed his announcers to "avoid the military cliches: the blitzes, the sacks, the throwing bullets." Rothman's network, ESPN, canceled a pay-per-view ad for college football games promising "Saturday soldiers fighting for every touchdown."

Ray Brown, a left guard for the San Francisco 49ers, told reporters he would no longer cast himself as a soldier. "Football is nothing like war, nothing like battle," he said. "If I've ever used that analogy, I apologize."

Not every sportsperson was ready to swear off the war talk. "What a numbskull notion," wrote Bob Wolfley in the Milwaukee Journal Sentinel. "These comparisons are natural. It should not be a source of guilt, or a reason to alert the sensitivity storm troopers."

Wolfley's idea that sports-as-war metaphors are "natural" found plenty of support. Arguing against "a preemptive strike on our own vocabulary," Boston Globe columnist Jan Freeman declared that sports were "invented precisely to serve as ritualized battles," making the battlefield language both inevitable and appropriate.

Rubbish, says Kenn Finkel. "You can see where the war cliches come from, but does that make it right?"

A longtime sports editor at newspapers including the New York Times and Miami Herald, Finkel calls the sports-as-war idea "a pretty big stretch. It's part of the jargon, but that doesn't mean it's part of the game."

Finkel has campaigned for years to excise war cliches from sportswriting. He keeps a file of the worst offenders, including this pearl from a basketball writer:

> Bodies were flying in the Laker-Clipper skirmish last night — as if both teams had marched into a mine field. After being repulsed for years like Cossacks charging a machine gun nest, the Clippers were good and ready to change dog tags with the Lakers. But, though they've lost some comrades to boot hill in this battle of a basketball season, the Lakers still run this neighborhood.

429

Finkel is convinced that "any use of a war metaphor is overuse." For one thing, he says, "it's bad writing." For another, "It's tasteless. There are people who've lost people and friends and families in war."

"The war metaphors were never appropriate," Ray Ratto agreed in the *San Francisco Chronicle*, "and all you needed to discover that was to use one around someone who had actually been in Vietnam, or Korea, or one of the theaters of World War II."

If you ask the nation's foremost authority on metaphor, there's more at stake here than writing badly or offending veterans. George Lakoff, professor of cognitive linguistics at the University of California at Berkeley, has written widely on the ways in which metaphors shape our understanding of the world and influence our actions. He believes that equating sports and war warps our view of both.

"When you understand sports as war," Lakoff says, "you have a deficient frame" for comprehending an actual war like the one that began in September. "You wind up getting a view of war that doesn't have most of the horrors of war. You don't think in terms of body parts, blood and guts, widows, years of being crippled, starvation, refugees. So you say, 'Let's go to war,' and it sounds like we're going to play video games."

Lakoff believes that the way we see war these days — primarily on television — only reinforces the simplistic notions we draw from sports.

"The Gulf War looked like a video game when you watched it on TV," Lakoff says. "Nobody realized what was being bombed. Nobody realized that the result on the civilian population would be overwhelming, staggering, after the bombing stopped.

"The assumption becomes: If war is a game, if war is a sport, then once the war stops, the effects of it stop."

Do sports fans really confuse their favorite games with war? It certainly looked that way on October 7, the Sunday when the United States and Great Britain began to bomb Afghanistan. At Lowe's Motor Speedway in Concord, North Carolina, video images of the attack were flashed across the stadium scoreboard while race cars continued to speed around the track below. The crowd roared its approval. So did the football fans in Atlanta's Georgia Dome, where a public-address announcer interrupted the first quarter of the Falcons-Bears game to announce the attacks. Fans rose, applauded and chanted "U-S-A! U-S-A!" in much the same way they would cheer their team.

The reaction came as no surprise to Alfie Kohn, author of *No Contest: The Case against Competition*. Rather than providing a safe outlet for "natural" aggressions, he argues that sports create aggressive behavior.

"People are rarely killed on football fields," Kohn says. "But we know from empirical research that competition makes people more aggressive. You learn with sports to follow directions in order to defeat other people who are attempting to defeat you. Studies have shown a positive correlation among cultures that are warlike and those that have competitive sports."

After all, Kohn notes, it was President Eisenhower — a legendary general in World War II — who made the famous declaration: "The true mission of American sports is to prepare young people for war."

> *"The true mission of American sports is to prepare young people for war."*

Whether or not they agree with Eisenhower, sportspeople have so thoroughly absorbed the sports-as-war idea that the metaphors don't seem likely to go away for good — no matter how many proclamations are made to the contrary. After all, they outlasted World War II and Vietnam.

"Americans love to move metaphors around," says Paul Dickson, baseball writer and author of *War Slang.* "It's the way we think. And if you choose the wrong one, it seems like you can't stop it."

Kenn Finkel reluctantly agrees. "You can't stomp out cliches," says the man who has spent years trying to do just that. "Writers reach back and use them because they're easy. Rather than sit there and stare at the computer screen, you reach for what's easy."

As an editor, Finkel often questioned writers' use of war terms — to little effect. "You tell them, 'You've got a gratuitous use of war metaphors in your story,' and they just stare at you. They don't realize it at all what they're doing when they call passes bombs."

Oddly, some sportswriters have defended their use of war slang on similar grounds. The overfamiliarity of sports terms like "bombs," "blitzes," and "bullets," they argue, takes the sting out of the original concepts. "We have used the metaphors so regularly and so often that they are dead," Wolfley wrote. "They are ingrained. These comparisons have lost their electricity."

Finkel enthusiastically disagrees with what Lakoff calls the "dead metaphor hypothesis."

"Have these terms lost their significance?" Finkel asks rhetorically.

"Ask the people in Kabul if 'bomb' has lost its significance! Ask the people in a Greyhound bus station!"

Or ask Bruce Rollinson, football coach at Mater Dei High School in Orange County, California. On September 12, Rollinson was walking down a hallway when he overheard an assistant coach talking to a player about the upcoming game. We don't want to get "bombed" by our opponent on Friday night, the coach was saying — until he caught himself and there was a brief, uncomfortable silence. "In sports, we always draw parallels to war," Rollinson reflected afterward. "But these days, we have to be a little bit guarded."

For the moment, most everyone in hallways, on sports pages, and on television is guarding against military jargon. The exceptions — like a

Sports Illustrated story about baseball pitchers, headlined "Armed and Dangerous" — have begun to stick out, where they used to be the norm. Certainly, no newspaper would think of headlining a story about this year's baseball World Series the way one New York daily did last October: "War!"

Alfie Kohn, for one, holds out hope that the language of sports won't be the only thing that changes.

"Tough times can make people dig in their heels, wave the flag and fall back on the usual 'us-versus-them' paradigm in all areas of life," he says.

"However, a stark reminder of where competition leads might be just what we need to rethink our basic assumptions and our state religion, which is trying to defeat other people."

DISCUSSION

1. In the aftermath of the September 11 attacks, says Moser, it has become far more difficult to accept our sports culture's reliance on war metaphors as an unremarkable given. What, according to Moser, has changed? What is it about this particular event that has made our long-standing recourse to such language seem less OK? Do you share this view?

2. It is quite possible, writes Moser, that the prevalence of war metaphors in sports has led us to accept, even celebrate, violence as a normal part of our lives. Conversely, however, it is also possible that such language may well offer a safer surrogate for violence: an outlet for channeling it in less harmful directions. Which of these views seems more plausible to you? Do you think that both could be true? How or how not?

3. One key question underlying Moser's essay has to do with where our cultural penchant for aggression actually comes from. Does the violent character of such sports as football or boxing simply reflect a more endemic tendency toward aggression in our culture at large? Or do such spectacles (as well as the language we use to describe them) in fact create this tendency? How do you answer this question? Do competitive or violent sporting spectacles actually make people more aggressive? If so, how? If not, why not?

WRITING

4. Moser criticizes the sports-as-war metaphor on several levels. Write an essay in which you discuss each of the reasons Moser finds these metaphors distasteful, and why. In your opinion, which, if any, of these arguments presents the most pressing reason for dispensing with these metaphors? Why?

5. The Scenes and Un-Scenes feature for this chapter (p. 434) presents an array of images showing the marriage of sports and violence. Write an essay in which you discuss how the sports-as-war metaphor is present not only in the way we *talk* about sports, but also in the way we *watch* them. Do you think the visual presentation of the sports-as-war metaphor is weaker than when it's spoken? Why or why not?

6. Moser and Chris Hedges (p. 368) both share an interest in what Moser calls "dead metaphors": words that by virtue of being repeated over and over again lose their capacity to convey the reality or truth of what they purport to describe. Choose one of the war words from the sports world that Moser cites and discuss the ways it functions, in your view, as an example of a dead metaphor. In what contexts and for what reasons does it usually get invoked? And in what ways does it, through sheer overuse, obscure or deaden our sense of what war actually is? How do you think Hedges would evaluate the same term? How much of your own view do you think Hedges would share? Are there aspects of combat that he would argue this term does accurately capture?

Scenes and Un-Scenes:
We Are the Champions

Virtually every major sport in our culture makes use of its own set of militaristic or combat-related vocabulary to convey the nature of the contest and elevate or dramatize competition. Losing teams "take a beating" and winning teams "slaughter" the competition. Quarterbacks throw "long bombs," unless they're "sacked" first. It almost doesn't seem possible to make sense of sports in our culture without reference to the role violence plays, even if that violence appears largely in the language used to describe something as ordinary as throwing a ball. Visually, the sports-as-war metaphor is seen everywhere from the Olympics to movies to advertising. However, it is also the case that virtually every sport has recently experienced some controversy or scandal related to a moment when things have gotten a little bit *too* violent. Whether they involve the on-court brawls that have marred the NBA or the recent spate of life-endangering concussions in the NFL, off-field crimes or on-field infractions, these moments remind us that things may not be as clear-cut as they first appear. When we closely examine sports as a form of combat, what rules are we asked to accept regarding the limits of conflating sports and war? What messages do popular visual media send when they present images that liken a sports venue to a battlefield?

▶▶ *When the 1980 U.S. hockey team came from behind to beat the seemingly unbeatable team from the USSR, the game grew to represent to many Americans a triumph of the American way of life, of democracy over communism. Dubbed "The Miracle on Ice," the match resonated with another theme common to sports tales: the underdog. Scoring what was widely considered one of the greatest upsets in Olympic history (the Soviets had not lost a gold medal in ice hockey in the previous twenty-one Olympics), the triumph of an underappreciated and over-matched American team was celebrated by Americans of all stripes as a vindication for the "little guy": a potent affirmation of the grit, hope, and determination that supposedly defined the essential American character. (See next page.)*

▲▲ Cold War anxiety was given the Hollywood treatment in Rocky IV, where Sylvester Stallone as the title character defeats Soviet boxer Ivan Drago in a climactic against-all-odds final bout. As the classic underdog, the character Rocky Balboa has come to stand within the public imagination as the quintessential American as well: a living embodiment of the never-say-die resiliency believed to characterize the national temper. Viewed through the experiences of this emblematic underdog, fighting becomes not only a laudable form of self-defense but a kind of moral crusade as well: a heroic defense of the values and "ways of life" all Americans supposedly cherish.

▲▲ Denounced by sports fans and commentators alike, the recent spates of on-the-court brawls in the NBA are viewed not as manifestations of our most commonly held values and ideals but as symptoms of the problems plaguing our society at large. Unlike their feel-good counterparts, these spectacles don't lend themselves to any sentimental David versus Goliath, "good guys" versus "bad guys" type of framework. Behind all the grunting and punching that goes on here, we are told, there is no idealism, no higher moral purpose. Instead, we just have a bunch of people breaking the rules and slugging it out. What is it about this kind of fight that makes it exempt from the valorizing and mythologizing enjoyed by the previous examples?

All his life, Phil Weston has dreamed
of being on a winning team.
Phil... your time has come.

Will Ferrell   Robert Duvall

Kicking & Screaming

MAY 13

▲▲ It is often a very thin line in sports that separates the "noble battle" from the
all-out brawl. Indeed, the question of how to tell "good" fights from "bad" has
increasingly been taken up, debated, and even satirized in our popular culture. The
2005 Will Ferrell comedy Kicking and Screaming makes light of the phenomenon of
soccer parents, those who take their children's sporting events a little too seriously.
Ferrell's character is a children's soccer coach who becomes so obsessed with
victory that he encourages naked aggression and bad sportsmanship. In the end,
what does a film like this have to say about how seriously we take sports as a form
of combat?

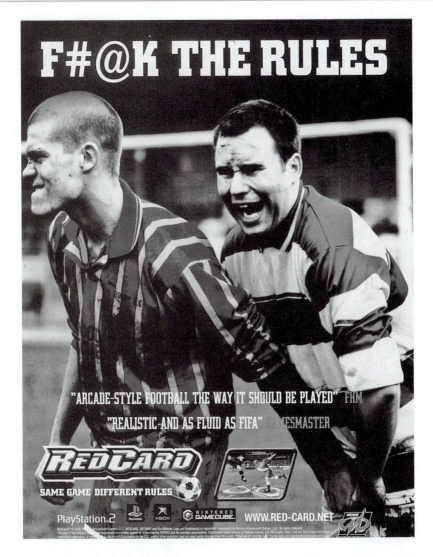

There are other moments, however, when hyper-competition and no-holds-barred violence get presented in our popular culture as something empowering. In the above example, the willingness to win at all costs, to disregard all rules is promoted as its own kind of ideal. Recycling the age-old conception of sports as a kind of masculine proving ground, ads like this one posit violence as the surest means for proving one's strength — and, by extension, one's worthiness as a true winner. What do you make of this proposition? How empowering does this type of violence seem to be?

DISCUSSION

1. Choose one of these images that in your view offers an example of the ways "good guys" and "bad guys" typically get defined in our culture. What are the differences in appearance or behavior that you note? Why do you think they are presented this way?

2. Choose one of the images you think offers a vision or definition of a "good fight." What specific ideals or benefits do you associate with it? What positive effects does it imply that fighting can achieve? What useful lessons does it suggest this kind of fighting teaches? Do you share this view?

3. Choose one of the images you think offers a vision or definition of a "bad fight." What specific problems or dangers does it associate with its example? What negative effects does it imply fighting in this way will have?

WRITING

4. Choose one of the previous images and write an essay in which you discuss how it visually portrays American values of valor, patriotism, or resolve. Does the image seem like a good example of these values to you, or is it in some way critical? How do these values relate to our ideals about how we should (or should not) fight?

5. In "Make Metaphor No More?" (p. 428) Bob Moser covers several of the reasons why the sports-as-war metaphor has been criticized in sports writing. Write an essay in which you argue how Moser might respond to this series of images. In your opinion, is the visual metaphor of sports-as-war as problematic as the metaphors often used in sports writing? Why or why not? How might you recompose these images so that the combat metaphor is removed? Would the image be as powerful?

6. How do you think Gerard Jones (p. 400) would respond to these images? Based on his own argument about media and violence, what sorts of lessons would he draw from the depictions of violence these examples present? Choose a couple of the images and present a discussion of how you think Jones would respond to and/or assess its messages. What kind of effect would he likely believe this image would have on its audience? What kind of script would he suggest it might write?

Putting It into Practice:
Community Conflicts

Now that you've read the chapter selections, try applying your conclusions to your own life by completing the following exercises.

DISSECTING VIOLENCE AS NEWS   Watch an episode of your local evening news and take notes on the way that violence is covered in the media, whether it is verbal conflict, violent crime, or war coverage. What words are used to describe the story? What images are shown? Do any particular types of conflict receive weightier treatment than others? Use your notes to write a brief essay about what you think the rules are that govern how the media discusses violence. If you were in charge, would you change these rules? Why?

PERSONAL CONFLICT   Choose a moment from your own experience where you engaged in fighting that you felt was "right" (that is, justified, useful or beneficial, perhaps even enjoyable). Describe this experience in as specific terms as possible. What factors made fighting in this moment seem OK? Next, choose a moment from your own experience where you engaged in fighting you felt was "wrong" (that is, unjustified, unnecessary, harmful or counterproductive, upsetting). What are the key differences between this experience and the previous one? Using these two contrasting experiences as your guide, come up with what, for you, seem to be the rules for differentiating an acceptable from an unacceptable form of fighting.

FLAME WAR   As Katy Vine illustrates in "Love and War in Cyber-space" (p. 380), the Internet has become a new battleground. With the rise of social networking sites like Facebook and MySpace, we have more opportunities than ever to take our aggression out on others over the Web. Write an essay in which you discuss what the appeal of virtual fighting might be. How does the Internet change the dynamics of a fight? Have you ever engaged in fighting over the Internet?

er Mrs. Wood
: A+ — Excellent, Independent work,
rage; B—Satisfactory Work of Average
s Passing But Can Be Improved, D—
—Absolute Failure.
Days
Deportment
English
Mathematics
Social Science
Spelling
History
5.
6.

6 **How We**

LEARN

Introduction

SCHOOL RULES

If you were to create your own school, what would it look like? What kinds of courses would get taught? What kind of work would get assigned, and how would it be evaluated? What sorts of activities and routines would organize daily classroom life? What roles would you script for teachers and students? As you consider all this, think too about what such a school would *not* look like: what sorts of lessons would never get taught, what rules would never get written, what kinds of teachers and students you would never see. After you've considered these questions, ask yourself a final one: How much of your experience at school has ever measured up to this ideal?

Everybody Knows That . . .

— *Detroit, Michigan, rules posted on a classroom door at Guyton Elementary School, part of the Detroit public school system*

It is difficult to think of an environment in contemporary life more rule-bound than school. If you doubt the validity of this claim, take a moment to compile a mental list of all regulations by which a typical school day is organized. We all know firsthand that once we walk into the classroom, precious few activities are really up for debate. In ways that are perhaps a bit more explicit than elsewhere, school is a world defined by very firm boundaries and governed by very clear requirements. Rules tell us what kinds of homework we have to complete and what kinds of tests we have to take, decree which courses are mandatory and which ones are optional, mandate the number of hours per week and the number of weeks per semester we need to spend at school. In some cases, in fact, rules even set standards for what we can wear or how we can talk. Underlying and justifying these many regula-tions is one final expectation: that we look on the rigid organization of school life as something both indispensable and nonnegotiable, an essential compo-nent of a quality education. Without things like homework and pop quizzes, standardized testing and attendance policies, graduation requirements and semester schedules, P.E. and recess, we are supposed to believe, real learning simply wouldn't happen.

But what exactly is *real* learning? And who should be given the authority to decide this? Do all the expectations and instructions we are called on to follow at school really turn us into better educated people? While school is

444

one of the few genuine touchstones in our lives — one of only a handful of institutions with which we all have had some degree of personal experience — it remains one of the most problematic as well. Because so many of the day-to-day decisions are taken out of our hands, it doesn't always feel as if the education we spend so many years pursuing actually belongs to us. We may wonder whether there is a logical connection between the tests we take and the grades we receive or between our personal opinions about a poem or short story and the views espoused by a professor in lecture, but given the way school is typically set up, there isn't a whole lot we can do about it. No matter what ideas we have about what rules should and should not govern our school experiences, we also know that subordinating these decisions to somebody else is part of our jobs.

For a particularly vivid illustration, take the example of grading. Grades are absolutely essential, so goes the conventional thinking, because they alone offer educators a reliable and verifiable way of assessing students' work. Without grades, how would we ever know if students were measuring up? But notice the unspoken assumptions that lie beneath this anxious query, most prominently among them the conviction that grades are accurate barometers of student ability and achievement. To believe in the validity and necessity of grading, we also have to believe that the standards on which they rest — the standards that differentiate, say, A work from C work — are grounded in a fair and universally applicable understanding of what good work involves. Nor do the assumptions stop here. We could easily probe the implications of

> ### *Everybody Knows That . . .*
>
> a. The Honor Code is an undertaking of the students, individually and collectively:
> 1. that they will not give or receive aid in examinations; that they will not give or receive unpermitted aid in class work, in the preparation of reports, or in any other work that is to be used by the instructor as the basis of grading;
> 2. that they will do their share and take an active part in seeing to it that others as well as themselves uphold the spirit and letter of the Honor Code.
>
> *— From the Stanford University Honor Code*

> ### *Everybody Knows That . . .*
>
> "I recognize the great work that some of our urban districts are doing, in fact I cited them in my remarks today. They are blazing the trail, they're the folks that are not in denial; they are working hard to close the achievement gap and are seeing some of the best progress.
>
> But I would say that no small part of that is due to No Child Left Behind, to this annual measurement, to paying attention to every child, every year, and to prescribing a cure, an instructional cure if you will, so that we can get kids on grade level by 2013–14, as the law requires."
>
> *— Secretary of Education Margaret Spellings on The NewsHour with Jim Lehrer, PBS, April 7, 2005*

this grading norm even further, posing questions about the ultimate wisdom of any system that so conspicuously emphasizes competition and rank. Does an arrangement that compels students to focus so much attention on the external markers of achievement really offer the best way to encourage meaningful learning? This question might well lead us to rethink the kinds of authority that typically get vested in teachers: the authority not only to grade student work, but also to evaluate, assess, and judge more generally. Posing these kinds of questions not only challenges some of the rules by which school conventionally operates, but, even more fundamentally, also starts the process of unlearning the core lessons that have taught us what a worthwhile education is.

In many ways, this unlearning process is already taking place. Education is one of the most contentiously debated issue of our time. We argue over the merits of public versus private schooling, over the limits of free speech on campus, over the place of religious belief in the classroom, over how to best utilize the educational resources of the Internet. Educational issues anchor our debates about multiculturalism, about economic and social class, about free speech. Whether it involves a court case adjudicating the merits of teaching intelligent design or a state initiative to require school uniforms, a dispute over online university accreditation or protests regarding a college's financial ties to companies that exploit their workers, school-related issues and controversies remain at the very center of our national life. So engrossing and encompassing a topic has education become that we could easily extend the scope of this investigation well beyond the walls of the classroom. The other chapters in this book help illustrate the argument that our larger culture itself is a classroom in which we are all pupils.

Taken together, the readings assembled in this chapter provide some sense of how richly diverse and broadly encompassing the issue of education is. Alissa Quart begins this chapter with an examination of the popularity of educational products for babies and what this says about the competitive desire some parents have to breed geniuses. Several writers examine some discrete aspect of our contemporary schooling practices. Alfie Kohn, for example, calls into question the conventional wisdom regarding grades and grading, while Michael Berube examines the dynamics of classroom conflict and attempts to refute some of the most common and politically charged objections leveled these days against higher education as a liberal conspiracy. Whereas Kohn and Berube criticize specific aspects of formal schooling, former teacher John Taylor

Everybody Knows That . . .

"This textbook contains material on evolution. Evolution is a theory, not a fact, regarding the origin of living things. This material should be approached with an open mind, studied carefully, and critically considered."

Approved by
Cobb County Board of Education
Thursday, March 28, 2002

— *Sticker added to Cobb County, Georgia, science textbooks*

Gatto argues that we ought to dismantle the entire system. In a personal comment on the educational system, bell hooks recounts her experiences navigating the educational and the social boundaries she encountered as a working-class student of color. Looking at the role of technology in education, reporter Brigid Schulte writes an eye-opening account of plagiarism that surveys the online resources students so often use these days and how drastically this material has altered the ways students think about and define cheating. Jonathan Kozol's essay catalogs the insidious ways that business language and business logic has come to underlie much of what happens in our elementary classrooms. Looking outside the campus altogether, Steve Salerno wonders about the sort of instruction undertaken by the army of self-help writers and gurus now prominent in our culture, asking whether this burgeoning industry teaches lessons that are not only dubious but harmful as well.

"EVERYBODY KNOWS THAT" EXERCISE

Choose one of the images or quotations featured in the margins on the previous pages and answer the following questions:

1. What does this image or quotation ask you to believe?
2. What are the particular ideas, values, or attitudes it invites us to accept as *normal*?
3. What would it feel like to act on or act out these norms in our personal lives?

Rule *Maker* > > > > > > > Rule *Breaker*

" *The United States increasingly needs what the best of higher education has to offer:* graduates who contribute positively to economic development through increased private and public revenues, greater productivity, increased consumption, more workforce flexibility, and decreased reliance on government financial support. . . . 'What do students really learn?' and 'What's the value-added?' are questions increasingly being asked across America."

— CHARLES MILLER AND CHERYL OLDHAM, THE SECRETARY OF EDUCATION'S COMMISSION ON THE FUTURE OF HIGHER EDUCATION, 2005

" *Is this, really, what it all comes down to? Is future productivity, from this point on, to be the primary purpose of the education we provide our children? Is this to be the way in which we decide if teachers are complying with their obligations to their students and society? . . . [T]here must be something more to life as it is lived by six-year-olds or ten-year-olds, or by teenagers for that matter, than concerns about 'successful global competition.'"*

— EDUCATION WRITER AND ACTIVIST, JONATHAN KOZOL, 2005

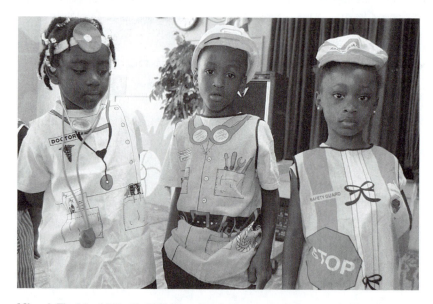

Miami, Florida, Little Haiti Edison Park Elementary School Career Day student uniforms

THE U.S. DEPARTMENT OF EDUCATION VS. JONATHAN KOZOL

When it comes to something as fundamental as education, it would be reassuring if there were a consensus on exactly what our national priorities and objectives should be. Unfortunately, though, this is far from the case. Over the last several years, in fact, the public discussion of this question has increasingly pitted two antithetical educational models against each other. The quotation from the Secretary of Education's Commission on the Future of Higher Education articulates the first model: The goal of schooling is to prepare students to become productive workers and contributors to America's market-driven economy. Jonathon Kozol sums up the second model: The goal of education is to make students into critical thinkers, to foster a familiarity with a diverse range of viewpoints, and to instill an appreciation for how varied and complex the world around us truly is. While terms such as *critical thinking* and *intellectual inquiry* loom large for defenders of the liberal arts ideal, the most prominent catchwords in the market-based lexicon include *productivity, workforce preparedness*, and *efficiency.* Within these competing vocabularies, we can get a fairly clear sense of the ways each side defines what education is as well as what it is for. Envisioning school as a kind of preprofessional training ground, the first model defines education as an economic resource, a set of discrete skills whose value is measured in terms of usefulness in the marketplace. Casting school as the setting for disinterested inquiry, the liberal arts model defines the nature and value of learning intrinsically, independent of any vocational purpose to which it might be put. What does it mean to be truly educated? How do we define legitimate or valuable knowledge? What are the rules by which our competence and skills, our abilities and intelligence, should really be measured?

FIND THE RULES: Write an brief essay in which you list all the ways you normally hear education described — in the news, in your classes, in your personal relationships with friends and families. Which of the two models represented by the quotations in this feature do these descriptions seem to align with?

MAKE YOUR OWN RULES: Write an essay in which you argue in favor of one of the characterizations of education featured here. Is there any way to reconcile these points of view so that a definition of education can encompass both models? How is that possible?

ALISSA QUART

The Baby Genius Edutainment Complex: The New Smart Baby Products

Is it really such a great thing to be called "gifted"? What do we even mean by this term, and how has it come to wield such influence over the ways parents and educators think about childhood learning? Turning a skeptical eye toward the burgeoning market for baby-education material, social critic Alissa Quart uncovers the different anxieties and aspirations that stand behind our culture's current preoccupation with youngsters and "high achievement." "Where," she asks, "is all this aggressive early learning taking us?" Quart is the author of two books, *Branded: The Buying and Selling of Teenagers* (2003) and *Hothouse Kids: The Dilemma of Gifted Children* (2006), from which this selection is taken. She has contributed articles and opinion pieces to publications including *New York Magazine*, the *New York Times, Elle*, and *Atlantic Monthly*. She is a graduate of Brown University and the Columbia University School of Journalism.

"She's ten months old, for God's sake," I said. "I know," Seymour said. "They have ears. They can hear." The story Seymour read to Franny that night, by flashlight, was a favorite of his, a Taoist tale. To this day, Franny swears that she remembers Seymour reading it to her. — J. D. Salinger, "Raise High the Roof Beam, Carpenters"

ONE DVD IS FULL OF IMAGES OF CHILDREN BIG AND SMALL, ALL holding violins, recorders, guitars, and cellos — while a song in the background insists that when playing music, children should "Do your best! And never less!" Another contains images of toddlers on a putting green or wandering around a basketball court and a baby with a golf ball, all set to bouncy music with words like *teamwork* flashing on the screen, in the hopes of inspiring a generation of toddler athletes. Another features a puppet called Vincent van Goat that introduces an infant to six primary colors and then to the colors as they appear in van Gogh's paintings *The Starry Night* and *What Fields with Reaper at Sunrise*. Yet another DVD contains colorful, high-contrast imagery of babies playing with blocks and balloons, counting tomatoes, and sibilating words in English, French, and Spanish.

These infant and toddler DVDs may be cute or even visually striking, but their selling point is that they offer the youngest viewer — intended age sometimes as young as newborn and up — a great deal more. The *Brainy Baby Left and Right Brain* DVD set, from a company whose motto heralds "a little genius in the making," claims to "engage your child's whole brain (logic and creative) to help boost your baby's intellect." The *Right Brain* disc features classical music and focuses on "cognitive skills," among them "Rhymes, Spatial Reasoning, and Imagination, Intuition, and more!" The *Left Brain* disc has bright visuals, patterns, and shapes in red, black, and white, with letters of the alphabet, and voiceovers offering words in Spanish and French. The *Baby Prodigy* DVD claims to do nothing short of giving a child "A Head Start in Life!" The disc's back copy reads, "Did you know that you can actually help to enhance the development of your baby's brain? The first 30 months of life is the period where a child's brain undergoes its most critical stages of evolution . . . together we can help to make your child the next Baby Prodigy!" The *So Smart!* two-disc set, suggested for infants of nine months and up, features Mozart and Vivaldi and interactive alphabet games the infant can play on the television using the remote control, while the *V. Smile* video game system promotes itself with the catchphrase "Turn Game Time into Brain Time."

Perhaps the best known of these products is the Baby Einstein series, which offers promotional materials swaddled in the rhetoric of stimulation: the word *multi-sensory* appears frequently. These DVDs tend to feature the alphabet or musical scales or colors, demonstrated through toys and lights and, of course, classical music. In fact, almost all of the company's DVDs are named after a crew of infantilized dead white male geniuses: *Baby Galileo*, *Baby Shakespeare*, *Baby Wordsworth*, and *Baby Van Gogh*. The Baby Einstein PR rep explains the product name by saying, "Albert Einstein exemplifies someone who was truly curious about the world around him." Her remark unwittingly undercuts the very premise of the series, suggesting not that babies can be made into Einsteins but that Einstein remained, in some sense, a baby. Additionally, I couldn't help but recall that Albert Einstein was not an early bloomer.

These videos are part of a DVD and toy fad that I call the Baby Genius Edutainment Complex. What I mean by the word *complex* here is two things. The first is as in "military-industrial complex": as Webster's has it, "a whole made up of complicated or interrelated parts," and "a group of obviously related units of which the degree and nature of the relationship is imperfectly known." The second is the psychological sense of the word: an exaggerated reaction to a situation. The complex is the first stage of the

> *The complex is the first stage of the American passion for raising gifted children, reflecting the faith that . . . bright children can be invented.*

American passion for raising gifted children, reflecting the faith that, exposed to enough media, typically in tandem with equally stirring classes, bright children can be invented, and that precocity is the best insurance policy for one's children. The complex is also composed of products and companies now promising to urge on children's precocity.

This complex is relatively new. Until 1997, there were no Baby Einstein videos. By 2003, 32 percent of our nation's infants owned at least one Baby Einstein video. Ten percent of kids aged six months to two years have a television remote designed for children, according to a 2003 report by the Henry J. Kaiser Family Foundation, *Zero to Six: Electronic Media in the Lives of Infants, Toddlers, and Preschoolers.*[1] Forty-two percent of children in this age group watch a videotape or a DVD each day. According to the 2005 Kaiser report *A Teacher in the Living Room? Educational Media for Babies, Toddlers, and Preschoolers,*[2] on the average babies six months to three years spend an hour watching TV and forty-seven minutes a day on videos or computers, all despite the American Academy of Pediatrics' 1999 recommendation of no screen time at all for babies under two and no more than an hour or two of highly educational screen media for children ages two and older.[3] No wonder, then, that developmental videos and DVDs in 2004 brought in profits of $100 million. That same year, videos and DVDs for preschool-age children earned $500 million. (From 2003 to 2004, overall sales of educational toys increased by 19 percent.)

One boon to the producers of children's DVDs is that the parent consumer appears more willing to buy rather than rent them because of their "repeatability" — that is, infants and young children, unlike adults, enjoy watching the same DVD over and over again. (The irony here is that babies and toddlers like doing a lot of different kinds of things over and over again, in a level of repetition that adults might find intolerable, especially repeated actions with objects that are bright and shiny.) Chasing this opportunity, studios such as Warner Brothers have spent the last decade adding children's programming with an educational component into the mix. Baby Einstein is owned by Disney. The toy companies have also gotten into the act: Fisher-Price, a major DVD producer, is a subsidiary of Mattel. For the nation's biggest companies, the incentive to get into the edutainment DVD market is as clear as phonics. It's clear for smaller companies as well: as Dennis Fedoruk, president of Brainy Baby, says, "There's a bumper crop of new kids each month, after all."

But the impetus behind the Baby Genius Edutainment Complex's acceleration has not been just savvy marketing. The popularity of DVDs with classical music, pinwheels, and colorful imagery coincided with — and was also incited by — theories of infant and childhood learning that became fashionable in the early 1990s. As Liz Iftikhar, founder and president of Baby BumbleBee, puts it, the kid vid biz emerged on the back of the Mozart effect.

The phenomenon called the Mozart effect made its first appearance in a study done by Gordon Shaw and Frances Rauscher in 1993.[4] One group of college students listened to ten minutes of a Mozart sonata, while another group didn't. Then both groups took a paper-folding-and-cutting test. Those who had listened to the music reportedly performed better than those who had not. Shaw and Rauscher concluded that listening to Mozart improved the students' very short-term spatial thinking. A second study in 1995 yielded similar findings.

The benefits of listening to Mozart soon became folk wisdom, and Mozart became even more synonymous with early learning and precocity. From the start of the renown of the Mozart effect and the tendency to refer to children with gifts as "little Mozarts," I recall being somewhat disturbed by any ambition to be Mozartian. While we can all imagine little Mozart playing blindfolded before Emperor Joseph, it is quite clear that the infant prodigy was raised by his father to be a high-rent stage show, "scattering his notes," as the music historian Paul Metzner puts it, all around Europe, and that he grew up to be a wildly creative yet also unstable young man whose incandescent exertions ultimately brought him physical deterioration and an early death. Nevertheless, the two Mozarts coexist, the parental fantasy and the Enlightenment wreck.[5]

Soon the Mozart effect study's college students morphed into infants in the imaginations of kid marketers, parents, and Zell Miller, then governor of Georgia, who pushed his state to send a Mozart CD to every newborn. The idea that classical music played to infants, or even fetuses, would improve their ability to reason fed into the pitches of edutainment video companies, which in 1995 started to make ostensibly stimulating videos for babies, usually with a classical music component. One businessman, Don Campbell, even trademarked the term *Mozart Effect* in order to better sell "educational" CDs and books for infants. And the pitch has broadened beyond the music of the prodigious Wolfgang Amadeus — some of the newer videos are accompanied by the sonorous strains of Beethoven, and some offer random noise.

The catch to all these CDs and baby edutainment videos is that no psychologists, musicians, or musicologists have been able to duplicate the Mozart effect that Shaw and Rauscher described. Kenneth Steele, professor of psychology at Appalachian State University, was one of the scholars who tried. In 1997, a few of his graduate students conducted similar experiments and failed to reproduce the results.[6] Steele presumed at first that the Mozart effect was the result of individuals' arousal after listening to music. But he did not discover this to be the case. Then Steele himself tried, and he wasn't able to replicate the results, either. He eventually became the effect's greatest critic, publishing half a dozen papers decrying it, chief among them "Prelude or Requiem for the 'Mozart Effect'?" published with coauthors in *Nature* magazine in 1999. To date, the Mozart effect has failed to replicate in scientific settings at least three dozen times. Many additional scholars have noted that if any such effect does exist, it could well be due to the increased arousal that music can cause, or to the testing conditions.

None of this scholarly debunking has stymied the spread of the Baby Genius Complex. In fact, the complex has only expanded since the middle 1990s. Now it includes mind-enhancing baby formulas: giftedness has become digestible. In 2003 a fatty acid, DHA, suddenly made news as a wonder ingredient in baby formulas. DHA-ARA oils (docosahexaenoic acid and arachidonic acid), extracted from microbial sources such as algae and fungus, are supposed to help formulas replicate breast milk more closely than non-DHA formulas, thus increasing infant intelligence. Now a host of formulas offer DHA-ARA: Similac Advance, Nestle Good Start, Supreme with DHA and ARA, and Bright Beginnings. The Bright Beginnings pitch tells parents that the lipids added "are associated with mental and visual development." Enfamil A+ claims to be "the only formula clinically proven to result in higher early mental development scores."

Apparently, the creation of baby geniuses begins not at birth, but in the womb. Expecta Lipil, a pill for pregnant women, offers DHA in a prenatal form. There are also auditory prenatal enrichment products. Brent Logan, inventor of BabyPlus and author of *Learning before Birth: Every Child Deserves Giftedness*,[7] hawks the prenatal BabyPlus system, a speaker unit that pregnant women are supposed to place in a fabric pouch that is then strapped to their abdomens: the unit gives off sixteen "scientifically designed rhythmic sounds that resemble a mother's heartbeat," according to the BabyPlus company. "The rhythm of the sounds increases incrementally and sequentially as the pregnancy progresses. The BabyPlus sound pattern introduces your child to a sequential learning process, built upon the natural rhythms of their own environment."

In describing his product to me, Logan promises that BabyPlus's "auditory exercises" will produce a higher-than-average IQ. The key to his pitch is the logical technique of inversion: he mentions in an interview that infants in Romania and Russia who are deprived suffer as adults, and thus infants in America who are enriched by a product like his will blossom. BabyPlus's ad copy claims that "babies and children enriched with BabyPlus are more relaxed at birth, with eyes and hands open, crying little," that they "reach their milestones earlier" and "have longer attention spans."

> **"Babies and children enriched with BabyPlus are more relaxed at birth, with eyes and hands open, crying little."**

BabyPlus may be a far-out product, but like so many others, it uses parents' fears that their child might not hit milestones early or at the "normal time." Like the edutainment DVDs, it is first in a series of products claiming to promote child development and a timely march of the infant toward multilingualism and early spatial acumen. For instance, just to make sure progress is indeed timely, there is the Time Tracker, a lighted test-timer for children aged four and up. Once you could get by with an egg timer or a stopwatch. But in the age of edutainment mass culture, that's not good enough. The Time Tracker is a plastic object shaped like a large cucumber standing on its end. It has red, yellow, and green stripes that can be programmed to light up after a certain amount of time has passed, accompanied by six sound effects. I bought it and programmed it. I was struck by a number of things regarding Time Tracker. For starters, there was the product's relative popularity — on Amazon.com it was in the top 2,000 the last time I checked. Second, I found the extension of time management — now such a concern among adults, as documented by a number of sociologists who study time use, and parents — to the toys of the youngest children meaningful. I was also struck by its similarity to a number of other objects: a lighted joystick, a miniature of the spaceship in *Close Encounters or the Third Kind*, and finally and somewhat disturbingly, although also somewhat amusingly, a sex toy.

The claims made by the producers of Baby Genius Edutainment DVDs and brain-feeding formulas may at times seem absurd. But the impulses that usher parents into the complex and drive them to purchase these products are utterly sincere, and the wish to raise flourishing children is so old it is practically biblical.

As Peggy Madsen, a parent of two in Colorado, put it to me, "Giftedness is a gift you can give." Madsen has always been terrifically determined that her children be the very smartest, and she continues to champion the use of flash cards to inspire early reading. She has written about wandering around the house, naming objects, when her children were still newborns, watching their eyes intently to make sure they understood. She believes it is thanks to her efforts that her children began attending college when they were thirteen.

The ambition to give "giftedness" may have quite a history, but other aspects of the complex are new. Today's complex yokes together two concepts of infant betterment — that those skills and aptitudes not provided through genetics can be worked at and developed, and that one must do so by a certain age, or the jig is up. Only in the last ten years have parents been inundated with flash cards, DVDs, toys, and games that promise to provide "just the right level" of stimulation. Parents are much more receptive to these ideas and pitches today because they are more anxious about their children's futures, which precocious achievement may assure.

One need only look at the history of toys to learn that educational stimulation has not always been the primary aim of children's and infants' playthings. Through the nineteenth century, children tended not to play with manufactured things. Toys were handcrafted and usually homemade, and most children had few or even no toys in the cupboard. Only the wealthy had a number of toys, and these were quite different from contemporary playthings. Diminutive replicas of women, babies, and furniture enabled children to engage the larger world at their own level, that of small bit players. Many children's toys were indistinguishable from the miniatures included in the reliquaries of the adult dead. Such toys were meant to help pass the time, not to create genius.

Early manufactured toys and games were a good index for how Americans conceived of childhood, and also of parents' more general wishes and impulses.[8] The game Monopoly, for example, first produced in 1883, was an Industrial Revolution training ground whose promotional material described it as the site of "the struggle between Capital and Labor." In fact, "One of the most important changes in the play of children from large group ring games to small group board games represented the embourgeoisement of our society," writes Stephen Kline, a professor of media studies at Simon Fraser University, in his book *Out of the Garden*. For instance, the beginning of the twentieth century saw a rise of mass-produced toys dedicated to solitary play. Lincoln Logs (invented by John Lloyd Wright, son of architect Frank), boxes of crayons (first produced by Crayola in 1903), and Erector sets (introduced in 1913) all signaled an increase in time spent indoors for children in newly prosperous families.

Some of these toys for solitary play were the earliest precursors of the DVDs and similar products sold by today's edutainment complex. Initially, Parker Bros., Playskool, and Milton Bradley were three toy companies specializing in "education games." A notion of playthings as maturational devices for children was on the rise, but it remained very different from the ideas behind today's ostensibly intelligence-enhancing toys. These maturational playthings did not claim to promote a child's achievement or mental gain: they could simply be dolls that taught mothering, for example. (In an article in a toy trade magazine in 1927, dolls were termed an "Antidote to Race Suicide" in that they would encourage white girls to reproduce.) The teddy bear emerged in Brooklyn, New York, in 1902 and soon became faddish. It, too, was thought to have maturational benefits, but not in the sense of making children or toddlers faster learners. Rather, teddy bears were thought to be objects that spurred children's emotional growth. Teddy bears also have the benefit of being tactile, tangible, and manipulatable in a way that today's Baby Genius Edutainment Complex's DVDs and videos are not. DVDs, when playing on a screen, are by definition untouchable and mechanical. They encourage infants and toddlers to think while watching images on a box, rather than to invent and imagine a story around an object like a toy bear.

One of the aspects of the Baby Genius Edutainment Complex, the study of play and playthings' relationship to the development of children, also began in the late nineteenth century. Anthropologists started studying children's games as a sort of living folklore. One study of 15,000 kids in Cleveland in 1913 discovered that of a number of possible activities, "3171 were just fooling" while "531 were playing with kites," a bit of historical data that strikes me as particularly interesting in light of our contemporary attitudes toward children's mental development, where the "just fooling" time, seen as wasteful, has shrunk. At the turn of the century, toys were being used in kindergartens. The educator Maria Montessori used toys to teach math concepts, and promoted the enlightened notion that child pupils would be less obdurate about learning if work was more

> **The "just fooling" time, seen as wasteful, has shrunk.**

playlike, because when they were playing they were actively engaged.[9] Montessori's ideas soon caught on among some educators. But the nature of toys was also debated, with academics championing free play and high-quality materials. In 1920, a professor at Columbia University's Teachers College informed a group of businessmen in the toy industry that they should make toys of better quality that appealed to the imagination — a plea not always heeded by manufacturers.

Complaints about toys stifling imagination rather than charging it have become ever more urgent with regard to the toys and DVDs of today. In an insolent, sparkling essay on the subject first collected in 1957 in the book *Mythologies*, the cultural critic Roland Barthes decried his era's playthings as products of "chemistry not nature."[10] He was horrified that there were "dolls which urinate" and other toys "meant to prepare the little girl for the causality of housekeeping, to 'condition' her to her future role as mother." These toys, Barthes wrote, "are meant to produce children who are users, not creators." He was paraphrasing what was to become a central tenet of scholars of play: self-directed play is seen as superior play, and toys where children can improvise and imagine are privileged over those that are passive and preprogrammed. Prefabricated toys of this kind condemned the child to feel, Barthes wrote, that "he does not invent the world, he uses it; there are prepared for him, actions without adventure, without wonder, without joy. He is turned into a little stay-at-home householder who does not even have to invent the mainsprings of adult causality; they are supplied to him readymade: he has only to help himself, he is never allowed to discover anything from start to finish."

After Barthes, the psychologist Erik Erikson's insights into toys and development complicated the study of playthings. Erikson wrote of the earliest and most primitive play in a child's life, "autocosmic play," where infants play with their own bodies, and going on to a toy "microsphere" or "the small world of manageable toys," which is "a harbor" for the child's ego.[11] Ultimately, according to Erikson, the toy "thing-world" expands into the "macrosphere" of group play, or play with other children. Erikson kept underlining the point that play and play with toys is a part of identity, and the children's world of manageable toys should be shaped or intervened with as little as possible to avoid any disruption in their social learning.

At least in Barthes's era, children's playthings were still primarily tactile in character. Today's DVDs tend to be images of toys emanating from a television screen in programs with goofy pedantry. Still, Barthes's notion of toys as totems of a prescribed and manufactured adult world held some truth, and would only become more true with time. Already by the middle of the last century, toys had become less arcadian. They were creations devoted to novelty and expendability — in other words, trendy and makeshift: yo-yos and Davy Crockett hats and the like. In fact, today's nostalgia for a simpler time, for a time when childhood meant frolicking in more innocent pastoral climes — romping through the yard rather than through parents' DVD collections — may be an attractive construction, but it is also almost always misleading, a sort of sentimentality for an idyllic childhood that may have existed a century ago rather than one or two generations past. Beginning as early as the 1950s, toys suddenly became spin-off gear from television shows or children's films: when a child wasn't watching television, she might well be playing with action figures or other toys based on television programs, products that would allow her to re-create, in her own home, scenes from her favorite series. Along with the ever more calculated nature of children's toys, there was inevitably an increase of market-driven toy testing and research conducted by toy manufacturers.

This isn't to say that the "maturational" ambitions of toys vanished. For instance, the construction toy Lego advertised itself as an "instructive game." And in 1969, the ultimate maturational television program, *Sesame Street* debuted, with a line of educational toys following in its wake.[12] The lessons of *Sesame Street* were strongly influenced by the educational philosophy of Maria Montessori, and from the beginning *Sesame Street's* producers, the Children's Television Workshop, made a huge effort at outreach to young children and their families in low-income areas. The show was, in fact, considered to be an extension of the 1960s "War on Poverty," funded in part by the Department of Healt0h, Education, and Welfare, as if it were a social program.

But in a certain sense, the early debates that swirled around *Sesame Street* are echoed today in the debates over the Baby Edutainment Complex. *Sesame Street's* critics argued that young children benefit from imaginary play rather than watching television. Similarly, the edutainment DVDs for infants regularly run afoul of the American Academy of Pediatrics, which suggests that there should be no television watching at all for children under two. But there is a crucial difference between edutainment DVDs and *Sesame Street*. *Sesame Street* was not intended for babies (until now, that is, as a *Sesame Street* infant DVD line is readied for release), while today's DVDs are made explicitly for children two and under.

Companies are making these products because parents want them. Parents want them because they are concerned about their children's mental lives, thanks to the hard-sell marketing. There are deeper reasons, too, for parents' greater receptivity to such products and toys. One is a contemporary mania for infant betterment and precocity. Another is an increasing fashion for gizmos and technological improving devices for people of all ages, starting in infancy. A third reason is harder to prove but seems to me to be widespread: adults' tendency to project themselves into infant and toddler experience, as an antidote to their inability to remember that time, and perhaps to remember much of childhood at all, given the pressure to live in the future rather than the past. The gap between adults' projections onto infants' viewing experience and the true nature of that experience is large — is the baby learning or just taking in a set of bright two-dimensional images that makes little sense? And if the infant is learning from the edutainment DVD, wouldn't she learn from any repetitive experience, since infants learn through repetition? DVDs are just easier to repeat than other experiences.

This is part of how the Baby Edutainment Complex is the beginning of the movement to invent gifted children: it starts with parental wishes and hopes, one of which is that the infant is getting as much out of a DVD as his parents. It's also part of another aspect of childhood that will be covered in more depth elsewhere in this book — directed play has trumped free play. This is one unspoken reason why babies are now the audience for educational products. According to Brainy Baby president Dennis Fedoruk, parents are concerned about their infants' mental lives. "Parents know about that preschool window of opportunity — it's very narrow," he says. "Parents want to maximize results their children without causing their children trouble. Listen, you can't turn back the hands of time. Once they enter kindergarten they can't have the window of opportunity any longer. It's too late."

> **"Parents want to maximize results in their children without causing their children trouble."**

Similarly, CEO and founder of the Athletic Baby Company Karen Foster tells me that her *Athletic Baby Golf* and *Athletic Baby All-Star* DVDs help parents give a head start to their kids, so that when they are actually old enough to play a sport or even to walk, "they will succeed at it." She likens her DVDs' potential effect to the effect of his father on Tiger

Woods: "Everyone has heard about Tiger's imprinting from an early age by his father. . . . The earlier the age, the more successful they will be." Foster gives the standard edutainment-complex line: if infant deprivation creates negative effects, inversely, "enriching" products must automatically produce a positive effect. She mentions the child obesity epidemic frequently, as if her *Athletic Baby* DVDs are a sure cure. Even as many researchers tie obesity to sedentary habits, Foster wants parents to sit their babies down in front of a DVD to prevent — well, to prevent them from sitting around. By this logic, adults would be encouraged to keep in shape by watching the NFL on TV each Sunday afternoon.

The makers of the smart-baby formulas also sell their products by promising bright children. "The difference between the children who received formulas containing this ingredient and other children can be observed from each group's reading of one line on the eye chart," claimed Angela Tsetsis, director of marketing for Martek, the company that produces the "smart" fatty acid and sells it to the companies that use it in their baby formulas. "At eighteen months, we looked at the mental acuity of babies who have received the nutrient, and those babies scored higher."

"BabyPlus helps with imprinting," Brent Logan, the inventor, claims. "And soon, the imprinting window shuts off for the pre-infants and it is too late. When they are pre-nates, they are in an unusual different time and they are learning in a different mode." Logan and BabyPlus are extremes in the edutainment market — Logan does an unironic star turn in a British television documentary program entitled *Brave New Babies*, which he proudly sends me. But his prenatal interventionist ideology is not a fringe belief. Real mothers are buying his product. Rather than a radical maneuver, Logan's move into prenatal marketing seems like the next logical step.

All of these are pitches that could make a parent nervous enough to run out and buy the product. But are any of them accurate? To better understand the answer to this question, one needs to first cleave the popular ideas of infant "crucial stages," "brain cell death," "windows of time," and "brain plasticity" (today's scientized buzzword for "ability to learn") from the science and cultural history underlying them.

The notion that the first three years are key ones for emotional and intellectual development isn't new. Americans have long sought to command and control natural processes so as to accelerate them. This is part of our faith in man's ability to harness nature and to use time shrewdly. As Benjamin Franklin said, time is money, and the stuff life is made of. Child development pioneer Jean Piaget was famously disturbed by Americans' fixation on their children's educational velocity.[13] A story was told to me anecdotally by Charles Nelson, a professor of pediatrics at Harvard Medical School, of Piaget's tour of American universities in the middle of the last century. When the Swiss psychologist described the cognitive stages children pass through as they mature, his American listeners asked him how they could make their children go through those stages faster. (Piaget was displeased.) In 1964, those who founded Head Start, a federally funded program for disadvantaged preschool children, emphasized the urgent nature of education in the earliest years, an undertaking that was seen as determining these children's entire futures.

In the last decade or so, a focus on early development and the necessity of intervention for disadvantaged children, once a social welfare plank, fueled a popular awareness (and sometimes misunderstanding) of the crucial period from zero to three. Vociferous celebrity advocates for infants, a White House conference on the subject, and the Mozart effect theory ultimately gave rise to a rash of baby products promising infant precocity.

As John Bruer recounts in his clear-headed derogation of the early enrichment movement, *The Myth of the First Three Years*, texts from the 1990s like *Rethinking the Brain* tended to suggest that critical periods pervade all areas of learning.[14] In the mid-1990s, the actor Rob Reiner's national "I Am Your Child" campaign, with its slogan "The first years last forever," disseminated the zero-to-three worldview. Reiner claimed at the time that parents who don't read to their children in those first three years were diminishing the growth potential of their brains, and that by the age of ten "your brain is cooked and there's nothing much you can do." While Reiner and his campaign claimed to address an infant's intellectual development, Bruer notes correctly that it was theories of emotional attachment as outlined by child psychologists in the late 1950s, '60s, and '70s — most famous among them the legendary British child psychologist John Bowlby — that gave Reiner's campaign its true ballast. A second event that egged the craze onward was the 1997 White House Conference on Child Development, which emphasized the effect of early childhood events on the development of a child's intelligence. A third element was a series of studies on rats and enrichment conducted by Mark Rosenzweig at the University of California, Berkeley, and William Greenough at the University of Illinois in the 1970s and '80s.[15] Both researchers looked at how rats' brains benefit from experience. They conducted studies on the brains of rats raised in enriched environments with toys and with other rats — cages akin to the rats' natural habitat — versus the brains of rats in bare cages more akin to prison cells. The rats in the enriched cages were found to have more dendritic area in certain regions of the brain: basically, these rats were more mentally enhanced than their deprived colleagues. This research was ultimately absorbed by the popular press and applied to infants and children.

And then there was the Mozart effect.

But in the years since the middle 1990s, scholars have cast aspersions on the credence of zero-to-three as an absolute time frame. William Greenough of rat-enrichment fame was a vehement critic of the new overemphasis on early learning: he argued that his research supported the idea that the brain continues to be plastic after infancy, rather than the opposite conclusion that the time for development is limited. Indeed, many in the neuroscientific community now dismiss the idea that adult brains lose plasticity, viewing the brain as an entity that continually remodels itself. The trend in current research is to study in earnest how individuals execute cognitive tasks from ages six to ninety, and observe mental dynamics across the life span.

"It's important to point out that windows of development do not slam shut, as the earliest versions of 'Parents' Action for Children' and the 'Birth to Three' movement suggested," says Bradley Schlaggar, a pediatric neurologist at Washington University. "When the development windows are thought to slam shut, a parent may feel that he or she must try again with the next child. While the motivation was very justifiable — a desire to make sure every child had access to good nutrition — the message was so harsh."

Schlaggar and other neurologists, cognitive scientists, psychologists, and child development specialists I spoke with questioned the idea that educational toys or DVDs accomplish what their makers claim. As Professor Charles Nelson, a professor at Harvard Medical School and a preeminent scholar of the infant brain, puts it, "There is no proof of the value of the early enrichment toys and videos in terms of brain science." Nelson also consulted for Mead Johnson for a year regarding "smart" food additives and says that while DHA and ARA have been shown to improve babies' auditory and retina responses, they have not been shown to improve reading skills.

Scholars have also argued that the idea of hard and fast "critical periods" is overplayed. For one thing, there is a difference between brain functions that are "experience-expectant" and bound by critical periods, and those that are "experience-dependent" and not so bound. Experience-expectant means, for example, that the brain requires exposure to light so that vision can develop properly. This experience does, in fact, need to take place at a particular point in the development of all infants. Experience-dependent learning, by contrast, is how an infant or child learns things individual to her environment — reading or weaving or dumpling-making. This sort of learning is less time-governed. As John Bruer puts it, "critical periods are less likely to exist for traits and behaviors that are unique to the experiences of individuals, social groups, or cultures."

According to Fred Dick, a developmental cognitive neuroscientist and a lecturer in psychology at the University of London, starting to learn second or even third languages early can be a good thing. But early doesn't mean infancy. Furthermore, teaching a child language with another child may be preferable to using videos, because a normal environment with another child "holds more information than any multimedia film."

Experts tell me that today's edutainment DVDs or language-blurting toys are generally untested in how effective they are in teaching children a second language. The DVDs tend to offer only disconnected French or Spanish words; additionally, a child must be exposed to a language continuously to acquire it. Studies have shown that the ability to learn the grammar of a second language begins to decline in puberty — quite a while after the age of three. And ultimately, says Dick, one can be a successful language learner well into adulthood. "It's not as easy, but I can take up a new language when I am twenty," says Michael Merzenich, a neuroscientist at the University of California and a preeminent expert on brain plasticity. "It's not as easy *not* because I am less plastic, but because I became so damn proficient at my native language."

Many infant DVDs are hawked with questionable promises about time-limited opportunities for learning. Some head straight for the parental panic button, selling themselves by gesturing at the specter of "infant brain cell death." Charles Zorn, a neuropsychological education specialist, told me that he often has to reassure parents that numbers of brain cells are not a measure of a child's intelligence, knowledge, or ability to learn. The brain deliberately makes too many, then lets a bunch wither; the specific ones that wither depend on the environment the newborn

> *Some head straight for the parental panic button, selling themselves by gesturing at the specter of "infant brain cell death."*

encounters. In fact, cell death is actually a part of the learning process. "When you learn to read, you are killing cells to create a pathway," he says.

Indeed, reducing infant brain cell death is counterproductive; cell death is the main way the nervous system refines its circuits. One scholar used the example of a toddler flying an airplane and asked rhetorically; Wouldn't you rather a trained adult pilot it, even if the toddler may have more exuberant brain cells?

Academics who study cognition also question the value of prenatal enrichment products. Gary Marcus, a professor of psychology at New York University and author of *The Birth of the Mind*, says that while it is possible to learn something in the womb, it also isn't good to give a fetus too much stimulation. And given the paucity or long-term research on the subject, it's hard to gauge what would be overstimulating, says Marcus: "We don't know enough about early brain development to say."

In truth, scant neurobiology is dedicated to gifted children, and there are also few studies on the value of edutainment videos. The 2005 Kaiser Family Foundation report *A Teacher in the Living Room*,[16] underlines the point I have heard time and again from researchers of infant brain development and education on the effect of the bright baby videos: there is little adequate scholarship on these products' value over time.

What researchers *can* comfortably assert is that a false set of assumptions is at work. According to the blurry logic I described earlier, the total neglect of orphans is shown to be bad, and therefore superstimulation must be good. This is a false conflation, says Nelson; deprived infants who benefit from a move to an ordinary environment are being used to indicate the benefits of enrichment to children who grow up in ordinary or even "super" environments. "For many infants, there's an a priori enrichment in their daily lives," says Nelson. "What they see in *Baby Einstein*, and all of the edutainment DVDs, exists in the baby's ordinary environment." As long as you don't put a child in a closet, nutritionally deprive him, or cause trauma to his developing brain, he will naturally learn.

The proposition is that, say, if disadvantaged children are helped by exposure to age-appropriate enrichment, then advantaged children will be even more enriched by exposure to supersonic educational stimuli. Data on the value of early learning intervention for disadvantaged kids is also mapped onto the value of pumped-up learning for advantaged children, including a study in which three-year-olds in Early Head Start programs performed significantly better cognitively, linguistically, and emotionally than a similarly disadvantaged control group not enrolled in Early Head Start.[17] But just because a child who lacks the ordinary stimulation of an everyday childhood and gets a great deal of negative stimulation may experience permanent damage, that does not mean that more stimulation is better for all kids. To put it in hothouse terms, a lack of water will kill an orchid — but so will a flood. Nevertheless, the makers of baby edutainment use a blurry syllogism in their efforts to beguile parents: Deprivation is bad; therefore, the opposite of deprivation is good.

The final criticism that researchers have made of the Baby Genius Edutainment Complex goes beyond the fact that the DVDs are not as educational as they claim: their widening use may actually prevent more effective learning from taking place. A University of Massachusetts researcher had one sample group of infants learn to use a puppet from a live person, while the other learned by watching a DVD.[18] The tots who received live instruction learned to use the puppet immediately, but the infant video-watchers had to repeat their viewing six times before they learned the same skill. A number of scholars have also started to investigate whether the millions of infants and children who have grown up watching educational videos have actually been damaged by their new orientation to the television. One such scholar, Rhonda Clements, a professor of education at Manhattanville College and the former president of the American Association for the Child's Right to Play, recently conducted a study that found that 70 percent of the sample's mothers said that they themselves played every day outdoors when they were children, typically tag, hopscotch, and jumping rope, as compared with 31 percent of their children.[19] And of the mothers who said their children played outdoors, only 22 percent played for three hours at a time or longer. The study concluded that today's level of indoor activity and play, even if it involves "learning," is deleterious to the children's young bodies and minds. (The study was financed by the detergent maker Wisk — perhaps in an effort to promote an increase in dirt and grass stains.)

But despite negative findings about time spent watching DVDs indoors, and the fuzziness of the edutainment product makers' claims, even the most sophisticated parents can be drawn to the Baby Edutainment Complex.

"There are some guarantees with these products," says Lynne Varner, a forty-two-year-old newspaper writer and mom who resides in Seattle. "There aren't guarantees in the world. My son may not see all the colors in the prism every day. He may go outside and see a green tree one day and a roaring bus the next day, but I have to hope that nature and life offer everything to him. I want our child to always be doing something that stimulates him. And so does everyone I know."

Varner's accumulation of educational toys started with Baby Einstein and grew from there to Baby BumbleBee toys purchased at the Imaginarium and the now-defunct Zany Brainy. The stores and products made reassuring guarantees that her kid was going to be smart, she says: Baby Einstein markets itself this way to the "überparents" she knows in Seattle and Palo Alto.

"I do believe that the brain has a certain clump of neurons firing, and that by the time he is five it will be too late," one women, an educated professional who is an avid consumer of these products, told me. "It sounds panicky, I know, but if those neurons are dying off . . . you have to get in there during the first three years. If my baby doesn't use it with a stimulating game or class, he is going to lose it." But her baby's neurons are going to die no matter what she does. They're supposed to die.

On Amazon.com, reviewers likewise emphasize that the videos are part of their responsibility to adequately enhance and stimulate their children. One writes about *Brainy Baby Left Brain*, "I come from a Montessori background and have very high standards regarding my child's education. I am discriminating about what I expose her to. The formative years are a crucial time in every child's development. . . . Now that she is three years old, she enjoys the more cognitive lessons in the video (even though it is all review for her!). . . . No longer do parents have to tolerate the use of mindless videos to 'occupy' their young ones. We now have the opportunity to actually EDUCATE our babies with a video. The child will LEARN something while watching this."

Another reviewer writes, "My 1-year-old is growing into a Brainy Baby, himself! How many 18-month-olds can tell you what an orangutan is, or the difference between a circle and an oval, or that the color of our van is 'silver'? My son could — from watching these videos!"

Of course, parents don't entirely trust the pitches from the companies. The Seattle mom recognizes that many of the pitches she receives for toys play upon her worst fears — that her children's brains will stop growing, that her children will become adults who fall through the cracks. "Unless something cataclysmic happens, our children won't be prisoners, or even drug addicts," says the mom. But she still buys *Baby Einstein*, Leapster, and the rest.

Many parents buy these products even as they remain skeptical about their claims. In 2004, I attended an educational-toy party in New York. The party's emcee, the self-proclaimed "Discovery Toy Lady," was named Simone Weissman. Weissman is an enthusiastic woman with curly hair, a loud girlish voice, and a more-than-passing resemblance to Bette Midler. She sold her products Tupperware-style: plastic toys, plush toys, and flash cards in a sea of primary colors, laid out before her on a table in a sunset-suffused thirtieth-floor apartment. The partygoers, women of thirty or fortyish, wore stretchy comfort clothes — not a plunging shirtdress in sight. As they drank wine, a wailing baby provided the party's sound track from behind a set of screens. While the baby cried, Discovery Toy Lady Weissman pointed out the products that provoke "fine and gross mental skills." She moved on to a toy that used to be merely sentimental: a stuffed bear. But this teddy was named Classical Casey, and played famous melodies from six classical composers. He wasn't sold as being all about love: he also strengthened an infant's "sensory capacities," Weissman said. The mothers looked on, seemingly unimpressed by Classical Casey. No one reached for their purses, even when she showed the group flash cards called Think It Through Tiles. The cards, Weissman said, were good for studying for the ERBs — the Educational Records Bureau test for private preschool admission, tests that are given to children as young as three.[20] The mothers

> **This teddy was named Classical Casey, and played famous melodies from six classical composers.**

at this particular party weren't planning on sending their children to private schools, but upon hearing that other mothers were using these flash cards and had seen great improvement in their children's scores, they perked up. They didn't want to fail to do due diligence for their kids. Weissman said that the cards' buyers wanted their children to have an edge. "These moms worry that their children aren't doing the right things, you know?" she said.

But doing things "right" isn't the whole story. It seems to me that the Baby Genius Edutainment Complex exists, in part, out of a deeper fear than that of infants losing their learning opportunities. It responds to adults' fear of children's boredom. The edutainment products are, at bottom, meant to reduce unproductive boredom.

But what exactly is boredom, especially in infancy and childhood? The psychotherapist and writer Adam Phillips writes in *On Kissing, Tickling, and Being Bored* that the bored child is waiting "for an experience of anticipation" and that being bored, rather than an inadequacy, is an opportunity and perhaps even a capacity: boredom is "a developmental achievement for the child."[21]

"It is one of the most oppressive demands of adults that the child should be interested," writes Phillips, "rather than take time to find what interests him. Boredom is integral to the process of taking one's time." But taking one's time and waiting for desire or interest to return goes against the grain of the new improved infancy, and the regimen of infant stimulation.

Talking about childhood boredom is not boring — I find this out discoursing on dullness in the sun-filled office of Dona Matthews, coauthor of *Being Smart about Gifted Children: A Guidebook for Parents and Educators* and the director of Hunter College's Center for Gifted Studies and Education. Matthews is fifty-something, clad in a stripy sweater. Her office has the upbeat atmosphere common to those who work with children: a blue plate full of bright orange nectarines, an orchid, a colorful poster, and Matthews herself, with a bright smile and winningly tousled hair. "Parents are always saying, 'My kids are bored or understimulated,'" she says. "Sometimes it is a parent-induced boredom, where the parents are centered on entertaining the child." Like many in the gifted business, Matthews has the air of a Boomer Vivant. "Boredom is essential. It's important to encourage children to find things to do, and a commonality with others. We call it do-nothing time. It is necessary to be bored to find out what you really want to do." Buddhists call it non-doing.

There are even experts who argue that a certain amount of boredom is important for kids' development. Fred Dick, the developmental cognitive neuroscientist, notes that babies' emotional states tend to change, and thus an infant's caregivers should attend to a child but should not feel obliged to provide *constant* stimulation to their children.

One specialist in gifted education suggests that an adult finger can be just as stimulating for an infant as the whirling dervish of rainbows on a *Baby Einstein* DVD. Charles Zorn, the neuropsychological educational consultant, suggests that parents who aren't sold on the need for stimulating DVDs can see that the perfect educational baby toys are everywhere: keys on a chain. They jingle. Babies get excited, are aurally and visually stimulated, and learn to identify a shape that will have lifelong application. Others suggest playing with a broom and dustpan.

Such simple pleasures, which adults find boring — and this is part of it: our inability, as adults, to remember how easily we were entertained during our own infancies — are often just what infants need. Their systems are ready for simplicity, not for a deluge of diffuse stimuli.

Why the aversion to boredom? It belongs to a larger fear of emptiness, a fascination with whirring cities, technologies, a distrust of the "dull" repetitions of experience. As Patricia Meyer Spacks writes in her book of literary criticism, *Boredom*, "The diagnoses (self-diagnoses and evaluations by others) of middle class adolescents and housewives as sufferers from boredom exemplify the imaginative functions boredom serves in our culture. . . . The claim of boredom now locates the causes of conduct firmly outside the self."[22]

"If sleep is the apogee of physical relaxation," writes philosopher and cultural critic Walter Benjamin, "boredom is the apogee of mental relaxation. Boredom is the dream bird that hatches the egg of experience. A rustling in the leaves drives him away. His nesting places — the activities that are intimately associated with boredom — are already extinct in the cities and are declining in the country as well."[23]

Indeed, a number of childhood edutainment products are equivalent to a mechanical rustling in the leaves, a buzzing, bleeping thing called computerized enrichment that drives away the dream bird that could otherwise have hatched the egg of true human experience. What is that experience for infants? Perhaps it's keys on a chain. Perhaps it's what they see between the rails of their cribs. But it is also letting the infant alone with her thoughts, her own developing self, rather than providing external stimulus.

The fight against boredom, the insistence on external stimulation whenever possible, is clearly tied to a concern about time. This concern — or, perhaps, fear — drives the Baby Genius Edutainment Complex: the fear that time is being wasted, that windows of development are slamming shut, that time for learning is running out.

In the Baby Genius Edutainment Complex, the palliative for childish boredom or time-wasting is always a new product, and it can seem that price is no object. In effect, these products are mostly intended for the reasonably well off. The Time Tracker, for instance, costs $35. BabyPlus runs $150. The Leapster Multimedia Learning System is $70. The LeapPad Plus Writing and Microphone System is $59.99. The by now classic Baby Einstein videos — *Baby Mozart, Baby Bach, Baby Beethoven, Baby Einstein Language Nursery*, and Baby Einstein Language Discovery Cards — come as a special set at a cost of $69.99.

Like a number of other elements of precociously gifted childhood, which may include private school admissions, overstructured activity, proto-professional training, and participation in competitions, edutainment products are the first items in a two-tiered system where children are divided into have and have-less. The infants inculcated with the early reading DVDs and flash cards are supposed to ultimately deploy their precocious knowledge to get ahead of other reasonably affluent children.

The paradox is that infants whose parents have the wherewithal to purchase these products are most likely already ahead of other children. Of course, some of the products, like "smart" baby formulas, are marketed to working-class parents as well — taking advantage, perhaps, of parents who also want to help their children succeed but don't have the money to send them to private schools or live in a place with good public schools or spend a lot of time with them because they have to work. In the United States, breast-feeding rates are rising, and the formula market is shrinking. The smart-baby formulas have thus offered formula manufacturers a much-needed edge. Marion Nestle, professor of food studies at New York University, told me that this is why the formula companies now "do everything they can get away with to convince moms that breast-feeding is inconvenient or impossible. They fought hard for permission to add the new nutrients because they can use them as an additional sales strategy." Now a large share of formulas contain them, up to 50 percent of baby formulas by some counts, and mothers of all social classes are buying them. The smart formulas' popularity seems to me to indicate that many of the mothers who can't afford the classes and the schools and the tutors, or even DVDs and toys, still want to imagine that they are "giving" their children the gift of giftedness.

The DVDs and the range of toys are just the beginning of the expenditure. After all, the educational-kid-toy-and-video industry is the equivalent of a gateway drug into the larger giftedness culture, the first stop on the voyage on which children of America are shaped into champions.

NOTES

[1]Henry J. Kaiser Family Foundation, *Zero to Six: Electronic Media in the Lives of Infants, Toddlers, and Preschoolers* (Washington, D.C.: Henry J. Kaiser Family Foundation, 2003).

[2]Henry J. Kaiser Family Foundation, *A Teacher in the Living Room? Educational Media for Babies, Toddlers and Preschoolers* (Washington, D.C.: Henry J. Kaiser Family Foundation, 2005).

[3]"American Academy of Pediatrics Media Education Policy Statement," *Pediatrics*, August 2, 1999. For data on the big business of baby edutainment videos, see G. Khermouch, "Brainier? Maybe. Big Sales? Definitely," *BusinessWeek*, January 12, 2004.

[4]One original pro-Mozart effect article is by F. H. Rauscher, G. L. Shaw, and K. N. Ky, "Music and Spatial Task Performance," *Nature* 365 (1993).

[5]The 1982 film *Amadeus* is one of the few vehicles to portray Mozart as the disturbed Enlightenment wreck.

[6]See K. M. Steele, J. D. Brown, and J. A. Stoecker, "Failure to Confirm the Rauscher and Shaw Description of Recovery of the Mozart Effect," *Perceptual and Motor Skills* 88 (1999); and K. M. Steele, K. E. Bass, and M. D. Crook, "The Mystery of the Mozart Effect: Failure to Replicate," *Psychological Science* 10 (1999).

[7]Brent Logan, *Learning before Birth: Every Child Deserves Giftedness* (New York: Authorhouse, 2003).

[8]I have relied on a number of books on toys here. One good reference is Bernard J. Mergen, *Play and Playthings: A Reference Guide* (New York: Greenwood Press, 1982). The truly perspicacious one is by Stephen Kline's, *Out of the Garden: Toys, TV, and Children's Culture in the Age of Marketing* (New York: Verso, 1995). See also Antonia Fraser, *A History of Toys* (London: Spring Books, 1972); and Colin. Heywood, *A History of Childhood: Children and Childhood in the West from Medieval to Modern Times* (New York: Polity Press, 2001).

[9]She was also, however, critical of the toy industry. As Maria Montessorri writes in *The Absorbent Mind* (New York: Owl Books, 1995), "But in those countries where the toy making industry is less advanced, you will find children with quite different tastes. They are also calmer, more sensible, and happy."

[10]See Roland Barthes, *Mythologies* (New York: Hill and Wang, 1972).

[11]The necessary classic by Erik H. Erikson, *Toys and Reasons: Stages in the Ritualisation of Experience* (London: Marion Boyars, 1978), republished as *Childhood and Society* (New York: W. W. Norton, 1993).

[12]James Day, *The Vanishing Vision: The Inside Story of Public Television* (Berkley and Los Angeles: University of California Press, 1995). See also James Ledbetter, *Made Possible By: The Death of Public Broadcasting in the United States* (Verso, 1998); and Heather Hendershot, *Saturday Morning Censors: Television Regulation before the V-Chip (Console-Ing Passions)* (Durham, N.C.: Duke University Press, 1999).

[13]Some Piaget books I read while writing this included *Psychology of Intelligence* (New York: Routledge, 2001), and *The Child's Conception of the World: A 20th-Century Classic of Child Psychology* (Sturgeon Bay, Wis.: Littlefield Adams, 1976).

[14]John Bruer, *The Myth of the First Three Years: A New Understanding of Early Brain Development and Lifelong Learning* (New York: Free Press, 2002).

[15]William Greenough et al., "Effects of Rearing Complexity on Dendritic Branching in Frontolateral and Temporal Cortex of the Rat," *Experimental Neurology* 41, no. 2 (1973).

[16]Kaiser Foundation, *"Teacher in the Living Room."*

[17]Similarly, the Abecedarian Project, which began in the 1970s, assigned some low-income families in Chapel Hill, North Carolina, to a high-quality child-care setting, while some were not so assigned. At age twenty-one, the participants assigned to a high-quality setting were discovered to have significantly higher mental test scores than the control group.

[18]Daniel R. Anderson's study was referenced in Tamar Lewin, "See Baby Touch a Screen, but Does Baby Get It?" *New York Times*, December 15, 2005. I looked at Anderson's earlier work about toddlers as well; see K. L. Schmitt and D. R. Anderson, "Television and Reality: Toddlers' Use of Visual Information from Video to Guide Behavior," *Media Psychology* 4 (2002).

[19]Rhonda Clements, "An Investigation of the Status of Outdoor Play," *Contemporary Issues in Early Childhood Education* 5, no. 1 (2004).

[20]The best account of the history of American achievement tests that I have read, and, I believe, the best that exists, is Nicholas Lemann's *The Big Test: The Secret History of the American Meritocracy* (New York: Farrar, Straus and Giroux, 2000).

[21]Adam Phillips, *On Kissing, Tickling, and Being Bored: Psychoanalytic Essays on the Unexamined Life* (Cambridge, Mass.: Harvard University Press, 1994); this is a remarkably good book from one of the most enjoyable and smart writers on this subject.

[22]Patricia Meyer Spacks, *Boredom: The Literary History of a State of Mind* (Chicago: University of Chicago Press, 1996). This stirringly un-dull book makes one point, among others: that a few great novelists even recommended boredom as a proper antidote to vice.

[23]Walter Benjamin, *Illuminations* (New York: Schocken, 1969).

DISCUSSION

1. Take a moment to consider the essay's title. How do you understand the term *edutainment*? What conception of learning, what definition of the ideal pupil, does it conjure in your mind?

2. One of the central ideas underlying the so-called baby genius industry is that giftedness is something that can be cultivated, trained, even invented: in Quart's words, that the "skills and aptitudes not provided through genetics can be worked out and developed." What do you make of this hypothesis? Is giftedness something that can be taught? If so, what are some of the forms this kind of instruction might take?

3. Quart also levels the charge that the emphasis placed on achievement and giftedness in these toys and games robs children of their childhood. What do you think Quart means by this? What aspects of childhood do these baby genius products seem to erase? And what, in your view, is the true cost of this loss?

WRITING

4. Quart clearly suggests there is a close relationship between the baby genius industry and the particular question of social status. Much of the appeal of these products, it seems, rests on the implied promise that they will help children eventually reach a higher marker of social achievement than would otherwise be likely: a prestigious job, a degree from a top college, a comfortable level of income, and so on. Log on to the home page of one of the companies marketing baby genius products and write an essay in which you analyze the ways this website scripts a particular formula or recipe for status enhancement. What particular (social, financial, professional) reward or payoffs does this company seem to promise? What steps does it map for achieving them?

5. According to Quart, how does the baby genius industry define what makes a child gifted? Write a brief essay in which you compare this definition with your own definition of giftedness. What do the two definitions have in common? What are the key differences?

6. Choose one example of the promotional language used to market a baby education product that Quart excerpts (p. 450). Write an essay in which you discuss the ways this piece of sales talk can be viewed as part of a larger social script, one designed to teach children how best to spend their time. What does it encourage kids to spend their time doing? What activities does this excerpt suggest kids should consider most important? Least important? Next, compare this list to the educational priorities Jonathan Kozol (p. 530) argues for in his essay. What different standards and norms does each seem to promote?

ALFIE KOHN
From Degrading to De-grading

Are grades really necessary? Do they truly offer us an accurate, meaningful measure of student ability or achievement? Couldn't we have a quality education without them? Answering this final question with an emphatic, "yes!," Alfie Kohn makes the case that grades are not only irrelevant but actually antithetical to learning. Kohn has published eleven books on education and parenting, including *No Contest: The Case against Competition* (1986), *Unconditional Parenting: Moving from Rewards and Punishments to Love and Reason* (2005), and, most recently, *The Homework Myth: Why Our Kids Get Too Much of a Bad Thing* (2006). His articles have appeared in *Phi Delta Kappan*, the *Journal of Education*, the *Nation*, and the *Harvard Business Review*. As a public speaker he has lectured school groups and corporations against competition in education. He has also appeared on the *Today* show and the Oprah Winfrey show. The essay that follows was originally published in *High School Magazine*.

Y OU CAN TELL A LOT ABOUT A TEACHER'S VALUES AND PERSONALITY just by asking how he or she feels about giving grades. Some defend the practice, claiming that grades are necessary to "motivate" students. Many of these teachers actually seem to enjoy keeping intricate records of students' marks. Such teachers periodically warn students that they're "going to have to know this for the test" as a way of compelling them to pay attention or do the assigned readings — and they may even use surprise quizzes for that purpose, keeping their grade books at the ready.

Frankly, we ought to be worried for these teachers' students. In my experience, the most impressive teachers are those who despise the whole process of giving grades. Their aversion, as it turns out, is supported by solid evidence that raises questions about the very idea of traditional grading.

THREE MAIN EFFECTS OF GRADING

Researchers have found three consistent effects of using — and especially, emphasizing the importance of — letter or number grades:

1. Grades tend to reduce students' interest in the learning itself. One of the best-researched findings in the field of motivational psychology is that the more people are rewarded for doing something, the more they tend to lose interest in whatever they had to do to get the reward (Kohn 1993). Thus, it shouldn't be surprising that when students are told they'll need to know something for a test — or, more generally, that something they're about to do will count for a grade — they are likely to come to view that task (or book or ideal) as a chore.

While it's not impossible for a student to be concerned about getting high marks and also to like what he or she is doing, the practical reality is that these two ways of thinking generally pull in opposite directions. Some research has explicitly demonstrated that a "grade orientation" and a "learning orientation" are inversely related (Beck, Rorrer-Woody, and Pierce 1991; Milton, Pollio, and Eison 1986). More strikingly, study after study has found that students — from elementary school to graduate school, and across cultures — demonstrate less interest in learning as a result of being graded (Benware and Deci 1984; Butler 1987; Butler and Nisan 1986; Grolnick and Ryan 1987; Harter and Guzman 1986; Hughes, Sullivan, and Mosley 1985; Kage 1991; Salili et al. 1976). Thus, anyone who wants to see students get hooked on words and numbers and ideas already has reason to look for other ways of assessing and describing their achievement.

2. Grades tend to reduce students' preference for challenging tasks. Students of all ages who have been led to concentrate on getting a good grade are likely to pick the easiest possible assignment if given a choice (Harter 1978; Harter and Guzman 1986; Kage 1991; Milton, Pollio, and Eison 1986). The more pressure to get an A, the less inclination to truly challenge oneself. Thus, students who cut corners may not be lazy so much as rational; they are adapting to an environment where good grades, not intellectual exploration, are what count. They might well say to us, "Hey, you told me the point here is to bring up my GPA, to get on the honor roll. Well, I'm not stupid: The easier the assignment the more likely that I can give you what you want. So don't blame me when I try to find the easiest thing to do and end up not learning anything."

3. Grades tend to reduce the quality of students' thinking. Given that students may lose interest in what they're learning as a result of grades, it makes sense that they're also apt to think less deeply. One series of studies, for example, found that students given numerical grades were significantly less creative than those who received qualitative feedback but no grades. The more the task required creative thinking, in fact, the worse the performance of students who knew they were going to be graded. Providing students with comments in addition to a grade didn't help: The highest achievement occurred only when comments were given *instead* of numerical scores (Butler 1987; Butler 1988; Butler and Nisan 1986).

In another experiment, students told they would be graded on how well they learned a social studies lesson had more trouble understanding the main point of the text than did students who were told that no grades would be involved. Even on a measure of rote recall, the graded group remembered fewer facts a week later (Grolnick and Ryan 1987). And students who tended to think about current events in terms of what they'd need to know for a grade were less knowledgeable than their peers, even after taking other variables into account (Anderman and Johnston 1998).

MORE REASONS TO JUST SAY NO TO GRADES

The preceding three results should be enough to cause any conscientious educator to rethink the practice of giving students grades. But there's more.

Grades aren't valid, reliable, or objective. A B in English says nothing about what a student can do, what she understands, where she needs help. Moreover, the basis for that grade is as subjective as the result is uninformative. A teacher can meticulously record scores for one test or assignment after another, eventually calculating averages down to a hundredth of a percentage point, but that doesn't change the arbitrariness of each of these individual marks. Even the score on a math test is largely a reflection of how the test was written: what skills the teacher decided to assess, what kinds of questions happened to be left out, and how many points each section was "worth."

> **A B in English says nothing about what a student can do, what she understands, where she needs help.**

Moreover, research has long been available to confirm what all of us know: Any given assignment may well be given two different grades by two equally qualified teachers. It may even be given two different grades by a single teacher who reads it at two different times (for example, see some of the early research reviewed in Kirschenbaum, Simon, and Napier 1971). In short, what grades offer is spurious precision — a subjective rating masquerading as an objective evaluation.

Grades distort the curriculum. A school's use of letter or number grades may encourage a fact- and skill-based approach to instruction because that sort of learning is easier to score. The tail of assessment thus comes to wag the educational dog.

Grades waste a lot of time that could be spent on learning. Add up all the hours that teachers spend fussing with their grade books. Then factor in the (mostly unpleasant) conversations they have with students and their parents about grades. It's tempting to just roll our eyes when confronted with whining or wheedling, but the real problem rests with the practice of grading itself.

Grades encourage cheating. Again, we can either continue to blame and punish all the students who cheat — or we can look for the structural reasons this keeps happening. Researchers have found that the more students are led to focus on getting good grades, the more likely they are to cheat, even if they themselves regard cheating as wrong (Anderman, Griesinger, and Westerfield 1998; Milton, Pollio, and Eison 1986).

Grades spoil teachers' relationships with students. Consider this lament, which could have been offered by a teacher in your district: "I'm getting tired of running a classroom in which everything we do revolves around grades. I'm tired of being suspicious when students give me compliments, wondering whether or not they are just trying to raise their grade. I'm tired of spending so much time and energy grading your papers, when there are probably a dozen more productive and enjoyable ways for all of us to handle the evaluation of papers. I'm tired of hearing you ask me, 'Does this count?' And, heaven knows, I'm certainly tired of all those little arguments and disagreements we get into concerning marks which take so much fun out of the teaching and the learning . . ."(Kirschenbaum, Simon, and Napier 1971, p. 115).

Grades spoil students' relationships with one another. The quality of students' thinking has been shown to depend partly on the extent to which they are permitted to learn cooperatively (Johnson and Johnson 1989; Kohn 1992). Thus, the ill feelings, suspicion, and resentment generated by grades aren't just disagreeable in their own right; they interfere with learning.

The most destructive form of grading by far is that which is done "on a curve," such that the number of top grades is artificially limited: No matter how well all the students do, not all of them can get an A. Apart from the intrinsic unfairness of this arrangement, its practical effect is to teach students that others are potential obstacles to their own success. The kind of collaboration that can help all students to learn more effectively doesn't stand a chance in such an environment. Sadly, even teachers who don't explicitly grade on a curve may assume, perhaps unconsciously, that the final grades "ought to" come out looking more or less this way: a few very good grades, a few very bad grades, and the majority somewhere in the middle.

The competition that turns schooling into a quest for triumph and ruptures relationships among students doesn't only happen within classrooms, of course. The same effect is witnessed schoolwide when kids are not just rated but ranked, sending the message that the point isn't to learn, or even to perform well, but to defeat others. Some students might be motivated to improve their class rank, but that is completely different from being motivated to understand ideas. (Wise educators realize that it doesn't matter how motivated students are; what matters is *how* students are motivated. It is the type of motivation that counts, not the amount.)

EXCUSES AND DISTRACTIONS

Most of us are directly acquainted with at least some of these disturbing consequences of grades, yet we continue to reduce students to letters or numbers on a regular basis. Perhaps we've become inured to these effects and take them for granted. This is the way it's always been, we assume,

> *It's rather like people who have spent all their lives in a terribly polluted city and have come to assume that this is just the way air looks.*

and the way it has to be. It's rather like people who have spent all their lives in a terribly polluted city and have come to assume that this is just the way air looks — and that it's natural to be coughing all the time.

Oddly, when educators are shown that it doesn't have to be this way, some react with suspicion instead of relief. They want to know why you're making trouble, or they assert that you're exaggerating the negative effects of grades (it's really not so bad — cough, cough), or they dismiss proven alternatives to grading on the grounds that our school could never do what other schools have done.

The practical difficulties of abolishing letter grades are real. But the key question is whether those difficulties are seen as problems to be solved or as excuses for perpetuating the status quo. The logical response to the arguments and data summarized here is to say: "Good heavens! If even half of this is true, then it's imperative we do whatever we can, as soon as we can, to phase out traditional grading." Yet, many people begin and end with the problems of implementation, responding to all this evidence by saying, in effect, "Yeah, yeah, yeah, but we'll never get rid of grades because . . ."

It is also striking how many educators never get beyond relatively insignificant questions, such as how many tests to give, or how often to send home grade reports, or what number corresponds to what letter. Some even reserve their outrage for the possibility that too many students are ending up with good grades, a reaction that suggests stinginess with A's is being confused with intellectual rigor.

COMMON OBJECTIONS

Let's consider the most frequently heard responses to the above arguments — which is to say, the most common objections to getting rid of grades.

First, it is said that students expect to receive grades and even seem addicted to them. This is often true; I've taught high school students who reacted to the absence of grades with what I can only describe as existential vertigo. (*Who am I if not a B+?*) But as more elementary and even some middle schools move to replace grades with more informative (and less destructive) systems of assessment, the damage doesn't begin until students get to high school. Moreover, elementary and middle schools that *haven't* changed their practices often cite the local high school as the reason they must get students used to getting grades regardless of their damaging effects — just as high schools point the finger at colleges.

Even when students arrive in high school already accustomed to grades, already primed to ask teachers, "Do we have to know this?" or "What do I have to do to get an A?", this is a sign that something is very wrong. It's more an indictment of what has happened to them in the past than an argument to keep doing it in the future.

Perhaps because of this training, grades can succeed in getting students to show up on time, hand in their work, and otherwise do what they're told. Many teachers are loath to give up what is essentially an instrument of control. But even to the extent this instrument works (which is not always), we are obliged to reflect on whether mindless compliance is really our goal. The teacher who exclaims, "These kids would blow off my course in a minute if they weren't getting a grade for it!" may be issuing a powerful indictment of his or her course. Who would be more reluctant to give up grades than a teacher who spends the period slapping transparencies on the overhead projector and lecturing endlessly at students about Romantic poets or genetic codes? Without bribes (A's) and threats (F's), students would have no reason to do such assignments. To maintain that this proves something is wrong with the kids — or that grades are simply "necessary" — suggests a willful refusal to examine one's classroom practices and assumptions about teaching and learning.

"If I can't give a child a better reason for studying than a grade on a report card, I ought to lock my desk and go home and stay there." So wrote Dorothy De Zouche, a Missouri teacher, in an article published in February . . . of 1945. But teachers who *can* give a child a better reason for studying don't need grades. Research substantiates this: When the curriculum is engaging — for example, when it involves hands-on, interactive learning activities — students who aren't graded at all perform just as well as those who are graded (Moeller and Reschke 1993).

Another objection: It is sometimes argued that students must be given grades because colleges demand them. One might reply that "high schools have no responsibility to serve colleges by performing the sorting function for them" — particularly if that process undermines learning (Krumboltz and Yeh 1996, p. 325). But in any case the premise of this argument is erroneous: Traditional grades are not mandatory for admission to colleges and universities.

MAKING CHANGE

A friend of mine likes to say that people don't resist change — they resist being changed. Even terrific ideas (like moving a school from a grade orientation to a learning orientation) are guaranteed to self-destruct if they are simply forced down people's throats. The first step for an administrator, therefore, is to open up a conversation — to spend perhaps a full year just encouraging people to think and talk about the effects of (and alternatives to) traditional grades. This can happen in individual classes, as teachers facilitate discussions about how students regard grades, as well as in evening meetings with parents, or on a website — all with the help of relevant books, articles, speakers, videos, and visits to neighboring schools that are further along in this journey.

The actual process of "de-grading" can be done in stages. For example, a high school might start by freeing ninth-grade classes from grades before doing the same for upperclassmen. (Even a school that never gets beyond the first stage will have done a considerable service, giving students one full year when they can think about what they're learning instead of their GPAs.)

Another route to gradual change is to begin by eliminating only the most pernicious practices, such as grading on a curve or ranking students. Although grades, per se, may continue for a while, at least the message will be sent from the beginning that all students can do well, and that the point is to succeed rather than to beat others.

Anyone who has heard the term *authentic assessment* knows that abolishing grades doesn't mean eliminating the process of gathering information about student performance — and communicating that information to students and parents. Rather, abolishing grades opens up possibilities that are far more meaningful and constructive. These include narratives (written comments), portfolios (carefully chosen collections of students' writings and projects that demonstrate their interests, achievements, and improvement over time), student-led parent-teacher conferences, exhibitions, and other opportunities for students to show what they can do.

Of course, it's harder for a teacher to do these kinds of assessments if he or she has 150 or more students and sees each of them for forty-five to fifty-five minutes a day. But that's not an argument for continuing to use traditional grades; it's an argument for challenging these archaic remnants of a factory-oriented approach to instruction, structural aspects of high schools that are bad news for reasons that go well beyond the issue of assessment. It's an argument for looking into block scheduling, team teaching, interdisciplinary courses — and learning more about schools that have arranged things so each teacher can spend more time with fewer students (e.g., Meier 1995).

The real problem is that almost all kids . . . will come to focus on grades and, as a result, their learning will be hurt.

Administrators should be prepared to respond to parental concerns, some of them completely reasonable, about the prospect of edging away from grades. "Don't you value excellence?" You bet — and here's the evidence that traditional grading *undermines* excellence. "Are you just trying to spare the self-esteem of students who do poorly?" We are concerned that grades may be making things worse for such students, yes, but the problem isn't just that some kids won't get A's and will have their feelings hurt. The real problem is that almost all kids (including yours) will come to focus on grades and, as a result, their learning will be hurt.

If parents worry that grades are the only window they have into the school, we need to assure them that alternative assessments provide a far better view. But if parents don't seem to care about getting the most useful information or helping their children become more excited learners — if they demand grades for the purpose of documenting how much better their kids are than everyone else's — then we need to engage them in a discussion about whether this is a legitimate goal, and whether schools exist for the purpose of competitive credentialing or for the purpose of helping everyone to learn (Kohn 1998; Labaree 1997). Above all, we need to make sure that objections and concerns about the details don't obscure the main message, which is the demonstrated harm of traditional grading on the quality of students' learning and their interest in exploring ideas.

High school administrators can do a world of good in their districts by actively supporting efforts to eliminate conventional grading in elementary and middle schools. Working with their colleagues in these schools can help pave the way for making such changes at the secondary school level.

IN THE MEANTIME

Finally, there is the question of what classroom teachers can do while grades continue to be required. The short answer is that they should do everything within their power to make grades as invisible as possible for as long as possible. Helping students forget about grades is the single best piece of advice for those who want to create a learning-oriented classroom.

When I was teaching high school, I did a lot of things I now regret. But one policy that still seems sensible to me was saying to students on the first day of class that, while I was compelled to give them a grade at the end of the term, I could not in good conscience ever put a letter or number on anything they did during the term — and I would not do so. I would, however, write a comment — or, better, sit down and talk with them — as often as possible to give them feedback.

At this particular school I frequently faced students who had been prepared for admission to Harvard since their early childhood — a process I have come to call "Preparation H." I knew that my refusal to rate their learning might cause some students to worry about their marks all the more, or to create suspense about what would appear on their final grade reports, which of course would defeat the whole purpose. So I said that anyone who absolutely had to know what grade a given paper would get could come see me and we would figure it out together. An amazing thing happened: As the days went by, fewer and fewer students felt the need to ask me about grades. They began to be more involved with what we were learning, because I had taken responsibility as a teacher to stop pushing grades into their faces, so to speak, whenever they completed an assignment.

What I didn't do very well, however, was to get students involved in devising the criteria for excellence (what makes a math solution elegant, an experiment well designed, an essay persuasive, a story compelling) or in deciding how well their projects met those criteria. I'm afraid I unilaterally set the criteria and evaluated the students' efforts. But I have seen teachers who were more willing to give up control, more committed to helping students participate in assessment and turn that into part of the learning. Teachers who work with their students to design powerful alternatives to letter grades have a replacement ready to go when the school finally abandons traditional grading — and are able to minimize the harm of such grading in the meantime.

ADDENDUM: MUST CONCERNS ABOUT COLLEGE DERAIL HIGH SCHOOL LEARNING?

Here is the good news: College admissions practices are not as rigid and reactionary as many people think. Here is the better news: Even when that process doesn't seem to have its priorities straight, high schools don't have to be dragged down to that level.

Sometimes it is assumed that admissions officers at the best universities are eighty-year-old fuddy-duddies peering over their spectacles and muttering about "highly irregular" applications. In truth, the people charged with making these decisions are often just a few years out of college themselves, and after making their way through a pile of interchangeable applications from 3.8-GPA, student-council-vice-president, musically accomplished hopefuls from high-powered traditional suburban high schools, they are desperate for something unconventional. Given that the most selective colleges have been known to accept homeschooled children who have never set foot in a classroom, secondary schools have more latitude than they sometimes assume. It is not widely known, for example, that hundreds of colleges and universities don't require applicants to take either the SAT or the ACT.

Admittedly, large state universities are more resistant to unconventional applications than are small private colleges simply because of economics: It takes more time, and therefore more money, for admissions officers to read meaningful application materials than it does for them to glance at a GPA or an SAT score and plug it into a formula. But I have heard of high schools approaching the admissions directors of nearby universities and saying, in effect, "We'd like to improve our school by getting rid of grades. Here's why. Will you work with us to make sure our seniors aren't penalized?" This strategy may well be successful for the simple reason that not many high schools are requesting this at present and the added inconvenience for admissions offices is likely to be negligible. Of course, if more and more high schools abandon traditional grades, then the universities will have no choice but to adapt. This is a change that high schools will have to initiate rather than waiting for colleges to signal their readiness.

At the moment, plenty of admissions officers enjoy the convenience of class ranking, apparently because they have confused being better than one's peers with being good at something; they're looking for winners rather than learners. But relatively few colleges actually insist on this practice. When a 1993 survey by the National Association of Secondary School Principals asked eleven hundred admissions officers what would happen if a high school stopped computing class rank, only 0.5 percent said the school's applicants would not be considered for admission, 4.5 percent said it would be a "great handicap," and 14.4 percent said it would be a "handicap" (Levy and Riordan 1994). In other words, it appears that the absence of class ranks would not interfere at all with students' prospects for admission to four out of five colleges.

Even more impressive, some high schools not only refuse to rank their students but refuse to give any sort of letter or number grades. Courses are all taken pass/fail, sometimes with narrative assessments of the students' performance that become part of a college application. I have spoken to representatives and all assure me that, year after year, their graduates are accepted into large state universities and small, highly selective colleges. *Even the complete absence of high school grades is not a barrier to college admission*, so we don't have that excuse for continuing to subject students to the harm done by traditional grading.

> *It takes more time . . . for admissions officers to read meaningful application materials than it does for them to glance at a GPA or an SAT score.*

REFERENCES

Anderman, E. M., T. Griesinger, and G. Westerfield. 1998. "Motivation and Cheating During Early Adolescence." *Journal of Educational Psychology* 90: 84–93.

Anderman, E. M., and J. Johnston. 1998. "Television News in the Classroom: What Are Adolescents Learning?" *Journal of Adolescent Research* 13: 73–100.

Beck, H. P., S. Rorrer-Woody, and L. G. Pierce. 1991. "The Relations of Learning and Grade Orientations to Academic Performance." *Teaching of Psychology* 18: 35–37.

Benware, C. A., and E. L. Deci. 1984. "Quality of Learning With an Active Versus Passive Motivational Set." *American Educational Research Journal* 21: 755–65.

Butler, R. 1987. "Task-Involving and Ego-Involving Properties of Evaluation: Effects of Different Feedback Conditions on Motivational Perceptions, Interest, and Performance." *Journal of Educational Psychology* 79: 474–82.

Butler, R. 1988. "Enhancing and Undermining Intrinsic Motivation: The Effects of Task-Involving and Ego-Involving Evaluation on Interest and Performance." *British Journal of Educational Psychology* 58: 1–14.

Butler, R., and M. Nisan. 1986. "Effects of No Feedback, Task-Related Comments, and Grades on Intrinsic Motivation and Performance." *Journal of Educational Psychology* 78: 210–16.

De Zouche, D. 1945. "'The Wound Is Mortal': Marks, Honors, Unsound Activities." *The Clearing House* 19: 339–44.

Grolnick, W. S., and R. M. Ryan. 1987. "Autonomy in Children's Learning: An Experimental and Individual Difference Investigation." *Journal of Personality and Social Psychology* 52: 890–98.

Harter, S. 1978. "Pleasure Derived from Challenge and the Effects of Receiving Grades on Children's Difficulty Level Choices." *Child Development* 49: 788–99.

Harter, S., and M. E. Guzman, 1986. "The Effect of Perceived Cognitive Competence and Anxiety on Children's Problem-Solving Performance, Difficulty Level Choices, and Preference for Challenge." Unpublished manuscript, University of Denver.

Hughes, B., H. J. Sullivan, and M. L. Mosley, 1985. "External Evaluation, Task Difficulty, and Continuing Motivation." *Journal of Educational Research* 78: 210–15.

Johnson, D. W., and R. T. Johnson. 1989. *Cooperation and Competition: Theory and Research*. Edina, Minn.: Interaction Book Co.

Kage, M. 1991. "The Effects of Evaluation on Intrinsic Motivation." Paper presented at the meeting of the Japan Association of Educational Psychology, Joetsu, Japan.

Kirschenbaum, H., S. B. Simon, and R. W. Napier. 1971. *Wad-Ja-Get?: The Grading Game in American Education*. New York: Hart.

Kohn, A. 1992. *No Contest: The Case Against Competition*. Rev. ed. Boston: Houghton Mifflin.

Kohn, A. 1993. *Punished by Rewards: The Trouble with Gold Stars, Incentive Plans, A's, Praise, and Other Bribes*. Boston: Houghton Mifflin.

Kohn, A. 1998. "Only for My Kid: How Privileged Parents Undermine School Reform." *Phi Delta Kappan*, April: 569–77.

Krumboltz, J. D., and C. J. Yeh. 1996. "Competitive Grading Sabotages Good Teaching." *Phi Delta Kappan*, December: 324–26.

Labaree, D. F. 1997. *How to Succeed in School Without Really Learning: The Credentials Race in American Education*. New Haven, Conn.: Yale University Press.

Levy, J., and P. Riordan. 1994. *Rank-in-Class, Grade Point Average, and College Admission*. Reston, Va.: NASSP. (Available as ERIC Document 370988.)

Meier, D. 1995. *The Power of Their Ideas: Lessons for America from a Small School in Harlem*. Boston: Beacon.

Milton, O., H. R. Pollio, and J. A. Eison. 1986. *Making Sense of College Grades*. San Francisco: Jossey-Bass.

Moeller, A. J., and C. Reschke. 1993. "A Second Look at Grading and Classroom Performance: Report of a Research Study." *Modern Language Journal* 77: 163–69.

Salili, F., M. L. Maehr, R. L. Sorensen, and L. J. Fyans Jr. 1976. "A Further Consideration of the Effects of Evaluation on Motivation." *American Educational Research Journal* 13: 85–102.

DISCUSSION

1. Kohn has some pointed things to say about the connection that is often presumed to exist between traditional grading and student motivation. More specifically, he questions the long-standing educational norm that says students who do not receive grades have no incentive to work. What do you think of this claim? Is it valid? How does your own view compare to Kohn's?

2. Kohn's critique of conventional grading practices rests in part on his assertion that, no matter how minutely calculated, every letter or number grade is a subjective and arbitrary assessment. Do you agree? Can you think of an example from your own school experiences that either confirms or confounds this argument?

3. "Perhaps," Kohn speculates, "we've become inured to [the] effects [of grades] and take them for granted. This is the way it's always been, we assume, and the way it has to be. It's rather like people who have spent all their lives in a terribly polluted city and have come to assume that this is just the way air looks — and that it's natural to be coughing all the time." What do you make of this analogy? To what extent does it seem valid to think of our contemporary approach to grading as a kind of pollution? Does this analogy capture any aspect of your own educational experiences?

WRITING

4. Write a personal essay in which you either support or refute Kohn's argument about grading using anecdotes from your experience as a student. Do you view grading in a negative or positive light? Why or why not? Make sure to structure your argument by addressing Kohn's multiple points directly.

5. Kohn writes about the need to move a school "from a grade orientation to a learning orientation." What do you think he means by labeling the shift this way? How, according to Kohn, does grading make it harder to focus on learning? Write an essay in which you discuss what the characteristics of these two orientations are. Do you think it's possible to have an educational system that emphasizes both?

6. Write an essay in which you discuss how Kohn might use Brigid Schulte's "The Case of the Purloined Paper" (p. 524) as evidence for his argument against grading. How do you think Kohn would argue that non-grade-based assignments would help solve the problem of plagiarism?

MICHAEL BERUBE
Reasonable Disagreements

We hear a lot these days about how college campuses have become hotbeds of liberal thinking and liberal politics. But is this really the case? Undertaking to dismantle the charge of "political correctness" so often leveled these days against colleges and universities, Michael Berube offers a ringing defense of the values that undergird the so-called liberal education. Along the way, he poses hard questions about the goals and responsibilities of teaching (his own and others) as well as what it is we should really expect from contemporary education. Berube teaches American literature and cultural studies at Penn State University. His books include *Public Access: Literary Theory and American Cultural Politics* (1994), *The Employment of English: Theory, Jobs, and the Future of Literary Studies* (1998), *Rhetorical Occasions: Essays on Humans and the Humanities* (2006), and *What's Liberal about the Liberal Arts? Classroom Politics and "Bias" in Higher Education* (2006). In 2006, conservative writer David Horowitz included Berube in his *100 Most Dangerous Academics in America* for being part of what Horowitz called the left-wing academy. Beginning in 2004, Berube wrote an award-winning blog about education, literary theory, and disability studies. In 2007, he stopped publishing at his own site and joined Crooked Timber, a group blog run by several academics.

T HE CLASS STARTED OFF INNOCUOUSLY ENOUGH. WE WERE IN THE fifth week of an undergraduate honors seminar in postmodernism and American fiction, reading Ishmael Reed's 1972 novel, *Mumbo Jumbo*, and I was starting to explain how the novel is built on a series of deliberate anachronisms. I began with Abdul Hamid's encounter with PaPa LaBas at a rent party (the novel is set in New York during the Harlem Renaissance), where Hamid delivers a tirade that presages the rise of the Nation of Islam and the antiwar protests of the late 1960s:

> This is the country where something is successful in direct proportion to how it's put over; how it's gamed. Look at the Mormons. . . . The most fundamental book of the Mormon Church, the Book of Mormon, is a fraud. If we Blacks came up with something as corny as the Angel of Moroni, something as trite and phony as their story that the book is the record of ancient Americans who came here in 600 B.C. and perished by A.D. 400, they would deride us with pejorative adjectival phrases like "so-called" and "would-be." They would refuse to exempt our priests from the draft, a privilege extended to every

White hayseed's fruit stand which calls itself a Church. But regardless of the put-on, the hype, the Mormons got Utah, didn't they?[1]

Most of my students had no idea why Hamid would go off on the Mormons; for them, the passage was just so much mumbo jumbo. I explained briefly that Muhammad Ali's refusal to fight in Vietnam had been incendiary in the late 1960s but eventually led the United States to reconsider its criteria for conscientious-objector status; that the comparison between the Church of Jesus Christ of Latter-Day Saints and the Nation of Islam was a fairly common one when Reed wrote the novel; and that one nationalist group, the Republic of New Africa, had called for the creation of a separate black nation based in five Southern states, as partial reparation for slavery.[2]

At that point, John, a large white student in the back of the room, snorted loudly and derisively. "That's completely ridiculous!" he exclaimed. Startled, the students in the front rows turned to look at John. "It may seem ridiculous to you, yes," I replied, "and for the record, I don't believe there was any possibility that the Republic of New Africa was going to become a reality. I don't endorse it myself. But it was proposed, and some black nationalists pointedly compared their relation with the US government to that of the Mormons."

But John was just getting started. These people are not Africans, he insisted. They are African-*Americans*. The whole "Africa" thing is a charade; racial separatism and identity politics are tearing this country apart; people have to realize that if they live in this country, no matter how they got here, they are Americans first, and something-Americans second.

Apparently, we had touched a nerve. I pointed out, gently but I hoped not patronizingly, that whatever any of us might feel about the various projects of black nationalism, we are dealing here with a character in a novel — a character, I hastened to add, whose reductive brand of nationalism is ultimately undermined in the course of the narrative. It only makes sense to try to understand what he might be trying to say, and there's no reason to assume that his remarks are endorsed by the author — or by the professor who assigned the book. And now let's move on to another example of anachronism in *Mumbo Jumbo* . . .

The other students in the class — of various colors and genders, some of them born on other continents, some of them first-generation college kids from rural Pennsylvania, none of them African-American — didn't respond directly to John's outburst. They were more interested in the novel's use of anachronism, and uncertain (as so many other readers have been) about whether to take seriously the novel's various conspiracy theories about Warren Harding's death, about the demise of the Harlem Renaissance, about the role of the Freemasons in American history, and about the rise of Western culture itself. For the moment, the Republic of New Africa had been forgotten once again — but John simmered throughout the rest of the hour, clearly upset that no one had addressed his comment.

I've dealt with students like John before and I'm sure I'll see them again, no matter what class I'm teaching. But that semester was different; it was the fall of 2001, and students' nerves and political opinions were especially raw. I negotiated any number of delicate exchanges that semester, many of which were indirectly related to the events of September 11. And in the years since, as conservative students and pundits have begun to mount campaigns against what they perceive as liberal "bias" in American universities, I've had many occasions to wonder whether I've always dealt with students like John in the best possible way. Although I'm a fairly opinionated and outspoken liberal-progressive writer outside the classroom, I keep most of my political opinions to myself when I enter the classroom, and only very rarely do I encounter an undergraduate student who's familiar with my writings for *Dissent* or the *Nation* or major-city newspapers. Nor do I pry into my students' personal beliefs; ordinarily, I neither know nor care where my students stand on abortion, the minimum wage, genocide in Rwanda or Sudan, war in Iraq, the regressive Social Security tax, or the policies of the World Bank. But this time I thought I should engage John more thoroughly, precisely because he sensed that the class had deliberately ignored him and (as I learned later) he assumed that I was antagonistic to him as well.

> As conservative students and pundits . . . mount campaigns against what they perceive as liberal "bias" . . . I've had many occasions to wonder whether I've always dealt with students like John in the best possible way.

So after class that day, I talked to John at some length as we wandered through the noontime campus swarms. He was insistent that membership in the American community requires one to subordinate his or her ethnic or national origin, and that he himself wanted to be understood not as an American of Russian or Polish or German "extraction," but simply as an American among other Americans. And he was just sick and tired of African-Americans refusing to do the same.

I replied by telling John something like this: "Your position has a long and distinguished history in debates over immigration and national identity. It's part of the current critique of multiculturalism, and to a point I have some sympathy with it, because I don't think that social contracts should be based on cultural homogeneity." Deep breath. "That said," I went on, "I have to point out that the terms under which people of African descent might be accepted as Americans, in 1820 or 1920 or whenever, have been radically different from the terms under which your ancestors, whoever they were, could be accepted as Americans. You're right to insist that you shouldn't be defined by your ancestry, but, unfortunately, most African-Americans — who, by the way, fought and died for integration for many generations — didn't have that option. And it shouldn't be all that surprising that, when African-Americans finally *did* have the option of integrating into the larger national community, some of them were profoundly ambivalent about the prospect."

I didn't press the point that Reed's novel is itself profoundly ambivalent about that profound ambivalence; I thought that we were now on terrain that had little to do with the textual details of *Mumbo Jumbo*, and I was simply trying to come to an understanding with a student who clearly felt very strongly about one of the social issues raised in class. We parted amicably, and I thought that though he wasn't about to agree with me on this one, we had, at least, made our arguments intelligible to each other. And I thought that as a professor, I had an obligations — both a professional obligation and a "liberal" one, that is, liberal in the tradition of John Stuart Mill — to make some kind of reasonable accommodation for the airing of opinions that may differ not only from my own but also from the views of most of my other students.

But the dynamic of the class had been changed. From that day forward, John spoke up often, sometimes loudly, sometimes out of turn. He had begun to conceive of himself as the only countervailing conservative voice in a classroom full of liberal-left think-alikes, and he occasionally spoke as if he were entitled to reply to every other student's comment — in a class of seventeen. He was forceful, intelligent, and articulate. Sometimes he was witty, and he was knowledgeable about science fiction; his expertise was always welcome, because I'd assigned the class three strikingly disparate examples of the genre (by Philip K. Dick, Ursula LeGuin, and William Gibson). Often, however, he was obstreperous and out of bounds.

His obstreperousness presented me with not one problem but two. It would have been a relatively simple matter to put the brakes on — to speak to him, in class or afterward, in such a way as to let him know that he was not, in fact, entitled to comment on every other student's comment. But I did not want to contribute to his growing sense of lonely opposition. The layout of the classroom itself didn't help matters.

> *I did not want to contribute to his growing sense of lonely opposition.*

Ordinarily, small seminars are held around seminar tables, so that all students can speak to one another and to me simultaneously; but in this long and shallow room (three rows deep, eight or nine seats wide), all the seats faced the front desk, and when John would speak from the back row, I would sometimes be treated to a silent chorus of eye-rolling among students in the first two rows. I had to be careful not to endorse any such eye-rolling by look or gesture, yet at the same time I did not want to glare at the eye-rolling students in such a way as to let John know that they were blowing him off. His sixteen classmates were not, in fact, a unified left-liberal bloc; some of them were recognizably left of center, but not all. In the weeks after September 11, my students sounded off on an extraordinary range of questions, including the question of whether that day marked the death of postmodernism, as the *New York Times*'s Edward Rothstein had suggested (in an essay I distributed to the class a few days after its publication).[3] As a result, I knew more about my students' politics than I ordinarily do, and they learned more about mine than they ordinarily would have. I knew my class contained a handful of people adamantly opposed to military action against the Taliban in Afghanistan (in most cases, that put them to the left of me, though I believe a couple of my students opposed war on religious grounds and could not be easily pegged as left or right), a handful of people who wanted to redraw the Middle East from scratch in the manner of Paul Wolfowitz, and a handful of people who called themselves libertarians but whose politics didn't go much beyond keep-your-laws-off-my-bong.

Actually, some students agreed with John about one thing or another but were simply annoyed that he was taking up so much class time. They began sending me e-mail messages and speaking to me privately about how they did not want John to set the parameters for class discussion. One student complained that she was wasting time trying to think of things that John wouldn't reply to; another said that he found anti-porn feminism obnoxious, just as John did, but couldn't stand it when people dismissed feminism so sweepingly as to render suspect other people's more careful critiques (his own, for example). If I directly asked John to cool it, then he would undoubtedly feel silenced and I would be in the position of validating what was perhaps, for him, a stifling liberal hegemony over classroom speech; if I failed to restrain him, I would in effect be allowing him to dominate the class, thereby silencing the other students who'd taken the time to speak to me about the problem.

For the remaining weeks of the semester, I tried to split the difference. John spoke more often than any other student, but I did not recognize him every time he asked; when students criticized his remarks, implicitly or explicitly, I did not validate their criticisms but I did try to let them speak in rough proportion to their numbers. On the class listserv, I aimed for a similar compromise — at one particularly tense point, I wrote to the other sixteen students to ask them not to reply to every single one of John's dismissive comments about the syllabus or his fellow students' contributions to the weekly listserv discussions. For a while, order was restored.

* * *

One of the flaws in my approach was that it left John completely unaware of how much the rest of the class and I were doing to accommodate him — to ensure that he would continue to contribute to our discussions, in class and online, and to ensure among ourselves that his contributions would not become the focal point of discussion. (That second imperative was practically self-negating, insofar as the sentence "Don't pay so much attention to John" necessarily pays attention to John.) I'll admit that John's obliviousness to his classmates' complaints — and to my behind-the-scenes attempts to rein in those complaints — afforded me a few moments of aggravation, in which I gave in to the temptation to think of myself as the preternaturally patient professor who stays up late at night trying to figure out ways of making sure that Every Voice Is Heard. Gradually, then, another flaw in my approach revealed itself to me: I was increasingly thinking of John as a problem to be *managed* somehow: By mid-semester, then, I decided to treat John as I would any other talkative, engaging student; I would learn more about him and the various predispositions, tastes, enthusiasms, and aversions he brought to class. I knew as much about five or six of my other students — enough to know that one was a passionate civil libertarian profoundly shaken by the attacks of September 11, another was smitten to the core by the work of James Joyce, another was fluent in German and found it easier to read post-Nietzschean German philosophy in the original, another was a promising poet from a blink-and-you'll-miss-it small town in the mountains, another was a prizewinning fiction writer who wanted to work in publishing after graduation, and so on. What was up with John?

One thing I found puzzling was that although he held a good deal of the syllabus in contempt — informing the listserv that Thomas Pynchon's *The Crying of Lot 49* is full of "the sort of prose that gives writers a bad name" and opening his comment on Ishmael Reed by writing, "Dear Sir: Please translate your novel *Mumbo Jumbo* into something resembling English. Thank you. P.S. Grammar can be your friend if you are kind to it" — he was a cyberpunk fan, and cyberpunk is not normally a genre in which one finds well-crafted prose or well-rounded characters. At one point, I found myself telling John that his complaints about post-modern novels, from the convolutions of Pynchon to the plotlessness of DeLillo's *White Noise*, were common to many readers of contemporary American fiction, but that few of those readers would then proceed, as he did, to name William Gibson's *Neuromancer* as their favorite item on the syllabus. Insofar as his dislike for Pynchon, Reed, and DeLillo wasn't rooted, as it is for so many readers, in a preference for plausible characters and/or the high seriousness of George Eliot or William Faulkner, I wasn't sure what to make of it — nor did I understand why he'd signed up for a course called "postmodernism and American fiction" in the first place. Another student told me she'd taken the course because it had three science fiction books on the syllabus, and she was merely tolerating the rest of the material. Perhaps John's motivations were similar; at any rate, I made a mental note not to emphasize science fiction quite so much in the future if it was attracting students who didn't like reading anything else.

I also learned a thing or two — but only a thing or two — about why race was such a volatile topic for John. Penn State had weathered an exceptionally unpleasant spring in 2001, just before I arrived on campus; dozens of students had received anonymous racist letters and e-mail messages, and the leader of the Black Student Caucus had received direct death threats. In May of that year, the *Chronicle of Higher Education* reported on the incidents and Penn State's attempt to defuse the crisis and address the concerns — more accurately, the outrage — of minority students and faculty:

> Trouble began in mid-April, when Daryl Lang, a reporter who covers diversity issues for the student newspaper, *The Collegian*, received a letter filled with profanity and racial slurs. The letter instructed Mr. Lang to forward an enclosed letter to LaKeisha Wolf, president of the university's Black Caucus. The letter to Ms. Wolf contained direct death threats. "I could have killed you 10 times by now," the letter reads. "This is a white academy in a white town — in a white country and by god it's going to stay that way, nigger bitch."[4]

Many students rallied in sympathy with the Black Caucus and Penn State's African-American students, who make up a paltry 4 percent of the overall student population, forming what they called a "village" in the student center. But most students, I heard from various sources, had no idea what was going on. And, sure enough, there were also those who insisted that the protestors were overplaying their hand, and one professor, a Christian conservative in the education school, even went so far as to suggest that the death threats were a hoax and that the campus was in fact facing "a Tawana Brawley situation," referring to the young black New York woman who in 1987 baselessly charged that she had been assaulted and raped by a group of white men. John informed me, in one of our after-class conversations, that he had had some kind of run-in with one of the African-American campus demonstrators that spring, in which he emphatically told the demonstrator he was not a racist.

It was not hard to imagine that whatever took place between John and the demonstrator might have been quite ugly, and I could also imagine (extending the principle of charity) that the demonstrator might possibly have given John some reason to feel defensive, angry, or even threatened. Yet I couldn't shake the feeling that, although John and students like him might occasionally feel wary or uncomfortable in some areas of campus (and perhaps in classes like mine), they aren't in any real danger. Every once in a while, in the wake of the 2000–01 demonstration (even to this day), the local campus conservatives like to point to all the things they think the Penn State administration does for black students; one recent flier complained that there is a Paul Robeson Center on the campus (and Robeson was a Communist!), whereas the campus conservatives have to meet in a classroom. After I finished shaking my head at the sheer foolishness of the complaint — did these kids really think that the HUB–Paul Robeson Center, which is simply a student-union building used by absolutely everyone at Penn State, was established

> *I wondered just how many of my conservative white students . . . would prefer to be black at Penn State, black in the United States.*

as the headquarters of a black-activist organization? — I wondered just how many of my conservative white students, if given the chance, would prefer to be black at Penn State, black in the United States.

I didn't fault John for bringing his predispositions, tastes, enthusiasms, and aversions into our classroom. Nor did I mind the fact that his political and cultural beliefs informed his response to the material. I did think — and still think — that he sometimes used the novels as springboards for political editorializing, and that his response to Abdul Hamid in *Mumbo Jumbo* was a fairly clear example of how not to do literacy criticism. Still, I can't deny that I quite often invite students to comment on the broader social or cultural implications of the literary works they read; avoiding broader social and cultural questions seems to me to be yet another example of how not to do literary criticism. So it's not as if I would ever chastise a student for suggesting, for example, that Hamid's speech about Mormonism is, just possibly, a tad snide and unfair, just as I would not chastise a student who objected to Reed's portrayal of the nationalist Hamid as something of a huckster and a hypocrite.

Besides, there was a still larger issue at stake, inasmuch as some of John's comments were clearly directed specifically to me: to what extent should my own beliefs be an explicit part of my teaching? This is not a rhetorical question. It is something I weigh every time I walk into the classroom, regardless of the rapport I have or have not established with a group of students. Literature professors have an exceptionally wide range in this regard, since their subject matter covers most of the known world from history to psychology to physics, and in some cases (such as science fiction, including the cyberpunk variety) features of worlds not yet known to history or psychology or physics. Mimesis, after all, is a staggeringly capacious thing: literature is capable of addressing every conceivable personal, social, cultural, and political question humans have posed to themselves since the invention of written language, as well as depicting forms of language, behavior, and social organization that do not exist outside of the imaginative worlds created by written language. So when people tell me I should focus my teaching on "literature" rather than on personal, social, cultural, or political questions, I always stop to ask them what, exactly, they imagine literature to be about.

Even if I were not working in literary study, with its capaciousness and its uncontainable mimesis, I cannot begin to imagine what it would be like to be a teacher without beliefs, or what it would be like to be a teacher whose beliefs about the world did not inform his work and his very demeanor. And yet one of my beliefs is this: the classroom is an intimate, quasi-public, quasi-private space, and it would be an abuse of my position if I were to treat my students as captive audiences who need to be educated about the rightness of affirmative action or the wrongness of Republican fiscal policy. I would be selling students short if my classes did not reflect some of my beliefs about literary theory or feminism or postmodernism or multiculturalism, since I have spent my entire adult life studying such things and am familiar with a wide range of opinions about them, quite apart from my own; just as I am duty-bound to make this argument or that under my own name when it is relevant to the material, so too am I duty-bound to inform students of some of the most cogent critiques of the positions I favor. But it is not my job to change students' minds about this policy or that, this person or that, by the end of the semester. I can hope to affect the way my students apprehend the world, and I especially hope to affect the way they approach the possibility that some forms of interpretive disagreement may not in fact be negotiable. But when I hear leftist professors here and there arguing that their students watch six hours of Fox News every day and that it's therefore their job to expose them to the "other side" for an hour, I tend to imagine that their classes sound, to some students, more like a seventh hour of Fox News than the voice of liberation. It is a skewed notion of dissent to think that one's classroom should be deployed as the counterweight to conservatism in the rest of the culture; it is a poor conception of rhetoric that leads a professor to speak as if everyone in the room agrees with him or her; and it is a curious form of pedagogy to conduct oneself as if one's lectures could simply and suddenly cause the scales to fall from the eyes of a roomful of Republican undergraduates.

Good teaching involves all kinds of ventriloquism. Sometimes I speak in my own voice; sometimes I refer students to a general consensus (Faulkner's career goes downhill after *Go Down, Moses*) or a generally accepted set of historical facts (there was almost no market for African-American fiction before the era of the Harlem Renaissance); and sometimes I present interpretations I disagree with or actively dislike in order to present lesser-known sides of a ten-sided question, or simply to stir things up. Like liberal New York University professor Siva Vaidhyanathan, I often find myself being a classroom contrarian in the hope that it will make my students sharper. "Most often," Vaidhyanathan writes,

> at liberal places like Wesleyan, the University of Wisconsin, and New York University, I find myself playing devil's advocate. I take positions for the sake of challenging lazy lefty thought. I have voiced approval of Starbucks, Barnes and Noble, and Wal-Mart and made the occasional hemp-clothing-wearing student defend her criticisms of them. I have asked pointed questions that indicate support for television and Web censorship. I have argued against peer-to-peer file sharing. In a course on multiculturalism in which every student had inchoate positive feelings about pluralism, I spent the entire semester breaking it down and exposing its weaknesses. I tried to turn feelings into thoughts and encouraged them to abandon some opinions and strengthen others. Somebody had to do it.[5]

Yes, somebody has to do it. And for most teachers, it's all in a day's work.

Late in the semester, we read Richard Powers's 1988 novel, *Prisoner's Dilemma*. Part of it is set during World War II and involves a character's fantasia about how Walt Disney turns out to be an American of Japanese ancestry. Appalled by the 1942 federal order to intern Japanese-Americans living in the United States, Disney manages to get two of his employees out of the camps so that they can help him work on a top-secret film project, which will not only win this war but prevent all future wars. I noted that Powers is asking whether it is right to fight a totalitarian enemy by employing totalitarian tactics, and I pointed to passages in which he adduces the internment camps as examples of the game-theory problem known as the prisoner's dilemma (hence the title of the novel).[6] In the prisoner's dilemma, two prisoners are prevented from communicating with each other, and each is given the following options: if you confess and the other guy follows suit, you both get ten years; if you keep quiet and the other guy does the same, you both get two years; if you keep quiet and the other guy squeals, you get the chair and he goes free. At first, each prisoner thinks, well, this is simple enough; I should keep quiet, and the other guy should keep quiet. But then the problem appears to him in another way: if I keep quiet, I get two years or I get the chair; if I squeal, I go free or I get ten years. Clearly, then, I do better when I squeal. And since the other prisoner reasons the same way, they each get ten years, or five times the sentence they'd have gotten if they had kept quiet. You can play with the parameters, but that's the classic version. Almost invariably, prisoners choose to confess, even though mutual trust in the other's steadfastness is clearly the way to go if they want to (a) stay alive and (b) keep their jail time to a minimum. Powers's point is that a world without mutual trust would be a world of unending world war; as the novel unfolds, the prisoner's dilemma becomes a metaphor not only for the Japanese-American internment camps but also for the postwar nuclear era of mutually assured destruction, and for one family's attempt to come to terms with the legacy of that era.

Because it was the fall of 2001, internment camps were a hot topic. The two previous times I had taught the novel, in 1995 and 1999, my students had never heard about the imprisonment of Japanese-Americans during World War II, or about the confiscation of their property. But after the debates about the Patriot Act and the detainees in Guantánamo, almost everyone in the class had heard about the World War II camps. Realizing, then, that everything we said in class about World War II would have sharp resonance for the world after September 11, I mentioned that Powers has been criticized for apparently suggesting a kind of moral equivalence between Nazi concentration camps and US internment camps — since the latter, however outrageous and indefensible they were in a putatively democratic nation, were not part of a program of genocide. *Prisoner's Dilemma* refers at one point to "roundups far more hideously evil than the local one," thus distinguishing between the Holocaust and the Japanese-American internment, but this has not deflected criticism of Powers on that score. So I asked the class what they thought of the critique.

John wasn't having any of it. There's no moral equivalence here at all; Powers is out of his mind, and even Powers's critics have gone wrong in implicitly agreeing to parse out the different forms of moral wrong at stake — because, and let's get this much straight, the internment camps were justified. Far from being outrageous and indefensible, they were a reasonable security precaution in a desperate time and, furthermore, the detainees were treated quite well.

At that point, I have to admit, I was flummoxed. I've never lost my composure in a classroom, but I was so stunned that I almost blurted out, "You've got to be kidding." Even if I had, though, I'm not sure John would have heard me, because the entire classroom was immediately in a minor uproar. Everyone from the pacifists to the drug-law libertarians to the undecideds chimed in at once to criticize — to say, collectively and incoherently, OK, pal, this time you've gone too far. "You know nothing about the Japanese who were imprisoned." "You know nothing about the Constitution." "You're forgetting that the United States actually issued an apology to the internees, as well as financial reparations," students said. For a few seconds, it looked and sounded as if John's classmates wanted to argue him right out of the room.

So, instead of blurting, I whistled. Loud. "All right. Wait a minute." The following silence was punctuated by a few low murmurs. "The object here isn't to pile on," I said over them. "This is, in fact, one of the things the novel wants us to debate."

"But John," I added, turning to him, "I do want to remind you that you spoke up quite forcefully, earlier this semester, on behalf of the belief that we're all Americans first, and that our national and ethnic origins shouldn't matter. Didn't the internment camps violate that principle?"

No, he said, because here we were dealing with the possibility of treason during wartime, and some Japanese-Americans had, indeed, been in touch with relatives in Japan in ways that threatened national security. Fine, I said, I believe you're quite mistaken about that, and I will be happy to direct you to sources that will challenge you,[7] but suffice it to say for now that you reject one of the premises of the novel, somewhat more emphatically than Powers's harshest critics. Now, let's take this to the rest of the class. Does the prisoner's dilemma apply to World War II in the ways Powers suggests? John here says that the camps were justified; the threat of treason must be met with mass internment. How does Powers treat this argument?[8]

We got through the novel, of course — we didn't lose any lives, and no one was injured. It was only literary criticism, after all. But the class had been completely derailed. John was confirmed in his isolation and sense of opposition, his classmates took to even more severe eye-rolling and head-shaking at his remarks, and, by December, when

> **John was confirmed in his isolation and sense of opposition.**

we got to Colson Whitehead's 1999 novel *The Intuitionist*, a whimsical allegory about race relations and the history of elevator inspection,[9] John was complaining that there were no good white characters in the novel. By that point, even I had had enough, and I told him, via e-mail, that his complaint was not only unwarranted on its face but thoroughly beside the point. In this class, I said, we are not in the business of pursuing reductive identity-politics enterprises like looking for "positive images" in literature, regardless of what group images we might be talking about.

When the semester was over, I wondered whether John's story was the stuff of which right-wing legends are made. Would he remember the seminar as the class in which his right to free speech and debate was trampled by politically correct groupthink, even though he spoke more often than any other single student? He couldn't possibly contend that I'd graded him on the political content of his remarks, because he had received an A for the course. But there was no question that he felt embattled, that he didn't see any contradictions in his argument about the internment camps, and that he had begun to develop an aggressive-defensive "I'm not a racist, but these people . . ." mode of speaking about not only black literary characters but black writers and critics as well. In the last couple of weeks of the term, I found myself speaking to him almost solicitously, as if to say, "You know, if you understand so little about how some of your remarks might be taken by members of racial minorities, and yet you say so much about them, you could be in for some rough times. You might want to read a manual on tact."

But who am I to say such things? For all I know, John might be able to craft a life in which he can deride African-American ambivalence about integration and defend Japanese-American internment camps without ever confronting anyone who disagrees with him. More than that, he might be able to build an entire career out of saying things that I and most of my friends and colleagues would find repugnant. After all, Dinesh D'Souza wrote an entire book on what he called the "civilizational differences" between blacks and whites, defending "rational discrimination" and insisting that "the American slave *was* treated like property, which is to say, pretty well,"[10] and it didn't stop him from winning sinecures at the American Enterprise Institute and the Hoover Foundation, or from being hired by CNN in 2004 as a news analyst. And Michelle Malkin has managed to write a shameful book, *In Defense of Internment*,[11] that advances John's argument about the Japanese-American camps even though the claim that the camps were justified by political necessity has repeatedly been shot down by every reputable historian and journalist, to the point at which it verges on being one of those "interpretations" that no sane person countenances, any more than we countenance the "interpretation" that reports of the Holocaust have been wildly overblown by the international Jewish lobby. And yet, despite offering what her publisher proudly and ignorantly calls a "ringing justification" for the Japanese-American internment camps, Malkin remains a widely published syndicated columnist. Clearly, then, my standards for reasonable discourse, at least when it comes to race, are not universally shared. I can set the tone for my own classroom, but I don't have any business advising John how to talk about anything once he completes my course.

Reflecting on that course years later, I've come to see that only a small, intense class can produce the kind of dynamic we dealt with that semester — where I often felt compelled to restrain students from criticizing someone whose arguments I myself found obnoxious, and where I had to weigh carefully, seven days a week, what things I could say to students in the quasi-public, quasi-private space of the classroom, and what things I should reserve for face-to-face after-class discussions or follow-up e-mail messages. Because of the syllabus, and because of September 11, students wanted to talk after class, on off days, on e-mail, with a professor who would converse with them on all matters local and global. Few critics of academe — and even fewer critics of liberal-left professors — have any idea what kind of work that entails, which is one reason, surely, why headlines like "Conservative Student Punished by Stalinist Campus Orthodoxy" strike those of us who teach as so surreal.

496

Over my twenty years in teaching, I've had many conservatives in my classes. I like to imagine that I've even had one or two Stalinists, too. I've had many intelligent, articulate students who behaved as if they had a right to speak more often and at greater length than anyone else in the room; I've had versions of Reese Witherspoon's character in *Election* and Hermione Granger in the *Harry Potter* series, who knew the answers to every question ever asked; I've had my share of blurters with very little sense of social boundaries, a few of whom may genuinely have had some degree of Asperger's syndrome, with various autistic or antisocial symptoms. To all such students — indeed, to all students, those with disabilities and those without — I try to apply the standard of disability law: I make reasonable accommodation for them. Needless to say, that doesn't mean that I treat non-disabled students as disabled; it simply means that I try to take each student on his or her own terms. The beautiful thing about the standard of "reasonable accommodation" is that it is a universal imperative (everyone should be accommodated, within reason) that requires one to acknowledge individual idiosyncrasies (not every accommodation will take the same form). It offers a liberal vision of society that I find particularly appealing, both in the classroom and out. The challenge, however, lies in making reasonable accommodation for students whose standards of reasonableness are significantly different from yours. Few aspects of teaching are so difficult — and, I think, so rarely acknowledged by people who don't teach for a living.

Some of my friends tell me I think too much about students like John, and that, in his case, I overaccommodated a disruptive student precisely because I was too worried about exacerbating his sense of grievance. They're probably right on both counts, but then again, I think I have plenty of reason to worry these days. Over the past five years, conservatives' complaints about American universities — long a feature of conservative culture, at least since the publication of William F. Buckley's 1951 *God and Man at Yale* — have reached a fever pitch. The predominance of liberals on college faculties is taken as proof that conservatives are actively discriminated against in hiring and tenure decisions; commentators like David Horowitz and Stanley Kurtz are calling for direct governmental oversight of professors, programs, and even individual course reading lists; and a network of student complaint is being built, via groups such as Noindoctrination.org and Students for Academic Freedom, to allow conservative students to report on the doings and teachings of liberal professors — or, more accurately, professors who offend conservatives' political sensibilities in one way or another. It is a dicey time to be a liberal college professor. If you don't have tenure, as two-thirds of us do not,[12] you had better be very careful about what you say and to whom you say it.

I have written this [piece] not only to offer a reply to academe's conservative critics but also to offer curious readers a look into the classroom dynamics of undergraduate courses in contemporary literature and culture, since these are some of the most widely derided and maligned courses in the literature of conservative complaint. But this [piece] is not a string of defenses and denials. On the contrary, it is about liberal "bias" in my own teaching; it is about how classroom discussion is framed, and how I try to frame it. It is also about some of the odd fantasies people (including college students) have about college campuses, and the wrenching personal transformations that either do or don't occur on them. Finally, it is about what it's like to teach young men and women in large public universities in Pennsylvania and Illinois, in the rural middle of otherwise populous states in a complexly divided and fractious democracy. My desire is inescapably that of a veteran and inveterate teacher: I want to explain. In the course of explaining, I will undoubtedly do some special pleading, for I feel that I am working under special circumstances, at a time when both my institution and my faith in reasoned debate are challenged in unprecedented ways. I want to explain not merely because my liberal colleagues and I are under attack from an organized and ascendant conservative movement, but because I believe that liberal education is fundamental to the future of democracy in ways many of us have not fully realized. The United States is the home of the world's only experiment in mass higher education, and even those aspects of American higher education that consist of career training and narrow professional tracking nevertheless contribute to the formation of a credentialed (as opposed to a hereditary or a clerical) class of people who, ideally, should be able to understand cultural values and cultural conflict in New Guinea and in New Orleans. Even the vocational side of college education, in other words, has some cosmopolitan potential. However, this [piece] is concerned primarily with the nonvocational aspects of American higher education — the ones that have to do with the imperative to foster rational debate regardless of its ends.

One of the things at stake on my end of the campus is the very ideal of independent intellectual inquiry, the kind of inquiry whose outcomes cannot be known in advance and cannot be measured in terms of efficiency or productivity. There is no mystery why so many conservative commentators loathe liberal campuses; it is not simply that conservatives control all three branches of government and a good deal of the mass media, and are striking out at the few areas of American cultural life they do not dominate. That much is true, but it fails to capture the truly radical nature of the conservative attacks on academe, for these are attacks not simply on the substance of liberalism (in the form of specific fiscal or social policies stemming from the Progressive Era, the New Deal, and the Great Society) but on procedural liberalism itself, on the idea that no one political faction should control every facet of a society. Radical conservatives' hatred of procedural liberalism, with its checks, balances, and guarantees that minority reports will be incorporated into the body politic, can be seen in House Republicans' rewriting of the rules of their chamber so that Democrats cannot offer amendments, propose legislation, or challenge committee chairs; in Senate Republicans' attempts to establish a similar tyranny of the majority in their chamber, by eliminating the filibuster except in "extraordinary circumstances"; in conservative pundits' defenses of a secret National Security Agency program of domestic spying authorized by the president without legislative or judicial oversight, in direct violation of the Constitution; and in the radical right's increasingly venomous and hallucinatory attacks on a judicial branch most of whose members were in fact appointed by Republicans. What animates the radical right, then, is not so much a specific liberal belief about stem-cell research here or hate-crimes legislation there, but rather the very existence of areas of political independence that do not answer directly and favorably to the state. Independent journalists, independent judges, independent filmmakers, independent professors — all are anathema to the radical right.

There are some forms of conservatism that are absolutely essential to my conception of liberalism. Because I cannot have and do not seek unanimity in political and cultural matters (I have been told that a political party made up of people who agree with me about everything could comfortably conduct its meetings in a phone booth), I believe that the liberal ideal consists in engaging my most stringent interlocutors, so long as we share an underlying commitment to open-ended rational debate. This means that I am open to all manner of reasonable challenges to my beliefs with regard to abortion, affirmative action, taxation and public-sector spending, stem-cell research, disability law, feminism, international relations, nationalism and citizenship, love, hate, war, and peace. But it also means that I inevitably come into conflict with certain kinds of conservatives who value "reason" very differently than I do, and as a result I invariably produce what one of my conservative interlocutors once called a "moral mist" in the classroom, in which (as he put it) certain positions are tacitly understood to be more virtuous than others, and students who want to argue for one of the less virtuous positions understand that they will, in effect, have to argue twice — once to make their point, and once to make the point that they are entitled to make their point.

What do I mean by "moral mist"? Just this: most conservative students should have no problem with my courses, and, in the past, my conservative students have fared just fine. (The postmodernism seminar offers them little in the way of support, however, because conservative intellectuals and artists haven't contributed much to the debates about postmodernism except to wish the whole thing into the ash heap of history.) I do not hold forth on the superiority of Keynesian to Hayekian economics, and only rarely am I moved to say anything about the creation of the social welfare state, so for the most part I don't produce the kind of moral mist that economic libertarians and conservatives would find noxious. And though I am an agnostic myself, I never speak ill of Christianity, Judaism, Islam, or any organized religion, so there is no sense in which any religious student should feel that he or she has to argue twice in my classroom. But on race and sexuality, invariably, my syllabus, my comments, and my very demeanor cannot help but cue students that some forms of social conservatism will indeed have to make their arguments twice in order to be heard. Cultural conservatives of the sort who feel oppressed because their classroom environments do not always permit them to say that homosexuality is a sin and/or a curable disease will surely find my classrooms less than ideal. Likewise, students who defend the Japanese internment camps can expect to be challenged, especially when their remarks appear to contradict remarks they've made earlier in the semester. The practice of critical thinking, after all, is not contentless; it can and does challenge unreasoning prejudice of all kinds, and without it neither the Enlightenment nor the contemporary university is thinkable. And insofar as it places additional moral burdens on certain kinds of conservatives whose opposition to homosexuality stems from deeply held religious belief, yes, this kind of critical thinking can appear to such students to be a form of prejudice in itself.

> **The practice of critical thinking . . . can and does challenge unreasoning prejudice of all kinds.**

This conundrum, forged in the gap between procedural liberalism's openness to debate and substantive liberalism's opposition to racism, sexism, and homophobia, seems to me one of the most difficult moral and intellectual quandaries any liberal teacher has to face. In the "political correctness" debates of yesteryear, it sometimes took the form of the mind-bending charge that liberals were the truly intolerant forces in American society, because they failed to tolerate certain forms of intolerance that were grounded in conservative religious belief. This phrasing of the problem has befuddled more than one liberal, leaving such liberals not only befuddled but committed to finding better (and more liberal) ways of including the voices of people whose most cherished aim is to silence us forever. Liberals are required to foster and practice a kind of critical pluralism with regard to social and cultural disputes, but they are not and should not be required to promote — or protect from criticism — the views of radicals and authoritarians who construe all forms of liberalism either as treason to the republic or as grounds for eternal damnation.

The rise of the authoritarian right thus gives me reason to suspect the motives of conservatives who call for governmental regulation of professorial speech; I think that such conservatives are less interested in "fair and balanced" campuses than in campuses that can be compelled, quickly and painlessly, to toe the party line. And yet. . . . the rise of the authoritarian right is not merely an academic affair. The university is one of the last remaining areas in American life dominated by liberals — and dominated by a most curious kind of liberal, namely, liberal intellectuals who are committed both to substantive and procedural liberalism, to a form of pluralism and reasoned debate that does not always culminate in liberal *conclusions*. It is no overstatement, therefore, to say that the right's attacks on American universities are attacks on one of the critical institutions of democracy.

NOTES

This chapter is an extensively revised version of an essay that first appeared in the *Chronicle of Higher Education*, December 5, 2003, under the title, "Should I Have Asked John to Cool It? Standards of Reason in the Classroom": B5–7, http://chronicle. com/free/v50/i15/15h00701.htm.

[1] Ishmael Reed, *Mumbo Jumbo* (New York: Atheneum, 1972), 38.

[2] For a brief introduction to the Republic of New Africa, see William L. Van Deburg, *New Day in Babylon* (Chicago: University of Chicago Press, 1992), 144–49.

[3] Edward Rothstein, "Attacks on US Challenge Postmodern True Believers," *New York Times*, September 22, 2001: A17.

[4] Eric Hoover, "Death Threats and a Sit-In Divide Penn State," *Chronicle of Higher Education*, May 11, 2001: A43, http://chronicle.com/weekly/v47/i35/35a04301.htm. The "Christian conservative" quoted in the report is Professor David Warren Saxe.

[5] Professor Vaidhyanathan posted his remarks on Eric Alterman's MSNBC *Altercation* weblog on May 4, 2005, at http://www.msnbc.msn.com/id/7720654/#050504.

[6] Throughout the novel, Powers treats the internment camps as forms of "tit for tat," an abrogation of freedom undertaken in the name of freedom. One such passage reads as follows:

> Disney sits at his drawing board and wrestles up a pen and ink cell of the Mouse. "What do you say to fighting fire with fire?" he mumbles to the image. With a few deft strokes, he blows a talk bubble above Mickey's head reading, "That makes a *big* fire, Walt." Disney puts his pens down and sighs. He knows the size of the blaze we are up against. He has heard Murrow's London broadcasts. He has seen what the Imperial Navy accomplished in the Philippines. He knows about roundups far more hideously evil than the local one. Terminally evil. And other than retaliation he cannot think of a weapon large enough to put this fire out.

Richard Powers, *Prisoner's Dilemma* (New York: Harper Perennial, 1988), 176.

[7] At the time, I was thinking of Michi Weglyn, *Years of Infamy: The Untold Story of America's Concentration Camps* (New York: Morrow, 1976; repr., Seattle: University of Washington Press, 1996). Today, I would add Eric L. Muller, *Free to Die for Their Country: The Story of the Japanese American Draft Resisters in World War II* (Chicago: University of Chicago Press, 2001); Greg Robinson, *By Order of the President: FDR and*

the Internment of Japanese Americans (Cambridge, MA: Harvard University Press, 2003); and David Neiwert, Strawberry Days: How Internment Destroyed a Japanese American Community (New York: Palgrave, 2005).

[8]In a variety of ways, one of which involves comparing the treatment of Americans of Japanese ancestry with that of Americans of Italian or German ancestry:

> Walt rubs his ears for hours, wondering if Huston and Capra, at this very minute making documentaries and cheer films for the army, are having half as much difficulty overcoming the technical obstacles to believability as he. Capra's making Why We Fight. Disney must make the far more problematic and unpopular Why We Shouldn't Have To. It occurs to him that Capra is a first-generation Italian. We're at war with the Eye-ties too, right? What are THEY doing walking around free while we're locked up? The suggestion is clear: national security is not separable from budding hatred. (Powers, Prisoner's Dilemma, 218.)

I don't imagine that I have to elaborate on the resonance of the final sentence for debates over national security after September 11. All I can say is that I didn't plan things that way; I drew up my syllabus many months before the attacks, and had planned to discuss the experimental aspects of Prisoner's Dilemma, in which an apparently realistic novel turns out to be both a Nabokovian hall of mirrors and a quasi-autobiographical account of a midwestern family.

[9]Colson Whitehead, The Intuitionist (New York: Anchor, 1999). I have since written an essay on the novel, titled "Race and Modernity in Colson Whitehead's The Intuitionist," in The Holodeck in the Garden: Science and Technology in Contemporary American Fiction, ed. Peter Freese and Charles B. Harris (Normal, IL: Dalkey Archive Press, 2004), 163–78.

[10]Dinesh D'Souza, The End of Racism: Principles for a Multiracial Society (New York: Free Press, 1995), 147.

[11]Michelle Malkin, In Defense of Internment: The Case for "Racial Profiling" in World War II and the War on Terror (Washington, DC: Regnery, 2004).

[12]See, e.g., Ana Marie Cox "More Professors Said to Be Off Tenure Track," Chronicle of Higher Education, July 6, 2001: A12: "John Lee, president of JBL Associates, a group in Bethesda, MD., that analyzed the data for the [National Education Association], says the drop to 32 percent from 35 percent of all faculty members (full- and part-time) who hold tenure 'is mostly due to the increased number of part-timers, and the great number of professors working at institutions that don't offer tenure.'" The Chronicle report is available online (for subscribers) at http://chronicle.com/weekly/v47/i43/43a01201.htm; the NEA report is available at http://www.nea.org/he/heupdate/vol7no.3.pdf. The most recent and comprehensive data set on faculty employment (through fall 2003) is available from the National Center for Education Statistics and can be found in the IPEDS Dataset Cutting Tool, National Center for Education Statistics (accessed January 3, 2006), http://nces.ed.gov/ipedspas/dct/download/index.asp?Year=2003&Survey=9.

DISCUSSION

1. One of the key questions Berube's essay raises has to do with the issue of free speech within the classroom. How do we distinguish legitimate debate — what Berube calls "reasonable disagreement" — from the kinds of argument or difference of opinion that should not be allowed? Where does Berube seem to draw this line? How does it compare with the line you would draw?

2. Berube talks a good deal about what it means to "bring one's politics into the classroom," either as a teacher or a student. "To what extent," he asks, "should my own beliefs be an explicit part of my teaching?" Where do you weigh in on this question? In what circumstances or under what conditions is it valid to talk about one's personal politics in class?

3. Berube worries throughout this essay that his response to John's classroom behavior serves only to exacerbate the sense of isolation this self-described conservative student may already feel. What, in your view, are the risks or problems of finding (or feeling) oneself isolated within the class? What are the best ways to redress this situation?

WRITING

4. What would you do if presented with the same dilemma posed by Berube's student, John? Write an essay in which you describe what choices you would have made, the things you would have said (and not said). Do you think the way Berube handled the situation with John was correct? What would you have done differently? Your essay should cite Berube and, if applicable, include anecdotes from episodes in your classes where you were exposed to dissent.

5. Much of Berube's essay is devoted to dispelling what he calls the "myth of liberal bias" within the modern university. Write a personal essay in which you argue whether, based on your experience, this myth is in fact real. Based on how Berube explains his own dilemma in dealing with his conservative student, to what degree do you believe that personal politics belong in the classroom?

6. What similarities can you find between Berube's discussion of political viewpoints in his classes and bell hooks's (p. 515) remembrance of the impact of race and class in higher education? Write an essay in which you compare what these authors have to say about the broad-ranging subject of diversity. How does each seem to define the term? What are the central problems that they address that prevent real diversity from being accepted? Do they see any solutions?

Then and Now: *Monkeying Around with Science*

1925

In 1925, John Thomas Scopes was arrested and indicted on charges that he violated the recently passed Butler Act, which made it a criminal offense in Tennessee for any public schoolteacher to teach the scientific theory of evolution. Americans across the nation paid attention to the ensuing trial (known as the Scopes Monkey Trial), which was a calculated effort by the American Civil Liberties Union (ACLU) to overturn the Butler Act. The ACLU, like some Americans, believed that teaching religious beliefs such as creationism had no place in public school science classes. Though Scopes was found guilty, eventually the U.S. Supreme Court ruled in *Epperson v. Arkansas* (1968) that banning the teaching of evolution was unconstitutional because it violated the Establishment Clause of the First Amendment, which prohibits laws establishing a state religion.

Creationism has been at the forefront of debate once again, this time in Kansas and Pennsylvania. In 2006, school boards in those two states sought the side-by-side teaching of the theory of evolution with that of intelligent design, which argues that certain features of life are best explained by the presence of an intelligent cause (that is, the God of the Old Testament).

2005

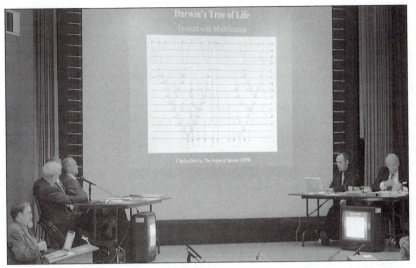

The images here show the drastic differences in approach in arguing for the teaching of a divine creator in science classes. The image on the left, showing anti-evolution protestors during the Scopes trial, is overtly religious. The second, showing pro-intelligent design scientists from the Discovery Institute at a debate in Kansas, signals nothing of a religious nature. At the same time, has anything here really changed? Is intelligent design truly scientific, or is it creationism dressed in scientific language? How does this debate potentially redefine what is science? How does it blur the line between traditional religious belief and scientific inquiry?

WRITING

1. Part of the argument for intelligent design asks us to redefine what science is, that is, to consider possible supernatural in addition to natural causes in scientific inquiry. Write an essay in which you argue whether you think this is possible. How does this new definition change your perception of what science is? Since scientific fact traditionally relies on experimental proof and the supernatural often requires faith without that proof, what do you think it would mean to include both these points of view under the label *science*?

2. What do you think the rules are in our culture regarding how we treat conflicts between science and religion? How does the battle for inclusion of intelligent design in the science curriculum arguably an attempt to appease both sides? Do you think it works in that regard? Why or why not?

Against School

Does boredom define the modern experience of being a student? And if so, who or what is to blame for this? Posing the provocative question "do we really need school?" long-time educator and educational critic John Taylor Gatto offers a stinging rebuke to the practices and assumptions that underlie what passes for modern education. Gatto was born in Monongahela, Pennsylvania, and before becoming a schoolteacher and educational critic he held a number of jobs, including scriptwriter, taxi driver, and hot dog vendor. In 1991 he was named New York State Teacher of the Year. His books include *Dumbing Us Down: The Hidden Curriculum of Compulsory Schooling* (1992), *Different Kind of Teacher: Solving the Crisis of American Schooling* (2000), and, most recently, *The Underground History of American Education* (2001). He is now retired from teaching and is working on a documentary about compulsory education called *The Fourth Purpose*. The following piece originally appeared in the September 2003 issue of *Harper's*.

I TAUGHT FOR THIRTY YEARS IN SOME OF THE WORST SCHOOLS IN Manhattan, and in some of the best, and during that time I became an expert in boredom. Boredom was everywhere in my world, and if you asked the kids, as I often did, why they felt so bored, they always gave the same answers: They said the work was stupid, that it made no sense, that they already knew it. They said they wanted to be doing something real, not just sitting around. They said teachers didn't seem to know much about their subjects and clearly weren't interested in learning more. And the kids were right: their teachers were every bit as bored as they were.

Boredom is the common condition of schoolteachers, and anyone who has spent time in a teachers' lounge can vouch for the low energy, the whining, the dispirited attitudes, to be found there. When asked why they feel bored, the teachers tend to blame the kids, as you might expect. Who wouldn't get bored teaching students who are rude and interested only in grades? If even that. Of course, teachers are themselves products of the same twelve-year compulsory school programs that so thoroughly bore their students, and as school personnel they are trapped inside structures even more rigid than those imposed upon the children. Who, then, is to blame?

We all are. My grandfather taught me that. One afternoon when I was seven I complained to him of boredom, and he batted me hard on the head.

He told me that I was never to use that term in his presence again, that if I was bored it was my fault and no one else's. The obligation to amuse and instruct myself was entirely my own, and people who didn't know that were childish people, to be avoided if possible. Certainly not to be trusted. That episode cured me of boredom forever, and here and there over the years I was able to pass on the lesson to some remarkable students. For the most part, however, I found it futile to challenge the official notion that boredom and childishness were the natural state of affairs in the classroom. Often I had to defy custom, and even bend the law, to help kids break out of this trap.

The empire struck back, of course; childish adults regularly conflate opposition with disloyalty. I once returned from a medical leave to discover that all evidence of my having been granted the leave had been purposely destroyed, that my job had been terminated, and that I no longer possessed even a teaching license. After nine months of tormented effort I was able to retrieve the license when a school secretary testified to witnessing the plot unfold. In the meantime my family suffered more than I care to remember. By the time I finally retired in 1991, I had more than enough reason to think of our schools — with their long-term, cell-block-style, forced confinement of both students and teachers — as virtual factories of childishness. Yet I honestly could not see why they had to be that way. My own experience had revealed to me what many other teachers must learn along the way, too, yet keep to themselves for fear of reprisal: if we wanted to we could easily and inexpensively jettison the old, stupid structures and help kids take an education rather than merely receive a schooling. We could encourage the best qualities of youthfulness — curiosity, adventure, resilience, the capacity for surprising insight — simply by being more flexible about time, texts, and tests, by introducing kids to truly competent adults, and by giving each student what autonomy he or she needs in order to take a risk every now and then.

But we don't do that. And the more I asked why not, and persisted in thinking about the "problem" of schooling as an engineer might, the more I missed the point: What if there is no "problem" with our schools? What if they are the way they are, so expensively flying in the face of common sense and long experience in how children learn things, not because they are doing something wrong but because they are doing something right? Is it possible that George W. Bush accidentally spoke the truth when he said we would "leave no child behind"? Could it be that our schools are designed to make sure not one of them ever really grows up?

Do we really need school? I don't mean education, just forced schooling: six classes a day, five days a week, nine months a year, for twelve years. Is this deadly routine really necessary? And if so, for what? Don't hide behind reading, writing, and arithmetic as

Do we really need school?

a rationale, because 2 million happy homeschoolers have surely put that banal justification to rest. Even if they hadn't, a considerable number of well-known Americans never went through the twelve-year wringer our kids currently go through, and they turned out all right. George Washington, Benjamin Franklin, Thomas Jefferson, Abraham Lincoln? Someone taught them, to be sure, but they were not products of a school system, and not one of them was ever "graduated" from a secondary school. Throughout most of American history, kids generally didn't go to high school, yet the unschooled rose to be admirals, like Farragut; inventors, like Edison; captains of industry like Carnegie and Rockefeller; writers, like Melville and Twain and Conrad; and even scholars, like Margaret Mead. In fact, until pretty recently people who reached the age of thirteen weren't looked upon as children at all. Ariel Durant, who co-wrote an enormous, and very good, multivolume history of the world with her husband, Will, was happily married at fifteen, and who could reasonably claim that Ariel Durant was an uneducated person? Unschooled, perhaps, but not uneducated.

We have been taught (that is, schooled) in this country to think of "success" as synonymous with, or at least dependent upon, "schooling," but historically that isn't true in either an intellectual or a financial sense. And plenty of people throughout the world today find a way to educate themselves without resorting to a system of compulsory secondary schools that all too often resemble prisons. Why, then, do Americans confuse education with just such a system? What exactly is the purpose of our public schools?

Mass schooling of a compulsory nature really got its teeth into the United States between 1905 and 1915, though it was conceived of much earlier and pushed for throughout most of the nineteenth century. The reason given for this enormous upheaval of family life and cultural traditions was, roughly speaking, threefold:

1. To make good people.

2. To make good citizens.

3. To make each person his or her personal best.

These goals are still trotted out today on a regular basis, and most of us accept them in one form or another as a decent definition of public education's mission, however short schools actually fall in achieving them. But we are dead wrong. Compounding our error is the fact that the national literature holds numerous and surprisingly consistent statements of compulsory schooling's true purpose. We have, for example, the great H. L. Mencken, who wrote in the *American Mercury* for April 1924 that

> the aim of public education is not to fill the young of the species with knowledge and awaken their intelligence. . . . Nothing could be further from

the truth. The aim . . . is simply to reduce as many individuals as possible to the same safe level, to breed and train a standardized citizenry, to put down dissent and originality. That is its aim in the United States . . . and that is its aim everywhere else.

Because of Mencken's reputation as a satirist, we might be tempted to dismiss this passage as a bit of hyperbolic sarcasm. His article, however, goes on to trace the template for our own educational system back to the now vanished, though never to be forgotten, military state of Prussia. And although he was certainly aware of the irony that we had recently been at war with Germany, the heir to Prussian thought and culture, Mencken was being perfectly serious here. Our educational system really is Prussian in origin, and that really is cause for concern.

The odd fact of a Prussian provenance for our schools pops up again and again once you know to look for it. William James alluded to it many times at the turn of the century. Orestes Brownson, the hero of Christopher Lasch's 1991 book, *The True and Only Heaven*, was publicly denouncing the Prussianization of American schools back in the 1840s. Horace Mann's "Seventh Annual Report" to the Massachusetts State Board of Education in 1843 is essentially a paean to the land of Frederick the Great and a call for its schooling to be brought here. That Prussian culture loomed large in America is hardly surprising, given our early association with that utopian state. A Prussian served as Washington's aide during the Revolutionary War, and so many German-speaking people had settled here by 1795 that Congress considered publishing a German-language edition of the federal laws. But what shocks is that we should so eagerly have adopted one of the very worst aspects of Prussian culture: an educational system deliberately designed to produce mediocre intellects, to hamstring the inner life, to deny students appreciable leadership skills, and to ensure docile and incomplete citizens in order to render the populace "manageable."

It was from James Bryant Conant — president of Harvard for twenty years, WWI poison-gas specialist, WWII executive on the atomic-bomb project, high commissioner of the American zone in Germany after WWII, and truly one of the most influential figures of the twentieth century — that I first got wind of the real purposes of American schooling. Without Conant, we would probably not have the same style and degree of standardized testing that we enjoy today, nor would we be blessed with gargantuan high schools that warehouse 2,000 to 4,000 students at a time, like the famous Columbine High in Littleton, Colorado. Shortly after I retired from teaching I picked up Conant's 1959 book-length essay, "The Child, the Parent, and the State," and was more than a little intrigued to see him mention in passing that the modern schools we attend were the result of a "revolution" engineered between 1905 and 1930. A revolution?

He declines to elaborate, but he does direct the curious and the uninformed to Alexander Inglis's 1918 book, *Principles of Secondary Education*, in which "one saw this revolution through the eyes of a revolutionary."

Inglis, for whom a lecture in education at Harvard is named, makes it perfectly clear that compulsory schooling on this continent was intended to be just what it had been for Prussia in the 1820s: a fifth column into the burgeoning democratic movement that threatened to give the peasants and the proletarians a voice at the bargaining table. Modern, industrialized, compulsory schooling was to make a sort of surgical incision into the prospective unity of these underclasses. Divide children by subject, by age-grading, by constant rankings on tests, and by many other more subtle means, and it was unlikely that the ignorant mass of mankind, separated in childhood, would ever re-integrate into a dangerous whole.

Inglis breaks down the purpose — the actual purpose — of modern schooling into six basic functions, any one of which is enough to curl the hair of those innocent enough to believe the three traditional goals listed earlier:

1. The adjustive or adaptive function. Schools are to establish fixed habits of reaction to authority. This, of course, precludes critical judgment completely. It also pretty much destroys the idea that useful or interesting material should be taught, because you can't test for reflexive obedience until you know whether you can make kids learn, and do, foolish and boring things.

2. The integrating function. This might well be called "the conformity function," because its intention is to make children as alike as possible. People who conform are predictable, and this is of great use to those who wish to harness and manipulate a large labor force.

3. The diagnostic and directive function. School is meant to determine each student's proper social role. This is done by logging evidence mathematically and anecdotally on cumulative records. As in "your permanent record." Yes, you do have one.

4. The differentiating function. Once their social role has been "diagnosed," children are to be sorted by role and trained only so far as their destination in the social machine merits — and not one step further. So much for making kids their personal best.

5. The selective function. This refers not to human choice at all but to Darwin's theory of natural selection as applied to what he called "the favored races." In short, the idea is to help things along by consciously attempting to improve the breeding stock. Schools are meant to tag the unfit — with poor grades, remedial placement, and other punishments — clearly enough that their peers will accept them as inferior and effectively bar them from the reproductive sweepstakes. That's what all those little humiliations from first grade onward were intended to do: wash the dirt down the drain.

6. The propaedeutic function. The societal system implied by these rules will require an elite group of caretakers. To that end, a small fraction of the kids will quietly be taught how to manage this continuing project, how to watch over and control a population deliberately dumbed down and declawed in order that government might proceed unchallenged and corporations might never want for obedient labor.

That, unfortunately, is the purpose of mandatory public education in this country. And lest you take Inglis for an isolated crank with a rather too cynical take on the educational enterprise, you should know that he was hardly alone in championing these ideas. Conant himself, building on the ideas of Horace Mann and others, campaigned tirelessly for an American school system designed along the same lines. Men like George Peabody, who funded the cause of mandatory schooling throughout the South, surely understood that the Prussian system was useful in creating not only a harmless electorate and a servile labor force but also a virtual herd of mindless consumers. In time a great number of industrial titans came to recognize the enormous profits to be had by cultivating and tending just such a herd via public education, among them Andrew Carnegie and John D. Rockefeller.

There you have it. Now you know. We don't need Karl Marx's conception of a grand warfare between the classes to see that it is in the interest of complex management, economic or political, to dumb people down, to demoralize them, to divide them from one another, and to discard them if they don't conform. Class may frame the proposition, as when Woodrow Wilson, then president of Princeton University, said the following to the New York City School Teachers Association in 1909: "We want one class of persons to have a liberal education, and we want another class of persons, a very much larger class, of necessity, in every society, to forgo the privileges of a liberal education and fit themselves to perform specific difficult manual tasks." But the motives behind the disgusting decisions that bring about these ends need not be class-based at all. They can stem purely from fear, or from the by now familiar belief that "efficiency" is the paramount virtue, rather than love, liberty, laughter, or hope. Above all, they can stem from simple greed.

There were vast fortunes to be made, after all, in an economy based on mass production and organized to favor the large corporation rather than the small business or the family farm. But mass production required mass consumption, and at the turn of the twentieth century most Americans considered it both unnatural and unwise to buy things they didn't actually need. Mandatory schooling

> **School didn't have to train kids in any direct sense to think they should consume nonstop, because it did something even better: it encouraged them not to think at all.**

was a godsend on that count. School didn't have to train kids in any direct sense to think they should consume nonstop, because it did something even better: it encouraged them not to think at all. And that left them sitting ducks for another great invention of the modem era — marketing.

Now, you needn't have studied marketing to know that there are two groups of people who can always be convinced to consume more than they need to: addicts and children. School has done a pretty good job of turning our children into addicts, but it has done a spectacular job of turning our children into children. Again, this is no accident. Theorists from Plato to Rousseau to our own Dr. Inglis knew that if children could be cloistered with other children, stripped of responsibility and independence, encouraged to develop only the trivializing emotions of greed, envy, jealousy, and fear, they would grow older but never truly grow up. In the 1934 edition of his once well-known book *Public Education in the United States*, Ellwood P. Cubberley detailed and praised the way the strategy of successive school enlargements had extended childhood by two to six years, and forced schooling was at that point still quite new. This same Cubberley — who was dean of Stanford's School of Education, a textbook editor at Houghton Mifflin, and Conant's friend and correspondent at Harvard — had written the following in the 1922 edition of his book *Public School Administration*: "Our schools are . . . factories in which the raw products (children) are to be shaped and fashioned. . . . And it is the business of the school to build its pupils according to the specifications laid down."

It's perfectly obvious from our society today what those specifications were. Maturity has by now been banished from nearly every aspect of our lives. Easy divorce laws have removed the need to work at relationships; easy credit has removed the need for fiscal self-control; easy entertainment has removed the need to learn to entertain oneself; easy answers have removed the need to ask questions. We have become a nation of children, happy to surrender our judgments and our wills to political exhortations and commercial blandishments that would insult actual adults. We buy televisions, and then we buy the things we see on the television. We buy computers, and then we buy the things we see on the computer. We buy $150 sneakers whether we need them or not, and when they fall apart too soon we buy another pair. We drive SUVs and believe the lie that they constitute a kind of life insurance, even when we're upside-down in them. And, worst of all, we don't bat an eye when Ari Fleischer tells us to "be careful what you say," even if we remember having been told somewhere back in school that America is the land of the free. We simply buy that one too. Our schooling, as intended, has seen to it.

Now for the good news. Once you understand the logic behind modern schooling, its tricks and traps are fairly easy to avoid. School trains children to be employees and consumers; teach your own to be leaders and adventurers. School trains children to obey reflexively; teach your own to think critically and independently. Well-schooled kids have a low threshold for boredom; help your own to develop an inner life so that they'll never be bored. Urge them to take on the serious material, the grown-up material, in history, literature, philosophy, music, art, economics, theology — all the stuff schoolteachers know well enough to avoid. Challenge your kids with plenty of solitude so that they can learn to enjoy their own company, to conduct inner dialogues. Well-schooled people are conditioned to dread being alone, and they seek constant companionship through the TV, the computer, the cell phone, and through shallow friendships quickly acquired and quickly abandoned. Your children should have a more meaningful life, and they can.

First, though, we must wake up to what our schools really are: laboratories of experimentation on young minds, drill centers for the habits and attitudes that corporate society demands. Mandatory education serves children only incidentally; its real purpose is to turn them into servants. Don't let your own have their childhoods extended, not even for a day. If David Farragut could take command of a captured British warship as a pre-teen, if Thomas Edison could publish a broadsheet at the age of twelve, if Ben Franklin could apprentice himself to a printer at the same age (then put himself through a course of study that would choke a Yale senior today), there's no telling what your own kids could do. After a long life, and thirty years in the public school trenches, I've concluded that genius is as common as dirt. We suppress our genius only because we haven't yet figured out how to manage a population of educated men and women. The solution, I think, is simple and glorious. Let them manage themselves.

DISCUSSION

1. Gatto repeatedly associates conventional compulsory schooling with entrapment. To what extent does this reflect your feelings and experiences? Has school ever made you feel trapped?

2. Gatto draws a distinction between helping children "take an education" and "receive a schooling." How do you understand the difference between the two? In your view, which of these phrases defines the superior model of education? Why?

3. "Childishness and boredom," writes Gatto, are too often "the natural state of affairs in the classroom." To what extent do you think this is true? And what factors account for why these things have come to stand as our current educational norms? What, in your view, would it take to denaturalize them — to get teachers and students to regard them as something other than "just the way school is"?

WRITING

4. At the heart of the problems around contemporary schooling, argues Gatto, is its compulsory nature. Think back on your experiences in school. How much of what typically defined your role was compulsory? What are some of the scripts (for how to act, talk, even think) that were required? Write an essay that argues in favor of or against the validity of implementing these particular requirements. What educational goals did they seem designed to accomplish, and were they worth it?

5. Gatto lists the three objectives that, he contends, we typically assume underlie contemporary education: "to make good people," "to make good citizens," "to make each person his or her personal best." Create a lesson plan that, in your view, would actually help fulfill these goals. What activities or assignments would it include? What would be the roles for teachers and students? Then, in an additional paragraph, sketch out an analysis or assessment of the ways this lesson plan would rewrite the script that you think more typically characterizes the modern classroom.

6. Much of Gatto's critique revolves around the charge of standardization. Modern American schools, he says, have become "factories" bent on mass-producing unimaginative, conformist, mediocre students. How do you think Alfie Kohn (p. 472) would respond to such a statement? Write an essay in which you compare each author's opinion on the state of education. What are the key problems each sees? Do you ultimately agree with their assessments of the education system? Why or why not?

BELL HOOKS

Learning in the Shadow of Race and Class

How does one's race and class affect one's experience of school? To what extent is modern education shaped by the unspoken norms connected to these two questions? Recounting her own experiences at one of America's elite institutions of higher education, bell hooks examines some of the core assumptions, ideals, and double standards that go into scripting the ideal "minority" student. As a writer and scholar, hooks focuses on the intersections of race, class, and gender. She is the author of over thirty books, including *Talking Back: Thinking Feminist, Thinking Black* (1989), *Teaching to Transgress* (1994), *Rock My Soul: Black People and Self-Esteem* (2002), and *Outlaw Culture: Resisting Representations* (2006). Most recently, hooks published a book of poems, *When Angels Speak of Love* (2007). She was born Gloria Jean Watkins in Hopkinsville, Kentucky. Currently, hooks is a Distinguished Professor of English at City College in New York. The following essay first appeared in the November 17, 2000 issue of *The Chronicle of Higher Education*.

A S A CHILD, I OFTEN WANTED THINGS MONEY COULD BUY THAT MY parents could not afford and would not get. Rather than tell us we did not get some material thing because money was lacking, mama would frequently manipulate us in an effort to make the desire go away. Sometimes she would belittle and shame us about the object of our desire. That's what I remember most. That lovely yellow dress I wanted would become in her storytelling mouth a really ugly mammy-made thing that no girl who cared about her looks would desire. My desires were often made to seem worthless and stupid. I learned to mistrust and silence them. I learned that the more clearly I named my desires, the more unlikely those desires would ever be fulfilled.

I learned that my inner life was more peaceful if I did not think about money, or allow myself to indulge in any fantasy of desire. I learned the art of sublimation and repression. I learned it was better to make do with acceptable material desires than to articulate the unacceptable. Before I knew money mattered, I had often chosen objects to desire that were costly, things a girl of my class would not ordinarily desire. But then I was still a girl who was *unaware of class*, who did not think my desires were

> **I was still a girl who was unaware of class, who did not think my desires were stupid and wrong.**

stupid and wrong. And when I found they were, I let them go. I concentrated on *survival*, on making do.

When I was choosing a college to attend, the issue of money surfaced and had to be talked about. While I would seek loans and scholarships, even if everything related to school was paid for, there would still be transportation to pay for, books, and a host of other hidden costs. Letting me know that there was no extra money to be had, mama urged me to attend any college nearby that would offer financial aid. My first year of college, I went to a school close to home. A plain-looking white woman recruiter had sat in our living room and explained to my parents that everything would be taken care of, that I would be awarded a full academic scholarship, that they would have to pay nothing. They knew better. Still they found this school acceptable.

After my parents dropped me at the predominately white women's college, I saw the terror in my roommate's face that she was going to be housed with someone black, and I requested a change. She had no doubt also voiced her concern. I was given a tiny single room by the stairs — a room usually denied a first-year student — but I was a first-year black student, a scholarship girl who could never in a million years have afforded to pay her way or absorb the cost of a single room. My fellow students kept their distance from me. I ate in the cafeteria and did not have to worry about who would pay for pizza and drinks in the world outside. I kept my desires to myself, my lacks, and my loneliness; I made do.

I rarely shopped. Boxes came from home, with brand-new clothes mama had purchased. Even though it was never spoken, she did not want me to feel ashamed among privileged white girls. I was the only black girl in my dorm. There was no room in me for shame. I felt contempt and disinterest. With their giggles and their obsession to marry, the white girls at the women's college were aliens. We did not reside on the same planet. I lived in the world of books. The one white woman who became my close friend found me there reading. I was hiding under the shadows of a tree with huge branches, the kinds of trees that just seemed to grow effortlessly on well-to-do college campuses. I sat on the "perfect" grass reading poetry, wondering how the grass around me could be so lovely, and yet, when daddy had tried to grow grass in the front yard of Mr. Porter's house, it always turned yellow or brown and then died. Endlessly, the yard defeated him, until finally he gave up. The outside of the house looked good, but the yard always hinted at the possibility of endless neglect. The yard looked poor.

Foliage and trees on the college grounds flourished. Greens were lush and deep. From my place in the shadows, I saw a fellow student sitting alone weeping. Her sadness had to do with all the trivia that haunted our day's classwork, the fear of not being smart enough, of losing financial aid (like me she had loans and scholarships, though her family paid some), and boys. Coming from an Illinois family of Czechoslovakian immigrants, she understood class.

When she talked about the other girls who flaunted their wealth and family background, there was a hard edge of contempt, anger, and envy in her voice. Envy was always something I pushed away from my psyche. Kept too close for comfort, envy could lead to infatuation and on to desire. I desired nothing that they had. She desired everything, speaking her desires openly, without shame. Growing up in the kind of community where there was constant competition to see who could buy the bigger better whatever, in a world of organized labor, of unions and strikes, she understood a world of bosses and workers, of haves and have-nots.

White friends I had known in high school wore their class privilege modestly. Raised, like myself, in church traditions that taught us to identify only with the poor, we knew that there was evil in excess. We knew rich people were rarely allowed into heaven. God had given them a paradise of bounty on earth, and they had not shared. The rare ones, the rich people who shared, were the only ones able to meet the divine in paradise, and even then it was harder for them to find their way. According to the high-school friends we knew, flaunting wealth was frowned upon in our world, frowned upon by God and community.

The few women I befriended my first year in college were not wealthy. They were the ones who shared with me stories of the other girls flaunting the fact that they could buy anything expensive — clothes, food, vacations. There were not many of us from working-class backgrounds; we knew who we were. Most girls from poor backgrounds tried to blend in, or fought back by triumphing over wealth with beauty or style or some combination of the above. Being black made me an automatic outsider. Holding their world in contempt pushed me further to the edge. One of the fun things the "in" girls did was choose someone and trash their room. Like so much else deemed cute by insiders, I dreaded the thought of strangers entering my space and going through my things. Being outside the in crowd made me an unlikely target. Being contemptuous made me first on the list. I did not understand. And when my room was trashed, it unleashed my rage and deep grief over not being able to protect my space from violation and invasion. I hated the girls who had so much, took so much for granted, never considered that those of us who did not have mad money would not be able to replace broken things, perfume poured out, or talcum powder spread everywhere — that we did not know everything could be taken care of at the dry cleaner's, because we never took our clothes there. My rage fueled by contempt was deep, strong, and long lasting. Daily it stood as a challenge to their fun, to their habits of being.

Nothing they did to win me over worked. It came as a great surprise. They had always believed black girls wanted to be white girls, wanted to possess their world. My stony gaze, silence, and absolute refusal to cross the threshold of their world was total mystery; it was for them a violation they needed to avenge. After trashing my room, they tried to win me over with apologies and urges to talk and understand. There was nothing about me I wanted them to understand. Everything about their world was overexposed, on the surface.

One of my English professors had attended Stanford University. She felt that was the place for me to go — a place where intellect was valued over foolish fun and games and dress up, and finding a husband did not overshadow academic work. I had never thought about the state of California. Getting my parents to agree to my leaving Kentucky to attend a college in a nearby state had been hard enough. They had accepted a college they could reach by car, but a college thousands of miles away was beyond their imagination. Even I had difficulty grasping going that far away from home. The lure for me was the promise of journeying and arriving at a destination where I would be accepted and understood.

All the barely articulated understandings of class privilege that I had learned my first year of college had not hipped me to the reality of class shame. It still had not dawned on me that my parents, especially mama, resolutely refused to acknowledge any difficulties with money because her sense of shame around class was deep and intense. And when this shame was coupled with her need to feel that she had risen above the low-class backwoods culture of her family, it was impossible for her to talk in a straightforward manner about the strains it would put on the family for me to attend Stanford.

All I knew then was that, as with all my desires, I was told that this desire was impossible to fulfill. At first, it was not talked about in relation to money, it was talked about in relation to sin. California was an evil place, a modern-day Babylon where souls were easily seduced away from the path of righteousness. It was not a place for an innocent young girl to go on her own. Mama brought the message back that my father had absolutely refused to give permission.

I expressed my disappointment through ongoing unrelenting grief. I explained to mama that other parents wanted their children to go to good schools. It still had not dawned on me that my parents knew nothing about "good" schools. Even though I knew mama had not graduated from high school, I still held her in awe.

When my parents refused to permit me to attend Stanford, I accepted the verdict for awhile. Overwhelmed by grief, I could barely speak for weeks. Mama intervened and tried to change my father's mind, as folks she respected in the outside world told her what a privilege it was for me to have this opportunity, that Stanford University was a good school for a smart girl. Without their permission, I decided I would go. And even though she did not give her approval, mama was willing to help.

My decision made conversations about money necessary. Mama explained that California was too far away, that it would always "cost" to get there, that if something went wrong, they would not be able to come and rescue me, that I would not be able to come home for holidays. I heard all this, but its meaning did not sink in. I was just relieved I would not be returning to the women's college, to the place where I had truly been an outsider.

There were other black students at Stanford. There was even a dormitory where many black students lived. I did not know I could choose to live there. I went where I was assigned. Going to Stanford was the first time I flew somewhere. Only mama stood and waved farewell as I left to take the bus to the airport. I left with a heavy heart, feeling both excitement and dread. I knew nothing about the world I was journeying to. Not knowing made me afraid, but my fear of staying in place was greater.

I had no idea what was ahead of me. In small ways, I was ignorant. I had never been on an escalator, a city bus, an airplane, or a subway. I arrived in San Francisco with no understanding that Palo Alto was a long drive away — that it would take money to find transportation there. I decided to take the city bus. With all my cheap overpacked bags, I must have seemed like just another innocent immigrant when I struggled to board the bus.

This was a city bus with no racks for luggage. It was filled with immigrants. English was not spoken. I felt lost and afraid. Without words the strangers surrounding me understood the universal language of need and distress. They reached for my bags, holding and helping. In return, I told them my story — that I had left my village in the South to come to Stanford University and that, like them, my family were workers.

On arriving, I called home. Before I could speak, I began to weep as I heard the faraway sound of mama's voice. I tried to find the words to slow down, to tell her how it felt to be a stranger, to speak my uncertainty and longing. She told me this is the lot I had chosen. I must live with it. After her words, there was only silence. She had hung up on me — let me go into this world where I am a stranger still.

Stanford University was a place where one could learn about class from the ground up. Built by a man who believed in hard work, it was to have been a place where students of all classes would come, women and men, to work together and learn. It was to be a place of equality and communalism. His vision was seen by many as almost communist. The fact that he was rich made it all less threatening. Perhaps no one really believed the vision could be realized. The university was named after his son, who had died young, a son who had carried his name but who had no future money could buy. No amount of money can keep death away. But it could keep memory alive.

Everything in the landscape of my new world fascinated me, the plants brought from a rich man's travels all over the world back to this place of water and clay. At Stanford University, adobe buildings blend with Japanese plum trees and leaves of kumquat. On my way to study medieval literature, I ate my first kumquat. Surrounded by flowering cactus and a South American shrub bougainvillea of such trailing beauty it took my breath away, I was in a landscape of dreams, full of hope and possibility. If nothing else would hold me, I would not remain a stranger to the earth. The ground I stood on would know me.

Class was talked about behind the scenes. The sons and daughters from rich, famous, or notorious families were identified. The grown-ups in charge of us were always looking out for a family who might give their millions to the college. At Stanford, my classmates wanted to know me, thought it hip, cute, and downright exciting to have a black friend. They invited me on the expensive vacations and ski trips I could not afford. They offered to pay. I never went. Along with other students who were not from privileged families, I searched for places to go during the holiday times when the dormitory was closed. We got together and talked about the assumption that everyone had money to travel and would necessarily be leaving. The staff would be on holiday as well, so all students had to leave. Now and then the staff did not leave, and we were allowed to stick around. Once, I went home with one of the women who cleaned for the college.

Now and then, when she wanted to make extra money, mama would work as a maid. Her decision to work outside the home was seen as an act of treason by our father. At Stanford, I was stunned to find that there were maids who came by regularly to vacuum and tidy our rooms. No one had ever cleaned up behind me, and I did not want them to. At first I roomed with another girl from a working-class background — a beautiful white girl from Orange County who looked like pictures I had seen on the cover of *Seventeen* magazine. Her mother had died of cancer during her high-school years, and she had since been raised by her father. She had been asked by the college officials if she would find it problematic to have a black roommate. A scholarship student like myself, she knew her preferences did not matter and, as she kept telling me, she did not really care.

Like my friend during freshman year, she shared the understanding of what it was like to be a have-not in a world of haves. But unlike me, she was determined to become one of them. If it meant she had to steal nice clothes to look the same as they did, she had no problem taking these risks. If it meant having a privileged boyfriend who left bruises on her body now and then, it was worth the risk. Cheating was worth it. She believed the world the privileged had created was all unfair — all one big cheat; to get ahead, one had to play the game. To her, I was truly an innocent, a lamb being led to the slaughter. It did not surprise her one bit when I began to crack under the pressure of contradictory values and longings.

Like all students who did not have seniority, I had to see the school psychiatrists to be given permission to live off campus. Unaccustomed to being around strangers, especially strangers who did not share or understand my values, I found the experience of living in the dorms difficult. Indeed, almost everyone around me believed working-class folks had no values. At the university where the founder, Leland Stanford, had imagined different classes meeting on common ground, I learned how deeply individuals with class privilege feared and hated the working classes. Hearing classmates express contempt and hatred toward people who did not come from the right backgrounds shocked me.

To survive in this new world of divided classes, this world where I was also encountering for the first time a black bourgeois elite that was as contemptuous of working people as their white counterparts were, I had to take a stand, to get clear my own class affiliations. This was the most difficult truth to face. Having been taught all my life to believe that black people were inextricably bound in solidarity by our struggles to end racism, I did not know how to respond to elitist black people who were full of contempt for anyone who did not share their class, their way of life.

> **I did not know how to respond to elitist black people who were full of contempt for anyone who did not share their class, their way of life.**

At Stanford, I encountered for the first time a black diaspora. Of the few black professors present, the vast majority were from African or Caribbean backgrounds. Elites themselves, they were only interested in teaching other elites. Poor folks like myself, with no background to speak of, were invisible. We were not seen by them or anyone else. Initially, I went to all meetings welcoming black students, but when I found no one to connect with, I retreated. In the shadows, I had time and books to teach me about the nature of class — about the ways black people were divided from themselves.

Despite this rude awakening, my disappointment at finding myself estranged from the group of students I thought would understand, I still looked for connections. I met an older black male graduate student who also came from a working-class background. Even though he had gone to the right high school, a California school for gifted students, and then to Princeton as an undergraduate, he understood intimately the intersections of race and class. Good in sports and in the classroom, he had been slotted early on to go far, to go where other black males had not gone. He understood the system. Academically, he fit. Had he wanted to, he could have been among the elite, but he chose to be on the margins, to hang with an intellectual artistic avant-garde. He wanted to live in a world of the mind where there was no race or class. He wanted to worship at the throne of art and knowledge. He became my mentor, comrade, and companion.

Slowly, I began to understand fully that there was no place in academe for folks from working-class backgrounds who did not wish to leave the past behind. That was the price of the ticket. Poor students would be welcome at the best institutions of higher learning only if they were willing to surrender memory, to forget the past and claim the assimilated present as the only worthwhile and meaningful reality.

Students from nonprivileged backgrounds who did not want to forget often had nervous breakdowns. They could not bear the weight of all the contradictions they had to confront. They were crushed. More often than not, they dropped out with no trace of their inner anguish recorded, no institutional record of the myriad ways their take on the world was assaulted by an elite vision of class and privilege. The records merely indicated that, even after receiving financial aid and other support, these students supply could not make it, simply were not good enough.

At no time in my years as a student did I march in a graduation ceremony. I was not proud to hold degrees from institutions where I had been constantly scorned and shamed. I wanted to forget these experiences, to erase them from my consciousness. Like a prisoner set free, I did not want to remember my years on the inside. When I finished my doctorate, I felt too much uncertainty about who I had become. Uncertain about whether I had managed to make it through without giving up the best of myself, the best of the values I had been raised to believe in — hard work, honesty, and respect for everyone no matter their class — I finished my education with my allegiance to the working class intact. Even so, I had planted my feet on the path leading in the direction of class privilege. There would always be contradictions to face. There would always be confrontations around the issue of class. I would always have to reexamine where I stand.

DISCUSSION

1. Take a few moments to consider the title of this piece. What are the shadows that, according to hooks, most directly affect or shape her experiences of school? To what extent do these shadows operate in her life as powerful, unspoken scripts, drawing the lines around the particular role she felt allowed to play?

2. As hooks relates, she became familiar with the standards and expectations being placed on her in college largely by indirection and inference. The norms and scripts to which she was expected to conform, she makes clear, remained invisible and unspoken. How would you put some of these norms and scripts into words? What script would you write?

3. For hooks, the prospect of succeeding in school revolved around the experience of loss: giving up connections and relationships that had formerly defined how she viewed herself. In your experience, has anything similar defined your relationship to school?

WRITING

4. Race and class, hooks argues, are the unspoken norms that structure everyday college life, the invisible scripts that set the boundaries around what different types of students are encouraged or allowed to expect from school. Write an essay in which you analyze how hooks makes this argument. How does she present her own experience as a student as an example? What unspoken (or spoken) scripts about schooling, education, race, or class does hooks expose in her writing?

5. For hooks, there is a complicated relationship between education and desire. Write an essay in which you analyze how this relationship works, according to hooks. Describe the particular role imposed on hooks as a black working-class student, and assess the particular ways this role seems designed to set boundaries around the educational designs and desires she was allowed to have.

6. On page 506, John Taylor Gatto lists Alexander Inglis's six basic functions of modern schooling. Write an essay in which you analyze these functions with regard to whether any of them also appear in hook's assessment of education. How do you think hooks would respond to Gatto's critique of the educational system? Would any of Gatto's suggestions alleviate the issues of race and class that hooks faced?

The Case of the Purloined Paper

When it comes to plagiarism, where does borrowing end and cheating begin? And what do we do when students and teachers retain widely different conceptions of what plagiarism involves? Taking up this tricky question, journalist Brigid Schulte offers an overview of current attitudes about academic "cheating" — how we define it, why and when we argue over it, and what this entire discussion says about the changing nature of our educational norms. Brigid Schulte is a journalist who writes for the Metro section of the *Washington Post*. Her work has also appeared in *American Journalism Review*. The selection that follows first appeared in the *Washington Post* on September 23, 2002.

NANCY ABESHOUSE IS EXCITED ABOUT TEACHING HER ADVANCED Placement literature class at Springbrook High School in Montgomery County, Maryland. These are her best students, the class is rigorous enough to count for college credit, and the activity she has planned is one of the intellectual highlights of the year: She's had the class read Henry James's *The Turn of the Screw*. They've had to write a paper on whether the main character, the governess, really saw ghosts or was just imagining things.

But it turns out not to be such a highlight. The discussion falls flat. Everyone in the class has the same opinion — that James didn't believe in ghosts and was parodying sexually repressed Victorian society. And most of the papers include variations on the same sentence: "Unable to express her desires, she imagines that she sees the ghosts of luckier souls who did express their desires."

After the students file out, Abeshouse is more than suspicious. She goes to her computer, logs on to the Internet, and types bits of the telltale sentence into the search engine Google. Up it comes on SparkNotes.com, a hipper, online version of Cliffs Notes. "I wanted them to go through an intellectual exercise. And they just wanted the answer," Abeshouse says later. "By our standards, it's cheating. By theirs, it's efficiency."

A teacher for 22 years, Abeshouse has battled the run-of-the-mill copiers and cheaters, and in recent years even the ones who merely change the typeface and turn in their friend's homework. Usually she gives students zeros or sends them to the principal's office for a lecture on plagiarism. This time, since these students are among the best, she wants to teach them a lesson. She downloads the SparkNotes summary of *The Turn of the Screw* — which, she says, has an "anti-intellectual, cynical, what's-the-bottom-line tone." Then she prints copies of an analysis from a top journal, using letters James wrote to his publisher about the book and historical references to the era. She gives them both to her students and hopes they notice the difference. Or care.

Lately, Abeshouse has become nearly obsessed with how easy the Internet makes it for students to cheat and get away with it. "I've just found a Web site that posts International Baccalaureate-style essays. In different languages," she says, sadly triumphant. But what she may not realize is that the *Turn of the Screw* incident is just one skirmish in the ongoing cold war of high-tech cheating. "It's like an arms race," says Joe Howley, a student in an elite Montgomery County magnet program who says he watched widespread cheating from the sidelines. "And teachers are always playing catch-up."

Donald McCabe is the founding president of the Center for Academic Integrity at Rutgers University, and his research shows that "academic integrity" is fast becoming an oxymoron. And not just in colleges, where cheating is rampant, he says.

McCabe is finding that cheating is starting younger — in elementary school, in fact. And by the time students hit middle and high school, cheating is, for many, like gym class and lunch period, just part of the fabric of how things are. It isn't that students have become moral reprobates. What has changed, says McCabe, is technology. It has made cheating so easy. The vast realms of information on the Web are so readily available. Who could resist?

> **Cheating is, for many, like gym class and lunch period, just part of the fabric of how things are.**

Not many do. In McCabe's 2001 survey of 4,500 high school students from 25 high schools around the country, 74 percent said they had cheated at least once on a big test. Seventy-two percent reported serious cheating on a written work. And 97 percent reported at least one questionable activity, such as copying someone else's homework or peeking at someone else's test. More than one-third admitted to repetitive, serious cheating.

And few appeared to feel shame. "You do what it takes to succeed in life," wrote one student. "Cheating is part of high school," said another. Fifteen percent had turned in a paper bought or copied from Internet sources. More than half said they had copied portions of a paper from the Web without citing the source. And 90 percent were indiscriminate copiers, plagiarizing from the Net, from books, magazines, even the old low-tech standard, the World Book encyclopedia.

"Students were certainly cheating before the Internet became available. But now it's easier. Quicker. More anonymous," McCabe says. "I can't tell you how many high school students say they cheat because others do and it goes unpunished. Being honest disadvantages them."

Besides, most people get away with it. It's easy for students to stay at least one step ahead of their teachers. When teachers began noticing that students would copy from the Internet or from one another and simply change the typeface, students quickly moved on. They discovered the wonders of Microsoft Word's AutoSummarize feature, which can take an entire page and shorten it to highlight the key points.

They think "that we don't know as much about technology as they do," says Carol Wansong, who just retired from teaching high school. "And, of course, we don't. They were born with it."

Even if students are caught, the consequences can be negligible. At some colleges, students who plagiarize are expelled. But a high school student caught plagiarizing may just get a zero for that particular assignment. Often, he or she will be given a chance to make it up for at least partial credit. And there's no mention of it on the all-important transcript that gets sent to colleges. At Bardstown High School in Kentucky last year, 118 seniors were caught copying and pasting from the Internet. Sometimes entire short stories were lifted. The punishment? One essay on the evils of plagiarism. No National Honor Society memberships were pulled, and one of those caught cheating remained the class valedictorian.

Plagiarism — a derivative of the Latin word for kidnapping — literally means to steal someone else's words or credit for them. According to the rules of scholarship, if you borrow someone else's words, you put them in quotation marks. If you use someone else's idea, you acknowledge it in your essay or in a footnote.

All this cheating raises an uncomfortable question: Are successful, educated parents putting too much pressure on their children in the belief that going to an elite school buys entree into the good life and attending a lesser school will leave you at a disadvantage?

At Walt Whitman High School in Bethesda, Maryland, students answered the question for themselves after a low–tech cheating scandal — the student government president was caught with 150 answers to a final exam hidden in his baseball cap — raised the issue. A junior who wasn't involved in the scandal told the school newspaper that some parents "are under the impression that if you don't do well and your grades aren't top, you'll be lying in a gutter somewhere for the rest of your life."

To Wansong, who taught rigorous International Baccalaureate classes, it's not just that parents put pressure on their children to achieve, it's the attitude that the end justifies whatever means necessary. In the past, she says, she would find one or two students plagiarizing their research project. But in recent years, with the advent of the Internet, it's been more like 12 or 14. "They showed no remorse when they were caught," she says. "I had students look me right in the eye and say, 'I don't see what the big deal is.' And their parents didn't, either."

That attitude echoed loudly in Kansas last year. When teacher Christine Pelton failed more than two dozen students for plagiarizing from the Internet, their parents complained. The students were given credit for the work. And Pelton quit. (The superintendent who had told Pelton to restore the grades, however, recently resigned.)

One Washington area high school magnet program student who plagiarized multiple sources for an essay on *Macbeth* said he knew what he did was wrong but that he didn't feel had about it. "Remorse," he said, "just slows you down."

John Barrie, a Berkeley biophysics graduate student, wrote software he intended to help students peer-review each other's work. Instead, they were selling each other's papers on the quad. So he rewrote the program to catch plagiarism. And now, that program has become a booming business, with some of the toniest names in public and private schools paying for its services. Turnitin.com scans 10,000 papers a day, half of them from middle and high school students. One-third are plagiarized from the Web. And most, Barrie says, come from high-achieving kids in top-performing schools.

Students responded by shifting tactics. They began taking a sentence here, a paragraph there, in what Barrie calls "mosaic" plagiarism. The students in Abeshouse's class need not have relied solely on SparkNotes. A quick Net search on Henry James and *The Turn of the Screw* yields obscure essays such as "A Ghost Story" or a "Delve into a Neurotic Mind?"

Barrie says Turnitin.com's software can detect anything copied from the Net down to an eight-word string. What it won't catch is students who crib the ideas, not the words.

One Maryland high school student was stuck on the Hamlet paper due in her AP lit class. So she went to the Internet and found the perfect essay from a site that offered them for free. "I took a good idea that wasn't given much effort in the online paper and put it into my paper with correct grammar and clear sentence structure. Added a little quote. Touched up the final thought. And took credit for it," she wrote in an e-mail. "Is that wrong?"

> **"I took a good idea that wasn't given much effort in the online paper and put it into my paper with correct grammar and clear sentence structure. . . . Is that wrong?"**

Well, yes. "If all a student has done is taken big quotes or paraphrased and more or less pasted together others' opinions, by academic standards, that's plagiarism," Abeshouse says.

For teachers like Abeshouse, the next tactical move in the cheating war is to change the way they teach. Abeshouse has students write more during class. She asks for rough drafts of term papers, annotated bibliographies, summaries of contents, evaluation of sources. "We don't ask them to summarize a book anymore. Now we ask for comparisons, personal responses, evidence of themes," she says. "Any teacher that says, 'The term paper is due four weeks from now' is asking for the kiss of death."

But who will win the wider conflict in the cheating game is anyone's guess. "It's naive to think that once a student has a high school or a Harvard diploma that all of a sudden they become an ethical person," Barrie says. "Where that leads you to is a very ugly society in the future."

His stolen *Macbeth* paper long forgotten, the magnet student eagerly packs to go off to a top university. He had applied to six universities, and, with his high grades, had been accepted at all six. With scholarships. "It's highly conceivable I'll cheat," he says matter-of-factly. He has no qualms that he will do whatever it takes to succeed.

DISCUSSION

1. The original derivation for plagiarism, Schulte informs us, is "kidnapping": literally, to "steal someone else's words." How valid is it to define contemporary plagiarism in terms of this original meaning?

2. Cast yourself in the role of a teacher or an administrator whose job is to devise a new policy for dealing with online plagiarism. What should this policy be? How should *cheating* get defined? What punishments or consequences would you assign for these infractions? And what incentives, conversely, would you proffer to encourage students to "do the right thing"?

3. One of Schulte's central premises is that the rise in incidents of plagiarism reflects less a decline in the morality of current students than the influence of new technology designed to make the copying and borrowing of others' work easier to do. Do you agree with this contention?

WRITING

4. As Schulte writes, there are clear differences in the ways that teachers and students define plagiarism. Write a list of all the "borrowings" you think should be considered permissible. Then, write a second list of "borrowings" that you think cross the line into cheating. Write an essay in which you analyze the different levels of borrowing, and explain what principles or rules you used in making your distinction between borrowing and cheating.

5. One of the most enduring norms of contemporary schooling involves what Schulte calls the bottom-line approach to classroom work: an approach that forgoes the real intellectual work of critical thinking in favor of finding only the so-called right answer. Write an essay in which you describe some type of school assignment that, in your view, encourages or even requires this kind of approach. What does the assignment look like? What work does it require students to undertake? And in what particular ways does it seem designed to discourage critical thinking? How would you change this assignment to foster a more satisfying approach to learning?

6. One of the points Schulte emphasizes is that what most teachers see as cheating, students see as efficiency. How do you think Jonathan Kozol (p. 530) would respond to this statement? Write an essay in which you look at Schulte's examination of cheating as part of the larger issue Kozol writes about.

JONATHAN KOZOL
Preparing Minds for Markets

Whether we want to admit it, many of our public schools play a formative role in shaping how children come to see themselves as workers. Presenting an eye-opening account of the ways that corporate logos and workplace terminology have permeated our modern classrooms, Jonathan Kozol offers a spirited critique of the work-related scripts children today are often compelled to take up. Kozol is a writer and educator best known for his works on inequality in American education. He graduated from Harvard University and was awarded a Rhodes Scholarship to study at Magdalen College, Oxford. Rather than finishing at Oxford, however, he moved to Paris to work on a novel. When he returned to the United States, he began teaching in the Boston public schools, but he was fired for teaching a Langston Hughes poem that was not in the curriculum. His experiences in Boston's segregated classrooms led to his first book, *Death at an Early Age* (1967), which won the National Book Award. His other books include *Savage Inequalities* (1991), *Amazing Grace* (1995), and, most recently, *Letters to a Young Teacher* (2007). The following selection is from *The Shame of the Nation*, published in 2006.

THREE YEARS AGO, IN COLUMBUS, OHIO, I WAS VISITING A SCHOOL IN which the stimulus-response curriculum that Mr. Endicott was using in New York had been in place for several years.[1] The scripted teaching method started very early in this school. ("Practice Active Listening!" a kindergarten teacher kept repeating to her children.) So too did a program of surprisingly explicit training of young children for the modern marketplace. Starting in kindergarten, children in the school were being asked to think about the jobs that they might choose when they grew up. The posters that surrounded them made clear which kinds of jobs they were expected to select.

"Do you want a manager's job?" the first line of a kindergarten poster asked.

"What job do you want?" a second question asked in an apparent effort to expand the range of choices that these five-year-olds might wish to make.

But the momentary window that this second question seemed to open into other possible careers was closed by the next question on the wall. "How will you do the manager's job?" the final question asked.

The tiny hint of choice afforded by the second question was eradicated by the third, which presupposed that all the kids had said yes to the first. No written question asked the children: "Do you want a lawyer's job? a nurse's job? a doctor's job? a poet's job? a preacher's job? an engineer's job? or an artist's job?" Sadly enough, the teacher had not even thought to ask if anybody in the class might someday like to be a teacher.

In another kindergarten class, there was a poster that displayed the names of several retail stores: JCPenney, Wal-Mart, Kmart, Sears, and a few others. "It's like working in a store," a classroom aide explained. "The children are learning to pretend that they're cashiers."

Work-related themes and managerial ideas were carried over into almost every classroom of the school. In a first grade class, for instance, children had been given classroom tasks for which they were responsible. The names of children and their tasks were posted on the wall, an ordinary thing to see in classrooms everywhere. But in this case there was a novel twist: All the jobs the kids were given were described as management positions!

There was a "Coat Room Manager" and a "Door Manager," a "Pencil Sharpener Manager" and a "Soap Manager," an "Eraser, Board, and Marker Manager," and there was also a "Line Manager." What on earth, I was about to ask, is a "Line Manager"? My question was answered when a group of children filing in the hallway grew a bit unruly and a grown-up's voice barked out, "Who is your line manager?"

In the upper grades, the management positions became more sophisticated and demanding. In a fourth grade, for example, I was introduced to a "Time Manager" who was assigned to hold the timer to be sure the teacher didn't wander from her schedule and that everyone adhered to the prescribed number of minutes that had been assigned to every classroom task.

Turning a corner, I encountered a "HELP WANTED" sign. Several of these signs, I found, were posted on the walls at various locations in the school. These were not advertisements for school employees, but for children who would be selected to fill various positions as class managers. "Children in the higher grades are taught to file applications for a job," the principal explained — then "go for interviews," she said, before they can be hired.

> "Children in the higher grades are taught to file applications for a job."

According to a summary of schoolwide practices she gave me, interviews "for management positions" were intended to teach values of "responsibility for . . . jobs."

In another fourth grade class, there was an "earnings chart" that had been taped to every child's desk, on which a number of important writing skills had been spelled out and, next to each, the corresponding earnings that a child would receive if written answers he or she provided in the course of classroom exercises such as mini-drills or book reports displayed the necessary skills.

"How Much Is My Written Answer Worth?" the children in the class were asked. There were, in all, four columns on the "earnings charts" and children had been taught the way to fill them in. There was also a Classroom Bank in which the children's earnings were accrued. A wall display beneath the heading of the Classroom Bank presented an enticing sample of real currency — one-dollar bills, five-dollar bills, ten-dollar bills — in order to make clear the nexus between cash rewards and writing proper sentences.

Ninety-eight percent of children in the school were living in poverty, according to the school's annual report card; about four-fifths were African-American. The principal said that only about a quarter of the students had been given preschool education.

At another elementary school in the same district, in which 93 percent of children were black or Hispanic, the same "HELP WANTED" posters and the lists of management positions were displayed. Among the positions open to the children in this school, there was an "Absence Manager," a "Form-Collector Manager," a "Paper-Passing Manager," a "Paper-Collecting Manager," a "Paper-Returning Manager," an "Exit Ticket Manager," even a "Learning Manager," a "Reading Manager," a "Behavior Manager," and a "Score-Keeper Manager." Applications for all management positions, starting with the second graders, had to be "accompanied by references," according to the principal.

On a printed application form she handed me — "Consistency Management Manager Application"[2] was its title — children were instructed to fill in their name, address, phone number, teacher, and grade level, and then indicate the job that they preferred ("First job choice. . . . Why do you want this job? Second job choice. . . . Why do you want this job?"), then sign and date their application. The awkwardly named document, the principal explained, originated in a program aimed at children of minorities that had been developed with financial backing from a businessman in Texas.

The silent signals I'd observed in the South Bronx and Hartford were in use in this school also. As I entered one class, the teacher gave his students the straight-arm salute, with fingers flat. The children responded quickly with the same salute. On one of the walls, there was a sign that read "A Million Dollars Worth of Self-Control." It was "a little incentive thing," the teacher told me when I asked about this later in the afternoon.

As I was chatting with the principal before I left, I asked her if there was a reason why those two words "management" and "manager" kept popping up throughout the school. I also summoned up my nerve to tell her that I was surprised to see "HELP WANTED" signs within an elementary school.

"We want every child to be working as a manager while he or she is in this school," the principal explained. "We want to make them understand that, in this country, companies will give you opportunities to work, to prove yourself, no matter what you've done."

I wasn't sure of what she meant by that — "no matter what you've done" — and asked her if she could explain this. "Even if you have a felony arrest," she said, "we want you to understand that you can be a manager someday."

I told her that I still did not quite understand why management positions were presented to the children as opposed to other jobs — being a postal worker, for example, or construction worker, or, for that matter, working in a field of purely intellectual endeavor — as a possible way to earn a living even if one once had been in trouble with the law. But the principal was interrupted at this point and since she had already been extremely patient with me, I did not believe I had the right to press her any further. So I left the school with far more questions in my mind than answers.

When I had been observing Mr. Endicott at P.S. 65, it had occurred to me that something truly radical about the way that inner-city children are perceived was presupposed by the peculiar way he spoke to students and the way they had been programmed to respond. I thought of this again here in these classes in Ohio. What is the radical perception of these kids that underlies such practices? How is this different from the way most educated friends of mine would look at their own children?

"Primitive utilitarianism" — "Taylorism in the classroom" — were two of the terms that Mr. Endicott had used in speaking of the teaching methods in effect within his school. "Commodification" — "of the separate pieces of the learning process, of the children in themselves" — is the expression that another teacher uses to describe these practices. Children, in this frame of reference, are regarded as investments, assets, or productive units — or else, failing that, as pint-sized human deficits who threaten our competitive capacities. The package of skills they learn, or do not learn, is called "the product" of the school. Sometimes the educated child is referred to as "the product" too.

These ways of viewing children, which were common at the start of the last century, have reemerged over the past two decades in the words of business leaders, influential educators, and political officials. "We must start thinking of students as workers . . . ," said a high official of one of the nation's teachers unions at a forum convened by *Fortune* magazine in 1988.[3] I remember thinking when I read these words: Is this, really, what it all comes down to? Is future productivity, from this point on, to be the primary purpose of the education we provide our children? Is this to be the way in which we will decide if teachers are complying with their obligations to their students and society? What if a child should grow ill and die before she's old enough to make her contribution to the national economy? Will all the money that our government has spent to educate that child have to be regarded as a bad investment?

Admittedly, the economic needs of a society are bound to be reflected to some rational degree within the policies and purposes of public schools. But, even so, most of us are inclined to ask, there must be *something* more to life as it is lived by six-year-olds or ten-year-olds, or by teenagers for that matter, than concerns about "successful global competition." Childhood is not merely basic training for utilitarian adulthood. It should have some claims upon our mercy, not for its future value to the economic interests of competitive societies but for its present value as a perishable piece of life itself.

Listening to the stern demands we hear for inculcating worker ideologies in the mentalities of inner-city youth — and, as we are constantly exhorted now, for "getting tough" with those who don't comply — I am reminded of a passage from the work of Erik Erikson, who urged us to be wary of prescriptive absoluteness in the ways we treat and think about our children. "The most deadly of all possible sins" in the upbringing of a child, Erikson wrote, derive too frequently from what he called "destructive forms of conscientiousness."[4] Erikson's good counsel notwithstanding, the momentum that has led to these utilitarian ideas about the education of low-income children has been building for a long, long time and, at least in public discourse as it is presented in the press and on TV, has not met with widespread opposition. Beginning in the early 1980s and continuing with little deviation right up to the present time, the notion of producing "products" who will then produce more wealth for the society has come to be embraced by many politicians and, increasingly, by principals of inner-city schools that have developed close affiliations with the representatives of private business corporations.

> *The notion of producing "products" who will then produce more wealth for the society has come to be embraced by many politicians and . . . principals.*

"Dismayed by the faulty products being turned out by Chicago's troubled public schools," the *Wall Street Journal* wrote in 1990, "some 60 of the city's giant corporations have taken over the production line themselves," a reference to the efforts that these corporations had invested in creation of a model school in a predominantly black neighborhood that was intended to embody corporate ideas of management and productivity. "I'm in the business of developing minds to meet a market demand," the principal of the school announced during a speech delivered at "a power breakfast" of the top executives of several of these corporations. "If you were manufacturing Buicks, you would have the same objectives," said a corporate official who was serving as the school's executive director.[5]

Business jargon has since come to be commonplace in the vocabularies used within the schools themselves. Children in the primary grades are being taught they must "negotiate" with one another for a book or toy or box of crayons or a pencil-sharpener — certainly not a normal word for five- or six-year-olds to use. In many schools, young children have been learning also to "sign contracts" to complete their lessons rather than just looking up and telling Miss O'Brien they will "try real hard" to do what she has asked.

Learning itself — the learning of a skill, or the enjoying of a book, and even having an idea — is now defined increasingly not as a process or preoccupation that holds satisfaction of its own but in proprietary terms, as if it were the acquisition of an object or stock-option or the purchase of a piece of land. "Taking ownership" is the accepted term, which now is used both by the kids themselves and also by their teachers. Most people like to think they "get" ideas, "understand" a process, or "take pleasure" in the act of digging into a good book. In the market-driven classroom, children are encouraged to believe they "own" the book, the concept, the idea. They don't *engage* with knowledge; they possess it.

In the Columbus schools, as we have seen, children are actively "incentivized" (this is another term one hears in many inner-city schools) by getting reimbursements for the acquisition of a skill in terms of simulated cash. At P.S. 65 in the South Bronx, I was shown another Classroom Bank, out of which a currency called "Scholar Dollars" was disbursed. Some of these things may be dismissed as little more than modern reembodiments of ordinary rituals and phrases known to schoolchildren for decades. We all got gold stars in my elementary school if we brought in completed homework; many teachers give their students sticky decals with a picture of a frog or mouse or cat or dog, for instance, as rewards for finishing a book report or simply treating one another with politeness. Most Americans, I think, would smile at these innocent and pleasant ways of giving children small rewards. But would they smile quite so easily if their own children were provided earnings charts to calculate how much they will be paid for learning to write sentences?

Some of the usages that I have cited here ("ownership," "negotiate," for instance) have filtered into the vocabularies of suburban schools as well, but in most of these schools they are not introduced to children as the elements of acquisitional vocabulary and are more likely to be used, unconsciously perhaps, as borrowings from language that has come to be familiar in the world of pop psychology — "learning to 'take ownership' of one's emotions," for example. It is a different story when they are incorporated into a much broader package of pervasive corporate indoctrination.

535

Very few people who are not involved with inner-city schools have any idea of the extremes to which the mercantile distortion of the purposes and character of education have been taken or how unabashedly proponents of these practices are willing to defend them. The head of a Chicago school, for instance, who was criticized by some for emphasizing rote instruction which, his critics said, was turning children into "robots," found no reason to dispute the charge. "Did you ever stop to think that these robots will never burglarize your home?" he asked, and "will never snatch your pocket books. . . . These robots are going to be producing taxes. . . ."[6]

Would any educator feel at ease in using terms like these in reference to the children of a town like Scarsdale or Manhasset, Glencoe or Winnetka, or the affluent suburban town of Newton, Massachusetts, in which I attended elementary school and later taught? I think we know this is unlikely. These ways of speaking about children and perceiving children are specific to the schools that serve minorities. Shorn of unattractive language about "robots" who will be producing taxes and not burglarizing homes, the general idea that schools in ghettoized communities must settle for a different set of goals than schools that serve the children of the middle class and upper middle class has been accepted widely. And much of the rhetoric of "rigor" and "high standards" that we hear so frequently, no matter how egalitarian in spirit it may sound to some, is fatally belied by practices that vulgarize the intellects of children and take from their education far too many of the opportunities for cultural and critical reflectiveness without which citizens become receptacles for other people's ideologies and ways of looking at the world but lack the independent spirits to create their own.

> These ways of speaking about children and perceiving children are specific to the schools that serve minorities.

Perhaps the clearest evidence of what is taking place is seen in schools in which the linkage between education and employment is explicitly established in the names these schools are given and the work-related goals that they espouse. When badly failing schools are redesigned — or undergo "reconstitution," as the current language holds — a fashionable trend today is to assign them names related to the world of economics and careers. "Academy of Enterprise" or "Corporate Academy" are two such names adopted commonly in the renaming of a segregated school. Starting about ten years ago, a previously unfamiliar term emerged to specify the purposes these various academies espouse. "School-to-work" is the unflinching designation that has since been used to codify these goals, and "industry-embedded education" for the children of minorities has now become a term of art among practitioners.

Advocates for school-to-work do not, in general, describe it as a race-specific project but tend instead to emphasize the worth of linking academic programs to the world of work for children of all backgrounds and insisting that suburban children too should be prepared in school for marketplace demands, that children of all social classes ought to have "some work experience" in high school, for example. But the attempt at even-handedness in speaking of the ways that this idea might be applied has been misleading from the start. In most suburban schools, the school-to-work idea, if educators even speak of it at all, is little more than seemly decoration on the outer edges of a liberal curriculum. In many urban schools, by contrast, it has come to be the energizing instrument of almost every aspect of instruction.

Some business leaders argue that this emphasis is both realistic and humane in cases, for example, where a sixteen-year-old student lacks the skills or motivation to pursue a richly academic course of study or, indeed, can sometimes barely write a simple paragraph or handle elementary math. If the rationale for this were so defined in just so many words by the administrators of our schools, and if it were not introduced until the final years of secondary education at a point when other options for a student may appear to be foreclosed, an argument could certainly be made that school-to-work is a constructive adaptation to the situation many teenage students actually face.

But when this ethos takes control of secondary education almost from the start, or even earlier than that, before a child even enters middle school, as is the case in many districts now, it's something very different from an adaptation to the needs of students or the preferences they may express. It's not at all an "adaptation" in these cases; it's a prior legislation of diminished options for a class of children who are not perceived as having the potential of most other citizens. It's not "acceding" to their preferences. It's manufacturing those preferences and, all too frequently, it's doing this to the direct exclusion of those options other children rightly take as their entitlement.

There are middle schools in urban neighborhoods today where children are required, in effect, to choose careers before they even enter adolescence. Children make their applications to a middle school when they're in the fifth grade. . . . [A] South Bronx middle school [bears] Paul Robeson's name. "Robeson," however, as I subsequently learned, wasn't the complete name of this school. "The Paul Robeson School for Medical Careers and Health Professions" was the full and seemingly enticing designation that it bore; and, sadly enough, this designation and the way the school described itself in a brochure that had been given to the fifth grade students in the local elementary schools had led these girls into believing that enrolling there would lead to the fulfillment of a dream they shared: They wanted to be doctors.

"An understanding and embracement of medical science and health," said the brochure in a description of the school's curriculum, "is developed through powerful learning opportunities. . . . To be successful at the Paul Robeson School . . . , a student is expected to be highly motivated to broaden their horizons." Not many ten-year-olds in the South Bronx would likely know that this description represented an outrageous overstatement of the academic offerings this middle school provided. Unless they had an older sibling who had been a student there, most would have no way of knowing that the Robeson School, perennially ranking at the lowest level of the city's middle schools, sent very few students into high schools that successfully prepared a child for college and that any likelihood of moving from this school into a medical career, as these girls understood the term, was almost nonexistent.

"It's a medical school," another child, named Timeka, told me when I asked her why she had applied there. "I want to be a baby doctor," she explained, a goal that a number of the girls had settled on together, as children often do in elementary school. But the program at the Robeson School did not provide the kind of education that could lead her to that goal. A cynic, indeed, might easily suspect it was designed instead to turn out nursing aides and health assistants and the other relatively low-paid personnel within a hospital or nursing home, for instance, all of which might be regarded as good jobs for children with no other options, if they continued with their education long enough to graduate; but even this was not the usual pattern for a child who had spent three years at Robeson.

Timeka went from Robeson to another of those "industry-embedded" schools,[7] a 97 percent black and Hispanic school called "Health Opportunities," in which only one in five ninth graders ever reached twelfth grade and from which Timeka dropped out in eleventh grade.[8] I had known Timeka since she was a jubilant and energetic eight-year-old. I used to help her with her math and reading when she was in the fourth grade. She was smart and quick and good with words, and very good in math. If she had gone to school in almost any middle-class suburban district in this nation, she'd have had at least a chance of realizing her dream if she still wanted to when she completed high school. And if she changed her mind and settled on a different dream, or many different dreams, as adolescents usually do, she would have been exposed to an array of options that would have permitted her to make a well-informed decision. The choice of a career means virtually nothing if you do not know what choices you may actually have.

> **The choice of a career means virtually nothing if you do not know what choices you may actually have.**

"In recent years, business has taken ownership of school-to-work . . . ," according to an advocate for these career academies.[9] National and regional industry associations, he reports, are "linking students" to "standards-driven, work-based learning opportunities while they are in school" and then, he says, providing students with job offers from participating businesses. One such program has taken place for several years at a high school in Chicago where an emphasis on "Culinary Arts" has been embedded in curriculum.[10] A teacher at the school, where 98 percent of students are black or Hispanic (many of Mexican descent), told me of a student she had grown attached to when she taught her in eleventh grade. The student, she said, showed academic promise — "I definitely thought that she was capable of going on to college" — so she recommended her to be admitted to a senior honors class.

It was a big school (2,200 students) and the teacher said she didn't see this girl again until the following September when she happened to run into her during a class break on an escalator in the building, and she asked her if she'd been admitted to the honors class. The student told her, "No," she said. "I couldn't figure out why." Then, she said, "I realized she'd been placed in Culinary Arts."

Students, she explained, were required "to decide on a 'career path' at the end of freshman year," and "once you do this, your entire program is determined by that choice." Technically, she said, a student could select a college education as "career path," but this option, she reported, wasn't marketed to many of the students at the school as forcefully as were the job-related programs. The career programs in the upper-level grades, moreover, were blocked out "as a double period every day," the teacher said, which made it harder for the students in these programs who so wished to take an honors class or other academic classes that appealed to them.[11]

The program in culinary arts, in which the students were prepared to work in restaurant kitchens, had been set up in coordination with Hyatt Hotels, which offered jobs or internships to students on completion of their education.[12] The program was promoted to the students so effectively that many who initially may have had academic goals "appear to acquiesce in this" — "they will defend it, once they've made the choice," she said — even though some recognize that this will lead them to a relatively lower economic role in later years than if they somehow found the will to keep on and pursue a college education. "If you talk with them of college options at this point," and "if they trust you," said the teacher, "they will say, 'Nobody ever told me I could do it.' If you tell them, 'You *could* do it,' they will say, 'Why didn't someone tell me this before?'"

She told me she felt torn about expressing her concern that college education as a possible career path for such students was, in her words, either "not presented" or else "undersold," because she said there were outstanding teachers in the work-related programs and she did not want to speak of them with disrespect or compromise their jobs. At the same time, she clearly was upset about this since she spoke with deep emotion of the likelihood that "we may be trapping these young ones" in "low-paying jobs."

The teacher's story of her brief encounter with her former student reminded me of the disappointment I had felt about Timeka. The teacher seemed to blame herself to some degree, wishing, I guess, that she could have remained in closer touch with this bright student in the months since she had been a pupil in her class, perhaps believing that she might have intervened somehow on her behalf. The teacher didn't speak of a career in cooking in a restaurant, or work in a hotel, with any hint of condescension or disparagement. She was simply cognizant of other possibilities her student might have entertained; and she was saddened by this memory.

NOTES

[1] I visited these schools in November 2002, following a preliminary visit in October 2001.

Poverty and racial data for both schools described: School Year Report Cards, Columbus City School District, 2003–2004 (race and poverty data from 2002–2003).

[2] This document, part of a self-described "comprehensive classroom management program" known as "Consistency Management and Cooperative Discipline" is published by Project Grad USA, based in Houston, Texas.

[3] Albert Shanker, Americas Federation of Teachers, cited in *Fortune*, November 7, 1988.

[4] *Young Man Luther*, by Erik Erikson (New York: Norton, 1962).

[5] *Wall Street Journal*, February 9, 1990.

[6] "Learning in America," a MacNeil/Lehrer Production, PBS, April 3, 1989.

[7] Clara Barton High School for Health Professionals (95 percent black and Hispanic) had 633 ninth graders and 301 twelfth graders in 2002–2003. Graphic Arts Communications High School (94 percent black and Hispanic) had 1,096 ninth graders and 199 twelfth graders. Metropolitan Corporate Academy (98 percent black and Hispanic) had 90 ninth graders and 55 twelfth graders, of whom 34 graduated in 2003. Metropolitan Corporate Academy was conceived as a partnership with the financial firm Goldman Sachs, which provided mentors and internships for students. A school's reliance on resources from the private sector carries risks of instability, however. After serious layoffs at Goldman Sachs in 2002, according to Insideschools, an online service of Advocates for Children, "the number of mentors was cut in half." (Annual School Reports for all three schools, New York City Public Schools, 2002–2003 and 2003–2004; Insideschools 2002.)

[8] Of 294 ninth graders in the fall of 1999, only 60 remained as twelfth graders in 2003. White students made up 1.6 percent of the school's enrollment of 665. (Annual School Report for Health Opportunities High School, New York City Public Schools, 2002–2003; Common Core of Data, National Center for Education Statistics, U.S. Department of Education, 1999–2000 and 2002–2003.)

[9] Tim Barnicle, director of the Workforce Development Program at the National Center on Education and the Economy, Washington, D.C., in a letter to *Education*

Week, February 3, 1999. "The most viable school-to-work partnerships," Mr. Barnicle writes, are "tied to high academic standards . . . , supported by business and industry partners that provide students with technical skills needed to succeed in a job. . . ." He concedes that "too often school-to-work" has not been "viewed as being connected to higher academic performance in the classroom," but nonetheless believes that career-embedded schools, if properly conceived, can improve retention and increase "access to postsecondary education."

[10]The program is sited at the Roberto Clemente High School. For racial demographics, see Illinois School Report Card for Roberto Clemente Community High School, 2002, and Roberto Clemente Community High School Profile 2003–2004, Chicago Public Schools, 2004.

[11]Interview with teacher (unnamed for privacy concerns), July 2003, and subsequent correspondence in 2004 and 2005.

[12]"Project Profile, Roberto Clemente Community Academy," Executive Service Corps of Chicago, 2002–2003. An early evaluation of the program is provided in "The Millennium Breach, the American Dilemma, Richer and Poorer," a report by the Milton S. Eisenhower Foundation and the Corporation for What Works, Washington, D.C., 1998.

DISCUSSION

1. For many minority or low-income children in the United States today, school is primarily a dress rehearsal for one's future life on the job — what Kozol refers to as "vocational" or "utilitarian" learning. What do you think of this educational model? Are the market-driven roles Kozol describes the ones best for children to practice and master in school?

2. What do you make of the phrase "school-to-work"? In your view, does it suggest an approach to education that is legitimate or even useful? Does it reflect the way we're usually taught to think about education? Can you think of an alternative term that would suggest an educational approach that is preferable?

3. Kozol describes visiting one kindergarten classroom in which posters of different retail stores (JCPenney, Wal-Mart, Kmart, Sears) were displayed. "'It's like working in a store,?' a classroom aide explained. 'The children are learning to pretend that they're cashiers.'" What, in your opinion, is either good or bad about this kind of educational setting? This particular lesson? Are these types of roles worth modeling?

WRITING

4. Here is a list of the job titles to which the students in the classroom Kozol observes can aspire: coat room manager; door manager; pencil sharpener manager; eraser, board, and marker manager. Write an essay in which you assess the particular kind of learning environment this classroom seems to offer. What rules and what roles are present for students and teachers alike? Do you find anything redeeming about this classroom model? Why or why not?

5. "A fashionable trend today," Kozol writes, "is to assign [schools] names related to the world of economics and careers" — names like "Academy of Enterprise" or "Corporate Academy." Write an essay in which you analyze how this might or might not represent a shift in the way we think about the purposes of education. How would you go about arguing in favor of this market-oriented approach to education? What advantages or benefits of this model would you play up?

6. While they focus on different aspects of this phenomenon, Kozol and Alissa Quart (p. 450) share an interest in the ways that corporate or commercial culture has insinuated itself into the ways we educate our children. Write an essay that focuses on the commonalities that link these two essays. Despite their differences, how might you talk about their commentaries as kindred or related critiques?

Hopelessly Hooked on Help

Few of us these days remain untouched by the self-help movement: a vast universe of advice, how-to manuals, and twelve-step programs designed to remedy every disorder or challenge we face. But what really stands behind the growth of this industry? What needs does it address, whose interests does it serve, and (above all) does it really work? Delving beneath the surface of the self-help and actualization movement (SHAM), journalist Steve Salerno trains a skeptical eye on the "life lessons" these sorts of programs impart to the American public. Salerno is a freelance writer and reporter whose articles have appeared in *Harper's,* the *New York Times Magazine,* the *Wall Street Journal,* and *Sports Illustrated.* In 2005, he published *SHAM: How the Self-Help Industry Made America Helpless,* from which the following is excerpted. Salerno has taught writing and journalism at Indiana University and at several small colleges in Pennsylvania.

It's okay to eat meatloaf. — Sample inspirational thought from It's Okay to Be Happy, *by J. F. Mulholland*

Compared to the possibilities in life, the impossibilities are vastly more numerous. What I don't like to hear adults tell people your age is that you can be president or anything else you want to be. That's not even remotely true. The truth is that you can run for president, and that's all. . . . In our wonderfully free society, you can try to be just about anything, but your chances of success are another thing entirely. — Marilyn vos Savant, recognized by the Guinness Book of World Records *for Highest IQ, responding to a young person's letter in her* Parade *column, March 2, 2003*

I N TWENTY-FOUR YEARS AS A BUSINESS WRITER AND AN INVES-tigative journalist, I have covered all kinds of "money stories." I have written about boondoggles on bankers' row and sleight of hand at Seventh Avenue fashion houses. I've written about the gyrations of the stock market as well as the myriad forces that surround, yet never quite explain, investing itself. I've written about money as it relates to sales, money as it relates to sports, money as it relates to music, money as it relates to love. It's safe to say that if it involves money, combined with some form of human aspiration, I've probably written about it.

Never, during all that time and reporting, have I encountered an industry whose story reads quite like the one at the heart of this book. It's a story that represents the *ultimate* marriage of money and aspiration (although the money invested so exceeds the fulfillment of the aspirations that the marriage probably should be annulled). Never have I covered a phenomenon where American consumers invested so much capital in every sense of the word — financial, intellectual, spiritual, temporal — based on so little proof of efficacy. And where they got such spotty, it not nonexistent, returns.

For more than a generation, the Self-Help and Actualization Movement — felicitously enough, the words form the acronym SHAM — has been talking out of both sides of its mouth: promising relief from all that ails you while at the same time promoting nostrums that almost guarantee nothing will change (unless it gets worse). Along the way, SHAM has filled the bank accounts of a slickly packaged breed of false prophets, including, but by no means limited to, high-profile authors and motivational speakers, self-styled group counselors and workshop leaders, miscellaneous "life coaches," and any number of lesser wisemen-without-portfolio who have hung out shingles promising to deliver unto others some level of enhanced contentment. For a nice, fat, nonrefundable fee.

Self-help is an enterprise wherein people holding the thinnest of credentials diagnose in basically normal people symptoms of inflated or invented maladies, so that they may then implement remedies that have never been shown to work. An entire generation of baby boomers searching desperately for answers to the riddle of midlife has entrusted itself to a select set of dubious healers who are profiting handsomely, if not always sincerely, from that desperation.

The self-help movement has not been a wholesale failure. Surely it provides some help to some people (albeit no more so than sugar pills provide help to some patients in controlled studies of investigational drugs). Here and there a marriage is saved, a parenting dilemma solved, a mental-health problem identified and eventually corrected as a result of advice imparted in a self-help product. Here and there. But for the most part, SHAM does not do what it promises. It is the emperor's new life plan.

That's actually being charitable about it. To describe SHAM as a waste of time and money vastly understates its collateral damage. To date, the industry has escaped intense scrutiny because even those who doubt its effectiveness regard self-help as a silly but benign pursuit, an innocuous vice that plays to the Jerry Springer set, and even then is taken to heart by only a small number of perpetual victims and defenseless dupes. Self-help's best-known critics — like Wendy Kaminer, author of *I'm Dysfunctional, You're Dysfunctional* — have mostly played it for laughs, offering up their barbs with a wink and a smile.

That is, in fact, SHAM's stealth weapon, the sinister secret of its success: Everyone underestimates it. You may think Dr. Phil is the greatest thing since sliced bread, or you may chortle at his braggadocio and his sagebrush sagacity. But almost no one *worries* about Dr. Phil. Like the rest of SHAM, he slips under the radar.

Self-help is everywhere and yet it's nowhere, seldom recognized for what it is: a contributing factor (at a minimum) to many of the problems now plaguing our society. It is almost impossible to reckon the full magnitude of what SHAM has done to America besides take its money— though [I] will try. Whether you follow self-help's teachings or not, you have been touched by it, because SHAM's effects extend well beyond the millions of individual consumers who preorder Phil McGraw's latest book or attend Marianne Williamson's seminar-style love-ins. The alleged philosophies at the core of the movement have bled over into virtually every area of American social conduct and day-to-day living: the home, the workplace, the educational system, the mating dance, and elsewhere. Corporations spend billions of dollars each year on SHAM speakers, boot camps, wilderness outings, and any number of similar programs; increasingly they incorporate SHAM's beliefs into office protocols, mandating "enlightened" policies that add cost, offer no documented benefit, and may even work as *dis*incentives for quality, productivity, and morale. SHAM rhetoric has recently infected health care, too, spawning an aggressive new wing of alternative medicine that shoos people away from proven mainstream treatments by persuading them that they can cure themselves through sheer application of will.

> **Self-help is . . .
> a contributing
> factor . . . to many of
> the problems now
> plaguing our society.**

In the most macro, cultural sense, the ongoing struggle between SHAM's two polar camps . . . has parsed the meanings of right and wrong, good and bad, winning and losing, while attaching entirely foreign connotations to once commonly understood terms like *family, love, discipline, blame, excellence,* and *self-esteem.* The implications of this for legislation, the judicial system, and public policy are about what you'd expect. One camp, *Victimization,* has eroded time-honored notions of personal responsibility to a probably irrecoverable degree, convincing its believers that they're simply pawns in a hostile universe, that they can never really escape their pasts (or their biological makeup). The other camp, *Empowerment,* has weaned a generation of young people on the belief that simply aspiring to something is the same as achieving it, that a sense of "positive self-worth" is more valuable than developing the talents or skills that normally win recognition from others. Those in this second category tend to approach life as if it were an endless succession of New Year's resolutions: It's always what they're *going* to do. Meanwhile, the months and years pass.

And the self-help onslaught continues. As the *New York Times* has reported, SHAM gurus aim to be in their followers' "kitchen cupboards, medicine chests, and gym bags, as well as their heads, coaching them to peak performance, 24/7."

It somewhat embarrasses me to admit that for a long time self-help slipped under my radar as well. For decades I have been tracking the self-help movement without fully realizing its place in the zeitgeist, even though I've written often about its component parts. My first book, in 1985, described the "mainstreaming" of veteran sales and motivational trainers like Tom Hopkins and Zig Ziglar, both of whom were then beginning to expand their brands; they were subtly turning their antennae away from hard-core salesmanship to the much airier patter of mass-market training, with its exponentially greater target audience. Their efforts signaled the beginning of what we now call "success training" or, in its more intensive, small-group settings, "life coaching."

During the late 1980s and 1990s I wrote separate magazine pieces about:

TONY ROBBINS. Today he's the Eighty Million Dollar Man (per year). Back at the beginning of his career, customers were paying as little as $50 apiece to learn how to "focus" enough to be able to walk over hot coals pain free (a bit of gimmickry that the debunker James Randi tells us has nothing to do with mental preparation and everything to do with the principles of heat conduction).

TOMMY LASORDA. By the mid-1990s the former Los Angeles Dodgers manager had become a huge draw on the banquet circuit, commanding at least $30,000 an hour for imparting such philosophical gems as "Ya gotta want it!"

THE PECOS RIVER LEARNING CENTER. At Pecos River, otherwise rational corporate citizens fully expected to buttress their self-confidence and negotiating skills by falling backward off walls and sliding down the side of a mountain on a tether.

PETER LOWE. In 1998 I covered one of the barnstorming impresario's weekend-long success-fests for the *Wall Street Journal*. I guesstimated the two-day take at $1.4 million, plus ancillaries. We'll get to the ancillaries in a moment.

In reporting these and other stories, I never quite recognized all those trees as a forest. I also watched, but didn't quite apprehend, as scholarship and complex thought fell to the wayside amid the influx of simple answers delivered via bullet points, as logic and common sense took a backseat to sheer enthusiasm and even something akin to mass hysteria.

What brought everything into focus for me was a career move of my own in mid-2000. For the ensuing sixteen months, I served as editor of the books program associated with *Men's Health* magazine, the glamour property in the vast better-living empire that is Rodale. In addition to publishing such magazines as *Prevention, Organic Gardening,* and *Runner's World,* Rodale had become the premier independent book publisher in the United States largely through its aggressive and ingenious mail-order books program. The company conceived, wrote, printed, and sold millions of self-help or other advice books each year. Thus, my experience there gave me a bird's-eye view of the inner workings of the self–help industry. Rodale's professed mission statement, as featured on its corporate Web site at the time of my arrival, was simple: "To show people how they can use the power of their bodies and minds to make their lives better."

At considerable expense, Rodale undertook extensive market surveys, the results of which dictated each business unit's editorial decisions. In the case of self-help books specifically, the surveys identified the customers' worst fears and chronic problems, which we were then supposed to target in our editorial content. One piece of information to emerge from those market surveys stood out above all others and guided our entire approach: *The most likely customer for a book on any given topic was someone who had bought a similar book within the preceding eighteen months.* In a way that finding should not have surprised me. People read what interests them; a devoted Civil War buff is going to buy every hot new book that comes out on the Civil War. Pet lovers read endlessly about pets.

But the Eighteen-Month Rule struck me as counterintuitive — and discomfiting — in a self-help setting. Here, the topic was not the Civil War or shih tzus; the topic was showing people "how they can use the power of their bodies and minds to make their lives better." Many of our books proposed to solve, or at least ameliorate, a problem. If what we sold worked, one would expect lives to improve. One would not expect people to need further help from us — at least not in that same problem area, and certainly not time and time again. At some point, people would make the suggested changes, and those changes would "take." I discovered that my cynicism was even built into the Rodale system, in the concept of *repurposing* — reusing chunks of our copyrighted material in product after product under different names, sometimes even by different authors.

> **If what we sold worked, one would expect lives to improve.**

Worse yet, our marketing meetings made clear that we counted on our faithful core of malcontents. (Another important lesson in self-help theology: SHAM's answer when its methods fail? You need more of it. You *always* need more of it.) One of my Rodale mentors illustrated the concept by citing our then all-time best-selling book, *Sex: A Man's Guide.* This individual theorized that the primary audience for *Man's Guide* did *not* consist of accomplished Casanovas determined to polish their already enviable bedroom skills. Our buyers were more likely to be losers at love — hapless fumblers for whom our books conjured a fantasy world in which they could imagine themselves as ladies' men, smoothly making use of the romantic approaches and sexual techniques we described. Failure and stagnation, thus, were central to our ongoing business model.

Failure and stagnation are central to all of SHAM. The self-help guru has a compelling interest in *not* helping people. Put bluntly, he has a potent incentive to play his most loyal customers for suckers.

Yet it's even worse than *that*. Much of SHAM actively fans the fires of discontent, making people feel impaired or somehow deficient as a prelude to (supposedly) curing them. One striking example comes from no less an insider than Myrna Blyth, a former *Ladies' Home Journal* editor. In her 2004 book, *Spin Sisters: How the Women of the Media Sell Unhappiness — and Liberalism — to the Women of America*, Blyth repents for her own role in an industry that was supposed to help women grow but instead wreaked incalculable harm on the psyches of its devoted followers. What women's magazines mostly have done, argues Blyth, is create and implant worry, guilt, insecurity, inadequacy, and narcissism that did not exist in women before the magazines came along.

PAYING THE (PIED) PIPERS

The American love affair with self-help is unmistakable in the sheer size of the SHAM fiscal empire. Granted, the movement's total cash footprint defies down-to-the-penny measurement. There's just too much of it out there, perpetrated to an increasing degree by independent life coaches or poor-man's Tony Robbinses giving small-ticket motivational speeches at the local Ramada Inn. But just what we know for sure is staggering. According to Marketdata Enterprises, which has been putting a numerical face on major cultural trends since 1979, the market for self-improvement grew an astonishing 50 percent between 2000 and 2004. This substantially exceeds the already robust annual growth figures Marketdata forecast in 2000. Today, self-improvement in all its forms constitutes an $8.56 billion business, up from $5.7 billion in 2000. Marketdata now expects the industry to be perched at the $12 billion threshold by 2008.

Remember — this is only what we can document. And it does not include the broader social and political costs, which we'll discuss separately.

Between thirty-five hundred and four thousand new self-help books appeared in 2003, depending on whose figures you use and precisely how you define the genre. The higher figure represents more than double the number of new SHAM titles that debuted in 1998, when wide-eyed social commentators were remarking at self-help mania and what it signified about the decline of premillennial Western civilization. Together with evergreens like *Codependent No More*, Melody Beattie's seminal 1987 tract on overcoming self-destructive behaviors, these books accounted for about $650 million in sales, according to Simba Information, which tracks publishing trends.

Self-help was well represented on best-seller lists in 2004, anchored by a spate of musings from the Family McGraw (Dr. Phil and son Jay); Rick Warren's *The Purpose Driven Life*; Joel Osteen's spiritually tinged *Your Best Life Now: 7 Steps to Living at Your Full Potential*; Greg Behrendt's cold shower for lovelorn women, *He's Just Not That into You*; and actualization demigod Stephen R. Covey's *The 8th Habit: From Effectiveness to Greatness*. The last is a sequel to Covey's blockbuster work, *The 7 Habits of Highly Effective People*, which remains a postmodern classic, as do Tony Robbins's various tomes about that giant who slumbers within you and the six dozen separate *Chicken Soup* books now in print. Stephen Covey, too, has a son, Sean, and Sean Covey has his very own best seller, *The 7 Habits of Highly Effective Teens*. Freshly minted guru-authors appear like clockwork each year.

They almost have to, if the demand is to be met. In fact, by 1983, so substantial were sales figures for books of this genre that the lofty *New York Times Book Review*, which for decades fought the good fight on behalf of books written by actual writers, threw in the towel and added another category, "Advice Books," to its distinguished best-seller list. In an accompanying announcement, *Times* editors explained that without this new category even the most compelling works of authentic nonfiction — memoirs, exposés, biographies, think pieces, and the like — might never appear on their own best-seller list. They were being swept aside by this massive wave of self-improvement. Ten years later, a study quoted in *American Health* magazine said that self-help addicts — and *addict*, evidence suggests, is the right word — continue to buy books "long after their shelves are stocked." *Publishers Weekly* put it this way in October 2004: "Self-help books are a Teflon category for many booksellers. No matter the economy or current events, the demand is constant."

Another cultural signpost: A fair percentage of these book-buying transactions take place at the five thousand New Age bookstores now spread throughout the United States. (Industry sources thought the New Age trend had peaked a few years ago, when the number of stores hit four thousand.) Thus it should come as no surprise that the fastest-growing self-help sectors are also the softest and least utilitarian. Sales of inspirational, spiritual, and relationship-oriented programs and materials constitute a third of overall SHAM dollar volume and are tracking upward. The more brass-tacks stuff — business and financial materials, tactical training — constitute 21 percent and are tracking down. Americans seem to think it's more important to get along than to get ahead.

For today's budding self-help star, the usual progression is to parlay one's pseudoliterary success into a thriving adjunct career on TV or radio, on the lecture circuit, or at those intensive multimedia seminars known to the industry as "total immersion experiences." According to Nationwide Speakers Bureau founder Marc Reede, whose specialty is booking engagements for sports celebrities, "personal-improvement experts" account for no small part of the 9,000 *percent* increase in membership in the National Speakers Association since 1975. Just the top dozen speakers grossed $303 million in 2003; their fees generally ran between $30,000 and $150,000 per speech. More than a decade after her ethereal book *A Return to Love* dominated best-seller lists, Marianne Williamson's personal appearances still sell out as quickly as Springsteen concerts. Mass-market single-day presentations by Tony Robbins must be held in basketball arenas and convention centers. He attracts upwards of ten thousand fans at $49 a head — still a bargain-basement price for salvation when compared to his weeklong Life Mastery seminar at $6,995. "You have to have something for all the market segments," Robbins once told me. "You can't ignore the folks who can only afford a quick dose of inspiration." By 1999, more than a decade of having something for all market segments had paid off big-time for Robbins; *Business Week* pegged his annual income at $80 million.

It was the lure of such lucre that sparked the mainstreaming phenomenon among Hopkins, Ziglar, and other training specialists from fields closely allied to sales and motivation. Ziglar, the author of arguably the most successful "crossover" book ever written, *See You at the Top*, now preaches to thousands of eager disciples at his sky's-the-limit tent revivals. (Herewith a free sample of the indispensable advice Ziglar offers to husbands: "Open your wife's car door for her." And, as an added bonus, a bit of all-purpose wisdom: "You have to *be* before you can *do,* and you have to *do* before you can *have.*") Suze Orman followed Ziglar's lead as well as his advice and soared to the top: Starting with a background in institutional finance, she mastered the art of talking about money in a way that sounded as if she was really talking about "something more meaningful." She then threw in a dollop of spirituality

> **"You have to be *before* you can do, and you have to do *before* you can have."**

for good measure and became a touchstone for millions of women who'd always felt unwelcome at the financial party.

A truly hot SHAM artist may franchise himself. Relationships guru John Gray presides over just a handful of the estimated five hundred monthly "Mars and Venus" seminars that bear his imprimatur. The rest he entrusts to a cadre of handpicked stand-ins who can parrot his kitschy trademark material. And then there are the barnstormers, like the aforementioned Peter Lowe, who took the seminar industry to another level by packaging a number of speakers into themed motivational road shows. His evangelical tours teamed an improbable rotating cast of eclectic presenters, ranging from former United Nations ambassador Jeane Kirkpatrick to actor Edward Asner to professional football coach Mike Shanahan. They also featured a formidable, at times almost overwhelming, menu of ancillary products.

Ah, the ancillaries. All major seminarists reap a substantial added windfall from their so-called ancillary products: the $10 workbooks, the $19 videos and DVDs, the $49 series of CDs and cassettes for the car, to give you that all-important motivational jolt during the commute to work. To keep the good vibes flowing once you're ensconced at your desk with your misanthropic boss hovering over you, there are the inspirational trinkets, like those $29 paperweights engraved with uplifting slogans. Robbins occasionally takes time out from his usual seminar patter to hawk unrelated products — like QLink, a pendant that, he says, will protect you from cell-phone radiation, electromagnetic pulse, and other types of harmful ambient energy. The pendant costs anywhere from $129 for the bare-bones model to $839 for a version finished in brushed gold — the perfect complement for one's newly gilded self-image. Tom Hopkins, at one time the unquestioned dean of trainers in the field of real-estate sales, now depends on his low-cost success seminars to generate sales of his ancillary goods. The modest fee for the seminar is Hopkins's loss leader for an array of high-margin products.

Topping it all off are the miscellaneous do-it-yourself "personal-enhancement" products and "revolutionary new technologies!" sold via infomercial. Dale Beyerstein, a philosophy professor who has written extensively on pseudoscience, argues that the customary formula calls for taking a modicum of legitimate research and "piggybacking" onto it — that is, extending and misapplying its conclusions in a way that's just plausible enough to skirt criminal sanctions by the Federal Trade Commission or the U.S. Postal Service. The hubris of some of these pitches — not to mention the contempt for the consumer — almost defies description. For a while during the 1980s, a company called Potentials Unlimited was selling subliminal audiotapes to cure deafness.

Which begs the question: What has America gotten in return for its $8.56 billion investment?

The answer: There is no way of knowing. So much money, so few documented results.

Yes, SHAM gurus have no trouble producing the obligatory testimonial letters, the heartrending anecdotal stories of women who found the courage to leave abusive men or men who found the courage to face up to the demons within. But in any meaningful empirical sense, there is almost no evidence — at all — for the utility of self-help, either in theory or in practice. There's only one group of people we can prove benefit from the books: the authors themselves.[1]

For example, as Martin Seligman, a past president of the American Psychological Association, told *Forbes* in 2003, though some of Tony Robbins's preachments may be worth listening to, they remain altogether untested — despite the unambiguously rosy claims made for Robbins's material and the quasi-scientific pretense of the material itself.

Actually, that's not quite true. A growing body of evidence *challenges* SHAM's ability to do what it says. For one thing, despite all the talk of personal empowerment, limitless potential, and a world in which glasses are always at least half full, Americans have become ever more dependent on chemical modification. Almost four decades after Thomas A. Harris's landmark self-help tract *I'm OK — You're OK*, we live in a culture in which some of the most profitable products made are named Prozac, Paxil, and Xanax. Evidently a great many Americans don't think they're all that "OK." In the final analysis, it's not the thousands of seminars or millions of books with their billions of uplifting words that Americans seem to count on to get them through the day. *It's the drugs.*

That's no great shock to Archie Brodsky, a senior research associate for the Program in Psychiatry and the Law at Harvard Medical School. "Psychotherapy has a chancy success rate even in a one-on-one setting over a period of years," observes Brodsky, who coauthored (with Stanton Peele) *Love and Addiction*. "How can you expect to break a lifetime of bad behavioral habits through a couple of banquet-hall seminars or by sitting down with some book?"

Brodsky alludes to twelve-step recovery meetings, which don't often feature celebrity speakers or hordes of pricey ancillary products but do have a strong and loyal following nonetheless. The twelve-step movement developed as an outgrowth of Alcoholics Anonymous and now encompasses programs for a staggering range of problems, whether compulsive shopping, or loving too easily or too much, or overeating. These days, if it's a problem for someone, somewhere, it's a treatable disorder. And a support group likely exists for it. At the apex of the Recovery phenomenon, in 1992, *American Demographics* reported that twelve million Americans belonged to at least one of the nation's five hundred thousand support-group chapters.

Americans for some reason assume that Recovery groups work, when in fact there is little or no hard evidence of their ability to help people recover from anything, as this book will document. Consider, for the time being, this one fact: The results of a 1995 study conducted by Harvard Medical School indicated that alcoholics have a better chance of quitting drinking if they *don't* attend AA than if they *do*. Americans seldom hear about such results, in part because AA and its sister organizations have actively opposed independent research that could test their programs' effectiveness.

> **A 1995 study conducted by Harvard Medical School indicated that alcoholics have a better chance of quitting drinking if they don't attend AA than if they do.**

The dearth of good science can be recognized throughout SHAM. In her revealing book *PC, M.D.: How Political Correctness Is Corrupting Medicine*, psychiatrist Sally Satel complains bitterly about the faulty (or nonexistent) research underlying the nostrums and home remedies that contemporary SHAM artists preach. "We have a generation of healers who unflinchingly profess to know everything that's good for everybody," Satel told me in an interview. "They make no distinctions between science, pseudoscience, and pure fantasy. They liberally dispense their dubious prescriptives as if they'd been blessed by an NIH double-blind study." Tony Robbins, for example, contends that diet is an integral part of a successful lifestyle — not an eyebrow-raising notion, except that he goes on to counsel his audiences on the "energy frequency" of popular foods. The energy frequency of Kentucky Fried Chicken, for example, is "3 megahertz." Satel knows of no such food term and has no idea what it could possibly mean in any case. I checked with Yale University's Dr. Kelly Brownell, one of the nation's foremost experts on diet and nutrition. He was similarly mystified.

This is not to say that all SHAM rhetoric is patently false. In fact, there are whole categories of self-help precepts that can't possibly be disputed. That's because they're *circular* — the guru who espouses them is saying the same thing in different ways at the beginning and end of a sentence. The conclusion merely restates the premise.

Here's a perfect illustration, from Phil McGraw's *New York Times* number one best seller *Self Matters*: "I started this process by getting you to look at your past life, because I believe that the best predictor of future behavior is past behavior. That being true, the links in the chain of your history predict your future." The "that being true" makes it sound as if McGraw is rousing to some profound conclusion. But he isn't. The part after "that being true" merely repeats what he said in the first sentence, with slightly altered wording. It's not a conclusion at all. It's what logicians call a tautology. I am reminded of Larry Bird's priceless response to an interviewer who besieged the Indiana Pacers executive with statistics. The reporter demanded to know what Bird made of them and what they implied about the Pacers' chances in an upcoming play-off series. "All I know," Bird replied wearily, "is that we win 100 percent of the games where we finish with more points than the other guy."

Other SHAM kingpins, or ambitious pretenders, achieve a certain contrived plausibility by using puffed-up, esoteric-sounding jargon. In August 2004, Dan Neuharth, PhD, the author of *Secrets You Keep from Yourself: How to Stop Sabotaging Your Happiness*, told the readers of the magazine *First for Women* that "avoidance is a knee-jerk response to a core fear that threatens your ego." Translation: We avoid things we're really afraid of.

Far too often, the SHAM leaders delivering these pompous philosophies of life and living have no rightful standing to be doing any such thing. "There's a tendency on the reader's part to think these people are unimpeachable authorities speaking gospel truth," says Steven Wolin, a professor of psychiatry at George Washington University. "That's hardly the case." In truth, writes Wendy Kaminer in *I'm Dysfunctional, You're Dysfunctional*, the only difference between a self-help reader and a self-help writer may be "that the writer can write well enough to get a book deal." In Kaminer's view, the end result is that consumers make sweeping changes in their lives based on "something their aunt or auto mechanic could have told them."

By the time the most powerful woman in American media plucked him from obscurity and conferred the Oprah Touch, Phil McGraw had given up on clinical psychology, in part because, he later said, he was "the worst marital therapist in the history of the world." But McGraw, at least, holds a degree to practice what he now preaches. As we'll see, others of similar SHAM stature hail from far less convincing backgrounds; they proclaim themselves "relationship therapists" or "dating coaches," made-up specialties that require no particular licensing yet *sound* credible, thus duping unsuspecting patrons by the millions. At meetings of Alcoholics Anonymous and other support groups, the leader's sole credential may consist of his being in recovery from whatever the specific addiction is. Society, again, seems to think this makes good sense. I would ask two questions: Isn't it possible that fellow sufferers are a bit too close to the problem to lead effectively and impartially? And if your problem was, say, that the electrical fixtures in your house were acting funky, would you really want a workshop taught by some other homeowner who couldn't get his lights to work right (and who, by his own admission, still *had the problem*)? Or would you want a trained electrician?

In today's SHAM marketplace, individuals who stumbled into celebrity sans talent, or who managed to "conquer adversity" entirely by accident, now collect hefty fees for talking up their experiences as if they'd planned the whole thing out as an inspirational crucible. Get stuck on a mountain for a while, lose some body parts, and *presto!* — instant motivational icon. I refer to Beck Weathers, the Texas pathologist who lost his nose, his right hand and part of his left hand, and nearly his life in the notorious May 1996 Mount Everest disaster that was chronicled in Jon Krakauer's *Into Thin Air*. Weathers, now in his late fifties, travels the lecture circuit, expounding on the theme of "surviving against all odds." You wonder, though: How many people live in situations that are truly analogous to what Beck faced up on the mountain? For that matter, what role did any of Weathers's own actions play in his survival? According to Krakauer, Weathers was like a hapless pinball bounced around the mountaintop for sixteen hours, and he almost surely would have died if others hadn't helped him down the treacherous slopes at significant risk to themselves, and if his wife had not arranged for a dangerous helicopter rescue. (To be blunt about it, Weathers probably had no business being up on that mountain in the first place, as Krakauer himself strongly implies.) So what do we learn from a Beck Weathers? Tellingly, he informs his admiring audiences that "Everest, in many ways, was one of the best things to happen to me." At $15,000 per speech, he's not kidding. Even pathologists don't make that kind of money.

The bizarre case of Beck Weathers boldfaces the huge question mark that punctuates so much of SHAM doctrine and its myriad applications. The sitcom *Seinfeld*, in the famous words of its creator and title character, was a "show about nothing." Much the same could be said of SHAM. To a disconcerting degree, it is an $8.56 billion social crusade about nothing. It is a religion whose clerics get very, very rich by stating the obvious in a laughably pontifical fashion. As Anne Wilson Schaef, best known for her book *Co-Dependence: Misunderstood — Mistreated*, informs us in a later work, *Living in Process*, "Life is a process. We are a process. The Universe is a process."

To which a cynic might add: Making airy, asinine statements meant to impress or hoodwink gullible people is also a process.

NOTE

[1]On their hilarious cable TV program *Bullshit*, confirmed skeptics Penn and Teller made this point succinctly. Referring to self-styled guru Hale Dwoskin and his so-called Sedona Method, which promises to solve a cornucopia of problems for its followers, they remarked, "If the problem is that you have $295 too much, he can help you."

DISCUSSION

1. Salerno spends a good deal of time documenting the financial rewards that many of the "self-help gurus" have reaped for their efforts. What difference does this fact make? Does it affect your own views concerning the validity or effectiveness of these programs?

2. One of the core tenets underlying the self-help movement, writes Salerno, is "victimization." Can you think of a self-help program that endeavors, either overtly or implicitly, to teach participants to view themselves as victims? In this particular case, is doing so a helpful or harmful thing to do?

3. Here is a partial list of the self-help titles Salerno includes in his essay: *The 7 Habits of Highly Effective People, Codependent No More, Self Matters, Secrets You Keep from Yourself: How to Stop Sabotaging Your Happiness.* Look over these titles. What ideas or assumptions do they seem to share? Taken together, what kind of a social role do they invite readers to adopt?

WRITING

4. Think about the self-help movement as a kind of adult education. Write an essay in which you compare some of the details of the self-help movement that Salerno writes about to some more widely known educational practices that you are aware of. How do you think the structure of these programs might be designed to mimic the ways we're used to being "schooled"? How are they different?

5. According to Salerno, many of the messages embedded in self-help texts focus on the idea of empowerment. Write an essay in which you summarize the idea of empowerment as Salerno defines and assesses it. How does this compare to the dominant thinking about education as its own form of empowerment? Do you think the self-help form of empowerment, with its promises of subsequent success, is related to empowerment as an educational ideal? How or how not?

6. Both Salerno and Alissa Quart (p. 450) write about the power of aspiration in motivating us to seek education. Write an essay in which you discuss what messages our culture sends that encourage us to be educated. How, according to Salerno and Quart, are these messages incorporated into marketing pitches for educational products? Do you think these promises are realistic?

Scenes and Un-Scenes:
Looking at Learning

How do we define what learning looks like? What a good education looks like? Underneath every definition of the ideal school, every vision of the perfect teacher or model student, there lies an even more fundamental vision: of what it means to be truly educated. Think for a moment about all of the different material that gets proffered and promoted in our culture that, in one way or another, claims to answer this question. There are all of the advice books, offering parents and educators "expert" instruction on how to enhance kids' learning. There are all of the "enrichment" games, toys, and programs currently on the market. There are all of the TV shows — from *Sesame Street* to *Mr. Rogers* — that model the proper way of "doing school." Whatever its individual purview, each of these can be understood as an effort to script out for us the standards and ideals that define "real" education. Each of the following examples invites you to conduct this kind of analysis: to decode the vision of learning, the model of schooling each presents.

▶▶ *Though school environments like the one pictured here are less and less the norm (with the advent of pods and grouping), nonetheless this stereotype of school remains relevant. How many scripts can you spot here regarding teacher authority, student interaction, learning styles, and so on? (See next page.)*

▲▲ Much debate on U.S. education focuses not only on what is taught, but also on the environment in which it is taught including concerns about school security. What do images like this make you think about learning environments today? How does this shift the norm from the previous photo?

▲▲ We are much more likely today to think of educational environments as diverse. This photo shows a mother homeschooling her children. What strikes you as inherently different about this environment versus those that we more commonly associate with school?

▲▲ *Films for teenagers have always used school as a central locale for their stories to unravel. Why do you think this is? How closely do the portrayals of school made in television or film reflect your experiences as a student? How do these movies present education? What factors of education do they ignore?*

◄◄ *Photos like this one show how our culture values even the youngest children learning before they enter formal schooling. How does this photo present the learning process? Are there any elements of this photo you would alter to reflect criticism of pushing children into formal learning too soon (such as those discussed by Alissa Quart, p. 450)?*

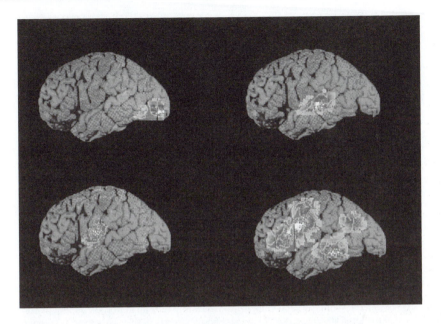

This photo shows activity in the brain during the learning process. Without being able to see an environment or context for the learning process shown here, how does this change your impression of what learning looks like?

DISCUSSION

1. Which of these images best captures your experiences in school? Which of them would you most want to use as a model or template for rewriting the scripts by which your experiences as a student unfolded?

2. Do you think any of these depictions promote messages that are problematic or dangerous to follow?

3. Are there any educational ideals that you think this collection of images leaves out? If so, what are they? And what, in your view, makes them so valuable?

WRITING

4. Choose a television show or movie that sketches a portrait of modern school life. How does it depict school? What specific aspects of schooling (for example, school rules, teacher or student behavior, and so on) get idealized? Which satirized? Write an essay in which you analyze the practices and standards this portrait presents as the ideal. How do they compare with the images of school or learning shown in this feature?

5. Make a list of all the different aspects of contemporary education that you think this collection could critique. Then write an essay in which you identify a particular question or issue that does not get raised or referenced in this collection. What is it, and what in your view makes it an important aspect of our educational life to focus on? Can you find an image of this issue that you would include to better balance this set?

6. Choose one of the images above, one whose depiction clearly lays out an alternative model of schooling. Then choose the writer in this chapter whose own critique of conventional education most closely mirrors this model. Write an essay in which you compare and contrast the specific features within each of these alternative visions.

Putting It into Practice: **Educational Scripts**

Now that you've read the chapter selections, try applying your conclusions to your own life by completing the following exercises.

QUIZZING TEACHERS   Prepare an interview questionnaire about attitudes toward teaching and education, and ask an instructor, teacher, or education major you know to complete it. Here are some suggested questions: *What do you like most about teaching? Least? What are the biggest challenges you face as an educator? What do you believe is the purpose of education? What do you believe is most important for your students to know?* Feel free to ask any other questions you might think of. When you get his or her answers, write an essay in which you analyze the responses based on what you think are the most common ways we think of education in our culture. How do the answers reflect this common thinking? Where do they differ? Do any of the responses echo the critiques or anxieties of any of the authors in this chapter?

DOING YOUR HOMEWORK   Choose some educational issue or controversy that is currently being publicly debated: school board election, referendum on funding, and so on. First, research this issue as thoroughly as you can. What are the keys points of disagreement? What questions or issues does it involve? What people, organizations, or interest groups are on each side? If you were asked to pick a side in the debate, which would it be, and why? Then attend one of the public meetings in which this debate is being conducted and write up a description of your observations.

GRADE THE IMPACT   Choose one of the educational issues discussed by the writers included in this chapter and write a personal essay in which you discuss how this issue has impacted your life as a student. What new insight have you gained by reading further about this issue? How do you view your education differently? If you could, what would you change about your education?

7 How We
TALK

Introduction

PUTTING IT INTO WORDS

Picture this: you're at a weekend party, surrounded by friends, class-mates, and acquaintances, when suddenly a person you don't recognize approaches, clearly interested in striking up a conversation. Assuming you are interested in conversing as well, what is your next move? And how do you make this decision in the few seconds you have available? What, for example, are your options for how to introduce yourself? What sorts of topics are OK to broach? The tone of voice or type of body language acceptable to adopt? And once things are underway, where do you go from there? What kinds of conversation do people typically transition into? And what are the conventions for ending them when you decide to be done? As you consider these questions, you might even make two lists: the first containing all the words or phrases, gestures, and topics that you think are permissible to use in a situation like this, and the second itemizing all those that aren't. Looking over lists such as these reminds us that talk — like so many other aspects of our daily lives — is something defined and constrained by particular norms.

This scenario merits our attention because it underscores how much of our everyday language is borrowed. Whether we are entirely aware of it or not, a good deal of what we say has already been said many times before. Many of the statements we make are really *restatements*: repetitions or reenactments of dialogue that has been written out long before we arrived on the scene. It isn't that hard, after all, to come up with at least one cliché that, in a given situation, it seems as if "everybody" says. And while it may be amusing, this fact is also important because when we use language that has been used before, we are expressing views that similarly have come from somewhere else. And if this sort of thing happens a lot, if we mouth sentiments simply because doing so has become the convention or norm, then in a certain sense we really aren't choosing our words at all. Rather, our words are choosing for us — scripting not just the particular words we are supposed to use but also the ideas we are allowed to express. Intuitively at least, this is something most of us already understand. We may not always acknowl-edge it openly, but on some level we know that many of the day-to-day situations we find ourselves in are defined by a limited repertoire of things considered acceptable to say. And yet, we don't always think about what this really means. Once we confront this reality more squarely, in fact, a number of frequently overlooked questions push their way to the forefront. For one, where does all this "canned" language come from? Who or what is responsible for scripting the lines we so often speak in our daily lives? And why do we choose this language rather than something else? Is it because there simply aren't any other words that capture our feelings, convey our ideas, or express our attitudes quite as well? Or do all of these kinds of canned phrases and scripted conversations serve some larger social purpose?

Everybody Knows That . . .

"Gitmo, Combined Celebrity Names (i.e., "Brangelina"), Awesome, Gone/ Went Missing, Pwn or Pwned, Now Playing in Theaters, We're Pregnant, Undocumented Alien, Armed Robbery/ Drug Deal Gone Bad, Truthiness, Ask Your Doctor, Chipotle, i-Anything, Search, Healthy Food, Boasts"

— Lake Superior State University's annual list of banished words, 2007

However we answer these questions, there is little doubt that the standards and norms around our public speech are things we are *taught.* From talk show hosts to sportscasters, political pundits to radio shock jocks, stand-up comedy acts to public service announcements, we hardly lack for examples that model for us the expected or acceptable ways to talk. Nor is there any shortage these days of the venues through which we are supposed to channel all this talk: from cell phones to e-mail, radio shout-outs to political commercials, letters-to-the-editor to personal ads. What isn't immediately clear is whether all this material sets comparably firm boundaries around how we think. Indeed, what makes an investigation into our culture's myriad talk-related scripts so provocative is the possibility that these guidelines leave at least some room for improvisation and revision.

In this sense, the presence of cliché illustrates the relationship we have to many of our culture's talk-related scripts as a kind of cultural ventrilo- quism: a process in which our larger culture speaks through us, in which we merely read lines and espouse views scripted for us. There are other moments, however, where it makes more sense to regard these scripts as occasions for improvisation: a process in which we recite prescribed lines in order to take them over, revising their accepted or conventional meanings to suit our own purposes. What makes the entire question even more com- plicated, of course, is that, depending on the circumstances we find our- selves in, either possibility is more likely to seem valid. To be sure, it almost become a cliché in itself to think of our speech as something fundamentally personal and private. Our talk, we like to believe, is the means by which we express ourselves and through which we affirm our unique individuality. After all, what is more intrinsic to us, more exclusively and entirely our own, than our own voice? As we've begun to see, however, this conceit may well underplay how complexly entwined our voice is with social roles and social scripts.

Each of the selection authors in this chapter tries to makes sense of the guidelines our various forms of expression conventionally adhere to and of the larger purpose these scripts seem designed to serve. Each author hazards an answer to the same basic question: Why do we talk the way we do? Some of the writers answer this question by focusing on the different rhetorical forms our contemporary talk most often adheres to. Using the question of argument as a cultural lens, Deborah Tannen inaugurates this chapter by itemizing the various scripts that our public disputes tend most often to follow these days — from political mudslinging to television talk shows. Pursuing a similar focus, Stephen Miller uses argument to pose a set of questions concerning the fate of conversation in American public life, asking whether our current enthusiasm for confrontation and conflict has succeeded in making the thoughtful, reciprocal dialogue a relic of the past. Completing this trio is an essay by Geoffrey Nunberg, whose history of *liberal* as a favorite pejorative term connects this rhetorical analysis to a more explicitly political context. Other writers undertake such rhetorical analyses by using the language of role-playing and script writing. Exploring some of the more typical forms joking has come to take, Peter Hyman both marvels at and warns against what he sees as our unchecked enthusiasm for modeling our own talk along the lines of the most popular stand-up comedians. Shifting from comedy to sex, Sheelah Kolhatkar tracks the particular formulae and stereotypes that college sex advice columns follow in dispensing their advice. Other selections meanwhile delve beneath the surface of all this talk to investigate some of the underlying forces (political, economic, technological) that both motivate and mold it. This is the goal that lies behind Jeff Sharlet's provocative exposé of Clear Channel, a media conglomerate whose increasingly monopolistic grip over commercial radio threatens to

Everybody Knows That . . .

"Congress shall make no law respecting an establishment of religion, or prohibiting the free exercise thereof; or abridging the freedom of speech, or of the press; or the right of the people peaceably to assemble, and to petition the Government for a redress of grievances."

— *First Amendment to the U.S. Constitution*

standardize not only the kinds of music played, but also the types of ideas or views expressed on the public airwaves. Carl Elliott looks at the role technology plays in shaping and limiting public voice, detailing his visit to an "accent reduction" business, a burgeoning field that trades on our faith in technology to refashion not only our voices but our very identities as well.

"EVERYBODY KNOWS THAT" EXERCISE

Choose one of the quotations featured in the margins on the previous pages and answer the following questions:

1. What does this quotation ask you to believe?
2. What are the particular ideas, values, or attitudes it invites us to accept as *normal*?
3. What would it feel like to act on or act out these norms in our personal lives?

Rule Maker > > > > > > > > Rule Breaker

“ (b) **Policy.** — A member of the armed forces shall be separated from the armed forces under regulations prescribed by the Secretary of Defense if one or more of the following findings is made and approved in accordance with procedures set forth in such regulations: . . .

(2) That the member has stated that he or she is a homosexual or bisexual, or words to that effect, unless there is a further finding, made and approved in accordance with procedures set forth in the regulations, that the member has demonstrated that he or she is not a person who engages in, attempts to engage in, has a propensity to engage in, or intends to engage in homosexual acts.”

— FROM TITLE 10, SUBTITLE A, PART II,
CHAPTER 37, § 654 OF THE U.S. ARMED SERVICES
CODE, COMMONLY REFERRED TO AS THE
“DON'T ASK, DON'T TELL” POLICY

“ [Steve] Ralls [director of communications for the Servicemembers Legal Defense Network] says that even in wartime, as DADT [Don't Ask, Don't Tell] discharges decline, lesbian and gay servicemembers still have to take great care and use discretion. Phone calls by overseas troops are monitored, for example, so saying “I love you” to someone of the same sex can start an investigation. And, he says, while attitudes toward gays and lesbians may be more tolerant among younger recruits, gay and lesbian soldiers are still harassed and illegally targeted for investigation.”

— “LIFE DURING WARTIME” BY SEAN BUGG,
METRO WEEKLY, MARCH 25, 2004

THE U.S. MILITARY VS. SERVICEMEMBERS LEGAL DEFENSE NETWORK

Enacted in 1993 by President Bill Clinton, the “Don't Ask, Don't Tell” policy has recently returned as a widely debated topic as the U.S. wars in Iraq and Afghanistan continue. Touted as a compromise policy that allows gays and lesbians to serve in the military provided they do not discuss or act on their sexuality, “Don't Ask, Don't Tell” has been criticized on both sides, by parties who believe that allowing gays and lesbians to serve threatens unit cohesion and by the gay and lesbian community, who view the policy as blatant discrimination that does nothing to protect the military careers of gays and lesbians. What do you think it would mean to live by this policy as a gay soldier? How does this policy put clear limitations around what you can say about who you are? As a broader consideration, how does Don't Ask, Don't Tell offer a case study or template for how Americans in general are allowed to talk publicly about homosexuality? The question of what it means to be "out," after all, extends far beyond the military.

FIND THE RULES: Are there any contradictions that you can find in a supposedly nondiscriminatory policy that places a caveat on itself that gay servicemembers should not disclose their sexuality?

MAKE YOUR OWN RULES: In your opinion, should the "Don't Ask, Don't Tell" policy be overturned? Why or why not? What policy would you put in its place that would appease one side's fears about maintaining unit cohesion while allowing gay and lesbian servicemembers to serve without fear of discharge?

DEBORAH TANNEN

Fighting for Our Lives

Arguing is one of the most essential and ubiquitous aspects of contemporary talk. From political pundits to radio shock jocks, argument has established itself as one of the principal ways we now talk with and at each other. But is it necessarily a good thing, Deborah Tannen asks, that we now live in a world where this type of "us verses them" approach has become an enshrined cultural norm? Tannen is a linguist best known for her books about the differing communication styles of men and women. These include *You Just Don't Understand* (1990), which was at the top of the *New York Times* bestseller list for eight months, and *Talking from 9 to 5* (1994), about communication in the workplace. Her most recent book is *You're Wearing That? Understanding Mothers and Daughters in Conversation* (2006). Tannen got her undergraduate degree from Binghamton University and did graduate work at Wayne State University before finishing her PhD in linguistics at the University of California–Berkeley. She currently teaches sociolinguistics at Georgetown University. The selection that follows is from *The Argument Culture* (1998).

THIS IS NOT ANOTHER BOOK ABOUT CIVILITY. "CIVILITY" SUGGESTS A superficial, pinky-in-the-air veneer of politeness spread thin over human relations like a layer of marmalade over toast. This book is about a pervasive warlike atmosphere that makes us approach public dialogue, and just about anything we need to accomplish, as if it were a fight. It is a tendency in Western culture in general, and in the United States in particular, that has a long history and a deep, thick, and far-ranging root system. It has served us well in many ways but in recent years has become so exaggerated that it is getting in the way of solving our problems. Our spirits are corroded by living in an atmosphere of unrelenting contention — an argument culture.

The argument culture urges us to approach the world — and the people in it — in an adversarial frame of mind. It rests on the assumption that opposition is the best way to get anything done: The best way to discuss an idea is to set up a debate; the best way to cover news is to find spokespeople who express the most extreme, polarized views and present them as "both sides"; the best way to settle disputes is litigation that pits one party against the other; the best way to begin an essay is to attack someone; and the best way to show you're really thinking is to criticize.

Our public interactions have become more and more like having an argument with a spouse. Conflict can't be avoided in our public lives any more than we can avoid conflict with people we love. One of the great strengths of our society is that we can express these conflicts openly. But just as spouses have to learn ways of settling their differences without inflicting real damage on each other, so we, as a society, have to find constructive ways of resolving disputes and differences. Public discourse requires *making* an argument for a point of view, not *having* an argument — as in having a fight.

The war on drugs, the war on cancer, the battle of the sexes, politicians' turf battles — in the argument culture, war metaphors pervade our talk and shape our thinking. Nearly everything is framed as a battle or game in which winning or losing is the main concern. These all have their uses and their place, but they are not the only way — and often not the best way — to understand and approach our world. Conflict and opposition are as necessary as cooperation and agreement, but the scale is off balance, with conflict and opposition overweighted. In [*The Argument Culture*], I show how deeply entrenched the argument culture is, the forms it takes, and how it affects us every day — sometimes in useful ways, but often creating more problems than it solves, causing rather than avoiding damage. As a sociolinguist, a social scientist, I am trained to observe and explain language and its role in human relations, and that is my biggest job here. But I will also point toward other ways for us to talk to each other and get things done in our public lives.

THE BATTLE OF THE SEXES

My interest in the topic of opposition in public discourse intensified in the years following the publication of *You Just Don't Understand*, my book about communication between women and men. In the first year I appeared on many television and radio shows and was interviewed for many print articles in newspapers and magazines. For the most part, that coverage was extremely fair, and I was — and remain — indebted to the many journalists who found my ideas interesting enough to make them known to viewers, listeners, and readers. But from time to time — more often than I expected — I encountered producers who insisted on setting up a television show as a fight (either between the host and me or between another guest and me) and print journalists who made multiple phone calls to my colleagues, trying to find someone who would criticize my work. This got me thinking about what kind of information comes across on shows and in articles that take this approach, compared to those that approach topics in other ways.

At the same time, my experience of the academic world that had long been my intellectual home began to change. For the most part, other scholars, like most journalists, were welcoming and respectful in their responses to my work, even if they disagreed on specific points or had alternative views to suggest. But about a year after *You Just Don't Understand* became a best-seller — the wheels of academia grind more slowly than those of the popular press — I began reading attacks on my work that completely misrepresented it. I had been in academia for over fifteen years by then, and had valued my interaction with other researchers as one of the greatest rewards of academic life. Why, I wondered, would someone represent me as having said things I had never said or as having failed to say things I had said?

The answer crystallized when I put the question to a writer who I felt had misrepresented my work: "Why do you need to make others wrong for you to be right?" Her response: "It's an argument!" Aha, I thought, that explains it. When you're having an argument with someone, your goal is not to listen and understand. Instead, you use every tactic you can think of — including distorting what your opponent just said — in order to win the argument.

Not only the level of attention *You Just Don't Understand* received but, even more, the subject of women and men, triggered the tendency to polarize. This tendency to stage a fight on television or in print was posited on the conviction that opposition leads to truth. Sometimes it does. But the trouble is, sometimes it doesn't. I was asked at the start of more than one talk show or print interview, "What is the most controversial thing about your book?" Opposition does not lead to truth when the most controversial thing is not the most important.

> **This tendency to stage a fight on television or in print was posited on the conviction that opposition leads to truth.**

The conviction that opposition leads to truth can tempt not only members of the press but just about anyone seeking to attract an audience to frame discussions as a fight between irreconcilable opposites. Even the Smithsonian Institution, to celebrate its 150th anniversary, sponsored a series of talks billed as debates. They invited me to take part in one titled "The Battle of the Sexes." The organizer preempted my objection: "I know you won't be happy with this title, but we want to get people interested." This is one of many assumptions I question in this book: Is it necessary to frame an interchange as a battle to get people interested? And even if doing so succeeds in capturing attention, does it risk dampening interest in the long run, as audiences weary of the din and begin to hunger for more substance?

THOUGHT-PROVOKING OR JUST PROVOCATIVE?

In the spring of 1995, Horizons Theatre in Arlington, Virginia, produced two one-act plays I had written about family relationships. The director, wanting to contribute to the reconciliation between Blacks and Jews, mounted my plays in repertory with two one-act plays by an African-American playwright, Caleen Sinnette Jennings. We had both written plays about three sisters that explored the ethnic identities of our families (Jewish for me, African-American for her) and the relationship between those identities and the American context in which we grew up. To stir interest in the plays and to explore the parallels between her work and mine, the theater planned a public dialogue between Jennings and me, to be held before the plays opened.

As production got under way, I attended the audition of actors for my plays. After the auditions ended, just before everyone headed home, the theater's public relations volunteer distributed copies of the flyer announcing the public dialogue that she had readied for distribution. I was horrified. The flyer announced that Caleen and I would discuss "how past traumas create understanding and conflict between Blacks and Jews today." The flyer was trying to grab by the throat the issue that we wished to address indirectly. Yes, we were concerned with conflicts between Blacks and Jews, but neither of us is an authority on that conflict, and we had no intention of expounding on it. We hoped to do our part to ameliorate the conflict by focusing on commonalities. Our plays had many resonances between them. We wanted to talk about our work and let the resonances speak for themselves.

Fortunately, we were able to stop the flyers before they were distributed and devise new ones that promised something we could deliver: "a discussion of heritage, identity, and complex family relationships in African-American and Jewish-American culture as represented in their plays." Jennings noticed that the original flyer said the evening would be "provocative" and changed it to "thought-provoking." What a world of difference is implied in that small change: how much better to make people think, rather than simply to "provoke" them — as often as not, to anger.

It is easy to understand why conflict is so often highlighted: Writers of headlines or promotional copy want to catch attention and attract an audience. They are usually under time pressure, which lures them to established, conventionalized ways of expressing ideas in the absence of leisure to think up entirely new ones. The promise of controversy seems an easy and natural way to rouse interest. But serious consequences are often unintended: Stirring up animosities to get a rise out of people, though easy and "provocative," can open old wounds or create new ones that are hard to heal. This is one of many dangers inherent in the argument culture.

FOR THE SAKE OF ARGUMENT

In the argument culture, criticism, attack, or opposition are the predominant if not the only ways of responding to people or ideas. I use the phrase "culture of critique" to capture this aspect.[1] "Critique" in this sense is not a general term for analysis or interpretation but rather a synonym for criticism.

It is the *automatic* nature of this response that I am calling attention to — and calling into question. Sometimes passionate opposition, strong verbal attack, are appropriate and called for. No one knows this better than those who have lived under repressive regimes that forbid public opposition. The Yugoslavian-born poet Charles Simic is one. "There are moments in life," he writes, "when true invective is called for, when it becomes an absolute necessity, out of a deep sense of justice, to denounce, mock, vituperate, lash out, in the strongest possible language."[2] I applaud and endorse this view. There are times when it is necessary and right to fight — to defend your country or yourself, to argue for right against wrong or against offensive or dangerous ideas or actions.

What I question is the ubiquity, the knee-jerk nature, of approaching almost any issue, problem, or public person in an adversarial way. One of the dangers of the habitual use of adversarial rhetoric is a kind of verbal inflation — a rhetorical boy who cried wolf: The legitimate, necessary denunciation is muted, even lost, in the general cacophony of oppositional shouting. What I question is using opposition to accomplish *every* goal, even those that do not require fighting but might also (or better) be accomplished by other means, such as exploring, expanding, discussing, investigating, and the exchanging of ideas suggested by the word "dialogue." I am questioning the assumption that *everything* is a matter of polarized opposites, the proverbial "two sides to every question" that we think embodies open-mindedness and expansive thinking.

> *I am questioning the assumption that everything is a matter of polarized opposites . . . that we think embodies open-mindedness and expansive thinking.*

In a word, the type of opposition I am questioning is what I call "agonism." I use this term, which derives from the Greek word for "contest," *agonia*, to mean an automatic warlike stance — not the literal opposition of fighting against an attacker or the unavoidable opposition that arises organically in response to conflicting ideas or actions. An agonistic response, to me, is a kind of programmed contentiousness — a prepatterned, unthinking use of fighting to accomplish goals that do not necessarily require it.[3]

HOW USEFUL ARE FIGHTS?

Noticing that public discourse so often takes the form of heated arguments — of having a fight — made me ask how useful it is in our personal lives to settle differences by arguing. Given what I know about having arguments in private life, I had to conclude that it is, in many cases, not very useful.

In close relationships it is possible to find ways of arguing that result in better understanding and solving problems. But with most arguments, little is resolved, worked out, or achieved when two people get angrier and less rational by the minute. When you're having an argument with someone, you're usually not trying to understand what the other person is saying, or what in their experience leads them to say it. Instead, you're readying your response: listening for weaknesses in logic to leap on, points you can distort to make the other person look bad and yourself look good. Sometimes you know, on some back burner of your mind, that you're doing this — that there's a kernel of truth in what your adversary is saying and a bit of unfair twisting in what you're saying. Sometimes you do this because you're angry, but sometimes it's just the temptation to take aim at a point made along the way because it's an easy target.

Here's an example of how this happened in an argument between a couple who had been married for over fifty years. The husband wanted to join an HMO by signing over their Medicare benefits to save money. The wife objected because it would mean she could no longer see the doctor she knew and trusted. In arguing her point of view, she said, "I like Dr. B. He knows me, he's interested in me. He calls me by my first name." The husband parried the last point: "I don't like that. He's much younger than we are. He shouldn't be calling us by first name." But the form of address Dr. B. uses was irrelevant. The wife was trying to communicate that she felt comfortable with the doctor she knew, that she had a relationship with him. His calling her by her first name was just one of a list of details she was marshaling to explain her comfort with him. Picking on this one detail did not change her view — and did not address her concern. It was just a way to win the argument.

We are all guilty, at times, of seizing on irrelevant details, distorting someone else's position the better to oppose it, when we're arguing with those we're closest to. But we are rarely dependent on these fights as sources of information. The same tactics are common when public discourse is carried out on the model of personal fights. And the results are dangerous when listeners are looking to these interchanges to get needed information or practical results.

Fights have winners and losers. If you're fighting to win, the temptation is great to deny facts that support your opponent's views and to filter what you know, saying only what supports your side. In the extreme form, it encourages people to misrepresent or even to lie. We accept this risk because we believe we can tell when someone is lying. The problem is, we can't.

Paul Ekman, a psychologist at the University of California, San Francisco, studies lying. He set up experiments in which individuals were videotaped talking about their emotions, actions, or beliefs — some truthfully, some not. He has shown these videotapes to thousands of people, asking them to identify the liars and also to say how sure they were about their judgments. His findings are chilling. Most people performed not much better than chance, and those who did the worst had just as much confidence in their judgments as the few who were really able to detect lies. Intrigued by the implications of this research in various walks of life, Dr. Ekman repeated this experiment with groups of people whose jobs require them to sniff out lies: judges, lawyers, police, psychotherapists, and employees of the CIA, FBI, and ATF (Bureau of Alcohol, Tobacco, and Firearms). They were no better at detecting who was telling the truth than the rest of us. The only group that did significantly better were members of the U.S. Secret Service. This finding gives some comfort when it comes to the Secret Service but not much when it comes to every other facet of public life.

TWO SIDES TO EVERY QUESTION

Our determination to pursue truth by setting up a fight between two sides leads us to believe that every issue has two sides — no more, no less: If both sides are given a forum to confront each other, all the relevant information will emerge, and the best case will be made for each side. But opposition does not lead to truth when an issue is not composed of two opposing sides but is a crystal of many sides. Often the truth is in the complex middle, not the oversimplified extremes.

We love using the word "debate" as a way of representing issues: the abortion debate, the health care debate, the affirmative action debate — even "the great backpacking vs. car camping debate."[4] The ubiquity of this word in itself shows our tendency to conceptualize issues in a way that predisposes public discussion to be polarized, framed as two opposing sides that give each other no ground. There are many problems with this approach. If you begin with the assumption that there must be an "other side," you may end up scouring the margins of science or the fringes of lunacy to find it. As a result, proven facts, such as what we know about how the earth and its inhabitants evolved, are set on a par with claims that are known to have no basis in fact, such as creationism.[5]

> *If you begin with the assumption that there must be an "other side," you may end up scouring the margins of science or the fringes of lunacy to find it.*

The conviction that there are two sides to every story can prompt writers or producers to dig up an "other side," so kooks who state outright falsehoods are given a platform in public discourse. This accounts, in part, for the bizarre phenomenon of Holocaust denial. Deniers, as Emory

University professor Deborah Lipstadt shows, have been successful in gaining television airtime and campus newspaper coverage by masquerading as "the other side" in a "debate."

Appearance in print or on television has a way of lending legitimacy, so baseless claims take on a mantle of possibility. Lipstadt shows how Holocaust deniers dispute established facts of history, and then reasonable spokespersons use their having been disputed as a basis for questioning known facts. The actor Robert Mitchum, for example, interviewed in *Esquire*, expressed doubt about the Holocaust. When the interviewer asked about the slaughter of six million Jews, Mitchum replied, "I don't know. People dispute that."[6] Continual reference to "the other side" results in a pervasive conviction that everything has another side — with the result that people begin to doubt the existence of any facts at all.

THE EXPENSE OF TIME AND SPIRIT

Lipstadt's book meticulously exposes the methods used by deniers to falsify the overwhelming historic evidence that the Holocaust occurred. That a scholar had to invest years of her professional life writing a book unraveling efforts to deny something that was about as well-known and well-documented as any historical fact has ever been — while those who personally experienced and witnessed it are still alive — is testament to another way that the argument culture limits our knowledge rather than expanding it. Talent and effort are wasted refuting outlandish claims that should never have been given a platform in the first place. Talent and effort are also wasted when individuals who have been unfairly attacked must spend years of their creative lives defending themselves rather than advancing their work. The entire society loses their creative efforts. This is what happened with scientist Robert Gallo.

Dr. Gallo is the American virologist who codiscovered the AIDS virus. He is also the one who developed the technique for studying T-cells, which made that discovery possible. And Gallo's work was seminal in developing the test to detect the AIDS virus in blood, the first and for a long time the only means known of stemming the tide of death from AIDS. But in 1989, Gallo became the object of a four-year investigation into allegations that he had stolen the AIDS virus from Luc Montagnier of the Pasteur Institute in Paris, who had independently identified the AIDS virus. Simultaneous investigations by the National Institutes of Health, the office of Michigan Congressman John Dingell, and the National Academy of Sciences barreled ahead long after Gallo and Montagnier settled the dispute to their mutual satisfaction. In 1993 the investigations concluded that Gallo had done nothing wrong. Nothing. But this exoneration cannot be considered a happy ending. Never mind the personal suffering of Gallo, who was reviled when he should have been heralded as a hero. Never mind that, in his words, "These were the most painful years and horrible years of my life." The dreadful, unconscionable result of the fruitless investigations is that Gallo had to spend four years fighting the accusations instead of fighting AIDS.[7]

The investigations, according to journalist Nicholas Wade, were sparked by an article about Gallo written in the currently popular spirit of demonography: not to praise the person it features but to bury him — to show his weaknesses, his villainous side. The implication that Gallo had stolen the AIDS virus was created to fill a requirement of the discourse: In demonography, writers must find negative sides of their subjects to display for readers who enjoy seeing heroes transformed into villains. The suspicion led to investigations, and the investigations became a juggernaut that acquired a life of its own, fed by the enthusiasm for attack on public figures that is the culture of critique.

METAPHORS: WE ARE WHAT WE SPEAK

Perhaps one reason suspicions of Robert Gallo were so zealously investigated is that the scenario of an ambitious scientist ready to do anything to defeat a rival appeals to our sense of story; it is the kind of narrative we are ready to believe. Culture, in a sense, is an environment of narratives that we hear repeatedly until they seem to make self-evident sense in explaining human behavior. Thinking of human interactions as battles is a metaphorical frame through which we learn to regard the world and the people in it.

All language uses metaphors to express ideas; some metaphoric words and expressions are novel, made up for the occasion, but more are calcified in the language. They are simply the way we think it is natural to express ideas. We don't think of them as metaphors. Someone who says, "Be careful: You aren't a cat; you don't have nine lives," is explicitly comparing you to a cat, because the cat is named in words. But what if someone says, "Don't pussyfoot around; get to the point"? There is no explicit comparison to a cat, but the comparison is there nonetheless, implied in the word "pussyfoot." This expression probably developed as a reference to the movements of a cat cautiously circling a suspicious object. I doubt that individuals using the word "pussyfoot" think consciously of cats. More often than not, we use expressions without thinking about their metaphoric implications. But that doesn't mean those implications are not influencing us.

At a meeting, a general discussion became so animated that a participant who wanted to comment prefaced his remark by saying, "I'd like to leap into the fray." Another participant called out, "Or share your thoughts." Everyone laughed. By suggesting a different phrasing, she called attention to what would probably have otherwise gone unnoticed: "Leap into the fray" characterized the lively discussion as a metaphorical battle.

Americans talk about almost everything as if it were a war. A book about the history of linguistics is called *The Linguistics Wars*. A magazine article about claims that science is not completely objective is titled "The Science Wars." One about breast cancer detection is "The Mammogram War"; about competition among caterers, "Party Wars" — and on and on in a potentially endless list.[8] Politics, of course, is a prime candidate. One of innumerable possible examples, the headline of a story reporting that the Democratic National Convention nominated Bill Clinton to run for a second term declares, "DEMOCRATS SEND CLINTON INTO BATTLE FOR A 2D TERM."[9] But medicine is as frequent a candidate, as we talk about battling and conquering disease.

Headlines are intentionally devised to attract attention, but we all use military or attack imagery in everyday expressions without thinking about it: "Take a shot at it," "I don't want to be shot down," "He went off half cocked," "That's half the battle." Why does it matter that our public discourse is filled with military metaphors? Aren't they just words? Why not talk about something that matters — like actions?

Because words matter. When we think we are using language, language is using us. As linguist Dwight Bolinger put it (employing a military metaphor), language is like a loaded gun: It can be fired intentionally, but it can wound or kill just as surely when fired accidentally. The terms in which we talk about something shape the way we think about it — and even what we see.

> *The terms in which we talk about something shape the way we think about it — and even what we see.*

The power of words to shape perception has been proven by researchers in controlled experiments. Psychologists Elizabeth Loftus and John Palmer, for example, found that the terms in which people are asked to recall something affect what they recall. The researchers showed subjects a film of two cars colliding, then asked how fast the cars were going; one week later, they asked whether there had been any broken glass. Some subjects were asked, "About how fast were the cars going when they bumped into each other?" Others were asked, "About how fast were the cars going when they smashed into each other?" Those who read the question with the verb "smashed" estimated that the cars were going faster. They were also more likely to "remember" having seen broken glass. (There wasn't any.)

This is how language works. It invisibly molds our way of thinking about people, actions, and the world around us. Military metaphors train us to think about — and see — everything in terms of fighting, conflict, and war. This perspective then limits our imaginations when we consider what we can do about situations we would like to understand or change.

Even in science, common metaphors that are taken for granted influence how researchers think about natural phenomena. Evelyn Fox Keller describes a case in which acceptance of a metaphor led scientists to see something that was not there. A mathematical biologist, Keller outlines the fascinating behavior of cellular slime mold. This unique mold can take two completely different forms: It can exist as single-cell organisms, or the separate cells can come together to form multicellular aggregates. The puzzle facing scientists was: What triggers aggregation? In other words, what makes the single cells join together? Scientists focused their investigations by asking what entity issued the order to start aggregating. They first called this bosslike entity a "founder cell," and later a "pacemaker cell," even though no one had seen any evidence for the existence of such a cell. Proceeding nonetheless from the assumption that such a cell must exist, they ignored evidence to the contrary: For example, when the center of the aggregate is removed, other centers form.

Scientists studying slime mold did not examine the interrelationship between the cells and their environment, nor the interrelationship between the functional systems within each cell, because they were busy looking for the pacemaker cell, which, as eventually became evident, did not exist. Instead, under conditions of nutritional deprivation, each individual cell begins to feel the urge to merge with others to form the conglomerate. It is a reaction of the cells to their environment, not to the orders of a boss. Keller recounts this tale to illustrate her insight that we tend to view nature through our understanding of human relations as hierarchical. In her words, "We risk imposing on nature the very stories we like to hear."[10] In other words, the conceptual metaphor of hierarchical governance made scientists "see" something — a pacemaker cell — that wasn't there.

Among the stories many Americans most like to hear are war stories. According to historian Michael Sherry, the American war movie developed during World War II and has been with us ever since. He shows that movies not explicitly about war were also war movies at heart, such as westerns with their good guy–bad guy battles settled with guns. High Noon, for example, which became a model for later westerns, was an allegory of the Second World War: The happy ending hinges on the pacifist taking up arms. We can also see this story line in contemporary adventure films: Think of Star Wars, with its stirring finale in which Han Solo, having professed no interest in or taste for battle, returns at the last moment to destroy the enemy and save the day. And precisely the same theme is found in a contemporary low-budget independent film, Sling Blade, in which a peace-loving retarded man becomes a hero at the end by murdering the man who has been tormenting the family he has come to love.

PUT UP YOUR DUKES

If war provides the metaphors through which we view the world and each other, we come to view others — and ourselves — as warriors in battle. Almost any human encounter can be framed as a fight between two opponents. Looking at it this way brings particular aspects of the event into focus and obscures others.

Framing interactions as fights affects not only the participants but also the viewers. At a performance, the audience, as well as the performers, can be transformed. This effect was noted by a reviewer in the *New York Times*, commenting on a musical event:

> **Showdown at Lincoln Center:** Jazz's ideological war of the last several years led to a pitched battle in August between John Lincoln Collier, the writer, and Wynton Marsalis, the trumpeter, in a debate at Lincoln Center. Mr. Marsalis demolished Mr. Collier, point after point after point, but what made the debate unpleasant was the crowd's blood lust; humiliation, not elucidation, was the desired end.[11]

Military imagery pervades this account: the difference of opinions between Collier and Marsalis was an "ideological war," and the "debate" was a "pitched battle" in which Marsalis "demolished" Collier (not his arguments, but him). What the commentator regrets, however, is that the audience got swept up in the mood instigated by the way the debate was carried out: "the crowd's blood lust" for Collier's defeat.

This is one of the most dangerous aspects of regarding intellectual interchange as a fight. It contributes to an atmosphere of animosity that spreads like a fever. In a society that includes people who express their anger by shooting, the result of demonizing those with whom we disagree can be truly tragic.

But do audiences necessarily harbor within themselves a "blood lust," or is it stirred in them by the performances they are offered? Another arts event was set up as a debate between a playwright and a theater director. In this case, the metaphor through which the debate was viewed was not war but boxing — a sport that is in itself, like a debate, a metaphorical battle that pitches one side against the other in an all-out effort to win. A headline describing the event set the frame: "AND IN THIS CORNER . . . ," followed by the subhead "A Black Playwright and White Critic Duke It Out." The story then reports:

> the face-off between August Wilson, the most successful black playwright in the American theater, and Robert Brustein, longtime drama critic for the *New Republic* and artistic director of the American Repertory Theatre in Cambridge, Mass. These two heavyweights had been battling in print since last June. . . .
>
> Entering from opposite sides of the stage, the two men shook hands and came out fighting — or at least sparring.[12]

Wilson, the article explains, had given a speech in which he opposed Black performers taking "white" roles in color-blind casting; Brustein had written a column disagreeing; and both followed up with further responses to each other.

According to the article, "The drama of the Wilson-Brustein confrontation lies in their mutual intransigence." No one would question that audiences crave drama. But is intransigence the most appealing source of drama? I happened to hear this debate broadcast on the radio. The line that triggered the loudest cheers from the audience was the final question put to the two men by the moderator, Anna Deavere Smith: "What did you each learn from the other in this debate?" The loud applause was evidence that the audience did not crave intransigence. They wanted to see another kind of drama: the drama of change — change that comes from genuinely listening to someone with a different point of view, not the transitory drama of two intransigent positions in stalemate.

To encourage the staging of more dramas of change and fewer of intransigence, we need new metaphors to supplement and complement the pervasive war and boxing match metaphors through which we take it for granted issues and events are best talked about and viewed.

MUD SPLATTERS

Our fondness for the fight scenario leads us to frame many complex human interactions as a battle between two sides. This then shapes the way we understand what happened and how we regard the participants. One unfortunate result is that fights make a mess in which everyone is muddied. The person attacked is often deemed just as guilty as the attacker.

The injustice of this is clear if you think back to childhood. Many of us still harbor anger as we recall a time (or many times) a sibling or playmate started a fight — but both of us got blamed. Actions occur in a stream, each a response to what came before. Where you punctuate them can change their meaning just as you can change the meaning of a sentence by punctuating it in one place or another.

Like a parent despairing of trying to sort out which child started a fight, people often respond to those involved in a public dispute as if both were equally guilty. When champion figure skater Nancy Kerrigan was struck on the knee shortly before the 1994 Olympics in Norway and the then-husband of another champion skater, Tonya Harding, implicated his wife in planning the attack, the event was characterized as a fight between two skaters that obscured their differing roles.[13] As both skaters headed for the Olympic competition, their potential meeting was described as a "long-anticipated figure-skating shootout."[14] Two years later, the event was referred to not as "the attack on Nancy Kerrigan" but as "the rivalry surrounding Tonya Harding and Nancy Kerrigan."[15]

By a similar process, the Senate Judiciary Committee hearings to consider the nomination of Clarence Thomas for Supreme Court justice at which Anita Hill was called to testify are regularly referred to as the "Hill-Thomas hearings," obscuring the very different roles played by Hill and

Thomas. Although testimony by Anita Hill was the occasion for reopening the hearings, they were still the Clarence Thomas confirmation hearings: Their purpose was to evaluate Thomas's candidacy. Framing these hearings as a two-sides dispute between Hill and Thomas allowed the senators to focus their investigation on cross-examining Hill rather than seeking other sorts of evidence, for example by consulting experts on sexual harassment to ascertain whether Hill's account seemed plausible.

SLASH-AND-BURN THINKING

Approaching situations like warriors in battle leads to the assumption that intellectual inquiry, too, is a game of attack, counterattack, and self-defense. In this spirit, critical thinking is synonymous with criticizing. In many classrooms, students are encouraged to read someone's life work, then rip it to shreds. Though criticism is one form of critical thinking — and an essential one — so are integrating ideas from disparate fields and examining the context out of which ideas grew.

> *Opposition does not lead to the whole truth when we ask only "What's wrong with this?"*

Opposition does not lead to the whole truth when we ask only "What's wrong with this?" and never "What can we use from this in building a new theory, a new understanding?"

There are many ways that unrelenting criticism is destructive in itself. In innumerable small dramas mirroring what happened to Robert Gallo (but on a much more modest scale), our most creative thinkers can waste time and effort responding to critics motivated less by a genuine concern about weaknesses in their work than by a desire to find something to attack. All of society loses when creative people are discouraged from their pursuits by unfair criticism. (This is particularly likely to happen since, as Kay Redfield Jamison shows in her book *Touched with Fire*, many of those who are unusually creative are also unusually sensitive; their sensitivity often drives their creativity.)

If the criticism is unwarranted, many will say, you are free to argue against it, to defend yourself. But there are problems with this, too. Not only does self-defense take time and draw off energy that would better be spent on new creative work, but any move to defend yourself makes you appear, well, defensive. For example, when an author wrote a letter to the editor protesting a review he considered unfair, the reviewer (who is typically given the last word) turned the very fact that the author defended himself into a weapon with which to attack again. The reviewer's response began, "I haven't much time to waste on the kind of writer who squanders his talent drafting angry letters to reviewers."[16]

The argument culture limits the information we get rather than broadening it in another way. When a certain kind of interaction is the norm, those who feel comfortable with that type of interaction are drawn to participate, and those who do not feel comfortable with it recoil and go elsewhere. If public discourse included a broad range of types, we would be making room for individuals with different temperaments to take part and contribute their perspectives and insights. But when debate, opposition, and fights overwhelmingly predominate, those who enjoy verbal sparring are likely to take part — by calling in to talk shows, writing letters to the editor or articles, becoming journalists — and those who cannot comfortably take part in oppositional discourse, or do not wish to, are likely to opt out.

This winnowing process is easy to see in apprenticeship programs such as acting school, law school, and graduate school. A woman who was identified in her university drama program as showing exceptional promise was encouraged to go to New York to study acting. Full of enthusiasm, she was accepted by a famous acting school where the teaching method entailed the teacher screaming at students, goading and insulting them as a way to bring out the best in them. This worked well with many of the students but not with her. Rather than rising to the occasion when attacked, she cringed, becoming less able to draw on her talent, not more. After a year, she dropped out. It could be that she simply didn't have what it took — but this will never be known, because the adversarial style of teaching did not allow her to show what talent she had.

POLARIZING COMPLEXITY: NATURE OR NURTURE?

Few issues come with two neat, and nearly opposed, sides. Again, I have seen this in the domain of gender. One common polarization is an opposition between two sources of differences between women and men: "culture," or "nurture," on one hand and "biology," or "nature," on the other.

Shortly after the publication of *You Just Don't Understand*, I was asked by a journalist what question I most often encountered about women's and men's conversational styles. I told her, "Whether the differences I describe are biological or cultural." The journalist laughed. Puzzled, I asked why this made her laugh. She explained that she had always been so certain that any significant differences are cultural rather than biological in origin that the question struck her as absurd. So I should not have been surprised when I read, in the article she wrote, that the two questions I am most frequently asked are "Why do women nag?" and "Why won't men ask for directions?" Her ideological certainty that the question I am most frequently asked was absurd led her to ignore my answer and get a fact wrong in her report of my experience.

Some people are convinced that any significant differences between men and women are entirely or overwhelmingly due to cultural influences — the way we treat girls and boys, and men's dominance of women in society. Others are convinced that any significant differences are entirely or overwhelmingly due to biology: the physical facts of female and male bodies, hormones, and reproductive functions. Many problems are caused by framing the question as a dichotomy: Are behaviors that pattern by sex biological or cultural? This polarization encourages those on one side to demonize those who take the other view, which leads in turn to misrepresenting the work of those who are assigned to the opposing camp. Finally, and most devastatingly, it prevents us from exploring the interaction of biological and cultural factors — factors that must, and can only, be understood together. By posing the question as either/or, we reinforce a false assumption that biological and cultural factors are separable and preclude the investigations that would help us understand their interrelationship. When a problem is posed in a way that polarizes, the solution is often obscured before the search is under way.

WHO'S UP? WHO'S DOWN?

Related to polarization is another aspect of the argument culture: our obsession with ratings and rankings. Magazines offer the 10, 50, or 100 best of everything: restaurants, mutual funds, hospitals, even judges. Newsmagazines tell us Who's up, Who's down, as in *Newsweek*'s "Conventional Wisdom Watch" and *Time*'s "Winners and Losers." Rankings and ratings pit restaurants, products, schools, and people against each other on a single scale, obscuring the myriad differences among them. Maybe a small Thai restaurant in one neighborhood can't really be compared to a pricey French one in another, any more than judges with a vast range of abilities and beliefs can be compared on a single scale. And timing can skew results: Ohio State University protested to *Time* magazine when its football team was ranked at the bottom of a scale because only 29 percent of the team graduated. The year before it would have ranked among the top six with 72 percent.

After a political debate, analysts comment not on what the candidates said but on the question "Who won?" After the president delivers an important speech, such as the State of the Union Address, expert commentators are asked to give it a grade. Like ranking, grading establishes a competition. The biggest problem with asking what grade the president's speech deserves, or who won and who lost a campaign debate, is what is not asked and is therefore not answered: What was said, and what is the significance of this for the country?

AN ETHIC OF AGGRESSION

In an argument culture aggressive tactics are valued for their own sake. For example, a woman called in to a talk show on which I was a guest to say, "When I'm in a place where a man is smoking, and there's a no-smoking sign, instead of saying to him 'You aren't allowed to smoke in here. Put that out,' I say, 'I'm awfully sorry, but I have asthma, so your smoking makes it hard for me to breathe. Would you mind terribly not smoking?' Whenever I say this, the man is extremely polite and solicitous, and he puts his cigarette out, and I say, 'Oh, thank you, thank you!' as if he's done a wonderful thing for me. Why do I do that?"

I think this woman expected me to say that she needs assertiveness training to learn to confront smokers in a more aggressive manner. Instead, I told her that there was nothing wrong with her style of getting the man to stop smoking. She gave him a face-saving way of doing what she asked, one that allowed him to feel chivalrous rather than chastised. This is kind to him, but it is also kind to herself, since it is more likely to lead to the result she desires. If she tried to alter his behavior by reminding him of the rules, he might well rebel: "Who made you the enforcer? Mind your own business!" Indeed, who gives any of us the authority to set others straight when we think they're breaking rules?

Another caller disagreed with me, saying the first caller's style was "self-abasing" and there was no reason for her to use it. But I persisted: There is nothing necessarily destructive about conventional self-effacement. Human relations depend on the agreement to use such verbal conventions. I believe the mistake this caller was making — a mistake many of us make — was to confuse *ritual* self-effacement with the literal kind. All human relations require us to find ways to get what we want from others without seeming to dominate them. Allowing others to feel they are doing what you want for a reason less humiliating to them fulfills this need.

Thinking of yourself as the wronged party who is victimized by a law-breaking boor makes it harder to see the value of this method. But suppose you are the person addicted to smoking who lights up (knowingly or not) in a no-smoking zone. Would you like strangers to yell at you to stop smoking, or would you rather be allowed to save face by being asked politely to stop in order to help them out? Or imagine yourself having broken a rule inadvertently (which is not to imply rules are broken only by mistake; it is only to say that sometimes they are). Would you like some stranger to swoop down on you and begin berating you, or would you rather be asked politely to comply?

As this example shows, conflicts can sometimes be resolved without confrontational tactics, but current conventional wisdom often devalues less confrontational tactics even if they work well, favoring more aggressive strategies even if they get less favorable results. It's as if we value a fight for its own sake, not for its effectiveness in resolving disputes.

> **Current conventional wisdom often devalues less confrontational tactics even if they work well.**

This ethic shows up in many contexts. In a review of a contentious book, for example, a reviewer wrote, "Always provocative, sometimes infuriating, this collection reminds us that the purpose of art is not to confirm and coddle but to provoke and confront." This false dichotomy encapsulates the belief that if you are not provoking and confronting, then you are confirming and coddling — as if there weren't myriad other ways to question and learn. What about exploring, exposing, delving, analyzing, understanding, moving, connecting, integrating, illuminating . . . or any innumerable verbs that capture other aspects of what art can do?

THE BROADER PICTURE

The increasingly adversarial spirit of our contemporary lives is fundamentally related to a phenomenon that has been much remarked upon in recent years: the breakdown of a sense of community. In this spirit, distinguished journalist and author Orville Schell points out that in his day journalists routinely based their writing on a sense of connection to their subjects — and that this sense of connection is missing from much that is written by journalists today. Quite the contrary, a spirit of demonography often prevails that has just the opposite effect: Far from encouraging us to feel connected to the subjects, it encourages us to feel critical, superior — and, as a result, distanced. The cumulative effect is that citizens feel more and more cut off from the people in public life they read about.

The argument culture dovetails with a general disconnection and breakdown of community in another way as well. Community norms and pressures exercise a restraint on the expression of hostility and destruction. Many cultures have rituals to channel and contain aggressive impulses, especially those of adolescent males. In just this spirit, at the 1996 Republican National Convention, both Colin Powell and Bob Dole talked about growing up in small communities where everyone knew who they were. This meant that many people would look out for them, but also that if they did something wrong, it would get back to their parents. Many Americans grew up in ethnic neighborhoods that worked the same way. If a young man stole something, committed vandalism, or broke a rule or law, it would be reported to his relatives, who would punish him or tell him how his actions were shaming the family. American culture today often lacks these brakes.

Community is a blend of connections and authority, and we are losing both. As Robert Bly shows in his book by that title, we now have a *Sibling Society*: Citizens are like squabbling siblings with no authority figures who can command enough respect to contain and channel their aggressive impulses. It is as if every day is a day with a substitute teacher who cannot control the class and maintain order.

The argument culture is both a product of and a contributor to this alienation, separating people, disconnecting them from each other and from those who are or might have been their leaders.

WHAT OTHER WAY IS THERE?

Philosopher John Dewey said, on his ninetieth birthday, "Democracy begins in conversation." I fear that it gets derailed in polarized debate.

In conversation we form the interpersonal ties that bind individuals together in personal relationships; in public discourse, we form similar ties on a larger scale, binding individuals into a community. In conversation, we exchange the many types of information we need to live our lives as members of a community. In public discourse, we exchange the information that citizens in a democracy need in order to decide how to vote. If public discourse provides entertainment first and foremost — and if entertainment is first and foremost watching fights — then citizens do not get the information they need to make meaningful use of their right to vote.

Of course it is the responsibility of intellectuals to explore potential weaknesses in others' arguments, and of journalists to represent serious opposition when it exists. But when opposition becomes the overwhelming avenue of inquiry — a formula that *requires* another side to be found or a criticism to be voiced; when the lust for opposition privileges extreme views and obscures complexity; when our eagerness to find weaknesses blinds us to strengths; when the atmosphere of animosity precludes respect and poisons our relations with one another; then the argument culture is doing more damage than good.

I offer [these thoughts] not as a frontal assault on the argument culture. That would be in the spirit of attack that I am questioning. It is an attempt to examine the argument culture — our use of attack, opposition, and debate in public discourse — to ask; What are its limits as well as its strengths? How has it served us well, but also how has it failed us? How is it related to culture and gender? What other options do we have?

I do not believe we should put aside the argument model of public discourse entirely, but we need to rethink whether this is the *only* way, or *always* the best way, to carry out our affairs. A step toward broadening our repertoires would be to pioneer reform by experimenting with metaphors other than sports and war, and with formats other than debate for framing the exchange of ideas. The change might be as simple as introducing a plural form. Instead of asking "What's the other side?" we might ask instead, "What are the other sides?" Instead of insisting on hearing "both sides," we might insist on hearing "all sides."

Another option is to expand our notion of "debate" to include more dialogue. This does not mean there can be no negativity, criticism, or disagreement. It simply means we can be more creative in our ways of managing all of these, which are inevitable and useful. In dialogue, each statement that one person makes is qualified by a statement made by someone else, until the series of statements and qualifications moves everyone closer to a fuller truth. Dialogue does not preclude negativity. Even saying "I agree" makes sense only against the background assumption that you might disagree. In dialogue, there is opposition, yes, but no head-on collision. Smashing heads does not open minds.

There are times when we need to disagree, criticize, oppose, and attack — to hold debates and view issues as polarized battles. Even co-operation, after all, is not the absence of conflict but a means of managing conflict. My goal is not a make-nice false veneer of agreement or a dangerous ignoring of true opposition. I'm questioning the *automatic* use of adversarial formats — the assumption that it's *always* best to address problems and issues by fighting over them. I'm hoping for a broader repertoire of ways to talk to each other and address issues vital to us.

NOTES

[1]I first introduced this term in an op-ed essay, "The Triumph of the Yell," The *New York Times*, Jan. 14, 1994, p. A29.

[2]Charles Simic, "In Praise of Invective," *Harper's*, Aug. 1997, pp. 24, 26–27; the quote is from p. 26. The article is excerpted from *Orphan Factory* (Ann Arbor: University of Michigan Press, 1997). I am grateful to Amitai Etzioni for calling this article to my attention.

[3]Both the term "agonism" and the phrase "programmed contentiousness" come from *Walter Ong, Fighting for Life*. Ong, Walter J. *Fighting for Life: Contest, Sexuality, and Consciousness* (Ithaca, NY.: Cornell University Press, 1981).

[4]Steve Hendrix, "Hatchback vs. Backpack," The *Washington Post Weekend*, Mar. 1, 1996, p. 6.

[5]See, for example, Jessica Mathews, "Creationism Makes a Comeback," The *Washington Post*, Apr. 8, 1996, p. A21.

[6]Lipstadt, *Denying the Holocaust*, p. 15. Lipstadt cites *Esquire*, Feb. 1983, for the interview with Mitchum. Lipstadt, Deborah. *Denying the Holocaust: The Growing Assault on Truth and Memory* (New York: Free Press, 1993).

[7]See Nicholas Wade, "Method and Madness: The Vindication of Robert Gallo," The *New York Times Magazine*, Dec. 26, 1993, p. 12, and Elaine Richman, "The Once and Future King," *The Sciences*, Nov.–Dec. 1996, pp. 12–15. The investigations of Gallo were among a series of overly zealous investigations of suspected scientific misconduct — all of which ended in the exoneration of the accused, but not before they had caused immense personal anguish and professional setbacks. Others similarly victimized were Gallo's colleague Mika Popovic, immunologist Thereza Imanishi-Kari, and her coauthor (not accused of wrongdoing but harmed as a result of his defense of her) Nobel Prize winner David Baltimore. On Popovic, see Malcolm Gladwell, "Science Friction," The *Washington Post Magazine*, Dec. 6, 1992, pp. 18–21, 49–51. On Imanishi-Kari and Baltimore, see The *New Yorker*, May 27, 1996, pp. 94–98ff.

[8]Randy Allen Harris, *The Linguistics Wars* (New York: Oxford University Press, 1993); "The Science Wars," *Newsweek*, Apr. 21, 1997, p. 54; "The Mammogram War," *Newsweek*, Feb. 24, 1997, p. 54; "Party Wars," *New York*; June 2, 1997, cover. The

subhead of the latter reads, "In the battle to feed New York's elite, the top caterers are taking off their white gloves and sharpening their knives."

[9]The *New York Times*, Aug. 29, 1996, p. A1.

[10]Keller, *Reflections on Gender and Science*, p. 157. Keller, Evelyn Fox. *Reflections on Gender and Science* (New Haven: Yale University Press, 1985). Another such case is explained by paleontologist Stephen Jay Gould in his book *Wonderful Life* about the Burgess shale — a spectacular deposit of 530-million-year-old fossils. In 1909, the first scientist to study these fossils missed the significance of the find, because he "shoehorned every last Burgess animal into a modern group, viewing the fauna collectively as a set of primitive or ancestral versions of later, improved forms" (p. 24). Years later, observers looked at the Burgess shale fossils with a fresh eye and saw a very different reality: a panoply of life forms, far more diverse and numerous than what exists today. The early scientists missed what was right before their eyes because, Gould shows, they proceeded from a metaphoric understanding of evolution as a linear march of progress from the ancient and primitive to the modern and complex, with humans the inevitable, most complex apex. Accepting the metaphor of "the cone of increasing diversity" prevented the early scientists from seeing what was really there.

[11]Peter Watrous, "The Year in the Arts: Pop & Jazz/1994," The *New York Times*, Dec. 25, 1994, sec. 2, p. 36.

[12]Jack Kroll, "And in This Corner . . . ," *Newsweek*, Feb. 10, 1997, p. 65.

[13]Though Harding was demonized somewhat more as an unfeminine, boorish "Wicked Witch of the West" (George Vecsey, "Let's Begin the Legal Olympics," The *New York Times*, Feb. 13, 1994, sec. 8, p. 1.), Kerrigan was also demonized as cold and aloof, an "ice princess."

[14]Jere Longman, "Kerrigan Glides Through Compulsory Interview," The *New York Times*, Feb. 13, 1994, sec. 8, p. 9.

[15]Paul Farhi, "For NBC, Games Not Just for Guys; Network Tailors Its Coverage to Entice Women to Watch," The *Washington Post*, July 26, 1996, p. A1.

[16]The *Washington Pass Book World*, June 16, 1996, p. 14.

DISCUSSION

1. According to Tannen, we now resort to militarized language (that is, the terminology of warfare, combat, and conflict) to conduct our most prominent public debates. Can you think of an example of the ways this kind of rhetoric frames the discussion of a current public issue? In your view, does such language help or hinder the conduct of this debate?

2. One of Tannen's central claims is that our current emphasis on conflict interferes with our ability to fully understand pressing social and political issues. Do you agree? Can you think of any circumstances in which this kind of emphasis might enhance our understanding?

3. What aspect of Tannen's discussion do you personally find most useful? Do any of the specific points she raises clarify, or even change, the ways you might argue in your own life?

WRITING

4. Choose an issue that is typically presented within our media as polarizing: an issue about which, we are told, there is no middle ground. What are the central points of conflict? What positions or viewpoints define the two sides? What areas of agreement or middle ground may have been overlooked?

5. Write an essay in which you discuss two or three of the types or techniques of argument that Tannen defines. Where in your life do you see examples of them? How does each example cause you to personally react? Which do you find most effective, and why?

6. To what extent is there overlap between Tannen's evaluation of argument and Geoffrey Nunberg's (p. 607) discussion of liberalism? Do you think Nunberg would point to "argument culture" as a contributing factor in the demonization of the term *liberal*? Why or why not?

STEPHEN MILLER

The Ways We Don't Converse Now

What is the state of conversation in America? Is it a dying art? A relic of the past? Or has it simply assumed new guises and come to adhere to a different set of norms? Surveying the vast landscape of our contemporary media culture, Stephen Miller offers an overview of some of the forms that "talk" most often takes these days. Sketching a vivid portrait of their chief dynamics, he wonders aloud about whether the ways we talk these days still fulfills the definition of conversation. Miller is a freelance writer and a contributing editor for the *Wilson Quarterly*. His essays have also appeared in the *Times Literary Supplement*, *Partisan Review*, and *Sewanee Review*. Miller's latest book, from which the following is excerpted, is *Conversation: The History of a Declining Art* (2006). He has also published *Special Interest Groups in American Politics* (1983), *Excellence and Equity: The National Endowment for the Humanities* (1984), and *Three Deaths and Enlightenment Thought: Hume, Johnson, Marat* (2001).

I N GERALD GREEN'S NOVEL *THE LAST ANGRY MAN* (1983) THE MAIN character, an elderly Brooklyn doctor, is angry because he cares deeply about the community, and he thinks too many people, especially young doctors, care only about themselves. His anger signifies that he is a good man; he is not selfish and apathetic. For many Americans anger is a good thing. Why shouldn't they be angry about fundamentalist Republicans or secularist Democrats, about corrupt businessmen or greedy trial lawyers? To paraphrase John Ruskin: Tell me what you are angry about, and I will tell you what your politics are.

According to the comedian Janeane Garofalo, there is more anger on the Right than on the Left. "On the left," she says, "you've got a person who is more willing to engage in conversations that have context and nuance." But angry left-wing books and angry right-wing books sell equally well, so the politically angry are on both ends of the political spectrum.

The ancients said that anger is an enjoyable passion. "A certain pleasure accompanies anger," Aristotle says. In the *Iliad* Achilles speaks of "that gall of anger that swarms like smoke inside of a man's heart / and becomes a thing sweeter to him by far than the dripping of honey." The ancients argued that in certain circumstances anger is appropriate as an energizing force — a way of promoting action. But they also argued that anger clouds the mind. Renaissance writers on conversation agreed.

Bacon offers advice on "how the natural inclination and habit [disposition] to be angry may be attempered and calmed."

Have Americans become angrier about politics since the terrorist attacks of 9/11? Americans have often been angry about politics — as Mrs. Trollope, Dickens, and Tocqueville pointed out. The United States has had two civil wars. We forget that the Revolutionary War was a civil war; many Americans were loyalists — including William Franklin, Benjamin Franklin's son. (He was the royal governor of New Jersey before he was arrested.) Gordon Wood notes that "the two times Franklin met his son . . . in the summer of 1775 [their conversation] ended in shouting matches loud enough to disturb the neighbors." In 1784, William, who was living in London after serving two years in a Connecticut prison and four years as president of the Board of Associated Loyalists, tried to effect a reconciliation with his father, who headed the American delegation to France, but Ben Franklin put off a meeting with him. "I ought not to blame you for differing in Sentiment with me in Public Affairs," the father said. But he did blame him.

Contemporary America is not on the edge of civil war, but it is reasonable to assume that Americans have become angrier since 9/11. "Grief and disappointment," Hume says, "give rise to anger." (There is a lot of anger in the book of Job. Job's wife is angry with God. Job is angry with his friends; the friends are angry with Job.) In late 2003 a report from the Pew Research Center said: "National unity was the initial response to the calamitous events of 11 September 2001, but that spirit has dissolved amid rising political polarization and anger." Bozza, the biographer of Eminem, offers a similar assessment (in the jaunty language of a pop music critic): "In a post 9/11 world, Eminem is less shocking, and understandably so. . . . The violence and hate in Eminem's music . . . is the soundtrack of the times: America is angry, poor, out of work, misunderstood, and gunning for revenge."

Political anger seems to have increased after the U.S. invasion of Iraq in March 2003. Godfrey Hodgson, a British historian, said American politics has become "viciously polarized." *Washington Post* columnist David Ignatius referred to the "vituperative e-mails" he gets from both conservatives and liberals. Senator John McCain told a television reporter: "I've never seen such anger [in Congress]."

Nowadays there is a lot of fuel to keep political anger burning. We can listen to talk radio, view Web sites that provide us with information and commentary on the stupidities of those on the Right (or the Left), and exchange e-mails (and e-mailed articles) with like-minded persons. Political anger is being stoked by publishers who are eager to publish political tirades, which generally sell well. One publisher said recently: "We want people to feel their blood pressure rise when they read our books."

Are Americans increasingly living in what I call anger communities? Anger communities often are preoccupied with their political opponents. To paraphrase a line by Yeats: "More substance in their enmities, than in their loves." Jeanne Marie Laskas, a columnist for the *Washington Post*, says: "We the people never seem to have discussions anymore; we all just rant to our like-minded friends with our like-minded rhetoric."

Anger communities are similar to what Cass Sunstein calls a feuding group. In *Why Societies Need Dissent* (2003), Sunstein says: "One of the characteristic features of feuds is that members of feuding groups tend to talk only to one another, or at least to listen only to one another, fueling and amplifying their outrage." Political anger is a time-saver: one reads only news and opinion that confirm one's views. Almost seventy years ago Paul Valéry said that the vast amount of news that citizens are barraged with every day would have a negative effect on our intelligence. "The daily output of vast quantities of published matter, the flood of printing and broadcasting, wash over our judgments and impressions from morning to night, mangling and mixing them, making of our brains truly a gray matter in which nothing stands out, nothing can last." Valéry was wrong: the vast amount of information does not make us opinionless; it makes it easier for us to have strong opinions, since there is information to confirm almost any thesis.

> *The vast amount of information does not make us opinionless; it makes it easier for us to have strong opinions, since there is information to confirm almost any thesis.*

Because many Americans get angry when discussing politics, it makes sense to avoid conversations about politics. Anne Applebaum, a *Washington Post* columnist, warns against discussing politics at dinner parties. "Anyone who has ever even invited guests of opposing political persuasions over to dinner will know how quickly it can all go wrong. . . . A chilly, polite dinner is more bearable than one that ends with guests stomping out the door."

In Johnson's club politics and religion rarely were discussed, but club members had solid conversations about many other subjects — literature, the nature of the passions, political economy. Nowadays people rarely read the same books or even go to the same movies. Moreover, the fear of getting into an argument about politics and the fear of hurting someone's feelings may be having a chilling effect on solid conversation in general — not only political conversation. At dinner parties I've attended the topics of conversation mainly were restaurants, vacations, and health — all safe subjects.

To engage in small talk is often enjoyable and it certainly is "polite," but a steady diet of conversation about food, vacations, and health is tedious. "Politeness," La Rochefoucauld says, "is essential in social life, but it should have limits; it becomes a kind of slavery when it is excessive." An advertisement in the *New Yorker* for the French liqueur Grand Marnier, which has a Web site that sponsors an Internet chat group, asks: "Isn't there more to talk about than how many carbs you ate today?"

Yet it is hard to avoid saccharine politeness when the alternative is often the angry venting of opinions. Judith Martin says that "she would be only too happy to welcome the return of substantive conversation at dinner parties; goodness knows she is weary of hearing people talk about the food. But conversation requires listening respectfully to others and engaging in polite give-and-take, rather than making speeches and impugning others' motives and judgment."

Is Martin alluding to a new kind of social anxiety: the fear of angry confrontation on social occasions? A woman told Theodore Zeldin that dinner-party conversations are unpleasant because her guests usually are "egos shouting." She said that she prefers to watch conversations on television or listen to conversations on the radio. Since Zeldin is an English historian, the woman he quoted probably is English, but I suspect that many Americans would agree with her, which is why many spend more time watching television talk shows or listening to radio talk shows than having a solid conversation.

ENJOYING ERSATZ CONVERSATION

Television talk shows offer a variety of ersatz conversations. I call them ersatz conversations because they are semiscripted performances that are concerned with winning and influencing viewers and boosting audience ratings, which are of primary importance to all television stations, including noncommercial ones. Many television talk shows also have a secondary purpose — to promote the products of their celebrity guests, who are invited to plug a new television series, a new movie, a new book, a new CD, even a new line of cookware.

For the politically angry there is also another form of ersatz conversation: talk radio. In the United States there are 1,300 talk radio stations, most of them with right-wing hosts. The leading talk radio host is Rush Limbaugh, who sounds off to roughly 20 million listeners on 580 stations. On the opposite end of the political spectrum is Randi Rhodes, a popular South Florida talk show host whose ratings in her listening area are higher than Limbaugh's. Jason Zengerle writes that Rhodes is proof that "a liberal talk radio host can be just as bombastic, hyperbolic, and plain old nasty as a conservative one." Talk radio, Zengerle says, "is the quintessential 'arena for angry minds.'" (The phrase "arena for angry minds" is from Richard Hofstadter's seminal essay "The Paranoid Style in American Politics.")

There are angry minds on television as well. They appear on political talk shows where pundits with opposing views yell at each other. Michael

Kinsley of the *Los Angeles Times* has called them "shoutfests." Are such shows popular? *Crossfire*, the most famous, was cancelled in January 2005 after a twenty-three-year run. CNN president Jonathan Klein said he wanted to move CNN away from what he called "head-butting debate shows." His description of *Crossfire* was accurate. Two men sat across a table — one "from the Left," the other "from the Right." They began a conversation about a political question, but it soon became overheated. A bell then sounded — ending the round. One pundit, now looking at the camera rather than at his "opponent," announced another topic. Another round began.

According to Kinsley, *Crossfire* "didn't cause the ideological divisions in this country. It reflected them. Sometimes it reflected them so well that people got angry, and they shouted. But that anger was usually genuine." To my mind, the anger didn't seem genuine, for the two pundits had no trouble switching from being angry to calmly introducing a commercial break. Alessandra Stanley, the television critic for the *New York Times*, says that "real anger is as rare on television as real discussion."

The cancellation of *Crossfire* does not mean that such political talk shows are unpopular. Similar shows can be found on several stations. Kinsley, who defends such programs, acknowledges that they have a rigid formula. "The conceit that there are exactly 2.0 sides to every question, one 'left' and one 'right,' is a genuine flaw of 'Crossfire'-type shows."

Oprah, a famous daily talk show, has nothing to do with anger and very little to do with political questions. Oprah Winfrey — her last name is rarely used — is a billionaire who has been called "the world's most influential voice" and "one of the most influential women of the 20th century." Her program appears in more than 200 domestic and 130 foreign markets.

When the show comes on the air we see the word Oprah against a swirling yellow and white background. In a voice-over Oprah describes the contents of the day's program. Then we see Oprah walking down an aisle in the studio theater while the predominantly female audience cheers and applauds. There are close-ups of women who look inspired by the sight of her. (Seeing Oprah grab outstretched hands as she walks, I recall the medieval notion of the king's healing touch.) Oprah signals for quiet and begins discussing the first topic of the day. There is a brusque, no-nonsense quality about her. Though she smiles a lot and makes fun of herself, mugging before the camera and occasionally switching into a comic accent, her main purpose is serious: she wants to help women improve their lives.

Oprah's guests usually are people who have an interesting story to tell, especially a story about triumphing over adversity. The stories are fleshed out with video clips. One show was devoted to people who survived a life-threatening ordeal. The first guest was a man who suffered a gunshot at close range. After the audience viewed a videotape of the shooting, the man described what he felt after being shot, and he talked about how the shooting changed his life. He said he now rarely complains about anything. And he appreciates little things much more. He is grateful to be alive. On the same program other survivors — a man who was buried in an avalanche, a woman who was impaled on a fence — talked about their ordeals. A doctor in the audience who wrote a book about these survivors answered several questions about the nature of pain.

Oprah's guests often promote a new book. On one show Hillary Clinton discussed her autobiography. On another show a successful business-woman talked about the book she wrote: *Powerful Inspirations: 8 Lessons That Will Change Your Life.* Another program was mainly about women who run a successful business while managing a young family. The audience received a gift from each businesswoman — a shrewd way of marketing a new product.

Oprah asks questions and gives answers. One can't imagine a guest saying: "No, Oprah, I don't see it that way." The viewers of *Oprah* want her to give them advice. A blurb for one of her books says she offers "timeless wisdom and savvy advice" — including ten commandments for lifelong success. Oprah believes she has helped people improve their lives. "People have told me their lives have changed because of me. I take away from this the sense that I'm on the right track."

> One can't imagine a guest saying: "No, Oprah, I don't see it that way."

The talk show called *Dr. Phil* — Phil McGraw is Oprah's male counterpart — is also a blend of advice and inspiration. Oprah and Dr. Phil take an instrumental view of conversation. They want to motivate people — to get them to take control of their lives. They are the Dale Carnegies of television — telling viewers how to make the most of their lives.

Ellen DeGeneres, the host of the *Ellen DeGeneres Show*, is not in the advice business. She has only one purpose: to cheer her viewers up. When the show opens, a voice-over says: "Don't get mad, get glad." Then we see the predominantly female audience whistling, clapping, and even dancing in the aisles. DeGeneres once told an interviewer: "There's so much energy in this world that's negative and so much hate; I think I'm actually helping put out good energy."

DeGeneres — who achieved a degree of notoriety a few years ago by declaring on *Ellen*, a television sitcom she starred in, that she was a lesbian — is a good comic, even when her material is weak. Her awkward and hesitant way of speaking is effective. She occasionally looks surprised, as if she doesn't know why she said what she just said, and then she smiles. In effect, she says to her viewers: "I'm a goofy woman who is having a good time. Why not take your mind off things by watching this mindless show?"

Though DeGeneres is amusing, the conversations she has with her celebrity guests usually are insipid — mainly because the guest and the host trade compliments. Interviewing the actor James Caan, DeGeneres says she likes the new NBC show Caan appears in (*Las Vegas*). Caan then says he likes her show. Caan looked uncomfortable when he made this comment, as if he knew that no one would believe that he watches a morning talk show whose viewers mainly are women.

(Celebrity promotion is not new. In the late 1950s I was a guest on a popular morning radio talk show. I was chosen to be on the show because a friend of my mother's was the show's producer. The other guests included a popular pianist, a movie star, a gossip columnist, and two other celebrities. The pianist performed a lively number, and the other celebrity guests complimented him. Then the host turned to me; he wanted to know what the students at the college I attended thought about the pianist. Without thinking I blurted out: "I've never heard of him." Everyone glared at me and after the show they ignored me. I had broken the iron law of talk shows, which is: never say anything negative about a celebrity guest.)

DeGeneres's show tries to appear informal, as if it were put together at the last minute. DeGeneres's opening monologue conveys a sense of casualness. She flits from one subject to another. Each time I saw the show she was dressed in pants and sneakers — as if she had come to the studio after grocery shopping or working out at a gym. Despite the air of casualness, the show is carefully scripted. DeGeneres does an opening comic monologue that lasts about ten minutes, then she dances for a minute or two, sits down in a chair, takes a sip from a coffee mug, and chats with a young man who is the on-stage disc jockey. The chat leads her into the second part of her monologue, which usually has to do with someone who has written to the show or some event from a previous show. After a commercial break the first of three guests appears.

Describing the week's guests, the show's Web site frequently uses the phrase "chats with" or "chats about," but the guests mainly serve as straight men for DeGeneres, who often responds to their remarks with humorous questions. If she makes a remark that is slightly witty (or if she looks at the audience in a funny way), the audience whoops it up, applauding and whistling. Though the show is pure fluff, it is impossible to dislike DeGeneres, who has a great deal of antic charm.

The View, which airs at the same time as DeGeneres's show, is more like a conversation than any other daytime talk show on commercial television. (It was the recipient of the 2003 Daytime Emmy Award for "Outstanding Talk Show.") When the title comes on, we hear the studio audience applauding and yelling while a voice-over describes the highlights of the day's program. Then we see headshots and the names of five women. The women walk onto a set that looks like a dining room, with a living room in the backdrop. On the table there are flowers, coffee mugs, and newspapers — suggesting that the women will be talking about the news of the day.

When I watched the show for two weeks the only woman I was familiar with was Barbara Walters, the show's producer, who appears three days a week. The other regulars are Joy Behar, a stand-up comic, actress, and author; Star Jones Reynolds, an African-American lawyer and former prosecutor who has been a television analyst for many high-profile trials; Meredith Vieira, who is a former television journalist (she is the moderator); and Elisabeth Hasselbeck, the youngest member, who has been a participant on the television show *Survivor*. (She is also married to a professional football player.)

According to the program's Web site, *The View* is an "original forum where real women discuss relevant, everyday issues and share their daily no-holds-barred opinions and lively, colorful conversations." By using the term "real women," the Web site implies that the hosts of the show are accomplished women who are knowledgeable about current affairs. Yet by saying that the women "share" their opinions, the Web site implies that it is a women's show — one in which the guests are supposed to avoid the blunt disagreement that is de rigueur on male-dominated political talk shows.

The Web site is misleading, since only the first segment of the show — "Hot Topics" — attempts to be a conversation. (The rest of the show consists of celebrity interviews or tips for women about buying clothing or preparing a meal.) In three respects the "Hot Topics" segment sounds like conversation. First, there is good-humored disagreement — even what might be called raillery. (DeGeneres occasionally disagrees with her guests, but the disagreement is part of her comic routine.) Secondly, the talk jumps rapidly from one subject to another, though I am certain the women know in advance what topics they are going to discuss. Third, occasionally several people talk at the same time, though not for long. In other words, the show edges toward the disordered world of real conversation, where people are always interrupting people.

The Web site says that the "dynamic" women have conversations about "the most exciting events of the day." On one show someone referred to the 2004 presidential race but the discussion centered on whether the taller candidate usually wins. After a brief conversation about the HBO series *The Sopranos*, the women discussed McDonald's announcement that it would no longer be serving a Double Big Mac, which led to a discussion of whether there should be tax credits for those who get medical treatments to fight obesity. The lengthiest discussion was about the Oscars. On another day the "hot topic" was gay marriage. Four of the five women seemed to be making pitches for recognizing gay marriage. Notwithstanding its claim to be about the "exciting events of the day," *The View* is mainly chitchat about celebrity culture.

Finally, there are the "trash TV" talk shows. The most popular is the *Jerry Springer Show*. The show implies that real conversation is angry confrontation. Springer says in his autobiography: "Our best shows . . . were those where there was real personal conflict, real issues of confrontation." In a veiled criticism of other talk shows, Springer says: we show "real people honestly responding to something they felt deeply about at the moment." The operative word is real.

Springer's show, which has been called "nuts and sluts," is always vulgar and occasionally violent, though the violence is not allowed to get out of hand. The show is as much about the audience as it is about the guests — or about the interaction between the audience and the guests. The mood is set at the opening: we hear the audience screaming "Jerry, Jerry!" — they are told to do so — while we see a disclaimer that the show might not be appropriate for children. The screaming continues while the show's contents are previewed. Then there are shots of the audience, which is composed mostly of young men and women. When the announcer introduces Jerry Springer, the audience, which is still yelling, stands up. The audience stops shouting and for thirty seconds Springer shakes hands with people. Then he announces the theme of the show.

A show I watched, "Hot-headed Hookers," featured four prostitutes who were confronted by people who wanted them to stop hooking: an angry stepmother, two angry boyfriends, an angry husband. Most of the guests acted foolishly, especially the first two prostitutes, who repeatedly bared their breasts and shouted obscenities. The shows are taped in advance, so the obscenities are blipped out and the bare breasts are blurred.

When the first "hot-headed hooker" walked onto the set — a heavy-set blonde woman in her late twenties or early thirties dressed in a halter and a skirt — the audience taunted her. She pranced about — defiantly announcing that she was a truck stop hooker who charges forty dollars for ten minutes. While she talked she bared her breasts and butt and yelled at the men in the audience. The audience yelled back, daring her to reveal more. Several women in the audience taunted her, and one bared her breasts, saying: "Here's what good breasts look like." After allowing the antics to go on for a few minutes, Springer asked the guest several questions and then said it was time for a commercial.

The next prostitute was also a proud and defiant exhibitionist. An attractive African-American woman who was a stripper before she became a prostitute, she said she was a high-class whore who charges two hundred dollars. She repeatedly bared her breasts and traded insults with members of the audience. Springer asked her if she would give up prostitution if her boyfriend asked her to do so. She replied that she wouldn't; she needed the money. The woman couldn't focus on Springer's questions because the audience kept shouting crude remarks about her aging body. She answered them as crudely as they addressed her. Finally, the boyfriend came out — seemingly angry because she is a prostitute though she claimed that he was not angry the day before. She traded obscenities with him, and then another man came out — the boyfriend's brother, who apparently was the woman's pimp, and the men started pushing and shoving each other. The audience egged them on.

During the course of his shows, Springer generally keeps a low profile. If the guests become violent, the show's security crew intervenes. Springer doesn't urge the guests to be outrageous. That is the audience's job. In his autobiography Springer says: "The talk show is my job. I love it. It's great fun to do. I meet fascinating people, it pays well." Yet when the guests act up Springer often looks as if he'd rather be somewhere else. At the end of the show Springer sits on a stool and offers what he calls a "Final Thought." He ends with his signature line: "Till next time, take care of yourself and each other." Take care of yourself and each other? The show encourages its guests to trash each other.

> *Take care of yourself and each other? The show encourages its guests to trash each other.*

In his autobiography Springer offers a number of justifications for his show. He says the unpaid guests volunteer to be on the show, so he is not exploiting them. He also says he does not approve of their conduct. Nevertheless, he brags that when the show stopped editing out the obscenities and the violence "viewership went through the roof. For the first time in ten years, *Oprah* was surpassed as the number-one talk show in America. Suddenly, everybody was talking *Jerry*."

Senator Joseph Lieberman and the conservative cultural critic William Bennett have criticized Springer's show as well as other so-called trash TV shows. They argue, among other things, that such shows undermine civility. Many observers agree with their assessment. One critic says of the *Jerry Springer Show*: "America's new No. 1 show gives us butting heads — the perfect visual metaphor for the breakdown of communication, if not civilization." But the show is not very different from the acts of many rappers and performance artists.

What is insidious about Springer's show is that it advertises itself as "real" when it has nothing to do with reality. It is a carefully designed composite of two aspects of America's conversational landscape: the in-your-face side and the non-judgmental side. We see people shouting at each other and we hear Springer trying to be a therapist. The guests on Springer's show are often crude and coarse, yet it is hard not to feel sympathy for some of them when they struggle to express themselves. Watching a boyfriend talking incoherently to a former girlfriend, I thought of a famous sentence in *Madame Bovary*: "None of us can ever express the exact measure of his needs or his thoughts or his sorrows; and human speech is like a cracked kettle on which we tap crude rhythms for bears to dance to, while we long to make music that will melt the stars."

What is the appeal of the *Jerry Springer Show*? Some viewers may be moved by the plight of the people on the show, but the antics of the guests provoke laughter in the studio audience. The people in the audience are like the eighteenth-century Londoners who visited Bedlam, an institution for the mentally ill, in order to gape and laugh at the patients. Bedlam — the nickname for Bethlehem Hospital — was a tourist attraction. The novelist Samuel Richardson quotes a young lady who visited the place: "The distemper'd fancies of the miserable patients most unaccountably provoked mirth, and loud laughter" among the visitors.

At the opposite end of the television talk show spectrum from the *Jerry Springer Show* are several programs that feature lengthy interviews with writers, politicians, policymakers, and scientists. In serious interview shows the interviewer plays an active part, and the guests are given enough time to respond cogently. Nevertheless, these shows are mainly interviews.

Dick Cavett, who was a writer for the *Jack Paar Show*, which aired from 1957 to 1962, reports that when he asked Paar what the secret was in doing such a show, Paar replied: "Don't make it an interview, kid. Make it a conversation." According to John J. O'Connor, a former television critic for the *New York Times*, Paar had "an uncanny ability to listen carefully and actually engage in clever and often witty conversation." When Paar died in January 2004, Tom Shales, television critic for the *Washington Post*, said that Paar's "true art was the art of conversation. . . . To be on Paar's show, your talk had to be witty, amusing, wry, insightful, even educational; guests weren't booked just because they had movies opening or TV series premiering." Paar, he says, "developed his own repertory company of zany conversationalists." Even if Paar was as good a conversationalist as O'Connor and Shales say he was, Paar was mainly concerned with winning viewers. No matter how clever and witty television conversations are, they still are ersatz conversations.

Watching witty and charming people bantering on television talk shows (I am not talking about the people on the *Jerry Springer Show*), viewers may occasionally ask themselves: "Why can't the people I know — family, friends, colleagues — be more like these people?" In the ersatz conversible world one rarely meets irritable or tedious people. (One does meet angry people.) So why not tune in the ersatz world and tune out — as much as possible — the real world?

I have not mentioned television's morning talk–news shows, which regularly attract an audience of roughly eleven million Americans. According to Lee Siegel, the television critic for the *New Republic*, the growing popularity of these shows "might . . . be owed to the heightened

American nervousness about 'reality.' The prospect of spending eight to ten hours with real, live, untelevised and uncontrollable humans makes more and more people hasten back as fast as they can into the tube world in which they happily concluded the previous evening." Siegel's point is the same as mine: the ersatz conversible world has many attractions.

No one — except people who suffer from acute social anxiety disorder — wants to live only in the ersatz conversible world. Yet millions of Americans (and millions of people in all advanced industrial nations) spend a great deal of time in that world because it is one they can control. (According to a recent poll, 54 percent of Americans frequently watch television during dinner.) They can choose the kind of ersatz conversation that suits their mood. They can watch people sounding off at political questions, relating inspiring stories, chitchatting about celebrities, telling amusing anecdotes, or cursing their boyfriends. In the ersatz conversible world everything is predictable. Oprah will always be inspirational, Ellen DeGeneres will always be goofy, Jerry Springer will always be nonjudgmental.

> **Millions of Americans (and millions of people in all advanced industrial nations) spend a great deal of time in that world because it is one they can control.**

There is another reward to watching, or listening to, ersatz conversations. We can insult someone risk-free. Watching a television talk show or listening to a radio talk show, we can comment on the remarks the guests make without worrying about whether we are being rude or boring or misinformed. I often rant at my television set — telling various guests on the *Lehrer News Hour* that they don't know what they are talking about.

Watching ersatz conversation is like talking to one's dog. Dogs do not answer back. (And dogs, unlike most people, give us undivided attention when we say something — unless they see a squirrel.) I read somewhere that talking to a dog or cat on a regular basis is likely to lower one's blood pressure. Watching ersatz conversation may have the same effect, which is perhaps why the Englishwoman said to Zeldin: "I really enjoy other people having conversations for me."

The ersatz conversible world is expanding. In January 2005 I read that new television talk shows are in the works for next year. In April 2005 I saw an ad in the *New Yorker* for a new program called "Dinner for Five." It shows a cartoon of three people in a living room with a television set. One person says: "With 'Dinner for Five'" we don't really need stimulating conversation of our own."

In Miller's view, there are two basic categories into which contemporary talk falls: discussion and rant. How do you understand the difference between these terms? Which better conforms to the idea of what conversation should be?

2. As its title suggests, Miller is interested not only in how we converse, but also in how we do not converse. What are some of the most typical ways, according to Miller, that we no longer talk? What topics no longer seem to get broached? What conversational rules seem never to be observed? And do you think it makes any difference?

3. How would you define the ideal conversation? What script would it follow? What topics? What roles for each participant?

WRITING

4. Miller talks a good deal about how effective a marketing tool anger can be in the world of talk show culture. What do you think the principal attraction of anger is? What are the pleasures and payoffs of shows that showcase dysfunction and conflict, name calling and "sparks"? Choose one such example from our current crop of talk shows that, in your view, markets anger as a kind of product. Write an essay in which you analyze the ways this show attempts to promote its presentation of strife or conflict as a pleasurable spectacle. What is your personal response to such a sales pitch? Does your personal response conform to or deviate from the script that the show seems to create for its viewers?

5. One of the hallmarks of our contemporary talk culture, Miller contends, is the ubiquity of what he calls ersatz conversations: "semiscripted performances that are concerned with winning and influencing viewers and boosting audience ratings." But what is it exactly that determines whether a conversation is scripted or genuine? Fake or real? Choose a show that, in your view, fits Miller's definition of an ersatz conversation. Write an essay about this show in which you assess whether the "semiscripted" form of talk it showcases comes across convincingly as real, making sure to use examples from the show and quotes from Miller. How does this example compare to your experience of what it means to converse?

6. To what extent are Miller's observations about "talk culture" related to Deborah Tannen's (p. 572) discussion of "argument culture"? Write an essay in which you assess the parallels between these two discussions of how we talk as a culture.

GEOFFREY NUNBERG
Trashing the L-Word

What do you think of when you hear the word *liberal*? What type of person does it conjure? What set of attitudes? Is this a flattering or critical portrait? Recounting the varied and contentious history of this political label, linguist Geoffrey Nunberg tells the story of how *liberal* came to stand as one of our culture's preeminent pejorative terms. Nunberg is a senior researcher at the Center for the Study of Language and Information at Stanford University and a consulting professor in the Stanford Department of Linguistics. He also teaches at the University of California–Berkeley's School of Information. His popular works include *Going Nucular: Language, Politics, and Culture in Confrontational Times* (2004) and *Talking Right* (2006), from which this selection is drawn. His essays on language and culture have appeared in the *Atlantic, Fortune*, the *Los Angeles Times*, and the *New York Times.* Nunberg has also written a series of commentaries for the NPR program *Fresh Air*, which are collected in *The Way We Talk Now* (2001), and he serves as chair of the usage panel for the *American Heritage Dictionary.*

Given the aversion this word inspires in Democratic candidates, future civilizations sifting through the rubble may well conclude that "liberal" was a euphemism for "pederast" or "serial killer." — Timothy Noah, 1986[1]

IN 1960, THE *NEW YORK TIMES* SUNDAY MAGAZINE PUBLISHED AN article by the philosopher Charles Frankel called "A Liberal Is a Liberal Is a . . ." Frankel observed that it was hard to find a major figure in American politics who had not had a kind word to say about liberalism, from Hoover to Truman or Taft to Eisenhower. Indeed, he said, "anyone who today identifies himself as an unmitigated opponent of liberalism . . . cannot aspire to influence on the national political scene."

Frankel noted that even politicians who indulged in attacks on "liberals" were always careful to qualify the word. Southern conservatives complained about "Northern liberals," and usually added that they themselves were liberals in matters of social welfare. Even Senator McCarthy usually restricted himself to attacking "phony liberals," leaving open the inference, as Frankel put it, "that he had nothing against genuine liberals, if only he could find one."

Frankel's article was accompanied by a cartoon that showed a group of politicians labeled "Left-Wing Democrat," "Middle-Wing Democrat,"

"Right-Wing Republican," and so forth, all sitting at a table in front of a TV camera and applying makeup from jars bearing labels like "Liberal Cream," "Liberal #7," and "Do-It-Yourself Liberal Kit."

If that cartoon were run again today, the jars would all contain vanishing cream. Nowadays not even most politicians on the left wing of the Democratic party are willing to own up to being liberals. When someone presses them, they either dismiss the significance of labels in general or acknowledge the label defensively, the way Howard Dean did during the 2003 primary season: "If being a liberal means a balanced budget, I'm a liberal." (As Ann Coulter observes, for once accurately: "The surest sign one is dealing with a liberal is his refusal to grant meaning to the word 'liberal.'") And ordinary voters are equally wary of the label. Over recent decades, the number of Americans willing to describe themselves as liberals[2] has been hovering around 20 percent, with around 35 percent describing themselves as conservatives, and the rest opting for "moderate" or "middle of the road."

It's tempting to see the declining fortunes of the liberal label simply as a sign of the shift to the right among the American electorate: if people have rejected *liberal*, it must be because they've rejected liberalism. Granted, liberalism was never a precise doctrine, particularly in the postwar decades, when its tent was spread so wide. But however liberalism was defined, there's no question that its appeal began to diminish shortly after its high-water mark in the Kennedy years. It was partly the victim of a complacency born of its own successes. Already in 1955, Richard Hofstadter was writing that "the dominant force in our political life no longer comes from the liberals who made the New Deal possible."[3] But it was also challenged by the white backlash to civil rights legislation, the perceived failure of Great Society social programs, and the bitter divisions over the Vietnam War. Before long, liberalism was under assault from both the New Right and the New Left — it was just a few years after the Frankel article appeared that the folksinger Phil Ochs released "Love Me, I'm a Liberal," a sardonic catalog of liberal hypocrisies ("I love Puerto Ricans and Negroes /as long as they don't move next door").

By the late 1970s, liberalism was already associated with "profligacy, spinelessness, malevolence, masochism, elitism, fantasy, anarchy, idealism, softness, irresponsibility, and sanctimoniousness."[4] And then on August 14, 1988, Ronald Reagan made the stigma quasi-official when he told the 1988 Republican National Convention, "The masquerade is over. It's time to . . . say the dreaded L-word; to say the policies of our opposition are liberal, liberal, liberal."[5]

Rather than owning up to the label, the Democratic candidate Michael Dukakis tried to change the subject, responding that "the L-word of this campaign is 'leadership.'" That strategy suited the purposes of his opponent, George H. W. Bush, who made a running gag out of Dukakis's coyness about acknowledging the label. Dukakis, he said, had avoided appearing on *Wheel of Fortune* because "[h]e was afraid that Vanna might turn over the L-word." It wasn't until a few days before the election that Dukakis finally got around to saying, a little defensively, "Yes, I'm a liberal, in the tradition of Franklin Roosevelt and Harry Truman and John Kennedy." The declaration was treated as major news ("Dukakis Uses L-Word" was the page-one headline in

> **Liberals are four times as likely as conservatives to be described as "unapologetic" or "unabashed."**

the *Boston Globe*). But the damage was done by then, not just to the Dukakis campaign but to the liberal label, which would be branded from then on as "the L-word," according to the familiar formula we use when we want to pretend a word is unspeakable. By now, it's considered noteworthy when a politician admits to being a liberal. Even in supposedly "liberal" papers like the *New York Times* and the *Washington Post*, liberals are four times as likely as conservatives to be described as "unapologetic" or "unabashed." In this day and age, it's assumed that liberalism is something most people would have qualms about owning up to.

But if voters are reluctant to declare themselves liberals nowadays, they haven't bailed out on most of the views that defined liberalism in the past. By substantial margins, Americans feel that the Democrats would do a better job than the Republicans at taking care of the environment, making the tax system fair, safeguarding Social Security, and improving the health care system. In a 2003 CBS–*New York Times* poll, only 11 percent of respondents believed the president's tax cuts were very likely to create new jobs, which a lot of people would take as a central tenent of conservative faith. And the overwhelmingly negative response to the Bush administration's efforts to privatize Social Security in 2005 made it clear that Americans were not prepared to throw the most important achievements of the New Deal aside in the name of "the ownership society." In short, Americans seem to have a lot more misgivings about the liberal label than about liberal ideas. The real shift to the right has been among the Republican leadership and party activists, who have moved much farther to the right of the American mainstream than the Democrats have moved left.[6] And they've dragged political discourse along with them.

In fact, the whole idea of liberalism as a political doctrine sometimes seems to be beside the point these days. The word itself isn't used nearly as much as it used to be — today, the media talk about liberals a great deal more than they talk about liberalism.[7] And when *liberalism* comes up, it's usually in phrases like "West Side liberalism" or "Hollywood liberalism," where it suggests a social clique rather than a philosophical school — "Hollywood liberalism" isn't the same sort of thing as "Chicago economics." These days, it's as if being a liberal has less to do with a commitment to a particular –ism than with being a political fashion victim. What were once regarded as political ideals have become merely the ancillary signs of a decadent lifestyle.

The trashing of the liberal label is one of the most significant changes in the language of American politics in recent times. By now, most of the politicians who would have proudly called themselves liberals forty years ago have abandoned the name, if not the liberal worldview. Even those who identify with liberal principles are more likely to describe themselves as "progressives" — something like what the Ford Motor Company did in 1960 when it discontinued the Edsel line but continued to market the same car with a different grille and trim under the name of Galaxie. The fact is, the progressive label has been on something of a tear. It's used not just by activists who inherited the New Left's disdain for liberals, but by centrists and old-fashioned pols. It figures in the name of the Progressive Policy Institute of the centrist Democratic Leadership Council. And during the 2003 gubernatorial recall election, California governor Gray Davis said that he was confident he would prevail because "I don't think they're going to replace my progressive agenda with a conservative agenda" — this from a Democrat who was not exactly known for cruising in the party's left lane.

Progressive has its advantages: it conveys the right message to *Nation*-reading, Pacifica-listening voters without connoting anything negative to the majority of the electorate — to most, in fact, it doesn't connote much of anything at all. And the word clearly irks the right, as you can tell from the way conservative publications like *National Review* tend to set it in quotation marks, the form of passive resistance that's used by those who have allowed the other side to stake out the linguistic territory. Some conservatives have even tried to usurp the word. Shortly after the 2004 election, the Seattle *Post-Intelligencer*'s Julia Youngs wrote that "George W. Bush kept the presidency because he was the more progressive candidate." Bush's victory, she said, was a sign that voters repudiated the left's resistance to "progressive ideas" like proactive pursuit of terrorists, limitations on abortion, privatization of Social Security, and the flat tax.[8] If actual progressives could get past the butter-wouldn't-melt effrontery of that statement, they might find the appropriation of their label flattering.

Has *liberal* had its day? Seventy years is a pretty good run for a political label,[9] and perhaps some day *liberal* will be replaced by *progressive* or some other term, particularly if the nation has to undergo an upheaval comparable to the Great Depression. But labels have returned from near-oblivion before. Fifty years ago, *conservative* was on the ropes; in a 1949 editorial, the *Wall Street Journal* said:

> If a man eschews extreme fads in clothing himself, we say he is a conservative dresser and we are more inclined to employ him in our business or be seen in his company. If a banker is described as conservative most people are more inclined to trust their money to his care. But if a man is described as a "conservative" in politics then the reaction to him is very likely to be altogether different. He is likely to be suspected of wanting to cheat widows and orphans and generally to be a bad fellow who associates with a lot of other bad fellows. Consequently very few people will admit they are conservatives and if they are accused they will go to great lengths to prove otherwise. . . . [Conservatives] have been propagandized and bullied into believing that they must shun a word and the word is the very one that describes their attitude.[10]

You could write the same article today substituting *liberal* for *conservative* (though you might have trouble getting the *Journal* to print it). "Everyone has a good word for liberal benefactors and liberal helpings of potatoes. . . ."

Still, the liberal label still has its defenders, not just because of the tradition of thought it stands for, but because it would be a strategic error to abandon it.[11] For the present, the opposition between liberals and conservatives is too deeply etched in the language and on the media's split screens to be dropped anytime soon, particularly with the right hammering incessantly on the "elite liberals" theme. *Liberal* is the word that ordinary people use when they're talking about political polarities, and Democrats who avoid it in favor of *progressive* seem to confirm the widespread suspicion that liberals aren't talking the same language as other Americans, even when it comes to pronouncing their own name right.[12]

For as long as the Democrats refuse to come to terms with the liberal label, it will continue to dog them. As Dukakis learned, a candidate's reluctance to acknowledge the label may often strike voters as a sign of unwillingness to own up to his principles. And it's a fair bet that John Kerry's refusal to call himself a liberal helped him less among centrists than it hurt him among voters of all stripes who already had doubts about his constancy of principle.

What's worse, the Democrats' phobia about the liberal label has given the right free rein to define the word in its own terms, pushing the meaning of *liberal* to the political margins. There was a time when *liberal* and *leftist* were contrasting terms; now the right tends to use them interchangeably.[13] Not long ago, in fact, the Republican minority leader of the South Carolina Senate described a Democratic legislator as "one of the most liberal leftists that we have in the House"[14] — not an uncommon wording these days, which implies that *liberal* has actually outflanked

The more Democrats shun the liberal label, the easier it is for the right to demonize it.

leftist as a term for extreme political views. It's a vicious circle: the more Democrats shun the liberal label, the easier it is for the right to demonize it, making Democrats even more reluctant to wear it than before. If the flight from the liberal label continues, self-avowed liberals may wind up like the Celts of medieval Europe, driven to the peripheries of the continent by invading tribes.

This isn't a problem only for the left and center-left of the Democratic party. True, there are plenty of individual Democrats who see no need for the liberal label, and even some centrists who rejoice in its imminent passing. But in the end, the eclipse of the label has left the party groping for a unifying philosophical center to fill the role that the broad-tent conception of liberalism did from the time of FDR to the Kennedy era. Mid-twentieth-century liberalism may not have been a very precise or stirring philosophy, or even a philosophy at all. Lionel Trilling described it back in 1951 as "a large tendency rather than a concise body of doctrine."[15] But it did give Democrats a common touch point in a line of political tradition, just as conservatism does for today's Republicans.[16]

"In a representative government," Franklin Roosevelt said in 1941, "there are usually two general schools of political belief — liberal and conservative. . . . Since at least 1932, the Democratic Party has been the liberal party." Nowadays, to all but the right, the Democrats are merely the party formerly known as liberal. The absence of an ideological center haunts the party. Slogans like Clinton's "Opportunity, Responsibility, Community" may make for good photo backdrops, but they're too vague to provide the sense of party identity and tradition that a commitment to liberalism did in the past. A 2005 Democracy Corps survey found that 55 percent of voters said the Republicans know what they stand for, as opposed to only 27 percent who said the same thing of the Democrats.

You can see the problem reflected in the media, where Republicans are identified in terms of an ideological reference point far more often than Democrats are. Middle-of-the-road Republicans like George Pataki or Rudy Giuliani are usually described as "moderates," which locates them relative to the party's mainstream, but middle-of-the-road Democrats like Evan Bayh and Max Baucus tend to be called "centrists," which locates them relative to the broader political horizon.[17] In fact, the press identifies politicians as "mainstream Republicans" four times as often as it identifies them as "mainstream Democrats," and it is almost five times as likely to speak of Republicans as "true believers." In the public mind, *Republican* names a movement, whereas *Democrat* is only a ZIP code.

There's a certain self-delusion in Democrats' avoidance of the L-word; it suggests that they really haven't understood the magnitude of the linguistic shift that has taken place. Liberalism isn't like a brand of automobile that has fallen out of favor — it can't be reinvigorated simply by marketing it under a new name with a NASCAR-approved grille. The trashing of the liberal label is only the most obvious sign of a process that has rewritten whole pages of the American political dictionary, as familiar words have acquired new meanings that reflect a changed conception of what politics is about. Even if you could magically eradicate *liberal* from the collective consciousness, you wouldn't dispel all the fatuous stereotypes that have accumulated around the word or reverse the broader shifts of political meaning that they stand in for. In the end, this really isn't so much about reclaiming *liberal* as about redressing the shift in political language that the stigmatization of the liberal label stands in for. To understand what has happened to *liberal*, you have to understand how the right has rewritten the language of class.

NOTES

[1]Timothy Noah, "10 Political Words That Dare Not Speak Their Name," *New York Times*, November 19, 1986.

[2]The Harris poll notes that "it is hard to think of another set of attitudinal questions that have been so extraordinarily stable."

[3]Richard Hofstadter, "The Pseudo-Conservative Revolt," in Daniel Bell, ed., *The Radical Right* (Criterion, 1955), p. 63.

[4]Jonathan Rieder, *Canarsie: The Jews and Italians of Brooklyn Against Liberalism* (Harvard University Press, 1985), p. 6.

[5]*Liberal* was occasionally described as "the L-word" before that, but the designation usually had to be explained. Within a few months of Reagan's speech, however, Marty Nolan could write in the *Boston Globe*, "Throughout this presidential campaign, 'Massachusetts' ranks second (after the L-word) whenever George Bush wants to, as he says, 'talk dirty,'" without feeling the need to tell his readers just what the L-word was. Campaign Watch series: "Baker's Tight Ship," *Boston Globe*, October 21, 1988.

[6]See Jacob S. Hacker and Paul Pierson, *Off Center: The Republican Revolution and the Erosion of American Democracy* (Yale University Press, 2005), pp. 43–44.

[7]In press stories, *liberalism* is only about 60 percent as frequent relative to *conservatism* as it was in the early 1980s, though the ratio of *liberal* and *conservative* is largely unchanged.

[8]This isn't to deny that there are various themes in modern conservatism that echo the concerns of early twentieth-century Progressives for better and for worse. But that clearly isn't what Youngs is getting at — for her, "progressive" is just an adjectival form of *progress*.

[9]*Liberal* has had a long and complicated history as a political label since it was first used in the Napoleonic period, and various of its older meanings survive in phrases such as "liberal democracy" and "liberal Western values," not to mention in the names of various European parties and movements. But its modern American sense really begins in the New Deal period, when the opposition between liberals and conservatives was established. Some conservatives like to argue that modern liberals are not "true liberals" in this or that historical sense of the term, even as liberals charge that modern conservatives are untrue to the historical sense of *their*

name. This kind of essentialism has its polemical uses, but it serves no serious intellectual purpose. Talking about "the true meaning of *liberalism*" is as idle an exercise as talking about "the true meaning of *jazz*." For discussions of the development of the modern meanings of *liberal* and *liberalism*, see Ronald D. Rotunda, *The Politics of Language: Liberalism as Word and Symbol* (University of Iowa Press, 1986), and David Green, *The Language of Politics in America* (Cornell University Press, 1987).

[10]"Conservative," *Wall Street Journal*, March 17, 1949.

[11]"To surrender the label 'liberal' to history," Stephen Macedo writes, "would be a profound mistake, for the great tradition of liberal thinking deserves a better fate." *Diversity and Distrust: Civic Education in a Multicultural Democracy* (Harvard University Press, 2003), p. 8.

[12]Some on the right have taken to using *progressive* as a disparaging term — Bill O'Reilly likes to rail at "secular progressives." That might ultimately help to establish the label in general usage, but not exactly as a neutral replacement for *liberal*.

[13]On the Web, Martin Sheen and Susan Sarandon are more likely to be labeled leftists than Fidel Castro is.

[14]That wording is not uncommon. A letter-writer to the *Palm Beach Post*, October 19, 2001, decried the influence of "extremely liberal leftists" in academia.

[15]Lionel Trilling, *The Liberal Imagination: Essays on Literature and Society* (Viking Press, 1951), p. xi.

[16]*Republicanism* plays a similar role: people have used the term since the Reagan years to refer to the political philosophy of the Republicans. But there is no corresponding word *Democratism* for the Democrats.

[17]William Safire, "Iron Fist," *New York Times*, August 20, 2000. On the Web, "moderate Republican" outpolls "moderate Democrat" by 4-to-1, whereas "centrist Democrat" has a 3-to-1 edge over "centrist Republican." Many conservative Republicans dislike the implications of *moderate*. As Safire observed in 2000, "From a conservative's point of view, a moderate is the liberal's way of avoiding the pejorative tag of *liberal*. From a liberal's point of view, *moderate* is a friendly way of describing a Republican who is not a hard-core, reactionary, troglodyte kook." But Republicans aren't crazy about describing figures like Rudy Giuliani and George Pataki as "centrists," either, and the stigmatization of *liberal* has turned "liberal Republican" into a term of abuse within party circles. So even Bush's former press secretary Ari Fleischer found himself referring to "moderate Republicans" on some occasions.

DISCUSSION

1. What kind of person does the term *liberal* conjure in your mind? What kind of interests, attitudes, and lifestyle? What kind of person would you say this stereotype is defined against? What sorts of interests, attitudes, and lifestyles stand in our culture as the opposite? Do these labels seem accurate? Do you know many people who actually fit the stereotypes of each?

2. There is a marked difference, Nunberg writes, between public attitudes toward the liberal label and public attitudes toward the actual ideas of liberalism itself: "Americans seem to have a lot more misgivings about the liberal label than about liberal ideas." Why do you think this is the case? Can you think of another term or label that doesn't accurately define what it purports to describe?

3. *Liberal* stands as one of our political culture's most polarizing terms: a word that people use to create firm divisions between "us" and "them." Can you think of a word that does the opposite? That erases boundaries? That eases or reduces our sense of difference and antagonism?

WRITING

4. Write an essay in which you discuss all the words that come to your mind in association with the terms *liberal* and *conservative.* Do you personally identify with one term over another? What messages about each term have you read or seen in popular culture? In your opinion, are these terms useful labels? Why or why not?

5. Underlying Nunberg's analysis is an interest in how language itself (i.e., the words we use) can serve to create an idea or model of the enemy. Choose a controversy or debate currently unfolding and write an analysis of the ways each side uses language to create a version or vision of its enemy. What particular words get deployed? And how do they serve to evoke a particular image of the opposition? Do any of these strategies resemble those that Nunberg discusses?

6. Both Deborah Tannen (p. 572) and Stephen Miller (p. 594) discuss the role that conflict plays in how we talk at a conversational level. In your opinion, how do the strategies behind labeling an opponent that Nunberg discusses either reinforce or discredit the arguments of these two authors?

PETER HYMAN
Stop Them before They Joke Again

Somewhere along the line, "being funny" has gone from being a personal talent or individual penchant to an everyday, even universal, expectation. With our airwaves filled with a seemingly endless litany of stand-up comedians, talk show hosts, and sitcom characters, it has become increasingly commonplace for our own conversations to mirror or mimic the roles and scripts purveyed in our larger pop culture. For Peter Hyman, this has given rise to a situation in which we now *all* feel the need to be actors. Hyman writes articles, reviews, and humor pieces for the *New York Times*, the *New York Observer*, *Details*, the *San Francisco Chronicle*, and other publications. He previously worked for *Vanity Fair* and *Drill*. His first book, *Reluctant Metrosexual: Dispatches from an Almost Hip Life*, was published in 2004. Hyman also maintains a blog about current events and pop culture called Manufactured Dissent. The selection that follows originally appeared on State.com in 2006.

THE WHITE-COLLAR TEMPLE IBM IS USUALLY NOT A SOURCE OF POP-cultural memes. But this reputation may be receding, thanks to a trio of comedic videos topping the charts on YouTube. Shot in the mock-doc style of *The Office*, these parodies of internal training videos feature a group of sales executives as they pump themselves up with canned corporate wisdom and hawk million-dollar servers by cold-calling random names from the phone book. In other words, they make fun of IBM at its stodgy core. And while Steve Carell's job is probably safe, what is interesting about these shorts is that they were made by IBM using actual company executives, not paid actors or comedians.

Whatever one's opinion about the content of these videos — making mainframe servers funny is a challenge, no matter how much comedic coaching you buy — this scenario raises some interesting questions. Must everybody try to be funny these days? Are we now compelled, as a culture, to be comical, no matter the setting or the endeavor? And if so, what on earth gave rise to this troubling idea?

One possible culprit may be corporate America itself, where being funny is now seen as a valuable asset. Fortune 500 companies dole out big fees to comedy consultants who offer humor seminars and improv workshops — all in the name of improved productivity. But how exactly are funnier employees better for business? According to Tim Washer, a former improv performer who is now a communications executive at IBM, funniness helps foster team-building and, of course, learning how to "think outside the box." Never mind that, as Washer suggests, being funny can't really be taught. "Humor is binary," he says. "You're either funny or you're not." Still, thanks to coaches like Washer, when Joe BlackBerry leaves the office after a day of training, he goes out into the world armed with a PowerPoint primer on comedic timing and the notion that he's funny. And, at some point, he's going to try to prove this to you.

Another possible contributor is television and the fact that we mimic what we watch. There is more comedy being broadcast today than ever before, thanks to the full flowering of the *Seinfeld* effect (everyday existence is funny) and the comedic explosion inspired by the show. An endless array of cable offerings now besiege the populace daily with comedy in the form of hackneyed sitcoms (both rerun and original content), predictable stand-up routines, and clichéd cultural commentators in love with decades of the late 20th century. "So what?" you might say. "People are experiencing more comedy. It beats a kick in the teeth." But just as reality television blurs the line between entertainment and actual life, this avalanche of televised humor may be giving the viewing public the misguided idea that comedy is easy.

The comedic personalities garnering the most airtime tend to be regular folks (Who doesn't love Raymond? Or Kevin James from *King of Queens?*) speaking in a universal language of baseline observations ("Men and women often have different approaches to situations, especially when they are married!") about the most pedestrian aspects of life ("Hey, I fight with my spouse about the laundry/kids/in-laws as well . . . my world must be equally hilarious"), which makes comedy seem like an endeavor that the Everyman should undertake. The end result? The guy standing next to you in line at Starbucks sounds like a nondescript sitcom actor that even your TiVo can't stand.

A related cause could be the contemporary avoidance of sincerity. *Vanity Fair* editor Graydon Carter's post-9/11 declaration pronouncing the death of irony is, five years later, the misstatement of the millennium. From sneakers to cell-phone ring-tones to rain on your wedding day, *everything* is ironic. Or, more accurately, everything is sarcastic, the less-literary stepcousin of irony. Unlike irony, sarcasm can be printed on a T-shirt or written into every tenth line of an ESPN newscast with the generic (and easily aped) voice of mocking detachment that is so prevalent today.

What is the upside of being funny? Well, apart from getting noticed, it's safer to hide behind the mask of humor, especially in a culture skeptical of intellectualism. Andrew Stott, an English professor whose academic treatise *Comedy* explored the philosophy of humor, sees

> **It's safer to hide behind the mask of humor, especially in a culture skeptical of intellectualism.**

it like this: "Being funny is a means of avoiding scrutiny. It's a deeply con-cealing activity that invites attention while simultaneously failing to offer any detailed account of oneself. The reason humor is so popular today is that it provides the comfort of intimacy without the horror of actually being intimate." Thus, schlock-jock Opie & Anthony clones rule drive-time America while truth-tellers like Bill Hicks linger in relative obscurity.

This is not to say that avoiding honest discourse via humor is always a bad thing. When David Letterman came forth with his pitch-perfect Midwestern droll in early 1980s, the voice was a refreshing change from the Johnny Carson boy-that-President-Carter-is-indecisive school of joke-telling. But the Letterman tone has grown so prevalent that the comedic effect has long since been lost, leaving only the grating noise of a million imitators, all sounding like a tired Top Ten list.

If you've ever been at a party where some guy trying to tap a keg chimes in with a quip about how "it's all ball bearings nowadays" (a line stolen from the most over-referenced film of all time), then you have had firsthand experience with this crisis. Still, up until a few years ago, these situations were relegated to the realm of the interpersonal, which one could limit by sitting at home in the dark and avoiding all human contact. But this luxury no longer exists. For, as the IBM example illustrates, we are now mired in an era of instant mass self-expression. And, for all of the democracy the Internet engenders, it is possible to have too much *vox populi*, especially when the *populi* seem intent on using such tired punch lines and hacky premises.

The only solution is for some of us to voluntarily retire from the humor game. Let me be the first to forge a new reality by pledging never to try to be funny again. I can only hope that the executives at IBM read this and follow suit, if they're not already busy filming a sitcom pilot for Fox on some back lot in Studio City.

DISCUSSION

1. According to Hyman, virtually every joke we tell nowadays has its origins in our larger popular culture. Is there anything troubling about this idea? Does it matter that this aspect of our personal behavior may very well have been scripted by television or movies?

2. One of the most pervasive verbal norms these days, says Hyman, is irony. From self-conscious car commercials to cheeky ring tones on our cell phones, we are inundated with images and products that encourage us to cultivate an ironic attitude toward the world. How often do you adopt this view? Are there certain kinds of occasions or circumstances where it feels most natural?

3. What is the value or benefit of adopting a comic attitude toward business? What objectives do you think these tongue-in-cheek advertisements for big corporations are designed to achieve?

WRITING

4. Write an essay in which you analyze Hyman's use of humor in his essay criticizing everybody's desire to be funny. Do you think his approach is effective or hypocritical? Why? What are the possible benefits of using humor in everyday (stereotypically unfunny) settings? What are the possible downfalls? In your opinion, when is the use of humor most effective?

5. Write an essay in which you describe some of the stereotypes of serious business that pervade our popular culture. Considering some of the tools of humor that Hyman discusses, how would you go about satirizing or poking fun at these stereotypes? Are you yourself using any popular films, TV shows, or books as a model for creating this satire?

6. Hyman and Stephen Miller (p. 594) both organize their discussions around the assumption that media spectacles (whether stand-up comedy acts or confessional talk shows) are, by definition, script writers, supplying the rest of us with the instructions for how to talk in our own lives. Write an essay in which you either support or refute these authors' arguments.

Then and Now: *Talking Dirty*

Hays Code

III. Vulgarity
The treatment of low, disgusting, unpleasant, though not necessarily evil, subjects should always be subject to the dictates of good taste and a regard for the sensibilities of the audience.

IV. Obscenity
Obscenity in word, gesture, reference, song, joke, or by suggestion (even when likely to be understood only by part of the audience) is forbidden.

V. Profanity
Pointed profanity (this includes the words, God, Lord, Jesus, Christ — unless used reverently — Hell, S.O.B., damn, Gawd), or every other profane or vulgar expression however used, is forbidden.

— from the Production Code (also known as the Hays Code), adopted in 1930

PG – Parental Guidance Suggested

The label PG plainly states parents may consider some material unsuitable for their children, but leaves the parent to make the decision. Parents are warned against sending their children, unseen and without inquiry, to PG-rated movies. The theme of a PG-rated film may itself call for parental guidance. There may be some profanity in these films. There may be some violence or brief nudity. However, these elements are not considered so intense as to require that parents be strongly cautioned beyond the suggestion of parental guidance. There is no drug use content in a PG-rated film. The PG rating, suggesting parental guidance, is thus an alert for examination of a film by parents before deciding on its viewing by their children. Obviously such a line is difficult to draw. In our pluralistic society it is not easy to make judgments without incurring some disagreement. As long as parents know they must exercise parental responsibility, the rating serves as a meaningful guide and as a warning.

— Motion Picture Association of America (MPAA) website, "What Do the Ratings Mean?"
http://www.mpaa.org/FlmRat_Ratings.asp, still in use today.

When we look around at all the different kinds of talk that dominate our lives these days, it's tempting to feel as if we live in an era where all prohibitions, all limits, have been left behind. In a world where television talk show hosts regularly grill guests about the details of their sex lives, where self-help manuals urge their readers to divulge their personal stories of travail or abuse, where cable television comedians regularly punctuate their stand-up routines with four-letter vulgarities, it's easy to conclude that in this day and age only one rule remains in effect: the one telling us that "anything goes." But is this really the case? With the advent of talking motion pictures, Hollywood adopted the Production (or Hays) Code in 1930 as a way to enforce decency in movies. Today, its rules regarding the use of profanity seem utterly restrictive.

It could well be the case, however, that our own era's seeming absence of inhibition around language simply reflects the ways we have learned to follow different scripts — ones that, while perhaps less visible, structure our speech just as firmly. There's little question that nowadays we tend to look on the old rules governing what can and cannot be said on film and TV as quaint relics long since consigned to a bygone era. But our contemporary candor about this topic doesn't automatically mean that there aren't *other* guidelines, *other* norms that may have replaced them. If you read the Motion Picture Association of America's explanation of why certain movies are rated PG, you will no doubt notice an absence of specifics. But does that necessarily mean we have relaxed our standards of what can and cannot be said? Or has an outright ban on specific words been replaced by a tendency to consider these taboo words in context? Do you think what the Hays Code considered as profane would still be considered profane by the modern MPAA?

WRITING

1. Write an essay in which you compare and contrast what is seemingly *not* allowed between the Hays Code and the MPAA rating system. According to each system, who do you think is more responsible for policing the language allowed in films? Does one system seem more restrictive than the other? How so?

2. Recently, the MPAA rating system has been criticized by some in the film industry for being too vague. Write an essay in which you propose how the description for a PG rating could be revised to present a clearer picture of what should and should not be allowed, making sure to describe what your own beliefs are about what constitutes profanity.

SHEELAH KOLHATKAR

You Are Not Alone: College Newspapers Discover the Sex Column

What are the conventional rules in our culture around how we may and may not talk about sex? Long considered to be the ultimate taboo topic, sex now comprises one of the most commonplace subjects in our public conversation. Offering a case in point, Sheelah Kolhatkar takes stock of the rising popularity of sex advice columns on college campuses. What, she asks, are we to make of this recent development? Does the proliferation of such advice suggest that we've learned to shed old anxieties and hang-ups when it comes to the subject of sex? And if so, is all this newfound candor necessarily a good thing? Kolhatkar is a staff writer at the *Condé Nast Portfolio.* She was previously a staff writer at the *New York Observer*, where she covered publishing, media, and culture. Her writing has also appeared in the *Atlantic Monthly*, the *New York Times*, and *Elle.* Before pursuing a career in journalism, she worked on Wall Street as a hedge fund analyst. Kolhatkar holds a BFA from New York University and an MA from Stanford University. The selection that follows originally appeared in the November 2005 issue of *Atlantic Monthly.*

SOME HIGH-ACHIEVING STUDENTS COME TO COLLEGE WITH BIG plans: to edit the school newspaper or join the right sorority, to secure a slot at Wharton business school or a volunteer job in Africa. But a healthy number, mostly women, make their mark, and shock their parents, by starting a sex column.

Raunchy, clumsily titled, and almost universally cringe-inducing, sex columns have blossomed at universities across the country. Students at tiny Craven Community College, in the Bible Belt town of New Bern, North Carolina, briefly enjoyed "Between the Sheets"; the *Cornell Daily Sun* offered "Cornellingus"; there was "Behind Closed Doors" at William and Mary, "Love Bites" at Swarthmore, "Mouth to Mouth" at Emory. The list has grown dramatically, as if every school newspaper needs a baby pundit opining on subjects ranging from tantric sex to true love.

The dominant mode in such columns is a cheery, shock-the-bourgeoisie frankness. Plain old intercourse usually takes a back seat to Clintonian shenanigans ("On Valentine's Day, nothing says 'I love you' like oral sex," Claire Fuller wrote in Northern Arizona University's the *Lumberjack*, sparking a minor furor in Flagstaff), auto-eroticism ("I just bought my first vibrator," declared Katie Giblin — a "Biology concentrator," class of 2006 — in a column in the *Harvard Independent*), or exhibitionism ("Sex is exciting, but doing it where and when you're not 'supposed to' is even more exciting. It's a small taste of porn-stardom," Dave Franzese wrote last spring in "The Wednesday Hump," which runs in UC Santa Barbara's *Daily Nexus*).

The columns vary in their level of explicitness: the Ivy League and the state of California seem to be the best places to test the limits of good taste; the writing there occasionally takes on the clammy feel of "Penthouse Forum" letters, designed to make dorky freshmen feel like they're missing out on crazy erotic adventures. Some columns are written as naughty sex chronicles; others sound like an anatomy lecture; others are milder and more relationship-oriented. But in many respects most are basically the same.

The spirited "Sex on Tuesday," in Berkeley's *Daily Californian*, is credited with being one of the first collegiate sex columns (it made its debut in 1997), and it remains, in style and substance, typical of the genre. "Sex on Tuesday" was written during the past school year by a young woman named Sari Eitches, who appears full-figured and saucy in her author photo. Eitches seemed fully aware of the odd responsibility that comes with dishing out sex advice to randy twenty-year-olds, and like many of her peers, she tossed an occasional bone to the more staid sexperts at the university's health service, reminding people to use condoms and otherwise do their best to avoid sexually transmitted diseases. But these hints of sexual seriousness aside, her tone was breezy and all-knowing, her prose sprinkled with innuendo and euphemism, as she chided readers not to be prudish.

Indeed, prudishness is the only unforgivable sin for a sex columnist — and as a result there's constant pressure to see how far one can go. In a column titled "Some Like It Rough," printed in March, Eitches urged her readers, "Relax your idea of what constitutes sadomasochistic tendencies" and noted, "If you include not just getting whipped by a leather-clad dominatrix while attempting auto-asphyxiation, but also giving your partner a little hickey during a make-out session, this campus is just crawling with sadistic heathens." In an earlier entry she interviewed a female porn star about her methods of stimulating her leading men. And then there was the obligatory piece championing anal sex, titled . . . well, never mind.

In some ways college sex columnists are following in the footsteps of the first famous American sex-advice celebrity, the matronly Dr. Ruth Westheimer, whose radio program, *Sexually Speaking*, offered listeners wry expertise from 1980 to 1988, no matter how bizarre the query. (Westheimer also writes a column in which one typical response begins, "It is a bit shocking that, after all that has been written and said about sex, so many people remain sexually illiterate, but you are far from alone . . .")

But the junior sex columnists owe a greater debt to pop-sex writers such as Dan Savage; Anka Radakovich, who had a widely read column in *Details* magazine throughout the 1990s; and especially Candace Bushnell, whose meditations on the love lives of restless Manhattanites in the *New York Observer* column "Sex and the City" inspired the television show of the same name. Like Bushnell and her alter ego, Carrie Bradshaw, most collegiate sexologists write their columns as pseudo-diaries, drawing on personal experience to educate readers. And they, too, mix a jaded attitude toward the physical act itself with a wistful yearning for true love, and even a hint of disappointment. ("It is rare for college students to have sex with people they're genuinely in love with," lamented Miriam Datskovsky, a "Barnard College sophomore majoring in Human Rights and French," in the Columbia *Spectator*'s "Sexplorations" last April. "At the other end of the spectrum, random hook-ups allow us to have sex without intimacy.")

An important difference, though, separates Dr. Ruth and Bushnell from their undergraduate imitators: the writer of a college column usually has little experience and no special knowledge. You wouldn't know it from reading the columns, of course: they hint at a fantasy lifestyle filled with hangup-free sexual encounters, without the torment and awkwardness that usually accompany college relationships. After scanning columns from schools across the country, it's easy to come away thinking that torment and awkwardness went out with shoulder pads, and that America's college kids are busy vibrating and videotaping themselves into the stratosphere.

If anything, though, the opposite may be the case. Like harried alpha parents curling up with a *Sex and the City* DVD, or lonely divorcees thumbing through *Cosmopolitan*, college students seem to love nothing more than hearing about all the wild sex they might not be having. The number of sex columnists has gone up, but a 2004 survey showed little change in campus sexual activity over the previous four years. "I'm seeing more students abstaining than I did fifteen years ago," says Melinda Myers, a lecturer on human sexuality at Humboldt State University, in northern California, who wrote that school's sex column for many years. "On the other hand, they are more curious about it. They don't really want to have a lot of sex, but they want all the answers."

> **College students seem to love nothing more than hearing about all the wild sex they might not be having.**

And that's where the columnists come in — putting up a brave front, pretending to have knowledge and experience that they don't necessarily have. Natalie Krinsky, a former Yale *Daily News* columnist who made a name for herself with a much e-mailed piece about oral-sex etiquette, admits that her columns were loosely based on things she had overheard, adding that "people in college talk about sex ninety-five percent of the time" but "we always talk far more than we do, as a rule." Her column persona, too, bore at best a glancing relationship to reality. "I think that in my columns I was a lot more ballsy and sarcastic and confident than I necessarily am in real life, because I needed to be," she says. "You needed to be witty and poised, or at least appear that way, because you want to be relatable but you want to be credible."

Eitches had a similar experience at Berkeley. "At my school discourse about sex is very open in general," she says, "so in order for me to have something to write about, I did have to push the envelope a little bit and look for article topics that might surprise some people. I've been asked before, 'Why don't you write about an average college-student sex life, and things that pertain to that?' And I just didn't think that would be too interesting or fun to do research about. I think it was more, Oh, I'm curious to know what that's about." Eitches also says that she felt an obligation to address some more-obscure topics because students obviously had questions about things they'd heard or read about (she received many e-mailed queries), and didn't know whom else to ask.

The constant search for fresh material to satisfy a voyeuristic audience helps explain why reading these columns, especially in large batches, is so wearying. There are, after all, only so many ways to contort the human body; even the outlandish scenarios in the *Penthouse* letters all lead to the same short list of outcomes. In the words of one student sexpert, "You get to your fifth column and you're like, Oh, my God, how much else is there?"

So the search for novelty leads, paradoxically, to conformity. If Yale and the University of South Florida have vastly different social scenes, you wouldn't know it to read their sex columnists. While the micro-details may be different, students at both schools are revealed to be interchangeable consumers of the American university product, coping with bizarre roommates, drunken athletes, text-message flirting, rivers of alcohol. The faces change, but the sexual concerns remain the same: pornography and orgasms; the pros and cons of virginity and abstinence; sampling adult toys, "ex-sex," and sex with friends. And the columns return again and again to the oldest and most banal campus challenge: juggling a roommate and a sexual partner.

Even the columnists themselves have something fundamental in common: they're almost all women. It has been fashionable of late to suggest that documenting one's intimate life in explicit detail is somehow a realization of the feminist agenda — or at least the part of it that assumed that women were clueless in the bedroom until the sexual revolution came along. But writing as a woman about sex has become positively mainstream; it seems that there's no easier way for young women to get attention these days than by recounting their orgasms and those of their friends in either fictional or nonfictional form. (It's certainly the easiest way to attract a male readership, since men seem to prefer reading about sex when the author is a woman.) Meanwhile, established women writers with other areas of expertise complain of being called upon to discuss sex all the time.

The healthy demand for first-person sex writing can bring notoriety to female undergraduates on campus and in the world beyond. This spring, a year after graduating, Krinsky published a chick-lit novel based on her column, titled *Chloe Does Yale*, and now she plans to write screenplays; her success has made her a model for college-age women writers everywhere, inspiring further imitators at other schools and what seems like resigned acceptance by college administrators and parents that the genre is here to stay.

Given its conventions, it was a bold move when the student editor of the *Daily Nexus*, at UC Santa Barbara, appointed David Franzese, class of 2005, to produce the paper's sex column this past school year. For the most part Franzese demonstrated that a male columnist can be just as shallow about sex as his female counterparts. But in February he came up with one of the most radical sexual suggestions put forth all year: "That's right," he wrote, "I'm talking about having sex while you're sober for once."

DISCUSSION

1. Look over the essay's title for a moment. What does it mean for colleges to "discover" the sex column? What does the use of this term imply about the place such "sex talk" has traditionally occupied in campus life? In your view, is it surprising or not surprising that these columns would become so popular in this particular setting?

2. What standards underlie our culture's traditional taboos regarding how to talk about sex? And which of these taboos seem to get challenged by the advice columns Kolhatkar profiles? How do you view these challenges? In your view, is it a good thing that these prohibitions are being flouted? That scripts about how we should talk are being rewritten? Why or why not?

3. One of the possibilities raised by Kolhatkar's investigation is that explicit and graphic conversations about sex have become the new norm. In your own experience, does this seem to be the case? Has it now become largely acceptable, even expected, to talk about sex in our culture in these more open and explicit ways? And if so, how do you evaluate this development? Is it a change for the better? How or how not?

WRITING

4. As Kolhatkar notes, one of the assumptions behind this growing sex advice trend is that conversing openly and publicly about sex is liberating. According to this view, the popularity of columns such as these reflects an empowering change in our culture, signaling how much more open-minded this less inhibited sex talk actually makes us. Look over the topics that are discussed in these columns. What are some particular norms that these topics seem to challenge or rewrite? Do you find these changes liberating or empowering? Why or why not?

5. As Kolhatkar's discussion makes clear, the advice offered in these columns is designed to shape not just our personal behavior but our personal attitudes as well. Write an essay in which you analyze the ways you think these columns function as a blueprint for how we are supposed to think and talk about sex. What sorts of attitudes and assumptions do they seem to script as being most normal? Are these scripts the ones you want to follow in your life? Why or why not?

6. The Then and Now feature for this chapter (p. 620) compares the ways that restrictions on profanity in films has seemingly relaxed over time. Do you see a similar relaxation in our culture's ability to openly discuss sex in the examples that Kolhatkar discusses? Why or why not? In your opinion, what new boundaries govern the discussion of sex (as a medical problem, the domain of youth, part of a traditional marriage, and so on)? Do you believe that, as a culture, we are truly more comfortable with an open discussion of such a traditionally taboo topic?

JEFF SHARLET

Big World: How Clear Channel Programs America

We hear a good deal these days about the growing homogeneity within our public airwaves. When it comes to the music and news that gets broadcast, how much choice do we genuinely have? Uncovering the operations of Clear Channel, our country's premier commercial radio conglomerate, journalist Jeff Sharlet sheds light on the forces that have made possible such breathtaking consolidation in our modern media — as well as how this sea change has altered what we listen to. Sharlet is the editor of *Revealer*, an online review of news about religion, and a contributing editor to *Rolling Stone* and *Harper's*. His articles about religion, culture, and politics have appeared in the *Washington Post*, the *Chicago Reader*, *Nerve*, and *Salon*, among other publications. He is also the coauthor, with Peter Manseau, of *Killing the Buddha* (2004), which came out of their work from an online magazine of the same name. Sharlet has a book forthcoming called *Jesus Plus Nothing: How a Secret Brotherhood of Elite Believers Shaped the Faith and Politics of an Empire.* The selection that follows originally appeared in the December 2003 issue of *Harper's*.

ON JULY 17, 2002, AS A BAND CALLED THE BOILS WAS PREPARING TO play, seven men with badges, police officers, and agents of Philadelphia's Department of Licenses and Inspections, walked into the basement of the First Unitarian Church at Chestnut and Van Pelt. Nobody knows who tipped them off, but it was clear that someone wanted the Church, as the club in the basement was called, shut down. The show's promoter, Sean Agnew, had been booking acts there for six years, but before the night when the inspectors appeared his shows had not warranted a single official complaint. A tall, lean twenty-four-year-old with a stubbled undertaker's jaw and long, dark eyelashes, Agnew almost always wore a black mesh cap, with DORM SLUT scrawled on it graffitistyle in silver Sharpie, crammed over thick black hair. He was known locally, and in little music magazines around the country, as "DJR500." Agnew's shows were "straight-edge," which meant that drugs and alcohol were not welcome. A local paper had recently named him a man of the year, alongside 76ers guard Allen Iverson.

The Department of Licenses and Inspections does not keep records of complaints. All the deputy commissioner could tell Agnew was that someone had gone down to City Hall, pulled the Church's permit, and discovered that the Church was not zoned to hold gatherings for entertainment purposes. No bingo, no swing dancing, and definitely no Boils. The inspectors gave Agnew a red-and-white-striped "Cease Work/Operations" sticker to affix to the Church's door and declared the concert over.

Agnew got on stage and told everyone to go home; his friends circulated through the crowd, whispering that the show was moving to West Philadelphia, to a theater called The Rotunda. Soon Agnew cut a deal to produce all his concerts there, but he was able to put on only one more show before the Department of Licenses and Inspections shut that operation down as well. Someone had gone down to City Hall, pulled the theater's permit, and discovered that it was zoned for drama only. Then inspectors visited the record shop where Agnew sold his tickets, with the news that someone had gone down to City Hall, pulled the shop's permit, and found out that it wasn't zoned for selling tickets. A few days later the inspectors were back at the shop, looking for a box under the counter in which the store kept Agnew's mail — another violation, reported by yet another concerned citizen.

Although he had no evidence, Agnew's suspicions fell on Clear Channel Communications. Clear Channel controls almost every concert venue in and around Philadelphia — from the Theater of the Living Arts on South Street to the Tweeter Center in Camden — as well as six radio stations and nearly 700 billboards. The company's local viceroy, a man named Larry Magid, once ran the city's live-music scene as a private fiefdom. Now, since Clear Channel bought him out in 2000, he manages it as a corporate franchise. Clear Channel maintains a similar chokehold on live music in almost every major city in America, as well as in most of the small ones. Agnew, who had managed to book bands that could have made far more money playing Clear Channel theaters, suspected that he was grit in the machine.

"Four or five years ago," Agnew told me one day in the record shop, where he also works as a clerk, "there were a lot more people aware of corporate power." Now, he said, money so dominated the music scene that a lot of younger kids didn't even know what "selling out" meant. When I asked him what had kept him in business, he corrected me: "I don't consider what I got into a 'business.'" Many Philadelphia music fans had rallied to his defense, he explained. After the closures, Agnew sent out word to his email list, 8,000 people who had attended at least one of his shows, and within days 1,000 of them had written to City Hall. He rented a paid mailbox. He persuaded a lawyer to represent the Church pro bono, and soon the Church had a dance-hall permit, the record shop had a ticket-selling permit, and Agnew had more events scheduled than before he was shut down.

Whoever was behind the attempt to close the Church, nearly every concertgoer I talked to blamed Clear Channel. They adored Agnew for "standing up to the evil empire," as one musician put it. Agnew, a vegetarian who lives with a cat and thousands of obsessively organized records, is now the most authentic rock and roller in the city. When he walks down the street, people nod and smile and pat him on the back. DJR500 is huge, and one day soon Clear Channel might make him an offer.

Some people complain about Clear Channel because they miss their old, independent stations, some because Clear Channel stations shrink playlists and recycle an ever smaller number of songs. Musicians say touring has become a cross-country hopscotch from one Clear Channel venue to another, each more sterile than the last; their agents and managers say that if artists don't play when and where Clear Channel says, they will suffer less airplay or none. As journalists point out, Clear Channel has made commercial radio nearly reporting-free, believing that its syndication of Rush Limbaugh to as many stations as possible fulfills its mandate to provide news and political diversity. Evangelical Christians are distressed about radio firsts pioneered by Clear Channel DJs, such as torturing and killing live animals on the air (a chicken in Denver, a pig in Florida), but this can happen only where there's a DJ: Clear Channel has put hundreds of radio veterans out of work, replacing them with canned broadcasts tailored to sound local and live. Consumer advocates argue that such robot radio is the only efficiency Clear Channel has passed along to the public. In the last several years, they point out, the cost of "free" radio — in terms of time spent enduring ads — has spiked. Concert tickets have jumped from an average of $25 to more than $40, and radio advertising rates have risen by two thirds, pricing small businesses off the airwaves.

Clear Channel says that its enemies snipe simply because it's big, and this is probably true. No one had imagined that a radio company could get so big. When Clear Channel was founded in 1972, with one station bought by a San Antonio investment banker named L. Lowry Mays, federal law forbade a company from owning more than seven FM stations and seven AMs. By the 1990s, that cap had crept up to forty stations nationwide, no more than two per market. Then, in 1996, Congress passed the Telecommunications Act. Up to eight stations per market would be allowed, and as many overall as a company could digest. Within less than a year more than 1,000 mergers occurred; by 2000 four behemoths dominated the business. Today, Clear Channel rules.

Z-100 in New York? Clear Channel. K-BIG in L.A.? Clear Channel. KISS in Chicago? Clear Channel.

Z-100 in New York? Clear Channel. K-BIG in L.A.? Clear Channel. KISS in Chicago? Clear Channel. KISS, POWER, the FOX, and the ZONE are all Clear Channel brands, and the dozens of radio stations nationwide that bear one of those names take their orders from San Antonio, where Clear Channel's headquarters remain, in an unassuming limestone box next to a golf course. Rush Limbaugh is Clear Channel, and so are Dr. Laura, Casey Kasem, and Glenn Beck, the rising star of rant radio who organized the "Rally for America" prowar demonstrations.

Last June, when the FCC raised the caps on how much access to the American public any one media company could control — a move too crassly reminiscent of the days of robber barons for even the Republican-controlled House of Representatives, which voted 400–21 to roll it back — the one media company the commission hinted might actually be too big was Clear Channel. The recent debate in Congress over television ownership has focused on two numbers: 35 percent, which is the portion of American viewers to which a single TV-station owner can currently broadcast, and 45 percent, which strikes media giants as a more reasonable number. Clear Channel, meanwhile, reaches roughly 200 million people, or more than 70 percent of the American public. It owns 1,225 stations within the United States, or around 11 percent overall, and greater portions in major markets. It broadcasts from at least 200 more stations abroad, many clustered just south of the border like radio maquiladoras, and it owns or controls more live-music venues than any other company. In the first six months of 2003, Clear Channel sold more tickets than the forty-nine next largest promoters combined; in 2001, it claimed 70 percent of the total live-music take. The billboards that ring the stadiums, line the highways, clutter the skyline? Clear Channel owns most of those too.

As a business enterprise, Clear Channel is an experiment. It is giant and potentially unstable, more reliant on muscle than on financial Anesse, and to date only moderately profitable. A sort of Frankenstein's monster, it was built from the parts of once-dying industries and jolted into life by the 1996 Telecommunications Act. Supporters of the law say there was no choice; at the time, more than half the stations in the country were losing money. Opponents retort that Clear Channel is hardly a democratic solution. "I don't think there was anybody in Washington in 1996 who could have imagined that a few years later there'd be one company owning 1,200 stations," says Michael Copps, one of the two commissioners on the FCC's five-person board who opposed raising ownership caps. "We should never give anybody the ability to have that much power."

When I asked to interview Clear Channel's executives, a P.R. rep for the company told me that Clear Channel wouldn't talk to me, because it no longer needs the media: a Zen koan of consolidation. After the company learned that several underlings had talked nevertheless, radio CEO John Hogan agreed to speak with me on the phone. An amiable, forty-six-year-old former radio-ad salesman, he told me that "the key to radio is that it's a very personal, intimate medium." Hogan's first executive role was as the general manager of WPCH, a fully automated station in Atlanta known as "the Peach." Hogan made running the station sound like changing a diaper. "It was a 'beautiful music' station," he said. "You didn't have to make any decisions, all you did was put the tape on in the morning and you let it run for twenty-four hours and then you changed it the next day. There were no decisions to make, they were made for you. It was nice, you know, it was easy."

His idea of what radio is and can be does not seem to have changed since his days at the Peach. "People use radio 'cause it works," he told me. "If it stops working for 'em, they stop it." The "they" he was referring to were the advertisers. "For the first time ever, we can talk to advertisers about a true national radio footprint," he told me. "If you have a younger, female-skewing advertiser who wants access to that audience, we can give them stations in, you know, Boston and New York and Miami and Chicago, literally across the country. Los Angeles, San Francisco . . . We can take outdoor [ads] and radio, and drive people to live events and concerts and capture the excitement, the real visceral experience." The goal? "A different kind of advertising opportunity."

Hogan was promoted to radio CEO just over a year ago. He has tried to soften the company's image after several years of brutal acquisitions under the leadership of Randy Michaels, the former disc jockey who now manages the company's new-technologies division. Clear Channel wouldn't let me talk with Michaels, but not long after he left the radio division he gave a trade publication called *Radio Ink* an even blunter rationale for the company's push to dominate live music as it does radio. "People attending a concert are experiencing something with tremendous emotion," he said. "They're . . . vulnerable."

Across town from the Church, in a little club called the Khyber Pass, I went to see a show booked by Clear Channel's man in Philadelphia. The headliner was a band called The Dragons, best known for their album *Rock Like Fuck*, but the night belonged to the opening act, the Riverboat Gamblers, or, rather, to their singer, Teko. Tall, skinny, gruesomely pretty, he vibrated across the two-foot-high stage, shouting loud and hard. No one was there to see the bands; the crowd, maybe a hundred strong, was there to get drunk, or to take someone home. But everyone in the room — a cigar box painted matte black from top to bottom, beer on the floor and loose wiring dangling from the ceiling — pressed forward, chins bobbing, drunken eyes widening. Near the end of a song called "Hey, Hey, Hey," Teko jumped and landed on the two-step riser at the front of the stage. It slid away, sent him crashing onto his spine. His left hand clutched the mike, into which he continued to scream; his right hand, flailing to its beat even faster, had begun to bleed at the palm. Then he jolted off the floor, bit the mike, and launched into another song: "I get the feelin' you're gonna need a feedin'! Let's eat! Let's eat! Let's eat!"

A few minutes later, Clear Channel's man jammed himself into the edge of the crowd, grinning and rocking his head as the singer leaped from the stage and drove into the audience, swinging his bloody hand like a wrecking ball. Clear Channel's man loved it. Bryan Dilworth was a big man with small eyes and a head of thinning red hair that brought to mind Curly of the Three Stooges. He was in what he called "that moment." He grinned and rocked his head; he stopped scanning the room and actually watched the band. He elbowed me, nodding toward the Riverboat Gamblers, as if to say, "See? See?"

When the song ended, Dilworth stepped back from the crowd, returned to the bar in the next room, and ordered another Jameson's.

"Dude," he said. "That is what I'm fucking talking about."

Meaning the scene, the variables, "the combustibles": everything he claimed Clear Channel could never buy. That included himself. At various times, Dilworth told me he worked for Clear Channel, or didn't work for Clear Channel, or Clear Channel simply didn't matter. Sometimes he called Clear Channel "the evil empire"; sometimes he said it was the best thing that ever happened to his town. It was hard to know which Dilworth to believe: the one who took me up to the cluttered office of his private company, Curt Flood, two stories above the Khyber Pass, to play me tracks from one of his bands on a cheap boom box; or the one who took me on a tour of a Clear Channel hall and conceded that the paychecks that mattered came from Clear Channel, that he had a Clear Channel email address and a Clear Channel phone number, that he was in truth a Clear Channel "talent buyer" responsible for filling the calendars of a dozen Clear Channel venues around the city. At times Dilworth spoke of Clear Channel Philadelphia in the first person. "I am living proof," he told me more than once, "that Clear Channel Philadelphia is going to rock."

This flexibility was what made Dilworth such a valuable asset. Unlike Starbucks or Borders, Clear Channel does not build its empire from new franchises but rather goes from town to town and buys local operations. Clear Channel has Dilworths in every city with a scene, and what makes them so effective is precisely that their affiliation with the company is subject to doubt, even in their own minds. Dilworth develops "baby bands" in clubs like the Khyber on his own time and filters the most marketable of them to the more lucrative venues he books as his alter ego, a Clear Channel talent buyer. Such a double role appears to be part of the Clear Channel business plan, in which the independents who should be an alternative to Clear Channel instead become the company's farm team. As a result, live music is following the route taken by radio. Songs that sound the same are performed in venues that look the same and even have the same name: identically branded venues, all controlled by Clear Channel, brick-and-mortar embodiments of KISS, the FOX, and the ZONE.

> *Songs that sound the same are performed in venues that look the same and even have the same name.*

"Everything is so fucked," said Dilworth, another shot of Jameson's at his lips. "Music business my ass. Take the 'music' off and that's what it is." He drank the shot, and then he was talking about the Riverboat Gamblers again: Those dudes got it, they're going places, and Dilworth would take them there, Clear Channel all the way. That's not monopoly, said Dilworth, it's business in America. "Deregulation set this table a long time ago. I'm not taking a 'can't beat 'em then join 'em' attitude, but . . ." He trailed off, because, of course, he was.

Dilworth's contradictory relationship with Clear Channel extended even into his home life. His wife, Kristin Thomson, worked for the Future of Music Coalition, the leading activist group against consolidation. FMC's head, Jenny Toomey, had been a prominent witness against raising ownership caps during last winter's Senate hearings, at which she laid out a specific and compelling case for how Clear Channel has become a near monopoly. Thomson and Toomey had once been minor rock stars together, as the indie group Tsunami, and Dilworth thought his marriage to Thomson was a simple instance of "rocker dude meets rocker chick." He said they didn't talk about politics. Dilworth himself had given lectures for FMC on the music business. ("Fuck the art," he had advised a conference of musicians. "Put the hit first.") Thomson, for her part, felt that her husband wasn't like the rest of Clear Channel.

One night, when Dilworth and I were in his office, he showed me his first gold record, awarded for a small role he had played in the success of the band Good Charlotte. A very small role, he said; gold records get passed around freely when a record company sees a future in a relationship.

"A down payment?" I said.

"Yeah, man, it's like, a favor for a favor."

"What's the difference between that and payola?"

Dilworth guffawed and looked at me like I was the dumbest kid in school. "It's all payola, dude." Then his shoulders slumped and he stopped laughing.

What determines the course of music today is not a zeitgeist or a paradigm or anything that can be dismissed simply as fashion. It's not even greed. What matters now is the process. "Cross-selling." "Clustering." A confluence of car radios and concert halls, the drinks at the bar, the ticket that gets you in the door, the beat you dance to. "Anything you can do to be associated with the music, you try to do," a Clear Channel executive with forty years in radio told me. This is not entirely sinister, nor is it especially new. The music business, in its varied forms, has always depended on symbiosis. Clear Channel wants you to identify with the brand so fully that you don't recognize it as a brand at all but rather as yourself. The executive gave me an example. "Suppose you like Dave Matthews," he said. "We like Dave Matthews. We have Dave Matthews together."

To achieve this mind-meld, Clear Channel has designed itself as a self-contained, nationwide feedback loop, calibrating the tastes of its listeners and segmenting them into market-proven "formats." Today, Clear Channel operates in thirteen major music formats, and although some of these formats are nearly indistinguishable, they are nevertheless finely tuned: for example, listeners can choose between "AC" (Adult Contemporary) and "Hot AC," or among "CHR" (Contemporary Hits Radio), "CHR Pop," and "CHR Rhythmic." John Hogan, the radio division's CEO, boasted that in 2003 the company would make more than 2 million phone calls to survey its listeners, a process that would produce "around 10,000 local-audience research reports."

As these reports are generated, the company can respond rapidly. "If we have a CHR PD" — program director — "in, you know, Dayton, Ohio, who figures out a great way to package up a bit, or a great promotion, or comes up with something clever and innovative, we can almost instantaneously make it available to CHR radio stations across the country." (At the time of our interview, Clear Channel owned eighty-nine CHRs.) Then, for a given advertiser, the company can align all its CHRs to hit one "formatic target" — a demographic. Hogan suggested teenage girls. "A great advertiser would be the Crest Whitestrips. In the past, if Crest had wanted to use radio, they would have had to call a different owner in every market. There would have been no way to link together those stations with, you know, a common theme, or a common execution."

Such harmony extends to the company's concert business as well. "There's a lot of conference calling between cities," a booking agent named Tim Borror told me, "these former independents talking to one another, letting each other know what's going on." Another independent booking agent and a Clear Channel talent buyer, neither of whom would allow themselves to be named, confirmed this practice, adding that such calls take place almost on a weekly basis. The calls can launch a band or flatten it. "At a certain point, there's only one place to go — Clear Channel — and it doesn't matter whether or not they make you a fair offer," Borror said. "And pretty soon, they don't have to make you a fair offer. And they can decide what band is playing and what band isn't."

I asked John Hogan why I should believe that Clear Channel would never use its combined dominance of radio and live events to punish an artist — or a politician — who did not cooperate with the company. "I can't imagine a scenario where it would make any business sense at all," he replied. To use the power, he said, "would be to damage it." David T. "Boche" Viecelli, another booking agent, told me: "The thing people fear — legitimately fear — is that they're going to implement the threats they've intimated with radio airplay. It's not explicit. More often it's insinuation and innuendo."

> **Clear Channel is a system so pervasive that it relieves its participants — consumers, bands, employees, even executives — of the responsibility to object.**

Clear Channel doesn't have to actively be "the evil empire," because everyone knows that it could be. With so much of music and entertainment determined by, produced by, broadcast by, measured by, and defined by Clear Channel, the company need not exercise its control in order to wield it. Clear Channel is a system so pervasive that it relieves its participants — consumers, bands, employees, even executives — of the responsibility to object, and the ability to imagine why they would ever do so.

In Denver, Clear Channel owns half the rock stations on the dial, as well as the region's number-one station, the news/talk KOA. It owns the Fillmore, co-owns the Universal Lending Pavilion, controls the rights to the Pepsi Center, and in 2001 pried a sweetheart deal out of the city for booking shows at the legendary Red Rocks Amphitheatre, carved out of the stone of the Rocky Mountain foothills — as much of a temple as pop music can claim.

I went to Denver to meet Jesse Morreale, an independent promoter who is suing Clear Channel. Morreale is one of the biggest independents in the country, but he is also one of the last. He persuaded one of the so-called Big Four law firms in Denver to represent him, but even if they can prove that Clear Channel Radio and Clear Channel Entertainment work together to shut out other promoters and threaten artists who work with them, there's a good chance his company, Nobody in Particular Presents, will be out of business by the time the case reaches any kind of conclusion. For now, Morreale has been silenced; Clear Channel won a protective order from the court, and although Morreale was happy to complain, he could not give me particulars.

Nor would the minor rock stars who came through town while I was there. The leather-clad lead singer of Cradle of Filth, a death-metal band from England, assured me that he would "never" say anything against Clear Channel. A punk-pop threesome called the Raveonettes at first said they hadn't heard of Clear Channel, then admitted that they had, then offered me a beer and asked if we couldn't please instead talk about rock-and-roll music. A record-company agent clinked shots with me and said, "Rock 'n roll!" but when Morreale told him I was writing about Clear Channel, he asked for my notes. "I'm going to need those," he said, trying to sound official. I would have said no, but since all I had written down was "Fred Durst," and the guy looked like he might cry, I tore the page out and gave it to him.

The next morning, I was driving around Denver listening to the radio when I heard a prerecorded spoof ad for "Butt Pirates of the Caribbean." It consisted mainly of the DJ reading, in a sneering lisp, a list of actors he considered "homo." Which is to say, it was nothing unusual. I had been listening to Clear Channel radio all over the country and had found that gay jokes ran second only to "camel jockey" or "towel head" humor. Such slurs, I began to think, were simply the comedic equivalent of the mannered rock "rebellion" in the musical rotation. Like the knee-jerk distortion of a Limp Bizkit song, the fag gags of the local morning crew are there to assure listeners that someone, somewhere, is being offended by what they are pretending to enjoy.

Back at my hotel, I called the local Clear Channel headquarters and asked for the man in charge. I was surprised to get a call back from Clear Channel's regional vice president, Lee Larsen, who invited me out to see him that very morning.

Larsen, who looked to be in his mid-fifties, was not a formal man. He put his loafers up on the coffee table between us and his arms behind his head and told me to fire away: he loved to talk about radio. Larsen wore his sandy hair in a modest pompadour, and although he had some girth on him, his tall frame and thick shoulders made him look like a linebacker. He started on the air forty years ago but made his career as a manager. On a pedestal near the center of his office sat an antique wooden radio, flanked by Broncos helmets facing inward. When I asked him what he listened to, he replied with a long and diverse list of stations — none of them Clear Channel — that marked him as a man of broad but refined tastes. Nevertheless, he was a staunch believer in Giving the People What They Want. "This whole society," he said, "is based on majority rules." There is no such thing, he said, as "lowest common denominator"; there is only democracy, and in the music world Clear Channel is its biggest purveyor. The best thing about democracy, which he likened to a pizza, is that there is so much of it. "If I take one slice of the audience, and it's the biggest slice, and it's the 'lowest common denominator' slice, whatever you want to call it, guess what? There's lots of slices for the other guy." As evidence of this bounty, he gestured over his shoulder. At first I thought he wanted me to look at the view of the Rockies behind him, but it turned out he was thinking of the franchise-lined highways I'd driven to get there. "Who'd have thought there could be so many different fast-food restaurants as there are?"

There were those among us, he said, who would complain nonetheless. People "at odds with the masses." People who believe that "the mass in our country are stupid." People who would tell you that you "should read *Atlantic Monthly*, not *Time*." But that was all right. "You can have anything you want," he said. "You just can't have what you want everywhere." He smiled. "Some people don't like that." He leaned forward and patted the coffee table, a little gesture to let me know that he knew that I knew what he was talking about, that I was, with him, part of "the mass."

I asked him about "Butt Pirates of the Caribbean." He reared back and looked at me like I was Tipper Gore. In a gentle, rumbling tone, he asked, "What are you saying? That it should not have been on?"

"Well . . . ," I said, "switch 'Butt Pirates of the Caribbean' for something like, say, 'Jigaboos of Jamaica,' and I think you can see what I mean."

Larsen frowned. "I know clearly that you couldn't do a bit like that, that's ethnic. I know that, okay? Maybe, in the area you're talking about, that might still be open. Society's still trying to figure out the line there. If you took that bit and put it on a classical-music radio station and played it, well the people would be outraged. It's out of context." But there was a time and place for such things. "If every radio station was doing 'Butt Pirates,' then you would be saying, 'Well, what is this?' But they are not." At the station I had heard it on, he explained, "the talent must have felt that was within the bounds they could work within, and was something that the audience that was listening to their radio station could relate to."

I must have looked unconvinced, because Larsen seemed worried. "On the radio," he said, "the red light's on and you're talking. And you say something. Just like you do in real life. And you go" — he shaped his lips into an O and let his eyes bulge as he covered his mouth — "I. Wish. I. Hadn't. Said. That." He shrugged his shoulders, held up his palms in a "what can you do?" gesture. "But it's too late."

From Denver, I went to Oklahoma City to meet with former congressman Julius Caesar "J. C." Watts, who had recently been named to Clear Channel's board of directors. During the hour and a half we spent driving around and listening to the radio in his shiny new black Cadillac Escalade, the congressman referred to Americans as "dogs" five times. Not in the slang sense — Watts loathes what he calls that "hip-hop bebop rap" stuff — but in the idiom of business. He was trying to get at what business is all about. He wasn't concerned about Clear Channel's overwhelming control of live music, he said, because "the dogs are eating the dog food." He said that the reason talk radio is so conservative is that "the dogs ain't eating the dog food" offered by liberals: "You can't force bad dog food on people!"

A former football star for the Sooners and a Southern Baptist preacher at a church called Sunnylane, Watts has an easy manner that can nevertheless be disconcerting, as when he took both hands off the wheel at 75 miles an hour, turned, and gripped my arm, saying, "I'm ready to go to the American people with my dog food." Then he found a song he seemed to like, "Get Busy," by Sean Paul, and turned it up. It was hip-hop, but it did have a spiritual message: "From the day we born Jah ignite me flame/Gal a call me name and it is me fame/It's all good girl turn me on/Till the early morn'/Let's get it on."

The former fourth-ranking Republican in the House, Watts may be out of office at the moment (he chose not to run last year), but at age forty-five he still wields considerable power as chair of GOPAC, an organization designed to develop Republican candidates at the state level, and as the G.O.P.'s great black hope. When President Bush made his recent tour of Africa, he tapped Watts as a traveling companion. When Democratic fixer Vernon Jordan retired from Clear Channel's board, he pushed Watts, a man who considers LBJ to have been a "wild-eyed radical," as his replacement.

But I don't think Watts's connections — or his politics — are why he "aligns nicely," as Clear Channel CEO Lowry Mays put it, with the company. Rather, I suspect it has something to do with his mix of aggressive amiability and angry defensiveness. Watts often gets called an "Uncle Tom"; Clear Channel's radio and concert guys are sick of being called "sellouts." Watts thinks it's unfair that as a black man he should have to defend himself for also being a Republican; Clear Channel can't understand why people seem shocked when it competes as fiercely as it does. Both Watts and Clear Channel look at what they're doing as revolutionary, unsentimental, necessary. Watts thinks Clear Channel simply needs to do a better job of telling the American people — the dogs — what the company is.

We pulled into the parking lot of a motel next to a Denny's. Watts said, "In politics or in business, you're either on the offense or you're on the defense. If you're on the defense, you're losing." Clear Channel, he explained, had to hit back, and hard. "Jeff, I think today that people are concerned with" — he reached out and banged the dashboard speakers of his Escalade — "this. They don't care where it's coming from!" Then he turned the radio on again and tuned it to his daughter's favorite station and cranked it up. "Get Busy," by Sean Paul.

"Same song!" Watts shouted. "Thirty minutes ago! I couldn't have planned that in a thousand years!" To Watts, this was a good thing.

He said Clear Channel needed a great slogan, like Fox's "Fair and Balanced."

"You mean," I said, "something like 'Clear Channel: We Give You What You Want.'"

"Yeah!" Watts slapped my shoulder. "Yeah! Or maybe . . ." He paused to think, then held up his hands to frame his idea. "Clear Channel, Your Community, you know, Involvement, you know, Network, or, or Station, or Whatever . . ." An enemy says, 'Jeff, I don't want you to have what you have. You know, I'm gonna be a self-righteous income distributor. And I'm gonna balance this thing out.'" (Watts believes in balance, so long as it isn't, as he put it, "Communist," which, presumably, pre-1996 radio in America was.) "'And I'm gonna take from all those who're producing and give to those that aren't producing.'" He shook his head. "Uh-uh. When we get to the point where people are envious and we say, 'We're not gonna allow [consolidation] to happen'" — Watts clapped a hand over mine and shuddered — "that is a fiendish business."

Regulation of radio ownership — Watts's fiendish business — is rooted in the idea that the spectrum is a national resource, but as a reality the "public airwaves" are close to extinct. Even proponents of regulation now fight for it, perversely, in the language of business, touting ownership caps as a means to preserve the "marketplace of ideas." This phrase, or even the "free market of ideas," has become a rhetorical fixture of anti-consolidation activists, for whom it connotes a free and fair system by which ideas compete for the minds of the citizenry. Implicit in the phrase is that ideas compete in roughly the same manner as do brands of soap; that, given equal price and placement, the most effective ideas will win the day. By owning so many stations, the argument goes, Clear Channel reduces the number of songs, sounds, formats, and opinions from which American listeners can choose.

> **As a reality the "public airwaves" are close to extinct.**

But to so frame the argument is already to have lost. Media corporations want nothing more than to create new, popular formats with which to segment their audiences on advertisers' behalf. As advocates of deregulation never tire of pointing out, the "diversity" of U.S. radio content — in terms of average number of different formats available in each market — has increased with consolidation since 1996, not decreased. In fact, nothing resembles a "free market of ideas" so much as Clear Channel itself, where infinitesimal changes in ratings are tracked, mapped, and responded to; where Boston's successful new format can appear in San Diego overnight. This is what Lee Larsen means when he speaks of giving the people what they want. It is what J. C. Watts was trying to express when he jabbed the tuner on his radio and shouted, "This is democracy!" Clear Channel is a supermarket of ideas, which sells scores of different products all made in the same factory.

Activists fret that Clear Channel is foisting a right-wing agenda onto its listeners. To the contrary, the company seems to advance no ideology whatsoever; nor does it seem to advance any aesthetic that could be called good, bad, ugly, or beautiful. Perhaps the most instructive example here is the controversy over what has come to be called The List: the roster of songs that, immediately after September 11, were not supposed to be played on Clear Channel stations. The List's recommendations ranged from the obvious (AC/DC's "Shot Down in Flames") to the saccharine (Billy Joel's "Only the Good Die Young") to the grotesque (Van Halen's "Jump") to the unexpectedly poetic (Phil Collins's otherwise unremarkable "In the Air Tonight"). Antiwar activists pointed out that The List "banned" Cat Stevens's "Peace Train" and John Lennon's "Imagine," but ignored the fact that The List also proscribed Judas Priest's "Some Heads Are Gonna Roll" and the Clash's "Rock the Casbah," said to have been popular with U.S. pilots on bombing runs over Iraq during the first Gulf War.

Everyone seemed to see The List as the ultimate case of censorship by a corporate head office, but in fact The List came together just as might a great promotion by John Hogan's hypothetical program director in Dayton, Ohio. On his or her own initiative (nobody knows for certain where, or with whom, The List started), a Clear Channel PD drew up a list of songs; this PD emailed The List to a PD at another station, and he or she added more songs, and so on. When, eventually, The List was leaked to the press, Clear Channel pointed out that it was the work of independent program directors who were free to play — or not to play — whatever songs they liked.

Confusing The List for ideological censorship reflects a fundamental misunderstanding of the meaning of Clear Channel. It reflects the misguided notion that the company means anything at all. All the Clear Channel talent buyers, "on air personalities," news directors, and executives I spoke with shared a basic disregard for both the content of the product and its quality. The market would take care of those. Clear Channel's functionaries seemed to view the company as some marvelous but unfathomable machine with whose upkeep they had been charged. They knew only that it accomplished a miraculous task — satisfying the musical tastes of most of the people — and did not care to trouble themselves with how.

Bryan Dilworth swore to me he had nothing to do with Sean Agnew's show at the Church getting shut down. He said that any suggestion to the contrary was "Davy and Goliath bullshit." He claimed he walked into his boss's office and asked them if they had been involved. He told them he needed to know, because he would quit if they had. They swore innocence. I tried to confirm his story, but his bosses never returned my calls.

One Sunday I met Dilworth at his home in South Philly. His wife needed a nap, so we took his ten-month-old for a ride in his stroller. We walked through the Italian market, dead quiet at six on a Sunday evening, empty wooden stalls fronting pork shops and bakeries. We stopped to watch a group of boys on skateboards work a ramp they had set up in the street, performing for a video camera one of the kids was holding. Dilworth laughed. "The dudes who own those stores knew these kids were out here, skating on their stalls like that? They'd break their legs." This delighted him, all of it: the men who owned the stores who wouldn't give a damn for the law, the kids who took over the street who didn't give a damn for the owners. "This place is totally . . . this place," he said.

I asked him how that squared with his working for Clear Channel, which seemed dedicated to making every place the same. Dilworth didn't look at me but he smiled. His grin pushed his baby-fat cheeks up and made his eyes small.

"All of a sudden I'm supposed to be super-evil?" he said. "FUCK THAT."

"No, that's not what I meant," I said.

"FUCK THAT. I just wanted to make money doing something I liked. There are different opinions about how far down the road America is businesswise, but dude, whatever, it's too far gone for anything to change."

He bumped the stroller up over a curb, and the baby began to cry. We walked without talking for a few blocks, the clackety-clack of skateboard wheels fading behind us. But closer to home, both he and the baby mellowed. Dilworth stopped smiling, and his eyes stopped squinting.

"Then," he said, "there's that feeling in your spine, and it's all right." His voice went up in pitch and grew soft, as if he were embarrassed. He was talking about rock. "When the arc is just starting to arc? And you're saying this could be Van Halen, this could be Neil Young. It's like you're bearing witness. It's not, 'Ching-ching, here we go.' It's 'I saw it. It does exist.' There's something really there. It's not just a need for chaos. It's — yeah. That's what I want." His voice deepened again, and his pace evened out. The baby had nodded off. We stopped in front of Dilworth's stoop. "Clear Channel?" he said. "That's money. I need it to buy liquor and baby clothes."

DISCUSSION

1. In a few short sentences, Sharlet captures the true scope of Clear Channel's influence over the contemporary radio scene: "Z-100 in New York? Clear Channel. K-BIG in L.A.? Clear Channel. KISS in Chicago? Clear Channel." How do you react to a list like this? What vision of the public airwaves does it give you? And in your opinion, is there any downside to an arrangement in which radio stations across the country are owned and controlled by the same company?

2. "With so much of music and entertainment determined by, produced by, broadcast by, measured by, and defined by Clear Channel," writes Sharlet, "the company need not exercise its control in order to wield it. Clear Channel is a system so pervasive that it relieves its participants — consumers, bands, employees, even executives — of the responsibility to object, and the ability to imagine why they would ever do so." How would you assess the value, the helpfulness, of this sort of "relief"? Is it, in your view, a good thing for this attitude toward "objecting" to have become the norm?

3. Much of the Clear Channel's promotional language revolves around the cherished ideal of consumer choice. What kind of choice do you think a company like Clear Channel offers? What amount of variety? What degree of freedom?

WRITING

4. Write an essay in which you analyze the central conflicts in Sharlet's piece. What are the primary criticisms of Clear Channel, and why? How does Clear Channel argue against these criticisms? Ultimately, which side of the argument do you favor, and why?

5. On page 635, Sharlet discusses the ways that Clear Channel has divided the music market into formats. Write an essay in which you analyze these formats, proposing what type of music (artists, songs, and so on) might fit into them and what sort of listeners these formats might attract. What benefits or downfalls do you see in defining the music market this way? In your opinion, is this division of the music market appealing or arbitrary? Why?

6. "Clear Channel," writes Sharlet, "wants you to identify with the brand so fully that you don't recognize it as a brand at all but rather as yourself." What do you think he means by this? As a company, how do you think Clear Channel goes about obscuring itself as a brand? How do you respond to this as a corporate strategy?

'ect Voice

What is the relationship between our voice and our identity? While it may feel most natural to think of our voices as a immutable marker of who we are, the truth, as Carl Elliott points out, is that our voices are subject to a striking array of different kinds of change: from elocution training to regional accents, from vocal training to surgery. The factors or options we confront when it comes to how to talk raise thorny questions about what — when it comes to how we talk — constitutes evidence of the "real us." Carl Elliott teaches philosophy and bioethics at the University of Minnesota. He has published three books on the ethics of medical technologies: *Rules of Insanity: Moral Responsibility and the Mentally Ill Offender* (1996), *Philosophical Disease: Bioethics, Culture, and Identity* (1999), and *Better than Well: American Medicine Meets the American Dream* (2003), from which this selection is taken. He has also edited several collections of writing about medicine and ethics. Elliott completed a BS at Davidson College, an MD at the Medical University of South Carolina, and a PhD in Philosophy at the University of Glasgow in Scotland.

God talks like we do. — Lewis Grizzard, *Atlanta Journal-Constitution*

IN 1985, THE ENGLISH PHYSICIST STEPHEN HAWKING LOST HIS VOICE. Hawking suffers from amyotrophic lateral sclerosis, or ALS, a degenerative neurological illness. Over the years Hawking's illness had left his voice increasingly slurred and difficult to understand, but it was not until an episode of pneumonia forced him to have a tracheostomy that Hawking lost his voice completely. After the tracheostomy, Hawking could not speak at all. He could communicate only by raising his eyebrows when someone pointed to the correct letter on a spelling card.

Several years later, a computer specialist from California sent him a computer program called Equalizer. Equalizer allowed Hawking to select words from a series of menus on a computer screen by pressing a switch, or by moving his head or eyes. A voice synthesizer then transformed the words into speech. The computer was a vast improvement on the spelling card system, and for the most part, Hawking was also pleased with the voice synthesizer. "The only trouble," he wrote in a 1993 essay, "is that it gives me an American accent." Yet Hawking then went on to say that after years of using the voice synthesizer the American voice came to feel like his own. He started to identify with that voice, and feel as if it were really his. "I would not want to change even if I were offered a British-sounding voice," Hawking wrote. "I would feel I had become a different person."[1]

The anthropologist Gregory Bateson used to ask his graduate students if a blind man's cane is part of the man.[2] Most students would say no, that the limits of a person stop at his skin. But if Hawking is right, then the answer may be more complicated. For despite the fact that Hawking's "voice" was computer-synthesized, despite the fact that it came from a set of audio speakers rather than from his mouth, despite the fact that the synthesized voice sounded mechanical, robotic, and worse still, American, Hawking eventually came to feel that it was *his* voice. Hawking's identity, at least in his view, does not stop at the boundaries of his skin.

How exactly is a voice related to an identity? Many of us feel as if our voices are, in some vague and undefined way, *our* voices, an immutable part of who we are, but in fact our voices are changing all the time. The voice of a person at five years of age will sound different from the voice of the same person at age forty-five, and her voice will sound different again at age seventy-five. An Alabaman living in North Dakota probably will not speak with the same accent that he speaks with back in Tuscaloosa. A black American may sound different when speaking to other black Americans at home or at church than she does when speaking to white Americans at the office. Our voices even sound noticeably different to us from the inside, first-person standpoint than they sound to other people. For many of us, it still comes as a mild shock to hear our own voices on tape.

Hawking's remarks about his voice synthesizer reflect two tensions in modern identity that run through many debates over enhancement technologies. The first is a tension between the natural and the artificial, or more broadly, between what is *given* and what is *created*. The reason it initially sounds jarring to hear Hawking say he identifies so closely with a computer-generated voice is precisely because it has been generated by a computer, rather than by nature itself. Yet the fact that Hawking does identify with the computer-generated voice reflects something of the flexibility of modern identity. It is not uncommon these days for people to say they feel more like themselves while taking Prozac or typing in an online chat room, or that it was only after undergoing cosmetic surgery or taking anabolic steroids that their bodies began to look the way they were meant to look. Statements like these sound odd (and merit a deeper look) precisely because they confound what we expect to hear. We may expect to hear that an artificial technology makes a person feel *better* about herself, but we don't usually expect to hear that it makes her feel more *like* herself.

Related to this tension between the given and the created is a second tension, between the self as it feels from the inside and the self as it is presented to others. Most modern Westerners have some sense that there is a gap between self and self-presentation — between the self that sits alone in a room, thinking, and the self that hops up on stage to crack jokes and take questions from the audience. We also tend to think that the true self is the one that sits alone, a solitary self that endures over time, while the on-stage self is a mere persona, a type of useful role-playing that can be used or discarded as circumstances demand. But when Hawking the Englishman says he identifies with his American accent, and would feel like a different person with a British-sounding voice, he closes this gap between self and self-presentation. An accent is not a part of the self that sits silently in a room. It is a part of the self that is presented to others. By identifying so closely with his accent, Hawking is identifying less with his solitary self than with his self-presentation. This makes the gap between the two somewhat questionable.

> **An accent is not a part of the self that sits silently in a room. It is a part of the self that is presented to others.**

The voice is a good place to start thinking about identity, because many of us don't even think about our voices until we are made self-conscious about them. Those occasions of self-consciousness usually come when our identities are in flux or subject to challenge. If I am an adolescent boy, I will become self-conscious when my voice begins to deepen and crack. If I move to England, I will become self-conscious when the natives roll their eyes at my American accent. If I get sex-reassignment surgery and become a woman, I will become self-conscious when I still sound like a man. My voice is always distinctly *my* voice, but often I will not think of it as such until someone calls attention to my identity.

If you were listening to me speak these words, you would hear them spoken with a noticeable southern drawl. Some people might call it a twang, though I myself prefer the more flattering term "lilt," which was the term Lilli Ambro used when she heard me speak. Ambro runs an "accent-reduction clinic" in Greensboro, North Carolina called The Perfect Voice. Clients of The Perfect Voice come to Ambro for help in learning how to diminish, change, or erase their Southern accents. A speech pathologist by training, with a background in professional singing, Ambro is a southerner herself — a North Carolinian, educated at one of the very cradles of southern womanhood, Salem College. In fact, she speaks with more than a trace of a southern accent herself.

I had gotten in touch with Lilli Ambro after coming across a shelf of cassette tapes in a Berkeley bookshop aimed at helping recent Asian immigrants to the United States overcome their foreign accents. I had just spent several days with a research group talking about whether enhancement technologies were a form of liberation or self-betrayal, whether Prozac and sex-reassignment surgery help people change themselves or help them discover who they really are. Seeing these cassettes displayed in the bookshop, after walking out of the research meeting, the thought struck me that the purpose of an accent change is not really so different from many of the enhancement technologies we had been discussing. That thought eventually led me to The Perfect Voice, one of a number of accent-reduction clinics springing up throughout the South.[3]

Southerners have a complicated relationship with their accents, a complex mixture of pride and shame and fierce defensiveness. It's like a little brother who is a drunk or maybe a little crazy and therefore somewhat embarrassing — you are always shaking your head when his name is mentioned — but you can't really disown him because, well, damn it, he *is* family. Most southerners, when they talk to Yankees, will defend a southern accent as the most beautiful and melodic of all American accents, but deep down we are not really convinced this is true. Many of us modify our speech, often unconsciously, when we are around outsiders, and talk more southern in the company of one another. Some of us even learn to speak Yankee at work or when we are visiting up North. Many of us wish not so much to get rid of our southern accents as to get a *better* one, an accent that evokes a genteel, mythical old South rather than, say, *The Beverly Hillbillies*. Nobody explicitly teaches us this, but we somehow absorb the lesson that north of the Mason-Dixon line a southern accent generally codes for stupidity or simplemindedness. You can watch only so many movies and television shows featuring big-bellied southern sheriffs, sweaty fundamentalist preachers, and shotgun-carrying rednecks before the message sinks in. We learn early on that in certain settings, like universities, a southern accent needs to be moderated, if not effaced, or else you will not be taken seriously.

When I was growing up in Clover, our small corner of South Carolina, it would occasionally happen that someone in town would accomplish something worthy of attention from the local television news stations. The high school football team would make it to the upper state championships. A local preacher would accidentally burn down a church. Once, I remember, state law enforcement authorities staged an undercover sting operation and caught a local policeman stealing chocolate Easter eggs and frozen steaks from the grocery store. When these newsworthy events occurred, teams of television news reporters would make the trip down I-77 from Charlotte to investigate. Our moment of fame. In anticipation, we would all sit around the television and look at Clover through the lens of the television camera.

It was always a little embarrassing. The reporter would ask someone from Clover a question on camera, the Cloverite would answer, and my parents would immediately groan and shake their heads. "Why do they always pick these kinds of people to be on TV?" my father would say. "They sound like such hicks." It was true. They did sound like hicks. They would draw out their words in a country twang. They would say *insur-ance*, with the emphasis on the first syllable. *Greenville* became *Grainville*. *Here* became *hair* and *hair* became *hay-ur*. They sounded like one of those guys with overalls and a banjo on *Hee Haw*. Yet we never noticed this until we saw these people on television. Had we come across the very same people in the barbershop or the public library or in church, it would never have occurred to us that they had an accent. To be honest, their accents were probably no different from ours.

What interested me about this was the way the distinctiveness of our local accent was hidden from us until we pulled back and saw it — or rather listened to it — from the position of someone else. It was only by watching television, looking through the lens of the camera, that we were able to see what we ordinarily took for granted. What was most obvious to a television viewer, of course, was the way the local accents compared to the other ones on TV, which are all non-southern (that is to say, Yankee) accents. The television news reporters may well have been southerners themselves, but even southerners talk like Yankees when they are on TV. It is an unspoken convention: if you are on TV you talk like a Yankee. Everyone does. If you don't, you sound like a hick.

> **It is an unspoken convention: if you are on TV you talk like a Yankee. Everyone does. If you don't, you sound like a hick.**

Lilli Ambro told me that most of her clients at The Perfect Voice are people who have to do a lot of public speaking, like actors or certain kinds of businesspeople. One was, unsurprisingly, a television news reporter. Another was an aspiring actress whose acting coaches had advised her that to have a successful career she would need to be able to switch her southern accent on and off. All were southerners except one. The exception was a man from Pennsylvania running for local public office who wanted to reduce his northern accent in order to improve his chances for election. (This knife cuts both ways. In the South, a northern accent codes for arrogance and bad manners.) Most (though not all) of her clients were white. It goes without saying, perhaps, that most of these clients felt they needed to change their accents in order to succeed at work, and felt strongly enough about it that they were willing to pay $45/hour to undergo a successful "dialect change."

What sort of accents were these people trying to change? In her book on cosmetic surgery, sociologist Kathy Davis notes how difficult it was for her, as an outside observer, to guess exactly what feature of themselves the potential clients wanted cosmetic surgery for — that many of the women who wanted nose jobs did not have obviously large or misshapen noses, or that many of those who wanted breast reductions did not have obviously large or asymmetrical breasts. The "defects" that bothered them so much seemed to be exaggerated in their own eyes.[4] So I wondered aloud to Ambro whether there was a parallel in her work — whether it was ever difficult for an outsider to see exactly why these people wanted their accents changed. "No," she replied immediately; it was not hard to see why these people wanted to change. They all had very "strong" southern accents, she said. When I pressed her on what she meant by this, it became clear that most of her clients sounded like country folks or hillbillies. They were worried not so much about sounding southern as about sounding like hicks. Which made sense: this was the South, after all, where most people talk with southern accents. The worry in the South is not to get rid of your accent, like an expatriate southerner trying to pass in the North, but rather to transform it to a better one (which generally means something closer to what Ambro calls a "standardized American" accent). Ambro told me that she does not generally get clients who want to rid themselves of a Tidewater Virginia accent, say, or an old Charleston accent, or any of the accents that sound especially well bred to southern ears. Yet she did admit that she occasionally tried to convince some of her clients that accents that sounded objectionable to their own ears were actually quite lovely.

I have to confess that when I called Lilli Ambro, I was skeptical about the notion of accent-reduction clinics, notwithstanding Ms. Ambro's good intentions and her charming manners. Expatriate southerners like me are likely to worry excessively that distinctive features of the South are going to disappear; that in a vast consumerist sea, an age of generic TV news anchors speaking standardized American, southern accents will go the way of the corner barber shop and the porch swing. (Or, possibly even worse, that a southern accent will become a curiosity piece to be marketed to Yankees, like small-batch bourbon and alligator farms.) But what worried me most was the sense that by trying to change your accent, you are rejecting something of who you are. Unlike a Chinese or Cuban immigrant who speaks English with an accent, we southerners are raised to speak the way we do. It is our mother tongue. It is the first thing that non-southerners notice about us when we open our mouths. To try to speak like a northerner, quite honestly, strikes me as phoniness — perhaps necessary phoniness on occasion, and a kind of phoniness to which we are all prone, but phoniness nonetheless. This is also what rubs me the wrong way about some enhancement technologies especially those designed to efface markers of ethnicity. They look pretty close to fakery.

I once had a colleague at McGill University who spoke with a perfect upper-class English accent. It was only when I asked him what part of England he was from that I found out he was born and raised in Ontario.

He had spent a couple of years at Oxford as a student many decades previously. Apparently he had adopted an English accent while he was there, and had hung onto it ever since. I can't remember ever having met a southerner who would affect an Oxford accent (where I come from, Oxford is a town in Mississippi), or who would even feel inclined to try, but many southerners do try to talk standardized American, or what they think is standardized American, saying "you" instead of "y'all" and articulating their words very carefully. In the United Kingdom, the BBC has made a nod toward acknowledging the legitimacy of regional accents by occasionally substituting Scots-, Irish-, and Welsh-accented newsreaders for the traditional Englishmen. But in the United States, the newsreaders all speak as if they come from nowhere — which to a southern ear, usually sounds like somewhere up North. (A Tennessean I once met in Chicago told me that all Americans should hang on to their native accents or else we would all sound like we come from Indi-goddamn-ana.)

The newspaper piece that led me to The Perfect Voice was written for the *Greensboro News and Record* by a reporter with the southern-accented name of Parker Lee Nash. She is a self-described "southern girl, raised by bootleggers and Baptists," and her attitude toward The Perfect Voice could probably be best described as ironic and gently mocking. (She writes that to talk like a Yankee, you have to "open your mouth big and wide and relax your tongue so it flops up and down like a dog lapping water.") What interested me most about her article was the lighthearted remark she concluded with. After spending a day in accent-reduction classes, learning things like how to say "ham" in such a way that it does not contain two syllables, she concluded, "All the accent reduction classes in America can't take the Southern out of me. Thank the Lord."[5]

Implicit in that offhand remark, it seemed to me, was both the worry about an accent change — Am I trying to change who I am? — and the reassurance that this worry is misplaced ("No, being southern is about more than having a southern accent"). And so I began to wonder whether clients at an accent-reduction clinic had any mixed feelings about their change — whether they felt that putting on an accent was artificial, or a betrayal of their heritage.

When I put this question to Lilli Ambro, she proceeded (as southerners are inclined to do) to tell me a story. She once had a client who was a preacher. Or more precisely, he was a sort of junior preacher, an assistant to a more senior pastor in a local church. She wasn't sure what denomination, but it wasn't Presbyterian or Episcopalian — more likely it was Baptist, or some poor relation. This preacher was from out in the country and he had an appropriately countrified accent. His senior minister had told him that he needed to work on the way he spoke, or else the congregation wouldn't take him seriously. Hence his visit to The Perfect Voice. Interestingly enough, he did not last any longer than a lesson or two. The reason, he said, was because he felt that the accent-reduction classes were changing his personality. (Almost as an afterthought, Ambro added, "He never did pay his bill.")

As odd as this preacher's reaction initially sounded to me, I think I can understand it. To paraphrase Kurt Vonnegut, if you pretend for long enough, you may become what you are pretending to be. Yet when I mentioned the story to a colleague from the North, a philosopher at an Ivy League university, he was puzzled by the thought that anyone could feel that his identity was bound up in anything as trivial and incidental as an accent. Southerners, of course, usually understand the connection between accent and identity right away. So does anyone from the United Kingdom, where accent is a very public marker of social class, perhaps even the most important one. The British often confess to tremendous anxiety about accent, and what it reveals about social standing. And indeed, expatriates of all sorts in the United Kingdom are constantly made aware of their accents, and what the accent reveals about their geographical origins. I suspect that the thought that an accent is incidental to identity would occur mainly to people who have never had attention called to their own. . . .

In the vast museum of American consumerist oddities, accent-reduction clinics like The Perfect Voice probably merit little more than a small corner display. Yet there are at least two aspects to them that are worth thinking about more carefully, in light of the consumerist forces that drive the development of enhancement technologies. One is the way the language of illness is used to describe, however lightheartedly, the process of changing your accent. You do it at a clinic, and you are treated by a speech pathologist. In fact, you are not really changing your accent; you are "reducing" it, as if it had somehow ballooned out of control, like your weight or your blood sugar, and you need treatment in order to rein it back in.

The other thing to notice is just what is being sold at the accent-reduction clinic. Enhancement technologies are usually marketed and sold by taking advantage of a person's perception that she is deficient in some way. Accent reduction is no different. What is being sold at the accent-reduction clinic is old-fashioned, American-style self-improvement, and the yardstick on which the self-improvement is measured is social status and success at work. The accent-reduction clinic takes advantage of the perception (or perhaps the reality) that non-southerners see a southern accent as something to be hidden or overcome, and that even southerners themselves see certain kinds of southern accents as better than others. (The reason why it is better to talk like Scarlett

> **What is being sold at the accent-reduction clinic is . . . social status and success at work.**

and Rhett than those guys in the overalls in *Deliverance* is clear enough. But behind the more subtle gradations of accent is a peculiar sort of ancestor worship practiced by some white southerners that associates certain accents with a distinguished genealogy.) If The Perfect Voice is in any way representative, the people most inclined to change their accents are those whose success at work depends on the successful public presentation of themselves — actors, business people, news readers, and the occasional minister.

It is the relationship between public performance and the inner life that produces the mixed feelings that I suspect many southerners would have about an accent-reduction clinic. Southerners are quite familiar with public performance, of course; there is a good reason for all those self-dramatizing southern women in the plays of Tennessee Williams. But self-dramatization is one thing, and pretending to be a Yankee is another. Talking like a northerner would strike many southerners as a necessary evil at best, and at worst, a form of selling your birthright. It is a form of "passing," of hiding what is distinctive about your cultural identity. (The proper southern response to being made to feel ashamed of your accent, of course, is to exaggerate it.)

NOTES

[1]Stephen Hawking, *Black Holes and Baby Universes* (New York: Bantam Books, 1993), 26.

[2]N. Katherine Hayles, *How We Became Posthuman: Virtual Bodies in Cybernetics, Literature and Informatics* (Chicago: University of Chicago Press, 1999), 84.

[3]Parker Lee Nash, "My Fair Lady: Say Bye-Bye to Your Southern Accent," *Greensboro News and Record*, January 17, 1999; Woody Baird, "Learn to Take the South Out of Your Mouth, Y'all," *Palm Beach Post*, November 18, 1997; Art Harris, "Takin' the Drawl Outta Dixie," *Washington Post*, December 16, 1984.

[4]Kathy Davis, *Reshaping the Female Body: The Dilemma of Cosmetic Surgery* (New York: Routledge, 1995), 70.

[5]See Nash, "My Fair Lady."

DISCUSSION

1. Accent reduction is one of the many procedures Elliott gathers under the term *enhancement technology*: procedures (from dieting to plastic surgery) designed to improve our lives by altering one of the basic features of our physical selves. What do you think of this objective? Is there anything problematic about seeking to change this aspect of one's supposedly intrinsic self? What do you make of the notion of "overcoming" one's accent?

2. What are some of the words or expressions that characterize stereotypical speech in your area of the country? Is your area marked by a typical local accent? What are some of the assumptions made about people who speak with such an accent or dialect?

3. One of the central questions raised by Elliott's interest in "accent reduction" has to do with where the line separating self-presentation from impersonation should be drawn. Where does enhancement end and fakery begin? At what point do our concerns for making an impression lead us to put on an act that does not reflect who we truly are? Can you think of an experience from your life where this seemed to happen?

WRITING

4. Are there different areas in your life where you are inclined to modulate the way you speak? Write an essay in which you discuss how certain situations in your life influence the way you speak, whether it requires you to change your accent or your choice of words. What is each voice like? How specifically does each differ from each other? And what is it about each setting that accounts for these differences? According to Elliott, what factors in your environment might bring about this change?

5. Think about the various ways that an accent can mark us in the eyes of the general public. Accents, Elliott argues, play a major role in shaping the kinds of conclusions we draw about each other. We often focus on how someone else talks as if this were a definitive barometer of her or his character or worth. Choose a cultural product (for example, a television show, movie, or commercial) that, in your view, encourages us to do this. Write an analysis of the ways this product uses the issue of accent to define, label, or judge some group or category of people. What assumptions and associations does it encourage us to make? What particular stereotypes does it traffic in? And finally, how accurate or valid do you think this view is?

6. Compare Elliott's discussion of accents to what Stephen Miller (p. 594) has to say about our current media culture. How much does your opinion of different accents influence how you respond to conversation, either as a participant or onlooker? Are there particular mediums that trade on speech habits as part of their formula? How much confirmation of Elliott's thesis regarding accents do you think Miller would find in the talk shows, sitcoms, and news programs he surveys?

Scenes and Un-Scenes:
My Fellow Americans

Because they all claim to speak on behalf of the electorate at large, to be the "voice" of the people, politicians always face two separate challenges when it comes to the public statements they make. Not only do they have to articulate their views clearly and convincingly, they also have to find a way of casting these views as an expression of the larger public will. Put differently, they have had to figure out how to speak both *to* and *for* the American people. For generations, public figures of all stripes have sought to accomplish this goal by representing themselves as the embodiment or inheritor of "true" American values — a strategy that over the years has revolved as much around unspoken as spoken communication. Indeed, there is a long and storied tradition in American politics of using visual symbolism — from stagecraft to wardrobe to body language — as a vehicle for aligning oneself with those ideas and ideals considered to be uniquely, intrinsically American.

▲▲ As the nation was transformed by such developments as the feminist and civil rights movements, the prevailing definition of who constitutes a "true American" underwent pronounced changes. In the political realm, these changes are perhaps most visibly reflected in the dramatically enhanced diversity (both racial/ethnic and gender) among those candidates who now run for public office. Unlike FDR, this new generation of politicians faces a more complicated and delicate balancing act: how to use the same traditional patriotic trappings to challenge the traditional views concerning who gets to count as a "real" American. For Harold Ford Jr., an African American competing for a Tennessee senate seat in 2006, the challenge might have been how to square his own decidedly non-WASP background with some of the most traditional and conservative symbols of American identity. In what ways would you say Ford's self-presentation here revises the strategy modeled by FDR?

◄◄ Intended to reassure an anxious population shaken by the economic upheavals and social dislocations of the Great Depression, these "fireside chat" radio broadcasts not only allowed President Franklin Delano Roosevelt to keep the public abreast of his latest initiatives and decisions, but, perhaps even more importantly, they also offered the president an opportunity to present himself as the very embodiment of essential American values and ideals. News coverage of these broadcasts aided in this effort, regularly emphasizing FDR's patrician bearing and impeccable Yankee pedigree, key markers of a stereotypical "American-ness" that the president himself — through stagecraft, setting, and physical deportment — went to pains to reinforce as well.

▲▲ Nowhere is the question of who gets to count as a "real" American more urgently and contentiously debated these days than in discussions about domestic terrorism. For many in the Arab American community, the post September 11 era has been marked by unfounded and harmful suspicions concerning these citizens' supposedly dubious loyalty to the nation. In this photo, Connecticut senator Joe Lieberman, a prominent defender of the nation's "war on terror," engages with Arab American voters dressed in patriotic costumes. What, if anything, does this photo have to say about inclusiveness in America?

◄◄ So habituated have we become to seeing the prevailing definitions of "American-ness" challenged and debated that the effort has now become fodder for late-night comedians such as Stephen Colbert. Even in parody, however, it is still possible to discern the tensions and anxieties that continue to haunt this debate. Indeed, for many it is an open question whether such satiric efforts succeed more in undermin-ing or reinforcing traditional models of patriotic or national identity. Which effect would you say this image has?

◄◄ In this photo, Sean "P. Diddy" Combs uncovers what in many ways is at stake in these various efforts. As his T-shirt loudly declares, the most effective way to assert your "American-ness" — particularly for those who historically have had the franchise denied them — may well lie in the simple act of civic participation itself. What do you make of this alternative formulation? Does it offer a more or less compelling definition of being American?

DISCUSSION

1. Which of these patriotic portraits resonates most with you? Which offers or implies a definition of "being American" that you most identify with?

2. What are the limits or boundaries each image draws around its definition? According to the visual symbolism each employs, who does and does not seem to count as a "real American"?

3. What are the specific values, ideas, or attitudes that, in each case, get proffered as authentically American? Do you share this view? Are there other equally American values, ideas, or attitudes that get overlooked?

WRITING

4. In its own way, each of the images above can be read as a blueprint for American patriotism, issuing instructions for how best to show our "love of country." Choose one of these images and write an essay in which you describe and evaluate the particular patriotic script it seems designed to convey. What are the particular behaviors and attitudes it prescribes? And how do you think it would feel to play this role in your own life?

5. While definitions of "American-ness" have certainly become more expansive and diverse over the last several decades, it is nonetheless the case that certain attitudes and behaviors still remain "out of bounds." On the basis of what these images present to us, where does this boundary seem to be drawn? Write an essay in which you identify some of the activities, attitudes, and assumptions that this collection of images implicitly defines as "un-American." Then write a second paragraph in which you argue either in favor of or against drawing the boundary in this particular way.

6. How do you think Geoffrey Nunberg (p. 607) would respond to this set of images? In your opinion, would Nunberg see these images as proof that the use of symbolism in these images is designed to appeal to one sense of what it means to be American? Would Nunberg categorize these images as liberal or conservative? Why?

Putting It into Practice:
Speaking Out/ Talking Back

Now that you've read the chapter selections, try applying your conclusions to your own life by completing the following exercises.

MAKE YOUR VOICE HEARD   Pick a current events topic that is a source of recent public debate and write a persuasive speech in which you argue one view over the other. Your speech should not only state why your view is correct, but should also name the opposition's points and explain why they are wrong. Perform this speech for your class. Follow up by writing a brief reflective essay in which you discuss how writing your speech was different from delivering it in front of an audience. How is your experience as a speaker different from your experience as a writer?

SPEAKING ROLES   Write an analysis of the way some controversial issue or question gets addressed in one of your classes. What kinds of speaking roles do different students play? What role does the instructor play? On the basis of these roles, what would you say are the prevailing (if unspoken) expectations or rules governing this discussion? What seem to be the principal "dos" and "don'ts"? What new rules might you propose to change the conversation for the better?

STICKS AND STONES   On April 4, 2007, radio shock jock Don Imus caused a national outcry when he described the Rutgers University women's basketball team using racially insensitive language. This has opened up a national debate on exactly what artists and entertainers can get away with saying in every medium, from radio to television to music. While we live in a country that values free speech, what, in your opinion, are the boundaries (if any) that should be placed on our right to express ourselves freely? Use the Imus controversy or any recent scandal you can recall as a case study to argue what the parameters of free speech should be.

Catherine Newman. "I Do. Not.: Why I Won't Marry." From *The Bitch in the House: 26 Women Tell the Truth About Sex, Solitude, Work, Motherhood, and Marriage*, edited by Cathi Hanauer. Copyright © 2002 by Catherine Newman. Reprinted with the permission of the author.

Geoffrey Nunberg. "Trashing the L-Word." From *Talking Right: How Conversation Turned Liberalism into a Tax-Raising, Latte-Drinking, Sushi-Eating, Volvo-Driving, New York Times-Reading, Body-Piercing, Hollywood-Loving, Left-Wing Freak Show*. Copyright © 2006 by Geoffrey Nunberg. Reprinted by permission of Public Affairs, a member of Perseus Books Group.

Michael Pollan. "Big Organic." From *The Omnivore's Dilemma: A Natural History of Four Meals* by Michael Pollan. Copyright © 2006 by Michael Pollan. Used by permission of The Penguin Press, a division of Penguin Group (USA) Inc.

Francine Prose. "The Wages of Sin." From *Gluttony: The Seven Deadly Sins*. Copyright © 2003 by Francine Prose. Reprinted with the permission of Oxford University Press, Ltd.

Alissa Quart. "The Baby Genius Edutainment Complex: The New Smart Baby Products." From *Hothouse Kids: The Dilemma of the Gifted Child*. Copyright © 2006 by Alissa Quart. Reprinted with the permission of Penguin Group (USA) Inc.

Steve Salerno. "Hopelessly Hooked on Help." From *SHAM: How the Self-Help Movement Made America Helpless*. Copyright © 2005 by Steve Salerno. Used by permission of Crown Publishers, a division of Random House, Inc.

Rebecca Saxe. "Do the Right Thing: Cognitive Science's Search for a Common Morality." From *Boston Review* September/October 2005. Copyright © 2005 by Rebecca Saxe. Reprinted with permission.

Brigid Schulte. "The Case of the Purloined Paper." From the *Washington Post*, September 23, 2002. Copyright © 2002, The Washington Post. Reprinted with permission.

Loretta Schwartz-Nobel. "America's Wandering Families." From *Growing Up Empty: The Hunger Epidemic in America*. Copyright © 2002 by Loretta Schwartz-Nobel. Reprinted with the permission of HarperCollins Publishers, Inc.

Jeff Sharlet. "Big World: How Clear Channel Programs America." From *Harper's*, December 2003. Copyright © 2003 by Jeff Sharlet. Reprinted with the permission of the author.

Robert Sullivan. "How to Choose a Career That Will Not Get You Rich No Matter What Anyone Tells You." From *How Not to Get Rich, or Why Being Bad Off Isn't So Bad*. Copyright © 2005 by Robert Sullivan. Reprinted with the permission of Bloomsbury Publishing.

Deborah Tannen. "Fighting for Our Lives." From *The Argument Culture: Moving from Debate to Dialogue* by Deborah Tannen. Copyright © 1997 by Deborah Tannen. Used by the permission of Random House, Inc.

James Twitchell. "Two Cheers for Materialism." Adapted from *Lead Us Into Temptation: The Triumph of American Materialism*. Copyright © 1999 Columbia University Press. Reprinted with the permission of the publisher.

Louis Uchitelle. "The Consequences—Undoing Sanity." From *The Disposable American: Layoffs and Their Consequences*. Copyright © 2006 by Louis Uchitelle. Used by permission of Alfred A. Knopf, a division of Random House, Inc.

Katy Vine. "Love and War in Cyberspace." From *Texas Monthly*, February 2001. Reprinted with permission.

Judith Warner. "This Mess." From *Perfect Madness: Motherhood in the Age of Anxiety*. Copyright © 2005, 2006 by Judith Warner. Reprinted with the permission of Riverhead Books, an imprint of Penguin Group (USA) Inc.

Photo Credits

Index of Authors and Titles

Need help with writing and research?

Visit the Re:Writing Web site
bedfordstmartins.com/rewriting

Re:Writing is a comprehensive Web site designed to help you with the most common writing concerns. You'll find advice from experts, models you can rely on, and exercises that will tell you right away how you're doing. And it's all free and available any hour of the day. You can find help for the following situations at the specific areas of bedfordstmartins.com/rewriting listed below.

Need help with grammar problems?
> **Exercise Central**

Want to see what papers for your other courses look like?
> **Model Documents Gallery**

Stuck somewhere in the research process? (Maybe at the beginning?)
> **The Bedford Research Room**

Wondering whether a Web site is good enough to use in your paper?
> **Evaluating Online Sources Tutorial**

Having trouble figuring out how to document a source?
> **Research and Documentation Online**

Confused about plagiarism?
> **Avoiding Plagiarism Tutorial**

Want to get more out of your word processor?
> **Using Your Word Processor**

Trying to improve the look of your paper?
> **Designing Documents with a Word Processor**

Need to create slides for a presentation?
> **Preparing Presentation Slides Tutorial**

Interested in creating a Web site?
> **Mike Markel's Web Design Tutorial**

reduction. In each case, the interest is in exploring the ways "otherness" gets scripted: the norms and rules that encourage us not only to identify those supposedly not "like us," but also to denigrate them as inferior or lesser on this basis. You might ask your students to speculate about how Tannen would assess the accent reduction clinics Elliott showcases in his piece.

Kolhatkar and Hyman These writers are linked by their shared interest in so-called youth culture, more particularly in the ways the products, publications, and shows that cater to this demographic can purvey powerful norms around how we may and may not talk. Ask your students to speculate about what links the verbal norms under examination in each. Is there anything about the topics they raise or the dynamics they depict that make them seem a more natural fit for younger audiences? If so, what?

Sharlet and Elliott Each of these writers examines what we might call the commodification of public voice. In Sharlet's case, this revolves around the ways that different forms of artistic or political expression (for example, musical genres, the news) can be alternately marketed and bracketed by larger corporate forces. Elliott, meanwhile, chronicles the attempt to transform accent itself into a fungible and purchasable commodity.

Additional Suggestions for Clustering the Readings

Nunberg, Tannen, Miller Each of these writers explores some aspect of argumentation, looking at some of the topics and disputes that most dramatically polarize the American public. Each essay asks readers to think about where in our culture the line between "us" and "them" gets drawn. Each wonders about the implications of using words as weapons or instruments of power.

Elliott, Sharlet, Hyman, Kolhatkar Despite their differences, each of these writers tracks some effort to reduce, simplify, or even standardize the ways Americans talk. Whether it focuses on the effort of a media conglomerate to impose a single format for all its radio outlets (Sharlet), the growing tendency among young people to imitate the speech of stand-up comedians (Hyman), a program for eliminating regional or local accents (Elliott), or an enthusiasm among college students for particular sex advice clichés (Kolhatkar), in every case the focus is on the ways our options for how to talk and what to say are becoming increasingly circumscribed.

At Bedford/St. Martin's You Get More
More Resources to Support Your Teaching Needs

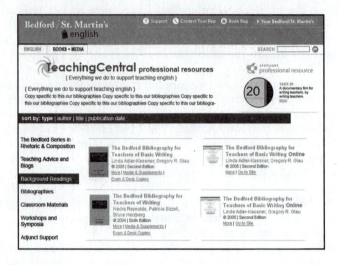

TeachingCentral
bedfordstmartins.com/teachingcentral

Visit TeachingCentral for a complete list of print and electronic teaching resources published by Bedford/St. Martin's—all available free to instructors. You'll find landmark works of reference, award-winning collections from our Series in Rhetoric and Composition, and practical advice for the classroom, along with handouts and assignments that you can download and adapt as needed.

Just-in-Time Teaching
bedfordstmartins.com/justintime

Free and expanding, Just-in-Time Teaching is *the* place to go for last-minute course materials—handouts, teaching tips, assignments, and more. Stop by before class to download background information on prominent writers, browse syllabi, print a handout about peer review, read tips on helping students with learning disabilities, or just see what's new.